High Stakes
and
Desperate Men

High Stakes
and
Desperate Men

CLASSICS OF ESPIONAGE

SELECTED

AND CONDENSED BY

THE EDITORS OF

THE READER'S DIGEST

THE READER'S DIGEST ASSOCIATION
Montreal, Sydney, Cape Town
Pleasantville, New York

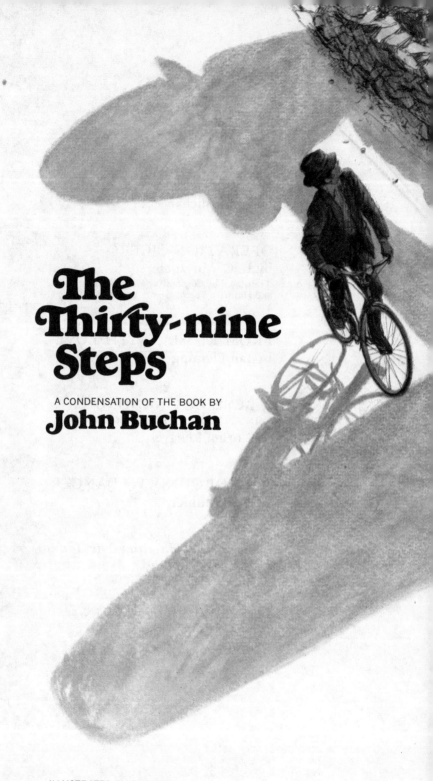

The Thirty-nine Steps

A CONDENSATION OF THE BOOK BY
John Buchan

ILLUSTRATED BY GUY DEEL

England 1914. A mood of uneasiness prevails. In Germany the Kaiser is rattling his sword and war drums are rumbling over the Continent. Into this setting comes Richard Hannay, an attractive young man but footloose and bored. An adventurer, some would say, and with enough money in his pocket to make gainful employment unnecessary. He was bound to get into trouble, and Scudder was trouble. First it was murder. Then, not only was Scotland Yard on Hannay's tail, but there was also that band of ruthless men known simply by the code name "Black Stone"— men who were determined to deal England a fatal knockout blow on the eve of war with Germany.

John Buchan, First Baron Tweedsmuir, was governor-general of Canada and the author of a long series of breathless thrillers including *Prester John* and *Greenmantle*. As a writer, however, he is known principally for *The Thirty-nine Steps*, later to become the unforgettable Alfred Hitchcock film classic.

CHAPTER 1

I RETURNED FROM the city about three o'clock on that May afternoon pretty well disgusted with life. I had been three months in the old country and was fed up with it. If anyone had told me a year ago that I would have been feeling like that, I should have laughed at him, but there was the fact. The weather made me liverish, the talk of the ordinary Englishman made me sick, I couldn't get enough exercise, and the amusements of London seemed as flat as soda water that has been standing in the sun. "Richard Hannay," I kept telling myself, "you have got into the wrong ditch, my friend, and you had better climb out."

It made me bite my lips to think of the plans I had been building up those last years in South Africa. I had got my pile—not one of the big ones, but enough; and I had figured out all kinds of ways of enjoying myself. My father had brought me out from Scotland at the age of six, and I had never been home since; so England was a sort of Arabian Nights to me, and I counted on staying there for the rest of my days. But from the first I was disappointed. In less than a month I was tired of seeing sights and I had had enough of restaurants and theaters and the racetrack. I had no real pal to go about with, which probably explains things. Plenty of people invited me to their houses, but they didn't seem much interested in me. They would ask me a question or two about South Africa and then get on to their own affairs. So here was I, thirty-seven years old, sound in wind and limb, with enough money to have a good time, yawning my head off all day. I had just about settled to clear out and get back to the veld, for I was the best-bored man in the United Kingdom.

That afternoon I had been worrying my brokers about investments, to give my mind something to work on, and on my way home I turned into my club to have a long drink and read the evening papers. They were full of the row in the Near East, and there was an article about Karolides, the Greek premier. I rather liked the chap. From all accounts he seemed the one big man in the show, and he played a straight game, too, which was more than could be said for most of them. I gathered that they hated him in Berlin and Vienna, but that we were going to stick by him. One paper even said he was the only barrier between Europe and Armageddon. I remember wondering if I could get a job in those parts. It struck me that Albania was the sort of place that might keep a man from yawning.

About six o'clock I went home, dressed, dined at the Café Royal, and then went to a music hall. It was a silly show, and I did not stay long. As I walked back to my flat, people surged past me on the pavements, busy and chattering, and I envied them for having something to do. At Oxford Circus I looked up into the clear night sky and I made a vow. I would give the old country another day; if nothing happened, I would clear out and go back to the veld.

My flat was near Portland Place, the second floor in a new apartment house behind Langham Place. There was a common staircase with a doorman and an elevator man at the entrance, but each flat was quite shut off from the others. I hate servants on the premises, so I had a fellow who came in by the day. He arrived before eight every morning, and departed at seven, for I never dined at home.

I was just fitting my key into the door, when I noticed a man at my elbow. I had not seen him approach, and the sudden appearance made me start. He was a slim man with a short brown beard and small gimlety blue eyes. I recognized him as the occupant of a flat on the top floor, with whom I had passed the time of day on the stairs.

"May I come in for a minute?" he said. He was steadying his voice with an effort, and his hand was pawing my arm.

I got my door open and motioned him in. No sooner was he over the threshold than he made a dash for my back room, where I smoke and write my letters. Then he bolted back.

"Is the door locked?" he asked feverishly, and he fastened the chain with his own hand. "I'm very sorry," he said humbly. "It's a liberty, but you look like a man who would understand. I've had you in mind in case things got troublesome. Will you do me a good turn?"

"I'll listen to you," I said. "That's all I'll promise." I was getting worried by the antics of this nervous little chap.

There was a tray of drinks on a table beside him, from which he made himself a stiff whisky and soda. He drank it in three gulps, and cracked the glass as he set it down.

"Pardon," he said. "I'm a bit rattled tonight. You see, at this moment I happen to be dead."

I sat down in an armchair and lit my pipe. "What does it feel like?" I asked, certain that I was dealing with a madman.

A smile flickered over his drawn face. "I'm not mad—yet. But I need help worse than any man ever needed it. I've been watching you, sir, and I reckon you're a cool customer. I reckon, too, you're an honest man. As I say, I need help, and I want to know if I can count you in."

"Get on with your yarn," I said, "and then I'll tell you."

He seemed to brace himself for a great effort and started on the queerest rigmarole. Here is the gist of it:

He was an American, from Kentucky, and after college, being pretty well off, he had started out to see the world. He wrote a bit, and acted as war correspondent for a Chicago paper, and spent a year or two in southeastern Europe. I gathered that he was a fine linguist and had gotten to know those parts pretty well. He spoke familiarly of many names that I remembered having seen in the newspapers.

He had played about with politics, he told me, because politics interested him. I read him as a sharp, restless fellow, who always wanted to get down to the roots of things. He'd gotten farther down than he wanted. By accident he had stumbled across a big subterranean movement engineered by very dangerous people. It fascinated him. He went deeper, and then got caught.

As for the conspiracy, I gathered that most of the people in it were the sort of educated anarchists that make revolutions, but that besides them there were also financiers who were playing for money. He told me some odd things that explained a lot that had puzzled me—things that happened in the Balkan War, why alliances were made and broken, and why certain men disappeared. The aim of the whole conspiracy was to get czarist Russia and Germany at loggerheads.

When I asked why, he said that the anarchists thought it would give them their chance. They looked to see a new world emerge. And the capitalists would make fortunes by buying up wreckage. Capital, he said, had no conscience and no fatherland. "And don't think," he ended, "that these fellows have played their last card. They haven't by a long sight. They've got the ace up their sleeves, and unless I can keep alive for a month, they are going to play it, and win."

"But I thought you were dead," I put in.

He smiled. "I'm coming to that, but I've got to put you wise to a lot of things first. If you read your newspaper, I guess you know the name of Constantine Karolides?"

I sat up at that, for I had been reading about the Greek premier that very afternoon.

"He's the man who has wrecked all their games. He's the one big brain in the whole show, and he happens also to be honest. Therefore he's a marked man. I found that out—not that it was difficult, for any fool could guess as much. But I also found out the way they are going to get him, and that knowledge is deadly. That's why I have had to die."

I mixed him another drink; I was getting interested in the beggar.

"They can't get him in his own country, for he has a bodyguard that would skin their grandmothers. But on the fifteenth of June he is coming to London. The British Foreign Office is giving a big international tea party on that date. Now, Karolides is the principal guest, and if these fellows have their way, he will never return to his admiring countrymen."

"That's simple, anyhow," I said. "You can warn him and keep him at home."

"And play their game?" he asked sharply. "If he does not come, they win, for he's the only man that can straighten out the tangle and thus prevent a war. And if his government is warned, he won't come, for he does not know how big the stakes will be on June fifteenth."

"What about the British government?" I asked. "They won't let their guests be murdered. Tip them off, and they'll take extra precautions."

"No good. They might stuff your city with detectives, and Constantine would still be a doomed man. These fellows are not playing this game for candy. They want a big occasion, with the eyes of all Europe on it. He'll be murdered by an Austrian, and there'll be plenty of evidence to show the connivance of Vienna and Berlin. It will all be an infernal lie, of course, but the case will look black enough to the world. I'm not talking hot air, my friend. I happen to know every detail, and I can tell you it will be the most finished piece of blackguardism since the Borgias. But it's not going to come off if there's a certain man alive right here in London on the fifteenth day of June. And that man is going to be your servant, me, Franklin P. Scudder."

I was getting to like the little chap. His jaw had shut like a rattrap, and there was the fire of battle in his gimlety eyes.

"Where did you get this story?" I asked.

"I got the first hint in an inn on the Achensee in Tirol. That set me inquiring, and I collected my other clues in a fur shop in the Galician quarter of Budapest, in a Strangers' Club in Vienna, and in a little bookshop off the Racknitzstrasse in Leipzig. I completed my evidence ten days ago in Paris. I can't tell you the details now; it's something of a history. When I was quite sure in my own mind, I judged it my business to disappear, and I reached this city by a mighty queer circuit. I left Paris a dandified young French-American, I sailed from Hamburg a Jewish diamond merchant, I left Bergen a cinema man, and I came here from Leith with a lot of pulpwood propositions in my pocket to put before the London newspapers. Till yesterday I thought I had muddied my trail, and I was feeling pretty happy. Then . . ."

The recollection seemed to upset him, and he gulped down some more whisky.

"Then last night I saw a man standing in the street outside this building. I watched him from my window, and I thought I recognized him. He came in and spoke to the doorman. Later I found a card in my mailbox. It bore the name of the man I want least to meet on God's earth."

I think that the look in my companion's eyes, the sheer naked fright on his face, convinced me of his honesty. My own voice sharpened as I asked him what he did next.

"I realized that I was as bottled as a pickled herring and that there was only one way out. I had to die. If my pursuers knew I was dead, they would go to sleep again."

"How did you manage it?"

"I told my valet that I was feeling bad, and I got myself to look like death. That wasn't difficult. I'm no slouch at disguises. Then I got a corpse of a man who had just died—you can always get a body in London if you know where to go—and brought it back here in a trunk. After that I went to bed and got my man to mix me a sleeping draft, and then told him to clear out. He wanted to fetch a doctor, but I swore and said I couldn't abide leeches. When I was left alone I started to fake up that corpse. He was my size and had died from drink, so I put some whisky about the place. The jaw was the weak point in the likeness, so I blew it away with a revolver. There are no neighbors on my floor, and I guessed I could risk a shot. I left the body in bed dressed in my pajamas, with a revolver lying on the bed-clothes and a considerable mess around. Then I got into some other clothes. It wasn't any use my trying to get into the streets. The men who are after me are pretty bright-eyed. There seemed nothing to do but make an appeal to you. I watched from my window till I saw you come home and then slipped down the stairs to meet you. . . ."

He sat blinking like an owl, fluttering with nerves and yet desperately determined.

It was the wildest sort of narrative, but I had heard steep tales before which had turned out to be true. Besides, I made a practice of judging the man rather than the story. However, I felt bound to verify his yarn if I could.

"Hand me your key," I said, "and I'll take a look at the corpse."

He shook his head. "I haven't got it. It's on my dressing table. I had to leave it behind to avoid raising suspicions. You'll have to take me on trust for the night. Tomorrow you'll get proof of the corpse right enough."

I thought for an instant.

"Right. I'll trust you for the night. I'll lock you in my back-room study and keep the key. Just one word, Mr. Scudder. I believe you're straight, but if so be you are not, I should warn you that I'm a handy man with a gun."

"Sure," he said, jumping up with some briskness, and he thanked me. Then he asked me to lend him a razor. I took him into my bedroom and turned him loose. In half an hour's time a figure came out that I scarcely recognized. Only his gimlety, hungry eyes were the same. He was shaved clean, his hair was parted in the middle, and he had cut his eyebrows.

Further, he carried himself as if he had been drilled, and was the very model, even to the brown complexion, of a British officer who had had a long spell in India. He had a monocle, too, and every trace of the American had gone out of his speech..

"My word! Mr. Scudder—" I stammered.

"Not Mr. Scudder," he corrected. "Captain Theophilus Digby, of the Seventh Gurkhas, presently home on leave. I'll thank you to remember that, sir."

I made him a bed in my study and sought my own couch, more cheerful than I had been for the past month. Things did happen occasionally in this God-forgotten metropolis!

I WOKE NEXT morning to hear my man, Paddock, making a row at the study door.

Paddock was a fellow I had done a good turn to out on the Selakwi, and I had hired him as my servant as soon as I got to England. He was not a great hand at valeting, but I could count on his loyalty.

"Stop that row, Paddock," I said. "There's a friend of mine sleeping in there." And I told Paddock how my friend was a great swell, that his nerves were overworked, and that he wanted absolute rest. Nobody was to know he was here, or he'd be besieged by communications from the India office and the prime minister, and his cure would be ruined.

Scudder played up splendidly when he came to breakfast. Paddock couldn't learn to call me sir, but he "sirred" Scudder as if his life depended on it.

After breakfast I left my guest with the newspaper and went into the city till lunch. When I got back, the doorman had a weighty face.

"Nawsty business 'ere this morning, sir. Gent in number fifteen been and shot 'isself. The police are up there now."

I ascended to number 15. A couple of bobbies and an inspector were busy making an examination. I asked a few idiotic questions, and they soon kicked me out. Then I found Scudder's valet and pumped him, but I could see he suspected nothing.

I attended the inquest the next day. A partner of some publishing firm gave evidence that the deceased, as an agent of an American business, had brought him pulpwood propositions. The jury found it a case of suicide while of unsound mind, and the few effects were handed over to the American consul. I gave Scudder a full account of the affair and it interested him greatly. He said he wished he could have attended. It would have been like reading one's own obituary.

The first two days he stayed with me he was very peaceful. He read and smoked and made jottings in a little black notebook, and every night we had a game of chess, at which he beat me soundly. I think he was nursing his nerves back to health. But on the third day I could see he was beginning to get restless. He made a list of the days till June 15 and ticked each off with a red pencil, making remarks in shorthand against them. I would find him sunk in a brown study, his eyes abstracted, and after these spells of meditation he was apt to be despondent.

That night he was very solemn.

"Say, Hannay," he said. "I think I should let you a bit deeper into this business. I should hate to go out without leaving somebody else to put up a fight." And he began to tell me in detail what I had only heard from him vaguely.

I did not give him very close attention. The fact is I was more interested in his own adventures than in his high politics. Karolides and his affairs were not my business. So a lot that Scudder said slipped clean out of my memory. I remember he was very clear that the danger to Karolides would not begin till he reached London, and would come from the highest quarters, where there would be no thought of suspicion. He mentioned the name of a woman—Julia Czechenyi. She would be the decoy, I gathered, to get Karolides away from his guards. He talked, too, about a Black Stone and a man who lisped, and he described very particularly somebody that he never referred to without a shudder—an old man with a young voice who could hood his eyes like a hawk.

He spoke a good deal about death, too—not that the safety of his own skin troubled him. "I reckon it's like going to sleep when you're tired out," he said, "and waking to find a summer day with the scent of hay coming in at the window."

Next day he was more cheerful and read the life of Stonewall Jackson most of the time. I went out to dinner with a mining engineer I had to see on business, and came back about half past ten, in time for our game of chess. When I pushed open the study door the lights were not lit, which struck me as odd. I wondered if Scudder had turned in already.

I snapped the switch, but there was nobody there. Then I saw something in the far corner which made me fall into a cold sweat.

My guest was lying sprawled on his back. There was a long knife through his heart, which skewered him to the floor.

I SAT DOWN IN A CHAIR and felt very sick. The poor, staring, white face on the floor was more than I could bear, and after a while I managed to get a tablecloth and cover it. Then I staggered to a cupboard, found some brandy, and swallowed several mouthfuls. I had seen men die violently before; indeed, I had killed a few myself in the Matabele War, but this cold-blooded indoor business was different.

Finally I managed to pull myself together. I shuttered and bolted all the windows and put the chain on the door. My wits were coming back to me, and it took me about an hour to figure the thing out.

I was in the soup—that was pretty clear. Any shadow of doubt I might have had about the truth of Scudder's tale was gone. Proof was lying under the tablecloth. The men who knew what he knew had found him, and had made certain of his silence. Yes; but he had been in my rooms for four days, and his enemies must figure that he had confided in me. So I would be the next to go. My number was up all right, tonight, or tomorrow, or the day after.

Then I had another thought. Supposing I called in the police now, or went to bed and let Paddock find the body and call them in the morning. What kind of a story was I to tell about Scudder? I had lied to Paddock about him. The whole thing looked desperately fishy. If I told the police everything Scudder had told me, they would simply laugh at me. The odds were a thousand to one that I would be charged with the murder. The circumstantial evidence was strong enough to hang me. Few people knew me in England; I had nobody who could come forward and swear to my character. Perhaps those secret enemies were counting on that. An English prison was as good a way of getting rid of me till after June 15 as a knife in my chest.

Besides, if I told the whole story now and by any miracle was believed, I would be playing their game. Karolides would stay at home, which was what they wanted. Somehow or other the sight of Scudder's dead face had made me a passionate believer in his scheme. He had taken me into his confidence, and I felt pretty well bound to carry on his work. You may think this ridiculous, but that was the way I looked at it. Now I am an ordinary fellow, no braver than most, but I hate to see a good man downed, and that long knife would not be the end of Scudder if I could take his place.

Somehow I must find a way to get in touch with the government people and tell them what Scudder had told me. I wished to heaven he had told me more, and that I had listened more carefully to the little he had told me. There was a big risk that I would not be believed, but I would have to chance that and meantime hope for something to happen to confirm my story in the government's eyes.

My first job, however, would be to vanish and stay vanished for the next three weeks. It was now May 24. That meant twenty days of hiding before I could venture to approach the powers that be. I reckoned that two sets of people would be looking for me—Scudder's enemies to put me out of existence, and the police for his murder. It was going to be a giddy hunt, yet the prospect comforted me. I had been slack so long that almost any chance of activity was welcome.

My next thought was whether Scudder had any papers about him to give me a better clue to the business. I drew back the tablecloth and searched his pockets, no longer shrinking from the body. There was nothing in the breast pocket, and only a few loose coins and a cigar holder in the vest. There was no sign of the little black book in which I had seen him making notes.

But as I looked up from my task I saw that some drawers in the writing table had been pulled out. Scudder, the tidiest of mortals, would never have left them in that state.

I went around the flat and found that everything had been ransacked—the insides of books, drawers, cupboards, even the pockets of the clothes in my wardrobe. There was no trace of the book.

After that I got out an atlas and looked at a map of the British Isles. My notion was to get off to some wild district—Scotland, perhaps—where my veldcraft would be of some use, for in a city I would be like a trapped rat. I had half an idea at first to act as a German tourist. My father had had German partners, and I had been brought up to speak the tongue fluently, not to mention my three years of prospecting for copper in German Damaraland.

But I came to the decision that I would be less conspicuous as a Scot. My people were Scottish and I could pass anywhere as an ordinary Scotsman. I fixed on Galloway as the best place to go to. It was the nearest wild part of Scotland, not overthick with population, from the look of the map. A search in Bradshaw informed me that a train left St. Pancras Station at 7:10, which would land me at a Galloway station in the late afternoon. That was well enough, but a more important matter was how I was to make my way to St. Pancras. I was pretty certain that Scudder's friends would be watching outside. I puzzled over this for a bit; then I had an inspiration, on which I went to bed and slept for two troubled hours.

I got up at four o'clock and opened my bedroom shutters. The faint light of a fine morning was flooding the skies, and sparrows had begun to chatter.

I hunted out an old tweed suit, a pair of strong nailed boots, and a flannel shirt. Into my pockets I stuffed a spare shirt, a cloth cap, and a toothbrush. I had drawn a sum from the bank two days before, in case Scudder should need money, and I put fifty pounds in a belt which I had brought back from Rhodesia. Then I had a bath and cut my long drooping mustache into a short stubby fringe.

Now came the next step. Paddock used to arrive punctually at 7:30 and let himself in with a key. But about 6:40, as I knew from bitter experience, the milkman would turn up with a great clatter of cans outside my door. I had seen him sometimes when I had gone out for an early ride. He was a young man about my height, with a scrubby mustache, dressed in white. On him I staked all my chances.

I went into the study, where the morning light was beginning to creep through the shutters. By this time it was getting on to 6:00. I put a pipe in my pocket and filled my pouch from a jar on the table by the fireplace. As I poked into the tobacco my fingers touched something hard, and I drew out Scudder's little black book.

It seemed a good omen. I lifted the cloth from his body and was amazed at the peace and dignity of the dead face. "Good-by, old chap," I said. "I'll do my best for you."

Then, fairly choking to get out of doors, I hung about in the hall waiting for the milkman. Six thirty passed, then 6:40. Finally at 6:46 I heard a rattle of cans outside. I opened the front door, and there he was, putting down my milk and whistling through his teeth. He jumped at the sight of me.

"Come in here a moment," I said. "I want a word with you." And I led him into the dining room. "I want you to do me a service. Lend me your cap and coat for ten minutes, and here's a sovereign for you."

At the sight of the gold coin he grinned broadly. "Wot's the gyme?" he asked.

"A bet," I said. "I haven't time to explain, but to win it I've got to be a milkman for the next ten minutes. All you have to do is stay here till I come back. You'll be a bit late, but you'll have that quid for yourself."

"Right-o!" he said cheerily. "I ain't the man to spoil a bit of sport. Here's the rig, guv'nor."

I stuck on his cap and his uniform coat, picked up the milk cans, and went whistling downstairs. The doorman told me to shut my jaw, which sounded as if my makeup was adequate.

At first I thought there was nobody in the street. Then I caught sight of a policeman a hundred yards down, and a loafer shuffling past on the other side. Some impulse made me raise my eyes to the house opposite, and there at a second-floor window was a face. As the loafer passed he looked up, and I fancied a signal was exchanged.

I crossed the street, whistling gaily and imitating the milkman's jaunty swing. Then I took the first side street, and turned left past some vacant land. There was no one about, so I dropped the milk cans behind a fence and sent the cap and coat after. I had just put on my own cap when a postman came around the corner. He answered my good-morning unsuspiciously.

At that moment a neighboring church clock struck seven. There was not a second to spare. As soon as I got to Euston Road I took to my heels and ran. At St. Pancras I had no time to get a ticket, let alone settle upon a destination. A porter directed me to a platform where the train was already in motion. Two station officials blocked the way, but I dodged them and clambered into the last car.

Three minutes later we were roaring through the northern tunnels. An irate conductor wrote out a ticket to Newtown Stewart, a place I had suddenly remembered, and then led me from the first-class compartment where I had ensconced myself to a third-class smoker, occupied by a sailor and a stout woman with a child. He went off grumbling, and as I mopped my brow I observed to my companions in my broadest Scots that it was a sore job catching trains.

"The impidence o' that man," said the woman bitterly. "He needit a Scottish tongue to pit him in his place. He was complainin' o' this wean no haein' a ticket and her no fower till August twelvemonth, and he was objectin' to this gentleman spittin'."

The sailor morosely agreed, and I started my new life in an atmosphere of protest against authority. I reminded myself that a week ago I had been finding the world pretty dull.

CHAPTER 2

As I TRAVELED north that day it was fine May weather. I didn't dare face the restaurant car, but I got a luncheon basket at Leeds. Also I got the morning papers, with news about starters for the Derby, and some paragraphs about how Balkan affairs were settling down. When I had read them I got out Scudder's little black book and studied it. It was filled with jottings, chiefly figures, though now and then a name was printed in—for example, Hofgaard, Luneville, Avocado, and especially the word Pavia.

Now I was certain that Scudder never did anything without a reason, and I was sure that there was a cipher in all this. That is a subject which has always interested me; I did a bit of code work myself once as intelligence officer at Delagoa Bay during the Boer War, and I used to count myself good at ciphers. This one looked like the numerical kind, where sets of figures correspond to alphabet letters, but any fairly shrewd person can decipher that sort after an hour or two's work, and I didn't think Scudder would have been content with anything so easy. You can make a pretty good numerical cipher if you have a key word to give you the sequence of the letters, so I fastened on the printed words. I tried for hours, but none of the words answered.

Then I fell asleep, and woke at Dumfries just in time to bundle out and get into the slow Galloway train. I traveled with half a dozen hill farmers who had come from the weekly market and whose mouths were full of prices and of talk about lambing. They had lunched heavily and were highly flavored with whisky, but they took no notice of me. We rumbled slowly into a land of little wooded glens and then to a great wide moor, gleaming with lochs and high blue hills.

By five o'clock the car had emptied and I was left alone, as I had hoped. I got out at the next station, a little place set in the heart of a bog. An old stationmaster was digging potatoes in his garden and, with his spade over his shoulder, sauntered to the train to take charge of a parcel. A child of about ten received my ticket, and I emerged on a white road that straggled over the brown moor.

It was a gorgeous spring evening, with every hill showing as clear as a cut amethyst. The air had the queer rooty smell of bogs, but it was fresh as mid ocean, and I actually felt lighthearted and swung along that road whistling. I might have been a boy out for a holiday tramp instead of a man of thirty-seven very much wanted by the police.

In a roadside planting I cut a walking stick of hazel, and presently struck off the highway up a bypath which followed a brawling stream. It was some hours since I had tasted food, and I was getting very hungry when I came to a shepherd's cottage set beside a waterfall. A brown-faced woman by the door greeted me with kindly shyness. When I asked for a night's lodging she said I was welcome to the bed in the loft, and soon she set before me a hearty meal of ham and eggs, scones, and thick sweet milk. At dark her man, a lean giant, came in from the hills. With the perfect breeding of moorland dwellers they asked no questions, but I could see they set me down as some kind of dealer, and I took some trouble to confirm their view. I spoke a lot about cattle, of which my host knew little, and I picked up from him a good deal about the local Galloway markets, which I tucked away in my memory for future use.

They refused any payment, and by six the next morning I had breakfasted and was striding south. My notion was to return to the railway line a station or two farther on from where I had alighted yesterday and to double back. I reasoned that that was the safest way, for the police would naturally assume I was heading away from London in the direction of some western port, if by now they had identified the fellow who had boarded the train at St. Pancras.

It was the same jolly, clear spring weather, and I was in better spirits than I had been for months. Over a long ridge of moorland I took my road, skirting the side of a high hill which the shepherd had called Cairnsmore of Fleet. Nestling curlews and plovers were crying everywhere. Green pastures were dotted with young lambs. I stepped out like a four-year-old. By and by I came to a swell of moorland which dipped to the vale of a little river, and a mile away in the heather I saw the smoke of a train.

The station, when I reached it, proved ideal for my purpose. The moor surged up around it and left room only for the single rail line, a waiting room, an office, and the stationmaster's cottage. There seemed to be no road to it from anywhere. In the small ticket office I paid the fare to Dumfries just as the eastbound train approached.

The only occupants of the car were an old shepherd and his dog. The man was asleep. On the cushion beside him was that morning's *Scotsman*. I seized on it eagerly.

There were two columns about the Portland Place murder, as it was called. My man Paddock had given the alarm and had the milkman arrested. Poor devil, he'd earned his sovereign. In the stop-press news I found a further installment of the story. The milkman had been released, I read, and the true criminal, about whose identity the police were reticent, was believed to have gotten away from London by one of the northern lines. I was named only as owner of the flat.

There was nothing else in the paper, nothing about foreign politics or Karolides or the things that had interested Scudder. I laid it down, and found that we were approaching the station at which I had gotten out yesterday. Three men were questioning the potato-digging stationmaster. I supposed that they were local police stirred up by Scotland Yard who had traced me as far as this one-horse siding. Sitting well back in the shadow, I watched them carefully. One was taking notes. The old potato digger seemed to have turned peevish, but the child who had collected my ticket was talking volubly.

As we moved away from the station my companion woke up. He fixed me with a wondering glance, kicked the dog, and inquired drunkenly where he was. Then his voice died away into a stutter, and sleep once more laid its heavy hand on him.

My plan had been to get out at some station down the line, but the train suddenly gave me a better chance, for it came to a standstill at the end of a culvert which spanned a brown-colored river. I looked out. Every car window was closed and no human figure appeared in the landscape. So I opened the door and dropped into a tangle of hazel which edged the line. Crawling through the thicket, I put a few hundred yards behind me. When I ventured to look back, the train had started again and was vanishing in the cutting.

I found myself in a wide semicircle of moorland ringed with high hills. There was not a sign or sound of a human being, only splashing water and the interminable crying of curlews. Yet, oddly enough, for the first time I felt the terror of the hunted. It was not the police that I thought of, but the other folk, who knew that I knew Scudder's secret and dared not let me live. Crouching low in the runnels of the bog, I started to run, and I ran till sweat blinded my eyes. The mood did not leave me till I had reached the rim of hills and flung myself panting on a ridge high above the brown river.

From my vantage ground I could scan the whole moor all the way to the railway line and south of it. But I could see nothing moving. Then I looked east beyond the ridge and saw a new kind of land-scape—shallow green valleys with fir trees and the faint lines of dust which hinted of highroads. Last of all I looked into the sky, and there I saw something that set my pulses racing. Low down in the south a small monoplane was climbing into the heavens.

I was as certain as if I had been told that that plane was looking for me, and that it did not belong to the police. For an hour or two I watched it from a pit of heather. It flew low along the hilltops and then in narrow circles back over the valley up which I had come. Finally it seemed to change its mind, rose to a great height, and flew away back to the south.

I did not like this espionage from the air; it made me think less well of the countryside I had chosen for refuge. These heather hills were no cover if my enemies were in the sky, and I began to look towards the green country beyond the ridge, where there would be woods and houses.

About six in the evening I came out of the moorland to a white ribbon of road which wound up the narrow vale of a stream. As I followed it the fields opened out into a plateau, and presently I reached a kind of pass, where a solitary house smoked in the twilight. The road swung over a bridge, and leaning on the parapet was a man. He was smoking a long clay pipe and studying the water.

He jumped around as my step rang on the stone, and I saw a pleas-ant, sunburned, boyish face. "Good evening to you," he said gravely.

The smell of woodsmoke and of some savory roast floated from the house. "Is that place an inn?" I asked.

"At your service," he said politely. "I am the landlord, sir, and I hope you'll stay overnight. To tell the truth I've had no company for a week."

Detecting an ally, I filled my pipe. "You're young to be an inn-keeper," I said.

"My father died a year ago and left the business to me. I live there with my grandmother. It's a slow job for a young man, and it wasn't my choice of profession."

"Which was?"

He actually blushed. "I want to write books," he said.

"Well, what better chance could you ask? Man, I've often thought an innkeeper would make the best storyteller in the world."

"Not now," he said. "Maybe in the old days when you had pilgrims and highwaymen and mail coaches on the road, but not now. Nothing comes here but cars full of fat women who stop for lunch, and a fisherman or two in the spring. There's no material in that. I want to see life, to travel, and write things, like Kipling and Conrad. But all I've done yet is to get some verses printed."

I looked at the inn, standing golden in the sunset against wine-red hills. "D'you think that adventure is found only in travel? Maybe you're rubbing shoulders with it at this very moment."

Sitting on the bridge in the soft May twilight, I pitched him a lovely yarn. It was true in essentials, too, though I altered details. I made out that I was a mining magnate from Kimberley, who had shown up a gang. They had pursued me across the ocean and had killed my best friend and were now on my tracks. I told the story well, if I say so myself. I described an attack on my life on the voyage home, and I made a really horrid affair of the Portland Place murder.

"You're looking for adventure!" I cried. "Well, you've found it."

"By God," he whispered, drawing his breath in sharply. "It's pure Conan Doyle."

"You believe me," I said gratefully.

"Of course I do." He held out his hand. "I believe everything out of the common and only distrust the normal." He was very young.

"I think they're off my track for the moment, but I must hide for a couple of days. Can you take me in?"

He caught my elbow eagerly and drew me towards the house. As I entered I heard from far off the throb of an engine. There silhouetted against the dusky west was my friend the airplane.

He gave me a room at the back of the inn with a fine outlook over the plateau, and an old woman brought me my meals. The next morning I sent him on his motor bicycle for the daily paper, which otherwise would arrive with the post in the late afternoon. I asked him to make note of any strangers, and to keep a lookout for cars and airplanes. Then I sat down in earnest to Scudder's notebook.

He came back at midday with the *Scotsman*. There was nothing in it except some further evidence from Paddock and the milkman, and a repetition of yesterday's statement that the murderer had headed north. But there was a long article, reprinted from *The Times*, about Karolides and the troubled state of affairs in the Balkans, though no mention of any visit to England. Then I got rid of the innkeeper for the afternoon, since I was getting very warm in my search for the cipher.

By an elaborate system of experiments I had pretty well discovered the nulls and stops. The trouble was the key word, and when I thought of the million-odd words that might have been used, it seemed hopeless. Suddenly the name Julia Czechenyi flashed across my mind. Scudder had said it was the key to the Karolides business, and it occurred to me to try it on his cipher.

It worked. The five letters of Julia gave me the position of the vowels. A was J, the tenth letter of the alphabet, and so represented by the Roman numeral X in the cipher; E was U = XXI, and so on. Czechenyi gave me the numerals for the principal consonants.

In half an hour I was reading with a whitish face and fingers that drummed on the table, when I glanced out the window and saw a big green open touring car coming up the glen towards the inn. It stopped at the door, and two men in raincoats got out.

Ten minutes later the innkeeper slipped into the room.

"Two chaps are looking for you," he whispered. "They're in the dining room below, having drinks. They asked about you and said they had hoped to meet you here. And they described you jolly well. I told them you'd been here last night and had gone off on a motor bicycle this morning, and one of them swore like a truck driver."

He excitedly described one as a dark-eyed thin fellow with bushy eyebrows. The other was always smiling, and lisped. Neither was any kind of foreigner; about this my young friend was positive.

I took a piece of paper and wrote some words in German on it as if it were a loose page from part of a private letter:

> . . . Black Stone. Scudder had got on to this, but he could not act for a fortnight. I doubt if I can do any good now, especially as Karolides is uncertain about his plans. . . .

"Take this down. Say it was found in my bedroom and ask them to return it to me if they overtake me."

Three minutes later I heard a car start up, and peeping from behind the curtain, I caught sight of the two figures. One was slim, the other sleek; that was the most I could make out.

The innkeeper appeared again. "Your piece of paper woke them up," he said gleefully. "The dark fellow went as white as death and cursed like blazes, and the fat one whistled and looked ugly. They paid for their drinks and wouldn't wait for change."

"Now then, I'll tell you what I want you to do," I said. "Get on your bicycle and go to Newtown Stewart, to the chief constable. Describe the two men and say you suspect them of having had something to do with the London murder. You can invent reasons. The two will be back, never fear. Not tonight, for they'll follow me, but tomorrow. Tell the police to be here bright and early."

He set off like a docile child, while I worked on Scudder's notes. When he came back we dined together, and in common decency I let him pump me about my adventures. I told him a lot of stuff about lion hunts and the Matabele War, thinking all the while what tame businesses those were compared to the present one. When he went to bed I sat up and finished Scudder's notes. Then I smoked in a chair till daylight, for I could not sleep.

At eight the next morning I saw two constables and a sergeant arrive. They entered the house. Twenty minutes later I saw from my window a second car come across the plateau from the opposite direction. It did not drive up to the inn, but stopped two hundred yards off in a patch of woods. Its occupants carefully reversed it before leaving it, and a minute or two later I heard their steps on the gravel outside the window. My plan had been to lie hidden in my bedroom and see what happened. I had a notion that, by bringing the police and my more dangerous pursuers together, something might work out of it to my advantage. But now I had a better idea. I scribbled a line of thanks to my host, opened the window, and dropped quietly into a gooseberry bush. Unobserved, I crossed the highroad to the big green car, standing spick-and-span in the morning sunlight, but with enough dust on it to tell of a long journey. I

jumped into the driver's seat and stole gently out onto the plateau. Almost at once the road dipped so that I lost sight of the inn, but the wind seemed to bring me the sound of angry voices.

CHAPTER 3

DRIVING THAT CAR for all it was worth over the crisp moor highway that shining May morning, I glanced back often over my shoulder and looked anxiously to every turning; but later I drove with a vague eye. For I was thinking desperately of what I had read in Scudder's notebook.

The fact was he had told me a pack of lies. All his yarns about the Balkans and the anarchists and the Foreign Office conference were eyewash. And yet not quite. I had staked everything on my belief in his story. Now here was his book telling me a different one, and instead of being once bit twice shy, I believed it absolutely. Why? I don't know.

But it rang desperately true, as the first tale had rung true also in spirit. June 15 was indeed to be a day of destiny, but a bigger destiny than the killing of a Karolides. It was so big that I didn't blame Scudder for keeping me out of the game and wanting to play a lone hand.

The whole story was in the notes—with gaps, you understand, which he would have filled from his memory. He listed his authorities, too, and had an odd trick of giving them all a numerical value and then striking a balance, which stood for the reliability of each stage in the yarn. The bare bones of the tale were all that was in the book—that, and one queer phrase which occurred half a dozen times inside brackets. "Thirty-nine steps" was the phrase, and at its last time of use it ran: "Thirty-nine steps—I counted them; high tide 10:17 p.m." I could make nothing of that.

As for the tale itself, the first thing I learned was that it was no question of preventing a war. That was coming, as sure as Christmas, had been arranged, said Scudder, ever since February 1912. And Karolides was a doomed man, all right, booked to hand in his checks on June 15, in two weeks and four days from that May morning.

The second thing was that this war would come as a big surprise to Britain. Karolides' death would set the Balkans by the ears, then Vienna would chip in with an ultimatum that Russia wouldn't like, and there would be bitter words. But Berlin would play peacemaker and pour oil on the waters, till suddenly she would find good cause for a quarrel, pick it up, and within hours let fly at us. That was the idea, and a pretty good one, too. Honey and fair speeches, then a strike in the dark. So while we were talking about Germany's goodwill and good intentions, our coast would be silently ringed with mines, and submarines would be waiting for every battleship.

But all this depended on a third thing, due to take place on June 15, when a very important man was coming over from Paris to get nothing less than a statement of the disposition of the British home fleet on mobilization. In spite of the nonsense talked in Parliament, there was a real working alliance between France and Britain, and the two general staffs met every now and then to make plans for joint action in case of war. But on June 15 others would be in London—others at whom I could only guess. Scudder called them collectively the Black Stone. They represented our foes, and the information destined for France, about the fleet's disposition, was to be diverted to their pockets. And it was to be used, remember—used a week or two later, with great guns and swift torpedoes, suddenly in the darkness of a summer night.

This then was the story I had deciphered in that back room of a country inn. This was the story that hummed in my brain as I swung the big open touring car from glen to glen.

My first impulse had been to write a letter to the prime minister, but a little reflection convinced me that that would be useless. Without proof, who would believe me? So I must just keep myself going, ready to act when things got riper, no light job with the police in full cry after me, and the Black Stone running swiftly on my trail.

Steering east by the sun, I presently came down from the moorlands and swung through old thatched villages, over lowland streams, and past gardens blazing with hawthorn and yellow laburnum. The land was so deep in peace that I could scarcely believe that somewhere behind me were those who wanted my life; or that in a month's time, unless I had the almightiest of luck, these round country faces would be pinched and staring, and men would be lying dead in English fields.

At midday I entered a long straggling village and had a mind to stop and eat. Halfway down the street by the post office stood a policeman. When he saw the car he advanced with raised hand and motioned me to stop.

I nearly was fool enough to obey. Then it dawned on me that my friends at the inn, desiring to see more of me, had wired a description of the car to villages through which I might pass. I released the brakes just in time; as it was, the policeman clawed at the hood.

I realized that main roads were no place for me, and turned into the byways. But it wasn't easy without a map, for I risked getting onto a farm road and ending in a duckpond or a stableyard, and I couldn't afford delay. I began to see what an ass I had been to steal their car. Still, if I left the big green brute and took to my feet, it would be discovered in an hour and I would have no head start in the race.

I struck up a lonely road which climbed over a pass. Evening was now drawing in, and I was furiously hungry, for I had eaten nothing since breakfast except a couple of buns I had bought from a baker's cart.

Just then I heard a noise in the sky, and lo and behold there was that infernal plane again, flying low, about a dozen miles south and coming rapidly towards me.

On a bare moor I was at its mercy. My only chance was to get to the leafy cover of the valley below. Down the hill I went like blue lightning. Soon I was on a road between hedges, and dipping to the deep-cut glen of a stream. Then came a bit of thick woods, where I slackened speed.

Suddenly on my left I heard the hoot of another car and realized to my horror that I was almost upon a couple of gateposts marking a private road. My horn gave an agonized roar, and I clapped on my brakes, but it was too late. A car was sliding in front of me. To avoid a wreck I did the only thing possible, and ran slap into the hedge on the right, trusting to find something soft beyond.

My car slithered through the hedge and then gave a sickening plunge forward. I saw what was coming, leaped up on the seat, and would have jumped out. But a branch of hawthorn got me in the chest, lifted me, and held me, while a ton or two of expensive metal slipped below me, bucked, pitched, and then dropped with an almighty smash fifty feet to the bed of the stream.

SLOWLY THE THORNS let go of me. As I scrambled to my feet a hand took my arm, and a badly scared voice asked if I was hurt. I found myself looking at a tall young man who kept on blessing his soul and whinnying apologies. For myself, once I got my wind back, I was rather glad than otherwise. This was one way of getting rid of the car.

"My blame, sir," I answered. "It's just lucky I haven't added homicide to my follies. That's the end of my Scottish motor tour, but it might have been the end of my life."

He studied his watch.

"You're an all right sort of fellow," he said. "Look, I can spare a quarter of an hour, and my house is only two minutes off. I'll see you clothed and fed. Where's your kit, by the way? In the car?"

"No, it's in my pocket," I said, brandishing a toothbrush. "I'm a colonial and travel light."

"A colonial!" he cried. "The very man I've been praying for. Are you by any chance a free trader?"

"I am," said I, without the foggiest notion what he meant.

He patted my shoulder and hurried me into his car. Minutes later we drew up before a comfortable-looking hunting lodge set among pine trees. He ushered me indoors to a bedroom and flung half a dozen suits before me, my own having been pretty well reduced to rags. I selected a blue serge, which differed conspicuously from my own garments. Then he haled me to the dining room, where the remnants of a meal stood on the table, and announced that I had just five minutes to eat. "Take a snack in your pocket, and we'll have supper when we get back. I've got to be at the Masonic Hall at eight o'clock."

While I had a cup of coffee and some cold ham, he stood on the hearthrug.

"You find me in the deuce of a mess, Mr.— By the by, you haven't told me your name. Twisden? Any relation of old Tommy Twisden of the Sixtieth? No. Well, you see I'm Liberal candidate for this part of the world, and I have a meeting on tonight at Brattleburn—that's my chief town, and an infernal Tory stronghold. I had the colonial ex-premier fellow, Crumpleton, coming to speak for me tonight, and had him tremendously advertised over the whole place. This afternoon I got a wire saying he has influenza, and here am I left to do the whole thing myself. I had meant to speak for ten minutes and must now go on for forty. I simply cannot do it. Be a good chap and help me. All you colonials have the gift of the gab—I wish to heaven I had it."

I had no ideas about free trade one way or the other, but my young gentleman was far too absorbed in his own difficulties to think how odd it was to ask a stranger who had just missed death by an ace to address a meeting for him on the spur of the moment. But necessity did not allow me to contemplate oddnesses or to pick and choose my supports.

"All right," I said. "I'm not much of a speaker, but I'll tell them a bit about Australia."

At my words the cares of the ages slipped from his shoulders and he was rapturous in his thanks. As we drove down dusty roads he poured out the simple facts of his history. He was an orphan; his uncle, a member of the Cabinet, had brought him up. After leaving Cambridge, he had been short of a job, and his uncle had advised politics. He had no preference in parties. "Good chaps in both," he said cheerfully. "I'm a Liberal, because my family have always been Whigs." But if he was lukewarm politically, he had strong views on other things. He jawed away about Derby entries, and he was full of plans for improving his shooting. Altogether a clean, decent, callow young man.

As we passed through a little town two policemen signaled us to stop and flashed their lanterns on us. "Beg pardon, Sir Harry," said one. "We've got instructions to look out for a car, and the description's not unlike yours."

"Right-o," said my host, while I thanked Providence for my safety. After that my host's mind began to labor heavily with his coming speech. His lips kept muttering and his eyes wandered. The next thing I knew we had drawn up outside a door and were being welcomed by some noisy gentlemen with rosettes.

The hall held about five hundred, women mostly, and a dozen or two baldheads. The chairman, a minister with a reddish nose, lamented Crumpleton's absence and gave me a testimonial as a "trusted leader of Australian thought." I hoped the police at the door took note of it. Then Sir Harry started.

He had a bushel of notes from which he read, and when he let go of them he fell into one prolonged stutter. Every now and then he remembered a phrase he had learned by heart, straightened his back, and gave it off like an old-time Shakespearean actor. The next moment he was bent double and crooning over his papers. He talked about the "German menace," and said it was all a Tory invention to cheat the poor of their rights and keep back peace and social reform. I thought of the little black book in my pocket! A lot Scudder's friends cared for peace and reform.

Yet I liked the speech. You could see the niceness of the chap shining through. Also it took a load off my mind. I mightn't be much of an orator, but I was a thousand percent better than Sir Harry. When it came my turn I simply told them all I could remember about Australia, praying no Australian was there. Altogether I was rather a success.

When we were in the car again, my host was in great spirits at having done his job. "A ripping speech, Twisden," he said. "Now, you're coming home with me. I'm all alone, and if you'll stop a day or two I'll show you some very decent fishing."

We had a hot supper—I needed it badly—and then drank grog in a big, cheery smoking room with a crackling wood fire. I thought the time had come for me to put my cards on the table.

"Listen, Sir Harry," I said. "I've something important to say to you, and I'm going to be frank. Where on earth did you get that poisonous rubbish you talked tonight?"

His face fell. "Was it as bad as that?" he asked ruefully. "I got most of it out of the *Progressive Magazine* and pamphlets. But you surely don't think Germany will ever go to war with us?"

"Ask that question in six weeks," I said. "Now, if you'll give me your attention for half an hour I'm going to tell you a story."

I can still see that bright room with the deers' heads and the old prints on the walls, Sir Harry hovering restlessly on the hearth and myself lying back in an armchair, speaking. I seemed to be another person, standing aside and listening to my own voice, and judging the reliability of my tale. It was the first time I had ever told it to anyone, and it did me no end of good. I skipped no detail.

"So you see," I concluded, "here in your house is the man wanted for the Portland Place murder. Your duty is to send for the police and give me up. I don't think I'll get very far. There'll be an accident and I'll have a knife in my ribs an hour or so after arrest. Nevertheless it's your duty, as a law-abiding citizen. Perhaps in a month's time you'll be sorry, but you have no cause to think of that."

He was looking at me with bright, steady eyes. "What was your job in Rhodesia, Mr. Hannay?" he asked.

"Mining engineer," I said. "I made my pile cleanly and I had a good time making it."

"Not a profession that weakens the nerves, is it?"

I laughed. "Oh, as to that, my nerves are good enough." I took a hunting knife from a stand on the wall and did the old Mashona trick of tossing it and catching it in my lips.

He watched with a smile. "I may be an ass on a platform, but I can size up a man. You're no murderer and you're no fool. I believe you're speaking the truth. I'm going to back you up. Now, what can I do?"

"First, I want you to write a letter to your uncle. I've got to get in touch with the government people sometime before the fifteenth of June."

He pulled his mustache. "That won't help you," he said. "This is Foreign Office business and my uncle would have nothing to do with it. Besides, you'd never convince him. No, I'll go one better. I'll write to the permanent secretary at the Foreign Office. He's my godfather and one of the best. What do you want?"

He sat at a table and wrote to my dictation. The gist of it was that if a man called Twisden (I thought I'd better stick to that name) turned up before June 15 he was to treat him kindly. Twisden would prove who he was by passing the word, Black Stone, and whistling "Annie Laurie."

"Good," said Sir Harry. "That's the proper style. By the way, you'll find my godfather—his name's Sir Walter Bullivant—down at his country cottage for Whitsuntide. It's close to Artinswell on the Kennet. That's done. Now, what's next?"

"Lend me the oldest tweed suit you've got. Anything will do, so long as the color is the opposite of the clothes I destroyed this afternoon. Then show me a map of the neighborhood. Lastly, if the police come asking about me, just show them the car in the glen. If the other lot turn up, tell them I caught the south express after your meeting."

He did, or promised to do, all these things. I shaved off the remnants of my mustache and got inside an ancient suit of what I believe is called heather mixture. The map gave me some notion of my whereabouts and told me what I wanted to know—where one could join the main railway to the south, and what wilderness areas lay near at hand.

At two o'clock he wakened me from sleep and led me blinking into the night. An old bicycle was handed over to me.

"Turn to the right up by the long fir woods," he enjoined. "By daybreak you'll be well into the hills. Then I should pitch the bicycle into a bog and take to the moors on foot. You can put in a week among the shepherds and be as safe as if you were in New Guinea."

I pedaled diligently up steep gravel roads till the sky paled. As the mists cleared before the sun, I found myself in a wide green world with glens falling on every side and a faraway horizon. Here at any rate I could get early news of my enemies.

CHAPTER 4

IN THE CREST of a pass I sat down and took stock of my position. Behind me the road climbed through a long cleft in the hills. Ahead was a flat space of maybe a mile pitted with bogholes and rough with tussocks, and then beyond it the road fell steeply down another glen to a plain whose blue dimness melted into the distance.

To left and right were round-shouldered green hills as smooth as pancakes, but to the south—that is, the left—there was a glimpse of high heathery mountains which I remembered from the map as the big knot of hill I had chosen for my sanctuary. I was on the central hill of a huge upland country, and could see for miles. In the meadows below the road, half a mile back, a cottage smoked—the only sign of human life. Otherwise there was only the calling of plovers and the tinkling of little streams.

It was now about seven o'clock, and as I waited, I heard once again the ominous throb in the air.

I sat quite still and hopeless while the sound grew louder. There was not enough cover to hide a tomtit in these bald green places. Then I saw a plane coming up from the east. It was flying high, but as I watched, it dropped several hundred feet and began to circle the knot of hill in narrowing rings, just as a hawk wheels before it pounces. Now it was flying very low, and now the observer on board caught sight of me. I could see someone examining me through glasses. Then suddenly the plane rose, and sped eastward again till it became a speck in the blue morning.

That made me do some savage thinking. My enemies had located me. The next thing would be a cordon around me. I didn't know what force they commanded, but I felt certain it would be sufficient. The plane had seen my bicycle, and might conclude that I would try to escape by the road. In that case there might be a chance on the moors to the right or left. I wheeled the bicycle away from the highway and plunged it into a moss hole where it sank among pond-weed and water buttercups. Then I climbed to a knoll which gave a view of the two valleys. Nothing stirred on the long white ribbon that threaded them.

Another time I should have liked this place, but now it seemed to suffocate me. The free moorlands were prison walls, and the keen hill air was the breath of a dungeon.

I tossed a coin—heads right, tails left—and it fell heads, so I turned north. In a little while I came to the brow of a ridge. I could see the highroad for maybe ten miles, and far down it something was moving that I took to be a car. Beyond the ridge I looked on a rolling green moor which fell away into wooded glens. Now, my life on the veld has given me the eyes of an eagle, and I could see away down the slope, a couple of miles off, several men advancing like a row of beaters at a shoot.

I dropped out of sight behind the skyline. That way was closed to me. I must try the bigger hills to the south. The car I had noticed was getting nearer, but it was still a long way off with some steep gradients before it. I ran hard, crouching low, and as I ran I kept scanning the brow of hill before me. Was it imagination or did I see figures moving—one, two, perhaps more?

If you are hemmed in on all sides in a patch of land, there is only one chance of escape. You must stay in the patch, and let your enemics search it and not find you.

I would have buried myself to the neck in mud or lain below water or climbed the tallest tree. But there was not a stick of wood, the bogholes were little puddles, and the stream was a slender trickle. There was nothing but short heather and bare hill and the white highway.

Then in a bend of the road, beside a heap of stones, I found the roadman.

He was a wild figure, with a week's beard on his chin and a pair of big horn-rimmed spectacles. He had just arrived on the job and was wearily flinging down his hammer. He looked at me with a fishy eye and yawned. Taking up the hammer finally, he struck a stone. Then he dropped the implement with an oath, and put both hands to his ears.

"Mercy on me, my heid's burstin'!" he cried. "I canna dae't. The surveyor maun just report me. I'm for my bed."

I asked him what was the trouble, though indeed it was clear enough.

"The trouble is that I'm no sober. Last nicht my dochter, Merran, was waddit, and they danced till fower in the byre. Me and some ithers sat down to the drinkin'—and here I am. Peety that I ever lookit on the wine when it was red!"

I agreed with him about bed.

"It's easy speakin'," he moaned. "But I got a postcaird yestere'en sayin' that the new road surveyor would be round the day. He'll come and he'll no find me, or else he'll find me drunk, and either way I'm a done man. I'll back to my bed and say I'm no weel, but that'll no help me, for they ken my kind o' no-weelness."

I had an inspiration. "Does the new surveyor know you?" I asked.

"No him. He's just been a week at the job."

"Where's your house?" I asked, and was directed by a wavering finger to the cottage by the stream.

"Well, back to your bed," I said, "and sleep. I'll take on your job for a bit and see the surveyor."

He stared at me; then his face broke into the vacant drunkard's smile. "You're the billy," he cried. "It'll be easy managed. I've finished that bing o' stanes, so you needna chap ony mair. Just take the barry, and wheel eneuch frae yon quarry doon the road to make anither bing."

I asked him his name.

"My name's Alexander Turnbull, and I've been seeven year at this trade, and twenty afore that herdin' on Leithen Water. My freends ca' me Specky, for I wear glasses. Just you speak the surveyor fair and ca' him sir, and he'll be fell pleased."

I borrowed his spectacles and filthy hat; stripped off my coat and vest, and gave them to him to carry home. I borrowed, too, his foul stump of a clay pipe. Without more ado he left me, and then I set to work to dress for the part. I opened my shirt collar to reveal a neck as brown as any tinker's. I whitened my boots and trouser legs with dust from the road, and hitched up my trousers, tying them with string below the knees. With a handful of dust I made a watermark around my neck, where Mr. Turnbull's Sunday ablutions might be expected to stop, and I rubbed a good deal of dirt on my cheeks.

The sandwiches Sir Harry had given me had gone off with my coat, but the roadman's lunch, tied up in a red handkerchief, was at my disposal. I ate several thick slabs of scone and cheese and drank a little cold tea. In the handkerchief was a local paper addressed to Mr. Turnbull—obviously meant to solace his midday leisure. I did up the bundle again, and put the paper conspicuously beside it.

My boots did not satisfy me, but by kicking among the stones I reduced them to the granitelike surface which marks a roadman's footgear. I broke one of the bootlaces and retied it in a clumsy knot and loosened the other so that my thick gray socks bulged over. The men I was matched against would miss no detail.

My toilet complete, I took up the barrow and began journeying to and from the quarry a hundred yards off. An old Rhodesian scout, Peter Pienaar, had once told me that the secret of playing a part was to think yourself into it. You could never keep it up, he said, unless you managed to convince yourself that you were *it*. So I switched all my thoughts to road mending. The little white cottage was my home. I recalled the years spent herding on Leithen Water, and made my mind dwell lovingly on sleep in a soft bed.

Still nothing appeared on that long white road. Now and then a sheep wandered off the heather to stare at me. A heron flopped down and started to fish in the stream, taking no notice of me, and on I went trundling my loads, growing so warm that the dust on my face changed into solid and abiding grit.

Suddenly a crisp voice spoke from the road. Looking up, I saw a little Ford two-seater, and a round-faced young man in a bowler.

"Are you Alexander Turnbull?" he asked. "I'm the new road surveyor. You have charge of the section from Laidlawbyres to the Riggs? Good! A fair bit of road, Turnbull, and not badly engineered. A little soft about a mile off, and the edges want cleaning. See you look after that."

Clearly my getup was good enough for the dreaded surveyor. I went on with my work, and towards noon I was cheered by a little traffic. A baker's van breasted the hill, and the man sold me a bag of gingersnaps which I stowed in my trouser pockets against emergencies. Then a shepherd passed with sheep, and disturbed me by asking loudly, "What hae become o' Specky?"

"In bed wi' the colic," I replied, and he passed on.

Just about midday a big car glided past and drew up a hundred yards away. Its three occupants descended as if to stretch their legs, and sauntered towards me.

Two of the men I had seen before from the window of the Galloway inn—one lean, sharp, and dark, and the other comfortable and smiling. The third was dressed in ill-cut knickerbockers and had the look of a countryman—a vet, perhaps, or a small farmer.

" 'Morning," said the third man. "That's a fine easy job o' yours."

I had not looked up on their approach, and now, when accosted, I slowly and painfully straightened my back, after the manner of roadmen; spat vigorously and regarded them before replying. I confronted three pairs of eyes that missed nothing.

"There's waur jobs and there's better," I said. "I wad rather hae yours, sittin' a' day on your hinderlands on thae cushions. It's you and your muckle cawrs that wreck my roads! If we a' had oor richts, you sud be made to mend what ye break!"

The third man was looking at the newspaper lying beside Turnbull's bundle. "I see you get your papers in good time," he said.

I glanced at it casually. "Aye. Seein' that that paper cam out last Saturday, I'm just fower days late."

He picked it up, glanced at the date, and laid it down again. The sleek smiling man had been looking at my boots, and a word in German called the speaker's attention to them.

"You've good taste in boots," he said. "These were never made by a country shoemaker."

"They were not," I said readily. "They were made in London. I got them frae the gentleman that was here last year for the shootin'. What was his name now?" And I scratched a forgetful head.

Again the sleek one spoke in German. "Let's get on," he said. "This fellow is all right."

They asked one last question. "Did you see anyone pass by early this morning? On a bicycle—or he might've been on foot."

I sensed my danger and pretended to consider deeply. "I wasna up very early," I said. "Ye see my dochter was merrit last nicht, and we keepit it up late. Since I cam up here there has been just the baker and a shepherd, besides you gentlemen."

One of them gave me a cigar, which I smelled gingerly and stuck in Turnbull's bundle. They got into their car and were soon out of sight.

My heart leaped with enormous relief, but I went on wheeling my stones. It was as well, for ten minutes later the car returned, one of the occupants waving to me as it passed on.

I finished Turnbull's bread and cheese, and considered my next step. I could not keep up this road-making business for long. A merciful Providence had kept Mr. Turnbull indoors, but if he appeared on the scene there'd be trouble. I figured that the cordon was still tight around the glen, and that if I walked in any direction I should meet with questioners.

But get out I must. No man's nerve could stand more than a day of being spied on.

I stayed at my post till five o'clock. By that time I had resolved to go to Turnbull's cottage at nightfall, then risk getting over the hills in the dark. But suddenly another car came up the road and slowed down a yard or two from me while the driver lit a cigarette.

By an amazing stroke of luck I knew him. His name was Marmaduke Jopley, and he was an offense to creation, a sort of stockbroker who did his business by toadying eldest sons and rich young peers and foolish old ladies. An adroit scandalmonger, Marmie would crawl a mile on his belly to anyone with a title or a million. I had had a business introduction to his firm when I came to London, and he had been good enough to ask me to dinner at his club. There he had pattered about his duchesses till his snobbery had made me sick. I asked a man afterwards why nobody kicked him, and was told that Englishmen reverenced the weaker sex.

Anyhow there he was now, nattily dressed, in a fine new car, obviously on his way to visit some of his fine friends. A sudden madness seized me, and in a second I had jumped into his car.

"Hello, Jopley," I sang out. "Well met, my lad!"

His chin dropped. "Who the devil are you?" he gasped.

"My name's Hannay," I said. "From Rhodesia, remember?"

"Good God, the murderer!" He choked.

"Just so. And there'll be a second murder, my dear, if you don't do as I tell you. Give me that coat of yours. That cap, too."

Blind with terror, he did as he was bid. Over my dirty trousers and shirt I put on his smart driving coat, and added his gloves as well as his cap to my getup, thereby transforming a dusty roadman into a neat motorist. Then I took the wheel, and with some difficulty turned the car around to go back the way it had come. The watchers, having seen it before, would probably let it pass unremarked.

"Now, Jopley," I said, "sit still and be a good boy. I mean you no harm. I'm only borrowing your car for an hour or two. But if you play any tricks, if you open your mouth, I'll wring your neck. Understand?"

I enjoyed that evening's ride. We ran eight miles down the valley, through a village or two, and I could not help noticing several strange-looking men lounging by the roadside. These no doubt would have had much to say to me had I been in other garb or company. As it was, they looked on incuriously. One touched his cap, and I responded graciously.

As darkness fell I turned up a side glen which led into an unfrequented corner of the hills. Soon villages were left behind, then farms. When we came to a lonely moor where night was blackening the sunset gleam in the bog pools, I stopped and obligingly restored the car and his belongings to Mr. Jopley.

"A thousand thanks," I said. "You're more use than I thought."

As I sat on the hillside, watching his taillights dwindle, I reflected on the various kinds of crime I had now sampled. Contrary to general belief, I was not a murderer, but I had become an unholy liar, a shameless impostor, and a highwayman with a marked taste for expensive cars.

CHAPTER 5

I SPENT THE NIGHT on a shelf of the hillside, in the lee of a boulder where the heather grew long and soft. It was a cold business, for my coat and vest were in Mr. Turnbull's keep. So were Scudder's little book, my watch, and—worst of all—my pipe and tobacco. Only my money accompanied me in my belt, and a few gingersnaps in my trouser pocket.

I ate some of these, and wormed deep into the heather for warmth. My spirits had risen, and I was beginning to enjoy this crazy game of hide-and-seek. So far I had been miraculously lucky, and that somehow gave me a feeling that I would pull through. My chief trouble was hunger. The gingersnaps merely emphasized an aching void. I lay there and tortured myself remembering all the good food I'd thought so little of in London. Paddock's crisp sausages and fragrant shavings of bacon, and shapely poached eggs—how often I'd turned up my nose at them! My soul lusted for the cutlets they did at the club, and a particular ham that stood on the cold table. My thoughts settled on a porterhouse steak and a quart of bitter. In longing hopelessly for these dainties, at last I fell asleep.

Shortly after dawn I awoke very cold and stiff. It took me a little while to remember where I was. First I saw the pale blue sky through a net of heather, then a big shoulder of hill, and then my own boots, which I had placed neatly in a blackberry bush. I raised myself on my arms and looked down into the valley. That one look set me lacing my boots in mad haste. Not more than a quarter of a mile off, men were spaced out on the hillside like a fan, beating the heather. Marmie had not been slow in seeking revenge, and the police had evidently called in local shepherds or gamekeepers to help look for me.

I crawled out of my shelf into the cover of a boulder, and from it gained a shallow trench which slanted up the mountain face. This led me into the narrow gully of a stream, by way of which I scrambled to the top of the ridge. From there, looking back, I saw that I was still undiscovered. My pursuers were patiently quartering the hillside and moving upwards.

Keeping behind the skyline, I ran for maybe half a mile till I judged I was above the uppermost end of the glen. Then I showed myself, and instantly was noted by one of the flankers, who passed word to the others. I heard cries coming up from below, and saw that the line of search had changed direction. I pretended to retreat over the skyline, but instead went back the way I had come, and in twenty minutes was again behind the ridge overlooking my sleeping place. From there I had the satisfaction of seeing the pursuit streaming up the hill on a hopelessly false scent. Before me was a choice of routes. I chose a ridge which made an angle with the one I was on, and soon put a deep glen between me and my enemies. The exercise had warmed my blood, and I was enjoying myself amazingly. As I went I breakfasted on the dusty remnants of the gingersnaps.

Knowing very little about the countryside, I hadn't a clue to what I was going to do next. I was well aware that those behind me would be familiar with the lie of the land, and that my ignorance would be a heavy handicap. In front of me a sea of hills rose high towards the south, but broke down northwards into broad ridges which separated wide and shallow dales. The ridge I had chosen seemed to sink after a mile or two to a moor lying like a pocket in the uplands. It seemed as good a direction to take as any.

My stratagem gave me a fair start—call it twenty minutes—and I had the width of a glen behind me before I saw the heads of my first pursuers. They hallooed at the sight of me, and I waved my hand. Two dived into the glen and began to climb my ridge, while the others kept their own side of the hill. I felt as if I were taking part in a schoolboy game of hare and hounds.

But very soon it began to seem less of a game. Looking back, I saw that only three men were following direct, and I guessed that the others were making a circuit to cut me off. My lack of local knowledge might very well be my undoing, and I resolved to get out of this tangle of glens to the pocket of moor I had seen from above.

To do so I had to increase my distance. I put on a great spurt and got off my ridge and down into the moor before any figures appeared on the skyline behind me. Crossing a stream, I came out on the high-road, which made a pass between two glens. In front of me was a big field of heather sloping up to a crest crowned with trees. By the road-side was a gate, from which a grass-grown track led over the first wave of the moor. I followed it, and after a few hundred yards—as soon as it was out of sight of the highway—the grass stopped and it became a respectable road. Clearly it ran to a remote dwelling, and I began to think of doing the same, since there were trees there—and that meant cover.

I did not follow the road, but a streambed which flanked it on the right, where bracken grew deep and high banks made a tolerable screen. It was well I did so, for no sooner had I gained the hollow than, looking back, I saw my pursuers topping the ridge from which I had descended.

After that I did not look back; I had no time. I ran up the stream-bed, crawling over open places, and wading for a while in shallow water. I passed a deserted cottage and an overgrown garden, and came to the edge of a plantation of firs. From there I saw the chimneys of a house off to my left. I approached it, crossing a rough lawn. It was an ordinary moorland farmhouse with a more pretentious whitewashed wing added. Attached to this wing was a glass veranda, and through the glass I saw the face of an elderly gentleman meekly watching me.

I stalked over a border of gravel and entered the house by the veranda door. Within was a pleasant room, glass on one side and a mass of books on the other. In the middle was a kneehole desk, and seated at it, with some papers before him, was the benevolent old gentleman. His face was round and shiny, and the top of his head was as bright and bare as a glass bottle. He never moved when I entered, but raised his placid eyebrows.

"You seem in a hurry, my friend," he said.

There was something so keen and knowledgeable about his eyes that I could not find a word to say, so I nodded towards the window, which revealed certain figures half a mile off.

"Ah, I see," he said, and took up a pair of field glasses. "A fugitive from justice, eh? Well, we'll go into the matter at our leisure. Meantime, I object to my privacy being broken in upon by clumsy rural policemen. Go into my study and you will see two doors facing you. Take the one to the left and c'ose it behind you. You will be perfectly safe."

And this extraordinary man took up his pen again.

I did as I was bid, and found myself in a little dark chamber which smelled of chemicals and was lit only by a tiny window high in the wall. The door swung behind me with a click like the door of a safe. Once again I had found an unexpected sanctuary.

No sound came to me in that dark place. I tried to be patient and to forget how hungry I was. Then I took a more cheerful view. The old gentleman could scarcely refuse me a meal. While my mouth was watering in anticipation, there was a click and the door opened.

I emerged into the sunlight to find the master of the house sitting in a deep armchair in the room he called his study, and regarding me with curious eyes.

"Have they gone?" I asked.

"They have gone. I convinced them that you had crossed the hill. I do not choose to have police come between me and one whom I

47

am delighted to honor. This is a lucky morning for you, Mr. Richard Hannay."

As he spoke his eyelids seemed to tremble and to fall a little over his keen gray eyes. In a flash Scudder's phrase came back to me, his phrase describing the man he most dreaded in the world: "An old man who could hood his eyes like a hawk." Then I saw that I had walked straight into the enemy's headquarters.

My first impulse was to throttle the old ruffian and make for the open air. But this impulse had been anticipated, for he smiled gently and nodded to the door behind me. I turned and saw two men-servants, who had me covered with pistols.

"I don't know what you mean," I said roughly. My wits were returning and I could think again. "Who are you calling Richard Hannay? My name's Ainslie."

"So?" he said, still smiling. "We won't quarrel about a name."

My clothes, at any rate, would not betray me. I put on my surliest face and shrugged.

"I suppose you're going to give me up after all, and I call it a damned dirty trick. My God, I wish I'd never seen that cursed car! Here's the money and be damned to you," and I flung four sovereigns on the table.

He opened his eyes. "Oh, no, I shall not give you up. My friends and I have a private settlement with you. You know a little too much, Mr. Hannay. You are a clever actor, but not quite clever enough."

He spoke with assurance, but I could see the dawning of a doubt in his mind. With one hand he was tapping his fingers on his knee.

"Oh, for God's sake," I cried, "everything's against me. I haven't had a bit of luck since I came onshore at Leith. What's the harm in a poor devil with an empty stomach picking up some money he finds in a bust-up car? That's all I done, and for that I've been chivvied for two days by those blasted bobbies over those blasted hills. I tell you I'm fair sick of it. You can do what you like, old boy! Ned Ainslie's got no fight left in him."

I could see that the doubt was gaining.

"Will you oblige me with the story of your recent doings?" he asked.

"I can't, guv'nor," I said in a real beggar's whine. "I've not had a bite to eat for two days. Give me a mouthful of food, and then you'll hear God's truth."

My hunger must have showed in my face, for he signaled to one of the men in the doorway. Some cold pie was brought and a glass of beer, and I wolfed them down like a pig—or rather like Ned Ainslie. In the middle of my meal he spoke to me suddenly in German, but I kept my face blank as a stone wall.

Then I told him my story—how I had come off a ship at Leith a week ago, and was making my way overland to my brother at Wigton. I had run short of cash—I hinted vaguely at a spree—and was pretty well on my uppers when I had come on a hole in a hedge, and, looking through, had seen a big car lying in a stream. I'd poked about to see what had happened, and had found four sovereigns lying on the floor. There was no sign of an owner, so I had pocketed the cash. But when I had tried to change a sovereign in a baker's shop the woman had cried to the police, and a little later the law had gotten after me.

"They can have the money back," I cried, "for a fat lot of good it's done me. Everyone's down on a poor man. Now if it had been you, guv'nor, that had found the quids, nobody would have troubled you."

"You're a good liar, Hannay," he said.

I flew into a rage. "Stop fooling, damn you! I tell you my name's Ainslie. I'd sooner have the police after me than you with your Hannays and your tricks. No, guv'nor, I don't mean that. I'm much obliged to you for the grub. But I'll thank you to let me go now the coast's clear."

It was obvious that he was badly puzzled. He had never seen me, and my appearance must have altered considerably from my photographs—if he had one of them.

"I do not propose to let you go. If you are what you say you are, you will soon have a chance to clear yourself. If you are what I believe you are—" He stopped and looked steadily at me, and that was the hardest ordeal of all. There was something weird and devilish in those eyes, cold, malignant, unearthly, and most hellishly clever. They fascinated me like the bright eyes of a snake, and I had a strong impulse to throw myself on his mercy. But I managed to stick it out and even to grin.

"You'll know me next time, guv'nor," I said.

Ignoring me, he rang a bell and a third servant appeared. "I want the Lanchester in five minutes," he said. "There will be three to lunch." Then he said in German to one of the other men, "Karl, put this fellow in the storeroom till I return. You will be answerable to me for his keeping."

I was marched out of the room with a pistol at each ear.

The storeroom was a damp chamber in what had been the old farmhouse. There was no carpet on the uneven floor, and it was black as pitch, for the windows were heavily shuttered. By groping I found that the walls were lined with boxes and barrels and sacks of some heavy stuff. I could hear my jailers shifting their feet as they stood guard outside.

I sat down in the chilly darkness in a very miserable frame of mind. No doubt the old boy had gone off to collect the two ruffians who had interviewed me yesterday as a roadman. They would remember me, for I was in the same rig. What was a roadman doing twenty miles from his beat, pursued by police? A question or two would put them on the track, and then what chance would I have? I began to think wistfully of the police, now plodding over the hills after my wraith; they at any rate were fellow countrymen and honest fellows.

The three would be back for lunch, so I hadn't more than a couple of hours to wait. It was simply waiting on destruction, for I could see no way out of this mess. I wished that I had Scudder's courage.

The only thing that kept me going was that I was pretty furious. The more I thought of this moorland house and its armed servants and the plot against Britain, the angrier I grew, and then I had to get up and move about. I tried the shutters, but they were locked. From outside came the faint clucking of hens. I groped among the sacks and boxes. I couldn't open the latter and the sacks seemed to be full of things like dog biscuits. But as I circumnavigated the room I felt a handle in the wall which seemed worth investigating.

It was to the door of a wall cupboard—what they call a press in Scotland—and it was locked. I shook it, and then, for want of something better to do, I got some purchase on the handle by looping my belt around it. I put out my strength and presently the thing gave with a crash which I thought would bring in my warders. I waited a moment, and then when no one came I started to explore the cupboard shelves. By luck I found a match in my trouser pocket, and I struck it. It went out in a second, but it showed me that there was a small stock of flashlights on one shelf. I picked up one and found it in working order.

With the light to help I investigated further. There were bottles and cases of queer-smelling stuff, probably chemicals for experiments, and coils of fine copper wire and bolts of a thin oiled silk. There was a box of detonators and a lot of cord for fuses. Then way at the back I found a stout brown cardboard box, and inside it a wooden case. I managed to wrench it open. Within lay half a dozen little gray bricks, each a couple of inches square.

I took one and found that it crumbled easily in my hand. Then I smelled it and put my tongue to it. After that I sat down to think. I hadn't been a mining engineer for nothing. I knew lentonite when I saw it.

With one of these bricks I could blow the house to smithereens. I had used the stuff in Rhodesia and knew its power. But the trouble was that my knowledge wasn't exact. I had forgotten the proper charge and the right way of preparing it, and I wasn't sure about the timing.

But it was a chance. It was also a mighty risk. Against that was absolute black certainty. I reckoned the odds were about five to one in favor of blowing myself up. Still, if I didn't use the stuff, I should very likely be occupying a six-foot hole in the garden by evening. The prospect was dark either way.

Remembrance of little Scudder decided me. I managed to set my teeth and choke back my doubts. Shutting off my mind, I pretended I was doing an experiment as simple as children's fireworks.

I got a detonator and attached it to a couple of feet of fuse. Then I took a quarter of a lentonite brick and buried it near the door, below one of the sacks, in a crack of the floor, fixing the detonator in it. For all I knew, half those boxes might hold dynamite. If the cupboard held such deadly explosives, why not the boxes? In that case there would be a glorious skyward journey for me and the German servants and about an acre of surrounding country. There was also a possibility that the detonation might set off the other bricks in the cupboard. The odds were horrible, but I had to take them.

I ensconced myself just below the windowsill and lit the fuse. Then

I waited. There was dead silence—except for the shuffle of heavy boots in the passage and the peaceful cluck of hens from out of doors. I commended my soul to my Maker, and wondered where I'd end up in five seconds.

A great wave of heat seemed to surge upwards from the floor and hang for a blistering instant in the air. Then the wall opposite me flashed into a golden yellow and dissolved with a rending thunder. Something dropped on me, catching the point of my left shoulder, and then I became unconscious.

My stupor can scarcely have lasted more than a few seconds. I felt myself being choked by fumes, and struggled out of the debris to my feet. Somewhere behind me I felt fresh air. The jambs of the window had fallen, and through the ragged hole smoke was pouring out to the spring noon. Stepping over the broken lintel, I found myself in a yard in a dense and acrid fog. I felt very ill, but could still move, and I staggered blindly away from the house.

There was a small wooden aqueduct leading to a mill at the other side of the yard, and into this I fell. The cool water revived me, and I had just enough wits left to think of escape. Squirming up the aqueduct on slippery green slime, I reached the mill wheel. Then I wriggled through the axle hole into the old mill and tumbled onto a bed of chaff. A nail caught the seat of my trousers, and I left a wisp of tweed behind me.

The mill had been long out of use. Ladders were rotten with age, and in the loft the rats had gnawed holes in the floor. Nausea shook me, and my left shoulder and arm seemed to be stricken with palsy. I looked out of the window and saw fog still hanging over the house and smoke escaping, and I could hear confused cries. But I had no time to linger; this mill was an obvious hiding place, and the search would begin as soon as they found that my body was not in the store-room. From another window I saw that on the far side of the mill there was an old stone dovecote. If I could reach it without leaving tracks, I might find a hiding place, for I argued that my enemies would conclude I had made for open country, and would go searching for me on the moor.

I crawled down the broken ladder and back over the mill floor, scattering chaff behind me to cover my tracks. Where the door hung on broken hinges I peeped out. Between me and the dovecote was a piece of cobbled ground, where no footmarks would show. Also the mill buildings mercifully hid it from any view from the house. I slipped across the cobblestones to the back of the dovecote and prospected a way of ascent.

That was a hard job. My shoulder and arm ached like hell, and I was sick and giddy and always on the verge of falling. But by using gaps in the masonry and a tough ivy root I finally got to the top. There was a little parapet, behind which I found space to lie down. Then I proceeded to go into an old-fashioned swoon.

I woke with a burning head and the sun glaring in my face. The smoke fumes seemed to have dulled my brain, and for a long time I lay motionless. Sounds came to me from the house—men speaking throatily and the throb of an idling car motor. Through a little gap in the parapet I got some perspective of the yard. I saw figures come out—a servant with his head bound up, and then a younger man. They moved towards the mill. One of them caught sight of the wisp of cloth on the nail, and cried out. They both went back to the house and brought two others to look at it. I noticed that all had pistols.

For half an hour they ransacked the mill. I could hear them kicking over barrels and pulling up planking. Then they came out and stood just below the dovecote, arguing fiercely and soundly berating the bandaged servant. I heard them fiddling with the dovecote door, and for one horrid moment I thought they were coming up. But they seemed to think better of it and went back to the house.

All that long blistering afternoon I lay baking on the rooftop. Thirst was my chief torment. And to make it worse I could hear the cool drip of water from the mill aqueduct. I watched the course of the little stream as it came in from the moor, and my fancy followed it up the glen to where it probably issued from an icy fountain fringed with cool ferns and mosses.

I had a fine view of the whole ring of moorland. I saw the car speed away with two occupants, and a man on a hill pony riding east. I judged they were looking for me, and wished them joy in their quest. But I saw something else more interesting. The farmhouse stood almost on the summit of a swell of moorland, and there was no higher point other than the big hills six miles off. The actual summit, as I'd noticed earlier, was feathered with trees—firs mostly, and a few ashes and beeches. On the dovecote I was almost on a level with the treetops and could see what lay beyond. The woods were not solid, but only a ring, and inside was an oval of green turf, for all the world like a big cricket field. I didn't take long to guess what it was. It was an airfield, and a secret one. The place had been most cunningly chosen. Anyone watching a plane descend here would think it had flown over the hill beyond the trees. Since the place was on top of a rise in the middle of a big amphitheater, observers from any direction would conclude it had passed out of view behind the hill. Only someone very close would realize that the plane had not gone over but had landed in the clearing. An observer with a telescope on one of the higher hills might have discovered the truth, but only shepherds went there, and shepherds do not carry spyglasses. Far away I could see a blue line I knew was the sea, and it made me furious to think that our enemies had this secret conning tower from which to rake our waterways.

Then I reflected that if their plane came back, the chances were that I would be discovered. So throughout the afternoon I lay and prayed for the coming of darkness. Finally the sun went down and a twilight haze crept across the moor. The plane was late. Dusk was far advanced when I saw it descend to its home in the woods. Lights twinkled for a bit and there was much coming and going from the house. Then night fell and silence.

Thank God it was a black night. The moon, in its last quarter, would not rise till late. Around nine o'clock, so far as I could judge, I started my descent. I was halfway down when I heard the back door of the house open and saw a lantern gleam against the mill wall. For agonizing minutes I hung from the ivy and prayed. Then the light disappeared, and I dropped as softly as I could onto the hard soil of the yard.

I crawled on my belly in the lee of a stone dike till I reached the fringe of trees surrounding the house. Had I known how, I would have tried to put the plane out of action, but I realized that any attempt to do so would probably be futile. Certain that there would be some kind of defense around the house, I went through the woods on hands and knees, feeling carefully every inch before me. Presently I came on a wire about two feet from the ground. Had I tripped over it, a bell in the house doubtless would have rung and I would have been captured.

A hundred yards farther on I found another wire cunningly placed on the edge of a small stream. Beyond that lay the moor, and soon I was deep in bracken and heather. Around the shoulder of a rise I found the little glen from which the millstream flowed. Minutes later, my face deep in the spring, I was soaking up pints of the blessed water. After that I did not stop till I had put half a dozen miles between me and that accursed farmhouse.

CHAPTER 6

A NATURAL THANKFULNESS for my escape was clouded by my severe bodily discomfort. Those lentonite fumes had fairly poisoned me, and baking for hours on the dovecote hadn't helped. I had a crushing headache. Also my shoulder seemed to be swelling and I had no use of my left arm.

My plan was to find Turnbull's cottage, recover my clothes and Scudder's notebook, and then to make for the main railway and get back to the south. The sooner I got in touch with the Foreign Office man, Sir Walter Bullivant, the better. I didn't see how I could get more proof than I had gotten already.

It was a wonderful starry night, and I had little difficulty with the road. Sir Harry's map had given me the lie of the land, and all I had to do was steer a point or two west of southwest to come to the stream where I'd met the roadman. In all these travels I never did know place names, but I believed this stream to be the upper waters of the river Tweed, and I calculated I must be about eighteen miles distant. That meant I could not get there before morning and so must lie up a day somewhere, for altogether I was no spectacle for God-fearing citizens to see on a highroad. I had no jacket, my trousers were badly torn, my face and hands were black from the explosion, and my eyes felt furiously bloodshot.

Very soon after daybreak I made an attempt to clean up in a brook, and then approached a shepherd's cottage, feeling the need of food. The shepherd was away from home, and his wife was alone, with no neighbor for miles. But she was a decent old body, and a plucky one. I told her that I'd had a fall, and like a true Samaritan she gave me a bowl of milk with a dash of whisky in it, and let me sit for a little by her kitchen fire. I don't know what she took me for— a repentant burglar, perhaps; for when I wanted to pay her and tendered a sovereign, the smallest coin I had, she shook her head and said something about "giving it to them that had a right to it." At this I protested so strongly that I think she believed me honest. She took the money and gave me a warm plaid for it and an old hat of her man's. She showed me how to wrap the plaid around my shoulders, and when I left her cottage I was the living image of the Scotsman you see in illustrations to Burns's poems. But at any rate I was more or less clad.

It was as well, for before midday the weather changed to a drizzle of rain. I found shelter below an overhanging rock, where a drift of dead bracken made a tolerable bed. There I managed to sleep till dusk, waking cramped and wretched, my shoulder gnawing like a toothache. I ate an oatcake and some cheese the old woman had given me, and set out again just before dark.

I pass over the miseries of that night among the wet hills. There were no stars to steer by, and I had to do my best from my memory of the map. Twice I lost my way, and I had some nasty falls into peat bogs. I had about ten miles to go, but my mistakes made it nearer twenty. The last stretch was completed with set teeth and a dizzy head, but by dawn I was knocking at Mr. Turnbull's door.

Turnbull himself opened to me—sober and something more than sober. He was primly dressed in an ancient but well-tended suit of black; he had shaved, he wore a linen collar, and in his left hand he carried a pocket Bible. At first he did not recognize me.

"Whae are ye that comes stravaigin' here on the Sabbath mornin'?" he asked.

I had lost all count of days. So the Sabbath was the reason for his strange decorum.

My head was swimming so wildly that I could not frame a coherent answer. But he recognized me and he saw that I was ill.

"Hae ye got my specs?" he asked.

I took them out of my trouser pocket and gave them to him.

"Ye'll hae come for your jacket and westcoat," he said. "Come in, bye. Losh, man, ye're terrible dune i' the legs. Haud up till I get ye to a chair."

I perceived I was in for a bout of malaria. I had a good deal of the fever in my bones, and the wet night had brought it out. Before I knew it, Mr. Turnbull was helping me off with my clothes, and putting me to bed in one of the two fold-up beds that lined the kitchen walls.

He was a true friend in need, that old roadman. His wife had died years ago, and since his daughter's marriage he lived alone. For the better part of ten days he did all the rough nursing I needed. When the fever had taken its course, and my skin was cool again, I found that the bout had more or less cured my shoulder. But it was a bad go, and though I was out of bed in five days, it took me some time to get back my legs.

He went out each morning, leaving me food for the day, and locking the door behind him; and came in in the evening to sit silent in the chimney corner. Not a soul came near us. He never bothered me with a question. Several times he brought me a two-day-old *Scotsman*, and I noticed that interest in the Portland Place murder seemed to have died down, since there was no mention of it.

One day he produced my belt from a locked drawer. "There's a heap o' siller in't," he said. "Ye'd better count it to see it's a' there."

He never even inquired my name. I asked him if anybody had been around making inquiries subsequent to my spell at road making.

"Aye, there was a man in a motor cawr. He speired whae had ta'en my place that day, and I said he maun be thinkin' o' my gude-brither frae the Cleuch that whiles lent me a haun'. He was a wersh-lookin' soul, and I couldna understand the half o' his English tongue."

I was getting pretty restless those last days, and as soon as I felt myself fit I decided to be off. That was on June 12, and as luck would have it a drover went past that morning taking some cattle to Moffat. He was a man named Hislop, a friend of Turnbull's, and he offered to take me with him.

I made Turnbull accept five pounds for my lodging, and a hard job I had of it. He grew positively rude when I pressed him, grunting something about "ae guid turn deservin' anither," and took the money at last without a thank-you. You would have thought from our leave-taking that we had parted in disgust.

Hislop was a cheery soul, who chattered all the way over the pass and down the sunny vale of Annan. But driving cattle is a slow job, and we took the better part of the day to cover a dozen miles. Had I not had such an anxious heart I should have enjoyed the shining blue weather, the brown hills, and the far, green meadows. But as the fateful fifteenth of June grew near, my difficulties weighed on me.

I got some dinner in a Moffat public house and then walked the two miles to the junction of the main railroad line. The southbound night express for England was due at midnight. When I caught it, the feel of third-class cushions and the smell of stale tobacco cheered me wonderfully. I now felt I was coming to grips with my job.

I was decanted at Crewe in the small hours and had to wait till six for a train to Birmingham. In the afternoon I changed to a local train which journeyed into the deeps of Berkshire, a land of lush water meadows and slow reedy streams. About eight o'clock in the evening, a weary and travel-stained being with a black-and-white plaid over his arm descended at the little station of Artinswell.

The road from the station led through a wood. After Scotland the air smelled heavy and flat, but infinitely sweet, for the chestnuts and lilac bushes were domes of blossom. Presently I came to a bridge, below which a clear, slow stream flowed between snowy beds of water buttercups. The water made a pleasant cool sound in the scented dusk, and I fell to whistling as I looked into its green depths. The tune which came to my lips was "Annie Laurie."

A fisherman came up from the waterside. As he neared me he, too, began to whistle "Annie Laurie." He was a huge man in untidy old flannels and a wide-brimmed hat, with a canvas bag slung on his shoulder. He nodded to me, and I thought I had never seen a shrewder or better-tempered face. He leaned his delicate ten-foot

split-cane rod against the bridge and looked at the water with me.

"Clear, isn't it?" he said pleasantly. "I'd back our Kennet water against any in the land. Look at that fellow! Four pounds, if he's an ounce! But the evening rise is over and you can't tempt 'em."

"I don't see him," I said.

"Look! There! A yard from the reeds, just above that rapid."

"I've got him now. You'd swear he was a black stone."

"So," he said, and whistled another bar of "Annie Laurie." "Twisden's the name, isn't it?" he added, his eyes still fixed on the stream.

"No," I said, forgetting my alias. "I mean yes."

"It's a wise conspirator that knows his own name," he observed, grinning broadly.

I straightened and looked at him, at his square cleft jaw and broad, lined brow and the firm folds of cheek, and began to think that here at last was an ally worth having.

Suddenly he frowned. "I call it disgraceful," he said, raising his voice. "Disgraceful that an ablebodied man like you should dare to beg. You can get a meal from my kitchen, but you'll get no money from me."

A dogcart was passing, driven by a young man who raised his whip to salute the fisherman. When he had gone, my ally picked up his rod.

"That's my house," he said, pointing to a white gate a hundred yards on. "Wait five minutes and then go round to the back door." And with that he left.

I found a pretty cottage with a lawn and a perfect jungle of guelder rose and lilac flanking the path. The back door stood open and a grave butler awaited me.

"This way, sir," he said, and he led me up a back staircase to a pleasant bedroom overlooking the river. There I found a complete outfit laid out, a suit, shirt, tie, shaving things, and hairbrushes, even a pair of shoes. "Sir Walter thought as how these would fit you, sir," said the butler. "He keeps some clothes 'ere, for he comes regular on the weekends. There's a bathroom next door, and I've prepared a 'ot bath. Dinner in 'alf an hour, sir. You'll 'ear the gong."

When he withdrew I looked at myself in the mirror and saw a wild, haggard fellow with a fortnight's ragged beard and dust in ears and eyes. I made a fine tramp, and here I was ushered by a prim butler into this house of gracious ease. And the best of it was that they did not even know my name. Resolving to take the gifts the gods provided, I shaved and bathed luxuriously, and then dressed, the clothes fitting me not so badly. By the time I had finished, the mirror showed a not unpersonable young man.

Sir Walter awaited me in a dusky dining room, where a little round table was lit with candles. The sight of him—so respectable and secure, the embodiment of law and all the conventions—took me aback and made me feel an interloper.

"I am more obliged to you than I can say, but I'm bound to make things clear," I said. "I'm an innocent man, but I'm wanted by the police. I've got to tell you this, and I won't be surprised if you kick me out."

He smiled. "That's all right. Don't let it interfere with your appetite. We can talk about these things after dinner."

I never ate a meal with greater relish. We drank a good champagne and had some uncommon fine port afterwards. I told Sir Walter about tiger fish in the Zambezi that bite off your fingers if you give them a chance, and we discussed sport up and down the globe, for he had hunted a bit in his day.

We went to his study for coffee, a jolly room full of books and trophies and untidiness and comfort. Then when the coffee cups were cleared away and our cigars lighted, my host swung his long legs over the side of his chair.

"I've obeyed Harry's instructions," he said, "and the bribe he offered was that you would tell me something to wake me up. I'm ready, Mr. Hannay." I noticed with a start that he called me by my proper name.

I began at the very beginning. I told about the night I had come back to find Scudder gibbering on my doorstep. I told him all Scudder had told me about Karolides and the Foreign Office conference, and that made him purse his lips and grin. Then I got to the murder, and he grew solemn again. He heard about the milkman and my time in Galloway, and my deciphering Scudder's notes at the inn.

"You've got them here?" he asked sharply, and drew a long breath when I whipped the little book from my pocket.

I said nothing of the contents. Then I described my meeting with Sir Harry, and the speeches at the hall. At that he laughed uproariously.

"Harry talked nonsense, did he? I quite believe it, though he's as good a chap as ever breathed. Go on, Mr. Hannay."

My day as roadman excited him. He made me describe the two fellows in the car very closely, and seemed to be raking back in his memory. He grew merry again when he heard of the fate of that ass, Jopley. But the old man in the moorland farmhouse worried him, and twice I had to describe his appearance.

"Bland and bald-headed and hooded his eyes like a bird . . . He sounds a sinister wildfowl! And you dynamited his house, after he had saved you from the police? Spirited piece of work, that!"

Presently I reached the end of my wanderings. He got up slowly and looked down at me.

"You may dismiss the police from your mind," he said. "You're in no danger from the law of this land."

"Have they got the murderer?" I cried.

"No. But for the last fortnight they have dropped you from their list of possibles."

"Why?" I asked in amazement.

"Principally because I received a letter from Scudder. I knew something of the man. He'd done several jobs for me. He was half crank, half genius, but wholly honest. His trouble was his partiality for playing a lone hand. It made him pretty well useless in any secret service—a pity, for he had uncommon gifts. I had a letter from him on the thirty-first of May."

"But he had been dead a week by then."

"It was written and posted on the twenty-third. He evidently did not anticipate dying so soon. His communications usually took a week to reach me, for they were sent undercover to Spain and then to Newcastle. He had a mania, you know, for concealing his tracks."

"What did he say?" I stammered.

"Nothing much. Merely that he was in danger, but had found shelter with a good friend, and that I would hear from him before the fifteenth of June. He gave me no address, but said he was living near Portland Place. I think his object was to clear you if anything happened. When I got it I went to Scotland Yard, went over the details of the inquest, and concluded that you were the friend. We made inquiries about you, Mr. Hannay, and found you were respectable. I thought I knew the motives for your disappearance—not only the police, the other one, too—and when I got Harry's scrawl I guessed at the rest. I have been expecting you anytime this past week. And now—let us have the notebook."

It took us a good hour to work through it. I explained the cipher, and he was quick to pick it up. He amended my reading on several points, but I had been fairly correct, on the whole. His face was very grave before he had finished, and he sat silent for a while.

"I don't know what to make of it," he said at last. "He is right about one thing—what is going to happen the day after tomorrow, on June fifteenth. How the devil can it have got known? That's ugly enough in itself. But all this about war and the Black Stone—it reads like some wild melodrama. If only I had more confidence in Scudder's judgment! The trouble is that he was romantic. He always wanted a story to be better than God meant it to be."

He stopped and I waited for him to continue.

"The Black Stone," he repeated. *"Der schwarze Stein.* And all this stuff about Karolides. That's the weak part of the tale, for I happen to know that Karolides is likely to outlast us both. There is no state in Europe that wants him gone. Frankly, Hannay, I don't believe that part of Scudder's story. There's some nasty business afoot, and he found out too much and lost his life over it. But I am ready to swear that it's ordinary spy work. A certain great European power makes a hobby of her spy system, and since she pays by piecework her blackguards are not likely to stick at a murder or two. They want our naval dispositions for their collection; but the dispositions will be pigeonholed—nothing more."

Just then the butler entered the room. "There's a call from London, Sir Walter. Mr. 'Eath wants to speak to you personally."

My host went off to the telephone.

He returned in five minutes with a white face. "I apologize to the shade of Scudder," he said. "Karolides was shot dead this evening at a few minutes after seven!"

CHAPTER 7

NEXT MORNING, AFTER eight hours of blessed sleep, I came down to breakfast to find Sir Walter decoding a telegram in the midst of muffins and marmalade. His fresh rosiness of yesterday seemed a little tarnished.

"I had a busy hour on the telephone after you went to bed," he said. "I got my chief to speak to the First Sea Lord and the war secretary, and they are bringing General Royer, the French assistant chief of state, over a day sooner. This wire clinches it. He will be in London at five today. Odd that the code word for a *sous-chef d'état-major* should be Porker."

He directed me to the hot dishes and went on.

"Not that I think it will do much good. If your friends were clever enough to find out the first arrangement, they are clever enough to discover any change. I would give my head to know where the leak is.

We believed there were only five men in England who knew about Royer's visit." While I ate he continued to talk, taking me, to my surprise, into his full confidence.

"Can't the naval dispositions be changed?" I asked.

"They could," he said. "But we want to avoid that if possible. They are the result of immense thought, and no alteration would be as good. Besides, on one or two points change is simply impossible. Still, perhaps something could be done, if it were absolutely necessary. But you see the difficulty, Hannay. Our enemies are not going to be such fools as to pick Royer's pocket or any childish game like that. They know that would put us on our guard and cause us to alter arrangements. Their aim is to get the details without any of us knowing, so that Royer will go back to Paris in the belief that the whole business is still deadly secret."

"Then we must stick by the Frenchman's side till he is home again," I said. "If they thought they could get the information in Paris, they would try there. So it means that they have some scheme on foot in London."

"Royer dines with my chief, and then comes to my house in London, where four people will see him—Whittaker from the Admiralty, myself, Sir Arthur Drew, and General Winstanley. The First Sea Lord is ill. At my house Royer will get a certain document from Whittaker, and after that he will be motored to Portsmouth, where a destroyer will take him to Le Havre. His journey is too important for the ordinary boat train. He will be attended every moment till he is safe back on French soil. The same with Whittaker till he meets Royer. That is the best we can do, and it's hard to see how there can be any miscarriage. But I don't mind admitting that I'm nervous. This murder of Karolides will play the deuce in the chancelleries of Europe."

After breakfast I drove with Sir Walter to town. It was a soft breathless June morning with a promise of sultriness later. We swung through little towns with freshly watered streets, and past the summer gardens of the Thames valley, and landed at his house in Queen Anne's Gate punctually at half past eleven.

The first thing Sir Walter then did was to take me around to Scotland Yard. There we saw a prim gentleman with a clean-shaven lawyer's face.

"I've brought you the Portland Place murderer," was Sir Walter's introduction.

The reply was a wry smile. "It would have been a welcome present, Bullivant. This, I presume, is Mr. Hannay, who for some days greatly interested my department."

"Mr. Hannay will interest it again. He has much to tell you, but for certain grave reasons his tale must wait twenty-four hours. Then, I can promise you, you will be entertained and edified. I want you to assure Mr. Hannay that he will suffer no further inconvenience."

Assurance was promptly given. "You can take up your life where you left off," I was told. "Your flat is waiting for you, and your man is still there. As you were never publicly accused, we considered that there was no need of a public exculpation. But on that, of course, you must please yourself."

"We may want your assistance later on, MacGillivray," Sir Walter said as we left.

Then he turned me loose.

"Come and see me tomorrow, Hannay. I needn't tell you to keep deadly quiet and lie low. If one of your Black Stone friends sees you, there might be trouble."

I felt curiously at loose ends. At first it was pleasant to be a free man, able to go where I wanted. I went to the Savoy and carefully ordered a very good luncheon, and then smoked the best cigar the house could provide. But I still felt nervous whenever anybody looked at me.

After that I took a taxi and drove several miles north of London. I walked back through fields and lines of villas and then slums and mean streets, and it took me nearly two hours. All the while my restlessness was growing worse. Great things, tremendous things, were happening or about to happen. Royer would be landing at Dover, Sir Walter would be making plans with the few people in England who shared the secret. And somewhere in the darkness the Black Stone was working. I felt a sense of danger and impending calamity, and I had the curious feeling, too, that I alone could avert it. But I was out of the game now. How could it be otherwise? Cabinet ministers and Admiralty lords and generals were not likely to admit me to their councils.

I actually began to wish that I could run into one of my enemies. I wanted enormously to have a vulgar fight, where I could hit out and flatten someone. I was rapidly getting into a very bad temper.

I didn't feel like going back to my flat. Instead I thought I would put it off till morning and go to a hotel for the night.

My irritation lasted through dinner at a restaurant in Jermyn Street. No longer hungry, I let several courses pass untasted, and the best part of a bottle of Burgundy did nothing to cheer me. An abominable restlessness possessed me. I felt that somehow I was needed to help this business through—that without me it would all go to blazes. I told myself it was sheer, silly conceit, that four or five of the cleverest people living, with all the might of Britain behind them, had the job in hand. Yet I couldn't be convinced. It seemed as if a voice kept speaking in my ear, telling me to be up and doing.

The upshot was that about half past nine I made up my mind to go to Queen Anne's Gate. When I entered that quiet thoroughfare it seemed deserted. But outside Sir Walter's house were three or four cars. I walked briskly up to the door. I had scarcely rung before it opened.

"I must see Sir Walter," I said to the butler. "My business is desperately important."

That butler was a great man. Without moving a muscle he held the door open, and then shut it behind me. "Sir Walter is engaged, sir, and I have orders to admit no one. Perhaps you will wait."

The house was old-fashioned, with a wide hall and rooms on both sides of it. At the far end was an alcove with a telephone and a couple of chairs, and there I was offered a seat.

Not long afterwards the butler admitted another visitor.

While he was taking off his coat I saw who it was. You couldn't open a newspaper or a magazine without seeing that face—the gray beard cut like a spade, the firm fighting mouth, the blunt square nose. I recognized the First Sea Lord, Lord Alloa.

He passed my alcove and was ushered into a room at the back of the hall. As the door opened I could hear low voices. Then it shut, and I was left alone again.

For twenty minutes I sat there, wondering what I was to do next. I was still perfectly convinced that I was needed, but had no idea when or how. I kept looking at my watch, and as the time crept on to half past ten I began to think that the conference must soon end. In a quarter of an hour Royer should be speeding along the road to Portsmouth.

Then I heard a bell ring and the butler appeared. The door of the back room opened, and the First Sea Lord came out. He walked past me, and in passing he glanced in my direction. For a second we looked each other straight in the face.

It was for only a second, but it was long enough to make my heart jump. I had never seen the great man before. He had never seen me. Yet in that fraction of time something sprang into his eyes, and that something was recognition. You can't mistake it. It is a flicker, a spark of light, a minute shade of difference. It came involuntarily, and in a moment it died, and he walked on. In a maze of wild fancies I heard the street door close behind him.

Quickly, I picked up the telephone book and looked up the number of his house. We were connected at once and a servant's voice answered.

"Is his lordship at home?" I asked.

"His lordship returned half an hour ago," said the voice, "and has gone to bed. He is not very well. Will you leave a message, sir?"

I rang off numbly. So my part in this business was not yet ended.

Not a moment could be lost. I marched boldly to the door of that back room and entered without knocking. Five surprised faces looked up from a round table. There was Sir Walter, and Drew, the war minister, whom I knew from photographs. There was a slim, elderly man, who was probably Whittaker, the Admiralty official, and General Winstanley, conspicuous from the long scar on his forehead. Lastly there was a short stout man with an iron-gray mustache and bushy eyebrows.

Sir Walter's face showed surprise and annoyance.

"This is Mr. Hannay, of whom I have spoken," he said to the company. "I'm afraid, Hannay, this visit is ill-timed."

"That remains to be seen, sir," I said. "For God's sake, gentlemen, tell me who went out a minute ago?"

"Lord Alloa," Sir Walter said, reddening with anger.

"No, it was not!" I cried. "It was someone made up to look like him. It was someone who recognized me, someone I have seen in the last month. He had scarcely left the doorstep when I rang up Lord

Alloa's house and was told he had come in half an hour before and had gone to bed."

"Who—who—" someone stammered.

"The Black Stone," I said, and I sat down in a chair and looked around at five badly scared gentlemen.

"NONSENSE!" SAID THE official from the Admiralty.

Sir Walter got up and left the room, while we stared blankly at the table. He came back in ten minutes with a long face. "I have spoken to Alloa," he said. "Had him out of bed—very grumpy. He went straight home after Mulross's dinner."

"But it's madness," broke in General Winstanley. "Do you mean to tell me that an impostor sat here beside me for half an hour, and that I didn't detect him?"

"You were too interested in other things to use your eyes," I said. "You took him for granted. Had it been anybody else you might have looked more closely, but it was natural for him to be here."

Then the short stout man, the Frenchman, spoke, very slowly and in good English.

"The young man is right. His psychology is good."

"But I don't see," went on Winstanley. "Their object was to get these naval dispositions without our knowing it. Well, it only required one of us to mention later to Alloa our meeting tonight for the whole fraud to be exposed."

Sir Walter laughed dryly. "The selection of Alloa shows their acumen. Which of us was likely to speak to him about tonight? Or was he likely to open the subject?" I remembered the First Sea Lord's reputation for taciturnity and shortness of temper.

"The thing that puzzles me," said the general, "is what good did his visit do? He could not carry away pages of figures and names in his head."

"That is not difficult," the Frenchman replied. "A good spy is trained to have a photographic memory. You noticed he said nothing, but went through these papers again and again. I think we may assume that he has every detail stamped on his mind. When I was younger I could do the same trick."

"Well, I suppose there is nothing for it but to change the plans," said Sir Walter ruefully.

Whittaker was looking grim. "I can't speak with absolute assurance, but I'm nearly certain we can't make any serious change unless we alter the geography of England."

"Another thing must be said." It was Royer who spoke. "I talked freely when that man was here. I told something of the military plans of my government. I was permitted to say so much, but that information will be worth millions to our enemies. No, my friends, I see no other way. The man who came here and his confederates must be taken and taken at once."

"Good God!" I cried. "And we have not a rag of a clue."

"Besides," said Whittaker, "there is the post. By this time the news will be on its way."

"No," said the Frenchman. "You do not understand the habits of the spy. He receives personally his reward, and delivers personally his intelligence. There is still a chance, *mes amis*. These men will have to cross the sea. Ships must be searched and ports watched. Believe me, the need is desperate."

Royer's grave good sense seemed to pull us together. But I saw no hope in any face, and I felt none myself. How within a dozen hours were we to lay hands on the three cleverest rogues in Europe?

Then suddenly I had an inspiration.

"Where is Scudder's book?" I asked Sir Walter. "Quick, man, I remember something in it."

He unlocked a desk drawer and gave it to me.

I found the place. " 'Thirty-nine steps'," I read, and again aloud, " 'Thirty-nine steps—I counted them; high tide ten seventeen p.m.' "

The Admiralty man was looking at me as if I had gone mad.

"Don't you see, we do have a clue!" I cried. "Scudder knew where these fellows are lying low—he knew where they plan to leave the country from; though he kept the name to himself. It is from someplace where high tide is at ten seventeen, and tomorrow is the day."

"They may have gone tonight," someone said.

"Not according to Scudder, and he's been right so far. They are working to a plan. Where the devil can I get a book of tide tables?"

Whittaker stood up. "It's a chance," he said. "Let's go to the Admiralty."

We got into two of the waiting cars—all but Sir Walter, who went to Scotland Yard—to "mobilize MacGillivray," he said.

WE MARCHED THROUGH empty corridors and big bare rooms where charwomen were busy, till we reached a little room lined with books and maps. A clerk was unearthed who brought us the Admiralty *Tide Tables*. I sat at a desk surrounded by the others. Somehow or other I had turned out to be in charge.

It was no good. There were hundreds of entries, and as far as I could see 10:17 might cover fifty places. We had to find some way to narrow possibilities. I put my head in my hands and thought. What

did Scudder mean by steps? Dock steps? But if he had meant that, I didn't think he would have mentioned the number. It must be some-place where there were several staircases and one marked out from the others by having thirty-nine steps.

Then I had a sudden thought and hunted up ship sailings. No boat left for the Continent at 10:17 p.m.

Why was high tide important? If it was a harbor, it must be some little place where the tide mattered, or else it was a heavy-draft boat. But no regular ship sailed at that hour, and somehow I didn't think they would travel by a big boat from a regular harbor. It had to be a little harbor where the tide did matter, or perhaps no harbor at all.

But if it was a little port, I couldn't see what the steps signified.

There were no sets of staircases at any harbor I had ever seen. It must be someplace which a particular staircase identified, and where the tide was full at 10:17. On the whole, it seemed to me that the place must be a bit of open coast. But the staircases kept puzzling me.

Then I gave the problem wider consideration. Whereabouts would a man be likely to leave for Germany, a man in a hurry who wanted a secret passage? Not from any of the big harbors. And not from the Channel or the west coast or the north of Scotland, for he was starting from London. I measured the distance on the map, and tried to put myself in the enemy's shoes. I would try for Ostend or Antwerp or Rotterdam and I would sail from somewhere on the east coast between Cromer and Dover.

All this was very loose guessing. I am no Sherlock Holmes. But I have always had a kind of instinct for puzzles. I have always used my brains as far as they went, and then after they came to a blank wall I have guessed, and usually my guesses have been fairly right.

So I set out all my conclusions on a piece of Admiralty paper.

Fairly Certain

(1) Place where there are several sets of stairs; one distinguished by having 39 steps.

(2) Full tide at 10:17 p.m. Leaving shore only possible at full tide.

(3) Steps not dock steps and so place probably not harbor.

(4) No regular ship at 10:17. Means of transport must be tramp (unlikely), yacht, or fishing boat.

There my reasoning stopped. I made another list, which I headed Guessed, but I was just as sure of the one as the other.

Guessed

(1) Place not harbor but open coast.

(2) Boat small—trawler, yacht, or launch.

(3) Place somewhere on east coast between Cromer and Dover.

It struck me as odd that I should be sitting at that desk with a Cabinet minister, a field marshal, two high government officials, and a French general watching me, while from the scribble of a dead man I was trying to drag a secret which meant life or death for us.

Sir Walter had joined us, and presently MacGillivray arrived. He had sent out instructions to watch the ports and railway stations for the three men I had described to Sir Walter—the old man who could hood his eyes like a hawk, the lean, dark younger man, and his sleek, smiling companion. Not that he or anybody else thought that that would do much good.

"Here's the most I can make of it," I said. "We have got to find a place where there are several staircases down to the beach, one of which has thirty-nine steps. I think it's a piece of open coast with biggish cliffs somewhere between the Wash and the Channel. Also it's a place where full tide is at ten seventeen tomorrow night."

Then an idea struck me. "Is there no inspector of coast guards or some fellow like that who knows the east coast?"

Whittaker said there was and that he lived in Clapham. He went off in a car to fetch him, and the rest of us sat about the little room. Finally at around one in the morning the coastguardsman arrived. The war minister cross-examined him.

"What places do you know on the east coast where there are cliffs, and where several sets of steps run down to the beach?"

The old fellow thought for a bit. "What kind of steps do you mean, sir? There are plenty of places with roads cut down through the cliffs, and most roads have a step or two in them. Or do you mean regular staircases—all steps, so to speak?"

Sir Arthur looked towards me. "We mean regular staircases," I said.

He reflected a minute or two. "I don't know that I can think of any. Wait a second. There's a place in Norfolk—Brattlesham—beside a golf course, where there are a couple of staircases to let the players get a lost ball."

"That's not it," I said.

"Then there are plenty of marine parades, if that's what you mean. Every seaside resort has them."

I shook my head. "It's got to be more secluded than that," I said.

"Well, gentlemen, I can't think of anywhere else. Of course, there's the Ruff—"

"What's that?" I asked.

"The big chalk headland in Kent, close to Bradgate. It's got a lot of villas on the top, and some of the houses have staircases down to a private beach. It's a very high-toned sort of place, and the residents like to keep to themselves."

I tore open the *Tide Tables* and found Bradgate. High tide there was at 10:27 p.m. on June 15.

"How can I find out what the tide is at the Ruff?" I cried excitedly.

"I can tell you that, sir," said the coastguardsman. "I once was lent a house there in this very month, and I used to go deep-sea fishing. The tide's ten minutes before Bradgate."

I closed the book and looked around.

"If one of those staircases has thirty-nine steps, I think we have solved the mystery, gentlemen," I said. "I want the loan of your car, Sir Walter, and a road map. If Mr. MacGillivray will spare me ten minutes, I think we can prepare something for tomorrow."

It was ridiculous of me to take charge like this, but they didn't seem to mind. After all, I had been in the show from the start. Besides, I was used to rough jobs, and they were too clever not to know it.

It was General Royer who gave me my commission.

"I for one," he said, "am content to leave the matter in Mr. Hannay's hands."

By half past three I was tearing past the moonlit hedgerows of Kent with MacGillivray's best man on the seat beside me.

CHAPTER 8

A PINK AND BLUE June morning found me at Bradgate looking from the Griffin Hotel over a smooth sea to the lightship on the Cock sands. A couple of miles farther south and much nearer shore a small destroyer was anchored. Scaife, MacGillivray's man, who had been in the navy, knew the boat. He told me her name and her commander's, and I sent off a wire to Sir Walter.

After breakfast, Scaife got from a house agent a key to the gates of the staircases on the Ruff. I walked with him along the sands, and sat down in a nook of the cliffs while he investigated the staircases. The place at this hour was quite deserted, and I saw nothing but sea gulls.

The job took him more than an hour, and when I finally saw him coming towards me, conning a bit of paper, my heart was in my mouth.

He read aloud the number of steps in the different stairs. "Thirty-four, thirty-five, thirty-nine, forty-two, forty-seven, and twenty-one," where the cliffs grew lower. I almost shouted.

We hurried back to the town and sent a wire to MacGillivray. I needed half a dozen men to be divided among different specified hotels. Then Scaife set out to prospect the house at the head of the thirty-nine steps.

He came back with news that both puzzled and reassured me. The house was called Trafalgar Lodge, and belonged to an old gentleman called Appleton—a retired stockbroker, the house agent said. Mr. Appleton was there a good deal in the summertime, and was in residence now—had been for the better part of a week. Scaife could pick up very little information about him, except that he was a decent old boy who paid his bills regularly and was always good for a fiver for a local charity. Scaife had penetrated to the back door of the house, pretending he was a salesman of sewing machines. Three servants were kept, a cook and two maids. The cook was not given to gossiping, and soon shut the door in his face, but Scaife said he was positive she knew nothing. Next door a new house was being built, which would give good cover for observation. The villa on the other side was to let, and its garden was rough and shrubby.

I borrowed Scaife's telescope, and before lunch went for a walk along the Ruff. I kept well behind the villas, and found a good observation point on the edge of the golf course. There I had a view of the line of turf along the cliff top, with seats placed at intervals and little square plots, railed in and planted with bushes, where the staircases descended to the beach. I saw Trafalgar Lodge very plainly, a red brick villa with a veranda, a tennis court behind, and in front the ordinary seaside garden full of marguerites and scraggy geraniums. An enormous Union Jack hung limply in the still air from a great flagstaff.

Presently I observed someone leave the house and saunter along the cliff. When I got my glasses on him I saw it was an old man, wearing white trousers, a blue serge jacket and a straw hat. He carried field glasses and a newspaper, and sat down on one of the iron seats to read. At intervals he would lay down the paper and turn his glasses on the sea. He looked for a long time at the destroyer. I watched him for half an hour, till he got up and went back to the house, probably for his lunch. Then I returned to the hotel for mine.

I wasn't feeling very confident. This decent commonplace villa was not what I had expected. The old man might be he of that horrible moorland farm, or he might not. He was exactly the kind of satisfied old bird you find in every suburb and every resort.

But after lunch as I sat on the hotel porch I saw something I had hoped for. A yacht, of about a hundred and fifty tons, came up from the south and dropped anchor opposite the Ruff. So Scaife and I went down to the harbor and hired a boatman for an afternoon's fishing.

We spent a peaceful afternoon, catching between us about twenty pounds of cod, and out in that dancing blue sea I took a cheerier view of things. At four o'clock, when we had fished enough, I made the boatman row us around the yacht, which lay like a delicate white bird, ready at a moment to flee. Scaife said she must be a fast boat from her build, and that she was pretty heavily engined.

Her name was *Ariadne*, as I discovered from the cap of one of the men who was polishing brasswork. I spoke to him and got an answer in the soft dialect of Essex. Another hand that came along also passed the time of day in an unmistakably English tongue. Our boatman had an argument with one of them about the weather, and for a few minutes we lay on our oars close to the bow.

Then the men suddenly disregarded us and bent their heads to their work as an officer came along the deck. He was a pleasant, clean-looking young fellow, and he put a question to us about our fishing in very good English. But there could be no doubt about him. His close-cropped head and the cut of his collar and tie never came out of England.

That did something to reassure me, but as we rowed back to Bradgate my obstinate doubts would not be dismissed. The thing that worried me was that my enemies knew that I had gotten my knowledge from Scudder. And it was Scudder who had given me the clue to this place. Now if the enemy thought that Scudder had this clue, why wouldn't they change their plans? Too much depended on their success for them to take any risks. The important question was how much they figured Scudder had known. If they suspected that someone was on their track, they would be fools not to run for cover. I wondered if the false Lord Alloa had noticed that I had recognized him. I did not think he had, and to that I clung. But the whole business had never seemed so difficult as that afternoon, when by all calculations I should have been rejoicing in assured success.

In the hotel I met the commander of the destroyer, to whom Scaife introduced me and with whom I had a few words. Then I decided to put in an hour or two watching Trafalgar Lodge.

I found a spot farther up the hill in the garden of the empty house. From there I had a full view of the court, on which two figures were having a game of tennis. One was the old man, whom I had already seen; the other was a younger fellow. They played with tremendous zest, and a more innocent spectacle would have been hard to conceive. They shouted and laughed, and stopped for drinks when a maid brought out two tankards on a tray. I rubbed my eyes and asked myself if I was not the biggest fool on earth. Mystery and darkness had hung about the men who hunted me over the Scottish moors. It had been easy to connect them with the knife that pinned Scudder to the floor, and with designs on the world's peace. But here were two guileless citizens, taking their innocuous exercise, soon to go indoors to a humdrum dinner, where they would talk of market prices and the latest cricket scores. I had been making a net to catch vultures and falcons. Instead, two plump thrushes had blundered into it.

Presently a third figure arrived, a young man carrying a golf bag. He strolled around to the tennis court and was welcomed riotously by the players. Evidently they were chaffing him, and their chaff sounded horribly English. Then the second man, mopping his brow with a handkerchief, announced that he must have a bath. I heard his very words—"I've got into a proper lather," he said. "This will bring down my weight and my handicap, Bob. I'll take you on tomorrow and give you a stroke a hole." You couldn't find anything much more English than that.

They all went into the house, and left me feeling a precious idiot, barking up the wrong tree. Were they acting? But if so, where was their audience? They didn't know I was sitting thirty yards away in a rhododendron. It was simply impossible to believe that these three hearty fellows were anything but what they seemed—three ordinary, innocent, suburban Englishmen.

And yet there were three of them; and one was old, and one was plump, and one was lean and dark; and their house chimed in with Scudder's notes; and half a mile off lay a yacht with at least one German officer. I thought of Karolides lying dead and all Europe trembling on the edge of an earthquake, and the men I had left behind me in London, who were waiting anxiously on the events of the next few hours. There was no doubt that hell was afoot somewhere. The Black Stone had won, and if it survived this June night it would bank its winnings.

There seemed only one thing to do—go forward as if I had no doubts, and if I was going to make a fool of myself, to do it handsomely. Never in my life have I faced a job with greater disinclination. I would rather have faced a charging lion with a popgun than enter the happy home of three cheerful Englishmen and tell them that their game was up and hear them laugh!

But suddenly I remembered something else that my old Rhodesian scout, Peter Pienaar, had once told me. He was the best scout I ever knew, and before he turned respectable he had often been on the windy side of the law. Peter had had a theory about disguises which had impressed me. He had said that, barring absolute certainties like fingerprints, mere physical traits were of very little use for identification if the fugitive really knew his business. He laughed at dyed hair and false beards and such childish follies. The only thing that mattered was what Peter called atmosphere. If a man could get into different surroundings from those in which he had been first observed, and—more important—really play up to these surroundings, behaving as if he had never been out of them, he could puzzle the cleverest detectives on earth. And he used to tell a story of how he once borrowed a black jacket and went to church and shared the same hymnbook with a man who was looking for him. If that man had seen him in decent company before, he would have recognized him; but he had only seen him snuffing the lights in a public house with a revolver.

Recollecting Peter's theory gave me the first real comfort I had had that day. A fool tries to look different; a clever man looks the same and *is* different.

Again, there was that other maxim of Peter's, which had helped me when I had been a roadman. "If you are playing a part, you will never keep it up unless you convince yourself that you are *it*." That would explain the game of tennis. Those chaps didn't need to act; they just turned a handle and slipped into another life, which came as naturally to them as the first. It sounds a platitude, but Peter used to say that it was the big secret of all famous criminals.

It was now near eight o'clock. I went back and saw Scaife to give him his instructions. I arranged with him how to place his men, and then I went for a walk, not feeling up to any dinner. I went around the deserted golf course, and then to a point on the cliffs farther north, beyond the line of the villas. On the little, newly made roads I met people coming back from tennis and the beach, and out at sea in the blue dusk I saw lights appear on the *Ariadne* and on the destroyer away to the south. Beyond the Cock sands I could see the bigger lights of ships making for the Thames. The whole scene was so peaceful and ordinary that my spirits sank more every second. It took all my resolution to stroll towards Trafalgar Lodge about half past nine. Scaife's men would be posted now, but there was no sign of them. The villa stood as open as a marketplace for anybody to observe. A three-foot railing separated it from the cliff road; the sound of voices revealed where its occupants were finishing dinner. Everything was as public and aboveboard as a charity bazaar. Feeling the greatest fool on earth, I opened the gate and rang the bell.

A man of my sort, who has traveled about the world in rough places, gets on perfectly well with two classes, what one might call the upper and the lower. He understands them and they understand him. I was at home with tramps and roadmen, and I was sufficiently at my ease with people like Sir Walter. But what fellows like me don't understand is the great comfortable, middle-class world, the people that live in villas and suburbs. He doesn't understand them, and he is as shy of them as of a black mamba. When a trim maid opened the door, I could hardly find my voice.

I asked for Mr. Appleton and was ushered in. My plan had been to walk straight into the dining room and by a sudden appearance wake in the men that start of recognition which would confirm my theory. But when I found myself in that neat hall, the place mastered me. There were the golf clubs and tennis rackets, the straw hats and walking sticks which you will find in ten thousand British homes. There was a grandfather clock ticking, and some polished brass warming pans on the walls, and a barometer, and a print of Chiltern winning the St. Leger. The place was as orthodox as an Anglican church. When the maid asked for my name I gave it automatically, and was shown into a study off the hall. That room was even worse. I hadn't time to examine it, but I could see some framed group photographs above the mantelpiece and I could have sworn they were English public school or college. I had only the one glance, for I then managed to gather my wits and go after the maid. But I was too late. She had already entered the dining room and given my name, and I had missed the chance of seeing how the three took it.

When I walked into the room the old man at the head of the table had risen and turned around to meet me. He was in evening dress—black tie, as was the other whom I called in my own mind the plump one. The third, the thin dark fellow, wore a blue serge suit and a soft white collar and the colors of some club or school.

The old man's manner was perfect. "Mr. Hannay?" he said hesitatingly. "Did you wish to see me? One moment, you fellows, and I'll rejoin you. We had better go to the study."

Though I hadn't an ounce of confidence in me, I forced myself to play the game. I pulled up a chair and sat down at the table.

"I think we have met before," I said, "and I guess you know my business."

The light in the room was dim, but insofar as I could see their faces they played their parts very well.

"Maybe, maybe," said the old man, seemingly mystified. "I haven't a very good memory. I'm afraid you must tell me your errand, for I really don't know it."

"Well, then," I said, and all the time I seemed to myself to be talking pure foolishness, "I have come to tell you that the game's up. I have here a warrant for the arrest of you three gentlemen."

"Arrest," said the old man, and he looked really shocked. "Arrest! Good God, what for?"

"For the murder of Franklin Scudder, in London, on the twenty-third day of last month."

"I never heard the name before," said the old man in a dazed voice.

One of the others spoke up. "That was the Portland Place murder. I read about it. Good heavens, you must be mad, sir! Where do you come from?"

"Scotland Yard," I said.

For a minute there was utter silence. The old man was fumbling with a nut on his plate, the very model of innocent bewilderment. Then the plump one spoke. He stammered a little, like a man picking his words.

"Don't get flustered, Uncle," he said. "It is all a ridiculous mistake, but we can easily set it right. It won't be hard to prove our innocence. I can show that I was out of the country on the twenty-third of May, and Bob was in a hospital. You were in London, but you can explain what you were doing."

"Right, Percy! Of course that's easy enough. The twenty-third! That was the day after Agatha's wedding. Let me see. What was I doing? I came up in the morning from Woking, and lunched at the club with Charlie Symons. Then— Oh, yes, I dined with the Fishmongers. I remember the punch didn't agree with me, and I was seedy next morning."

"I think, sir," said the young man, addressing me respectfully, "you will see you are mistaken. We want to assist the law like all Englishmen, and we don't want Scotland Yard to be making fools of themselves. That's so, Uncle?"

"Certainly, Bob." The old fellow seemed to be recovering his voice. "Certainly, we'll do anything in our power to assist the authorities. But—but this is a bit too much."

"How Nellie will chuckle," said the plump man. "She always said that you would die of boredom because nothing ever happened to you." And he began to laugh.

"By Jove, yes. Just think of it! What a story to tell at the club. Really, Mr. Hannay, I suppose I should be angry, but it's too funny! I almost forgive you the fright you gave me!"

It couldn't be acting, it was too confoundedly genuine. My heart went into my boots. I wanted to apologize and clear out. But I told myself I must see it through. The light from the dinner-table candles was not very good, and to cover my confusion I got up, walked to the door, and switched on the electric lights. The sudden glare made them blink, and I stood scanning the three faces.

Well, I made nothing of it. One was old and bald, one was stout, one was dark and thin. There was nothing in their appearance to prevent their being the three who had hunted me in Scotland, but there was nothing to identify them. They seemed exactly what they professed to be, and I could not have sworn to one of them. There in that pleasant dining room, with etchings on the walls, and a picture of an old lady above the mantelpiece, I could see nothing to connect them with the moorland desperadoes. There was a silver cigarette box beside me, and I saw that it had been won by Percival Appleton, Esq., of the St. Bede's Club, in a golf tournament. I had to keep firm hold of Peter Pienaar to prevent myself from bolting out of that house.

"Well," said the old man politely, "are you reassured by your scrutiny, sir? I hope you'll find it consistent with your duty to drop this ridiculous business. I make no complaint, but you see how annoying it must be to respectable people."

I shook my head.

"Oh, Lord," said the young man, "this is a bit too thick!"

"Do you propose to march us off to the police station?" asked the plump one. "I have a right to see your warrant. I realize you are only doing your duty. You'll admit it's horribly awkward. What do you propose to do?"

There was nothing to do except to call in my men and have them arrested or to confess my blunder and clear out. I felt mesmerized by the whole place, by the air of obvious innocence, and for a moment I was very near damning myself for a fool and asking their pardon.

"Meantime I vote we have a game of bridge," said the plump one. "It will give Mr. Hannay time to think things over. Anyway, we've been wanting a fourth. Do you play, sir?"

I accepted as if it had been an ordinary invitation at the club. We went into the study, where a card table was set up, and I was offered a drink. I took my place at the table in a kind of dream. The window was open and the moon was flooding the cliffs and sea with a great tide of yellow light. There was moonshine, too, in my head.

The three had recovered their composure and were talking easily—the kind of slangy talk you hear at any golf clubhouse. I must have cut a rum figure, sitting there knitting my brows, with my eyes wandering.

My partner was the young dark one. I play a fair hand at bridge, but I must have been rank bad that night. They saw that they had puzzled me, and that put them more than ever at ease. I kept looking at their faces, but they conveyed nothing to me. It was not that they looked different; they *were* different.

THEN SOMETHING AWOKE ME. The old man laid down his hand to light a cigar. He didn't pick it up at once, but sat back for a moment in his chair, with his fingers tapping his knees.

It was the movement I remembered when I had stood before him in the moorland farmhouse with the pistols of his servants behind me.

A little thing, lasting only a second, and the odds were a thousand to one that I might have had my eyes on my cards at the time and missed it. But I didn't, and in a flash the air cleared. A shadow lifted from my brain, and I looked at the three men with full and absolute recognition.

The clock on the mantelpiece struck ten.

The three faces seemed to change before my eyes and reveal their secrets. The young one was the murderer. Now I saw cruelty and ruthlessness where before I had only seen good humor. His knife I was certain had skewered Scudder to the floor. He had put the bullet in Karolides. Then I looked again at the plump man. He hadn't a face, only a hundred masks that he could assume when he pleased. He must have been a superb actor. Perhaps he had been Lord Alloa of the night before, perhaps not; it didn't matter. I wondered if he was the one who had first tracked Scudder and left his card. Scudder had said he lisped, and I could imagine how the adoption of a lisp might add terror.

But the old man was the pick of the lot. He was sheer brain, icy, calculating. Now that my eyes were opened I wondered how I had imagined benevolence. His jaw was like chilled steel, and his eyes had the inhuman luminosity of a bird's. I went on playing, and every second a greater hate welled up in my heart.

"Bob! Look at the time," said the old man. "You'd better think about catching your train. Bob's got to go to town tonight," he added, turning to me. The voice rang now as false as hell.

I looked at the clock. It was nearly half past ten.

"I am afraid you must put off your journey," I said.

"Oh damn!" said the young man. "I thought you had dropped that rot. I've got to go. You can have my address and I'll give any security you like."

"No," I said. "You'll stay."

I think they realized then that they had failed to convince me. Still, the old man spoke again.

"I'll go bail for my nephew. That ought to content you, Mr. Hannay." Was it imagination, or did I detect some halt in the smoothness of that voice?

There must have been, for, as I glanced at him, his eyelids fell in that hawklike hood which fear had stamped on my memory.

I blew my whistle.

In an instant the lights went out. A pair of strong arms gripped me around the waist, covering the pockets in which a man might be expected to carry a pistol.

"*Schnell, Franz, das Boot!*" cried a voice. "Hurry, Franz, the boat!" As it spoke my eyes were towards the window, and I saw two of my fellows emerge on the moonlit lawn.

The young dark man leaped for the window, was through it, and over the low fence before a hand could touch him. I grappled the old chap, and the room seemed to fill with figures. I saw the plump one collared, but my eyes were on the out-of-doors, where Franz was speeding over the road towards the railed entrance to the beach stairs. One man followed him, but he had no chance. The gate locked behind the fugitive, and I stood staring, with my hands on the old boy's throat, for such a time as a man might take to descend those steps to the sea.

Suddenly my prisoner broke from me and flung himself on the wall. There was a click as if a lever had been pulled. Then came a low rumbling far, far below the ground, and through the window I saw a cloud of chalky dust pouring up from the shaft of the stairway.

Someone switched on the light.

The old man was looking at me with blazing eyes.

"He is safe!" he cried. "You cannot follow him in time. He is gone. He has triumphed! The Black Stone has won victory!"

There was more in those eyes than any common triumph. They had been hooded like those of a bird of prey, and now they flamed with a hawk's pride. A white fanatic heat burned in them, and I realized for the first time the terrible thing I had been up against. This man was more than a spy; in his foul way he had been a patriot.

As the handcuffs clinked on his wrists I said my last words to him.

"I hope Franz will bear his triumph well. I ought to tell you that the *Ariadne* for the last hour has been in our hands."

THREE WEEKS LATER, as all the world knows, we went to war. I joined the army the first week, and owing to my Matabele experience got a captain's commission straight off. But I had done my best service, I think, before I put on khaki.

OPERATION
CICERO

Ankara 1943

OPERATION CICERO

A CONDENSATION OF THE BOOK BY

L. C. MOYZISCH

Translated by Constantine Fitzgibbon
and Heinrich Fraenkel

ILLUSTRATED BY ALLAN MARDON

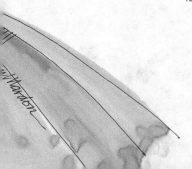

During the tense final phase of World War II, the German embassy in neutral Turkey paid a fortune for quantities of stolen "most secret" British documents—documents that revealed crucial Allied war plans to the enemy only a few days after they had been made.

It was the author, L. C. Moyzisch, an attaché at the German embassy, who effected these transactions, meeting regularly with a mysterious Albanian undercover agent employed as a valet at the British embassy and known by the code name "Cicero."

This amazing true spy story of World War II was acclaimed by *The New York Times* ". . . without doubt the most important, most bizarre and ironic single episode to come out of the cloak-and-dagger world of the last war."

CHAPTER 1

THE CICERO AFFAIR, or Operation Cicero, as we came to call it, was played out in Turkey, during the period between October 1943 and April 1944. It was perhaps the most spectacular single incident in that shadowy, secret, silent warfare that went on day and night for six long years; the struggle of brains to discover the enemy's intentions and thus to be in a position to frustrate them.

Cicero was a spy, and therefore this is in essence a spy story; yet the ramifications of Operation Cicero were so vast, and its details so fantastic, that it far transcends the normal secret service thriller. I never knew Cicero's real name, though he was responsible for the most hectic six months of my existence, a period during which, at times, I was nearly out of my mind with anxiety and which, at the end, almost cost me my life.

When Operation Cicero began, the war was reaching its huge and noisy climax. The Allies had landed in Italy. The Russians, who a year before had seemed to be facing disaster with German troops approaching Stalingrad and pouring into the Crimea, were now advancing. The air attacks on Germany proper were daily and visibly gathering weight. In fact Adolf Hitler's enormous war machine was just beginning to break up, while the even mightier power of the Allies was gathering strength for its decisive blows. In the hourglass of history the sand marking the life span of the Third Reich was fast running out. The German leaders refused to recognize it, even though Operation Cicero gave them quite precise knowledge of the enemy's power and intentions, knowledge such as no previous war leaders had probably ever received through secret service channels.

From the vantage point of Ankara the general picture of the war could perhaps be more clearly seen than from any other position. For Turkey occupied a unique position, politically almost equidistant from Germany, Russia and the Western powers. As an attaché at the German embassy in Ankara, I was naturally at the center of the ceaseless intrigues of wartime diplomacy, while my duties frequently took me to Istanbul—noisy, sweltering Istanbul—which at the time was the most important neutral city in the world.

The embassy at Ankara was undoubtedly Germany's best window on the outside world, and the position of ambassador there the most vital that the diplomatic service had to offer. Proof of this is provided by the fact that this appointment was held by Franz von Papen, a former chancellor of Germany and as subtle a politician as his country produced during the first half of the twentieth century.

Much of the trouble which it was von Papen's thankless task to smooth out was due to the fact that there were so many supreme chiefs in Berlin, each intent on controlling German foreign policy.

Our official authority was, of course, the Auswärtige Amt, the German Foreign Office, headed by the foreign minister, Joachim von Ribbentrop. But there were a great many other personalities and more or less official organizations active in matters of foreign policy.

In the first place there was the secret service of the Foreign Office itself. Then there was the huge secret service organization called the Sicherheitsdienst (Security Service), at this time being run by the very powerful SS General Ernst Kaltenbrunner, a notorious character subsequently condemned to death at Nuremberg. Also there was the Abwehr, the military intelligence division. There was also Heinrich Himmler's private secret service, which was finally incorporated in Kaltenbrunner's organization. Dr. Joseph Goebbels, too, through the Ministry of Propaganda, had his own secret service people and was apt to prove very jealous if any of the other organizations poached on what he regarded as his private preserve.

It was Dr. Goebbels' ministry that on one occasion caused us one of the most severe headaches we had to suffer as a result of the manifold activities of these unofficial makers of foreign policy.

One day, purely by chance, I was browsing around the German bookshop in Istanbul. As I glanced through a pile of books newly arrived from Germany, I was amazed to see a pamphlet entitled *"Türkisches Soldaten-Wörterbuch für den Feldgebrauch,"* which might be translated as "A Soldier's Guide to Turkey." It was a phrase book, containing such sentences as a German soldier might need while on active service in Turkey. It was an official booklet, one of a series. Books with almost identical phrases had been issued to German troops before the invasion of Norway, Holland, France, Yugoslavia and the other occupied countries.

My amazement soon turned to horror when I realized the implications of this book being on sale in Istanbul and the diplomatic crisis that was likely to ensue. I was even more apprehensive when the shop owner told me that out of his stock of one hundred copies, received from Berlin a day or two before, seven had already been sold.

I immediately bought the remaining ninety-three and took the night train back to Ankara, where I at once informed the ambassador. Herr von Papen was furious, and he, too, realized the implications of seven copies still being at large in Turkey.

We did not have to wait long for the expected reaction. At least one of the copies had reached Numan Menemencioglu, the Turkish foreign minister. A most unpleasant interview between the minister and the German ambassador was the result. Herr von Papen's position was not made any easier by the fact that a week or two earlier he had delivered to the head of the Turkish state a handwritten letter from Hitler, in which the latter professed eternal friendship and the keenest desire to spare Turkey the horrors of war.

On a visit to Berlin soon afterward I found that despite the imprimatur of the High Command, the Ministry of Propaganda was responsible for this blunder. This was typical of the way Dr. Goebbels played his game. It seemed that he did not approve of the policy of friendship with Turkey which was advocated by the German ambassador and temporarily endorsed by the Führer. So he hit upon the plan of having this book produced and dispatched to Istanbul and many other Turkish towns, though *not* to Ankara. He evidently hoped that a few copies would thus find their way into Turkish government circles before our embassy heard of the book and that Turko-German relations would deteriorate in consequence.

That was the sort of background against which von Papen had to work. It required all his abilities, and it was fortunate for us that he enjoyed the respect and confidence of the Turkish government and that they realized he had always used all his influence to prevent a German invasion of Turkey—at one time a very real danger.

It was common knowledge in diplomatic circles that the relationship between von Papen and Ribbentrop was anything but friendly. Time and again von Papen incurred the wrath of his chief and the Führer; his suggestions that the war might possibly be ended by negotiation they found particularly unpalatable.

On one occasion I happened to be at the Foreign Ministry in Berlin when von Papen had an unusually severe altercation with Ribbentrop. Von Papen ended it with these words: "There is only one other thing I wish to say, Herr Reichsaussenminister. It is very easy to start a war; it is infinitely more difficult to finish one. If you persist in your present attitude, you, sir, will never succeed in doing so. Good day, Herr Reichsaussenminister."

The strain between the ambassador and his foreign minister was not confined to verbal exchanges. Von Papen was actually spied on by agents of the intelligence services mentioned earlier. A particularly ludicrous example of this came to my attention when I was in Berlin, shortly before the start of Operation Cicero, in September 1943.

Through an intimate friend of mine in the German capital I had access to confidential reports about Turkey, most of which seemed to be written outside Turkey with a minimum of expert knowledge and a maximum of malevolent imagination. Safe behind the locked door of my friend's office, I was amusing myself by glancing through a file of these "highly confidential" reports. One of them quoted some "first-hand information from a thoroughly reliable source" about a meeting, which on a given day and at a specific place von Papen had had with Laurence Steinhardt and Sergei Vinogradov, the American and Russian ambassadors. This highly secret rendezvous between enemy ambassadors was supposed to have taken place when all three were allegedly out shooting near Ankara. According to the thoroughly reliable source, von Papen was accompanied by one of his attachés, who happened to be me. The report then went into considerable detail concerning the treasonable conversation that the three ambassadors had held.

When I read this amazing piece of fiction I was baffled. Then suddenly it all came back to me. The funny thing was that there was a grain of truth to the story, a tiny grain, to be sure, but one quite big enough for the author of the report to build his fables about top secret negotiations with the enemy around it.

We *had* gone shooting, and the meeting with the two enemy ambassadors had taken place. But the details were rather different from those in the report.

One day my chief had kindly invited my wife and me to accompany him on a duck shoot. Now shooting ducks near Ankara is not easy. On a lake near the city there are ducks in huge numbers, but the surrounding countryside is completely flat and open, with neither tree nor bush to provide cover. The ducks fly away long before one is within shotgun range, and so some way has to be found to deceive the birds.

Herr von Papen had thought out a very effective ruse. From the Ankara zoo he had borrowed four tame ducks. These we took with us in the car, each one trussed and fitted with a long piece of string. When we reached the lake, from which the wild ducks had flown off as usual, we threw the ducks we had brought with us into the water. They could then swim out as far as the strings allowed. Von Papen imagined they would act as decoys for the wild ones. Meanwhile, on the shore we dug a shallow hide where the ambassador, gun in hand, concealed himself, and I camouflaged him as best I could with branches and brambles that we had brought with us. Then, some three hundred yards away, I found a ditch and waited to see if von Papen's experiment would have any result. It did.

During the first few minutes nothing happened at all. Then, all of a sudden, two shots rang out in quick succession, echoing across the Anatolian plain. But they did not come from von Papen's hide. I saw him crawl out, covered with branches and brambles and gesticulating furiously. He had turned his back on the lake and the ducks and was shouting enragedly at two men who were standing some way off on a small hillock. They were obviously duck shooters, too. After a moment they disappeared. As I made my way toward von Papen I caught a glimpse of them. My wife, who had stayed in the car, saw them even more clearly. The ambassador told me, with extreme annoyance, what had happened.

"I'd hardly settled myself in the hide," he said, "when I heard a couple of shots behind me and was surrounded by a hail of pellets. As I jumped up I saw the two idiots silhouetted against the sun. I gave them a piece of my mind in every language I can lay my tongue to. Blasted poachers! Shooting at sitting birds! And they nearly got me, too, damn them! Just look at the mess."

The four ducks we had borrowed from the Ankara zoo were dead. Von Papen himself was bleeding freely behind one ear. "Would you recognize those damned poachers?" he asked me. "They passed close to you as they ran away. We should give their description to the police."

"I recognized them perfectly, sir. They happened to be your colleagues Mr. Steinhardt and Gospodin Vinogradov—the American and Russian ambassadors."

At no time did I see the ambassador so embarrassed as at that moment when he learned that he had called the American and Russian ambassadors poachers—and that was the mildest of the epithets he had used. He had completely forgotten his own injuries. Even so, he could not quite get over his horror at the shooting of sitting ducks.

For a day or so after this incident he was extremely worried about his inadvertent rudeness to his diplomatic colleagues; the fact that we were at war and that they were on the enemy side made it all somehow worse. Finally, with true diplomatic finesse, the ambassador solved his problem by calling personally on the Swedish and Swiss legations, taking the ministers into his confidence and asking them to seek a suitable opportunity for expressing his regret about the unseemly language he had used.

The fact remains that in the middle of World War II the German ambassador in Turkey was very nearly bagged by his enemy colleagues, along with four tame ducks from the Ankara zoo.

Such was the basis for the report of von Papen's treasonable conversation while out duck shooting. Comical though it might be, the fact that such reports were written and, presumably, taken seriously in certain circles in Berlin did not make his position any easier.

Apart from the ambassador the most important German diplomat in Ankara—and the only other one to be directly involved in the Cicero business—was Albert Jenke, the first secretary. He had a charming though ambitious wife, who incidentally was Ribbentrop's sister. Their presence in Ankara was perhaps not entirely fortuitous.

On the British side von Papen's opposite number was Sir Hughe Knatchbull-Hugessen, the British ambassador. A most distinguished man, he was highly thought of by our Turkish hosts, and there can be no doubt that he must have been one of the most able and conscientious ambassadors of the time. It was to be my lot to scrutinize most thoroughly innumerable documents from the files of the British embassy. Many of these, headed MOST SECRET, were annotated with marginal comments in Sir Hughe's own hand. I remember how von Papen, Jenke and I—nobody else on our side in Ankara ever managed to see this secret material—more than once expressed our admiration for the high professional standard of Sir Hughe's personal reports; a most expressive style, devoid of all superfluities.

CHAPTER 2

THOSE AUTUMN DAYS of 1943 in Ankara were strangely beautiful. The summer had been even hotter than usual, but by October the temperature was perfect and the daily sunshine gave us as much pleasure as did the incredibly blue sky stretching over the great expanse of the Anatolian plain. It seemed a very peaceful world, almost sarcastically so.

October 26 was at first no different from any other day. I dealt with various routine matters. I left the office early and, as I drove home, I certainly had no suspicion that before this day was over my whole life would have been changed.

I had decided to go to bed early. I read for a while, but soon switched off the light and was fast asleep when the telephone rang. It was Frau Jenke, the wife of the first secretary. There was a note of anxiety and urgency in her voice.

"Would you please come round to our flat at once? My husband wants to see you."

I said that I was already in bed and asked what it was all about, but Frau Jenke cut me short.

"It's urgent. Please come immediately."

My wife had waked up, too, and as I dressed we wondered what sort of a fool's errand this would turn out to be. It was probably some ridiculous signal from Berlin. That sort of thing had happened before. When I left the house I glanced at my watch. It was half past ten.

A few minutes' drive took me to the embassy, which, on account of its German style and also because it contained several buildings, was called by the Turks *Alman Köy*, the German village. The sleepy Turkish porter opened the big iron gate. A short walk brought me to where the Jenkes lived, and I rang the bell. Frau Jenke opened the door herself, apologizing in a few words for having disturbed my sleep.

"My husband's gone to bed, but he would like to see you first thing in the morning." Then she pointed to the door of the drawing room. "There's a strange sort of character in there. He has something he wants to sell us. You're to talk to him and find out what it's all about. And when you go, do please remember to shut the front door after you. I've sent the servants to bed."

She disappeared, and as I stood alone in the hall I wondered whether it was really part of an attaché's duties to have conversations in the dead of night with strange characters. At any rate I was determined to make this one as brief as possible.

I went into the drawing room. The heavy curtains were drawn and the only light came from two table lamps. In a deep armchair next to one of the lamps a man was seated, in such a way that his face was in shadow. He sat so still he might have been sleeping. But he was not. He got up and addressed me in French.

"Who are you?" he asked, with what seemed to me to be an anxious expression.

I told him that Jenke had instructed me to talk to him. He nodded and, judging by his expression, now fully visible in the light of the table lamp, seemed much relieved.

I guessed that he was in his early fifties. He had thick black hair brushed straight back from his forehead, which was fairly high. His dark eyes kept darting nervously from me to the door and back again. His chin was firm, his nose small and shapeless. Not an attractive face on the whole. Later, after I'd seen a great deal of him, it occurred to me to compare his face with that of a clown without his makeup on—the face of a man accustomed to disguising his true feelings.

There was a moment's silence while we eyed one another. I sat down and motioned him to do the same. Instead he tiptoed to the door, jerked it open, shut it silently again, and came back with evident relief to resume his seat in the armchair. He really did seem a strange sort of character.

Haltingly at first, and in his poor French, he began to speak. "I have an offer to make you, a proposition for the Germans. I ask your word that whether you accept it or not you won't ever mention it to anyone except your chief. Any indiscretion on your part would make your life as worthless as mine. I'd see to that if it was the last thing I did."

As he said this he made an unpleasant but unmistakable gesture, passing his hand across his throat. "Do you give me your word?"

"Of course I do. If I didn't know how to keep a secret I wouldn't be here now. Please be so good as to tell me what it is you want."

I made a show of looking at my wristwatch. He reacted at once.

"You'll have plenty of time for me once you know why I'm here. My proposition is of the utmost importance to your government. I am—" He hesitated, and I wondered if it were due to his difficulty in expressing himself in French or whether he wished to test my reaction. "I can give you extremely secret papers, the most secret that exist." He paused again for a moment, and then added, "They come straight from the British embassy. Well? That would interest you, wouldn't it?"

I did my best to keep my poker face. My first thought was that he was a petty crook out for some easy money. I would have to be careful. He seemed to have guessed what I was thinking, for he said, "But I'll want money for them, a lot of money. My work, you know, is dangerous, and if I were caught . . ." He repeated the unpleasant gesture with his hand across his throat, though this time, at any rate, it was not meant for me. "You've got funds for that sort of thing, haven't you? Or your ambassador has? Your government would provide it. I want twenty thousand pounds, English pounds sterling."

"Nonsense," I said. "Quite out of the question. It would have to be something extraordinarily important to be worth anything near that price. Besides, first I'd have to see these papers of yours. Have you got them with you?"

He leaned back so that his face was out of the light again. My eyes by now were accustomed to the dimness and I could see his expression. There was a superior smile on his unattractive face. I was not quite sure what to say. After all, I knew absolutely nothing about the fellow, save that he wanted an extremely large sum of money for

documents which purported to come from the British embassy. I
said nothing, and he soon began to speak again.

"I'm not a fool. I've spent years preparing for this day. I've worked
out all the details. Now the time has come to act. I'll tell you my
terms. If you agree, very well. If you don't . . ."

He leaned forward, out into the full glare of the lamp, and with
the thumb of his left hand pointed in the direction of the heavily curtained window. "If you don't, then I'll see if they'd like to have my
documents over there."

His thumb was pointing in the direction of the Soviet embassy.
There was a moment's silence, and then he added, hissing the words,
"You see, I hate the British."

I cannot recall what exactly I said in answer to the proposition,
but I do remember that at this moment, for the first time, it occurred
to me that the man might not be a crook after all. A fanatic perhaps?
Yet he was asking for a very great deal of money.

I offered him a cigarette, which he accepted gratefully, taking a few
deep pulls and then stubbing it out. He rose and went to the door
once again to make sure that there was no one listening. Then he
turned back and planted himself squarely in front of me. I got up, too.

"You'd like to know who I am, wouldn't you? My name is quite
unimportant and has no bearing. Perhaps I'll tell you what I do, but
first listen to me. I'll give you three days to consider my proposition.
You'll have to see your chief, and he'll probably have to get in touch
with Berlin. On the thirtieth of October, at three in the afternoon,
I'll telephone you at your office and ask you if you've received a letter
for me. I'll call myself Pierre. If you say no, you'll never see me again.
If you say yes, it'll mean that you've accepted my offer. In that case
I'll come to see you again at ten o'clock on the evening of the same
day. Not here, though. We'll have to arrange some other meeting
place. You'll then receive from me two rolls of film, containing
photographs of British secret documents. I'll receive from you the
sum of twenty thousand pounds in bank notes. You'll be risking
twenty thousand pounds, but I'll have risked my life. Should you approve of my first delivery you can have more. For each subsequent
roll of film I'll want fifteen thousand pounds. Well?"

I was inclined to think that the offer might be genuine, but I was
convinced that, in view of the exorbitant price he was asking, nothing

could come of it, particularly since he seemed to expect us to buy the papers sight unseen. I made a mental note to stress the inordinate risk in the memo that I would have to write about all this. I was certain the offer would be turned down.

Nevertheless, we agreed that he should telephone me at my office on October 30 at three o'clock. We also agreed that in the event of his offer being accepted we would meet near the toolshed at the end of the embassy garden.

Herr von Papen

Sir Hughe Knatchbull-Hugessen

Frau Jenke

Herr Jenke

Cicero

After these details had been arranged he asked me to switch out all the lights in the hall and on the stairs. He wished to leave the house in complete darkness. I complied with his request. When I came back to the drawing room he had put on his overcoat and his hat, which was pulled down over his eyes. It was past midnight by now.

I stood at the door to let him pass. He suddenly gripped my arm and whispered in my ear, "You'd like to know who I am? I'm the British ambassador's valet."

THE NEXT MORNING I had a slight headache and that dry feeling that comes after a sleepless night. By daylight I was inclined to revert to my original impression that the man was nothing but a trickster seeking to put one over on the gullible Germans.

After a long soak in my tub and some strong coffee I felt better. I told myself there was really no need for me to worry. I wouldn't have to make any decision—that was a matter for the ambassador, or Berlin. My job was merely to report what had taken place.

I reached my office very early that morning. My secretary had not yet arrived, and I was glad of the opportunity to draft my memo for the ambassador completely undisturbed.

As I signed it I began to wonder why the mysterious visitor, who claimed to be the British ambassador's valet, had gone to Jenke. But I did not have to wait long to discover the reason, which was to go a long way toward dispersing my doubts about the genuineness of the man's offer. While I waited for the ambassador to arrive, Herr Jenke telephoned and asked me to come over. Unlike me, both Herr and Frau Jenke had passed a very good night. I could see that Jenke was consumed with curiosity about the events of the previous evening.

"That strange sort of character of yours," I said to Frau Jenke, "he had a most remarkable offer to—"

"I know," Jenke interrupted. "I had a few words with him before you arrived. I thought you were the best man to deal with him. In my position I have to be careful about getting involved in anything of that sort."

"So you met the man," I said to Jenke. "Why do you think he picked on you?"

"I've met the man all right, and he knows me, too," said Jenke. "Some six or seven years ago, before I joined the diplomatic service, he worked for a while in our house. I haven't seen him since. I can't remember his name, but I did recognize his face when he came here last night. I suppose he wants money?"

"He most certainly does," I said. "To be exact he wants twenty thousand pounds sterling."

"What?" Herr and Frau Jenke exclaimed together. "Twenty thousand pounds!"

I nodded, but before I could say more the telephone rang. I had asked for an appointment with the ambassador as soon as he came in. He would see me now. Jenke came along, too.

We entered Herr von Papen's office together. It was a large room on the first floor, simply and tastefully furnished, with fine pictures on the walls. Behind his big desk sat the ambassador, gray-haired but still very handsome. He gazed at me with his striking blue eyes.

"Well, gentlemen, what have you been up to?"

"Last night," I said, "in Herr Jenke's house, I had a most remarkable conversation. With the British ambassador's valet."

"With whom?" asked Herr von Papen.

I repeated what I had said and handed him my memo. He put on his spectacles and, as he read, glanced at me once or twice over the top of them. When he had finished reading he pushed the paper to the far side of his desk, as if he wanted instinctively to have nothing to do with its contents. He got up, went to the window, opened it, and still without a word stood staring out over the open country to the line of mountains rising blue in the far distance. At last he turned toward us.

"What sort of valets do we employ in our embassy?"

I looked at the ambassador and then at Herr Jenke. No one said anything.

"What are we to do, sir?" I asked finally.

"I don't know. In any case the sum mentioned is far too large for us to be in a position to decide the matter here. Draft a signal for Berlin and bring it to me personally. I'll have another word with you then."

I went to my office, leaving Jenke with the ambassador. When I came back half an hour later Herr von Papen was alone. I held the draft of the signal in my hand.

"You realize what might be behind all this?" the ambassador asked.

"Well, sir, I suppose it might be a trap. They could let us have some documents, even genuine ones, and then bluff us later on with a bogus one. Even at best, that is if the man is genuine and it's not a British trap, we'd be involved in a most unpleasant scandal if the story ever came out."

"What impression did the man make on you personally?" von Papen asked.

"Not a particularly good one, sir, though by the end of the conversation I was inclined to believe his tale. He struck me as unscrupulous enough, and his hatred of the British, unless it's put on, would be an additional motive, quite apart from his obvious desire for money. On the whole he didn't strike me as an ordinary crook. Of course, all this is mere conjecture on my part."

"What do you think the British would do if one of our people made them a comparable offer?"

"I think they'd undoubtedly accept it, sir. In time of war no nation could afford to turn down such a proposition."

The ambassador reached for my draft signal and read it carefully. Then he took his green pencil—green was the ambassador's color, and no one else at the embassy when signing documents or initialing files was allowed to use it—and made a few small amendments, re-read the text, and finally signed it. Then he pushed it over to me. The piece of paper had now become an official document.

"Read it to me again," he said.

I did so:

"TO THE REICH FOREIGN MINISTER, PERSONAL

MOST SECRET

WE HAVE OFFER OF BRITISH EMBASSY EMPLOYEE ALLEGED TO BE BRITISH AMBASSADOR'S VALET TO PROCURE PHOTOGRAPHS OF TOP SECRET ORIGINAL DOCUMENTS. FOR FIRST DELIVERY ON OCTOBER THIRTIETH, TWENTY THOUSAND POUNDS STERLING IN BANK NOTES ARE DEMANDED. FIFTEEN THOUSAND POUNDS FOR ANY FURTHER ROLL OF FILMS. PLEASE ADVISE WHETHER OFFER CAN BE ACCEPTED. IF SO SUM REQUIRED MUST BE DISPATCHED BY SPECIAL COURIER TO ARRIVE HERE NOT LATER THAN OC-TOBER THIRTIETH. ALLEGED VALET WAS EMPLOYED SEVERAL YEARS AGO BY FIRST SECRETARY OTHERWISE NOTHING MUCH KNOWN HERE. PAPEN."

This signal was coded at once and dispatched by wireless before noon on October 27. It was on Ribbentrop's desk within the hour.

Nothing happened, and by the evening of October 28 I was con-vinced that the foreign minister, if he deigned to answer at all, would decide in the negative. It had happened more than once that the ambassador's suggestions had been turned down merely because they came from him, including some that might have gone a long way to help our country's cause.

October 28 was the eve of a great Turkish national festival, and that night all Ankara was floodlit. The next day I had almost forgot-ten about the answer that we were still awaiting from Berlin. In the early afternoon there was a military parade on the racecourse. When I returned to the embassy after the parade, I found a message that the ambassador wished to see me at once. I went to his office, where, without a word, he handed me a decoded signal. I read:

TO AMBASSADOR VON PAPEN, PERSONAL

MOST SECRET

BRITISH VALET'S OFFER TO BE ACCEPTED TAKING EVERY PRECAUTION. SPE-CIAL COURIER ARRIVING ANKARA 30TH BEFORE NOON. EXPECT IMMEDIATE REPORT AFTER DELIVERY OF DOCUMENTS. RIBBENTROP.

The matter had been decided for us.

On October 30, at three p.m. sharp, the telephone rang in my office. I think my heart skipped a beat as I snatched for the receiver. The voice at the other end sounded faint and far away.

"Pierre here. *Bonjour, monsieur.* Have you got my letter?"

"Yes."

"I'll see you tonight. *Au revoir!*"

I asked to see the ambassador. After a minute or two Fräulein Rose, his secretary, rang to say he was awaiting me. I went in at once.

"The valet's phoned, sir. I'm meeting him at ten tonight."

"Take care, my boy, not to let him fool you. Between you and me I don't care for this business at all. Above all we can't afford any scandal here. You have my instructions to go ahead, of course. But you must realize that if anything should go wrong, I'm afraid I shan't be able to protect you, and in fact I'd probably have to disclaim all knowledge of what you were doing. Let me warn you to be particularly careful about not mentioning this to anyone, *anyone.*"

"I've thought a great deal about it, sir," I said, "including the actual manner of handing over the money. I won't give it to him before I've had a chance of making sure that the stuff's genuine. Frankly, sir, I don't care for this sort of thing any more than you do. But I'm sure we'd have been wrong if we'd turned the offer down. Besides, it's not as though we were dipping into the British safe. The stuff's being brought to us. Anyway, it may still turn out to be a trick."

"Perhaps," said the ambassador. "Actually, I'm not quite sure whether I'd be altogether sorry if it were. Anyway, here's the money. You'd better count it."

Herr von Papen pulled out of his middle drawer an enormous bundle of bank notes, which he pushed across the desk to me. So the Berlin courier had arrived in time. I was astonished by that mass of bank notes, consisting as it did entirely of ten-, twenty- and fifty-pound notes, wrapped up in bundles. Could they not have found some of larger denomination in Berlin? To carry all this paper, one would have to cram one's pockets to bursting point. Only a small proportion of them seemed ever to have been in circulation. Somehow I felt vaguely suspicious about this.

The ambassador seemed to have guessed my thoughts. "Look altogether too new, these notes."

I shrugged my shoulders and began to count. It was £20,000 all right. I wrapped the whole lot up in the large front page of a newspaper which was lying on the ambassador's desk. As I was leaving, Herr von Papen accompanied me as far as the door.

"Remember, don't get me into trouble—or yourself, either."

Hugging my valuable parcel, I went downstairs and across the embassy gardens to my office. There I locked up the money in my safe.

Later that afternoon I sent for my secretary. Her real name—she is now happily married somewhere in Germany—is beside the point. As a matter of fact no one in the embassy ever called her by her real name. She was "Schnürchen" to everybody in the embassy, because her favorite expression was that everything in the office must *am Schnürchen gehen,* which is the German equivalent for everything being under control and in apple-pie order. Efficient, tidy, reliable and loyal—she was the perfect secretary. I knew I would have to hurt her feelings, but I had no choice in the matter. I didn't intend to take even the shadow of a risk.

"By the way, would you mind letting me have the other key to the safe? I'll take care of it from now on."

She gave me an astonished look. I could see that she resented this.

As a matter of fact Schnürchen got the key back a week later, and after that she kept it. For technical reasons this was unavoidable. Nor did she ever, at any time or in any way, betray the great trust I placed in her.

At ten minutes to ten that evening I was back in the embassy. I drew the curtains in my office and put out the lights in the hall, so that there was no chance of my visitor being seen from outside.

In the embassy cellar, where we had our darkroom, the photographer was ready. The man was an entirely trustworthy code clerk who in civilian life had been a professional photographer. If the valet really brought a roll of film, it was to be developed at once. As it happens, I am myself an amateur photographer, but I knew little about developing. That is why in the early stages of Operation Cicero I could not avoid employing the professional, but I think I managed to keep him from knowing what it was all about.

At two minutes to ten I was standing at the end of the embassy garden at the appointed meeting place near the toolshed. It was a dark night, and it seemed to me very suitable for the purpose in hand.

It was rather cold and absolutely still. I could almost hear the beating of my own heart. I had hardly waited a minute before I saw a person approaching me. My eyes tried to pierce the darkness. Then I heard his voice, speaking softly:

"It's me, Pierre. *Tout va bien?*"

CHAPTER 3

WE WALKED TOGETHER from the toolshed to the embassy in silence, and across the darkened hall into my room. When I switched on the light we were both, for the moment, dazzled by the glare.

He showed no trace of nervousness now, as he had done at our first meeting a few days before. He was apparently in the best of spirits and full of confidence.

He spoke first. "Have you the money?"

I nodded. He reached into his overcoat pocket and took out two rolls which I could see at a glance were 35-mm films. They lay in his open hand, but he withdrew it when I reached for them.

"First the money," he said calmly.

I went to my safe and opened it. I recall that I had a little trouble with the combination. My back was turned to him, and this added to my discomfort. When at last I had gotten the safe open and had reached in for the bundle, my hands were trembling.

I turned around. He stood in the same spot, his eyes fixed on the newspaper package I held, an expression of mingled curiosity and greed on his face.

I unwrapped the bank notes as I walked over to my desk. There I counted them, aloud and very slowly. Coming a little closer he counted them with me, for I could see his lips moving when I glanced up at him.

"Fifteen thousand . . . two fifty . . . five hundred . . . seven fifty . . . sixteen thousand . . ."

When I had finished I rewrapped the whole lot in the sheet of newspaper. This was the critical moment. I had to remain firm now in my decision not to pay him the money before I had made sure what it was I was buying.

"Give me the films," I said, putting my left hand on the money and holding out my right. He gave me both rolls, at the same time reaching out toward the bundle of notes.

"Not yet," I said. "You can have it as soon as I know what the films are like. You'll have to wait here while I develop them. Everything's ready. The money's all here; you've seen it and counted it yourself. If you won't agree to this you can have your film back at once. Well?"

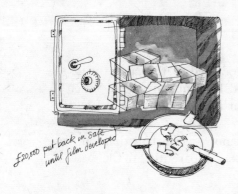

£20,500 put back in safe until film developed

"You're very suspicious. You should have more trust in me. But all right. I'll wait here."

I felt extremely relieved. Apparently it wasn't a trick after all. For the first time I felt that maybe the whole business would turn out all right. The sight of the money and my deliberately slow counting of it had had the effect I intended. He saw himself already in possession of a fortune, and he was not going to risk it all by being stubborn.

He stood there quite calmly while I locked the money back in the safe. He seemed to have considerably more confidence in me than I had in him.

I had fully recovered my composure by this time. "Cigarette?" I held out my case and he helped himself to several.

"They'll last me till you get back," he said coolly.

He sat down and began to smoke. I locked the door from the outside. The valet must have heard the key turn, but, somewhat to my surprise, he made no protest at being locked in like a prisoner. Then, with the two rolls of film in my pocket, I hurried to the darkroom, where the photographer was waiting.

He had made all the necessary preparations. The developer was ready and brought to the correct temperature. He put both the films into the developing tanks. I asked him to explain all his actions to me in detail, because in future I intended to do all this myself. Some ten minutes later the first tank was opened. I took out the spool and put it in the rinsing bath, and immediately afterward into the fixing bath. The second film followed.

Again some minutes passed, very slowly. At last the photographer said, "The first one should be ready by now."

He held one end of the film up against the viewing box.

In spite of the small size of the negatives I could clearly see the typescript. The photographs on both rolls seemed to be technically perfect. Then the two precious strips were dipped into the washing tank. I stood there watching it all impatiently. Another few minutes and we would know what it was that we were buying at such a high price.

I pegged the wet films onto a line. Now the little room was brightly lit by a hundred-watt bulb. Taking a strong magnifying glass I bent over the wet strip. I could read the writing quite clearly:

MOST SECRET

FROM FOREIGN OFFICE TO BRITISH EMBASSY, ANKARA

That, and the fact that the document bore a very recent date, was quite enough for me. I hurried the photographer out, locked the door carefully, and asked him to meet me there again in about fifteen minutes' time. Then I went up to my office.

When I came in my visitor was still sitting exactly as I had left him. Only the full ashtray indicated he had been waiting for some time. He seemed neither impatient nor irritated. All he said was, "Well?"

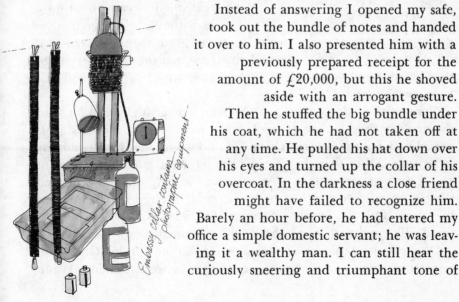

Embassy cellar contains photographic equipment—

Instead of answering I opened my safe, took out the bundle of notes and handed it over to him. I also presented him with a previously prepared receipt for the amount of £20,000, but this he shoved aside with an arrogant gesture. Then he stuffed the big bundle under his coat, which he had not taken off at any time. He pulled his hat down over his eyes and turned up the collar of his overcoat. In the darkness a close friend might have failed to recognize him. Barely an hour before, he had entered my office a simple domestic servant; he was leaving it a wealthy man. I can still hear the curiously sneering and triumphant tone of voice in which he spoke as he left me, clutching his precious package beneath his coat.

"*Au revoir, monsieur,*" he said. "Same time tomorrow."

When the photographer returned I managed, with his help, to make some adequate enlargements. Once I was sure I could carry on alone, I sent him off to bed. The two rolls consisted of fifty-two negatives, which I now proceeded to enlarge. Then, carrying the films and the prints, I went back to my office.

My emotions during the next few hours remain absolutely clear to me. Hour after hour, behind the locked door of my office, I read, sifted, made notes, read again. Gradually, as the night wore on, those secret documents threw a harsh light on much that, for me, had been confused and ill understood.

"Here, on my desk, were most carefully guarded secrets of the enemy...."

Here, on my desk, were most carefully guarded secrets of the enemy, both political and military—of incalculable value. There was nothing suspect about these documents. These were no plant. Out of the blue there had dropped into our laps the sort of papers a secret service agent might dream about for a lifetime without believing that he could ever get hold of them. Even at a glance I could see that the valet's service to the Third Reich was unbelievably important. His price had not been exorbitant.

None of these documents was older than a fortnight at most, and the majority bore a date of the last few days. They were all signals passed between the Foreign Office in London and the British embassy in Ankara. All of them bore in the top left-hand corner the imprint TOP SECRET or MOST SECRET. Apart from the date, they also showed the time at which they had been sent and received by the wireless operators. This was a technical point of great importance in helping the Berlin experts to break the British diplomatic cipher.

Of particular value for us were signals from the Foreign Office concerning relations and exchanges of opinion between London, Washington and Moscow. It was doubtless the extremely important position that Sir Hughe occupied, no less than the personal respect and confidence that he enjoyed in London, that led to his being so well informed about political and military affairs. I had clear proof of this in the batch of glossy photographs on my desk.

For a German those documents had an important and upsetting message to reveal. They clearly showed the determination, as well as the ability, of the Allies utterly to destroy the Third Reich in the comparatively near future. As I sat hunched over my desk for hour after hour, I saw the writing on the wall. This was not propaganda. The grim future that lay ahead of us was there for all to see.

I remember wondering whether the leaders of Germany, far away in Berlin or at the Führer's headquarters, would grasp the full significance of what was here revealed. Finally, exhausted by emotion as much as by anything else, I fell asleep over my desk, where my secretary's knock at the door next morning awakened me.

A few hours later I was sitting in the ambassador's little anteroom, on a sofa. I was very tired and unshaved. Fräulein Rose, the ambassador's secretary, was moving to and fro between the anteroom and the ambassador's office. While awaiting his arrival she was laying out the morning papers and mail. She obviously disapproved of my disheveled appearance.

In order to have something to do, I began to thumb through the fifty-two photographs in my folder. I held them in such a way that she could see only their backs.

"This must be important business for you to bother the chief so early in the morning. What have you got in that folder of yours?"

"Nothing for your chaste eyes, Rosie. Just some nudes—the bare facts, one might say."

"Now you're being coarse. You ought to be ashamed of yourself."

I was no longer listening to what she said. From sheer boredom I had begun to count the photographs—47 . . . 48 . . . 49 . . . 50 . . . 51. Surely it must have been due to Rosie's chatter that I had miscounted them! I started all over again—49 . . . 50 . . . 51.

In my office I had made sure that all fifty-two were there. As calmly as I could I counted them again. There were still only fifty-one.

"Fräulein Rose, would you mind helping me for a moment? Count them please, but don't turn them over."

She did so, while I stood and watched her. I was beginning to feel very frightened.

"Fifty-one," said Fräulein Rose.

It was appalling. Where could the other one be? Had I lost it? If so, it must have happened between my office and the ambassador's.

I grabbed the folder of photographs, put it under my arm, tore open the door and ran downstairs. At the front door I almost crashed into the ambassador, who was coming in. I did not stop or say a word. Herr von Papen looked at me as though he thought I had gone mad.

In the garden I examined every inch of the path I had taken. Nothing. I hurried into my office. My secretary was sitting calmly at her desk.

"Did I leave anything here? A photograph, for instance?"

"I haven't seen anything."

I searched through all my drawers, crept under the desk, lifted the carpet. Nothing. I must have dropped it on my way from my room to the ambassador's anteroom. Suppose somebody had already picked it up? God help us all if it got into the wrong hands. With a heavy heart I made my way slowly toward the ambassador's office.

Just before reaching the main gate I glanced around once more. Over there by the gate— I broke into a run.

It was the missing photograph all right, lying face down, showing nothing but its innocent white back. A few steps away stood the Turkish porter. He could not see it, since it was concealed from him by the half-open gate. Quite a few people must have passed that spot during the last twenty minutes. And only a few yards away was the great Boulevard Atatürk with its constant stream of pedestrians. A little gust of wind, and our secret would have been revealed to the world.

I picked it up, trying to look as unconcerned as possible, for the porter was watching me. Back in my room I counted the prints all over again. This time there were fifty-two. Then I set off once more to see the ambassador.

He received me with a smile. Evidently Fräulein Rose had told him all about the queer behavior of his attaché.

"Now, what about this valet of yours? Did you get rid of the twenty thousand pounds? From what Fräulein Rose tells me I gather you received a fine selection of bathing beauties in exchange?"

The ambassador was in a good mood this morning.

"I think, sir, you'll find my bathing beauties as exciting as I did." I handed him the folder. He took it and put on his spectacles.

"Fantastic," he murmured, almost at the first glance. As he turned over the glossy photos one by one I could see that he was growing more and more excited. As for me, I had a hard time to stop myself from falling asleep.

"Good heavens! Did you see this one?"

The ambassador's voice jerked me awake just as my eyes were about to close. He handed me one of the documents that gave precise details concerning the gradual infiltration of RAF personnel into Turkey. The figures were very considerable, far larger than anything we had suspected. "This doesn't look too good," said Herr von Papen. "Berlin won't like this one."

The ambassador then read a series of signals I had arranged in order early that morning, a breakdown of lend-lease equipment recently supplied to the Soviets. The volume was fantastic. This would certainly cause consternation at the Führer's headquarters.

Another document was a most important signal, intended for the British ambassador's eyes only, describing the state of relationships between London, Washington and Moscow. The Russians were insisting on an immediate second front, making it quite clear that they did not regard the Italian campaign as a sufficient contribution to Allied strategy. Moscow seemed to be not only impatient, but suspicious about the true intentions of her allies. That little item would suit Ribbentrop's purposes very well, convinced as he was of the ultimate collapse of what he had once called "the unholy alliance."

Von Papen kept on reading. From time to time he would shake his head or, speaking more to himself than to me, would mutter, "Fantastic! Unbelievable!"

Having made his first superficial study of the papers, he leaned back in his armchair. He seemed deep in thought and made no immediate comment on what he had read.

"Well, sir, what do you think?" I ventured to ask.

"If these documents are genuine, and I have no reason to doubt that they are, their value is inestimable. But we must still bear in mind the possibility of it all being an extremely clever trap. It's a great mistake ever to underestimate the British. The man's next delivery should help us to make up our minds on that point. Incidentally, when are you seeing him again?"

"Tonight at ten o'clock."

"The man must be working overtime. Let's hope he's not being rash. Where are you meeting him?"

"By the toolshed in the garden. He gets through the fence there and then I take him to my office."

"Who knows about this so far?"

"No one, sir, except you, Herr and Frau Jenke and myself."

"Your secretary?"

"No."

"Is she reliable?"

"Absolutely, sir."

He reached for the folder again and thumbed through the photographs. After a pause he said, "I'm certainly going to tighten up our own security regulations and make everyone on the staff conscious of them. If the British can get into this sort of mess, so can we. And . . ."

He fell silent. Then, after a while, he added, "Well, I'll have to inform the foreign minister about this. Meanwhile I'll keep the documents here. There are fifty-two of them, you say?"

Did I see a slight twinkle in his eye? Yet I felt a shiver at the sudden reminder that not so long ago there had only been fifty-one. "Yes, sir, fifty-two."

The ambassador was now having a look at the original rolls of film. Since neither he nor I were photographic experts, this inspection did not tell us anything.

"For purposes of correspondence the child must first be christened. We'll have to give the valet a code name. What shall we call him? Have you thought of a name?"

"What about Pierre?" I suggested. "That's what he calls himself on the telephone. I'm sure it's not his real name."

"No good, my boy. Very unimaginative. We've got to give him a code name that even he doesn't know. How about this? Since his documents are so very, very eloquent, let's call him Cicero."

10 o'clock meeting in embassy garden

CHAPTER 4

FTER A FEW HOURS' sleep I awoke entirely rested and ready to get
back to work. I had another talk with the ambasador, at which
Jenke was also present. Herr von Papen had devoted the greater part
of his day to a close study of the documents. He was now entirely
satisfied that they were genuine. The three of us discussed certain
points of technical interest.

How, in the first place, could a valet obtain access to such secret
documents?

Did he have an assistant? Was anyone else at the British embassy in
the know?

How exactly did he photograph the documents?

Did he himself select the ones worth reproducing? If so, how was
it that some of the documents we had so far received were of extreme
importance while others were relatively trivial?

Did he do the actual photographing inside or outside the British
embassy?

What, if any, were the man's motives, apart from his obvious desire
for money? Why did he hate the British? And how had he come to
enjoy the ambassador's confidence?

Why did he insist on being paid in sterling, a currency relatively
rare in Turkey and certainly far less popular than gold or dollars?
When he decided to go in for this dangerous work, would it not be
logical to assume that he was hoping for, or even expecting, a British
defeat? In the nature of things this would involve a depreciation of
British currency. Why then did he insist on sterling?

As the British ambassador's valet, he must speak fluent English.
Why, in talking to me, did he always choose French, which he spoke
very poorly indeed? I found this odd and scarcely credible.

All these questions I noted down for future discussions with Cicero.

At exactly ten that night I went to the toolshed in the garden.
Pierre, or Cicero, was already there. He greeted me like an old friend.
When we got to my office I locked the door. Cicero repeated the precautions he had gone through at Jenke's house, pushing the long curtains aside to make sure that there were no eavesdroppers. I let him
do so without comment. He seemed to be in no hurry. I sat down at

my desk. There was a chair for him opposite, which he finally took. There were cigarettes, and a decanter of whisky stood on a side table.

Cicero poured himself out a drink and then without a word placed two rolls of film on my desk. I took them and locked them in my drawer. I now had to explain to him that I had no more sterling at the moment, but that some was expected from Berlin in the very near future. I was a little anxious as to how he would take this, but he interrupted me after a few words. "*Ça ne fait rien.* You can give me the thirty thousand next time. I'll be back, you see. And I know that it'll be in your interests to keep me happy. Besides, I trust you."

It was gratifying to find that my word was worth £30,000. I drank his health and he returned the compliment.

"I was quite astounded last night by the technical quality of your work," I said, assuming a light conversational manner. "Do you do it alone, or have you an assistant? In either case you are obviously an expert photographer."

"I've been interested in photography for years. I have no one to help me. I do everything myself."

"He had picked the place with considerable shrewdness."

"Where do you do it? In the embassy, or somewhere else?"

"In the embassy, naturally."

"But how exactly do you take the photographs? And when? I'm most interested."

"Isn't it enough if I deliver the goods?" he asked, suddenly becoming sulky. "Maybe I'll tell you about how I work some other time, but not now."

There was clearly nothing more to be got out of him at the moment. When he was about to leave he asked me to get him a new camera.

← Drop Cicero at British embassy

"It was a big new Opel…."

"I've been working with a German Leica," he said. "I borrowed it from a friend. I'll have to return it fairly soon. Get me another one. You'd better have it sent from Berlin. Someone might have a record of the numbers of the cameras for sale here in Ankara."

He seemed to think of everything. But what he had told me was not satisfactory so far as the precise technicalities of his work were concerned. Still, I had no choice but to believe him when he said he did it all alone and that no one else knew anything about it.

It was nearly midnight by the time he left.

"When shall I see you again?" I asked.

"I'll ring you up when I have some new stuff, but I shan't come to your office anymore. It's too risky. We'll meet in the old part of the town in some dark street or other. You've got a car, I suppose?"

I nodded.

"We'd better arrange a meeting place tonight. Somewhere where you won't have to stop. Just drive along very slowly with your lights dimmed. As you reach the place, open the door of the car and I'll jump in. If there's anyone in sight ignore me, drive round the block and pick me up when the coast is clear. You'd better drive me to town now and we will fix on a place.

"There is just one other thing," he said. "In case your phone should be tapped—one never knows nowadays—I'll always name a date twenty-four hours later than the time I really mean. If I say I'm expecting you for bridge at such and such a time on the eighth it'll mean that I'll be waiting for you at that time on the seventh."

I went for the car while he waited in my office. My old Mercedes was being repaired, and I was temporarily using a car I had borrowed from a friend. It was a big new Opel, streamlined and in appearance very much like the numerous American cars used by the diplomatic corps. A few days later I bought this car, because it seemed particularly suitable for our purposes. By day I continued to drive the old Mercedes, which everyone in Ankara knew to be mine.

When I brought the Opel around that night he sat in the back seat and carefully drew the side curtains. Then, after directing me through the old part of the city, he told me to stop where there was a plot of wasteland between two houses. It was near a crossroads and quite unmistakable. He had picked the place with considerable shrewdness. "This," he said, "will be our meeting place for the time being. Now would you please drive me to the British embassy?"

I thought I must have misunderstood him.

"Surely you don't want me to take you to the British embassy of all places."

"Why not? That's where I live."

I could see, quite clearly silhouetted against the dark sky, the two buildings of the British embassy. It suddenly crossed my mind that this might be a trap. There was just one short straight stretch, then a sharp bend, and in a few seconds I would find myself opposite their main gate. Before I reached the corner I heard Cicero's voice behind me: "Go slowly now, but don't stop."

I took my foot off the accelerator. We were now rounding the corner and I had to watch the road. I heard a soft click. The back door had been closed almost noiselessly. I looked around. There was no sign of Cicero.

A few minutes later I pulled up at the gate of the German embassy. Everybody seemed to be asleep. The building was quite dark except for the Jenkes' flat. I knew that they were giving a small party. This suited me, for the Turkish porter who had opened the gate would obviously assume that I was one of their guests.

I got the two rolls of film and made my way downstairs to the darkroom. Early in the day I had bought a photography book, and now I mixed the developing and fixing solutions according to its instructions. After an hour's work I had the two strips of film neatly pegged between an electric heater and a ventilator.

Again the photographs were technically perfect. Excited and curious, I took the magnifying glass and, holding the still wet film against the light, tried to get a glimpse of the night's secrets. I could see very little. I would have to wait until they were dry. So I locked the room and went out into the dark garden.

There were still lights burning at the Jenkes', though it was getting on toward two o'clock. I went in and asked for some strong coffee. Jenke wanted to know my news and led me into a quiet corner of the drawing room. I told him that Cicero had been to see me again, but that he would have to wait until the afternoon to learn any more.

At close to three the party broke up. This was just the right time for me to be getting back to work. I said good-by to the other guests. No one noticed that I did not leave the embassy grounds.

Back in the darkroom at about three o'clock, I settled down at once to the job of enlarging. At about six o'clock I had forty new enlargements of secret British documents on my desk. By about eight I was superficially acquainted with their contents.

I locked them in my safe and left the embassy through the back door leading to the garden.

When I arrived home my wife, who had just gotten up, gave me a puzzled look. It was not too difficult to guess her thoughts.

"Work, my dear, nothing but work. I've been at the embassy all night, working all the time, apart from a little while at the Jenkes'. Are you satisfied?"

I think she was.

As for me, after this second night out of bed all I wanted was sleep. I asked my wife to call me at eleven o'clock. I felt completely refreshed after two and a half hours of sleep.

Just before twelve I entered the ambassador's office. In my briefcase were the forty documents. Among them were the first minutes of the Moscow conference that Anthony Eden and Cordell Hull had attended. The matters discussed at this conference were so confidential that Winston Churchill would only reveal them to the House of Commons in secret session.

During the next two weeks much of my daily work consisted of drafting and encoding signals for the ambassador to forward to Berlin. I was soon in a state of permanent exhaustion since, for reasons of security, I myself had to handle all the work connected with Operation Cicero that would normally have been done by the embassy clerks. Berlin added considerably to my troubles by sending me long lists of questions about Cicero to which they wanted full and immediate answers. The majority could only have been answered by a clairvoyant—which I, unfortunately, was not.

Above all they kept asking, over and over again, for precise information about Cicero's real name, his usual whereabouts and his antecedents. Not that these things were of the slightest importance. The value of the material he delivered was surely all that counted.

Parts of these interminable questionnaires were, of course, quite logical and absolutely justified, and I answered every one of them as best I could. One difficulty was that I could not even get in touch with Cicero to put the questions to him. I had to wait until he telephoned me, and that he would not do until he had resumed his photographic activities with some success.

From Berlin they reproached me for not having made some arrangement by which I could establish contact with Cicero. Suppose he never reported again? they asked. What would we do then?

The simple answer, of course, was that in that case Operation Cicero would be over. It was quite obvious that as long as Cicero saw a chance of getting money out of us he would do his best to get it. He would go on working for us just as long as he could manage to have access to British secret documents. If he should no longer be able to get at them, then neither my best efforts nor all the wealth of the Third Reich could do anything about it.

Such reasoning seemed logical enough to me, and I was not conscious of having made any mistakes so far. In Berlin they saw things differently.

It was particularly Kaltenbrunner, newly appointed chief of the Sicherheitsdienst, which was that part of the German secret service not controlled by the Foreign Ministry, who began to take an unpleasantly personal interest in Operation Cicero. Day after day we were inundated with signals from members of his large staff. By now, I felt quite sure, a dozen offices in Berlin must have had whole filing systems dealing with Cicero. Doubtless scores of more or less garrulous persons were in the know, most of them quite needlessly.

Finally one day, when I was particularly busy, I received yet another signal from Berlin asking me reproachfully why I had not yet found out Cicero's real name, age and place of birth. In a burst of irritation I replied: UNABLE SO FAR ASCERTAIN REAL NAME. COULD ONLY ESTABLISH IDENTITY ETCETERA FOR CERTAIN BY DIRECT INQUIRIES AT BRITISH EMBASSY. IF THIS DESIRED PLEASE SEND WRITTEN INSTRUCTIONS THAT EFFECT.

From then on I was spared further inquiries about Cicero's real name.

On November 4 a special courier arrived from Berlin. After I had signed his receipt, he handed me a small suitcase. When I opened it I found it filled with English bank notes, amounting to £200,000, all earmarked for Cicero.

On the next day I happened to be out of my office when I was wanted on the telephone. My secretary took the message, and later told me that a gentleman by the name of Pierre had invited me to play bridge at nine o'clock on November 6. That meant that same night, I thought, remembering the stipulated difference of twenty-four hours.

After dinner I got out the big Opel I had bought. On the seat beside me lay a paper parcel containing the £30,000 I owed Cicero for the last two films. I had some difficulty starting the car, and was a few minutes late when I turned into the dark street where I was to meet him.

"... he sat in the back seat and carefully drew the side curtains".

Noisy – £200,000 arrives from Berlin

About a hundred yards ahead I saw the sudden flicker of a torch. It was repeated twice. This could only be Cicero, and it struck me as careless, this melodramatic and unnecessary signal. The British were not likely to be there to see his childish histrionics, but then the Turkish police might be there.

I was driving very slowly by now. As I opened the back door I could distinctly make him out in the light of the dimmed headlights. He jumped into the slowly moving car, as agile as a cat. I could see him in the rearview mirror.

"Go toward the new part of the town. I get out soon."

I trod too hard on the accelerator, and the powerful car—I was not quite used to it yet—jumped forward. I went through streets and alleyways I had never seen before. A glance satisfied me that we were not being followed. Cicero gave me directions: "Left now . . . straight on . . . right . . ."

I did as I was told. Then I heard him say, "Have you got my thirty thousand pounds?"

"Yes."

"I've brought you another film. You'll like this one."

He passed forward a roll wrapped in newspaper. I put it in my pocket and handed him, over my shoulder, the parcel containing the money. In the little mirror I noticed how he hesitated a moment or so, probably wondering whether or not to count it. Finally he simply stuffed it under his overcoat. There was an expression of triumph on his face.

I turned down a dark alley and drove slowly round the block twice. I wanted to get him to talk.

"I have to ask you a few questions. Berlin wants to know your name and nationality."

There was a moment's silence as the car glided noiselessly down the dark and narrow street.

"My name is none of your business, or Berlin's either. If you've really got to know, you'll have to find it out for yourself, but you'd better be careful how you do it. One thing, though, you can tell Berlin—I'm no Turk, I'm an Albanian."

"You said once that you hated the British. Can you tell me why? Do they treat you badly?"

He didn't answer for a long time. I drove round the block again. I imagine the question upset him, for when he finally replied his voice was strained. In the darkness I could not see the expression on his face. "My father was shot by an Englishman."

I can still hear the way he said that. I remember that I was deeply moved at that moment. Perhaps here was a motive more noble than mere greed for money. For the first time, and for a few minutes only, I felt a fleeting sympathy for the man behind me. He had now relapsed into complete silence.

I did not put any further questions to him that evening. Cicero said coldly, "Take the first turning to the right and the second to the left."

I did as I was told. Suddenly I felt a touch on my shoulder.

"Slow down now, please. *Au revoir.*"

By about two in the morning I had finished my night's work. This time there were only some twenty enlargements of top secret British documents.

When I entered von Papen's office shortly after eleven and handed him the photographs, along with my report on what Cicero had told me the night before, he gave me a signal from Berlin to read. It was signed by Gustav von Steengracht, the secretary of state of the Foreign Ministry. The minister wished to see me in Berlin. I was to bring along all the Cicero material, both the original films and the enlargements. A seat had been reserved for me in the courier plane that left Istanbul on the morning of November 8.

I left Ankara by the night train the next day. Arriving at Istanbul, I drove straight out to the airport. The Junkers 52 was waiting for me.

We were soon flying over the Sea of Marmara, unbelievably blue in the early morning sunlight. Istanbul lay beneath us in all its glorious beauty. When we refueled at Sofia my name was called out over the loudspeaker system and I duly reported to the information desk. A tall young man in a gray military overcoat wanted to see my passport.

"I have instructions from SS General Kaltenbrunner to inform you that a special plane is waiting to take you to Berlin." I wondered at this sudden urgency to see the documents. "Please give me your ticket," he said impatiently. "I'll see to your luggage."

CHAPTER 5

THERE WAS A CAR waiting for me at the Berlin airport a few hours later. Even before I got into it I was told that Kaltenbrunner wished to see the Cicero documents immediately, before I showed them to Ribbentrop. Now I understood the special plane. I was soon to learn that this was the beginning of a fierce struggle between the foreign minister and the chief of the secret service.

I entered the imposing building at 101 Wilhelmstrasse, which has now long been a heap of rubble. There were sentries everywhere. I was escorted to a huge room, with an enormous desk in the middle. Behind it sat Kaltenbrunner. His face was much marked by dueling scars. His voice was deep and sonorous, and suited the man's bulky and powerful physique.

He wasted no time in getting to the point. The documents were immediately laid out on his desk. There were four other men in the room. I was not introduced to them.

"These documents," said Kaltenbrunner, "might prove to be of extreme importance if they are genuine. The gentlemen here are experts who will examine them from a technical point of view. As for you," and he turned to me again, "you are to tell us everything you know about Operation Cicero up to date. We have prepared a list of specific questions. Consider each one carefully before answering, and then answer as fully as you can. It's still possible the whole thing might be a very cunning enemy trap. Even the most minute detail might provide decisive evidence one way or the other."

One of the men now plugged in a recording machine. Then the four experts began to ask their questions. After an hour or so I begged to be allowed a short rest. Then they began again and it went on for another hour and a half.

In the meantime the rolls of film had been taken to the laboratory, and the results of the thorough examination were brought to Kaltenbrunner.

The photographs were taken with a small stop of a very strong lens at a distance of about four feet. Photoflood lamps in portable reflectors had been used. Of the films used, four were of American and one of German origin. They were all slightly underexposed; this, however, had not affected the legibility of the enlargements. Every one of the exposures was perfectly focused. It would appear that they had been made by an expert, but in a hurry. Taking into consideration what I had said, it seemed improbable though not impossible that one person could have taken the photographs unaided.

101 Wilhelmstrasse
"There were sentries everywhere."

This was the point that worried Kaltenbrunner more than others. If Cicero had not worked alone, the possibility of it all being a British plant was obviously much increased. Yet when Kaltenbrunner reached for one or another of the documents and considered once again the amazing importance of the information revealed, he seemed to have as little doubt as I had about their genuineness.

When there were no further questions to ask, because I had nothing further to tell, the four experts were dismissed. I was now alone with Kaltenbrunner.

"Take a seat."

The atmosphere became less formal. We both sat in comfortable armchairs, and I felt considerably more at ease when Kaltenbrunner, in his sonorous voice, resumed the conversation.

"I had you picked up by special plane at Sofia mainly because I wanted to see you before Ribbentrop does. I don't know whether you are aware of the fact that he is no friend of yours. You're too much one of von Papen's men for his liking. Ribbentrop will now try to claim all the credit for Operation Cicero. I don't intend to let him.

"Ribbentrop is still firmly convinced that the British sent the valet to you and that the whole thing is a plant. You can be quite sure he'll stick to that theory out of sheer pigheadedness. At any rate it'll take him a long time to change his mind. Meanwhile intelligence of incredible importance is simply rotting in his desk and being wasted. I intend to speak to the Führer personally about it, and I'll make it my business to arrange for Operation Cicero to be handled entirely by this department. So in future you'll take your instructions from me and from nobody else. You're not to accept any more money from the Foreign Ministry for paying Cicero. Incidentally, the two hundred thousand pounds you got the other day came from me. It arrived safely, I suppose?"

I told him that it had. I then made it quite clear that it was essential for me to be absolutely certain whom I should, and whom I should not, take my orders from. Otherwise the resultant strain and confusion were likely to endanger the whole business.

Kaltenbrunner reassured me that he would get the Führer to settle the matter of administrative control once and for all.

Then he began again questioning me about Cicero's character.

"You know the man," he said. "Do you really believe he's being honest with us?"

I shrugged my shoulders. Kaltenbrunner went on talking, I think more to himself than to me: "I think he's an adventurer. He's vain, ambitious and sufficiently intelligent to have raised himself out of the class into which he was born. He doesn't belong to that class anymore, but then he doesn't belong to the class above either, which he both loathes and admires. He may even be aware of that conflict in his emotions. He's lost all his roots. People like that are always dangerous. That is my opinion of what Cicero is."

"Admitting all that," said Kaltenbrunner, "couldn't he still be working for the British?"

"Possibly. I'm prejudiced on that particular point. I have no doubt whatever that, if he is, one day he'll give himself away. So far I haven't seen the slightest indication that he's anything other than what he pretends to be. I'm entirely convinced the man is genuine. Particularly after the chance remark he made about his father being shot by an Englishman."

"*Try to find out all you can about his father's death.*"

"*What?* Cicero's father shot by an Englishman? Why on earth didn't you report that? It might be the key to the whole thing!"

"But I did. In my last report. It went by diplomatic pouch to the Foreign Ministry."

Kaltenbrunner gave me a vicious look. "When did that signal leave Ankara?" He almost shouted the question.

"Day before yesterday."

"Then Ribbentrop has deliberately kept it from me." He spat out the words from between clenched teeth. He stubbed out his half-smoked cigarette in the ashtray with a violent gesture, and judging by the nasty glint in his eye he would have loved to put those strong hands around Ribbentrop's throat. He jumped to his feet. I was taken aback by this sudden loss of self-control. "What about the death of Cicero's father? Tell me!"

I repeated what Cicero had told me, and added, "It sounded to me as though he were telling the truth."

"But this is very important. It puts him in an entirely different light. Ribbentrop tried to cheat me of that information!"

He banged on the table with his fist. Then, becoming a little calmer, he said, "Try to find out all you can about his father's death. Don't skip any details. As for me, I'll certainly ask Herr von Ribbentrop what he means by not sending me your last report."

He went back to his desk and picked up the pile of photographs, which he handed me along with the rolls of film. I took them from him and began to count them immediately. I did not want to repeat my experience of having one missing.

Kaltenbrunner watched me with an expression of sardonic amusement. He said nothing until I had finished.

"When Ribbentrop sends for you, tell him that you've already seen me. As for your future reports on Operation Cicero, you'll receive my personal instructions when you get back to Ankara. When are you leaving, by the way?"

"I've no idea. I suppose that depends on the foreign minister. It was he who summoned me to Berlin."

Before I left the office I asked Kaltenbrunner to be so kind as to ring up Ribbentrop and to find out from him when he wished to see me. I felt that it would be far less unpleasant for me if Kaltenbrunner himself were to tell Ribbentrop that I had been to see him first. He did so, and I was told that the foreign minister would expect me at seven the following evening.

I left my briefcase with its valuable contents in Kaltenbrunner's office. He locked it up in his big desk. I felt that it would be safer there than in my hotel.

"I hope you don't have a valet," I said, attempting a joke.

Kaltenbrunner had no sense of humor.

"Your documents will be quite safe here," he replied frigidly.

Next morning I was told by telephone that my briefcase would be brought to me at my hotel at a quarter to seven that evening.

It was delivered to me in the hall of the Kaiserhof Hotel by two very important-looking gentlemen.

"We come from SS General Kaltenbrunner. We are to accompany you to see the foreign minister and be present at your meeting with him."

So that's it, I thought, but I said nothing.

Just before the stroke of seven Kaltenbrunner's bulldogs and I entered the Foreign Ministry in the Wilhelmstrasse. We were led to a small office where Secretary of State von Steengracht and Herr von Altenburg were waiting.

The one hundred and twelve top secret British documents again changed hands. The secretary of state looked at them one after the other and then passed them on to von Altenburg. As they glanced at them they both shook their heads, murmuring, just as von Papen had done, "Fantastic! . . . Incredible! . . ." Then they told me—as if I didn't already know—that the foreign minister was inclined to think that Cicero had been planted on us by the British with a view to tricking us in some manner yet to be disclosed.

"At first sight," said Herr von Steengracht, thumbing through the photographs, "they undoubtedly appear genuine enough. Look at this one!"

He handed me the photograph of a document giving detailed information about the Casablanca conference. "We actually can confirm the accuracy of this one. We happen to be quite well informed about Casablanca. Frankly, I can't imagine the British putting such an important piece of information into our hands simply as a decoy. This looks like the real thing to me. And if this document is as genuine as it appears, I see no reason to doubt that your valet has access to his ambassador's safe. He must be a most remarkable fellow."

"He's certainly no ordinary valet," I said, "nor, indeed, an ordinary man. He knows what he wants, his determination is enormous and, from what I've seen of him so far, he seems uncommonly intelligent and careful."

"So you believe in him?" asked Herr von Altenburg. "I mean, you rule out the possibility of his having been planted on us by the British?"

"I do. But I can't prove it. Not yet, at any rate."

Von Steengracht slowly put the photographs back into their folder.

"There's nothing else you can tell us, apart from what you've already reported?"

I shook my head.

Von Steengracht, after a brief glance in the direction of my two companions, said, "The foreign minister regrets he cannot see you himself today. The documents and the rolls of film will stay here. You are to remain available to be at the minister's disposal. I suppose we can reach you at the Kaiserhof at any time?"

That was the end of the interview. It was quite clear why I had not seen Herr von Ribbentrop personally. My two companions took me back to the nearby Kaiserhof. There I stayed, alone with my thoughts.

Two days later I received an urgent message summoning me at once to see Councillor Likus at the Foreign Ministry annex. When I got there I was told that the minister wished to see me immediately.

During the short drive to the ministry proper, Likus gave me some advice.

He said that Ribbentrop was in a foul temper and extremely annoyed about Kaltenbrunner's attitude. As for the Cicero documents, Ribbentrop had examined them personally. He was still convinced that the whole thing was a British trap. Recently, Likus went on, the minister had become more suspicious than ever on all subjects, which was a considerable nuisance to all his staff. I would be wise not to contradict him if I could possibly avoid it.

As we walked along the interminable corridors of the ministry toward Ribbentrop's anteroom, Likus gave me one further piece of advice. "Don't, for goodness' sake, mention von Papen's name if you can possibly help it. I've often seen him lose all control of himself when someone said a friendly word about von Papen."

Thus prepared, I was shown into the presence. Likus, who at that time seemed to be one of the few who enjoyed the minister's confidence, came, too. They were old friends—at any rate they had been at school together.

Ribbentrop got up as we came in. He remained behind his desk, his arms folded in the manner of Napoleon, his cold blue eyes fixed on me. This was the man who was responsible for the making of German foreign policy and who it is said once remarked, "History will recognize me as a greater Bismarck."

The initial silence was most oppressive. Likus, at last, made some conventional remark, and we all sat down around a table on which the Cicero documents were laid out. Ribbentrop reached for a few of them and toyed with them idly, holding them as if they were a hand of cards. Then he began to talk to me.

"So you have met this Cicero. What sort of man is he?"

I repeated what I had now said so often that I knew it almost by heart. Ribbentrop interrupted. "The man's clearly out for money. What I want to know is whether the documents are genuine. What are your views?"

"No more, sir, than what I have already reported. My personal opinion is—"

"I want facts," interrupted the minister. "I'm not interested in your personal opinions. They are hardly likely to relieve my considerable misgivings. What does Jenke think?"

"He agrees with me in believing that the documents are genuine and that the man came to us of his own initiative. Herr von **Papen** thinks so, too."

No sooner were the words out of my mouth than I realized I had made a mistake. At the mention of the ambassador's name Ribbentrop's expression became chillier and grew more arrogant than ever, his lips tightening to a thin line. Likus, behind his chief's back, gave me an exasperated look. Then Ribbentrop began to speak again, very slowly and in clipped sentences.

"I am asking you if these documents are genuine. If these alleged differences between London and Washington and Moscow are true, then I shall know what steps to take. That's all that matters. But I need facts, young man, facts—not personal opinions, your own or anybody else's. Do you feel capable of handling this assignment? Or shall I send someone else to Ankara?"

I was tempted to reply, Send someone else, sir, by all means. However, I just sat silent. If only he would get up, I thought, and announce that the interview was over.

It was Likus again who broke the painful silence.

"It can't be easy for Moyzisch to obtain cast-iron proof of the genuineness of the documents and the bona fides, if I may use the phrase, of the man in question. If Cicero works alone, it seems logical to assume that his documents are real ones. If, on the other hand, he has an assistant, that would be a point in favor of the plant theory, though even so it would hardly amount to evidence. May I make a suggestion?" And here Likus turned to me. "Perhaps you might devote your major efforts to clearing up that question?"

"A very good point, Likus," said his chief. "We'll bear it in mind." Then, turning, but without looking me straight in the face, Ribbentrop said, "First find out at all costs whether or not Cicero has someone to help him. What have you done so far along those lines?"

"Nothing, sir, except that I did put the question directly to Cicero. I depend, of course, entirely on his own statements. Should he be deceiving us I can only hope that he'll somehow give himself away."

Ribbentrop's hands were idly and nervously toying with the documents in front of him. Uncertainty and annoyance were clearly legible on his face as he glanced at the pile of glossy documents that so far was costing the Reich £65,000. With a sudden gesture he thrust the whole batch away from him, over to the far side of his desk. Almost inaudibly his lips formed the words, "Too good to be true."

Then he rose. "You are to stay in Berlin for the time being. I may want to see you again."

"But, sir, Cicero is waiting for me in Ankara, presumably with new documents."

"You are to stay in Berlin for the time being."

He gave me a curt nod. I was dismissed.

I found myself being kept on ice. The country might be heading for disaster; day by day thousands of men who had never wanted war might die in battle; night after night big cities might be reduced to rubble; all the time Cicero might be waiting to present the Third Reich with knowledge that might provide a last chance of saving Germany. Let him wait in Ankara while two high officials in Berlin went on with their petty quarrel.

A few days later, during this unnecessarily protracted stay in Berlin, I was invited to tea by the Japanese ambassador, Hiroshi Oshima. I had never met him before and I put his invitation down to the friendly relationship which I had with the Japanese embassy in Ankara.

Ambassador Oshima received me in his study. He was very interested in conditions in Turkey, which he described as a key point in global politics. He had a lot to say about the Berlin-Rome-Tokyo axis, expressing disappointment in the Italian end of it. While we had tea he glanced frequently at the huge world map that covered almost one complete wall of his study. Much later, when I took my leave, after asking me to convey his good wishes to his compatriots in Ankara he said, "Congratulations, incidentally, on your success."

As he said it there was a ghost of a chuckle in his voice and I seemed to see a knowing smile in his dark eyes. He was obviously referring to Cicero.

That was not all. I spent one of my last evenings in Berlin, with several other guests, at a house in a residential suburb. I realized as soon as I arrived that I was somehow regarded as a celebrity, the lion of the party. I felt the shadow of Cicero behind me.

I was not to be left in doubt for long as to what was expected of me. At first I feigned deafness, then pretended to be stupid, but my hosts, as persistent as they were indiscreet, soon asked me a direct question, "Won't you tell us something about Cicero?"

Initially I could see no way out, but then, ponderously and in my most serious manner, I gave them a lengthy disquisition on the life story of Marcus Tullius Cicero, the contemporary of Julius Caesar.

My flow of words was steady and extremely dull. I droned on and on, somewhat loudly perhaps, until I noticed that one by one my audience was slipping away. My host was the last one to accept my very broad hint.

On the morning of November 22 I was informed that the foreign minister had ordered me to return to Ankara. I left Berlin that same evening. It was lucky for me that I got to the Friedrichstrasse station well ahead of time. For to my surprise the train left before the scheduled time and went straight through two or three suburban stations where it was supposed to stop.

It was only at Breslau, in the middle of the night, that I learned the explanation. As our train was leaving Berlin toward the east, a strong force of British bombers was flying in from the west. It was the first of many giant raids to come. This was my last visit to Berlin before the end of the war.

CHAPTER 6

WHEN I REACHED Ankara I went straight to my office. My secretary told me that a Monsieur Pierre had telephoned repeatedly during my absence. He had left a message that he would probably ring again today. I nodded casually.

"Anything else?"

"Yes, there is."

Schnürchen had recently gotten married and she wanted a few days' leave to meet her husband in Istanbul. This would have to be unofficial.

"Granted," I said.

Then I went to see the ambassador, who wanted all the news from Berlin. He shook his head and grew more depressed as he listened to what I had to say. When I told him of Ambassador Oshima's parting words, he became really angry.

"Official doubts about the genuineness of the documents, that I can understand. But why the devil all the boasting about the very thing they profess not to believe in? Those gossiping idiots will land us in a first-class row here in Ankara yet."

Later that afternoon Cicero telephoned. He wanted to meet me at nine o'clock.

When he got in the car he seemed in the best of spirits. He had missed me, he said. I told him that I had gone to Berlin, entirely on his account. This sort of thing flattered him and he seemed pleased; however, he said that he had done one beautiful job during my absence, though he had not dared keep the film. Over fifty very highly classified documents—he couldn't be expected to carry the roll around with him indefinitely, could he? So finally he had simply exposed the film to the sunlight. He still had the roll and I would have to pay him for it at the normal rate.

"Quite out of the question," I replied. "What do you think they would say in Berlin if I went about buying blank films at fifteen thousand pounds?"

He shrugged his shoulders and dropped the subject for the time being.

I pulled up in front of a friend's house, where I had arranged to borrow a room for that evening. My friend had no clue as to who Cicero might be, and he discreetly left us as soon as he had shown us to the music room.

Cicero looked around him with some curiosity, examining the expensive and beautiful furniture. I handed him the £15,000 for the work he had brought me before I left for Berlin. He put two new rolls of film on a little table. Then he put the roll whose contents he had to spoil next to the other two. I picked it up and put it back in his pocket. While doing so my fingers touched something cold and metallic.

"So you carry a gun?" I asked.

"Just in case," he said, in a casual tone of voice. "I don't intend to let them catch me alive."

There were some sandwiches and a decanter on the table. Cicero helped himself and sat down beside me on the sofa. He evidently felt entirely at home. When he had finished eating he asked me for a cigar.

"Tell me about your father's death," I said, as I offered him my case.

"There is nothing to tell," he replied, his manner changing. From being cheerful he suddenly became glum. "Why do you keep on at me about my private life? If that's a German habit, all I can say is that I don't like it."

"I don't want to pry into your business. I've been told to ask you. In Berlin, for obvious reasons, they want to know more about the man who supplies them with such valuable information. You may call it Teutonic thoroughness if you like, but I assure you it's not just idle curiosity."

"Whatever you call it, I still don't like it. It's none of your business. I'm not your servant. I don't have to answer your questions. I risk my life getting you the documents. You pay me for them. That's all there is to it. I see no reason why I should do anything else for you. I don't want to talk about my past."

"I'd be the last man to try to make you. I had no idea there was any secret attached to your father's death."

"He was shot, and there's no secret about it. It was an accident while they were out shooting. My father had been hired as a beater. If that idiotic Englishman had learned how to handle a gun before going shooting, my whole life would have been different. I might have had a happy childhood. But who cares about the life of a poor Albanian? Now I've got some money, plenty of money, and plenty more to come, but . . ."

"Do you know the name of the Englishman who shot your father?" I asked, after a long pause.

"I know his name all right. I went to the authorities about it, and they gave me some money. Compensation for being an orphan! It was enough to get me to Turkey. It wasn't enough to stop me hating the British."

"Have you any other reason for hating them?"

"Plenty. They treat me badly. Not the ambassador, but some of the others. They don't regard servants as human, they seem to think that they are some sort of animal."

"Then why do you stay with them?"

"I enjoy swindling them. If I didn't stay, you wouldn't have their secret papers, would you? But I'll soon have had enough. Then I'll go somewhere where nobody knows me and where there are no Englishmen at all."

"Provided always they don't catch you first."

"I don't think they will. I've thought of everything, every little detail. And even if they do catch me, they won't take me alive."

It was nearly eleven when he left me. He declined my offer of a lift and seemed to be in a hurry.

I went back to the embassy and locked the rolls of film in my safe. My original fervor had been slightly dampened by my reception in Berlin; developing and enlarging would have to wait until morning. I walked home, thinking over what Cicero had said.

It seemed a fairly plausible story, and I was prepared to accept it. Yet there was an element of cheap melodrama about it that left me slightly skeptical, and I did not imagine that the story would make much impression in Berlin.

On the other hand I realized that to a European, brought up as I had been in Austria, the world of an Albanian mountaineer, with its blood feuds and its vendettas, was bound to appear strange. We never did discover whether the story of Cicero's father's death was true, or whether he invented it in order to have some less sordid reason than money for his treachery.

The next courier plane to Berlin carried some twenty new photographs. One concerning technical details affecting the interchange of messages between London and Ankara proved of immense value to the German secret service in helping them to break an important British code.

There was also the draft of a comprehensive report, almost entirely in the British ambassador's own tidy handwriting. It clearly revealed the British attempt to maneuver Turkey into a state of armed neutrality or nonbelligerency, to be followed by Turkish troop concentrations in Thrace designed to tie up as many German divisions as possible in Bulgaria. The first step was to be the breaking off of Turko-German diplomatic relations.

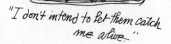

"I don't intend to let them catch me alive."

It was most revealing to see the enemy's intentions spelled out in detail by their most important representative. I was struck by Sir Hughe's lucid and sober assessment of the situation. He made no attempt to disguise the extent to which Turkish policy was being influenced by the personality of the German ambassador.

Drafts and documents of this sort might have provided an invaluable lesson for our German politicians, if they had been prepared to study the well-tried methods of British diplomacy and of British political activity abroad. Unfortunately our superiors in Berlin were entirely satisfied with themselves and with their own methods.

It was therefore in Ankara, rather than in Berlin, that Sir Hughe's draft was appreciated. "Neatly arranged and elegantly formulated," was von Papen's verdict, after he had carefully studied the document. And he added dryly, "Berlin won't like this very much."

With the documents I enclosed a covering note, reporting Cicero's story about his father's death. I also mentioned that he had been alarmed by my long absence in Berlin and that he had, in consequence, destroyed one roll of film containing reproductions which he claimed to have been particularly important. This I put in purely to annoy Ribbentrop. It was my small revenge for the treatment I had received in Berlin.

In reply a few days later I got a signal ordering me, in a peremptory fashion, to get Cicero to photograph those documents again.

During the last days of November I went to Istanbul. It was a nuisance making this long journey again, but Cicero, some time before, had asked me as a special favor to get him £5000 worth of United States dollars. It would be foolish for him to try to change such a substantial amount at one of the local banks; it would inevitably attract attention. He wanted those dollars urgently as he had been offered a profitable investment. In order to keep him in a good temper, I told him I would help him in this matter.

I therefore kept back £5000 from his next payment and took it to our own bank in Ankara, where I asked the manager if he could change that much sterling into dollars. The deal was soon made with an Armenian businessman, about to go abroad, who wanted to buy sterling for dollars.

I had almost forgotten about this transaction when the bank manager telephoned, obviously in considerable distress. He had just had a cable from Switzerland; apparently a Swiss businessman had bought the pound notes from the Armenian, had taken them to England and there had been told that they were counterfeit. The matter had been referred back to Ankara.

I immediately signaled Berlin and got back a most indignant reply, stating that it was utter nonsense to doubt the genuineness of money sent out by the Wilhelmstrasse. However, so as to avoid any breath of scandal, I was instructed to reimburse the Ankara bank out of embassy funds, the whole thing to be done discreetly. Berlin wished to hear no more about it.

While last in Berlin I had heard rumors that forged British bank notes, particularly of the larger denominations, were being printed in Germany for infiltration into neutral countries. I had asked various officials about this, and had on all occasions been given a categorical denial. This all came back to me now.

The business with the bank was settled without any fuss. All the same, I did not feel happy about it. It seemed most unlikely that the Wilhelmstrasse would make counterfeit money, and I could hardly believe that they would be so foolish as to jeopardize the whole of Operation Cicero by paying him in bad notes. But I wanted to make sure that the money I was giving him was genuine.

Therefore, I picked out samples from each of the many bundles of bank notes in my safe. In all they amounted to close on £10,000. These I took to the manager of the bank in Istanbul with which the German consulate general had its dealings, telling him that they had been offered to us for sale and that I had been told to make sure that they were good. After a couple of days, when I went to get them back, I was assured that they were perfectly all right. That, at least, was one thing less to worry about.

The first courier post in December contained a somewhat surprising item—a huge parcel of books, addressed to me, which turned out to be an almost complete library dealing with the more celebrated cases of espionage in the twentieth century. There were various white papers and official files, together with quite a few works

£5000 found to be counterfeit

135

of fiction. I had not ordered these books and had neither the time nor the desire to read them.

There was a covering note, in which I was more or less tactfully informed that a thorough study of these books would help me in handling Operation Cicero. I replied as civilly as I could that I had little time for fiction and that, so far as authentic cases went, I found it hard to detect any parallel between Operation Cicero and, say, the Mata Hari case. I suggested that if Berlin wished to help me in my work, they could not do better than to clear up the matter of to whom exactly I was responsible. An unofficial reply informed me that I had best be patient. Ribbentrop and Kaltenbrunner were still brawling.

After a while I received a communication from Berlin marked STRICTLY CONFIDENTIAL TO BE OPENED PERSONALLY. It contained a sharply worded order from Kaltenbrunner that I was no longer to inform Ambassador von Papen about anything to do with Operation Cicero. On no account was I to show him the actual documents.

I decided there and then not to obey these instructions when I felt that any document would be of value to Herr von Papen in his work. In fact I took the letter straight to the ambassador to ask his advice. Von Papen was extremely annoyed and upset by it. He said that if Kaltenbrunner's order were to be endorsed by Ribbentrop he would tender his resignation at once.

So far as I was concerned, my disobedience in this matter was to put me in a most unpleasant position a little later on.

December was Cicero's great period. Never before and never again did he deliver so much or such important material. There could no longer be the slightest doubt about his genuineness.

In Berlin they were at last beginning to see the value of it all. Every courier plane from Ankara carried fresh top secret British documents, documents so important that for a while even the private war between Ribbentrop and Kaltenbrunner took second place. Ribbentrop's personal attitude toward Operation Cicero seemed to be unchanged. He read the documents, but he never made the slightest effort to use the information he now possessed. Presumably he still had doubts as to whether or not the whole business was a British trick.

As for Cicero himself, he seemed a different man during that busy month. He was quite friendly now, even moderately talkative. When I asked him personal questions concerning his identity or his background, however, he made it quite clear that such matters were none of my business.

He was obviously very proud of his successes. What he liked best to talk about at our nocturnal meetings was his own future. He enjoyed thinking about the large house he was going to own in some pleasant country far away. He planned to have a great many servants. Sometimes his attitude reminded me of a child's exuberant excitement on Christmas Eve.

Cicero had changed considerably in appearance. He now wore well-cut suits of the best English cloth, and expensive shoes with crepe soles. One day, when he appeared wearing a large and flamboyant gold wristwatch, I thought it time I spoke to him.

"Don't you think your chief and other people might begin to wonder where the money is coming from to pay for all your new and obviously expensive possessions? Frankly, I think you're being a little rash."

Cicero looked at me thoughtfully. After a few moments he took off the wristwatch and asked me to keep it for him until he had a chance to take it to Istanbul and store it there with his other jewelry.

He was very fond of jewels. On one occasion he asked me to give him his usual £15,000 in the form of diamonds and other precious stones. He said he was afraid of arousing suspicion if he bought them himself.

I told him that it would seem equally suspicious if I were to buy £15,000 worth of diamonds. I did, however, finally agree to get him a couple of thousand pounds' worth. I felt that that was about the limit I could safely go in pretending I was buying presents for my wife.

Another noticeable change was in Cicero's fingernails. When I had first met him they had been bitten down to the quick. Now they were grown again. He even had them manicured. And this was not the only evidence to show that his earlier nervousness had completely left him. He had given up peeping behind curtains and jerking open doors. He was entirely self-assured, and I was even afraid that he might become careless.

Shortly after the Allied conferences in Cairo and Teheran were over, Cicero rang up and asked for a meeting. I had to attend an official dinner that evening, so I asked him to meet me a little earlier than usual.

At eight o'clock I was at our established meeting place, and with that curious, catlike agility of his he jumped into the slow-moving automobile. He seemed to be in rather a hurry. I passed him a fat bundle of money, which he stuffed right into his pocket while passing me two rolls of film. He said he would have some more for me in a few days' time, and at the next dark corner he slipped out of my car as quietly as he had entered it.

I did not want to be any later than necessary for the dinner party, so I drove straight there instead of first dropping the films at the embassy.

It was not a particularly pleasant dinner for me. I could not stop myself from putting my hand in my pocket every two minutes to make sure my rolls of film were still there. As soon as I decently could I made some excuse, took my wife home and went to the embassy. I had intended just to lock the films in the safe and leave the developing till the morning. But my curiosity was too strong, and I decided to do the job at once.

Finishing just as dawn was breaking, I found that I had in my possession complete minutes of the entire conferences at Cairo and at Teheran.

I worked on, all through the morning, writing a provisional report for the ambassador to forward to Berlin. Good old Schnürchen, when she came to my office at nine sharp, was probably surprised to see her chief at the typewriter, wearing a dinner jacket. Once again she showed her perfect diplomatic training: she made no comment.

With this delivery the sequence of events and development of Allied policy that was covered by the three recent meetings of Allied leaders became entirely clear to us. First there had been the Moscow conference, called by Stalin and attended by Eden and Cordell Hull; then came the Cairo talks of Roosevelt, Churchill and Chiang Kai-shek; and finally there was the great Teheran conference of the Big Three.

That morning, while I typed a résumé of what the batch of photographs on my desk told me, I realized with brutal clarity that what I was writing was nothing more or less than a preview of Germany's destruction. The Moscow conference had done the preparatory work; the Teheran conference had applied the finishing touches. Here a new world had been planned, whose premise was the utter blotting out of the Third Reich and the punishment of its guilty leaders. I never learned what effect these revelations had on the men whose personal fate had just been decided at Teheran. For myself I trembled with emotion at the vast historical perspective opened by these stolen documents.

I spent a very busy day drafting long signals. That evening I met Cicero again. He had yet another roll of film for me. This one contained only a few exposures, but at least one of them was of vital importance. We immediately wired Berlin that the head of the Turkish state had gone to Cairo to meet President Roosevelt and Prime Minister Churchill. Up to then none of us in Turkey, and certainly no one in Berlin, even suspected that President Ismet Inönü and the Turkish foreign minister had left Ankara.

Cicero now began to be more reckless. Every second or third day he produced fresh material. I had given him a brand-new Leica sent from Berlin, and I got him all the film he needed from Berlin, since it might have caused attention had he bought such quantities from the one photography shop in Ankara.

We were still in the second week of December when he telephoned once again asking me to meet him that night. As usual we drove aimlessly through the dark streets and alleys of Ankara, while from the back he handed over a roll of film and I passed him his money. This time, though, he gave me a small package in addition to the roll of film.

"Open it later," he said. "They will know what to do with it in Berlin."

I was about to ask him what it contained when I was blinded by the headlights of another car reflected in my rearview mirror.

Leaning out, I saw a long dark limousine some twenty yards behind us. I remember congratulating myself that I had taken care of my back license plate; it was bent and well coated with dried mud. Also the German make of my car was not easily discernible at night; at a superficial glance that big, streamlined Opel looked like one of the many new American cars so plentiful in Ankara.

I drove on slowly, waiting for the limousine to pass me, but it did not do so. I decided to draw in to the curb until it had gone by. The car behind stopped, too, still at a distance of about twenty yards. Now I really began to get worried. The other car's powerful headlights lit up the interior of the Opel. Cicero was evidently unaware of what was going on. He seemed merely to be bothered by the light, as he drew the curtains of the back window. At that moment I heard the other car's horn and saw in my mirror that it was slowly creeping up toward us.

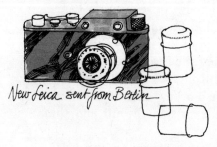

New Leica sent from Berlin

I was thoroughly frightened and drove off as fast as I could, putting on more and more speed, trying to shake off the car behind. I soon realized that it had at least as much speed as my Opel. Furthermore, I could not go full out, since I did not dare risk an accident. Meanwhile, the dark limousine kept close behind me, always at the same distance. I reduced speed to a mere crawl. So did the other car. I had no doubt in my mind that Cicero had been shadowed.

I went through a very narrow and dark alleyway, taking the corner rather slowly, and then suddenly accelerated as heavily as I could, tearing around another corner and then another one. It was no good. In the mirror I could still see the reflection of the dark limousine, twenty yards behind me.

While tearing around those street corners, I glanced at Cicero's reflection in the rearview mirror. He was hunched down in the seat, deadly white. He was aware now that his life was at stake.

"Can't you go faster?" His voice was a hoarse whisper.

It occurred to me to try and reach one of the great new highways that radiated out from Ankara over the plains. On one of them I could drive my big car flat out and I might be able to shake off the limousine. I realized at once that this plan was useless. The roads were marvelous, but there were no

£15,500 wrapped in newspaper

"I soon realized that it had at least as much speed as my Opel."

turnings. Whoever left on one of them had to come back the same way. The British, if it were they, would not even have to bother to chase me. They could simply wait until I came back.

I had no gun. I never carried one while I was in Ankara. There seemed no point, since I would certainly never fire the first shot and the second would be too late. But Cicero had a revolver. By now he was a nervous wreck, hunched there, chewing on his fingernails. For him to have a loaded gun in his pocket was, I thought, extremely dangerous for everyone concerned.

Once again I tried an old trick. I crossed an intersection very slowly. So did my pursuers. Then I raced around the corner and around another one and around still a third. It was touch and go. The car skidded on two wheels, screeching on the turns. Back in the straight I got the car under control again. Doubling around two more corners, I reached the great central boulevard of Ankara, where I accelerated to sixty and then seventy and seventy-five. Looking around I saw to my intense relief that there was no one behind me. I kept my foot pressed down, the accelerator flat against the floorboards. It was lucky that the boulevard, with its many crossings, was completely deserted at that hour of the night. We raced past the great iron gates of the German embassy.

"Take me to the British embassy," said the faint voice in the back seat.

I nodded and went straight on up the steep road. A solitary policeman jumped for his life. There was one more corner. With screaming brakes I went from sixty miles an hour to dead slow. We were a hundred yards from the British embassy. Without a word Cicero jumped out. The darkness swallowed him up.

I went back the same way. There was no other. I saw nobody, no pedestrians, no policeman, no cars, certainly no dark limousine.

It was only when I got to my office that I realized I was shaking all over. My shirt was soaked through and my hair, wet with perspiration, stuck to my forehead.

I put the new roll of film away in my safe, and poured myself a much needed drink. Then I broke the string on the small package. Wrapped in cotton wool and tissue paper was a hard object. It fell out of my still shaky fingers. I picked it up and found that it was a small black object; it had a waxy smell. I had no idea what it was and was about to put it in my drawer when I turned it over and saw on the back the clear imprint of two complicated keys.

Cicero had said they would know what to do with this object in Berlin; they certainly would. It was just a lump of ordinary cobbler's wax; the imprint was presumably that of the keys to the British ambassador's safe.

CHAPTER 7

THAT HECTIC AUTOMOBILE chase in the dead of night through the streets and back alleys of Ankara was the first indication we had that anybody on the outside knew anything about Operation Cicero. I have never really found out who was after us. I find it hard to believe that it was the British. If it was, then they did not know who was in my car with me, for if they had, Cicero could obviously have had no further access to the ambassador's safe. As it was, he continued to rifle it for some months to come.

I am inclined to think the dark limousine was a Turkish police car. My reason for this idea is a curious incident that occurred a few days later.

I was dining at the Jenkes' house. Among the guests were some senior officials of the Turkish Foreign Ministry. After dinner, one of these Turkish gentlemen suddenly said to me, "My dear Moyzisch, you seem to be an extraordinarily reckless driver. You ought to be more careful, you know, particularly at night."

He dropped this remark quite casually into the small talk. I needed all my presence of mind to conceal my real feelings. I smiled politely and thanked him for his well-meant advice.

What, I wondered, did the man really know? Though he could presumably explain the mystery of that chase, I obviously could not ask him to do so. If it had been a Turkish car, did they know who my passenger had been? I have puzzled over all this for a long time now. It seems unlikely that I shall ever find a satisfactory solution.

Cicero had been a nervous wreck when eventually he slipped out of my automobile that night; yet he must have regained his self-confidence almost immediately, for three days later I had another call from him. This time I took him to my friend's house.

He wanted to know if his lump of cobbler's wax had been sent to Berlin. He needed those keys urgently. They would enable him to do his photographing while his chief was away from the embassy. He would feel much safer working that way.

This was Cicero's evening off from the embassy, and he seemed to have plenty of time. Helping himself freely to drinks, sandwiches and cigars, he appeared to be in a most carefree and unreserved mood. In fact he was positively garrulous, boasting a good deal about his achievements, his ambitions and, above all, his cultured background. In the future he intended to devote himself to music. He would, he said, have done so earlier in life had circumstances permitted. He was very proud of his tenor voice, and he insisted on singing some arias from Leoncavallo's *I Pagliacci*. He had a pleasant, light voice; but what really struck me that night, as I sat there listening to him, was the change that came over his hard and ugly face as he sang. Music seemed to make a different man of him.

Cicero was mellow that evening, and the wine made him mellower. This gave me a good opportunity for discharging a recent instruction from Berlin, namely to cut the rate of payment per roll of film from £15,000 to £10,000. Somewhat to my surprise, Cicero readily agreed to this.

A day or two later he delivered a film which was to cause me endless worry and trouble. On the enlarged print of one of the documents a finger and a thumb were clearly visible, showing how the original had been held while the exposure was being made. There could be no doubt whatever that the fingers were Cicero's. He wore a rather conspicuous signet ring on his index finger, and that ring was clearly visible in the photograph. My first thought was that if the British should ever get hold of this print it would mean the end for Cicero.

The important point was that there seemed to be almost incontrovertible evidence that Cicero did have an assistant after all. And this, in its turn, would reopen all the old arguments about the genuineness of the material.

How Cicero photographed the documents had been one of the prime interests of Berlin from the start. Cicero had told me again and again that he held the Leica in one hand, using no tripod or any other form of support. With a finger of this hand he released the shutter and made the exposure. It would seem almost impossible to hold the camera and take the exposure with one hand without wobbling, and quite impossible at the same time to be holding the document to be photographed. Either Cicero had had a collaborator or he had misinformed me about his method.

As soon as they received the significant photograph in Berlin, they began inundating me with telegrams: why? how? with what? and so forth. They nearly drove me frantic. No one could possibly doubt the genuineness of the documents, since internal evidence, all our available external evidence, as well as subsequent events, bore them out. Suppose Cicero did have an accomplice, whom, for some reason, he did not mention. What difference did that make? To regard this minor point as the crux of the whole operation, to keep on asking irritating questions which only annoyed Cicero, seemed to me to be utter imbecility.

Wax imprint of keys to British ambassador's safe—

Then some bureaucrat had a brilliant idea. A trusted photographic expert, who could also speak French, was flown to Ankara. He brought with him a microphone and a long list of highly technical questions which I had to learn by heart.

Finally, after much persuasion, I managed to get Cicero to come to my office again. He did not want to do so, as he rightly considered it to be an entirely unnecessary risk. Still, eventually I got him there, where I asked him all the many technical questions which Berlin had thought up. Every word of this conversation was recorded by means of the specialist's hidden microphone.

Having seen Cicero safely off the premises, I returned to my office, where the Berlin expert was now waiting.

"There is only one thing I can say with absolute certainty," he said ponderously. "He lied about the photograph that shows his other hand. For that one, at least, he had an assistant. For all the others, there is just a possibility that your man might have made the exposures alone. I, however, would consider it most improbable."

I never saw the official report of our photographic expert. His visit had one satisfactory result from my point of view. Henceforth I was no longer pestered by telegrams which I was quite unable to answer.

That exciting month of December was still far from over. My last, and greatest, crisis of that year was caused indirectly by the ambassador. It got me into no end of trouble.

Shortly before Christmas, Cicero's delivery included a document dealing with recent developments in Anglo-Turkish relations. It showed that, in view of Germany's deteriorating military position, Ankara was prepared to yield to British demands for a much increased infiltration of military, naval and RAF personnel into Turkey. Figures were given. From the German point of view this was most important. In the circumstances I considered this a case where it was my duty to disobey Kaltenbrunner's instructions, and I showed Herr von Papen this grimly serious document.

The ambassador was very worried because of the probable reactions of Ribbentrop and his clique. When they learned about these developments they could be expected to react violently. One result might be that Ribbentrop's basically anti-Turkish attitude would be endorsed by the Führer and the high command, provoking reckless measures. In view of these possibilities, Herr von Papen decided to act at once. It was a bold step he took, and the results were far-reaching.

He asked for an immediate interview with M. Numan, the Turkish foreign minister. They had a long talk, alone together, and when the minister tried to dispel the German ambassador's suspicions concerning an imminent or indeed actual violation of neutrality, Herr von Papen did not hesitate to call his bluff. He did not, of course, actually quote any of the information derived from Cicero, but he did make it quite clear that he knew a great deal more than the Turkish government might imagine.

He had to do this. It was essential, from the German point of view, to let the Turks see that Germany was well aware of the nature of those highly confidential Anglo-Turkish staff talks. It was the diplomat's way of exercising pressure, the idea behind it being that the mere hint of German reprisals might make the Turks a little more cautious in their military commitments to the British. Von Papen certainly scored a bull's-eye by this determined *démarche*.

M. Numan was as experienced a diplomat as the German ambassador. He simply said that von Papen must have been misinformed. Finally, while not exactly denying that a few conversations might have been held by military experts in Ankara or London, he said that it would be wrong to attach any great importance to such talks. And again, just before the German ambassador left, the Turkish minister did his best to minimize the significance of a possible understanding with London.

The moment Herr von Papen had gone, M. Numan sent for the British ambassador. He told him every word of what von Papen had said. They both agreed that von Papen could not possibly be so well informed unless there were some high-level leakage, either on the British or on the Turkish side.

Sir Hughe immediately informed the Foreign Office in considerable detail about the conversation he had just had with the Turkish foreign minister. I imagine that this report caused considerable anxiety in Whitehall. Less than thirty hours after this signal had been sent to London, I held its photocopy in my hand. To this day I can remember the last sentence of Sir Hughe's report: "Von Papen evidently knows more than is good for him."

I had no illusions about the probable consequences of that particular document so far as I personally was concerned. The British signal made it quite clear that von Papen, when interviewing Numan, had information which Berlin would realize could only have been derived from the most recent Cicero documents. In the first week of December, as already stated, I had received strict orders from Kaltenbrunner to withhold all these documents from the ambassador. It would be apparent that I had deliberately disobeyed an order.

I thought of extracting that document. That would be quite useless, since Berlin would still have the negative, which they would immediately develop. I thought of concealing the existence of the whole roll. Yet I had to account for the £10,000 that it had cost us. I even toyed with the idea of replacing the money myself, but even if I had been able to raise that large sum in the very short time available, I would have had enormous difficulty in buying sterling. No, it was an impasse. With

I asked him many technical questions.

Conversation recorded

a heavy heart I sealed the documents in the usual envelope. I felt as though I were posting off my own death warrant.

For a while nothing happened at all. Kaltenbrunner's silence was far more unnerving than the most severe reprimand. After a week or so a courier brought me a letter TO BE OPENED PERSONALLY. It was a brief note, written on Kaltenbrunner's orders, curtly informing me that I would be held responsible for a gross breach of discipline in disobeying strict orders. Ribbentrop seemed to have nothing to say either on this or on the vital political issues involved. One could trust him not to back up his own people.

As for Cicero, he was suddenly in very great danger. It was evident that both at the British embassy in Ankara and in London suspicions were now aroused.

How far von Papen's *démarche* with the Turkish foreign minister ultimately affected the further course of Operation Cicero, I cannot say. It is certain, though, that once the suspicions of the British were aroused, they made intense efforts to find out where the German ambassador was getting his information.

TOWARD THE MIDDLE of December our press attaché, Seiler, had had to go to Sofia on official business. While there he went through the first of the American air raids on that city.

It was in the air-raid shelter of the German legation, during one of these raids, that Seiler first met Elisabet, who was to become deeply involved in Operation Cicero. Elisabet was not the girl's real name, but for the sake of her family I do not propose to reveal her identity.

Elisabet's father, a career diplomat of the old school, held a highly responsible position at the German legation in Sofia. Elisabet herself had some sort of secretarial job. She was high-strung; she took the raids very badly, and her parents felt that her nerves were near breaking point. Her father adored her, and he asked Seiler if he could possibly find some position for the girl either with the Ankara embassy or with the Istanbul consulate. He felt that it was essential for his daughter to have a rest in a neutral country.

When he got back to Ankara, Seiler told me about this. He knew that I was looking urgently for a second secretary, since Schnürchen, while closing the door of the office safe one day, had caught her thumb in it and could only type with one hand.

Elisabet sounded like exactly the sort of girl I was looking for—the daughter of a highly respected German diplomat, herself experienced in secretarial work and in the diplomatic service, an excellent linguist, and by reason of her background bound to be thoroughly reliable. In view of Operation Cicero the last consideration was far and away the most important.

I discussed the matter with the ambassador. He had no objection to Elisabet's transfer from Sofia to Ankara. He knew and respected her father. The transfer met with the approval of the chief of personnel at the Foreign Ministry in Berlin. The only person who might make difficulties about it was Kaltenbrunner; in view of Operation Cicero he, too, had to be consulted about all changes of personnel. Since there was a slight delay in receiving his approval, I wrote a long letter, pointing out that I could not handle all my work without some additional help.

In reply I received the offer of a male secretary to be sent from Berlin. The implication was obvious, and I did not care for the idea of having one of Kaltenbrunner's stool pigeons sent to spy on me. All I wanted was a reliable girl who could type and who had a fair knowledge of English and French.

The fact that I was responsible for Operation Cicero presumably put me in a fairly strong position. I finally did obtain Kaltenbrunner's consent, and so Elisabet, whom I had never seen, was transferred from Sofia to Ankara.

She arrived in the first week of January. I went to meet her at the station. The first impression she made on me was appalling. She struck me as perfectly dreadful. I am not, I think, unduly squeamish, but her appearance when she stepped off that train at Ankara was a shock. She was a platinum blonde in her middle twenties, of average height, with long, stringy, untidy hair. Her eyes were dull, with a sort of glazed expression. Her skin had an unhealthy grayish tinge.

I persuaded myself that her appearance was probably due to the long journey and the hard time she had had at Sofia. I took her to the small hotel where I had booked a room for her, and then to my house, where my wife had prepared supper for her.

My wife was equally taken aback by Elisabet. The girl had a most irritating way of trying to appear blasé and sophisticated. She seemed completely uninterested in this strange new city, built to order on a barren plain. She seemed, in fact, uninterested in everything. From the moment I met her, Elisabet was an enigma to me. She still is.

Seiler, who had spoken to me about her in the first place, told me that the Elisabet he saw in Ankara seemed a different person from the girl he had known in Sofia. Whatever the reason for this sudden change may have been, I never found it out.

The day after she arrived, Elisabet fell ill. Her only symptom, so far as I could see, was that her face swelled up in an alarming manner. I arranged for a doctor to attend her, and my wife went to see her; but the girl was quite unresponsive and apathetic, and silent to the point of rudeness. A few days later, when I went to call on her, I noticed on her bedside table some boxes of sleeping pills. It occurred to me then that the girl's state might be due to an exaggerated use of sedatives.

After ten days the doctor said she was well enough to start work. I gave her simple jobs, mainly translations from the British and French press. Her work proved thoroughly unsatisfactory, full of mistakes and oversights, and very untidily presented. This, at least, I did not expect, since she spoke English and French with scarcely a trace of a foreign accent.

She was a nuisance rather than a help in my office; yet, since I had asked so urgently that she be sent to me from Sofia, I felt I must make the best of it. Moreover, I still hoped that in time she might get over her lethargy and stop being so slovenly. To make her feel that she was being trusted and so to encourage her, I let her deal from time to time with slightly more confidential matters than mere press translations. Of course, I told her nothing about Cicero.

I thought that Elisabet would surely do something about her looks when she recovered from the exhaustion of her journey and of the Sofia raids. I was wrong. Finally, one day I asked my good friend Schnürchen to drop a tactful hint to the girl.

Elisabet, being highly sensitive, seemed to guess that the suggestion came originally from me. She resented it, though she did go to the hairdresser. When she came back she looked a different girl, and from then on, apart from occasional relapses, she seemed to go to the other extreme, spending a lot of time and money on her appearance. Still, she certainly made me aware of her resentment at my interference. For several days she would not speak to me at all.

I was too trusting in regard to Elisabet, and that was a serious mistake. A more serious one was my reluctance to interfere in her private life. I soon learned that she was having an affair with one of two Germans interned at Ankara, men I shall call Hans and Fritz. They had arrived in Turkey a few months before with a dramatic story of having bailed out over the Black Sea after being shot down by a superior force of Russian fighter planes. Investigation later proved they had deserted from the Luftwaffe. These young men were enjoying to the full the extremely decent internment conditions accorded by the Turks to combatants of all nations.

I cannot now remember which of the two Elisabet was reputedly seeing too often. That sort of gossip I have always hated and done my best to ignore. I felt that my secretary's private life was entirely her own affair and absolutely no concern of mine. I daresay in theory I was right. Had I been an ordinary businessman, there would have been no harm done. But ordinary businessmen do not often deal with men like Cicero.

After a time Elisabet took a flat in one of the many apartment houses in Ankara. Had I been a little more inquisitive, I might have found out in time that the apartment above Elisabet's was occupied by an employee of the British embassy.

A small pebble can start a landslide. Elisabet was to play a decisive part in Operation Cicero. She would probably never have become involved in it at all, at least certainly not in the role she ultimately assumed, if she had liked me. Looking back on it all now, I can see, I think, the occasion on which she started to dislike me, the exact moment at which the small pebble was dislodged. Granted she was a neurotic creature, even so it seems a most trivial incident.

One day I was dictating to her in my office. She had crossed her knees in such a way as to reveal a great deal of her shapely legs. This irritated me. After some minutes, as I passed her, I stopped and, with some joking remark, pulled down her skirt an inch or two. She blushed furiously. She said nothing, but at that moment I was quite certain that she hated me.

THE KEYS MADE in Berlin fitted the British ambassador's safe perfectly. Cicero told me that he could now do most of his work while his chief was out. He got a lot of material, but he never again approached the results achieved in December. There was a good reason for this. Conditions at the British embassy were not nearly so easy for Cicero as they had been.

He, of course, did not know the details of von Papen's talk with the Turkish foreign minister and the latter's subsequent conversation with Sir Hughe. But he certainly saw the practical results, for British security measures were immediately and rigorously tightened up.

As early as mid-January, Cicero told me, various men began arriving at the British embassy from London, apparently engaged on mysterious errands. It seemed obvious to me that they were doing a security checkup, and I guessed that the British authorities suspected that the leakage was somewhere inside their embassy. All the safes were being fitted with specially devised safety alarms.

It was a dangerous situation for Cicero. A wiser man would have called the whole thing off then and there. Cicero had already received well over £200,000 from me, which should have been enough to keep him in all the luxury he wanted for the rest of his life.

On January 14, 1944, any doubts Berlin might still have harbored about the genuineness of the documents were dispelled once and for all in a singularly ghastly manner. In an operation such as Cicero, one is apt to forget that the real stakes are the lives of human beings. On January 14 I was to be forcibly reminded of that fact.

Among the documents provided by Cicero in December was a copy of the minutes of military staff talks held during the Teheran conference. It had then been decided to start a series of heavy bombing attacks on the capitals of the Balkan countries allied to Germany— Hungary, Rumania and Bulgaria. The first city on the list was Sofia, and the raid was to take place on January 14. Thanks to Cicero, Berlin, as well as the German authorities in Sofia, knew of this plan well over two weeks before that date.

If this raid came off, Berlin informed me, it would be final proof of the genuineness of the Cicero documents; nothing less than the death of thousands of innocent civilians would convince Ribbentrop and Kaltenbrunner. It was an awful position to be in, knowing what was going to happen and quite unable to do anything to prevent it.

Late on January 14 I put through a call to the German legation at Sofia. The tension of waiting had become intolerable and I had to know what was going on there.

"The connection with Sofia is broken," said the Ankara operator.

It was not until early morning on the fifteenth that I finally got through. I spoke to an official at our legation who said, "We've just had the heaviest raid yet. The whole town's on fire. Very heavy casualties."

I wondered if Berlin was satisfied now. They had their proof. Cicero was genuine. Four thousand Bulgarians, men, women, and children, had vouched for it with their lives.

For a couple of weeks thereafter Cicero did not dare to touch the safe. He said that before attempting another job he would have to find out how the newly installed safety devices worked. Late in January he told me he had had a bit of luck. He happened to be in the next room, he said, while the ambassador was talking to security experts from London. By listening to what they said he had managed to pick up how the new devices worked.

I did not at the time tell Cicero that this was tacit admission that he had been lying when he had told me that he could speak no English. I had never really believed that. Obviously if he could follow a conversation which must have been of a highly technical nature, his mastery of English must be at least as good as I had always suspected it to be.

A few days later Cicero told me that the ambassador's safe had jammed. Experts and tools were flown out from England, and finally the safe was opened again. According to Cicero, he managed to be present while this was being done and thus saw exactly how these new security devices worked. He elaborated this extraordinarily unlikely tale with a highly involved description of the complex new arrangements for guarding the safe—electromagnetic devices, infrared rays and so on. I think he said all this merely to stress his own ingenuity in dealing with these new difficulties, and I suspect that a great part of it was made up.

His motive was plain enough. He maintained that the work was now so difficult and so dangerous that he must have at least double his present fee; that is, he wanted £20,000 per roll of film, each guaranteed to contain a minimum of fifteen exposures. I refused and we kept to the same price.

Now I realized why Cicero had lied to me about his knowledge of English. By telling me over and over again that he hardly knew a word of the language, he implied that he obviously could not judge the importance of the documents he photographed. Therefore, since he could not guarantee to deliver only the highest-level material, we would have to pay for all the rolls he brought us even if some of them should be of no interest to Berlin.

Up to February this issue had not arisen. In the early days, and particularly in December, almost everything that Cicero gave us was extremely valuable. Now, however, it was no longer easy, if indeed it was possible at all, for him to get at the really top secret documents, and so he began to make use of the scheme he had carefully planned from the very beginning.

One day he delivered a roll of film containing considerably more than the fifteen shots. After I had developed and enlarged it, I found that all it contained was a very long, and incidentally incomplete, statement of petty expenditures within the British embassy. Of course, it had no value for us whatsoever. Furthermore, I considered it most unlikely that the ambassador would keep this sort of thing in his private safe. For this roll Cicero demanded his usual £10,000.

I told him that I could not possibly pay for that sort of rubbish. Cicero insisted that I knew perfectly well that he couldn't understand English and, hence, that he had never been able to judge the value of what he photographed. Therefore, he demanded his usual payment.

New safety devices at British embassy

It seemed very simple to me. He had deliberately produced this worthless stuff to see if he could get away with it. If he could he would presumably go on doing so as long as the contents of the ambassador's safe were denied him.

I said that I would have to refer the matter to Berlin. I sent off the roll of film and the enlargements, with a covering letter explaining why I refused to pay. In a reply, which came by the next courier, I was curtly told to pay Cicero his £10,000 and informed that this roll had proved extremely valuable.

When I handed him the money he grinned broadly. I told him that I entirely disagreed with Berlin and that I was well aware of the game he was playing. He shrugged his shoulders and said that henceforth he would only select documents classified TOP SECRET, MOST SECRET or SECRET. His English, he explained, was good enough for him to recognize those words. From then on, as a matter of fact, we frequently spoke in English together.

At the end of January I went to Bursa, a famous Turkish watering place, for a rest. It was my first leave since arriving in Turkey. For at least a week I was determined to forget all about Cicero. I had hardly been there a day when a telephone call from Ankara put an end to my holiday.

An official had vanished from the Istanbul consulate. It was almost certain that he had deserted to the British. Since I had known the man, and the head of his department was a good friend of mine, I was required to return to Ankara at once. Also there was the question of whether the man's defection had had any repercussions on my own work. My department had been in close contact with the Istanbul consulate. I returned to Ankara that evening, deeply worried. That desertion, which was the first of a series, caused a considerable sensation. The man had occupied a key position in the Abwehr, the military intelligence division, and he had taken with him information that would prove of great value to Germany's enemies in Turkey.

Shortly afterward there was a second case of desertion, and within a few days a third.

Elisabet, usually so silent, worked herself up into quite a state over this. She said she could not understand how any German could go over to the enemy while his country was engaged in a life-and-death struggle. She regarded such behavior as the most despicable thing a man could do.

I was somewhat taken back by her vehemence. It was unusual for Elisabet to show any excitement, or even interest, about anything, and this sign that she was getting over her habitual indifference pleased me. Under the impact of these sensational events she became talkative. She told me one day about her two brothers, who were officers serving at the front, and she spoke at length about the duty of every noncombatant to help the soldiers who were risking their lives for Führer and Fatherland. Elisabet's little speech would have made an excellent leading article for one of Dr. Goebbels' newspapers.

At the office this sort of talk did not impress us very much. But I felt some satisfaction at seeing Elisabet show signs of vitality, even if they only took the form of parrotlike repetition of propaganda. It was a turn for the better and, what is more, it seemed to last. Elisabet began to accept invitations to parties. She even laughed sometimes. And once or twice she went so far as to make a joke herself. It seemed as though my hopes of winning her confidence were being realized. She came to my house on occasions now, and I arranged for her to be invited out by my colleagues. In fact, we went to a great deal of trouble to make the girl feel that she was liked and was one of us.

Yet there was always something strange about her. It was difficult not to be irritated by her sudden fits of behaving as though she were utterly bored. Many times at parties I saw a group of cheerfully talking people fall silent as Elisabet approached. Still, she did seem to be improving.

We would occasionally talk together, and once we had a short conversation which, in retrospect, seems to have considerable significance. We were alone in my office. I was drafting a report and she was busy translating an article from *The Times*. Suddenly she looked up and said, "Do you think Germany can still win the war?"

"Of course I do," I replied, somewhat abruptly.

"Why do you think so? The position looks very bad on all the fronts, doesn't it?"

I pushed my paper and pencil to one side and looked up at her.

"Yes, things do look bad. What with American matériel and Russian manpower, the war is theoretically lost, I agree. But there's still politics and diplomacy. A war is only finally lost when a country is defeated in those fields, too."

"And if that should happen?"

"Then it would be God's will. There'd be nothing we could do about it."

"But isn't there any way out?"

"I don't think so. It's as though we were all sitting in a very fast train headed for a crash. A man is as likely to break his neck by jumping out as by staying in. That is . . . if we are heading for a crash."

"How about the emergency brake?"

Elisabet was now looking me full in the face, something she had hardly ever done before. I could not make out what it was that she was getting at.

"What you are saying," I answered, "is equivalent to trying to stop the wheels of destiny. I personally would never presume to try that, merely for my own sake."

Elisabet went back to her work, but suddenly she asked, "What do you think about the Istanbul desertions?"

"Not much. They've jumped out of the train too late. After a man's been on one side all these years he should not change over now. I can respect a man who has always been against us, or who left us before our failure was apparent or even probable. To do so now seems to me undignified to say the least. On the other hand, I've no idea what private motives those deserters may have had."

"Aren't there rather a lot of Germans turning traitor just now? There've been similar cases in Stockholm and Madrid."

"So I've heard." I ended the conversation abruptly. It was a long time before I thought of it again.

When I arrived in my office the next morning I found Elisabet hunched over her desk, sobbing hysterically. There was nothing I could do. Schnürchen, when she came in, managed partially to calm the girl down. Elisabet never told either of us the reason for that sudden outburst of tears. I suggested she go home and rest.

She went without a word. In the afternoon she was back. She mumbled a few words of apology and went on with the unfinished translation on her desk. The result was very poor, full of typing errors and other mistakes.

I kept an eye on Elisabet for the rest of that afternoon. She would stare out of the window for minutes on end, sighing deeply. Once I noticed that she reached for the French dictionary while doing an English translation. It took her some time to notice her mistake.

Next day, though, she seemed entirely recovered. She was carefree and more cheerful than I had ever seen her before. Then, one day in March, Schnürchen came down with influenza. I was now left alone with Elisabet. I must admit that she worked very hard and far more conscientiously than usual. She was certainly trying to handle all the extra work, a great deal of which was quite unfamiliar to her.

The worst day of each week was always the one before the departure of the courier plane. It generally involved working until late in the night so as to have everything ready for the post that left at noon next day. Late in the afternoon on one of these busy days, when I had finished dictating, Elisabet volunteered to stay on and finish the work so that there would be no rush in the morning. I was very tired and appreciated her offer.

I went home and for the first time left her the key to the safe. I was so exhausted that I went straight to bed. But I could not sleep. Toward midnight I began to worry about having left the key with Elisabet. It was not that I suspected her of anything; I was merely afraid that she might forget to lock the safe properly or even lose the key on her way home.

There was no sense in my lying there fretting. I got up, dressed and drove to the embassy. A light still shone in my office. The heavy curtains were not drawn, and against the blind I could see Elisabet's shadow as she moved about.

When I entered the room she was seated at her typewriter. She jumped as I came in.

"It's high time you were in bed, Elisabet. Never mind if you haven't quite finished. We've got the whole morning tomorrow, you know."

"But I prefer working at night and I'm not a bit tired," she said.

I was in no mood to argue. I insisted on her knocking off at once. She got up reluctantly. The key was in the safe, and when all the papers had been put away I locked it. Then I put the key in my pocket.

Elisabet looked straight at me. "Don't you trust me? Your other secretary is allowed to keep the key."

"If I didn't trust you I shouldn't have let you have it in the first place. I'm taking it now merely because it worries me not to have it with me and I want to sleep peacefully tonight."

She said again that she was afraid I did not trust her. Two big tears rolled down her cheeks. There was a look in her eyes as though she were a dog I had unjustly beaten. It made me feel like a brute. We walked out to my car in silence. I offered to give her a lift home, but she declined it abruptly.

The next few days were uneventful. One day, during the luncheon break, Elisabet came into my office with two letters from her brother on the eastern front. She seemed to be deeply devoted to this brother and was always happy when she heard from him. Would I care to read the letters?

I did not want to hurt her feelings, so I took the letters, and began to read rather unwillingly. My mood soon changed. After only a few lines I was deeply impressed. Her brother knew how to express himself. This was the simple record of the feelings of an honest young man who was doing a grim job as well as he could and who was deeply worried about the future of his country and of the people and the home he loved.

I was sincerely moved. When I had finished reading I handed the letters back to Elisabet and thanked her for having allowed me to see them. A few minutes later she was again leaning on her typewriter, sobbing bitterly.

These sudden outbursts of tears and hysteria occurred every few days. Between them Elisabet kept an equally pointless and unbalanced appearance of cheerfulness. I never could make out what was the matter with her. Whatever it was, it interfered hopelessly with the work that had to be done in my office. Finally I felt compelled to go to the ambassador and tell him I had to get rid of Elisabet.

Herr von Papen was not inclined to cooperate. But when I pointed out the risk involved in having a hysterical girl in the office from which Operation Cicero was being handled, he became thoughtful. At last he promised to write a personal letter to Elisabet's father, who was now stationed in Budapest, telling him of her condition and asking him to come and take her away. She, of course, would know nothing about all this.

I was delighted with this diplomatic solution to the problem. He sent a letter to Elisabet's father by the next courier plane; it was a great load off my mind.

Meanwhile I was seeing much less of Cicero. He did produce a roll of film from time to time, but the material was nowhere near his former standard. Probably, since the tightening up of security measures by the British, important documents only remained in the ambassador's safe for as long as the ambassador was dealing with them. Cicero was therefore more dependent on luck than he had previously been.

Even so, he did at that time have one considerable success. For several weeks we had noticed that many of the recent documents were hinting at an important operation. Once I had come across a new code name, Operation Overlord. For a long time we had no indication as to what this Overlord might be. Nor was Berlin any the wiser, as I gathered from an urgent signal, repeated to most of the other embassies and legations, instructing all of us to find out at all costs what this code name meant.

I told Cicero that if, at any time, he heard Overlord mentioned in the British embassy, he was to memorize the exact context and report to me at once. He merely shrugged his shoulders. As usual, it was no use giving him orders.

For some time I had no clue as to the nature of Operation Overlord. Then one day I recalled another passage in a Cicero document, which I soon found in my file. It was a signal from London to the British ambassador in Ankara, insisting that certain Anglo-Turkish negotiations must be completed on or before May 15. I had a feeling that this might have some bearing.

Then there were other passages in the Cicero file, extracts from the minutes of the Moscow and Teheran conferences, showing that Churchill, under considerable pressure from the Kremlin, had committed himself to opening a second front in Europe in 1944.

Finally I was quite convinced that Operation Overlord was the code name for the second front. I immediately sent a signal to Berlin, giving my theory and the reasons that led up to it in detail. A week later I received a laconic reply: POSSIBLE BUT HARDLY PROBABLE.

That roll of film with the reference to Operation Overlord, delivered at the beginning of March, was Cicero's final delivery. It was not until the early hours of June 6, 1944, when the enormous Anglo-American armada appeared out of the dawn off the Normandy coast, that Germany received final confirmation of the mysterious code word's real meaning.

It seems ironic that the last piece of invaluable information supplied by Cicero should have been treated by Berlin with exactly the same lack of comprehension as all the others.

CHAPTER 9

I T WAS BOUND to happen sooner or later. Toward the end of March, Elisabet learned about Operation Cicero. I was in Istanbul on one occasion when the diplomatic bag from Berlin arrived in Ankara. Since Schnürchen was still away sick, Elisabet opened the correspondence addressed to my department. Generally great care was taken to put all messages referring to Cicero in a special envelope, addressed to me, and marked STRICTLY CONFIDENTIAL TO BE OPENED PERSONALLY. But on this one occasion Berlin had forgotten about the special envelope. In consequence Elisabet opened it and read the message.

I felt vaguely worried when I returned to Ankara and Elisabet gave me the contents of the courier's pouch. I felt more worried when she asked me, quite innocently, "Who is Cicero?"

I tried to ignore the question, but she repeated it.

"Listen," I said, when I saw that I could not very well avoid answering her. "There are certain matters I have to deal with entirely on my own. This is one of them. Please don't ask me any more questions because I shan't be able to answer them."

I read the message with particular attention. Berlin's carelessness in the matter of the envelope was very unfortunate, since the message in question made it quite clear to anyone who read it that Operation Cicero referred to something going on inside the British embassy. But I soon dismissed the incident from my mind.

A few days later, after office hours, I gave Elisabet a lift into town. She wanted to buy some things. When we reached Ankara's main shopping street, she asked me to accompany her while she bought lingerie. There was only one good shop of this sort in town. I had no particular desire to go with her, but she could speak no Turkish and she asked me to help her make her purchases.

She was a most difficult customer. The wretched attendant had piled up a regular mountain of materials on the counter while Elisabet was trying to make up her mind. She was still undecided which one to choose when a tinkle of the shop bell announced another customer. It was Cicero.

Of course I ignored him. He stood first behind me, and then next to Elisabet, and he, too, gave no indication that he had ever seen me before in his life. He ordered shirts, made to measure, very expensive silk shirts.

When he had finished, Elisabet was still not satisfied with the things she had been shown. My knowledge of Turkish is limited and I had difficulty in explaining to the attendant exactly what it was she wanted.

Cicero, who spoke perfect Turkish, offered to act as interpreter. He did it with considerable charm and adroitness, speaking to Elisabet in French. He took one piece after another of the flimsy materials lying on the counter and draped them on himself, as though he were a professional mannequin. Elisabet laughed, and soon they were joking as though they had known one another for years. I was feeling thoroughly uncomfortable, but I think the whole situation amused Cicero. He asked her if she was German, and when she said she was, he inquired politely if she enjoyed the life in Ankara.

"Very much indeed," she replied with a smile.

Cicero, after paying for his shirts from a huge roll of notes, took his leave of Elisabet with an accomplished, if somewhat exaggerated, bow. Then, while no one was looking, he gave me a broad wink. There was a knowing and cynical smile on his lips.

She, of course, had no idea that this friendly, elderly man was the Cicero about whom she had been questioning me. And neither he nor I suspected that a few days later, if it had not already happened, Elisabet was to decide the fate of both of us.

At length Herr von Papen received an answer from Elisabet's father. Personal circumstances prevented his collecting Elisabet until after Easter. It was not very long to wait.

One fine spring morning a small incident occurred to which I failed at the time to attach any significance. Work was slack, and Elisabet asked me politely if I could spare a few minutes for a friend of hers in the Luftwaffe, the man I have called Hans. She said he was looking for work.

She was evidently anxious to help the young man, and of course I remembered the gossip I had heard about her having an affair with one of them. I agreed to see him.

Next day both the fliers came to my office. It was the first time I had ever talked to them, though I knew them by sight. They sat down modestly, and even somewhat timidly, and wasted a lot of my time perorating about the Fatherland, a soldier's duties and their own particular desire to get back to the front and fight for the Führer. Unfortunately, having given their word to the ambassador, they could not escape from internment as otherwise they would most assuredly have done long ago.

Finally they came to the point and asked me if I could give them jobs. It didn't matter what it was, so long as they could make enough to pay for their cigarettes. Even that was a detail; all they really wanted was to make themselves useful and work for Germany. I let them finish their rather lengthy speech while I did my best to size them up. Then I gave them the only possible answer: there was nothing I could do for them.

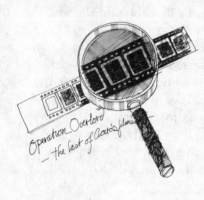

Operation Overlord
— The last of Cicero's films.

They left my office reluctantly. I was glad to see the last of them. I did not care for either of them. There was something definitely wrong about their manner—polite and even subservient though it had been.

Elisabet never mentioned the fliers to me again, but her behavior left not the slightest doubt in my mind that she deeply resented my refusal to help her friends.

A few days later there was another scene in the office, with Elisabet once again in floods of tears. This time I was, I suppose, a little to blame.

Schnürchen had been on leave for just over a week and Elisabet had done the extra work remarkably well. She turned out to be far more reliable than I had expected. I had to leave her in charge of the office for hours on end when the ambassador sent for me or I was attending official meetings. She always looked after everything quite satisfactorily in my absence. Incidentally, by now she was more or less well informed about the nature of Operation Cicero, though she knew nothing of the details.

Then Schnürchen came back and once again took over the main part of the work, as reliable and punctilious as ever. So Elisabet went back to her translations from the foreign press. Despite her excellent knowledge of languages, she had always been very bad at this sort of work. The reason was that she clearly disliked it. Her typescripts were full of errors, grammatical faults and simple mistakes in translation. I invariably had to correct them, which I usually did without comment.

But on that particular morning she produced a translation so hopelessly inadequate that I lost patience.

"I've no use for this sort of work," I said, showing my annoyance. "The thing's one mass of idiotic mistakes. I know perfectly well that you can do much better than this. You'll have to do it again."

I shoved the typescript back at her, and at once I realized the mistake I had made. I should not have lost my temper. After all, she would soon be gone.

Elisabet's face went white with anger. She took the typewritten pages, gave me a murderous look and left the room without a word. In the anteroom she savagely tore up the typescript into small pieces. Then she flung herself into an armchair and burst into tears.

I could hear her sobs from my office, and I went out to her. I had wanted to avoid a scene like this.

"Now listen, Elisabet," I said, with almost exaggerated calm, "do try to be more reasonable. We all have to put up with being scolded from time to time. Don't you think that the ambassador reprimands me when I do something wrong?"

"It's not that," she said, her voice muffled by tears. "It's the way you don't trust me. Nothing but those dull translations. I can't bear it anymore. Won't you let me do some proper work for you again?"

I had no idea what to do with this hysterical creature. I see now that the most sensible line would have been one of kindly firmness. But I was too irritated. Besides, I had tried that and there had been no end to these scenes.

"If you don't like your work here, you'd better go back to your old job in Sofia, if that's what you want. I'll see that it's arranged at once."

Elisabet raised her head; tears were still streaming down her face.

"So you want to get rid of me!" she whispered. Her voice was husky and her lips trembled.

Cicero file seen by Elisabet

"No, I don't want you to go," I lied, "but if you're unhappy here I shan't stop you."

Perhaps, I thought, she will say she would rather be in Sofia or with her father in Budapest. No such luck. All she did was turn on her heel, run out of the room and slam the door behind her. Half an hour later she was back. She apologized for her behavior. We were back exactly where we had been before.

On Monday, April 3, which was the first day of Easter week, Elisabet came into my office and asked, "Would it be possible for me to have a few days' leave over Easter to spend with my parents in Budapest? I know I'm not due for it, but you see my brother's getting leave and he'll be there, too."

I was delighted at her request, and had to use considerable self-control not to show it. Once she is in Budapest, I thought, her father can keep her there. But I knew Elisabet well enough to be sure that if I let her see how glad I was to have her go, she would change her mind and probably refuse to do so.

So I frowned and said, "Not a very good moment for you to go off. You've still got a lot of work outstanding."

"It'd make me so terribly happy if you'd let me. And I promise I'll get everything finished by Thursday."

"In that case," I said, my expression becoming less severe, "you can have your leave. You want to go on Thursday, you say?"

"The train that evening connects with the courier plane at Istanbul. Do you think it would be possible for me to get on it?"

"On the plane? I don't know," I said, still trying to look stern. "I'll see what I can do about getting you a seat."

When I told the ambassador about this stroke of good fortune he too was pleased. "Excellent," he said. "A perfect solution. You'd better send her father an explanatory letter by the same plane. I'll see to it she has a seat."

On Tuesday and Wednesday we did not see much of Elisabet in the office. She apologized politely, saying she still had a lot of shopping to do. I had no objections, even though she was clearly making no attempt to get her work finished before she left.

Once I saw her in town. She was carrying a large parcel.

"A new coat," she said with a smile. "For Easter in Budapest."

On Wednesday she came to the office for a few hours. As she worked at her translations she was humming cheerfully to herself. She would be back a week from today, she said. She wanted to promise me here and now that she would cause me no more trouble.

I bought the ticket to Istanbul for her. As usual the railway clerk maintained that all seats on the train were sold out, and I had to pay double for the ticket. I did so gladly. I would willingly have paid three times the amount to get rid of her so easily.

On the Thursday morning, that is, the sixth of April, 1944, Elisabet came to the office to say good-by to Schnürchen and me. I said I would see her off on the train that afternoon. She told me please not to bother. But I had left her train ticket at home. Furthermore, though I did not tell her this, I wanted to make sure she actually went.

"Then I shan't say good-by just yet," said Elisabet, "since I'll be seeing you again before I go."

By half past five I was at the station. The train was already standing at the platform, but there was still nearly half an hour before it was due to leave. I stood near the entrance of the station, with Elisabet's ticket in my pocket.

Five minutes before the train was due to leave I began to get nervous. Why can't that wretched girl be punctual? I thought.

Elisabet did not come. The train left without her. I was really worried now. I went straight from the station to her apartment, which she had recently been sharing with another girl from the embassy. It was this girl who answered the doorbell.

"Where is Elisabet?" I asked.

She told me Elisabet had left the apartment at three o'clock with two big trunks and a suitcase. I was by now completely nonplussed. I sat on her bed and tried to think where she could possibly have gone.

Might she have committed suicide? With Elisabet that was not impossible. But why had she taken all her luggage? Since three that afternoon no other train had left Ankara, so presumably she was still somewhere in the town.

I went back to the embassy and told Herr von Papen what had happened. I have seldom, if ever, seen him so angry.

"That's what you get for employing hysterical women in responsible positions," he said.

I said nothing, while he paced up and down his office. Then he said, "What are you going to do now?"

"I'll go on looking for her, and if I don't find her I suppose I'll have to tell Berlin and inform the Turkish police."

Von Papen shook his head. "Wait a bit before doing that. She may turn up. If we go to the Ankara police it might get into the papers, and we certainly don't want that sort of scandal here. If the worst comes to the worst, and we have to inform the police, I'll have a word with the foreign minister first myself."

I took my car out and hunted through every corner of Ankara. I sought out every acquaintance of Elisabet's I could think of. Over and over again I asked the question, "Have you seen my secretary by any chance?"

No one had.

Shortly before midnight I went to the hotel where the two German fliers were interned. When I had identified myself to the Turkish security officer, I was shown to the room occupied by Hans and Fritz.

I knocked sharply, and an irritated voice asked me what I wanted. I said who I was and that I must speak to them on an urgent matter. The door was unbolted by one of them wearing pajamas. At the far end of the room I could see the other one.

"Do you know where Elisabet is? She's completely vanished."

"Why should I? I haven't seen her for several days. Anyhow she's not in here. As you can see for yourself!"

With a sneer he opened the door fully, and ostentatiously stepped back so that I could see the whole room.

"Have you no idea where she might be?"

I looked him straight in the face. He glanced down at the floor, avoiding my eyes. There was something definitely shifty about him. My question had evidently taken him unawares, but he soon regained his surly composure.

"I just told you. I haven't seen your secretary for over a week. Do you doubt my word?"

A few days before, this man had humbly begged me to give him any sort of a job. There was nothing humble about him now. I turned away without a word. The door banged behind me.

What was I to do? I phoned our consulate at Istanbul and asked an official to meet the train that would get in from Ankara next morning. I gave him an exact description of Elisabet. Perhaps she had been on the train after all and for some obscure reason had chosen to hide from me.

ANKARA April 6, 1944
6 pm. train to Istanbul

— The train left without her—

At midnight the next train left Ankara. It did not go to Istanbul but to Adana. I searched this train, looking into every compartment. There was no trace of Elisabet. Then it occurred to me that maybe—provided she were still alive—she had motored out of Ankara and would get on this train at the first stop, which was about six or seven miles away. It was a farfetched idea, but I jumped into my car and drove furiously through the night. I reached the station a minute before the train pulled in. No one got on it at all.

There was nothing more I could do that night. I sat at home and tried to think. Where on earth could she be? Had she made the same choice as the Istanbul deserters? In that case it meant ruin for me and possibly even death.

Perhaps she had been involved in an accident. We would find out all about it in the morning. And yet, how about her luggage? Taking it all with her, she could not be intending to try to get to Budapest by plane, and was not planning to come back. Therefore . . . try as I might, I could not put the idea of desertion out of my mind.

At eight the next morning I went again to the apartment house where Elisabet had lived. Weary, anxious and full of forebodings, I trudged slowly up the stairs. I was so deep in thought that I went one floor higher than I meant to do. I rang the bell without looking at the door. No answer. I rang again. The front door of the next apartment was opened by a stout, elderly lady. She told me that the gentleman was not at home.

"What gentleman?" I asked.

Then I noticed the card tacked to the door. The flat belonged to a junior secretary at the British embassy. It seemed an unpleasant omen.

I felt more shaken than ever as I walked down the short flight to the floor below. I rang the right bell this time. All I learned was that Elisabet had not been back.

As soon as I thought he would be in his office I called on a senior official at the Turkish Ministry of the Interior, a friendly man whom I knew quite well. Sitting opposite him in his comfortable office, I told him all about Elisabet's disappearance. I asked him if the Turkish authorities could discreetly help me to find the girl, adding that von Papen was most anxious for nothing to appear in the papers.

He thought for some time before answering. Then he said, "I don't believe there's been an accident or suicide. If there had been I'd know of it by now. I'm afraid it's far more likely that your secretary has followed the example of the German deserters in Istanbul."

He saw me to the door. "I hope for your sake I'm wrong," he added.

When I got to my office an answer had come in from Istanbul. There had been no one on the train who in any way fitted my description of Elisabet.

I had no choice now. Berlin must be informed. I drafted the most difficult signal of my life, reporting that my secretary had vanished without trace and that, while the possibilities of suicide or accident could not yet be ruled out, it was equally possible that she had deserted to the British.

When I had dispatched this signal I knew very well that with every hour that passed her desertion was more of a probability.

An avalanche of excited signals began now to come in from Berlin, each of them asking questions I could not possibly answer. Needless to say, all these signals also contained a peremptory order to find the girl at all costs.

The days dragged by in a sort of nightmare. I was puzzled not to have heard from Elisabet's father, as he must have received my letter several days ago. On the fifth day after Elisabet's disappearance I received a signal from Kaltenbrunner's office, ordering me to report to Berlin at once. I was to fly by the next courier plane. I took the night train to Istanbul on April 12. My plane for Berlin was to leave on the fourteenth. I had a shrewd idea of what was waiting for me when I should get there.

As soon as I arrived in Istanbul I borrowed a friend's car and spent most of the day driving aimlessly through the streets of that great city. I hoped quite illogically that Elisabet might be there and that by some coincidence I might run into her. I did not.

The German courier plane arrived on the afternoon of the thirteenth. The next morning it would take me to Berlin.

In the consulate the mailbags were being sorted. I asked them to let me have a look to see if there was any mail for me. There were two further messages from Kaltenbrunner and one from the Foreign Ministry. In each I was severely reprimanded for Elisabet's disappearance. They all stressed the fact that it was due entirely to my urgent request that the girl had been transferred from Sofia in the first place.

I put the signals back in the bag, and was about to lock it up when I noticed a small brown envelope, also addressed to me. I opened it, and as I read the few lines hastily scribbled on a sheet of writing paper my hands began to tremble.

The message was from a friend of mine in the Foreign Ministry. It said that in certain high places I was suspected of having helped my secretary to escape. I would almost certainly be arrested as soon as I set foot on German soil.

CHAPTER 10

THE PLANE FOR BERLIN was leaving next morning. I walked about the streets of Istanbul for hours. There was no friend I could turn to for help or advice. Finally I thought of a temporary solution, or at least a postponement. Late that night I encoded a telegram to Berlin, informing my superiors that I had fallen ill and that my doctor had forbidden me to travel by air.

Back in my hotel, I took a long, cold shower in an attempt to clear my head. I was just turning off the water when the telephone rang. Still dripping wet, I reached for the receiver. From the other end of the line somebody spoke to me in English.

"I am calling you on behalf of the British. If you go to Berlin tomorrow you will almost certainly be shot. We want to give you a chance. Come over to us and save your life and the lives of your wife and children."

"Absolutely impossible." I hung up.

Instead of going to bed as I had originally intended, I began to dress again. Dead tired though I was, I could not possibly sleep. The telephone rang again. This time it was another voice, speaking German with a strong foreign accent.

"What you are about to do is mad. Think well before you make your decision. The British are humane. Come to the consulate and talk it over with Mr.——."

The voice mentioned a name I had heard frequently. I was trembling all over as I put the receiver down without a word.

A few minutes later it rang again.

"This is Dr. P—— speaking. You remember me, don't you?"

It was a fellow Viennese. I had never spoken to him, but we used to be on nodding terms.

"Listen," he said. "Listen carefully. I am authorized to make you one more offer, an offer to save your life. You have no need to be afraid of the consequences of anything you have done. The British know you are a decent sort and have merely carried out instructions. I can meet you tonight. I can tell you exactly what the British have to offer you. I have been with them for a long time now. Will you meet me?"

"I can't do it," I said. "Apart from anything else, there are practical and personal reasons why I can't. Most of my family is in Germany. Besides, to run out just now, when the ship's beginning to sink . . . No, I can't do it. Don't you understand?"

"Of course I do. But what about the future? What about your children? This opportunity won't be repeated. Besides, when Germany has lost the war you may find yourself held responsible for quite a few things if you stay where you are."

"I can't do it, Doctor. I daresay you mean well. Thank you."

I put back the receiver and ran downstairs. There were two or three men standing about in the hall. It seemed to me that they stared at me curiously as I walked past them to the little room that held the hotel switchboard.

"I don't want any more calls put through to my room tonight as I'm going to bed," I said.

I placed ten Turkish pounds on the chair beside the switchboard girl. She nodded.

Then I went back to my room. I was half undressed when the telephone rang again. Evidently someone had paid her more than I had.

At first I tried to ignore it, but as the ringing went on and on I finally picked up the receiver. It was still another voice. "If you go to Berlin you're finished. Think before it's too late."

I took out my pocketknife and cut through the telephone wire. As I did so I wondered whether I really did not want to listen to them anymore—or was I beginning to doubt my own powers of resistance?

I could not sleep. At two o'clock I walked down to the hall and used the porter's telephone to put through a long-distance call to my wife in Ankara. I told her not to let the children out of her sight for a minute and to keep all the doors of the house firmly locked until I got back. I would explain everything then. It had suddenly occurred to me that someone might try to kidnap my children. It seems a crazy idea, but those were crazy, melodramatic times.

Next morning the German courier plane took off for Berlin without me. I left Istanbul on the train to Ankara that night. It was an appalling trip.

When I got back I found that my secretary's flight had become common knowledge. Still, no one knew for certain where she had gone. On the second day after my return from Istanbul, Cicero rang up. He wanted to see me urgently. We met at my friend's flat at ten that night. He was plainly very nervous. He confirmed what I already knew but had not yet fully admitted.

"Your secretary's with the British," he said at once. I nodded. He added, "She's still in Ankara," and told me the address.

Then he asked, "What does she know about me?"

I really did not know. I could only guess. And what I did guess was not too pleasant. I said, after a pause, "She knows your code name, perhaps more."

He stared at me hard, his face white, gripping the back of the couch. "You're quite sure she hasn't taken any of the photographs with her?"

"Quite sure."

I could say that with certainty. I had counted them and they were all in my safe. This reassured Cicero slightly. I said, "You'd better get out of Ankara just as fast as you can."

He didn't answer. He just sat there on the couch, staring in front of him. At last he got up.

"I must be going now."

He stood in front of me, acute anxiety written all over his face. Now he seemed a beaten man with no resilience left in him. There was cold fear in his dark eyes. *"Au revoir, monsieur,"* he said.

For the first time I gave him my hand. He shook it limply. Then he quickly walked out of the house and vanished into the darkness. I never saw him again.

I did not go to my office for some time. In any case I was officially sick and unfit to travel. When I told the ambassador what had happened, omitting no details, he showed his usual sympathy and understanding.

I had been to the office once. My first action after my return to Ankara had been to examine the contents of my safe most thoroughly. There was nothing missing. Apparently the only thing Elisabet had been able to give the enemy was her knowledge, unless, of course, she had copied out certain documents.

During the night I received many calls to defect.

With nothing to do and deeply depressed as I was, I became really ill. For a few days I ran a temperature and was confined to my bed. When I got up again and looked into the mirror my face seemed completely changed. The hair around my temples showed the first few streaks of white.

There was no word from Berlin. I had reported that Elisabet was now known to be with the British, but I had received no reply. Nor was there any comment on my interrupted journey to Berlin or on my reporting sick. This silence was ominous. The account was still open; one day it would be presented to me. My record must seem very black to the people at home.

I had been on fairly good terms with the first Istanbul deserter as well as with the second and was a friend of their unfortunate departmental chief. I had urgently insisted on Elisabet's transfer to a neutral country, and I had neither foreseen nor prevented her defection to the enemy camp. Putting all this together I appeared in a highly suspicious light.

That was not all. For personal as well as for political reasons I had sided with Herr von Papen in almost all our internal squabbles and differences of opinion. That was certainly not in my favor either with Kaltenbrunner or with Ribbentrop. Perhaps worst of all, I had shown von Papen the Cicero documents, thereby deliberately disobeying a direct order.

After a couple of weeks I began going to my office again. I had the feeling that everyone was staring at me. Rightly or wrongly, I imagined them to be whispering behind my back. I began to feel, probably quite erroneously, that I was being cut or avoided.

One day, when I came home, the maid told me that there were two gentlemen waiting in the drawing room. I went in and found Hans and Fritz, who by now had quite given up their pretense of being two heroic airmen. They were simply two German deserters. The conclusive evidence had arrived from Berlin a few days before.

The airmen wasted no time in getting down to business. "We've come to see you on instructions from the British—"

I interrupted them. I asked them to leave my house and to tell me outside whatever it was that they had to say. Out in the street they began again.

"We have been instructed by the British embassy to ask you to put yourself at their disposal. You have nothing to fear from them. On the other hand, if you're fool enough to decline their offer, you'd better watch out."

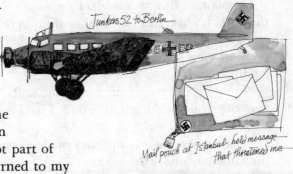

Junkers 52 to Berlin

Mail pouch at Istanbul held message that threatened me

I had no doubt that the direct threat contained in that last sentence was not part of their instructions. I returned to my house without a word.

My wife and I were dining that night at the Japanese embassy. Shortly before midnight I was summoned to the telephone. It was our maid. She urged me to come home at once. She rang off as soon as she had said this and before I could find out what the matter was.

I thought immediately of the children. From her tone of voice it sounded as though something terrible had happened. Without saying anything to my wife or my hosts, I jumped into my car and drove home at breakneck speed.

I ran up the stairs to the nursery four at a time. The children were sleeping peacefully. Mopping my forehead, I went down to the drawing room intending to give myself a stiff whisky and soda before asking the maid what the trouble was. To my surprise the lights were on. Then I saw, sitting on the sofa, a man I had known for many years.

"I must apologize for calling on you in this way and at this hour," he said. "But what I have to say is of extreme urgency. We know that you are no longer *persona grata* in Berlin. This is your last chance to safeguard your future. I know that other people have approached you and you've refused. I'm not asking you to desert, but to meet a member of the British embassy and talk the matter over with him. It commits you to nothing."

I had known this man for a long time. I had no idea that he had already changed sides. Did I really have to run away from my countrymen, frightened of being punished for something I had not done? I tried hard to convince my visitor that while I would do everything in my power to help shorten this horrible war, I would never desert to the enemy.

I explained this at considerable length, for I wanted to convince the British once and for all that they were wasting their time with me. I hoped that they would give up their attempts if I made my point of view sufficiently clear. When I had finished, their emissary got up.

"I understand your sentiments," he said. "I wish I thought I could persuade you to change your mind. I see I can't and, frankly, I almost like it better this way."

This was the last attempt they made to persuade me to give up my fundamentally hopeless position.

It had not been easy for me to resist their offers. It had cost me most of what nervous stamina I still had left. Therefore the next blow hit me all the harder.

One morning the courier bag from Berlin contained a letter for me: "You are herewith notified that an inquiry has been opened to establish the extent to which you are guilty of aiding and abetting your secretary's desertion to the enemy on April 6."

The same day I received a letter at home which contained a single sheet of white paper, folded in four. There was no address and no signature, just one line of German typescript: "In the British embassy everything is known about Cicero."

One detail struck me. There were two typing errors in a single line.

CHAPTER 11

THAT IS REALLY the end of Operation Cicero. The war soon entered its ultimate cataclysmic stage, and with the opening of the great final campaign in the east and west any possibility of a negotiated peace fast faded. Even had Cicero continued somehow to deliver his material, it seems doubtful if it would have been of any value to Germany once the final battles were joined.

My own predicament was solved for me by the breakdown of Turko-German relations. In May 1944 the Turks came to an agreement with the Allies which led, a few months later, to the severance of diplomatic relations between Turkey and Germany. During this period I managed to postpone going to Germany as I had been ordered.

From May to August I was engaged, together with other German officials in Turkey, in organizing the evacuation of the fairly large German colony still resident there. The Turks had informed us that they all had to leave by the end of August or be interned as hostile aliens. The German ambassador left on August 5, 1944, and three special trains were scheduled to transport the rest of the Germans before the end of the month.

I was by no means anxious to go back to Germany, and I had arranged to travel on the last of these trains. As it happened, this one never left Ankara. By then the Red Army, advancing through the Balkans, had cut the line somewhere between Sofia and Belgrade.

Thus, on August 31, my family and I, together with the other few remaining members of the embassy staff and the German colony, were interned. We were not put into a camp, but simply stayed on the embassy premises, the only change being that we were surrounded by a few strands of barbed wire, and Turkish sentries outside.

That internment was merely a temporary measure while we

awaited suitable transportation to Germany. We expected to go on a Swedish ship before the end of the year. Once again I was lucky; there was no Swedish ship available until the end of April, 1945. By then Hitler was dead and the Third Reich at its last gasp.

I and a few hundred other German diplomats put to sea at Istanbul. By the time we had reached Gibraltar the war was over. Since there was now no German government, there was also no German diplomatic service. We had, therefore, lost our immunity. A few of us were interned for quite some time by the British, first in England and later in the British Zone in Germany.

Having been interrogated, I was released and sent back to Vienna, which is my home. There I rejoined my wife and children, who had spent a part of the time in Sweden. Once or twice during the Nuremberg trials I was sent for by the court to give evidence. No charge was ever preferred against me and I am glad to say that I was sent back to civilian life with a clean record. I now live at a small place near Innsbruck in the Austrian Tirol, where I am export manager with a textile firm.

Ribbentrop and Kaltenbrunner were both condemned to death at Nuremberg and hanged. Herr von Papen, who was also a defendant at that celebrated trial, was completely acquitted.

What happened to the girl I have called Elisabet I do not know. She vanished completely, and to this very day even her family has no idea where she lives or, indeed, even if she is still alive.

Cicero vanished, too; shortly after our last interview he was no longer at the British embassy. Whether he was arrested or whether he got away in time, I have no way of knowing and I probably never shall. The archives of the British intelligence service might reveal what happened to him; they might, but they almost certainly will not.

If Cicero did get away with his money, he would not have been able to enjoy for long the life of extreme luxury that he had planned to live. He was intending to build a large house in some paradisiacal part of the globe where there were no Englishmen. Even if he found that remote, improbable place, the money he had received would hardly enable him to spend the rest of his life in anything larger than a comfortable cottage. He had received from me notes to the value of £300,000, or rather over a million dollars at the then rate of exchange, in bundles of ten-, twenty- and fifty-pound notes.

After Operation Cicero was over, I learned that nearly all these bank notes were forgeries. It seems probable that the first batch, sent by the Foreign Ministry, were genuine; but I have no doubt that the £200,000 sent by the Sicherheitsdienst were just as certainly "Made in Germany" as was the suitcase that carried them from Kaltenbrunner's office in Berlin to my safe in Ankara. Doubtless the subsequent consignments from him were equally bogus.

The people in Kaltenbrunner's forgery department were very clever at their job. The false notes were so well made that even bank managers fell for them. Our manager at Istanbul was not the only one to be taken in. It was only when they reached the Bank of England, and were examined by the experts of Threadneedle Street, that the truth was finally established.

If Cicero got away with his real, or noncounterfeit, earnings, what he took with him was presumably £20,000, $20,000 and £2000 worth of diamonds—less, of course, what he had already spent in Ankara on silk shirts and wristwatches; a fairly substantial sum, it is true, but only a little over one-tenth of the money he thought he had made.

Incidentally, this seems to me the explanation of why Berlin had no hesitation in paying £10,000 for the statement of petty expenses inside the British embassy. In fact they bought a worthless roll of film with worthless pieces of paper.

Thinking back over that exciting period of my life as dispassionately as I can, I cannot help detecting a touch of rather grim irony in the fact that most of the money paid to Cicero was counterfeit. It seems somehow symbolic of the whole business. This was the greatest sum of money ever demanded in the history of espionage—demanded, it is true, for the greatest value ever offered: documents giving precise, last-minute information on the most secret plans of the enemy. And the upshot of it all was that the money paid was a forgery and the information was never taken seriously enough to be used.

For here, to my mind, is historically the most important point about Operation Cicero. In the long run all that the German leaders learned from those documents was simply this: they were about to lose the war. And this unpleasant fact they refused to face.

It was the crucial period of the war, the turn of the tide. I hoped at the time that the almost fantastically complete and accurate information that was presented to the German leaders would make them realize that the alternatives for Germany were no longer victory or defeat, but defeat or utter annihilation.

I see now, of course, that Ribbentrop and the rest could not possibly have faced these consequences without destroying themselves. They knew that the Allies would never negotiate with them. So, at the cost of incalculable suffering to their country and, indeed, to the whole world, they decided to ignore the facts that Cicero had revealed to them.

That was the real reason for Berlin's prolonged suspicion of the documents, even when their genuineness was established beyond the shadow of a doubt. They trusted them well enough whenever the message happened to be one they wanted to hear. Ribbentrop attached immense importance to any evidence that the Cicero documents contained about a rift or a mere misunderstanding between the Eastern and Western allies. Yet he never initiated any diplomatic move to make use of such knowledge with a view to a possible negotiated peace on the eastern front.

I well remember how eagerly Berlin lapped up every detail about Churchill's serious illness during that winter. Churchill on his deathbed; that was what the Führer wanted to hear. Much more important, though less welcome, information contained in the same documents was brushed aside as meaningless or, more foolishly still, as something planted by the British.

Failure to face reality, to understand what the world was really like—that was perhaps the greatest single stupidity of the Nazi leaders. Their attitude toward Operation Cicero typified this. They were counterfeit patriots. It seems oddly suitable that they should have paid with counterfeit money for information they were incapable of using.

FROM RUSSIA,
WITH LOVE

ILLUSTRATED BY RICHARD HARVEY

From Russia, with Love

A CONDENSATION OF THE BOOK BY
Ian Fleming

At the highest level of Soviet intelligence a sinister plot is set in motion to shake the British Secret Service to its foundations. One of its top agents, 007, the redoubtable James Bond, is to be the victim of a murder so sensational that it will embarrass Her Majesty's government.

The bait that will lure the English operative into the trap prepared for him in Istanbul is the beautiful Tania. But waiting in the wings is the cold-eyed Granitsky, chief executioner for SMERSH, Soviet intelligence's most dreaded and secret department. And behind Granitsky is the malevolent, toadlike woman, Colonel Rosa Klebb, head of Otdyel II, in charge of operations and executions.

Ian Fleming's superagent, James Bond, has achieved worldwide fame in such novels and movies as *Casino Royale* and *Doctor No*. The London *Times* called *From Russia, With Love* Mr. Fleming's "tautest, most exciting and most brilliant tale."

CHAPTER 1

The naked man who lay splayed out on his face beside the swimming pool might have been dead.

He might have been drowned and fished out of the pool and laid out on the grass to dry while the police or the next of kin were summoned. Even the little pile of objects in the grass beside his head might have been his personal effects, meticulously assembled in full view so that no one should think that something had been stolen by his rescuers.

To judge by the glittering pile, this had been, or was, a rich man. It contained the typical membership badges of the rich man's club— a money clip, made of a Mexican fifty-dollar piece and holding a substantial wad of banknotes, a well-used gold Dunhill lighter, an oval gold cigarette case and a bulky gold wristwatch on a worn brown crocodile strap. It was a Girard Perregaux model designed for people who like gadgets, and it had a sweep-second hand and two little windows in the face to tell the day of the month, the month and the phase of the moon. The story it now told was two thirty on June 10 with the moon three-quarters full.

The garden in which the man lay was about an acre of well-kept lawn surrounded on three sides by thickly banked rosebushes from which came the steady murmur of bees. The sea boomed softly at the bottom of the cliff at the end of the garden. There was no view of the sea from the lawn. But from the upstairs bedrooms of the villa you could see a great expanse of blue water in front and, on either side, the upper windows of neighboring villas and the tops of trees—Mediterranean-type evergreen oaks, stone pines and an occasional palm tree.

The drowsy silence of early afternoon was broken by the sound of a car. It stopped in front of the villa, a car door slammed and the car drove on. The doorbell rang twice. At the noise of the bell and of the departing car, the naked man's eyes had for an instant opened very wide, as if the eyelids had pricked up like an animal's ears. The man immediately remembered where he was and the day of the week and the time of the day. The noises were identified. The eyelids drooped back over the very pale blue, inward-looking eyes.

A young woman carrying a small string bag and dressed in a white cotton shirt and a short blue skirt strode across the stretch of lawn towards the naked man. A few yards away from him, she dropped her bag and sat down and took off her shoes. Then she stood up and unbuttoned her shirt and took it off and put it, neatly folded, beside the bag. When she bent her arms to undo the side buttons of her skirt, small tufts of fair hair showed in her armpits. The impression of a healthy peasant girl was heightened by the chunky hips in faded blue stockinette bathing trunks and the thick short thighs that were revealed when she had stripped.

The girl put the skirt neatly beside her shirt, opened the string bag, took out a bottle, went over to the man and knelt on the grass beside him. She poured some liquid, a light olive oil scented with roses, between his shoulder blades and, after flexing her fingers like a pianist, began massaging the sternocleidomastoid and the trapezius muscles at the back of the man's neck.

It was hard work. The man was immensely strong and the bulging muscles at the base of the neck hardly yielded to the girl's thumbs even when the downward weight of her shoulders was behind them. She looked down at the round, smallish head on the sinewy neck. It was covered with tight red-gold curls that should have reminded her pleasantly of the formalized hair in the pictures she had seen of classical statues. But the curls were somehow too tight, too thickly pressed against each other and against the skull. They set her teeth on edge, and once again, as so often in the past, she wondered why she loathed this splendid body.

From the very first this man had been like a lump of inanimate meat. In two years he had never said a word to her. Neither his eyes nor his body had once shown the smallest interest in her. An occasional long shuddering yawn was the only sign that he had human reactions at all.

The masseuse tapped his arm. It was time for him to turn over. She got to her feet and stood, twisting her head slowly from side to side and flexing her shoulders. She went to her string bag and took out a hand towel and wiped the perspiration off her face and body. When she turned back to the man, he had already rolled over and now lay gazing blankly at the sky.

The girl glanced nervously at the red-brown face. Superficially it was handsome, with its full pink cheeks, upturned nose and rounded chin. But there was something cruel about the thin-lipped mouth, a pigginess about the wide nostrils in the upturned nose, and the blankness that veiled the pale blue eyes communicated itself over the whole face and made it look drowned and morguelike.

The masseuse worked up the arm to the huge biceps. Where had the man got these fantastic muscles from? Was he a boxer? What did he do with his formidable body? Rumor said this was a police villa. The two menservants were obviously guards of some sort, although they did the cooking and the housework. Regularly every month the man went away for a few days and she would be told not to come. From time to time she would be told to stay away for a week, or two weeks, or a month. Once, after one of these absences, the man's neck and the upper part of his body had been a mass of bruises, but she had never dared to ask anyone about him. When she had first been sent to the house, one of the menservants had told her that if she spoke about what she saw she would go to prison. And the chief superintendent back at the hospital had said the same thing. She would go to prison.

The telephone in the house started ringing. At once the man was up on one knee like a runner waiting for the gun. The ringing stopped. There was the mutter of a voice. One of the menservants showed briefly at the door and made a gesture of summons. Halfway through the gesture, the naked man was already running. The girl watched the brown back flash through the open glass door. Better not let him find her there when he came out again—doing nothing, perhaps listening. She got to her feet, took two steps to the concrete edge of the pool and dived gracefully in.

Although it would have explained her instincts about the man whose body she massaged, it was as well for the girl's peace of mind that she did not know who he was.

His real name was Donovan Grant, or "Red" Grant. But for the past ten years it had been Krassno Granitsky, with the code name of Granit.

He was the chief executioner of SMERSH, the official murder organization of the Soviet government, and at this moment he was receiving his instructions on the direct line from Moscow.

GRANT WENT TO his room and pulled a battered Italian suitcase from under the bed. He packed into it a selection of well-laundered cheap respectable clothes from the closet. Then he washed, hastily dressed in clothes as drab and nondescript as those he had packed, put on his wristwatch, pocketed his other belongings, picked up his suitcase, went down the stairs and out to a waiting car.

The villa was on the southeastern coast of the Crimea, about halfway between Feodosiya and Yalta. It was one of many official holiday dachas along the favorite stretch of mountainous coastline that is part of the Russian Riviera. Red Grant knew that he was immensely privileged to be housed there instead of in some dreary villa on the outskirts of Moscow. As the car taking him to the airport at Simferopol climbed up into the mountains, he thought that they certainly treated him as well as they knew how, even if their concern for his welfare had two faces.

At the airport he boarded a twin-engined Ilyushin 12 with twenty empty seats to choose from. Grant settled into the one nearest the hatch and fastened his seat belt. A short crackle of talk with the control tower came through the open door to the cockpit, and the two engines whined and coughed and fired. The plane turned quickly and, without further preliminaries, hurtled down the runway and up into the air.

Grant unbuckled his seat belt, lit a gold-tipped Troika cigarette and settled back to reflect comfortably on his past career and to consider the immediate future.

Donovan Grant was the result of a hasty midnight union between a German professional weight lifter and an Irish waitress of Belfast. His mother died of puerperal fever shortly after giving birth to the twelve-pound boy she named Donovan. He was reluctantly cared for by an aunt and grew up healthy and extremely strong, but very quiet. He had no friends. He refused to communicate with other children and when he wanted anything from them he took it with his fists. He made a name for himself boxing and wrestling at local fairs, where the bloodthirsty fury of his attack, combined with guile, gave

him victory over much older and bigger boys. When he left school he became a strong-arm man for some local smugglers. They paid him well for his work but saw as little of him as they could.

About this time his body began to feel strange and violent compulsions around the time of the full moon. When, in October of his sixteenth year, he first got "The Feelings," as he called them to himself, he went out and strangled a cat. This made him "feel better" for a whole month. In November it was a big sheep dog, and for Christmas he slit the throat of a cow, at midnight in a neighbor's shed. Then he took a chance and cut the throat of a sleeping tramp. He took to bicycling far and wide so that he came to distant villages in the dusk, when solitary people were coming home from the fields and girls were going out to their trysts. When he killed an occasional girl he did not "interfere" with her in any way. That side of things, which he had heard talked about, was quite incomprehensible to him. It was only the wonderful act of killing that made him feel better.

On his eighteenth birthday they took him for national service and he became a driver in the Royal Corps of Signals. The training period in England sobered him, or at least made him more careful when he had The Feelings. Now, at the full moon, he would take a bottle of whisky into the woods and drink it all down as he watched his sensations, coldly, until unconsciousness came. Then, in the early hours of the morning, he would stagger back to camp, only half satisfied, but not dangerous anymore.

Grant's transport section was rushed to Berlin about the time of the Corridor trouble with the Russians. In Berlin the constant smell of danger intrigued him and made him even more careful and cunning. He still got dead drunk at the full moon, but all the rest of the time he was watching and plotting. He liked all he heard about the Russians, their brutality, their carelessness of human life and their guile, and he decided to go over to them. But how? What could he bring them as a gift? What did they want? Then he was transferred to the coveted motorcycle dispatch service, and this could not have suited Grant better.

He waited a few days, and one evening when he had collected the day's outgoing mail from the Military Intelligence Headquarters he made straight for the Russian sector, waited with his engine running until the British control gate was opened to allow a taxi to pass, and then tore through the closing gate at forty and skidded to a stop beside the concrete pillbox of the Russian frontier post.

They hauled him roughly into the guardroom. A wooden-faced officer behind a desk asked him what he wanted.

"I want the Soviet Secret Service," said Grant flatly. "I have a lot of secret papers. Outside. In the leather bags on the motorcycle." He had a brainstorm. "You will get into bad trouble if they don't get to your secret service."

IT WAS HALF AN hour later, and the M.G.B. colonel was bored with the interview.

"So you would like to work in the Soviet Union, Mr. Grant?" The colonel had extracted from this rather unpleasant British soldier every military detail that could possibly be of interest. A few polite phrases to repay the man for the rich haul of secrets his dispatch bags had yielded, and then the man could go down to the cells and in due course be shipped off to some labor camp.

"Yes, I would like to work for you."

"And what work could you do, Mr. Grant? We have plenty of unskilled labor. We do not need truck drivers."

"I am an expert at killing people. I do it very well. I like it."

The colonel saw the red flame that flickered for an instant behind the very pale blue eyes. He thought, The man means it. He's mad as well as unpleasant. He looked coldly at Grant, wondering if it was worthwhile wasting food on him. Better perhaps have him shot. Or throw him back into the British sector and let his own people worry about him.

"You don't believe me," said Grant impatiently. This was the wrong man, the wrong department. "Who does the rough stuff for you here?" He was certain the Russians had some sort of a murder squad. Everybody said so. "Let me talk to them. I'll kill somebody for them. Anybody they like. Now."

The colonel looked at him sourly. Perhaps he had better report the matter. "Wait here." He got up and went into the next room. He picked up the receiver of the M.G.B. direct line to Moscow. When the military operator answered he said, "SMERSH." When SMERSH answered he asked for the chief of operations.

Ten minutes later he put the receiver back. What luck! A simple, constructive solution. Whichever way it went it would turn out well. If the Englishman succeeded, it would be splendid. If he failed, it would still cause a lot of trouble in the Western sector—trouble for the British because Grant was their man, trouble with the Germans because the attempt would frighten a lot of their spies, trouble with the Americans because they were supplying most of the funds for the Baumgarten ring and would now think Baumgarten's security was no good. Pleased with himself, the colonel walked back into his office and sat down again opposite Grant.

"In the British sector," he said, "there is a German called Dr. Baumgarten. He lives in Flat Five at Number Twenty-two Kurfürstendamm. Tonight, with your motorcycle, you will be put back into the British sector. Your number plates will be changed. Your people will be on the lookout for you. You will be given an envelope and a sharp knife of American manufacture. You will take the envelope to Dr. Baumgarten. It will be marked to be delivered by hand. In your uniform, and with this envelope, you will have no difficulty. You will say that the message is so private that you must see Dr. Baumgarten alone. Then you will kill him." The colonel paused. His eyebrows lifted. "Yes?"

"Yes," said Grant stolidly. "And if I do, will you give me more of this work?"

"It is possible," said the colonel indifferently. "First show what you can do, and then return to the Soviet sector. Good luck."

THE PLANE ROARED ON across the heartland of Russia. They had left behind them the blast furnaces of Stalino, the splash of light around Kharkov. The solid unbroken blackness below hid the great central steppe where grain was ripening in the darkness. Grant knew there would be no more oases of light until, in another hour, they would have covered the last three hundred miles to Moscow.

For by now Grant knew a lot about Russia. After the quick, neat, sensational murder of a vital West German spy, he had slipped back over the frontier, had been hustled into an empty M.G.B. plane and flown straight to Moscow.

At the end of a year of painstaking investigation Grant was given as clean a bill of political health as any foreigner can get in Russia. The spies had confirmed his story; he was totally uninterested in the politics or social customs of any country in the world, and the doctors and psychologists agreed that he was an advanced manic-depressive whose periods coincided with the full moon. They added that Grant was also a narcissist and asexual and that his tolerance of pain was high. These peculiarities apart, his physical health was superb and, though his educational standards were hopelessly low, he was as naturally cunning as a fox. Everyone agreed that Grant was an exceedingly dangerous member of society and that he should be put away.

When the dossier came before the head of personnel of the M.G.B., he was about to write "Kill him" in the margin when he had second thoughts. A great deal of killing had to be done in the U.S.S.R. as an instrument of policy. People who acted against the

state were enemies of the state, and the state had no room for enemies. They got killed. So many thousands a year had to be killed that
there was a shortage of executioners.

Then, too, executioners have a short life. They get tired of the
work. The soul sickens of it. Melancholy and drink take them, and a
dreadful lassitude. When the employer sees these signs he has no
alternative but to execute the executioner and find another one.

The head of personnel of the M.G.B. was aware of the problem.
He wrote a short, pungent note on Grant's papers, marked them
SMERSH Otdyel II and tossed them into his OUT tray.

Department 2 of SMERSH, in charge of operations and executions,
took over the body of Donovan Grant and changed his name to
Granitsky. The next two years were hard. In the Intelligence School
for Foreigners outside Leningrad, squashed tightly among the ranks
of Germans, Czechs, Poles, Balts, Chinese and Negroes, all with serious dedicated faces and pens that raced across their notebooks, Grant
struggled with subjects that were pure double Dutch to him.

There were courses in "General Political Knowledge"; lessons on
"The Class Enemy We Are Fighting," with lectures on capitalism and
fascism; weeks spent on "Tactics, Agitation and Propaganda," and
more weeks on the problems of minority peoples, colonial races, the
Negroes, the Jews. When they came to "Technical Subjects" he did
better. He was quick to understand the rudiments of codes and
ciphers, was good at communications and immediately grasped the
maze of contacts, fuses, couriers and mailboxes. He got excellent
marks for fieldwork, in which each student had to plan and operate
dummy assignments in the countryside around Leningrad. Finally,
in tests of vigilance, discretion, safety first, presence of mind, courage
and coolness, he got top marks out of the whole school.

At the end of the year the report that went back to SMERSH concluded: "Political value nil; operational value excellent"—which
was just what Otdyel II wanted to hear.

The next year was spent, with only two other foreign students,
among several hundred Russians at the School for Terror and Diversion at Kuchino, outside Moscow. Here Grant went triumphantly
through courses in judo, boxing, athletics, photography and radio.
Twice during this year an M.G.B. car came for him on the night of
the full moon and took him to one of the Moscow jails. There, with

a black hood over his head, he was allowed to carry out executions with various weapons. Electrocardiograms, blood pressure and other medical tests were applied to him before, during and after these occasions, but their purpose and findings were not revealed to him.

After that, Grant was allowed to go on minor operations in the satellite countries. These were beatings and simple assassinations of Russian spies and intelligence workers suspected of treachery or other aberrations. As a result, his usefulness became more officially recognized. For his excellent work he was granted Soviet citizenship and successive increases in pay. He was given the rank of major, and allotted the villa in the Crimea. Two bodyguards were attached to him, partly to protect him and partly to guard against the outside chance of his "going private," as defection is called in M.G.B. jargon. Once a month he was transported to the nearest jail and allowed as many executions as there were candidates available.

Naturally Grant had no friends. He was hated or feared or envied by everyone who came in contact with him. But, if he noticed the fact, he didn't care. The only individuals he was interested in were his victims. Then, of course, he had SMERSH. No one in the Soviet Union who has SMERSH on his side need worry about anything whatever except keeping the black wings of SMERSH over his head.

Grant was still thinking vaguely of how he stood with his employers when the plane started to lose altitude as it picked up the radar beam of Tushino Airport northwest of the red glow that was Moscow.

He was at the top of his tree, the chief executioner of SMERSH, and therefore of the whole of the Soviet Union. What could he aim for now? Further promotion? More money? Better techniques? Or was there perhaps some other man whom he had never heard of, in some other country, who would have to be set aside before absolute supremacy was his?

CHAPTER 2

SMERSH is a contraction of *Smiert spionam*, which means Death to spies. It is a name used only among Soviet officials. No sane member of the public would dream of allowing the word to pass his lips. The headquarters of SMERSH is a very large and ugly modern building on the Sretenka Ulitsa, a wide, dull street. Pedestrians keep their eyes to the ground as they pass the two sentries with submachine guns who stand on either side of the broad steps leading up to the big iron double door.

On the second floor, behind a soundproof door, there is a very large light room, fitted with a colorful Caucasian carpet of the finest quality. Across one corner of the room stands a massive oak desk, its top covered with red velvet under a thick sheet of plate glass. From the center of the desk, to form a T with it, a conference table, also covered with red velvet, stretches diagonally out across the room. Six straight-backed red leather chairs are drawn up to it. Ashtrays are on the table, and two heavy carafes of water, with glasses.

On one wall stands a large *televisor*, or TV set, concealing in its handsome oak cabinet a tape recorder which can be switched on from the desk. Microphones for the recorder stretch under the whole area of the conference table, the leads concealed in the legs of the table. On another wall, under a portrait of Army General Ivan Aleksandro-vitch Serov, chief of state security, is a bookcase containing the works of Marx, Engels, Lenin and Stalin, and books in all languages on espionage, counterespionage, police methods and criminology. Next to the bookcase stands a table on which are a dozen large leather-bound albums with dates stamped in gold on the covers. These contain photographs of Soviet citizens and foreigners who have been assassinated by SMERSH.

About the time Grant was landing at Tushino Airport, a tough-looking, thickset man of about fifty was standing at this table leafing through the volume for 1954. The head of SMERSH, Colonel General Grubozaboyschikov, known in the building as "G.," was dressed in a khaki tunic with a high collar, and dark blue cavalry trousers that ended in boots of soft black leather. On the breast of the tunic hung three rows of medal ribbons and the gold star of a Hero of the Soviet Union. The face was narrow and sharp. The eyes protruded like polished brown marbles below thick black brows. The skull was shaven clean and the tight white skin glittered in the light of the central chandelier.

One of the telephones on the desk buzzed softly. The man walked over and picked up the receiver of a telephone marked in white with the letters V.Ch., short for *vysokochastoty*, or high frequency. This telephone is served by a small exchange in the Kremlin, with connections to only fifty supreme officials and operated by professional security officers. Even they cannot overhear conversations, but every word spoken over its lines is automatically recorded.

"Yes?"

"Serov speaking. What action has been taken since the meeting of the Presidium this morning?"

"I have a meeting here in a few minutes' time, Comrade General. After that, if action is agreed upon, I shall have a meeting with my head of operations and head of plans. In case liquidation is decided upon, I have taken the precaution of bringing the necessary operative to Moscow. This time I shall myself supervise the preparations. We do not want another Khoklov affair."

"The devil knows we don't. Telephone me after the first meeting. I wish to report to the Presidium tomorrow morning."

"Certainly, Comrade General."

General G. put back the receiver and switched on the tape recorder. In a few minutes six men filed in and, with hardly a glance at the man behind the desk, took their places at the conference table. They were three senior officers, heads of their departments, and each was accompanied by an aide. In the Soviet Union no man goes alone to a conference. For his own protection, and for the reassurance of his department, he invariably takes a witness. This is important in case there is a subsequent investigation. No notes are taken at the conference and decisions are passed back to departments by word of mouth.

On the far side of the table sat Lieutenant General Slavin, head of the G.R.U., the intelligence department of the General Staff of the Army, with a full colonel beside him. The others round the table were Lieutenant General Vozdvishensky of R.U.M.I.D., the intelligence department of the Ministry of Foreign Affairs, with a middle-aged man in plain clothes, and Colonel of State Security Nikitin, head of intelligence for the M.G.B., the Soviet Secret Service, with a major at his side.

"Good evening, comrades."

A polite, careful murmur came from the three senior officers. Each one knew, and thought he was the only one to know, that the room was wired for sound, and each one had decided to utter the bare minimum of words consonant with good discipline and the needs of the state.

"Let us smoke." General G. took out a packet of cigarettes and lit one with an American Zippo lighter. There was a clicking of lighters round the table. "Comrades, General Serov, on behalf of the Presidium, has ordered me to make known to you certain matters of state policy. We are then to confer and recommend a course of action which will assist this policy. Our recommendation concerns a conspicuous act of terrorism to be carried out in enemy territory within three months."

Six pairs of expressionless eyes stared at the head of SMERSH, waiting.

"Comrades, the foreign policy of the U.S.S.R. has entered a new phase. Formerly, it was a 'hard' policy. This policy built up tensions in the West, notably in America. But the Americans are unpredictable people. They are hysterical. Our intelligence reports began to indicate that we were pushing America to the brink of an undeclared atomic attack on the U.S.S.R. We do not want such a war. So it was decided to change our methods, while maintaining our aims. A new policy was created—the 'hard-soft' policy. Geneva was the beginning of this policy. We were soft. China threatens Quemoy and Matsu. We are hard. We open our frontiers to a lot of newspapermen and actors and artists although we know many of them to be spies. Our leaders laugh and make jokes at receptions in Moscow. In the middle of the jokes we drop the biggest test bomb of all time. And so it goes on—the stick and then the carrot, the smile and then the frown. And the West is confused, their strategy disorganized. Tensions are relaxed before they have time to harden. Their common people laugh at our jokes, cheer our football teams and slobber with delight when we release a few prisoners of war whom we wish to feed no longer!"

General G. saw the eyes shining greedily round the table. The men were softened up. Now it was time for them to feel the new policy on themselves. Smoothly he leaned forward and raised his fist in the air. "But, comrades"—his voice was soft—"where has there been failure in carrying out the state policy of the U.S.S.R.? Who has all along been soft when we wished to be hard? Who has suffered defeats while victory was going to all other departments of the state? Who, with their stupid blunders, has made the Soviet Union look foolish and weak throughout the world? *Who?*"

The voice had risen almost to a scream. General G. glared at the pale, expectant faces. His fist crashed forward onto the desk. "The whole intelligence apparatus of the Soviet Union, comrades. It is we who are the sluggards, the saboteurs, the traitors! We!" His arm swept round the room. "All of us!" The voice became more reasonable. "Comrades, look at the record. First we lose Gouzenko and the whole of the Canadian operation and the scientist Fuchs, then the American operation is cleaned up, then comes the scandalous Khoklov affair, then Petrov and his wife in Australia—a bungled business if ever there was one! The list is endless—defeat after defeat, and the devil knows I have not mentioned the half of it."

General G. paused. He continued in his softest voice. "Comrades, I have to tell you that unless tonight we make a recommendation for a great intelligence victory, and unless we act correctly on that recommendation, if it is approved, there will be"—he paused and looked, with artificial mildness, down the table—"displeasure."

No one said a word for the defense. No one mentioned the countless victories of Soviet intelligence that could be set against the few mistakes. And no one questioned the right of the head of smersh, who shared the guilt with them, to deliver this terrible denunciation.

At the table the representative of the Ministry of Foreign Affairs, Lieutenant General Vozdvishensky, watched the smoke curl up from the tip of his long cigarette. General G.'s hard bulging brown eyes looked towards him. That is a deep one, thought General G. Let us put the spotlight on him and see how he shows up on the sound track.

"Comrades," General G. continued, "it is not just a question of blowing up a building or shooting a prime minister. Such bourgeois horseplay is not contemplated. The act of terrorism we recommend must do grave damage to enemy intelligence—hidden damage which the public will hear perhaps nothing of, but which will be the secret talk of government circles. But it must also cause a public scandal so devastating that the world will lick its lips and sneer at the stupidity of our enemies. Naturally governments will know that it is a Soviet *konspiratsia*. And the spies of the West will know it, too. They will marvel at our cleverness, and traitors and possible defectors will change their minds. But of course we shall deny any knowledge of the deed, and it is desirable that the common people of the Soviet Union should remain in complete ignorance of our complicity."

General G. paused and looked towards the foreign ministry representative again. "Comrade Lieutenant General Vozdvishensky, perhaps you would survey for us the relative importance of the Western intelligence services. We will then choose the one which is the most dangerous and which we would most wish to damage."

General Vozdvishensky was not dismayed by his task. He had been in intelligence, mostly abroad, for thirty years. He had helped train Sorge, the Soviet master spy, before Sorge went to Tokyo. He had been on the inside of the Burgess and Maclean operation and on countless other plots to penetrate the foreign ministries of the West. He was a professional spy to his fingertips and he was perfectly prepared to put on record his opinions of the rivals with whom he had been crossing swords all his life.

"In this matter," said General Vozdvishensky carefully, "one must not confuse the man with the office. Every country has good spies, and it is not always the biggest countries that have the most or the best. But secret services are expensive, and small countries cannot afford the coordinated effort which produces good intelligence. So we need not worry about these smaller countries. Italy can be dismissed. They are clever and active, but they do us no harm. The same can be said of Spain. In France, while we have penetrated most of their services, the Deuxième Bureau is still clever and dangerous. The head of it would be a tempting target and it would be easy to operate in France.

"England is another matter altogether. I think we all have respect for her intelligence service." There were grudging nods from everyone present, including General G. "They have notable successes. In certain types of operation, we are constantly finding that they have been there before us. Their agents are good. They pay them little money but they serve with devotion. It is curious that they play this game so well, for they are not natural conspirators." General Vozdvishensky felt that his remarks might be taken as too laudatory. He hastily qualified them. "Of course, most of their strength lies in the myth—in the myth of Scotland Yard, of Sherlock Holmes, of the

Secret Service. We certainly have nothing to fear from these gentlemen. But this myth is a hindrance which it would be good to set aside."

"And the Americans?" General G. inquired.

"The Americans have the biggest and richest service among our enemies. Technically, in such matters as radio and weapons and equipment, they are the best. But they have no understanding for the work. They get enthusiastic about some Balkan spy who says he has a secret army in the Ukraine. They load him with money with which to buy boots for this army. Of course he goes at once to Paris and spends the money on women. Americans try to do everything with money. Good spies will not work for money alone—only bad ones, of which the Americans have several divisions."

"They have successes, comrade," said General G. silkily. "Perhaps you underestimate them."

General Vozdvishensky shrugged. "They must have successes, Comrade General. You cannot sow a million seeds without reaping one potato. Personally I do not think the Americans need engage the attention of this conference."

"A very interesting exposition," said General G. coldly. "Comrade General Slavin?"

General Slavin had no intention of committing himself on behalf of the General Staff of the Army. "I have listened with interest to the words of Comrade General Vozdvishensky. I have nothing to add."

Colonel of State Security Nikitin felt it would do no great harm to make a modest recommendation that would probably tally with the inner thoughts of those present—and that was certainly on the tip of General G.'s tongue. "I recommend the English Secret Service as the object of terrorist action," he said decisively. "My department hardly finds them a worthy adversary, but they are the best of an indifferent lot."

"Is it agreed then, comrades?" General G., his thunder stolen, was annoyed.

There were careful, slow nods all round the table.

"I agree," said General G. "And now for the target within that organization. I remember Comrade General Vozdvishensky saying something about a myth upon which much of the alleged strength of the British Secret Service depends. Where does this myth reside?

We cannot destroy all its personnel at one blow. Does it reside in the head? Who is the head of the British Secret Service?"

Colonel Nikitin's aide whispered in his ear. This was a question the colonel could and perhaps should answer.

"He is an admiral. He is known by the letter M. We have a file on him, but it contains little. He does not drink very much. He is too old for women. The public does not know of his existence. It would be difficult to create a scandal round his death. And he would not be easy to kill. He rarely goes abroad. To shoot him in a London street would not be very refined."

"There is much in what you say, comrade," said General G. "But we are here to find a target who *will* fulfill our requirements. Have they no one who is a hero to the organization? Someone whose ignominious destruction would cause dismay? Myths are built on heroic deeds and heroic people. Have they no such men?"

There was silence round the table while everyone searched his memory. So many names to remember, so many dossiers, so many operations going on every day all over the world. Who was there in the British Secret Service? Who was the man who . . . ?

It was Colonel Nikitin of the M.G.B. who broke the embarrassed silence.

He said hesitantly, "There is a man called Bond."

General G.'s hand slapped down on the desk. "Comrade, there certainly is 'a man called Bond' as you put it." His voice was sarcastic. "James Bond. And nobody, myself included, could think of this spy's name! No wonder intelligence is under criticism. I recall that this Bond has at least twice frustrated the operations of SMERSH. That is," he added, "before I assumed control of the department. There was this affair in France, at that casino town. An excellent leader of the Party in France foolishly got into some money troubles. But he would have got out of them if this Bond had not interfered. Then there was some business about a treasure in the Caribbean. This Englishman smashed the whole organization and killed our man."

Colonel Nikitin broke in. "We had a similar experience in the case of the German rocket. It was a matter of high policy which could have borne decisive fruit. But again it was this Bond who frustrated the operation. There followed a period of serious embarrassment which was only solved with difficulty."

General Slavin felt that he should say something. The rocket had been an Army operation. "We asked for this man to be dealt with by your department, Comrade Colonel," he said icily. "I cannot recall that any action followed our request. If it had, we should not now be having to bother with him."

Colonel Nikitin's temples throbbed with rage. He controlled himself. "With due respect, Comrade General," he said in a loud, sarcastic voice, "the request was not confirmed by higher authority. Further embarrassment with England was not desired. In any case, if such a request had reached M.G.B., it would have been referred to SMERSH for action."

"My department received no such request," said General G. sharply. "Or the execution of this man would have rapidly followed. However, this is no time for historical researches. The rocket affair was three years ago."

Colonel Nikitin whispered hurriedly with his aide. He turned back to the table. "We have very little further information, Comrade General," he said defensively. "Perhaps there is more recent information in his file."

General G. picked up the receiver of the telephone nearest to him. He dialed a number. "Central Index? General Grubozaboyschikov here. The file of Bond—English spy. Emergency." He listened for the immediate "At once, Comrade General," and put back the receiver. "Comrades, from many points of view this spy sounds an appropriate target. He appears to be a dangerous enemy of the state. Also his loss will be felt by the Secret Service. But will it do more? Will it help to destroy this myth about which we have been speaking? Is this man a hero to his organization and his country?"

General Vozdvishensky spoke up. "The English are not interested in heroes unless they are footballers or cricketers or jockeys. This man Bond is unknown to the public. If he were known, he would still not be a hero. In England neither open war nor secret war is a heroic matter. They do not like to think about war."

Nikitin broke in. "English spies we have captured speak highly of this man. He is much admired, and is said to be a lone wolf, but a good-looking one."

There was a knock on the door, and an aide came in, placed a bulky file on the desk in front of the general and left. The file had a shiny black cover. In the top left-hand space there were the letters S.S. in white, and under them SOVERSHENNOE SEKRETNO, the equivalent of Top Secret. Across the center was neatly painted in white letters JAMES BOND, and underneath ANGLISKI SPION.

General G. opened the file and took out a large envelope containing photographs which he emptied onto the glass surface of the desk. He picked them up one by one, looking closely at them, sometimes through a magnifying glass which he took out of a drawer, and then

passing them across the desk to Nikitin, who glanced at them and handed them on.

The first, dated 1946, showed a dark young man sitting at a table outside a sunlit café. There was a tall glass beside him on the table and a cigarette between the fingers of the right hand resting on the table. The man didn't know that he was being photographed from a point about twenty feet away. The next, dated 1950, was a face and shoulders, blurred, but of the same man. Bond was looking with careful, narrowed eyes at something, probably the photographer's face, just above the lens. A miniature buttonhole camera, guessed General G. The third was from 1951. Taken from the left, quite close, it showed Bond in a dark suit, without a hat, walking down a wide empty street, as if he was going somewhere urgently. General G. reflected that it was probably taken from a car. The fourth and last, marked PASSPORT 1953, had been blown up to cabinet size. It must have been made at a frontier, or by the concierge of a hotel when Bond had surrendered his passport. General G. carefully went over the face with his magnifying glass.

It was a dark, clean-cut face, with a three-inch scar showing whitely down the sunburned skin of the right cheek. The eyes were wide and level under straight black brows. The hair was black, parted on the left, and carelessly brushed so that a thick black comma fell down over the right eyebrow. The longish straight nose ran down to a short upper lip below which was a wide and finely drawn but cruel mouth. The line of the jaw was straight and firm. A section of dark suit, white shirt and black knitted tie completed the picture.

General G. held the photograph out at arm's length. Decision, authority, ruthlessness—these qualities he could see. He passed the photograph down the table and turned to the file, glancing rapidly down each page and flipping brusquely on to the next. "He looks a nasty customer," he said grimly. "His story confirms it. I will read out some extracts. Then we must decide. It is getting late. 'All-round athlete; expert pistol shot, boxer, knife thrower; does not use disguises. Languages: French and German. Smokes heavily (special cigarettes with three gold bands). Vices: drink, but not to excess, and women. Not thought to accept bribes. Is invariably armed with a .25 Beretta automatic carried in a holster under his left arm. Magazine holds eight rounds. Has been known to carry a knife strapped to his left forearm; has used steel-capped shoes; knows the basic holds of judo. In general, fights with tenacity and has a high tolerance of pain.' "

General G. turned to the last page. " 'Conclusion. This man is a dangerous professional terrorist and spy. He has worked for the British Secret Service since 1938 and now holds the secret number 007 in that service. The double 0 numerals signify an agent who has killed and who is privileged to kill on active service. There are believed to be only two other British agents with this authority. If encountered in the field, full details to be reported to headquarters.' "

General G. shut the file decisively. "Well, comrades. Are we agreed?"

"Yes," said Colonel Nikitin loudly.

"Yes," said General Slavin in a bored voice.

General Vozdvishensky was looking down at his fingernails. He was sick of murder. He had enjoyed his time in England. "Yes," he said. "I suppose so."

General G. spoke into the internal office telephone. "Death warrant," he said harshly. "Made out in the name of James Bond." He spelled the names out. "Description: *Angliski spion*. Crime: Enemy of the state." He put the receiver back and leaned forward in his chair. "Thank you, comrades. That is all. I shall advise you of the decision of the Presidium on our recommendation. Good night."

When the conference had filed out, General G. picked up the V.Ch. receiver and asked for General Serov. He spoke quietly for five minutes. At the end he concluded: "And I am now about to give the task to Colonel Klebb and the planner, Kronsteen. We will discuss the outlines of a suitable *konspiratsia* and they will give me detailed proposals tomorrow. Is that in order, Comrade General?"

"Yes," came the quiet voice of General Serov. "Kill him. But let it be excellently accomplished. The Presidium will ratify the decision in the morning." The line went dead.

A moment later an aide opened the big door and stood in the entrance. "Comrade Colonel Klebb," he announced. A toadlike figure in an olive green uniform came into the room and walked with quick short steps to the nearest chair.

The head of Otdyel II, the department of SMERSH in charge of operations and executions, hitched up her skirts and sat down.

IN THE CHAMPIONSHIP CHESS game at Tournament Hall, Kronsteen, the champion of Moscow, playing against the champion of Georgia, was about to make his forty-first and final move. If he won this game he would be a contender for grand mastership.

In the pool of silence round the roped-off table there was no sound from the spectators, only the loud tripping feet of Kronsteen's clock. The two umpires sat motionless in their raised chairs. They knew that this was certainly the kill. Kronsteen had introduced a brilliant twist into the Meran Variation of the Queen's Gambit Declined.

There came a sigh from the crowded tiers. Kronsteen had slowly removed the right hand from his cheek and had stretched it across the board. Like the pincers of a pink crab, his thumb and forefinger had opened, then they had descended. The hand, holding a piece, moved up and sideways and down. Then the hand reached deliberately over and pressed down the lever at the bottom of his clock. His red pendulum went dead. At the same instant his opponent's pendulum came to life and started its loud, inexorable beat.

But now it was the end. The moments ticked by until, with five seconds to go on his clock, the opponent raised his whipped eyes no higher than the pouting lips of Kronsteen and bent his head in the brief, formal bow of surrender.

At the double ping of the umpire's bell, the crowded hall rose to its feet with a thunder of applause. Kronsteen stood up and bowed to his opponent, to the umpires, and finally, deeply, to the spectators. A man in plain clothes slipped under the ropes and handed him a white envelope. Kronsteen ripped it open with his thumb and extracted the anonymous sheet of paper. It said, in the large typewritten characters he knew so well, YOU ARE REQUIRED THIS INSTANT. No signature and no address. With the plainclothesman in his wake, he ducked under the ropes and fought his way coldly and rudely through the mass of his clamoring admirers towards the main exit.

Outside Tournament Hall stood a black limousine with its engine running. Kronsteen climbed into the back and shut the door. The plainclothesman jumped onto the running board and squeezed into the front seat. The driver crashed his gears and the car tore off down the street.

A few minutes later in General G.'s office, Kronsteen, head of the planning department of SMERSH, with the honorary rank of full colonel, took a chair and nodded acknowledgment of the brief pursed smile of Colonel Klebb. "Pass the photographs to him, Comrade Colonel," said General G. "The matter is as follows. . . ."

So it is another death, thought Kronsteen, as the general talked and he examined the dark ruthless face that gazed levelly at him from the blown-up passport photograph. While Kronsteen listened with half his mind to what the general was saying, he picked out the salient facts—English spy. Great scandal desired. No Soviet involvement. Expert killer. Weakness for women. Drinks. (But nothing is said about drugs.) Unbribable. (Who knows? There is a price for every man.) No expense would be spared. All equipment and personnel available from all intelligence departments. Success to be achieved within three months. Broad ideas required now. Details to be worked out later.

General G. fastened his sharp eyes on Colonel Klebb. "What are your immediate reactions, Comrade Colonel?"

The square-cut rimless glass of her spectacles flashed in the light of the chandelier as the woman looked across the desk at the general. The pale moist lips below the sheen of nicotine-stained fur over the mouth parted and started moving rapidly up and down as the woman gave her views. To Kronsteen, watching the face across the table, the opening and shutting of the lips reminded him of the jabber of a puppet. He wondered casually how much longer Rosa Klebb would last in her job—how much longer he would have to work with her.

Her rise, Kronsteen remembered, had begun with the Spanish Civil War, and the details were filed away in his memory like so many chess gambits. As a double agent she had been the right hand, and some sort of a mistress, they said, of her chief. Then, on the orders of Moscow, he was murdered and, it was rumored, murdered by her. From then on she had progressed slowly but straight up the ladder of power, surviving setbacks, surviving wars, surviving purges, until, in 1953, with the death of Beria, the bloodstained hands grasped the rung, so few from the very top, that was head of the operations department of SMERSH. In her late forties, she was short, about five feet four, and squat. Her dumpy arms and short neck, and the calves of the thick legs in the drab khaki stockings, were very strong for a woman.

The *tricoteuses* of the French Revolution, those women who sat and knitted and chatted while the guillotine clanged down, must have had faces like Rosa Klebb's, decided Kronsteen. The thinning orange hair scraped back to a tight, obscene bun; the shiny yellow-brown eyes that stared so coldly at General G. through the sharp-edged squares of glass; the wedge of thickly powdered nose; the wet trap of a mouth, opening and shutting as if it were operated by wires under the chin.

"Thank you, Comrade Colonel. Your review of the position is of value. And now, Comrade Kronsteen, have you anything to add?" General G.'s eyes stared fixedly across the desk into the fathomless brown pools below the bulging forehead.

Kronsteen slowly tilted back his head and gazed at the ceiling. His voice was extremely mild, but it had the authority that commands close attention.

"Comrade General, it was a Frenchman, Fouché, who observed that it is no good killing a man unless you also destroy his reputation. It will, of course, be easy to kill this man Bond. Any paid Bulgarian assassin could do it, if properly instructed. The second part of the operation, the destruction of this man's character, is more important and more difficult. At this stage it is only clear to me that the deed must be done away from England, and in a country over whose press and radio we have influence. If you ask me how the man is to be got there, I can only say that if the bait is important enough, he will be sent to seize it. To avoid the appearance of a trap, I would consider giving the bait a touch of eccentricity, of the unusual. The English treat the eccentric proposition as a challenge. I would rely partly on this reading of their psychology to have them send this important operator after the bait. We are then likely to require an assassin with a perfect command of the English language."

Kronsteen's eyes moved to the red velvet tabletop in front of him. Thoughtfully, as if this was the kernel of the problem, he added, "We shall also require a reliable and extremely beautiful girl."

CHAPTER 3

SITTING BY THE WINDOW of her one room and looking out at the serene June evening, at the distant onion spire of a church that flamed in the sunset like a torch above the ragged horizon of Moscow roofs, Corporal of State Security Tatiana Romanova thought that she was happier than she had ever been before.

Her happiness was not romantic. It was the quiet happiness of security, a word of praise she had had that afternoon, the smell of a good supper cooking on the electric stove, the prelude to *Boris Godunov* being played by the Moscow State Orchestra on the radio.

The room was a tiny box in a huge modern apartment building, the women's barracks of the state security departments. Built by prison labor, the fine eight-story building contained two thousand rooms, some, like hers on the third floor, nothing but square boxes with a telephone, hot and cold water, a single electric light and a share of the central bathrooms and lavatories. Others, on the two top floors, consisted of two- and three-room flats with bathrooms. These were for high-ranking women. But she was content with her lot. A salary larger than she could have earned in any other ministry; a room to herself; cheap food and clothes from the "closed shops" on the ground floor of the building; a monthly allocation of at least two ministry tickets to the ballet or the opera; a full two weeks' paid holiday a year. And, above all, a steady job with good prospects in Moscow.

Corporal Romanova left the chair by the window and went to examine the pot of thick soup that was to be her supper. It was nearly done and smelled delicious. She turned off the electricity and let the pot simmer while she washed and tidied. As she dried her hands, she examined herself in the big oval looking glass over the washstand.

One of her early boy friends had said she looked like the young Greta Garbo. What nonsense! And yet tonight she did look rather well. Fine dark brown silken hair brushed straight back from a tall brow and falling heavily down almost to the shoulders, there to curl slightly up at the ends; a good, soft pale skin with an ivory sheen at the cheekbones; wide-apart, level eyes of the deepest blue under straight natural brows and long lashes; a straight, rather imperious nose. What about the mouth? Was it too broad? She smiled at herself in the mirror. Yes, it was wide; but then so had Garbo's been. At least the lips were full and finely etched. There was the hint of a smile at the corners. No one could say it was a cold mouth!

In fact Corporal Tatiana Romanova was a very beautiful girl indeed, and was admired far beyond the confines of the English translation section of the M.G.B. Central Index. Apart from her face, she had faultless arms and breasts, and a tall, firm body that moved particularly well. She had been a year in the ballet school in Leningrad and had abandoned dancing as a career only when she grew an inch over the prescribed limit of five feet six. The school had taught her to hold herself well and to walk well. And she looked wonderfully healthy, thanks to her passion for figure skating, which she practiced all through the year at the ice rink.

The telephone rang harshly. She walked over and turned down the radio and picked up the receiver.

"Corporal Romanova?"

It was the voice of her section head. But out of office hours he always called her Tatiana or even Tania. What did this mean?

The girl was wide-eyed and tense. "Yes, comrade."

The voice at the other end sounded strange and cold. "In fifteen minutes, at eight thirty, you are required for interview by Comrade Colonel Klebb, of Otdyel Two. You will call on her in her apartment, Number Eighteen seventy-five, on the eighth floor of your building. Is that clear?"

"But, comrade, why? What is . . . What is . . ."

The odd, strained voice cut her short. "That is all, Comrade Corporal."

The girl held the receiver away from her face and stood for a moment, frozen. Should she call him back? No, that was out of the question. He had spoken as he had because he knew, and she knew, that every call, in and out of the building, was listened to or recorded. That was why he had not wasted a word.

The girl put her knuckles up to her open mouth and bit on them. What did they want her for? What had she done? Desperately she cast her mind back, scrabbling through the days, the months, the years. Had she made some terrible mistake in her work and had they just discovered it? Had she made some remark against the state, some joke that had been reported back? The girl glanced at the cheap watch on her wrist. Only seven minutes to go! A new panic seized her. She grabbed down her parade uniform from the clothes closet. On top of it all, whatever it was, to be late! She tore at the buttons of her white cotton blouse.

OUTSIDE THE CREAM-PAINTED door on the eighth floor, Tatiana waited until the voice told her curtly to come in. She opened the door and gazed into the eyes of the woman who sat behind the round table under the center light.

Colonel Klebb's eyes, staring through the square glass panes, moved all over her, like camera lenses. Somehow Tatiana managed to look bravely back.

"Comrade Corporal Romanova, sit down." She gestured to the chair across the table from her. "I have good reports of your work. Your record is excellent, both in your duties and in sport. The state is pleased with you."

Tatiana could not believe her ears. She blushed to the roots of her hair and then turned pale. She felt faint with reaction and stammered in a weak voice, "I am g-grateful, Comrade Colonel."

"Because of your excellent services you have been singled out for a most important assignment. It carries much responsibility. It bears a higher rank. I congratulate you on your promotion, Comrade Corporal, on completion of the assignment, to the rank of Captain of State Security."

This was unheard of for a girl of twenty-four! Tatiana sensed danger. "I am deeply honored, Comrade Colonel." She was unable to keep the wariness out of her voice.

Rosa Klebb grunted noncommittally. She knew exactly what the girl must have thought when she got the summons. The effect of her kindly reception, her shock of relief at the good news, her reawakening fears, had been transparent. This was a beautiful, guileless, innocent girl. Just what the *konspiratsia* demanded. "And now to business, comrade. There is much work to be done." She leaned forward. "Have you ever wished to live abroad?"

"No, comrade. I am happy in Moscow."

"You have never thought what it might be like living in the West —all those beautiful clothes, the jazz, the modern things?"

"No, comrade." She had truthfully never thought about it.

"And if the state required you to live in the West?"

"I would obey."

"Willingly?"

Tatiana shrugged her shoulders with a hint of impatience. "One does what one is told."

The woman paused. There was girlish conspiracy in the next question. "Are you a virgin, comrade?"

Oh, my God, thought Tatiana. "No, Comrade Colonel."

"How many men?"

Tatiana colored to the roots of her hair, and she stared defensively into the yellow eyes. "What is the purpose of these intimate questions, please, Comrade Colonel?"

Rosa Klebb straightened. Her voice cut back like a whip. "Remember yourself, comrade. You are not here to ask questions. You forget to whom you are speaking. Answer me!"

Tatiana shrank back. "Three men, Comrade Colonel."

"When? How old were you?" The hard gaze looked into the hunted blue eyes of the girl and commanded.

Tatiana was on the edge of tears. "At school. When I was seventeen. Then at the Institute of Foreign Languages. I was twenty-two. Then last year. I was twenty-three. It was a friend I met skating."

"Their names, please, comrade." Rosa Klebb picked up a pencil and pulled a pad towards her.

Tatiana covered her face with her hands. "No," she cried between sobs. "No, never, whatever you do to me. You have no right."

"Stop that nonsense." The voice was a hiss. "In five minutes I could have those names from you, or anything else I wish to know. You are playing a dangerous game with me, comrade. My patience will not last forever." Rosa Klebb paused. She was being too rough. "For the moment we will pass on. Tomorrow you will give me the names. No harm will come to these men. They will be asked one or two questions about you—simple technical questions, that is all. Now sit up and dry your tears."

Rosa Klebb got up and came round the table. She stood looking down at Tatiana. The voice became oily and smooth. "Come, come, my dear. You must trust me. Your little secrets are safe with me. And now, my dear, just one more intimate little question. Do you enjoy making love? Does it give you pleasure? Much pleasure?"

Tatiana answered in muffled tones, "Well, yes, Comrade Colonel. Naturally, when one is in love . . ." Her voice trailed away. What answer did this woman want?

"And supposing, my dear, you were not in love. Then would love-making with a man still give you pleasure?"

Tatiana bowed her head, trying to think, to be helpful, but she couldn't imagine such a situation. "I suppose it would depend on the man, Comrade Colonel."

"That is a sensible answer, my dear." Rosa Klebb opened a drawer, took out a photograph and slipped it across to the girl. "What about this man, for instance?"

Tatiana looked down warily at the handsome, ruthless face. She tried to think, to imagine. . . . "I cannot tell, Comrade Colonel. He is good-looking. Perhaps if he was gentle . . ." She pushed the photograph anxiously away from her.

"No, keep it, my dear. Put it up beside your bed and think of this man. The task for which you have been chosen from all the girls in Russia, Comrade Corporal, is a simple delightful duty, a real labor of love, as we say. It is a matter of falling in love. That is all. Just falling in love with this man."

"But who is he? I don't even know him."

Rosa Klebb's mouth reveled. This would give the silly chit of a girl something to think about. "He is an English spy."

"*Bozhe moy!*" Tatiana clapped a hand over her mouth as much to stifle the use of God's name as from terror. She sat, tense with shock, and gazed at Rosa Klebb through wide eyes.

"Yes," said Rosa Klebb, pleased with the effect of her words. "He is an English spy. Perhaps the most famous of them all. And from now on you are in love with him. So you had better get used to the idea. This is an important state matter for which you have been chosen as the instrument. For the next few weeks you will be most carefully trained until you know exactly what to do in all contingencies. You will be taught certain foreign customs. You will be equipped with beautiful clothes. You will be instructed in all the arts of allurement. Then you will be sent to a foreign country, somewhere in Europe. There you will meet this man. You will seduce him. In this matter you will have no silly compunctions. Your body belongs to the state. Since your birth, the state has nourished it. Now your body must work for the state. Is that understood?"

"Yes, Comrade Colonel." The logic was inescapable.

"You will accompany this man to England. There, you will no doubt be questioned. The English do not use harsh methods. We will supply you with certain answers which we would like to be given. You will probably be sent to Canada. That is where the English send a certain category of foreign prisoner. You will be rescued and brought back to Moscow." Rosa Klebb peered at the girl. She seemed to be accepting all this without question.

"What will happen to the man, Comrade Colonel?"

"That is a matter of indifference to us. We shall simply use him as a means to introduce you into England. The object of the operation is to give false information to the British. We shall, of course, comrade, be very glad to have your own impressions of life in England. The reports of a highly trained and intelligent girl such as yourself will be of great value to the state."

"Really, Comrade Colonel!" Tatiana felt important. Suddenly it all sounded exciting. She felt immensely grateful to the father figure that was the state, and proud that she would now have a chance to repay some of her debt.

IT WAS THE MORNING of the next day.

Colonel Klebb sat at her desk in the roomy office that was her headquarters in the underground basement of SMERSH. One wall was completely papered with a map of the Western Hemisphere. The opposite wall was covered with the Eastern Hemisphere. Every agent of SMERSH throughout the world was controlled from this room, and it was a vigilant and iron control.

One of the three telephones at her side purred softly. She picked up the receiver. "Send him in."

She turned to Kronsteen, who sat in an armchair up against the left-hand wall, under the toe of Africa. "Granitsky."

Kronsteen slowly turned his head and looked at the door.

Red Grant came in and closed the door softly behind him. He walked up to the desk and stood looking down into the eyes of his commanding officer. Kronsteen thought that he looked like a powerful mastiff waiting to be fed.

Rosa Klebb surveyed him coldly. "Are you fit and ready for work?"

"Yes, Comrade Colonel."

"Let's have a look at you. Take off your clothes."

Red Grant showed no surprise. He took off his coat and, after looking around for somewhere to put it, dropped it on the floor. Then, unselfconsciously, he took off the rest of his clothes, kicked off his shoes, and stood relaxed, his hands held loosely at his sides.

Rosa Klebb got to her feet and came round the desk. She studied the body minutely, prodding here, feeling there, as if she were buying a horse. She went behind the man and continued her minute inspection. Kronsteen saw her slip something out of her jacket pocket and fit it into her hand. There was a glint of metal. The woman came round and stood close up to the man's gleaming stomach, her left arm behind her back.

Suddenly, with terrific speed and the whole weight of her shoulder behind the blow, she whipped her left fist, loaded with heavy brass knuckles, round and exactly into the solar plexus of the man.

Whuck!

Grant let out a snort of surprise and pain. For a flash the eyes closed tight with agony. Then they opened again and glared redly down into the cold yellow probing eyes behind the square glasses. Apart from an angry flush on the skin, Grant showed no ill effects from a blow that would have sent any normal man writhing to the ground.

Rosa Klebb smiled grimly. She slipped the brass knuckles back in

her pocket and walked to her desk and sat down. She looked across at Kronsteen with a hint of pride. "At least he is fit enough," she said.

Kronsteen grunted.

Rosa Klebb sat back in her chair. "Comrade Granitsky, there is work for you. An important task that will earn you a medal." Grant's eyes gleamed. "You will be in a foreign country, and alone. The target is an English spy, a difficult and dangerous one. You would like to kill an English spy?"

"Very much indeed, Comrade Colonel." Grant's enthusiasm was genuine. He asked nothing better than to kill an Englishman. He had accounts to settle with the bastards.

"You will need many weeks of training and preparation. On this assignment you will be operating in the guise of an English agent. Your manners and appearance are uncouth. You will be placed in the hands of a certain Englishman we have here. A former *chentleman"*— the voice sneered—"of the Foreign Office in London. It will be his task to make you pass as some sort of an English spy. The operation will be around the end of August, but you will start your training at once. There is much to be done. Understood?"

"Yes, Comrade Colonel." Grant scrambled into his clothes and walked over to the door, buttoning his jacket. He turned. "Thank you, Comrade Colonel."

Rosa Klebb, writing up her note of the interview, didn't answer. Grant went out and the woman threw down her pen and sat back.

"And now, Comrade Kronsteen. Are there any points to discuss before we put the full machinery in motion?"

Kronsteen sat looking up at the ceiling, the tips of his fingers joined in front of him. The pulse of concentration beat in his temples. "This girl, Romanova. She was satisfactory?"

The woman said grudgingly, "She is very beautiful. She will serve our purpose. Her English is excellent. I have given her a certain version of her task and its object. She is cooperative. If she should show signs of faltering, I have the addresses of certain relatives, including children. I shall also have the names of her previous lovers. If necessary, it would be explained to her that these people will be hostages until her task is completed. She has an affectionate nature. Such a hint would be sufficient. But I do not anticipate any trouble from her."

"And this man Bond. Have we discovered his whereabouts?"

"Yes. The M.G.B. English network reports him in London. During the day he goes to his headquarters. At night he sleeps in his flat in a district of London called Chelsea."

"That is good. He will be available to go after our bait when they get the scent. Meanwhile, I have decided on Istanbul for the first contact. It is conveniently placed for us, with short lines of communication with Bulgaria and the Black Sea. It is relatively far from London. I am working out details of the point of assassination and the means of getting this Bond there, after he has contacted the girl. It will be either in France or very near it. We have excellent leverage on the French press. They will make the most of this kind of story, with its sensational disclosures of sex and espionage. It also remains to be decided when Granitsky shall enter the picture. These are minor details. We must choose the cameramen and the other operatives and move them quietly into Istanbul. The Cipher Department has agreed that there is no security objection to handing over the outer case of a Spektor machine. That will be attractive. The machine will go to the special devices section. They will handle its preparation." Kronsteen stopped talking.

He looked across into the watchful eyes of the woman. "I can think of nothing else at the moment, comrade," he said. "Many details will come up and have to be settled from day to day. But I think the operation can safely begin."

Rosa Klebb reached for one of the telephones and dialed a number. "Operations room," said a man's voice.

"Colonel Klebb speaking. The *konspiratsia* against the English spy Bond will commence forthwith."

CHAPTER 4

A<small>T SEVEN THIRTY</small> on the morning of Thursday, August 12, James Bond awoke in his comfortable flat in a square off the King's Road and was disgusted to find that he was thoroughly bored with the prospect of the day ahead. He reached out and gave two rings on the bell to show his housekeeper that he was ready for breakfast, then abruptly flung the single sheet off his naked body and swung his feet to the floor.

There was only one way to deal with boredom—kick oneself out of it. Bond went down on his hands and did twenty slow pushups. When his arms could stand the pain no longer, he rolled over on his back and did the straight leg lift until his stomach muscles screamed. He got to his feet, touched his toes twenty times and did chest exercises combined with deep breathing until he was dizzy. Panting with the exertion, he went into the big white-tiled bathroom and stood in the glass shower cabinet under very hot and then cold hissing water for five minutes.

At last, after shaving and putting on a sleeveless dark blue cotton shirt and navy blue tropical worsted trousers, he slipped his bare feet into black leather sandals and went into the long big-windowed sitting room with the satisfaction of having sweated his boredom, for the time being at any rate, out of his body.

His housekeeper, an elderly woman with iron gray hair, came in with the tray and put it on the table in the bay window, together with *The Times*, the only paper Bond ever read.

Breakfast was Bond's favorite meal of the day. When he was stationed in London it was always the same: strong coffee brewed in an American Chemex, of which he drank two large cups, black and without sugar; the single egg, boiled for three and a third minutes; two thick slices of whole wheat toast, a large pat of Jersey butter, strawberry jam, marmalade and Norwegian heather honey. The coffee pot and the silver on the tray were Queen Anne.

That morning, while Bond finished his breakfast with the honey, he pinpointed the immediate cause of his low spirits. To begin with, Tiffany Case, his love for so many happy months, had left him. He missed her badly and his mind still sheered away from the thought of her. And it was August, and London was hot and stale. He was due for leave, but he had not the energy or the desire to go off alone, or to try and find some temporary replacement for Tiffany to go with him. So he had stayed on in the half-empty headquarters of the Secret Service grinding away at the old routines, snapping at his secretary and rasping his colleagues.

At nine o'clock he walked out of his flat and down the steps to his car. As he pressed the self-starter and the twin exhausts of the Bentley woke to their fluttering growl, a curious bastard quotation slipped from nowhere into Bond's mind. "Those whom the Gods would destroy, they first make bored."

BOND HAD COMPLIMENTED his secretary on a new summer frock, and was halfway through the file of signals that had come in during the night, when the red telephone that could only mean M. or his chief of staff gave its soft, peremptory burr.

Bond picked up the receiver. "007."

"Can you come up?" It was the chief of staff.

"Any idea what it's about?"

The chief of staff chuckled. "Well, I have as a matter of fact. But you'd better hear about it from M."

As Bond put on his coat he had a feeling of certainty that the starter's gun had fired and that the dog days had come to an end. Even the ride up to the top floor in the lift and the walk down the long quiet corridor to M.'s office seemed to be charged with significance. And the eyes of M.'s private secretary had that old look of secret knowledge as she smiled up at him and pressed the switch on the intercom.

"007's here, sir."

"Send him in," said the metallic voice, and the red light of privacy went on above the door.

The room was cool, or perhaps it was the venetian blinds throwing bars of light and shadow across the dark green carpet that gave an impression of coolness. The quiet figure behind the big central desk sat in a pool of suffused greenish shade. In the ceiling directly above the desk, a big twin-bladed tropical fan slowly revolved. Bond sat down and looked into the tranquil, lined sailor's face that he loved, honored and obeyed.

M. picked his pipe out of the big copper ashtray and began to fill it. He said harshly, "You needn't answer this question, but it's to do with your, er, friend Miss Case. As you know, I don't generally interest myself in these matters, but I did hear that you had been, er, seeing a lot of each other since that diamond business. Even some idea you might be going to get married." He put the loaded pipe into his mouth and set a match to it.

Now what? wondered Bond. Damn these office gossips. He said gruffly, "Well, sir, there was some idea we might get married. But then she met some chap in the American embassy, and I gather she's going to marry him. We had too many rows. Probably my fault. Anyway, it's over now."

M. gave one of his brief smiles. "I'm sorry if it went wrong, James," he said. There was no sympathy in M.'s voice. As Bond's chief, the last thing he wanted was for Bond to be permanently tied to one woman's skirts. "Perhaps it's for the best. Had to know the answer before I told you what's come up. It's a pretty odd business. Be difficult to get you involved if you were on the edge of marrying."

M. leaned back in his chair and gave several quick pulls on his pipe to get it going. "This is what's happened. Yesterday there was a long signal in from Istanbul. Seems on Tuesday the head of Station T got an anonymous typewritten message which told him to take a round-trip ticket on the eight p.m. ferry steamer from the Galata Bridge to the mouth of the Bosporus and back. Head of T's an adventurous chap, and of course he took the steamer. He stood up for'ard by the rail and waited. After about a quarter of an hour a girl came and stood beside him, a Russian girl, very good-looking, he says, and after they'd talked a bit about the view and so on, she suddenly switched and in the same sort of conversational voice she told him an extraordinary story."

M. paused to put another match to his pipe. Bond interjected, "Who is head of T, sir? I've never worked in Turkey."

"Man called Kerim, Darko Kerim. Turkish father and English mother. Remarkable fellow. Been head of T since before the war. One of the best men we've got anywhere. Very intelligent and he knows all that part of the world like the back of his hand." M. dismissed Kerim with a sideways jerk of his pipe. "Anyway, the girl's story was that she was a corporal in the M.G.B. and had just got transferred to the Istanbul center as a cipher officer. She'd engineered the transfer because she wanted to get out of Russia and come over."

"That's good," said Bond. "Might be useful to have one of their cipher girls. But why does she want to come over?"

M. looked across the table at Bond. "Because she's in love." He paused and added mildly, "She says she's in love with you."

"In love with *me?*"

"Yes, with you. That's what she says. Her name's Tatiana Romanova. Ever heard of her?"

"Good God, no! I mean, no, sir." M. smiled at the mixture of expressions on Bond's face. "But what the hell does she mean? Has she ever met me? How does she know I exist?"

"Well," said M., "the whole thing sounds absolutely ridiculous. But it's so crazy that it just might be true. This girl is twenty-four. Ever since she joined the M.G.B. she's been working in their Central Index, the same as our Records. And she's been working in the English section of it. She's been there six years. One of the files she had to deal with was yours."

"I'd like to see that one," commented Bond.

"Her story is that she first took a fancy to the photographs they've got of you. Admired your looks and so on. She read up all your cases.

Decided that you were the hell of a fellow. You reminded her of the hero of a book by some Russian fellow called Lermontov. Apparently it was her favorite book. This hero chap liked gambling and spent his whole time getting in and out of scraps. One day the idea came to her that if only she could transfer to one of their foreign centers she could get in touch with you and you would come and rescue her."

"I've never heard such a crazy story, sir. Surely the head of T didn't swallow it."

"Now wait a moment." M.'s voice was testy. "Suppose you happened to be a film star instead of being in this particular trade. You'd get daft letters from girls all over the world about not being able to live without you and so on. Here's a silly girl doing a secretary's job in Moscow. Probably the whole department is staffed by women, like our Records. Not a man in the room to look at, and here she is, faced with your, er, dashing features on a file that's constantly coming up for review. And she gets what I believe they call a crush on these pictures just as secretaries all over the world get crushes on these dreadful faces in the magazines. Lord knows, these things happen."

Bond smiled. "Well, as a matter of fact, sir, I'm beginning to see there is some sense in it. There's no reason why a Russian girl shouldn't be just as silly as an English one. But she must have guts to do what she did. Does head of T say if she realized the consequences if she was found out?"

"He said she was frightened out of her wits," said M. "Spent the whole time on the boat looking round to see if anybody was watching. But wait. You haven't heard half the story." M. took a long pull at his pipe. "She told Kerim that this passion for you gradually developed into a phobia. She got to hate the sight of Russian men. In time this turned into dislike of the regime and particularly of the work she was doing for them and, so to speak, against you. So she applied for a transfer abroad, and since her languages were very good —English and French—in due course she was offered Istanbul if she would join the Cipher Department, which meant a cut in pay. To make a long story short, after six months' training, she got to Istanbul about three weeks ago. Then she sniffed about and soon got hold of the name of our man Kerim. He's been there so long that everybody in Turkey knows what he does by now. He doesn't mind, and it takes people's eyes off the special men we send in from time to time."

Bond commented, "The public agent often does better than the man who has to spend a lot of time and energy keeping under cover."

"So she sent Kerim the note. Kerim's first reactions were exactly the same as yours, and he fished around looking for a trap. But he simply couldn't see what the Russians could gain from sending this girl over to us. All this time the steamer was getting further and further up the Bosporus and the girl got more and more desperate as Kerim went on trying to break down her story. Then"—M.'s eyes glittered softly across at Bond—"came the clincher. She had a last card to play. And she knew it was the ace of trumps. If she could come over to us, she would bring her cipher machine with her. It's the brand new Spektor machine. The thing we'd give our eyes to have."

"God," said Bond softly, his mind boggling at the immensity of the prize. The Spektor! The machine that would allow them to decipher the top secret traffic of all. To have that, even if its loss was immediately discovered and the settings changed, or the machine taken out of service, would be a priceless victory, for he knew that, in the Russian Secret Service, loss of the Spektor would be counted a major disaster.

Bond was sold. At once he accepted all M.'s faith in the girl's story, however crazy it might be. For a Russian to take the appalling risk of bringing them this gift could only mean an act of desperation—of desperate infatuation if you liked. Whether the girl's story was true or not, the stakes were too high to turn down the gamble.

"But did she say how she could do it?"

"Not exactly. But Kerim says she was absolutely definite. Apparently she's on duty alone certain nights of the week and sleeps on a cot in the office. She seemed to have no doubts about it, although she realized that she would be shot out of hand if anyone even dreamed of her plan. She was even worried about Kerim reporting all this back to me. Made him promise he would encode the signal himself and send it on a one-time-only pad and keep no copy. Naturally he did as she asked. Directly she mentioned the Spektor, Kerim knew he might be on to the most important coup that's come our way since the war."

"What happened then, sir?"

"The steamer was coming up to a place called Ortaköy. She said she was going to get off there. Kerim promised to get a signal off that night. She refused to make any arrangements for staying in touch. Just said that she would keep her end of the bargain if we would keep ours. She said good night and mixed in the crowd going down the gangplank and that was the last Kerim saw of her."

Bond said nothing. He could guess what was coming.

"This girl will only do these things on one condition." M.'s eyes narrowed. "That you go out to Istanbul and bring her and the machine back to England."

Bond shrugged his shoulders. "Should be a piece of cake, sir. As far as I can see there's only one snag. Suppose that when she sees me in the flesh, I don't come up to her expectations."

"That's where the work comes in. That's why I asked those questions about Miss Case," said M. grimly. "It's up to you to see that you *do* come up to her expectations."

THE FOUR SMALL, square-ended propellers turned slowly, one by one, and became four whizzing pools. The low hum of the Viscount's turbojet engines rose to a shrill smooth whine, then to a banshee scream. With a jerk of released brakes, the ten-thirty B.E.A. Flight 130 from London to Rome, Athens and Istanbul gathered speed and hurtled down the runway and up into a quick, easy climb.

In ten minutes Bond unfastened his seat belt and lit a cigarette. He reached for the slim attaché case on the floor beside him and took out *A Coffin for Dimitrios* by Eric Ambler and put the case, which was very heavy in spite of its size, on the seat beside him. He thought how surprised the ticket clerk at London Airport would have been if she had weighed the case instead of letting it go unchecked as an "overnight bag."

Q Branch had put together this smart-looking little bag, ripping out the careful handiwork to pack fifty rounds of .25 ammunition, in two flat rows, between the leather and the lining of the spine. In each of the innocent sides there was a flat throwing knife, and the tops of their handles were concealed cleverly by the stitching at the corners. Despite Bond's efforts to laugh them out of it, Q's craftsmen had insisted on building a hidden compartment into the handle of the case, which, by pressure at a certain point, would deliver a cyanide death pill into his hand. (Bond had washed this pill down the lavatory.) More important was the thick tube of Palmolive shaving cream. The whole top of this unscrewed to reveal the silencer for the Beretta, packed in cotton wool. In case hard cash was needed, the lid of the attaché case contained fifty gold sovereigns. These could be poured out by slipping sideways one ridge of welting.

The plane sang steadily on above the endless sea of whipped-cream clouds that looked solid enough to land on if the engines failed. The clouds broke up and a distant blue haze, far away to their left, was Paris. For an hour they flew high over the burned-up fields of France until, after Dijon, the land turned from a pale to a darker green as it sloped up into the Juras.

Lunch came. Bond put aside his book and, while he ate, focused his mind on the immediate future—on this business, as he sourly described it to himself, of "pimping for England."

For he was on his way to seduce, and seduce very quickly, a girl whom he had never seen before, whose name he had heard yesterday for the first time. And all the while, however attractive she was, Bond's whole mind would have to be not on what she was, but on what she had—the dowry she was bringing with her—the cipher machine. It would be like trying to marry a rich woman for her money.

The plane slid into its fifty-mile glide towards Rome. Half an hour among the jabbering loudspeakers of Ciampino Airport, time to drink two excellent Americanos, and they were on their way again, flying steadily down towards the toe of Italy, and Bond's mind went back to sifting the minutest details of the coming rendezvous.

Was it all a complicated M.G.B. plot? Was he walking into some trap? God knew M. was worried about the possibility. Every conceivable angle of the evidence, for and against, had been scrutinized—not only by M., but also by a full-dress operations meeting of heads of sections that had worked all through the afternoon and evening before. But no one had been able to suggest what the Russians might get out of it. They might want to kidnap Bond and interrogate him. But why Bond? He was an operating agent carrying in his head nothing of use to the Russians except the details of his current duty and a certain amount of background information that could not possibly be vital. Or they might want to kill Bond, as an act of revenge. Yet he had not come up against them for two years. If they wanted to kill him, they had only to shoot him in the streets of London, or in his flat, or put a bomb in his car.

It was dusk and the half-moon rode clear and high above the lights of the town when, after a stop at Athens, the Viscount roared down the concrete airstrip on takeoff. They had only a ninety-minute flight to Istanbul, across the dark Aegean and the Sea of Marmara. An excellent dinner, with two dry martinis and a half bottle of Calvet claret, put Bond's worries about his assignment out of his mind and substituted a mood of pleased anticipation.

Then they were there and the plane's four propellers wheeled to a stop outside the fine modern airport at Yeşilköy, an hour's drive from Istanbul. Bond carried the heavy little attaché case through the passport check, and waited for his suitcase to come off the plane and be cleared by customs.

Outside the customs, a tall man with drooping black mustaches stepped out of the shadows. He wore a smart duster and a chauffeur's cap. He saluted and, without asking Bond his name, took his suitcase and led the way over to a gleaming black Rolls-Royce. When the car was gliding out of the airport, the man turned and said in excellent English, "Kerim Bey thought you would prefer to rest tonight, sir. I am to call for you at nine tomorrow morning. What hotel are you staying at, sir?"

"The Kristal Palas."

Behind them, in the dappled shadows of the airport parking place, Bond vaguely heard the crackle of a motor scooter starting up. The sound meant nothing to him and he settled back to enjoy the drive.

CHAPTER 5

JAMES BOND AWOKE EARLY in his dingy room at the Kristal Palas on the heights of Pera. When he had arrived the night before, to be greeted by a surly night concierge, and had briefly inspected the entrance hall with the flyblown palms, and the floor and walls of discolored Moorish tiles, he had half thought of going to another hotel. But inertia, and a perverse liking for the sleazy romance that clings to old-fashioned continental hotels, had decided him to stay.

Bond got out of bed, drew back the heavy red plush curtains, leaned on the iron balustrade and looked out over one of the most famous views in the world—on his right the still waters of the Golden

Horn, on his left the dancing waves of the unsheltered Bosporus, and, in between, the tumbling roofs, soaring minarets and crouching mosques of Pera. After all, his choice had been good. The view made up for everything—bedbugs, discomfort and the fact that only a thin stream of brownish liquid issued from the cold-water tap in the bathroom.

Punctually at nine the elegant Rolls came for him and took him through Taksim Square and down the crowded Istiklâl. The thick black smoke of the waiting steamers streamed across the first span of the Galata Bridge on the Golden Horn and hid the other shore, towards which the Rolls nosed forward through the bicycles and trams, the well-bred snort of the ancient bulb horn just keeping the pedestrians from under its wheels. Then the way was clear and the old European section of Istanbul glittered at the end of the broad half mile of bridge, with the slim minarets lancing up into the sky and the domes of the mosques crouching at their feet.

Across the bridge the car nosed to the right down a narrow cobbled street parallel with the waterfront and stopped outside a high wooden gate. A tough-looking watchman in frayed khaki came out and saluted. He opened the car door, gestured for Bond to follow him, and led the way through a small courtyard and on into a great vaulted warehouse. From the building's high circular windows dusty bars of sunshine slanted across a vista of bundles and bales of merchandise. There was a cool, musty scent of spices and coffee and, as Bond followed the watchman down the central passageway, a sudden strong wave of mint. At the end of the long warehouse was a raised platform, enclosed by a balustrade, where half a dozen young clerks were at work at high desks. Bond's guide led him past the clerks to the back of the platform, knocked on a fine mahogany door and, without waiting for an answer, opened it. He let Bond in and closed the door softly behind him.

"Ah, my friend. Come in. Come in." A very large man in a beautifully cut cream silk suit got up from a mahogany desk and, holding out his hand, came to meet Bond.

Darko Kerim, the head of Station T, had a wonderfully warm dry handclasp. The big hand had a coiled power that said it could easily squeeze your hand until it cracked your bones. Bond was six feet tall, but this man was at least two inches taller. Bond looked up into smiling blue eyes, watery and veined with red, the eyes of furious dissipation. The face was vaguely gypsylike in its fierce pride and in the heavy curling black hair and crooked nose. The impression of a vagabond soldier of fortune was heightened by the small thin gold ring in the lobe of the right ear. It was a dramatic face that radiated life. Bond let go the strong hand and smiled back at Kerim with a friendliness he rarely felt for a stranger.

"Thanks for sending the car to meet me last night."

"Ha!" Kerim was delighted. "You must thank our friends too. You were met by both sides. They always follow my car when it goes to the airport."

"Was it a Vespa or a Lambretta?"

"You noticed? A Lambretta. They have a whole fleet of them for their little men, mostly stinking Bulgars, who do their dirty work for them. But I expect this one kept well back. They don't get up close to the Rolls anymore since the day my chauffeur stopped suddenly, then reversed back as hard as he could. Messed up the paintwork and bloodied the bottom of the chassis but it taught them manners." Kerim went to his chair and waved to an identical one across the desk. Bond sat down and glanced round the room.

It was big and square and paneled in polished mahogany. A length of Oriental tapestry hung from the ceiling behind Kerim's chair, and light came from three high circular windows, which perhaps looked out over the Golden Horn. Bond could hear waves lapping at the walls below. In the center of the right-hand wall hung a gold-framed reproduction of Annigoni's portrait of Queen Elizabeth. Opposite, also imposingly framed, was a wartime photograph of Winston Churchill looking up from his desk like a contemptuous bulldog. A broad bookcase stood against one wall opposite a comfortably padded leather settee. On Kerim's littered desk in the center of the room were three silver photograph frames, and Bond caught a sideways view of the copperplate script of two Mentions in Dispatches and the Military Division of the O.B.E.

"Was it necessary to make my arrival so public?" Bond asked mildly. "The last thing I want is to get you involved in all this. Why send the Rolls to the airport? It only ties you in with me."

Kerim's laugh was indulgent. "My friend, I must explain. We and the Russians and the Americans have a paid man in all the hotels.

And we all have bribed officials of the secret police at headquarters. Also we all receive a carbon copy of the list of all foreigners entering the country every day by air or train or sea. Given a few more days I could have smuggled you in through the Greek frontier. But for what purpose? Your existence here has to be known to the other side so our friend can contact you. It is a condition she has laid down that she will make her own arrangements for the meeting. So why make things difficult for her?"

Bond laughed. "I take it all back. I'd forgotten the Balkan formula. Anyway, I'm under your orders here. You tell me what to do and I'll do it."

Kerim waved the subject aside. "First, let's talk of your comfort. How is your hotel? I was surprised you chose the Palas. It is little better than a disorderly house. And it's quite a haunt of the Russians. Not that that matters."

"It's not too bad. I just didn't want to stay at the Hilton or one of the other smart places."

"Money?" Kerim reached into a drawer and took out a flat packet of new green notes. "Here's a thousand Turkish pounds. Tell me when you've finished them and I'll give you as many more as you want. We can do our accounts after the game. What else? Cigarettes? Smoke only these. Diplomates. They're the best and not easy to get. Don't worry about your meals and your leisure. I will look after both. I wish to stay close to you while you are here. Now." He rang a bell on his desk. "In Turkey we cannot talk seriously without coffee or raki and it is too early for raki."

The door behind Bond opened. Kerim barked an order. When the door was shut, Kerim unlocked a drawer and took out a file. "My friend," he said grimly, "I do not know what to say about this case. It is most confusing. Does this girl really love her idea of you? Will she love you when she sees you? Will you be able to love her enough to make her come over?"

Bond made no comment. There was a knock on the door and the head clerk, a tall, swarthy man with a lean face and unexpected blue eyes, entered, put a china eggshell cup enclosed in gold filigree in front of each of them and went out. Bond sipped his coffee and put it down. It was good, but thick with grains. Kerim swallowed his at a gulp and fitted a cigarette into his holder and lit it.

"But there is nothing we can do about this love matter," Kerim continued, speaking half to himself. "We can only wait and see. In the meantime there are other things." He looked across at Bond, his eyes suddenly very hard and shrewd.

"There is something going on in the enemy camp, my friend. There are comings and goings. I have few facts"—he reached up a big index finger and laid it alongside his nose—"but I have this." He tapped the side of his nose as if he were patting a dog. "This is a good friend of mine and I trust him. If the stakes were not so big, I would say to you, 'Go home, my friend. Go home. There is something here to get away from.' "

Kerim sat back. The tension went out of his voice. He barked out a harsh laugh. "But we are not old women. And this is our work. So let us forget my nose and get on with the job. First of all, the girl has made no sign of life since my signal and I have no other information. But perhaps you would like to ask me some questions about the meeting."

"There's only one thing I want to know," said Bond flatly. "What do you think of this girl? Do you believe her story or not? Nothing else matters. If she hasn't got some sort of a hysterical crush on me, the whole business falls to the ground and it's some complicated M.G.B. plot we can't understand. Now. Did you believe the girl?" Bond's voice was urgent and his eyes searched the other man's face.

"Ah, my friend." Kerim shook his head. He spread his arms wide. "That is what I asked myself then, and it is what I ask myself the whole time since. But who can tell if a woman is lying about these things? Her eyes were bright—those beautiful innocent eyes. Her lips were moist and parted in that heavenly mouth. Her voice was urgent and frightened at what she was doing and saying. Her knuckles were white on the guardrail of the ship. But what was in her heart?" Kerim raised his hands. "God alone knows."

Coffee came again, and then more coffee, and the big room grew thick with cigarette smoke as the two men took each shred of evidence, dissected it and put it aside. At the end of an hour they were back where they had started. It was up to Bond to solve the problem of this girl and, if he was satisfied with her story, get her and the machine out of the country.

Kerim undertook to look after the administrative problems. As a first step he picked up the telephone and spoke to his travel agent and reserved two seats on every outgoing plane for the next week— by B.E.A., Air France, S.A.S. and Turkish Airlines.

"And now you must have a passport," he said. "One will be sufficient. She can travel as your wife. One of my men will take your photograph and he will find a photograph of some girl who looks more or less like her. As a matter of fact, an early picture of Garbo would serve. There is a certain resemblance. I will speak to the consul general. He's an excellent fellow who likes my little cloak-and-dagger plots. The passport will be ready by this evening. What name would you like to have?"

"Somerset. My mother came from there. David Somerset. And the girl? Let us say Caroline."

Kerim looked at his watch. "Twelve o'clock. Just time for the car to take you back to your hotel. There might be a message. And have a good look at your things to see if anyone has been inquisitive."

He rang the bell and fired instructions at the head clerk, who seemed to be some sort of chief of staff to Kerim. He stood with his sharp eyes on Kerim's and his lean head straining forward like a whippet's. Kerim led Bond to the door. There came again the warm powerful handclasp. "The car will bring you to lunch," he said. "A little place in the Spice Bazaar." His eyes looked happily into Bond's. "And I am glad to be working with you. We will do well together."

A NEW CONCIERGE WAS on duty at the Kristal Palas, a small obsequious man with guilty eyes in a yellow face. He came out from behind the desk, his hands spread in apology. "Effendi, I greatly regret. My colleague showed you to an inadequate room. It was not realized that you are a friend of Kerim Bey. Your things have been moved to Number Twelve. It is the best room in the hotel. In fact"—the concierge leered—"it is the room reserved for honeymoon couples. Every comfort. My apologies, effendi. The other room is not intended for visitors of distinction." The man executed an oily bow, washing his hands.

Bond looked the concierge in the eyes and said, "Oh." The eyes slid away. "Let me see this room. I may not like it. I was quite comfortable where I was."

"Certainly, effendi." The man bowed Bond to the lift. "But alas, the plumbers are in your former room. The water supply . . ." The voice trailed off. The lift rose about ten feet and stopped at the first floor. The concierge unlocked a high door and stood back.

Bond had to approve. The sun streamed in through wide double windows that gave onto a small balcony. The motif was pink and gray and the style was mock French Empire, battered by the years, but still with all the elegance of the turn of the century. There were fine Bokhara rugs on the parquet floor. A glittering chandelier hung from the ornate ceiling. The bed against the right-hand wall was huge. A large mirror in a gold frame covered most of the wall behind it. The adjoining bathroom was tiled and fitted with everything, including a bidet and a shower. Bond's shaving things were neatly laid out.

The concierge followed Bond back into the bedroom, and when Bond said he would take the room, bowed himself gratefully out. Bond again walked round the room. This time he carefully inspected the walls and the neighborhood of the bed and the telephone. Well, the story of the plumbers makes sense, he reflected. And, after all, there was no harm in having the best room in the hotel. Why not take the room? Why would there be microphones or secret doors? What would be the point of them? His suitcase was on a bench near the chest of drawers. He knelt down. No scratches round the lock. The bit of fluff he had trapped in the clasp was still there. He unlocked the suitcase and took out the little attaché case. Again no signs of interference. Bond locked the case and got to his feet.

He washed and went out of the room and down the stairs. No, there had been no messages for the effendi. The concierge bowed as he opened the door of the Rolls. Was there a hint of conspiracy behind the permanent guilt in those eyes? Bond decided not to care if there was. The game, whatever it was, had to be played out. If the change of rooms had been the opening gambit, so much the better. The game had to begin somewhere.

As the car sped back down the hill, Bond's thoughts turned to Darko Kerim. What a man for head of Station T! His size alone, in this country of furtive, stunted little men, would give him authority, and his giant vitality and love of life would make everyone his friend. He was a rare type of man, and Bond already felt prepared to add Kerim to the half dozen he took to his heart as real friends.

The car went back over the Galata Bridge and drew up outside the vaulted arcades of the Spice Bazaar. The chauffeur showed Bond a small arch in the thick wall. Turretlike stone steps curled upwards.

Bond climbed the cool stairs to a small anteroom, where a waiter took charge and led him through a maze of small, colorfully tiled, vaulted rooms to where Kerim was sitting at a corner table. Kerim greeted him boisterously, waving a glass of milky liquid in which ice tinkled.

"Here you are, my friend! Now, at once, some raki. You must be exhausted after your sight-seeing." He fired orders at the waiter. Bond sat down in a comfortable-armed chair and took the small tumbler the waiter offered him. He lifted it towards Kerim and drank it down. At once the waiter refilled his glass.

"And now to order your lunch. The waiter says the döner kebab is very good today. I don't believe him, but it can be. It is very young lamb broiled over charcoal with savory rice. Lots of onions in it. Or is there anything you prefer? A pilaf or some of those damned stuffed peppers they eat here? All right then. And you must start with a few sardines grilled *en papillote*. They are just edible." Kerim harangued the waiter, then sat back, smiling at Bond. "Any news?"

Bond shook his head. He told Kerim about the change of room and the untouched suitcase.

Kerim downed a glass of raki and wiped his mouth on the back of his hand. He echoed the thought Bond had had. "Well, the game must begin sometime. I have made certain small moves. Now we can only wait and see. We will make a little foray into enemy territory after lunch. I think it will interest you. Oh, we shan't be seen. We shall move in the shadows, underground." Kerim laughed delightedly at his cleverness. "And now let us talk about other things. How do you like Turkey? No, I don't want to know. What else?"

They were interrupted by the arrival of their lunch. Bond's sardines tasted like any other fried sardines. The kebab was good and tasted of smoked bacon fat and onions and with it Bond had a bottle of Kavaklidiere, a rich coarse Balkan Burgundy. Kerim ate a kind of steak tartare—a large flat hamburger of finely minced raw meat laced with peppers and chives and bound together with yolk of egg. He made Bond try a forkful. It was delicious.

"You ought to eat it every day," said Kerim earnestly. "It is good for those who wish to make much love. I also drink and smoke too much. But I am greedy for life. Perhaps they will put on my tombstone 'This Man Died From Living Too Much.' "

Bond laughed. "Don't go too soon, Darko," he said. "M. would be very displeased. He thinks the world of you."

"He does?" Kerim searched Bond's face to see if he was telling the truth, then laughed delightedly.

After a while Kerim looked at his watch. "Come, James," he said. "It is good that you reminded me of my duty. We will have coffee in the office. There is not much time to waste. Every day at three thirty the Russians have their council of war. Today you and I will do them the honor of being present at their deliberations."

CHAPTER 6

BACK IN THE COOL office Kerim opened a closet and pulled out sets of engineers' blue overalls. He stripped to his shorts and dressed himself in one of the suits, then pulled on a pair of rubber boots. Bond picked out a suit and a pair of boots that fitted him and put them on. With the coffee the head clerk brought in two powerful flashlights, which he put on the desk.

When the clerk had left the room Kerim said, "He is one of my sons—the eldest one. The others in there are all my children. The chauffeur and the watchman are uncles of mine. Common blood is the best security. And this spice business is good cover for us all. M. set me up in it. He spoke to friends of his in the City of London. I am now the leading spice merchant in Turkey. I have long ago repaid M. the money that was lent me. My children are shareholders in the business. They have a good life. When there is secret work to be done and I need help, I choose the child who will be most suitable. They all have training in different secret things. Some have already killed for me. They would all die for me—and for M." He picked up the flashlights and handed one to Bond. "And now to work."

Kerim walked over to the wide glass-fronted bookcase and put his hand behind it. There was a click and the bookcase rolled silently along the wall to the left. Behind it was a small door, flush with the wall. Kerim pressed one side and it swung inwards to reveal a dark tunnel with stone steps leading straight down. A dank smell, mixed with a faint zoo stench, came out into the room.

"You go first," said Kerim. "Go down the steps to the bottom and wait. I must fix the door."

Bond switched on his flashlight and stepped through the opening and went carefully down the stairs. The beam showed fresh masonry, and, twenty feet below, a glimmer of water. When Bond got to the bottom he found that the glimmer was a small stream running down a central gutter in the floor of an ancient stone-walled tunnel that sloped steeply up to the right. To the left the tunnel went on down-wards and would, he guessed, come out below the surface of the Golden Horn. Out of range of Bond's light there was a steady, quiet, scuttling sound, and in the blackness hundreds of pinpoints of red light flickered and moved. It was the same uphill and downhill. Twenty yards away on either side a thousand rats were looking at Bond, sniffing at his scent. Bond imagined the whiskers lifting slightly from their teeth. He had a quick moment of wondering what action they would take if his flashlight went out.

Kerim was suddenly beside him. "It is a long climb. A quarter of an hour. I hope you love animals." Kerim's laugh boomed hugely away up the tunnel. The rats scuffled and stirred. "Unfortunately there is not much choice. Rats and bats. Squadrons of them, divisions —a whole air force and army. And we have to drive them in front of us. Towards the end of the climb it becomes quite congested. Let's get started. The air is good. It is dry underfoot on both sides of the stream. Keep your light on my feet. If a bat gets in your hair, brush him away. It will not be often. Their radar is very good."

They set off up the steep slope. Clusters of bats hung like bunches of withered grapes from the roof and when, from time to time, either Kerim's head or Bond's brushed against them, they exploded twit-tering into the darkness. Ahead of them as they climbed there was the forest of squeaking, scuffling red pinpoints that grew denser on both sides of the central gutter. Occasionally Kerim aimed his flashlight forward and its beam shone on a gray field of fighting, tumbling bodies. An extra frenzy seized the rats, and those nearest jumped on the backs of the others to get away. All the while, as the pressure of the mass higher up the tunnel grew heavier, the frothing rear rank came closer.

The two men kept their flashlights leveled like guns on the rear ranks until, after a good quarter of an hour's climb, they reached their destination. It was a deep alcove of newly faced brick in the side wall of the tunnel. There were two benches on each side of a thick tarpaulin-wrapped object that came down from the ceiling of the alcove. They stepped inside.

"Watch," said Kerim.

There was a moment of silence. Further up the tunnel the squeak-

ing had stopped, as if at a word of command. Then suddenly the tunnel was a foot deep in a great wave of hurtling, scrambling gray bodies as, with a continuous high-pitched squeal, the rats turned and pelted back down the slope. For minutes the sleek gray river foamed by outside the alcove, until at last the numbers thinned and only a trickle of sick or wounded rats came limping and probing their way down the tunnel floor. The scream of the horde slowly vanished down towards the river, until there was silence except for the occasional twitter of a fleeing bat.

Kerim gave a noncommittal grunt. "One of these days those rats will start dying. Then we shall have the plague in Istanbul again. Sometimes I feel guilty for not telling the authorities of this tunnel so that they can clean the place up. But I can't so long as the Russians are up here." He jerked his head at the roof and looked at his watch. "Five minutes to go. They will be pulling up their chairs and fiddling with their papers. Sometimes the girl, Tatiana, comes in with a message and goes out again. Let us hope we will see her today. You will be impressed."

Kerim reached up and untied the tarpaulin cover and pulled it downwards. The cover protected the shining butt of a submarine periscope, fully withdrawn. Bond chuckled. "Where the hell did you get that from, Darko?"

"Turkish Navy. War surplus." Kerim's voice did not invite further questions. "Now Q Branch in London is trying to fix some way of wiring the damn thing for sound. It's not going to be easy. The lens at the top of this is no bigger than a cigarette lighter, end on. When I raise it, it comes up to floor level in their room. In the corner of the room where it comes up, we cut a small mousehole. We did it well. Once when I came to have a look, the first thing I saw was a big mousetrap with a piece of cheese on it." Kerim laughed briefly. "But there's not much room to fit a sensitive pickup microphone alongside the lens. And there's no hope of getting in again to do any more fiddling about with their architecture. The only way I managed to install this thing was to get my friends in the Public Works Ministry to turn the Russians out for a few days. The story was that the trams going up the hill were shaking the foundations of the houses. There had to be a survey. It cost me a few hundred pounds for the right pockets. The Public Works inspected half a dozen houses on either side of this one and declared the place safe. By that time, I and the family had finished our construction work. The Russians were suspicious as hell. I gather they went over the place with a fine-tooth comb when they got back, looking for microphones and bombs and so on. But we can't work that trick twice. Unless Q Branch can think up something very clever, I shall have to be content with keeping an eye on them."

Alongside the matrix of the periscope in the roof of the alcove there was a pendulous blister of metal, twice the size of a football. "What's that?" said Bond.

"Bottom half of a bomb—a big bomb. If anything happens to me, or if war breaks out with Russia, that bomb will be set off by radio control from my office. It is sad, but I fear that many innocent people will get killed besides the Russians."

Kerim glanced at his watch and bent down and gripped the handles on either side of the hooded eyepieces. Slowly he brought them up level with his face. There was a hiss as the glistening stem of the periscope slid up into its steel sheath in the roof of the alcove. Kerim gazed into the eyepieces and slowly inched up the handles until he could stand upright. He twisted gently, then centered the lens and beckoned to Bond, who moved over and took the handles.

"Have a good look," said Kerim. "Just six of them. You'd better get their faces in your mind. Head of the table is their resident director. On his left are his two staff. Opposite them are three new ones. The latest, who looks quite an important chap, is on the director's right. Tell me if they do anything except talk."

Bond's first impulse was to tell Kerim not to make so much noise. It was as if he were in the room with the Russians, sitting in a chair in the corner.

The wide, all-round lens, designed for spotting aircraft as well as surface ships, gave him a clear view of the director and his two colleagues—serious dull Russian faces. Bond could see less of the other three. Their backs were half towards him and only the profile of the nearest showed clearly. This man's jaw was badly shaved and the eye in profile was bovine and dull under a thick black brow. The only clues to the next man were an angry boil on the back of a fat bald neck, a shiny blue suit and rather bright brown shoes. He was motionless during the whole period that Bond kept watch, and apparently never spoke.

Now the man on the right of the resident director sat back and began talking. He had a strong, craglike profile with big bones and a jutting chin under a heavy brown mustache. This man puffed busily at a tiny wooden pipe. His profile had authority and Bond guessed that he was a senior man sent down from Moscow.

Bond's eyes were getting tired. He twisted the handles gently and looked round the office as far as the blurring jagged edges of the mousehole would allow. He saw nothing of interest—two filing cabinets, a hatstand by the door and a sideboard with a heavy carafe of water and some glasses. Bond stood away from the eyepiece, rubbing his eyes.

"If only we could hear," Kerim said, shaking his head sadly.

"It would solve a lot of problems," agreed Bond. "By the way, Darko, how did you come on this tunnel? What was it built for?"

"It's a lost drain from the Hall of Pillars up above us on the heights of Istanbul," Kerim said. "A thousand years ago it was built as a reservoir in case of siege, made to hold millions of gallons of water. I handed out some money to the Minister of Public Works and he closed the place for a week—'for cleaning.' We got into the tunnel not knowing where we'd come out. And of course it went straight down the hill—under the Street of Books where the Russians have their place, and out into the Golden Horn, by the Galata Bridge, twenty yards away from my warehouse. It took us a year and a lot of survey work to get directly under the Russians." Kerim laughed. "And now I suppose one of these days the Russians will decide to change their offices. By then I hope someone else will be head of T."

Kerim bent down to the rubber eyepieces. Bond saw him stiffen. Kerim said urgently, "The door's opening. Quick. Take over. Here she comes."

IT WAS SEVEN O'CLOCK on the same evening and James Bond was back in his hotel. He had had a hot bath and a cold shower. He thought that he had at last scoured the zoo smell of the tunnel out of his skin. Sitting naked except for his shorts at one of the windows of his room, he sipped a vodka and tonic and looked out at the sunset over the Golden Horn.

He was thinking of the tall beautiful girl with the dancer's long gait who had walked through the door of the drab Russian office with a piece of paper in her hand. She had stood beside her chief and handed him the paper. All the men had looked up at her. She had blushed and looked down. What had that expression on the men's faces meant? It was more than just the way some men look at a beautiful girl. They had shown curiosity. But what else? There had been slyness and contempt—the way people stare at prostitutes.

This girl was just one of the staff, with a corporal's rank, who was now going through a normal routine. Why had they all looked at her with this inquisitive contempt—almost as if she were a spy who had been caught and was going to be executed? Did they suspect her? Had she given herself away? But that seemed less likely as the scene played itself out. The resident director read the paper and the other men's eyes turned away from the girl and onto him. Then the resident director looked up at the girl and said something with a friendly, inquiring expression. The girl shook her head and answered briefly. The director said one word with a question mark on the end. The girl blushed deeply and nodded, holding his eyes obediently. The other men smiled encouragement, slyly perhaps, but with approval. No suspicion there. No condemnation. The scene ended with a few sentences from the director to which the girl seemed to say the equivalent of "Yes, sir." When she had left the room, the director said something and the men laughed heartily, as if what he had said had been obscene. Then they went back to their work.

Later, on their way back down the tunnel, and then in Kerim's office while they discussed what they had seen, Bond had racked his brains for a solution to this maddening bit of dumb show. Now, looking without focus at the dying sun, he was still mystified. Bond finished his drink and lit another cigarette. He put the problem away and turned his mind to the girl.

Tatiana Romanova. A Romanov. Well, she certainly looked like a Russian princess, or the traditional idea of one. The tall, fine-boned body that moved so gracefully and stood so well. The thick sweep of hair down to the shoulders and the wonderful Garboesque face with its curiously shy serenity. Was this the sort of girl to fall in love with a photograph and a file? How could one tell? Such a girl would have a deeply romantic nature. There were dreams in the eyes and in the mouth. At her age, twenty-four, the Soviet machine would not yet have ground the sentiment out of her. It could be true. Bond wanted it to be true.

The telephone rang. It was Kerim. "Nothing new?"

"No."

"Then I will pick you up at eight."

"I'll be ready."

Bond laid down the receiver and started to put on his clothes. Kerim had been firm about the evening. Bond had wanted to stay in his hotel room and wait for the first contact to be made—a note, a telephone call, whatever it might be. But Kerim had said no. The girl had been adamant that she would choose her own time and place. It would be wrong for Bond to seem a slave to her convenience. "That is bad psychology, my friend," Kerim had insisted. "She would despise you if you made yourself too available. From your face and your dossier she would expect you to behave with indifference—even with insolence. It is with an image she has fallen in love. Behave like the image. Act the part."

Bond had shrugged his shoulders. "All right, Darko. I daresay you're right. What do you suggest?"

"Live the life you would normally. Go home now and have a bath and a drink. If nothing happens, I will pick you up at eight. We will have dinner at the place of a gypsy friend of mine. A man called Vavra. He is head of a tribe, one of my best sources. Some of his girls will dance for you."

The telephone rang and Bond picked up the receiver. It was only the car. As he went down the few stairs and out to Kerim in the waiting Rolls, Bond admitted to himself that he was disappointed.

They were climbing up the far hill through the poorer quarters above the Golden Horn when the chauffeur half turned his head and said something in a noncommittal voice.

Kerim answered with a monosyllable. "He says a Lambretta is on our tail. It is of no importance. When I wish, I can make a secret of my movements. Often they have trailed this car for miles when there has been only a dummy in the back. A conspicuous car has its uses. They know this gypsy is a friend of mine, but I think they do not understand why. It will do no harm for them to know that we are having a night of relaxation."

Bond looked back through the rear window and watched the crowded streets. From behind a stopped tram a motor scooter showed for a minute and then was hidden by a taxi. Bond turned away. He reflected briefly on the way the Russians ran their centers—with all the money and equipment in the world—while the British Secret Service put against them a handful of adventurous, underpaid men, like this one, with his secondhand Rolls and his children to help him. Yet Kerim had the run of Turkey. Perhaps, after all, the right man was better than the right machine.

At half past eight they stopped on the outskirts of Istanbul at a dingy-looking open-air café with a few empty tables on the pavement. Behind it were the tops of trees over a high stone wall. They got out and the car drove off. They waited for the Lambretta, but its wasplike buzz had stopped and at once it was on its way back down the hill. All they saw of the driver was a glimpse of a short squat man wearing goggles.

Kerim led the way through the tables and into the café. It seemed empty, but a man stepped from behind the counter and, when he saw who it was, led them out through the back and across a stretch of gravel to a door in the high wall. After knocking once, the man unlocked the door and waved them through.

There was an orchard with plank tables dotted about under the trees. In the center was a circle of terrazzo dancing floor. On the far side, at a long table, about twenty people of all ages were sitting, eating. Children played in the grass behind the table. The three-quarter moon showed everything up brightly and made pools of membraned shadow under the trees.

Kerim and Bond walked forward. The man at the head of the table got up and came to meet them. He greeted Kerim with reserve, and stood for a few moments making a long explanation to which Kerim listened attentively, occasionally asking a question.

Vavra was an imposing, theatrical figure in Macedonian dress—white shirt with full sleeves, baggy trousers and laced soft leather top boots. His hair was a tangle of black snakes. A large downward-drooping black mustache almost hid the full red lips. The eyes were fierce and cruel on either side of a syphilitic nose. The moon glinted on the sharp line of the jaw and the high cheekbones. His right hand, which had a gold ring on the thumb, rested on the hilt of a short curved dagger in a leather scabbard tipped with silver filigree.

The gypsy finished talking. Kerim said a few complimentary words about Bond, at the same time stretching his hand out in Bond's direction. The gypsy stepped up to Bond and scrutinized him. He bowed abruptly. Bond followed suit. Vavra said a few words through a sardonic smile. Kerim laughed and turned to Bond. "He says if you are ever out of work you should come to him. He will give you a job— taming his women and killing for him. That is a great compliment to a *gajo*—a foreigner. You should say something in reply."

"Tell him that I can't imagine he needs any help in these matters."

Kerim translated. The gypsy politely bared his teeth. He said something and walked back to the table, clapping his hands sharply. Two women got up and came towards him. He spoke to them curtly and they went back to the table and picked up a large earthenware dish and disappeared among the trees.

"We have come on a bad night," Kerim explained to Bond. "The restaurant is closed. Some sort of family troubles which have to be solved in private. But I am an old friend and we are invited to share their supper. I hope you are good at eating with your fingers."

They walked over to the table. Two places had been cleared on either side of the head gypsy. Kerim gave what sounded like a polite greeting and they sat down. In front of each of them was a large plate of some sort of ragout smelling strongly of garlic, a bottle of raki and a cheap tumbler. Kerim poured himself half a tumblerful and everyone followed suit. Kerim added some water, raised his glass and made a short, vehement speech. Then all raised their glasses and drank. An old woman next to Bond passed him a long loaf of bread and said something. Bond smiled and said, "Thank you." He broke off a piece and handed the loaf to Kerim, who was picking through his ragout with thumb and forefinger.

The ragout was delicious but steaming hot. Bond winced each time he dipped his fingers into it. Everyone watched them eat, and from time to time the old woman dipped her fingers into Bond's stew and chose a piece for him.

When they had scoured their plates a silver bowl of water, in which rose leaves floated, and a clean linen cloth were put between Bond and Kerim. Bond washed his fingers and his greasy chin and turned to his host and dutifully made a short speech of thanks, which Kerim translated. The table murmured its appreciation. Vavra bowed towards Bond and said, according to Kerim, that he hated all *gajos* except Bond, whom he was proud to call his friend.

Boom!

The explosion lit the darkness behind the dance floor and a chunk of masonry sang past Bond's ear. Suddenly the orchard was full of running men and Vavra was slinking forward across the stone with his curved dagger held out in front of him. Kerim was following, a gun in his hand. The last of the women and children were already vanishing among the shadows.

Bond, the Beretta held uncertainly in his hand, followed slowly in Kerim's wake towards the wide breach that had been blown out of the garden wall. He wondered what the hell was going on.

The stretch of grass between the hole in the wall and the dance floor was a turmoil of fighting, running figures. It was only as Bond came upon the fight that he distinguished the squat, conventionally dressed Bulgars from the swirling finery of the gypsies. There seemed to be more of them than of the gypsies—almost two to one. As Bond peered into the struggling mass, a gypsy youth was ejected from it, clutching his stomach. He groped towards Bond, coughing terribly. Two small dark men came after him, their knives held low.

Instinctively Bond stepped to one side so that the crowd was not behind the two men. He aimed at their legs above the knees and the gun in his hand cracked twice. The two men fell, soundlessly, face downwards in the grass.

Two bullets gone. Only six left. Bond edged closer to the fight.

A knife hissed past his head and clanged onto the dance floor.

It had been aimed at Kerim, who came running out of the shadows with two men on his heels. The second man stopped and raised his knife to throw and Bond shot from the hip, blindly, and saw him fall. The other man turned and fled among the trees and Kerim dropped to one knee beside Bond, scrambling for his gun.

"Cover me," he shouted. "Jammed on the first shot. It's those bloody Bulgars. God knows what they think they're doing."

A hand caught Bond round the mouth and yanked him backwards to the ground. He felt a boot thud into the back of his neck. As he whirled over sideways in the grass he expected to feel the searing flame of a knife. But the men, and there were three of them, were after Kerim, crouching there beside him with his useless gun. As Bond scrambled to one knee he saw the squat black figures pile atop his friend, who sank down beneath them.

At the same moment that Bond leaped forward and brought his gun butt down on the round shaven head of one of the attackers, something flashed past his eyes and Vavra's curved dagger was growing out of the heaving back of another. Then Kerim was on his feet and the third man was running. Still another was standing in the breach in the wall shouting one word, again and again, and one by one the attackers broke off their fights and doubled over to the man and past him and out onto the road. There came the staccato firing of a squadron of Lambrettas, and Bond stood and listened to the swarm of wasps flying down the hill.

There was silence except for the groans of the wounded. Bond watched Kerim and Vavra walk among the bodies, occasionally turning one over with a foot. The other gypsies seeped back from the road and the older women came hurrying out of the shadows to tend their men.

Bond shook himself. What had it all been about? Ten or a dozen men had been killed. What for? Whom had they been trying to get? Not him, Bond. When he was down and ready for the killing they had passed him by and made for Kerim. Was it anything to do with the Romanova business? How could it possibly tie in?

Bond tensed. His gun spoke twice from the hip. The knife that had just been hurled at Kerim clattered harmlessly off his back. The figure that had risen from the dead twirled slowly round like a ballet dancer and toppled forward on his face. Bond ran forward. He had been just in time. The moon had caught the blade and he had had a clear field of fire.

Darko Kerim looked down at the twitching body. Turning to meet Bond, he grinned shamefacedly. "Now it is not good, James. You have saved my life too often. We might have been friends. Now the distance between us is too great. Forgive me, for I can never pay you back." He held out his hand.

Bond brushed it aside. "Don't be a damn fool, Darko," he said roughly. "My gun worked, that's all. Yours didn't. You'd better get one that does. For God's sake tell me what the hell this is all about. There's been too much blood splashing about tonight. I'm sick of it. I want a drink. Come and finish that raki." He took Darko's arm.

As they reached the table, littered with the remains of the supper, a piercing scream came out of the depths of the orchard. Bond put his hand on his gun. Kerim shook his head. "We shall soon know what they were after," he said gloomily. "My friends are finding out. I can guess what they will discover. I think they will never forgive me for having been here tonight. Five of their men are dead."

Bond added a dash of water to two tumblers of raki. They both emptied the glasses at one swallow. The head gypsy came up, wiping the tip of his curved dagger on a handful of grass. He sat down and accepted a glass of raki from Bond and started talking fast to Kerim, who listened attentively, occasionally interrupting the flow with a question.

Kerim turned to Bond. "My friend," he said dryly, "it is a curious affair. It seems the Bulgars were ordered to kill Vavra and as many of his men as possible. The Russians knew the gypsy had been working for me, so Vavra was a main target. I was another. The declaration of war against me personally I can also understand. But it seems that you were not to be harmed. You were exactly described so that there should be no mistake. Perhaps it was desired that there be no diplomatic repercussions. Who can tell?" Kerim looked puzzled and unhappy. "But now it is time we left these people. Vavra wishes you very well. He refuses to blame me for what has happened. He says that I am to continue sending him Bulgars. Ten were killed tonight. He would like some more. And now we will shake him by the hand and go. We are good friends, but we are also *gajos*. And I expect he does not want us to see his women weeping over their dead."

Kerim stretched out his huge hand. Vavra took it and looked into Kerim's eyes. For a moment his own fierce eyes seemed to go opaque. Then the gypsy let the hand drop and turned to Bond. The hand was dry and rough and padded like the paw of a big animal. Again the eyes went opaque. Letting go of Bond's hand, he spoke rapidly and urgently to Kerim, then turned his back on them and walked away towards the trees.

It was some time before Kerim spoke. Then he said, "The gypsy said we both have the wings of death over us. I am to beware of a son of the snows and you must beware of a man who is owned by the moon." He laughed harshly. "That is the sort of rigamarole they talk."

Kerim and Bond climbed through the breach in the wall. The Rolls stood, glittering in the moonlight, a few yards down the road opposite the café entrance.

Back at his hotel, Bond climbed the few stairs, unlocked his door, then bolted it behind him. Moonlight filtered through the curtains. He walked across the room and turned on the pink-shaded lights on the dressing table. He stripped off his clothes and went into the bathroom and stood for a few minutes under the shower. He cleaned his teeth and gargled with a sharp mouthwash to get rid of the taste of the day, turned off the bathroom light and went back into the bedroom.

Bond drew aside the curtains, opened wide the tall windows, and stood looking out across the great boomerang curve of water under the riding moon. The night breeze felt wonderfully cool on his naked body. He looked at his watch. It said two o'clock.

Bond gave a shuddering yawn and let the curtains drop back into place. He bent to switch off the lights on the dressing table. Suddenly he stiffened and his heart missed a beat.

There had been a nervous giggle from the shadows at the back of the room. A girl's voice said, "Poor Mr. Bond. You must be tired. Come to bed."

CHAPTER 7

BOND WHIRLED ROUND, crossed the room and turned on the pink-shaded light by the bed. There was a long body under the single sheet. Brown hair was spread out on the pillow. The tips of fingers showed, holding the sheet up over the face. Lower down the breasts stood up like hills under snow.

Bond laughed shortly. He leaned forward and gave the hair a soft tug. There was a squeak of protest from under the sheet. Bond sat down on the edge of the bed. After a moment's silence a corner of the sheet was cautiously lowered and one large blue eye inspected him. "You look very improper." The voice was muffled by the sheet.

"What about you! And how did you get here?"

"I walked down two floors. I live here too." The voice was deep and provocative. There was very little accent.

"Well, I'm going to get into bed."

The sheet came quickly down to the chin and the girl pulled herself up on the pillows. She was blushing. "Oh no. You mustn't."

"But it's my bed. And anyway you told me to." The face was incredibly beautiful.

"That was only a phrase. To introduce myself."

"Well, I'm very glad to meet you. My name's James Bond."

"Mine's Tatiana Romanova." She sounded the second *a* of Tatiana and the first *a* of Romanova very long. "My friends call me Tania."

There was a pause while they looked at each other, the girl with curiosity, Bond with cool surmise.

She was the first to break the silence. "You look just like your photographs." She blushed again. "But you must put something on. It upsets me."

"You upset me just as much. Anyway, what have *you* got on?"

She pulled the sheet a fraction lower to show a quarter-inch black velvet ribbon round her neck. "This."

Bond got up from the bed and went to put on one of the dark blue silk pajama coats he wore instead of pajamas. He came back to the bed and pulled up a chair beside it. He smiled down at her. "Well,

I'll tell you something. You're one of the most beautiful women in the world."

The girl blushed again. "Are you speaking the truth? I think my mouth is too big. Am I as beautiful as Western girls?"

"More beautiful," said Bond. "There is more light in your face. And your mouth isn't too big."

"What is that—'light in the face'? What do you mean?"

Bond meant that she didn't look to him like a Russian spy. She seemed to show none of the reserve of a spy. None of the coldness, none of the calculation. She gave the impression of warmth of heart. He searched for a noncommittal phrase. "There is a lot of gaiety and fun in your eyes," he said lamely.

Tatiana looked serious. "That is curious," she said. "No one speaks of fun and gaiety in Russia. I have never been told that before."

Gaiety? she thought. After the last two months? How could she be looking gay? And yet, yes, there was a lightness in her heart. Was she a loose woman by nature? Or was it something to do with this man she had never seen before? He was terribly handsome. Would he forgive her when they got to London and she told him that she had been sent to seduce him? Even been told the night on which she must do it and the number of the room? Surely he wouldn't mind very much. It was only a way for her to get to England and make those reports. Gaiety and fun in her eyes. Well, why not? He made it easy—made it fun, with a spice of danger. There was a wonderful sense of freedom being alone with a man like this and knowing that she would not be punished for it. It was really terribly exciting.

"You are very handsome," she said. "In fact you are like my favorite hero. He's in a book by a Russian called Lermontov. I will tell you about him one day."

One day? Bond thought it was time to get down to business.

"Now listen, Tania." He tried not to look at the beautiful face on the pillow. He fixed his eyes on the point of her chin. "What *is* all this about? Are you really going to come back to England with me?" He raised his eyes to hers. She had opened them wide again in that damnable guilelessness. It was fatal.

"But of course!"

Bond was taken aback by the directness of her answer. "You're not afraid?"

He saw a shadow cross her eyes. But it was not what he thought. She had remembered that she had a part to play. She was supposed to be frightened of what she was doing. Terrified. It had sounded so easy, this acting, but now it was difficult. How odd! She decided to compromise. "Yes. I am afraid. But not so much now. You will protect me. I know you will."

"Well, yes, of course I will." Bond thought of her relatives in Russia. He quickly put the thought out of his mind. "There's nothing to worry about. I'll look after you." And now for the question he had been shirking. He felt a ridiculous embarrassment. This girl wasn't in the least what he had expected. It was spoiling everything to ask the question. It had to be done.

"What about the machine?"

Yes. It was as if he had cuffed her across the face. Pain showed in her eyes, and the edge of tears.

She pulled the sheet over her mouth and spoke from behind it. "So that's what you want."

"Now listen." Bond put nonchalance in his voice. "This machine's got nothing to do with you and me. But my people in London want it." He remembered security. He added blandly, "It's not all that important. They know all about the machine and they think it's a wonderful Russian invention. They just want one to copy. Like your people copy foreign cameras and things." God, how lame it sounded!

"Now you're lying." A big tear rolled out of one wide blue eye and down the soft cheek and onto the pillow. She pulled the sheet up over her eyes.

Bond reached out and put his hand on her arm under the sheet. The arm flinched angrily away. "Damn the bloody machine," he said impatiently. "But for God's sake, Tania, you must know that I've got a job to do. Of course my people want it or they wouldn't have sent me out to bring you home with it. Just say one way or the other and we'll forget about it."

Tatiana dabbed her eyes with the sheet. Brusquely she pulled it down to her shoulders again. If only he had said that the machine didn't matter to him so long as she would come. But that was too much to hope for. And of course he was right. He had a job to do. So had she.

She looked up at him calmly. "I will bring it. Have no fear. But do not let us mention it again. And now listen." She sat up straighter on the pillows. "We must go tonight." She remembered her lesson. "It is the only chance. This evening I am on night duty from six o'clock. I shall be alone in the office and I will take the Spektor."

Bond's eyes narrowed. His mind raced as he thought of the problems. Where to hide her. How to get her out to the plane if the loss were immediately discovered. It was going to be a risky business. They would stop at nothing to get her and the Spektor back. Roadblock on the way to the airport. Bomb in the plane. Anything.

"That's wonderful, Tania." Bond's voice was casual. "We'll keep you hidden and then we'll take the first plane tomorrow morning."

"Don't be foolish." Tatiana had been warned that there would be some difficult lines in her part. "We will take the train. The Orient Express. It leaves at eleven fifteen tonight and I won't stay a minute longer in Istanbul than I have to. We will be over the frontier by early morning. You must get the tickets and a passport. I will travel with you as your wife." She looked happily up at him.

"But, Tania, that's crazy. They're bound to catch up with us somewhere. It's four days and five nights to London on that train."

"That's the only way I'll go," said the girl flatly. "If you are clever, how can they find out?"

Oh God, she thought. Why had they insisted on this train? But they had been definite. It was a good place for love, they had said. She would have four days to get him to love her. Then, when they got to London, he would protect her. Otherwise, if they flew to London, she would be put straight into prison. The four days were essential. And, they had warned her, we will have men on the train to see you don't get off. So be careful and obey your orders. She watched Bond's thoughtful face. She longed to reassure him that this was a harmless *konspiratsia* to get her to England: that no harm could come to either of them, because that was not the object of the plot.

"Well, I still think it's crazy," said Bond, wondering what M.'s reaction would be. "But I suppose it may work. I've got the passport. It will need a Yugoslav visa. I'll get the tickets and I'll have one of our men come along. Just in case. Your name's Caroline Somerset. Don't forget it. How are you going to get to the train?"

Karolin Siomerset. The girl turned the name over in her mind. "It is a pretty name. And you are Mr. Siomerset." She laughed happily. "That is fun. Do not worry about me. I will come to the train just before it leaves. It is the Sirkeci Station. I know where it is. So that is all. And we do not worry anymore. Yes?"

Suddenly Bond was disturbed at the girl's confidence. "Suppose you lose your nerve? Suppose they catch you?" A sharp tingle of suspicion ran down his spine.

"Before I saw you, I was frightened. Now I am not." Tatiana tried to tell herself that this was the truth. Somehow it nearly was. "I shall leave my things in the hotel and take my usual handbag to the office. I cannot leave my fur coat behind. I love it too dearly. But today is Sunday and that will be an excuse to come to the office in it. Tonight at half past ten I shall walk out and take a taxi to the station. And now you must stop looking so worried." Impulsively, she stretched out a hand towards him. "Say that you are pleased."

Bond moved to the edge of the bed. He took her hand and looked down into her eyes. God, he thought, I hope it's all right. I hope this crazy plan will work. Is this wonderful girl a cheat? Is she true? Is she real? The eyes told him nothing except that the girl was happy, and that she wanted him to love her. Tatiana's hand came up and round his neck and pulled him fiercely down to her. At first the mouth trembled under his and then, as passion took her, the mouth yielded into a kiss without end.

Above them, and unknown to both of them, behind the gold-framed false mirror on the wall over the bed, the two photographers from SMERSH sat close together in the cramped *cabinet de voyeur*, as, before them, so many friends of the proprietor had sat, on a honeymoon night in Room Number Twelve of the Kristal Palas. The viewfinders gazed coldly down on the passionate arabesques the two bodies formed, and the clockwork mechanism of the movie cameras whirred softly on and on as the breath rasped out of the open mouths of the two men and the sweat of excitement trickled down their bulging faces into their cheap collars.

UNDER THE ARC LIGHTS of Istanbul's main station, the long-chassied German locomotive waited quietly on Track Number Three, panting with the labored breath of a dragon dying of asthma. Each heavy breath seemed certain to be the last. Then came another. Wisps of steam rose from the couplings between the carriages and vanished quickly in the warm August air. A few minutes more, and the Orient Express would be thundering over the eighteen hundred miles of glittering steel track between Istanbul and Paris.

The heavy bronze cipher on the side of the dark blue coach said COMPAGNIE INTERNATIONALE DES WAGON-LITS ET DES GRANDS EXPRESS EUROPÉENS. Above the cipher, fitted into metal slots, was a flat iron sign that announced, in black capitals on white, ORIENT EXPRESS, and underneath, in three lines:

ISTANBUL	THESSALONIKE	BEOGRAD
VENEZIA	MILAN	
LAUSANNE	PARIS	

James Bond gazed vaguely at one of the most romantic signs in the world. For the tenth time he looked at his watch. Eleven six. His eyes went back to the sign. All the towns were spelled in the language of the country except Milan. Why not Milano? Bond took out his handkerchief and wiped his face. Where the devil was the girl? Had she been caught? Had she had second thoughts? Had he been too rough with her last night?

Eleven ten. The quiet pant of the engine had stopped. There came an echoing whoosh as the automatic safety valve let off the excess steam. A hundred yards away, through the milling crowd, Bond watched the stationmaster raise a hand to the engine driver and start walking slowly back down the train, banging the doors of the third-class carriages up front. Passengers, mostly peasants going back into Greece after a weekend with their relatives in Turkey, hung out of the windows and jabbered at the grinning crowd below.

The stationmaster came nearer. The brown-uniformed wagon-lit attendant tapped Bond on the arm. *"En voiture, s'il vous plaît."* Two rich-looking Turks kissed their mistresses—they were too pretty to be wives—and stepped onto the little iron pedestal and up the two tall steps into the carriage. There were no other wagon-lit travelers on the platform. The conductor, with an impatient glance at the tall Englishman, picked up the iron pedestal and climbed with it into the train.

There was no hurrying figure coming up the platform. High up above, the minute hand of the big illuminated station clock jumped forward an inch. Eleven fifteen.

A window banged down above Bond's head. Bond looked up. His immediate reaction was that the black veil was too wide-meshed. The intention to disguise the luxurious mouth and the excited blue eyes was amateurish.

"Quick."

The train had begun to move. Bond reached for the passing handrail and swung up onto the step. The attendant was still holding open the door. Bond stepped unhurriedly through. "Madam was late," said the attendant. "She came along the corridor. She must have entered by the last carriage."

Bond went down the carpeted corridor to the center compartment, Number Seven. The door was ajar. Bond walked in and shut it behind him. The girl had taken off her veil and her black straw hat. She was sitting in the corner by the window. A long, sleek sable coat was thrown open to show a natural-colored shantung dress with a pleated skirt, honey-colored nylons and a black crocodile belt and shoes. She looked composed.

"You have no faith, James."

Bond sat down beside her. "Tania," he said, "if there was a bit more room I'd put you across my knee and spank you. You nearly gave me heart failure. What happened?"

"What could happen?" said Tatiana innocently. "I said I would be here, and I am here. You have no faith. Since I am sure you are more interested in my dowry than in me, it is up there."

Bond looked casually up. Two small cases were on the rack beside his suitcase. He took her hand. He said, "Thank God you're safe." Something in his eyes, perhaps the flash of guilt as he admitted to himself that he had been more interested in the girl than the machine, reassured her. She kept his hand in hers and sank contentedly back in her corner.

As the train screeched slowly round Seraglio Point, the girl watched Bond's face with tenderness. What was this man thinking? What was going on behind those cold, level gray-blue eyes? Was he worrying about them both? Worrying about their safety? If only she could tell him that there was nothing to fear, that he was only her passport to England—he and the heavy case the resident director had given her that evening in the office. The director had said the same. "Here is your passport to England, Corporal," he had said, unzipping the bag. "A brand new Spektor. Be certain not to open the bag again or let it out of your compartment until you get to the other end. Or this Englishman will take it away from you and throw you on the dustheap. If you let them take this machine from you, you will have failed in your duty. Understood?"

There came a soft double knock on the door. Bond stood up. "That'll be my friend Kerim," he said. "I must talk to him. I won't be long. I shall be outside the door." He leaned forward and touched her hand. "We shall have all the night to ourselves. First I must see that you are safe." He unlocked the door and slipped out.

Darko Kerim's huge bulk was blocking the corridor. He was leaning on the brass guardrail, smoking and gazing moodily out towards the Sea of Marmara, which receded as the long train snaked away from the coast and turned inland and northwards. Bond leaned on the rail beside him. Kerim looked into the reflection of Bond's face in the dark window. He said softly, "The news is not good. There are three of them on the train."

"Ah!" An electric tingle ran up Bond's spine.

"It's three of the men we saw in that room. Obviously, they're on to you and the girl." Kerim glanced sharply sideways. "That makes her a double. Or doesn't it?"

Bond's mind was cool. So the girl had been bait. No, damn it. She couldn't be acting. It wasn't possible. The cipher machine? Perhaps after all it wasn't in that bag. "Wait a minute," he said, and turned and knocked softly on the door. He heard her unlock it and slip the chain. Then he went in and shut the door.

She smiled radiantly. "You have finished?"

"Sit down, Tatiana. I've got to talk to you."

Now she saw the coldness in his face and her smile went out. She sat down obediently with her hands in her lap.

Bond stood over her. Was there guilt in her face, or fear? No, only surprise and a coolness to match his own expression.

"Now listen, Tatiana." Bond's voice was deadly. "Something's come up. I must look into that bag and see if the machine is there."

"Take it down and look," she said indifferently, and examined the hands in her lap. So now it was going to come. What the director had said. They were going to take the machine and throw her aside, perhaps have her put off the train. Oh God! This man was going to do that to her.

Bond reached up and hauled down the heavy case and put it on the seat. He tore the zipper sideways and looked in. Yes, a gray japanned metal case with three rows of squat keys, rather like a typewriter. He held the bag open towards her. "Is that a Spektor?"

She glanced casually into the gaping bag. "Yes."

Bond zipped the bag shut and put it back on the rack. He sat down beside the girl. "There are three M.G.B. men on the train. We know they are from your center. What are they doing here, Tatiana?" Bond's voice was soft. He watched her, searched her with all his senses. She looked up. There were tears in her eyes, but there was no trace of guilt in her face. She only looked terrified of something.

She reached out a hand and then drew it back. "You aren't going to throw me off the train now you've got the machine?"

"Of course not," Bond said impatiently. "Don't be idiotic. But we must know what these men are doing. What's it all about? Did you know they were going to be on the train?" He tried to read some clue in her expression. He could only see a great relief. And what else? A look of calculation? Of reserve? Yes, she was hiding something. But what?

Tatiana seemed to make up her mind. She reached forward, put a hand on Bond's knee and, looking into his eyes, forced him to believe her. "James," she said, "I did not know these men were on the train. That is all I can tell you. Until we arrive in England, out of reach of my people, you must not ask me more. I have done what I said I would. I am here with the machine. Have faith in me. I am certain these men do not mean us harm. Have faith."

Was she so certain? Tatiana wondered. Had the Klebb woman told her all the truth? But she also must have faith in the orders she had been given. These men must be the guards to see that she didn't get off the train. They could mean no harm. Later, when they got to London, this man would hide her away out of reach of SMERSH and she would tell him everything he wanted to know. She had already decided this in the back of her mind. But God knew what would happen if she betrayed *Them* now. *They* would somehow get her, and him. She knew it. There were no secrets from these people. And *They* would have no mercy. So long as she played out her role, all would be well. Tatiana watched Bond's face for a sign that he believed her.

Bond shrugged his shoulders. He stood up. "I don't know what to think, Tatiana," he said. "You are keeping something from me, but I think it's something you don't realize is important. And I believe you think we are safe. We may be. I must talk to Kerim and decide what to do. Don't worry. We will look after you. But now we must be very careful."

Bond looked round. He tried the communicating door with the next compartment. It was locked. He decided to wedge it after the conductor had made up the beds and gone. He would do the same for the door into the passage. And he would have to stay awake. So much for the honeymoon on wheels! Bond smiled grimly to himself and rang for the conductor. Tatiana was looking anxiously up at him.

"Don't worry, Tania," he said again. "I will sit up tonight and watch. Perhaps tomorrow it will be easier. I will make a plan with Kerim. He is a good man."

The conductor knocked. Bond let him in and went out into the corridor. Kerim was still there gazing out. The train had picked up speed and was hurtling through the night, its harsh melancholy whistle echoing back from the walls of a deep cut, against the sides of which the lighted carriage windows flickered and danced.

Bond told Kerim of the conversation. It was not easy for him to explain why he trusted the girl as he did. He watched the mouth in the mirror of the window curl ironically as he tried to describe what he had read in her eyes and what his intuition told him. "James," Kerim said, "you are now in charge. This is your part of the operation. We have already argued most of this out today—the danger of the train, the possibility of getting the machine home in the diplomatic bag, the integrity of this girl. It certainly appears that she has surrendered unconditionally to you. At the same time you admit that you have surrendered to her. You have decided to trust her, perhaps only partially. But we didn't know we were to have an escort of three M.G.B. men, and I think that would have changed all our views. Yes?"

"Yes."

"Then the only thing to do is eliminate these three men. Get them off the train. Leave it to me. At least for tonight. This is still my country and I have certain powers in it. And plenty of money. I cannot afford to kill them. The train would be delayed. You and the girl might get involved. But I shall arrange something. Two of them have sleeping berths. The man with the mustache and the little pipe is next door to you—here, in Number Six." He gestured backwards with his head. "He is traveling on a German passport under the name of Melchior Benz, salesman. The dark one is in Number Twelve. He, too, has a German passport—Kurt Goldfarb, construction engineer. They have through tickets to Paris. I have seen their documents. I have a police card. The conductor made no trouble. He has all the tickets and passports in his cabin. The third man, the man with a boil on the back of his neck, turns out also to have boils on his face. A stupid, ugly-looking brute. I have not seen his passport. He is sitting up in the first class, in the next compartment to me. He does not have to surrender his passport until the frontier. But he has surrendered his ticket." Like a conjuror, Kerim flicked a yellow first-class ticket out of his coat pocket. He slipped it back and grinned proudly at Bond.

"How the hell?"

Kerim chuckled. "Before he settled down for the night, this dumb ox went to the lavatory. I was standing in the corridor and I suddenly remembered how we used to steal rides on the train when I was a boy. I gave him a minute. Then I walked up and rattled the lavatory door. I hung on to the handle very tight. 'Ticket collector,' I said in a loud voice. 'Tickets, please.' I said it in French and again in German. There was a mumble from inside. I felt him try to open the door. I hung on tight so that he would think the door had stuck. 'Do not derange yourself, monsieur,' I said politely. 'Push the ticket under the door.' There was more fiddling with the door handle. Then there was a pause and a rustle under the door. There was the ticket. I said, *Merci, monsieur,* very politely. I picked up the ticket and stepped across the coupling into the next carriage." Kerim airily waved a hand. "The stupid oaf will be sleeping peacefully by now. He will think that his ticket will be given back to him at the frontier. He is mistaken. The ticket will be in ashes and the ashes will be on the four winds." Kerim gestured towards the darkness outside. "I will see that the man is put off the train, however much money he has got. He will be told that the circumstances must be investigated, his statements corroborated with the ticket agency. He will be allowed to proceed on a later train."

Bond smiled. "You're a card, Darko. What about the other two?"

While they were talking, the conductor had come out of Number Seven. Kerim turned to Bond and put a hand on his shoulder. "Have no fear, James," he said cheerfully. "We will defeat these people. Go to your girl. We will meet again in the morning."

Bond watched the big man move off easily down the swaying corridor, his shoulders never touching the walls. Bond felt a wave of affection for the tough, cheerful professional spy.

THE TRAIN HOWLED ON through the night. Bond sat and watched the hurrying landscape and concentrated on keeping awake. The girl's head was warm and heavy on his lap. He cautiously lifted his wrist. Six fifteen. Only one more hour to the Turkish frontier.

The girl had insisted on sleeping like this. "I won't go to sleep unless you hold me," she had said. "I must know you're there all the time. It would be terrible to wake up and not be touching you. Please, James. Please, *dushka.*"

Bond had taken off his coat and tie and arranged himself in the corner with his feet up on his suitcase and the Beretta under the pillow within reach of his hand. She had made no comment about the gun. She had taken off all her clothes, except the black ribbon round her throat, and had pretended not to be provocative as she scrambled into bed and wriggled herself into a comfortable position. She had held up her arms to him. Bond had kissed her once, told her to go to sleep and then leaned back and waited icily for his body to leave him alone. Grumbling sleepily, she had settled herself, with one arm flung across his thighs. At first she had held him tightly, but her arm had gradually relaxed and then she was asleep.

Brusquely, Bond closed his mind to the thought of her and focused on the journey ahead. Whatever the orders of the three M.G.B. men, either they already knew Bond and Tatiana were on the train or they would soon find out. Their presence would be reported back to Istanbul, telephoned from some station, and by the morning the loss of the Spektor would have been discovered. Then what? Have the girl taken off the train as a thief? Or was that all too simple? And if it was more complicated—if all this was part of some Russian conspiracy—should he dodge it? Should he get the girl and the machine off the train at a wayside station, on the wrong side of the track, and hire a car and somehow get a plane to London?

Bond looked at his watch. Seven fifteen. They would soon be at Uzunköprü. What was going on down the train behind him? What had Kerim achieved? Bond sat back, relaxed. After all there was a simple answer. If they could quickly get rid of the three M.G.B. agents, they would stick to the train and to their original plan. He and Kerim were resourceful men. Kerim had an agent in Belgrade who was going to meet the train. There was always the embassy. Behind his reasoning, Bond calmly admitted to himself that he had an insane desire to play the game out and see what it was all about. It would be mad to run away and perhaps only escape one trap in order to fall into another.

The train gave a long whistle and began to slacken speed. With a jolt and a screech of couplings, the Orient Express slowed to walking speed and finally, with a sigh of vacuum brakes and a noisy whoosh of let-off steam, ground to a stop. The girl stirred in her sleep. Bond softly shifted her head onto the pillow and got up and slipped out of the door.

Uzunköprü was a typical Balkan wayside station—a façade of dour buildings, a dusty expanse of platform, some chickens pecking about and a few drab officials standing idly, unshaven, not even trying to look important. Up towards the cheap half of the train, a chattering horde of peasants with bundles and wicker baskets waited for the customs and passport control so that they could join the swarm inside. Across the platform from Bond was a closed door with a sign over it which said POLIS. Through the dirty window Bond caught a glimpse of the head and shoulders of Kerim.

"*Passeports. Douane!*"

A plainclothesman and two policemen in dark green uniforms entered the corridor. The wagon-lit conductor preceded them, knocking on the doors. At Number Twelve the conductor made an indignant speech in Turkish, holding out the stack of tickets and passports and fanning through them as if they were a pack of cards. When he had finished, the plainclothesman, beckoning forward the two policemen, knocked smartly on the door and, when it was opened, stepped inside. The two policemen stood guard behind him.

Bond edged down the corridor. He could hear a jumble of bad German. One voice was cold, the other frightened and hot. The passport and ticket of Herr Kurt Goldfarb were missing. Had Herr Goldfarb removed them from the conductor's cabin? Certainly not. Had Herr Goldfarb in truth ever surrendered his papers to the conductor? Naturally. Then the matter was unfortunate. An inquiry would have to be held. Meanwhile, it was regretted that Herr Goldfarb could not continue his journey. No doubt he would be able to proceed tomorrow. Herr Goldfarb was to get dressed. His luggage would be transported to the waiting room.

The M.G.B. man erupted into the corridor, his sallow face gray with fear. His hair was awry and he was dressed only in the bottom half of his pajamas. But there was nothing comical about his desperate flurry down the corridor. He brushed past Bond. At the door of Number Six he paused and pulled himself together. He knocked with tense control. The door opened on the chain and Bond glimpsed a thick nose and part of a mustache. The chain was slipped and Gold-farb went in. There was silence, during which the plainclothesman dealt with the papers of two elderly Frenchwomen in Nine and Ten, and then with Bond's.

The officer barely glanced at Bond's passport. He snapped it shut and handed it back to the conductor. "You are traveling with Kerim Bey?" he asked in French. His eyes were remote.

"Yes."

"*Merci, monsieur. Bon voyage.*" The man saluted. He turned and rapped sharply on the door of Number Six. The door opened and he went in.

Five minutes later the door was flung back. The plainclothesman, now erect with authority, beckoned the policemen. He spoke to them harshly in Turkish, then turned back. "Consider yourself under arrest, *mein Herr.* Attempted bribery of officials is a grave crime in Turkey." There was an angry clamor in Goldfarb's bad German. It was cut short by one hard sentence in Russian. A different Goldfarb, with madman's eyes, emerged and walked blindly down the corridor and went into Number Twelve. A policeman stood outside the door and waited.

"And *your* papers, *mein Herr.* Please step forward. I must verify this photograph." The plainclothesman held the green-backed Ger-man passport up to the light.

Reluctantly, his heavy face pale with anger, the M.G.B. man who called himself Benz stepped out into the corridor. The hard brown eyes looked straight into Bond's, ignoring him. The plainclothesman slapped the passport shut and handed it to the conductor. "Your papers are in order, *mein Herr.*" The plainclothesman saluted coldly and moved on down the corridor. The M.G.B. man went back into Number Six and slammed the door behind him.

Pity, thought Bond. One had got away.

Bond turned back to the window. A bulky man, wearing a gray homburg, and with an angry boil on the back of his neck, was being escorted through the door marked POLIS. Down the corridor a door slammed. Goldfarb, escorted by the policeman, stepped down off the train. With bent head, he walked across the dusty platform and dis-appeared through the same door.

The engine whistled, there was a jerk and a crescendo of explosive puffs from the engine, and once again the Orient Express began to move.

Bond pulled down the window, leaned out into the cool, sweet morning air and took a last look back at the Turkish frontier. Two birds down, he thought. Two out of three. The odds looked more respectable. He had made up his mind. He would stay on the train and see the thing through.

HOT COFFEE FROM THE little buffet at Pithion, a painless visit from the Greek customs and passport control and then the berths were folded away as the train hurried south towards the Gulf of Enez at the head of the Aegean.

Bond washed and shaved under the amused eyes of Tatiana. She approved of the fact that he put no oil on his hair. "I was told that many Europeans do that. We would not think of doing it in Russia. It dirties the pillows."

There came a knock on the door. It was Kerim. Bond let him in. Kerim bowed towards the girl. "What a charming domestic scene," he commented cheerfully, lowering his bulk into the corner near the door. "I have rarely seen a handsomer pair of spies."

Tatiana glowered at him. "I am not accustomed to Western jokes," she said coldly.

Kerim's laugh was disarming. "You'll learn, my dear. In England it is considered proper to make a joke of everything. I also have learned to make jokes. They grease the wheels. I have been laughing a lot this morning. Those poor fellows at Uzunköprü. I wish I could be there when the police telephone the German consulate in Istanbul. I fear the careers of your comrades have come to an end."

"How did you do it?" Bond knotted his tie.

"Money and influence. Five hundred dollars to the conductor. Some big talk to the police. It was lucky our friend tried a bribe. A pity that crafty Benz next door"—he gestured at the wall—"didn't get involved. I couldn't do the passport trick twice. We will have to get him some other way."

They were still talking when the train ground to a halt in the sun-baked station of Alexandroupolis. They had lunch in the restaurant car with the heavy bag under the table between Bond's feet. They saw the M.G.B. man called Benz on the platform buying sandwiches and beer from a buffet on wheels. Kerim suggested they ask him to make a fourth at bridge. Bond suddenly felt very tired and his tiredness made him feel that they were turning this dangerous journey into a picnic. Tatiana noticed his silence. She got up and said that she must rest. As they left they heard Kerim calling gaily for brandy and cigars.

Back in the compartment, Tatiana said firmly, "Now it is you who will sleep." She drew down the blind and shut out the hard afternoon light and the endless baked fields of maize and tobacco and wilting sunflowers. Bond wedged the doors and gave her his gun, then stretched out with his head in her lap and was immediately asleep.

The long train snaked along the north of Greece below the foothills of the Rhodope Mountains. Xanthe came, and Drama, and Serrai, and then they were in the Macedonian highlands and the line swerved due south towards Salonika.

It was dark when Bond awoke in the soft cradle of her lap. At once, as if she had been waiting for the moment, Tatiana took his face between her hands and looked down into his eyes and said urgently, "*Dushka*, how long shall we have this for?"

Bond gazed up into the beautiful, worried eyes. He cleared the sleep out of his mind. One had to face the fact that this girl was an enemy agent. After their arrival in London, intelligence would want to know what she could tell them. She would be taken away to "The Cage," that well-sentried private house near Guildford, where she would be put in a comfortable, well-wired room. The efficient men in plain clothes would talk with her, and the recorder would spin in the room below and the records would be transcribed and sifted for their grains of new fact—and, of course, for the contradictions they would trap her into. Perhaps they would introduce a stool pigeon—a nice Russian girl who would commiserate with Tatiana over her treatment and suggest ways of escape, of turning double, of getting harmless information back to her parents. This might go on for weeks or months. Then what? The changed name, the offer of a new life in Canada, the thousand pounds a year she would be given from the secret funds? And where would he be when she came out of it all? Perhaps the other side of the world. Or, if he was still in London, how much of her feeling for him would have survived the grinding of the interrogation machine? How much would she hate or despise the

English after going through all this? And how much would have survived of his own hot flame?

Tatiana was smiling down at him. "I will not ask any more foolish questions. But we must waste no more of these days."

An hour later, when Bond was standing in the corridor, Darko Kerim was suddenly beside him. He examined Bond's face. He said slyly, "You should not sleep so long. You have been missing the historic landscape of northern Greece. And it is time for the *deuxième service*."

"All you think about is food," said Bond. He gestured back with his head. "What about our friend?"

"He has not stirred. The conductor has been watching for me. I still feel disquiet. All is going well with our journey. And yet . . ." Kerim shook his head. "These Russians are great chess players. I have a feeling you and I and this girl are pawns on a very big board—that we are being allowed our moves because they do not interfere with the Russian game." Kerim paused. "I've made myself thirsty talking platitudes. Hurry the girl up and we will go and eat. But watch for surprises, I beg of you. Surprises are on the way for both of us. The gypsy said to watch out. Now I say the same. My nose"—he tapped it—"tells me so."

They finished their dinner as the train pulled into the hideous modern junction of Salonika. With Bond carrying the heavy little bag, they went back down the train and parted for the night. "We shall soon be disturbed again," warned Kerim. "There is the frontier at three fifteen. The Greeks will be no trouble, but those Yugoslavs like waking up anyone who is traveling soft. If they annoy you, send for me. Even in their country there are some names I can mention. I am in the second compartment in the next carriage. Tomorrow I will move into our friend Goldfarb's bed in Number Twelve."

Bond dozed wakefully as the train labored up the moonlit valley of the Vardar towards Yugoslavia. Tatiana again slept with her head in his lap. He thought of what Darko had said. He wondered if he should not send the big man back to Istanbul when they had got safely through Belgrade. It was not fair to drag him across Europe on an adventure that was outside his territory and with which he had little sympathy. He obviously suspected that Bond had become infatuated with the girl and wasn't seeing the operation straight anymore.

Well, there was a grain of truth in that, Bond admitted to himself.

Ten minutes after they had arrived at the Greek frontier station of Idomeni there was a knocking on the door. It woke the girl. Bond slipped from under her head and put his ear to the door. "Yes?"

"*Le conducteur, monsieur.* There has been an accident. Your friend Kerim Bey."

"Wait," said Bond fiercely. He fitted the Beretta into its holster and put on his coat. He tore open the door. "What is it?" he asked.

The conductor's face was yellow under the corridor light. "Come." He ran down the corridor towards the next carriage. Officials were clustered round the open door of the second compartment. They were standing, staring. The conductor made a path for Bond. Bond reached the door and looked in. The hair stirred softly on his head. Along the right-hand seat were two bodies. They were frozen in a ghastly death struggle that might have been posed for a film.

Underneath was Kerim, his knees up in a last effort to rise. The taped hilt of a dagger protruded from his neck near the jugular vein. His head was thrust back and the empty bloodshot eyes stared up at the light.

Half on top of him sprawled the heavy body of Benz, the M.G.B.

man, locked there by Kerim's left arm round his neck. Kerim's right arm lay across the man's back. The hand ended in a closed fist and the knob of a knife hilt, and there was a wide stain on the coat under the hand.

CHAPTER 8

THE ORIENT EXPRESS steamed slowly into Belgrade at five fifteen in the afternoon. There would be a six-hour delay while another section of the train came in from Bulgaria. Bond looked out at the crowds and waited for the knock on the door that would be Kerim's man. Tatiana sat huddled in her sable coat beside the door.

She had seen it all from the window—the long wicker baskets being brought out to the train, the flash of the police photographer's bulbs, the gesticulating *chef de train* trying to hurry up the formalities, and the tall figure of James Bond, straight and hard and cold as a butcher's knife, coming and going.

Bond had come back and had sat looking at her. He had asked sharp, brutal questions. She had stuck desperately to her story, knowing that now, if she told him everything, told him for instance that SMERSH was involved, she would certainly lose him forever. Now she sat and was afraid of what might have been behind the lies she had been told in Moscow.

There was a knock on the door. Bond got up and opened it. A tough cheerful man, with Kerim's blue eyes and a mop of tangled fair hair, exploded into the compartment.

"Stefan Trempo at your service." The big smile embraced them both. "They call me 'Tempo.' Where is the chief?"

"Sit down," said Bond. He thought to himself, This is another of Darko's sons. The man sat down carefully, his bright eyes staring at Bond with a terrible intensity in which there was fear and suspicion. His right hand slipped casually into the pocket of his coat.

When Bond had finished, the man stood up. He didn't ask any questions. He said, "Thank you, sir. Will you come, please? We will go to my apartment. There is much to be done." He walked into the corridor and stood with his back to them, looking out across the rails. When the girl came out he walked down the corridor without looking back. Bond followed the girl, carrying the heavy bag and his little attaché case.

It had started to drizzle. The station square, with its sprinkling of battered taxis and vista of dull modern buildings, was depressing. The man opened the rear door of a shabby Morris sedan. He got in front and took the wheel. They bumped their way over the cobbles and onto a slippery boulevard and drove for a quarter of an hour through wide, empty streets.

They stopped halfway down a cobbled side street. Tempo led them through a wide apartment-house door and up two flights of stairs that had the smell of cigarette smoke and cabbage. He unlocked a door and showed them into a two-room flat with nondescript furniture and heavy red plush curtains. On a sideboard stood a tray with several unopened bottles, glasses, and plates of fruit and biscuits—the welcome to Darko and Darko's friends.

Tempo waved vaguely towards the drinks. "Please, sir, make yourself and Madam at home. There is a bathroom. No doubt you would both like to have a bath. If you will excuse me, I must telephone!" The hard façade of the face was about to crumble. The man went quickly into the bedroom and shut the door behind him.

There followed two empty hours during which Bond sat and looked out of the window. From time to time he got up and paced to and fro. For the first hour Tatiana sat and pretended to look through a pile of magazines. Then she abruptly went into the bathroom and Bond vaguely heard water gushing into the bath.

At about eight o'clock Tempo came out of the bedroom. He told Bond that he was going out. "There is food in the kitchen. I will return in time to take you to the train. Please treat my flat as your own." He walked out and softly shut the door. Bond went into the bedroom, sat on the bed and picked up the telephone, then talked in German to the long-distance exchange. Half an hour later there was the quiet voice of M.

Bond spoke as a traveling salesman seeking instructions from his managing director. He said that his partner had taken sick.

"Very sick?"

"Yes, sir, very."

"How about the other firm?"

"There were three with us, sir. One of them caught the same thing.

The other two didn't feel well on the way out of Turkey. They left us at Uzunköprü—that's the frontier."

"So the other firm's packed up?"

Bond imagined M.'s face as he sifted the information. He wondered if the fan was slowly revolving in the ceiling, if M. had a pipe in his hand, if the chief of staff was listening in on the other wire.

"What are your ideas? Would you and your wife like to take another way home?"

"I'd rather you decided, sir. My wife's all right. The sample's in good condition. I'm still keen to finish the trip. Otherwise we shan't know what the possibilities are."

"Would you like one of our other salesmen to give you a hand?"

"It shouldn't be necessary, sir. Just as you feel."

"I'll think about it. So you really want to see this sales campaign through?"

Bond could see M.'s eyes glittering with the same perverse curiosity as he himself felt. "Yes, sir. Now that I'm halfway, it seems a pity not to cover the whole route."

"All right then. I'll think about giving you another salesman to lend a hand."

Bond put down the receiver. He sat and looked at it, suddenly wishing he had agreed with M.'s suggestion to give him reinforcements, just in case. At least they would soon be out of these damn Balkans and into Italy. Then Switzerland, France—among friendly people, away from the furtive lands.

And the girl, what about her? Could he blame her for the death of Kerim? Bond went back over everything, every expression, every gesture. No, he knew he couldn't put the blame on her. If she was an agent, she was an unconscious agent.

Later, after slivovitz and smoked ham and peaches, Tempo came and took them to the station. He said good-by, quickly and coldly, and vanished down the platform and back into his dark existence. Punctually at eleven fifteen the long train began its all-night run down the valley of the Sava.

Bond went along to the conductor's cabin to give him money and look through the passports of the new passengers. He knew most of the signs to look for in forged passports. The five new ones—three American and two Swiss—seemed innocent. The Swiss papers, favorites with the Russian forgers, belonged to a husband and wife, both over seventy. Bond finally passed them and went back to the compartment to prepare for another night with Tatiana's head on his lap.

Vinkovci came and Brod and then the ugly sprawl of Zagreb. The train hammered into the mountains of Slovenia. The girl awoke. They had a breakfast of fried eggs and hard brown bread and coffee that was mostly chicory. The restaurant car was full of cheerful English and American tourists. By early afternoon they would be over the frontier into Western Europe. We've made it, thought Bond with a lift of the heart. I really think we've made it.

He slept until Sežana. The hard-faced Yugoslav plainclothesmen came on board. Then Poggioreale came and the happy jabbering of Italian officials. And then they were loping easily down into Venice, towards the gay blue of the Adriatic.

When the train slid quietly into the gleaming station of Trieste, Bond pulled down the window. He gazed at the holiday crowd with an almost sensuous pleasure—the gaily dressed people passing towards the entrance, and the sunburned people, the ones who had had their holidays, hastening up the platform to get their seats on the train.

A shaft of sun lit up the head of one man who seemed typical of this happy, playtime world. The light flashed briefly on golden hair under a cap, and on a young golden mustache. There was plenty of time to catch the train, and the man walked unhurriedly. It crossed Bond's mind that he was an Englishman. Perhaps it was the rather well-used mackintosh, that badge of the English tourist, or it may have been the gray-flanneled legs, or the scuffed brown shoes. But Bond's eyes were drawn to him. He looks like an athlete, thought Bond, a professional tennis player going home after a round of foreign tournaments.

The man came nearer. Now he was looking straight at Bond. With recognition? Bond searched his mind. Did he know this man? No. He would have remembered those opaque eyes that stared out so coldly under the pale lashes. The eyes of a drowned man. But they had some message for him. What was it? Recognition? Warning?

Suddenly Bond knew who the man was. Of course! This man was from the service. M. had decided to send along an extra hand after all. That was the message of those queer eyes. How like M. to make absolutely sure!

To make the contact easy, Bond stood in the corridor. As the train began to move, he ran over the details of the code of the day, the few harmless phrases, changed on the first of each month, that served as a simple recognition signal between English agents. Suddenly the bronzed face was mirrored in the window.

"Excuse me. Could I borrow a match?"

"I use a lighter." Bond produced his battered Ronson and handed it over.

"Better still."

"Until they go wrong."

Bond looked up into the man's face, expecting a smile at the completion of the childish ritual.

The thick lips writhed briefly. There was no light in the very pale blue eyes. The eyes looked rather mad, in fact. But so they did in most of these men doing secret work abroad. One had to be a bit mad to take it on. Powerful chap, probably on the stupid side, but useful for this kind of guard work.

All this went through Bond's mind as he said, "Glad to see you. How did it happen?"

"Got a signal. Late last night. Personal from M. Shook me, I can tell you, old man."

Curious accent. What was it? Probably came from living too long abroad and talking foreign languages all the time. And that dreadful "old man" at the end. Shyness.

"Must have," said Bond sympathetically. "What did it say?"

"Just told me to get on the Orient this morning and contact a man and a girl in the through carriage. More or less described what you look like. Then I was to stick by you and see you both through to Gay Paree. That's all, old man."

Was there defensiveness in the voice? Bond glanced sideways. The pale eyes swiveled to meet his. There was a quick red glare in them, then the eyes were opaque again—the eyes of an introvert forever surveying the scene inside him. There's madness there all right, thought Bond, startled by the sight of it. One day he would certainly crack. "By the way, my name's James Bond. Traveling as David Somerset. And that's Caroline Somerset in there."

The man fished in his inside pocket and produced a battered wallet which seemed to contain plenty of money. He extracted a visiting card and handed it to Bond. It said CAPTAIN NORMAN NASH, and, in the left-hand bottom corner, ROYAL AUTOMOBILE CLUB.

"Well, Nash, come and meet Mrs. Somerset." Bond turned to the door, knocked softly and spoke his name. The door opened. Bond beckoned Nash in and shut the door behind him. The girl looked surprised.

"This is Captain Norman Nash. He's been told to keep an eye on us."

"How do you do." The hand came out hesitantly. The man touched it briefly. His stare was fixed. He said nothing. The girl gave an embarrassed little laugh. "Won't you sit down?"

"Er, thank you." Nash sat stiffly on the edge of the banquette. Silence fell. Nash obviously felt it was his turn to speak. He fished in his pocket and produced a newspaper clipping. It was from the front page of the *Corriere della Sera*. He handed it to Bond. "Seen this, old man?" The eyes blazed and died. The thick black lettering of the headlines said:

TERRIBILE ESPLOSIONE IN ISTANBUL
UFFICIO SOVIETICO DISTRUTTO

Bond couldn't understand the rest. He folded the clipping and handed it back. How much did this man know? Better treat him as a strong-arm man and nothing else. "Bad show," he said. "Gas main, I suppose." Bond saw again the obscene belly of the bomb hanging down from the roof of the alcove in the tunnel of rats, the wires that started off down the damp wall on their way back to the plunger in the drawer of Kerim's desk. Who had pressed the plunger yesterday afternoon when Tempo had got through? The head clerk? Or had they drawn lots and then stood round and watched as the hand went down and the deep roar had gone up in the Street of Books on the hill above? What time would it have been? About six o'clock. Had the daily meeting still been on? How many dead in the rest of the building? Friends of Tatiana's, perhaps.

Nash was looking at him. "Yes, I daresay it was a gas main," he said without interest.

A handbell tinkled down the corridor. "*Deuxième service. Prenez vos places, s'il vous plaît.*"

Bond said, "What about lunch?"

Nash was on his feet. "Had it, thanks, old man. And I'd like to have a look up and down the train. Is the conductor—you know . . . ?" He made a gesture of fingering money.

"Oh yes, he'll cooperate all right," said Bond. He reached up and pulled down the heavy little bag. Captain Nash stepped into the corridor, turned left and strode off.

After lunch it was the little room again, the smell of the sea coming through the half-open window, the drawn blind fluttering with the wind of the train, and the two whispering bodies on the banquette. As the train jolted into the echoing station of Venice, outside the vacuum of the tiny room there sounded a confusion of calls, metallic clanging and shuffling footsteps that slowly faded into sleep.

Padua came, and Vicenza, and then a fabulous sunset flickered gold and red through the cracks of the blind. Again the little bell came tinkling from outside the door. They woke. Bond dressed and went into the corridor. He looked out at the fading pink light over the Lombardy plain and thought of Tatiana and of the future. Nash's face slid up alongside his in the dark glass. "I think I've spotted one of the opposition, old man," he said softly.

Bond was not surprised. He had assumed that, if it came, it would come tonight. Almost indifferently he said, "Who is he?"

"Don't know what his real name is, but he's been through Trieste once or twice. Something to do with Albania. May be the resident director there. Now he's on an American passport. Calls himself a banker. In Number Six, right next to you. I don't think I could be wrong about him, old man." Bond glanced at the eyes in the big brown face. The red glare shone out again and was extinguished.

"Good thing you spotted him. This may be a tough night. You'd better stick by us from now on. We mustn't leave the girl alone."

"That's what I thought, old man."

They had dinner. It was a silent meal. Nash sat beside the girl and kept his eyes on his plate. He was clumsy in his movements. Halfway through the meal, he reached for the salt and knocked over Tatiana's glass of Chianti. He apologized profusely, then made a great show of calling for another glass and filling it.

Coffee came. Now it was Tatiana who was clumsy. She knocked over her cup. She had gone very pale and her breath was coming quickly. "Tatiana!" Bond half rose to his feet. But it was Captain Nash who jumped up and took charge.

"Lady's come over queer," he said shortly. "Allow me." He reached down and put an arm round the girl and lifted her to her feet. "I'll take her back to the compartment. You'd better look after the bag. And there's the bill. I can take care of her till you come."

"Don't worry, James. I lie down." Tatiana spoke with slack lips. Her head lolled against Nash's shoulder. He put one thick arm round her waist and maneuvered her quickly down the crowded aisle and out of the restaurant car.

Bond impatiently snapped his fingers for the waiter. Poor darling. She must be dead beat. Why hadn't he thought of the strain she was going through? He cursed himself for his selfishness. Thank heavens for Nash. Efficient sort of chap, for all his uncouthness. Bond paid the bill. He took up the heavy little bag and walked as quickly as he could down the crowded train.

He tapped softly on the door of Number Seven. Nash came out with his finger on his lips. He closed the door behind him. "Threw a bit of a faint," he said. "She's all right now. The beds were made up. She's gone to sleep in the top one. Been a bit much for the girl, I expect, old man."

Bond nodded and went into the compartment. A hand hung palely down from under the sable coat. Bond stood on the bottom bunk and gently tucked the hand under the corner of the coat. The hand felt very cold. The girl made no sound. Bond stepped softly down. Better let her sleep. He went into the corridor.

Nash looked at him with empty eyes. "Well, I suppose we'd better settle in for the night. I've got my book." He held it up. "*War and Peace*. Been trying to plow through it for years. You take the first sleep, old man. You look pretty flaked out yourself. I'll wake you up when I can't keep my eyes open any longer." He gestured with his head at the door of Number Six. "Hasn't shown yet." He paused. "By the way, you got a gun, old man?"

"Yes. Why, haven't you?"

Nash looked apologetic. " 'Fraid not. Got a Luger at home, but it's too bulky for this sort of job."

"Oh, well," said Bond reluctantly. "You'd better take mine. Come on in." They went in and Bond shut the door. He took out the

Beretta and handed it over. "Eight shots," he said softly. "Semiautomatic. It's on safe."

Nash took the gun and weighed it professionally in his hand. He clicked the safe on and off. He sat down near the window at the end of the bottom bunk. "I'll take this end," he whispered. "Good field of fire." He put his book down on his lap and settled himself.

Bond took off his coat and tie and laid them on the bunk beside him. He leaned back against the pillows and propped his feet on the bag with the Spektor that stood on the floor beside his attaché case. He picked up his book, but after a few pages found he was too tired. He laid the book down on his lap and closed his eyes. Could he afford to sleep? Was there any other precaution they could take?

The wedges! Bond felt for them in the pocket of his coat. He slipped off the bunk and knelt and forced them hard under the two doors. Then he settled himself again and switched off the reading light behind his head. The violet eye of the night-light shone softly down.

CHAPTER 9

THE LIGHT NUDGE AT his ankle woke Bond. He didn't move. His senses came to life like an animal's. Nothing had changed. There were only the usual noises of the train pounding out the kilometers.

What had awakened him? No sound came from the upper bunk. By the window, Captain Nash sat in his place, his book open on his lap, looking fixedly at Bond. Bond registered the intentness of the eyes. The lips parted. There was a glint of teeth.

"Sorry to disturb you, old man. I feel in the mood for a talk!"

What was there new in the voice? Bond put his feet softly down to the floor. Danger, like a third man, was standing in the room.

"Fine," said Bond easily. What had there been in those few words that had set his spine tingling? The idea came to Bond that Nash might have gone mad. His instincts about this man had been right. It would be a question of somehow getting rid of him at the next station. Where had they got to? When would the frontier come?

Bond lifted his wrist to look at the time. He tilted the watch face towards a strip of moonlight from the window. From the direction of Nash there came a sharp click, and Bond felt a violent blow on his wrist. Splinters of glass hit him in the face and his arm was flung back. He wondered if his wrist had been broken. He let his arm hang and flexed his fingers. They all moved.

The book was still open on Nash's lap, but now a thin wisp of smoke was coming out of the hole at the top of its spine and there was a faint smell of fireworks in the room. The saliva dried in Bond's mouth as if he had swallowed alum.

So there had been a trap all along. Captain Nash had been sent to him by Moscow. Not by M. And the M.G.B. agent in Number Six, the man with an American passport, was a myth. And Bond had given Nash his gun. He had even put wedges under the doors so that Nash would feel more secure. Bond shivered. Not with fear. With disgust.

Nash's voice was no longer a whisper, no longer oily. It was loud and confident. "Just a little demonstration to save argument, old man. I'm pretty good with this little bag of tricks the Russians dreamed up." He held the book up. "There are ten bullets in it—.25 dumdum, fired by an electric battery. You must admit the Russians are wonderful chaps for dreaming these things up, old man. Too bad that book of yours is only for reading."

"For God's sake stop calling me 'old man.' " This was Bond's first reaction to utter catastrophe—the reaction of someone in a burning house who picks up the most trivial object to save from the flames.

"Sorry, old man. It's gotten to be a habit. Part of trying to be a bloody gentleman. But let's get down to business. I expect you'd like to know what this is all about. We've got about half an hour before you're due to go, and I want to tell the famous Mr. Bond what a bloody fool he is."

"Yes," said Bond. "I'd like to know what it's all about. I can spare you half an hour." Desperately he wondered, Was there any way of putting this man off his stride? Upsetting his balance?

"Don't kid yourself, old man. You're going to die in half an hour. No mistake about it. I've never made a mistake or I wouldn't be chief executioner of SMERSH." There was a hint of pride in the voice.

SMERSH. So that was the answer—the worst answer of all. And this was their chief killer. Bond remembered the red glare that flickered in the opaque eyes. "Where does the girl come into all this?"

"Part of the bait." The voice was bored. "Don't worry. She won't butt in on our talk. Fed her a pinch of chloral hydrate when I poured her that glass of wine. She'll be out for the night. And then for every other night. She's to go with you."

"Oh really." Bond lifted his aching hand onto his lap, flexing the fingers to get the blood moving.

"Careful, old man. No tricks. If I don't like even the smell of a move, it'll be one bullet through the heart. That's what you'll be getting in the end. If you move it'll come a bit quicker. Remember your wristwatch. I don't miss. Not ever."

"Good show," said Bond carelessly. "But don't be frightened. You've got my gun. Remember? Get on with your story."

"Well," Nash went on, "SMERSH decided to kill you to bring Secret Service down a peg or two. Follow me?"

"Why choose *me?*"

"Don't ask me, old man. But they say you've got quite a reputation in your outfit. The way you're going to be killed has been three months cooking. This plan's a beaut. You see, old man, we've got quite a planner in SMERSH. Man called Kronsteen. Great chess player. And our head of operations is quite a character. I'd say she's killed more people than anyone in the world—or arranged for them to be killed. Yes, it's a woman. Rosa Klebb. Real swine of a woman. But she certainly knows all the tricks."

Rosa Klebb. So at the top of SMERSH there was a woman! If he could somehow survive this and get after her!

The flat voice in the corner went on. "Well, she found this Romanova girl. Trained her for the job. By the way, they got some nice pictures of you two." Nash tapped his coat pocket. "Whole reel of sixteen-millimeter. That's going into the girl's handbag. It'll look fine in the papers." Nash laughed. "They'll have to cut some of the juiciest bits, of course."

The change of rooms at the hotel. The honeymoon suite. The big mirror behind the bed. How well it all fitted! Bond felt his hands wet with perspiration. He wiped them down his trousers.

"Steady, old man. I told you not to move, remember?"

Bond put his hands back on the book in his lap. How much could he develop these small movements? "Did the girl know these pictures were being taken? Did she know SMERSH was involved in all this?"

Nash snorted. "Of course she didn't know about the pictures. Rosa didn't trust her a yard. Too emotional. The girl knew she was work-

ing for SMERSH, but all she was told was she had to get to London and
do a bit of spying there."

So, she had been as fooled as he had been, thought Bond. Why the
hell hadn't she told him that SMERSH was involved? Any hint would
have been enough—would have saved the life of Kerim, for instance.

Nash took a quick glance at his wristwatch. "In about twenty minutes we go into the Simplon Tunnel. That's where they want it done.
More drama for the papers. One bullet for you. Just one in the heart.
Then one in the back of the neck for her—with your gun—and out
the window she goes. Then one more for you with *your* gun. With
your fingers wrapped round it, of course. Plenty of powder on your
shirt. Suicide. That's what it'll look like at first. But there'll be two
bullets in your heart. That'll come out later. More mystery! Search
the Simplon again. Who was the man with the fair hair? They'll find
the film in her bag, and in your pocket there'll be a long love letter
from her to you—a bit threatening. It's a good one. SMERSH wrote it.
It says that she'll give the film to the newspapers unless you marry her.
That you promised to marry her if she stole the Spektor . . ." Nash
paused and added, "As a matter of fact, old man, the Spektor's booby-
trapped. When your cipher experts start fiddling with it, it's going
to blow them all to glory. Not a bad dividend on the side." Nash
chuckled dully. "And then the letter says that all she's got to offer you
is the machine and her body. Hot stuff, that part! The story's got
everything. Orient Express. Beautiful Russian spy murdered in
Simplon Tunnel. Filthy pictures. Secret cipher machine. Handsome
British spy with career ruined murders her and commits suicide. Old
man, it'll run for months!"

Yes, thought Bond. The French papers would give it such a send-
off, there'd be no press in the world that wouldn't pick it up. And the
Spektor! Would M.'s people have the sense to guess it was booby-
trapped? How many of the best cryptographers in the West would go
up with it? God, he must get out of this jam! But how?

The top of Nash's *War and Peace* yawned at him. Let's see. There
would be the roar as the train went into the tunnel. Then at once
the muffled click and the bullet. Bond's eyes measured the depth of
the shadow in his corner under the roof of the top bunk, remembering
exactly where his attaché case stood on the floor, guessing what Nash
would do after he had fired.

Bond said, "You took a bit of a gamble on my letting you team up at Trieste. And how did you know the code of the month?"

Nash said patiently, "We know your code of the month for every year. Every January you lose one of your small chaps somewhere—maybe Tokyo, maybe Timbuktu. SMERSH just picks one and takes him. Then they screw the code for the year out of him, and it's passed round to the centers. As for picking you up at Trieste, old man, I didn't. Rode down from Belgrade with you—in the front of the train. Got out as we stopped and walked back up the platform. You see, old man, we knew you'd call your chief—or the embassy or someone. Been listening in on that Yugoslav's telephone for weeks. Pity we didn't understand the code word your man Trempo shot through to Istanbul. Might have stopped the firework display, or anyway saved our chaps. But the main target was you, old man. You were in the killing bottle from the minute you got off that plane in Turkey. It was only a question of when to stuff the cork in."

Bond thought, We knew SMERSH was good, but we never knew how good. Somehow he must get the knowledge of that back. He *must*. Bond's mind raced round the details of his pitifully thin, pitifully desperate plan.

He said, "SMERSH seems to have thought things out pretty well. There's only one thing . . ." Bond let his voice hang in the air.

"What's that, old man?" Nash was alert.

"Not without a cigarette."

"Okay. Go ahead. But if there's a move I don't like, you'll be dead."

Bond slipped his right hand into his hip pocket. He drew out his broad gunmetal cigarette case. Took out a cigarette. Took his lighter out of his trouser pocket. Lit the cigarette and put the lighter back. He left the cigarette case on his lap beside the book, covering them casually with his left hand, as if to prevent them slipping off his lap. He had achieved his objective and hadn't been shot in the process. That was a start.

"You see." Bond described an airy circle with his cigarette to distract Nash's attention. His left hand slipped the flat cigarette case between the pages of his book. "You see, it looks all right, but what about you? What are you going to do after we come out of the Simplon? The conductor knows you're mixed up with us. They'll be after you in a flash."

"Oh that." Nash's voice was bored again. "I get off at Dijon and take a car to Paris. They won't catch up with me. Matter of fact, I've got a date at noon tomorrow—Room Two-oh-four at the Ritz Hotel, making my report to Rosa. She wants to get the kudos for this job. Then I turn into her chauffeur and we drive to Berlin."

The train had slowed at the Italian frontier, but now began to pick up speed. Bond tensed. In a few minutes it would come. What a way to die, if he was going to die. Through his own stupidity—blind, lethal stupidity. And lethal for Tatiana. And all the time SMERSH had been watching him go through his conceited paces, as it had been planned that he would. God, what a mess! If only . . . if only his tiny grain of a plan might work!

Ahead, the rumble of the train became a deep boom. A few more seconds. A few more yards.

The oval mouth between the white pages seemed to gape wider. In a second the dark tunnel would switch out the moonlight on the pages and the blue tongue would lick out for him.

"Sweet dreams, you English bastard."

The rumble became a great swift clanging roar.

The spine of the book bloomed flame and the bullet, homing on Bond's heart, flashed over its two quiet yards.

Bond pitched forward onto the floor and lay sprawled under the spectral eye of the violet night-light.

IT HAD ALL DEPENDED on the man's accuracy. Nash had said that Bond would get one bullet through the heart. Bond had taken the gamble that Nash's aim was as good as he said it was. And it had been.

Bond lay, as a dead man lies, totally collapsed, a broken doll with arms and legs outflung. He explored his sensations. Where the bullet had crashed into the book, his ribs were on fire. The bullet must have gone through the cigarette case and then through the other half of the book. He could feel the hot lead over his heart, burning inside his ribs. It was only a sharp pain in his head where it had hit the woodwork, and the scuffed toe cap of Nash's shoe against his nose, that said he wasn't dead.

Like an archaeologist, Bond explored the carefully planned ruin of his body. The position of the sprawled feet. The angle of the knee that would give purchase when needed. The right hand was within inches, when he could release the book, of the little attaché case—within inches of Q Branch's lateral stitching that held the flat-bladed throwing-knives, two-edged and sharp as razors. And his left hand, outflung in the surrender of death, rested on the floor and would provide upward leverage when the moment came.

Above him there sounded a long, cavernous yawn. The brown toe caps shifted as Nash stood up. In a minute, with Bond's gun in his right hand, Nash would climb onto the bottom bunk and reach up

and feel through the curtain of hair for the base of the girl's neck. Then the snout of the Beretta would nuzzle in after the probing fingers; Nash would press the trigger. The roar of the train would cover the muffled boom.

It would be a near thing. Bond desperately tried to remember simple anatomy. Where were the mortal places in the lower body of a man? The femoral artery down through the inside of the thigh. And the external iliac, or whatever it was called, across the center of the groin. If he missed both, it would be bad. Bond had no illusions about being able to beat this man in unarmed combat. The first violent stab of his knife had to be decisive.

The brown toe caps moved, pointing towards the bunk. One

brown shoe left the floor and stepped half across Bond. The vulnerable arch would be open above Bond's head.

Bond's muscles coiled like a snake's. His right hand flickered a few centimeters to the hard stitching on the edge of the case. Pressed sideways. Felt the narrow shaft of the knife. Drew it softly halfway out without moving his arm.

The brown heel lifted off the ground. The toe bent and took the weight.

Now the second foot had gone. Softly move the weight here, take the purchase there, grasp the knife hard so that it won't turn on a bone, and then . . . In one violent corkscrew of motion, Bond's body twisted up from the floor. The knife flashed.

The fist with the long steel finger, and all Bond's arm and shoulder behind it, lunged upwards. Bond's knuckles felt flannel. He held the knife in, forcing it further. A ghastly wailing cry came down to him. The Beretta clattered to the floor. Then the knife was wrenched from Bond's hand as the man gave a convulsive twist and crashed down.

Bond sidestepped towards the window, but a flailing hand sent him thudding onto the lower bunk. Before he could recover himself, up from the floor rose the terrible face, its eyes shining, the teeth bared. Slowly, agonizingly, the two huge hands groped for him.

Bond, half on his back, kicked out blindly. His shoe connected; but then his foot was held and twisted and he felt himself being pulled down. Soon the teeth would be at him. Bond hammered out with his free leg. It made no difference. He was going.

Suddenly Bond's scrabbling fingers felt something hard. Nash's book! How did the thing work? Would it shoot him or Nash? Desperately Bond held it out towards the great sweating face. He pressed at the base of the cloth spine. *Click!* Bond felt the recoil. *Click-click-click-click,* went the silencer. Now Bond felt the heat under his fingers. The hands on his legs were going limp. A terrible gurgling noise came from the throat. Then, with a slither, the body fell to the floor and the head crashed against the woodwork.

Panting through clenched teeth, Bond got to his feet and stepped over the sprawling legs of the dead man. He turned on the top light. What a shambles! The place looked like a butcher's shop. Then Bond stepped up and gently shook the shoulder of fur. There was no response. Had the man lied? Had he killed her with the poison?

Bond thrust his hand in against her neck. It was warm. Bond felt for the lobe of an ear and pinched it hard. The girl stirred sluggishly and moaned. Again Bond pinched the ear, and again. At last a muffled voice protested, "Don't." Bond talked to her, bullied her, cursed her, shook her. Finally she sat up and gazed vacantly at him. Bond pulled her legs out so that they hung down over the edge. Somehow he manhandled her down onto the bottom bunk.

Tatiana looked terrible—the upturned, sleep-drunk eyes, the tangle of damp hair. Bond got to work with a wet towel and her comb.

The galloping boom of the train began to change. With a final echoing roar the Orient Express sped out into the moonlight. Bond pulled at the edge of the blind. He saw warehouses and sidings. Lights shone brightly, cleanly on the rails. The lights of Switzerland.

Lausanne came and, an hour later, the French frontier at Vallorbe. Bond took their bags, one by one, to the end of the corridor and piled them against the exit. Then he went along to the conductor and told him that Madam was not well and that they would be leaving the train at Dijon. He gave the conductor a final tip. "My friend, the one with fair hair, is a doctor. He has been sitting up with us all night. I have put him to sleep in my bunk. The man was exhausted. It would be kind not to waken him until ten minutes before Paris."

"Certainement, monsieur."

The train began to slacken speed, and Bond went back to the compartment. He dragged Tatiana to her feet and out into the corridor and shut the door. At last they were down the steps and onto the hard, wonderful, motionless platform. A blue-smocked porter took their luggage. At that hour of the morning there were very few passengers awake. Only a handful in the third class saw a young man help a young girl away from the dusty carriage.

CHAPTER 10

THE TAXI DREW UP at the Rue Cambon entrance to the Ritz Hotel in Paris.

Bond looked at Nash's watch, now on his own wrist. Eleven forty-five. He must be dead punctual. He knew that if a Russian spy was even a few minutes early or late for a rendezvous the rendezvous was automatically canceled. He paid off the taxi and went through the door on the left that leads into the Ritz bar.

In the bar Bond ordered a double vodka martini. He drank it half down. He felt wonderful. Suddenly the last four days, and particularly last night, were washed off the calendar. Now he was on his own, having his private adventure. All his duties had been taken care of. The girl was sleeping in a bedroom at the embassy. The Spektor, still pregnant with explosive, had been taken away by the bomb disposal squad of the Deuxième Bureau. He had spoken to René Mathis, his old friend at the Deuxième, and the concierge at the Ritz had been told to give him a passkey and to ask no questions.

René had been delighted to find himself again involved with Bond. "Have confidence, *cher* James," he had said. "I will execute your mysteries. You can tell me the story afterwards. Two laundrymen with a large laundry basket will come to Room Two-oh-four at twelve fifteen. I shall accompany them dressed as the driver. We are to fill the laundry basket and take it to Orly and await an R.A.F. plane which will arrive at two o'clock. We hand over the basket. Some dirty washing which was in France will be in England. Yes?"

Bond finished his martini and walked out of the bar and up the steps to the concierge's lodge. The concierge looked sharply at him and handed over a key. Bond strolled over to the lift and got in and went up to the third floor. He walked softly down the corridor, looking at the numbers. Two hundred four. Bond knocked once.

"Come in." It was a quavering voice. An old woman's voice.

Bond tried the handle of the door. It was unlocked. He stepped in and shut it behind him.

It was a typical Ritz sitting room, extremely elegant, with good Empire furniture, white walls and wine-red carpet. In a pool of sunshine, in a chintz-covered chair beside a writing desk, a little old woman sat knitting. The eyes behind light-blue tinted bifocals examined Bond with polite curiosity. *"Oui, monsieur?"* The thickly powdered, rather puffy face under the white hair showed nothing but well-bred interest.

Bond's eyes flickered round the room. Had he made a mistake? Was this the wrong room? Should he apologize and get out? Could this little old woman possibly belong to SMERSH? She looked so exactly like the sort of rich widow one would expect to find sitting by herself in the Ritz, knitting. The old-fashioned black dress with the touch of lace at the throat and wrists, the thin gold chain that hung down over the shapeless bosom and ended in a folding lorgnette, the neat little feet in the sensible black-buttoned boots that barely touched the floor. It couldn't be Klebb! Bond had got the number of the room wrong. But now he would have to play the scene through.

"My name is Bond, James Bond."

"And I, monsieur, am the Countess Metterstein. What can I do for you?" The French was rather thick. She might be German Swiss. The needles tinkled busily.

"I am afraid Captain Nash has met with an accident. He won't be coming today. So I came instead."

Did the eyes narrow a fraction behind the pale blue spectacles?

"I have not the pleasure of the captain's acquaintance, monsieur. Nor of yours. Please sit down and state your business." The woman inclined her head an inch towards the high-backed chair beside the writing desk.

Bond walked across the room and sat down. Now he was about six feet away from her. The desk held a tall old-fashioned telephone with a receiver on a hook, and, within reach of her hand, an ivory-buttoned bell push. The black mouth of the telephone yawned at Bond politely.

Bond stared rudely into the woman's face, examining it. It was an ugly face, toadlike under the powder and the tight white hair. The eyes were such a light brown as to be almost yellow. The pale lips were wet and blubbery below the fringe of nicotine-stained mustache. Nicotine? Where were her cigarettes? There was no ashtray—no smell of smoke in the room. Bond glanced down at the shapeless length of beige wool the woman was working on. The steel needles. What was there odd about them? The ends were discolored as if they had been held in fire.

"*Eh bien, monsieur?*" Had she read something in his face?

Bond smiled. "It's no use," he said cheerfully, gambling. "You are Rosa Klebb. And you are head of Otdyel Two of SMERSH. You are a torturer and a murderer. You wanted to kill me and the Romanov girl. I am very glad to meet you at last."

The eyes had not changed. The woman reached out her left hand towards the bell push. "Monsieur, I am afraid you are deranged. I must ring for the *valet de chambre* and have you shown to the door."

Bond never knew what saved his life. Perhaps it was the flash of realization that no wires led from the bell push to the wall or into the carpet. Perhaps it was the sudden memory of the English "Come in" when the expected knock came on the door. But, as her finger reached the ivory knob, he hurled himself sideways out of the chair. As Bond hit the floor there was a sharp noise. His chair crashed to the floor, too, and out of the corner of his eye he saw a curl of smoke coming from the mouth of the "telephone."

Bond twisted over, tugging at the Beretta tucked into the waistband of his trousers. Then the woman was on him, the knitting needles glinting in her clenched fists. She stabbed downwards at his legs.

Bond lashed out with his feet and hurled her sideways. She had aimed at his legs! As he got to one knee, Bond knew what the colored tips of the needles meant. It was poison. Probably one of those German nerve poisons. All she had to do was scratch him, even through his clothes.

Bond was on his feet. He tugged furiously at his gun. The silencer had caught in his clothes. There was a flash of light, and Bond dodged. One of the needles rattled against the wall behind him and the dreadful chunk of woman, her white wig askew, her lips drawn back from her teeth, was on top of him.

Bond, not daring to use his naked fists against the needles, vaulted sideways over the desk.

Panting, Rosa Klebb scuttled round the desk, the remaining needle held forward like a rapier. Bond backed away, working at the stuck gun. The backs of his legs came against a small chair. He let go the gun and reached behind him and snatched it up. Holding it by the back, with its legs pointing like horns, he lunged to meet her.

The legs of the chair clutched the woman round the waist and over her shoulders. God, she was strong! She gave way, but only to the wall. There she held her ground, spitting at Bond over the top of the chair, while the knitting needle quested towards him like a long scorpion's sting.

Bond stood back a little, holding the chair at arm's length. He took aim and high-kicked at the probing wrist. The needle sailed away into the room and pinged down behind him. Now there was no way she could get out of the cage. Her arms, legs and head were free, but her body was pinned to the wall by the four chair legs.

"That's all, Rosa," Bond said. "The Deuxième will be here in a minute. In an hour or so you'll be in London. You won't be seen leaving the hotel. You won't be seen going into England. In fact very few people will ever see you again. From now on you're just a number on a secret file. By the time we've finished with you, you'll be ready for the lunatic asylum."

The wet, shapeless mouth lengthened in a grin. The pale eyes looking levelly into his were not defeated. "And where will you be when I am in the asylum, Mr. Bond?"

"Oh, getting on with my life."

"I think not, *Angliski spion.*"

Bond heard the click of the door opening behind him. His friend Mathis was there and the two laundrymen with him. Bond heard the creak of the laundry basket.

"You can take over now," said Bond over his shoulder. "I'll introduce you. Her name's Rosa. You'll like her. She's a big noise in SMERSH."

The woman's eyes were still locked on Bond. As she moved a little, shifting her weight, the toe of one shiny buttoned boot pressed under the instep of the other. From the point of its toe there slid forward half an inch of thin knife blade. Like the knitting needles, the steel had a dirty bluish tinge.

The two men came up and put the big square basket down.

"*Au revoir,* Rosa," said Bond.

"Farewell, Mr. Bond."

The boot, with its tiny steel tongue, flashed out. Bond felt a sharp pain in his right calf. He flinched and stepped back. The two men seized Rosa Klebb by the arms. The tongue of dirty steel had withdrawn into the leather. Now it was only a harmless bundle of old woman that was being lifted into the basket.

Mathis turned to Bond. "A good day's work, my friend. This evening we must have the best dinner in Paris. And I will find the loveliest girl to go with it."

Numbness was creeping up Bond's body. He felt very cold. He lifted his hand to brush his hair back. There was no feeling in his fingers. His hand fell heavily to his side.

Breathing became difficult. He clenched his jaws and half closed his eyes. Through his eyelashes he watched the basket being carried to the door. Now he had to gasp for breath. Again his hand moved up towards his cold face. He had an impression of Mathis starting towards him. He felt his knees begin to buckle. He said, or thought he said, "I've already got the loveliest . . ."

Bond pivoted slowly on his heel and crashed headlong to the wine-red floor.

I, BENEDICT
ARNOLD

I, Benedict Arnold

THE ANATOMY OF TREASON

A CONDENSATION OF THE BOOK BY

Cornel Lengyel

ILLUSTRATED BY DAVID BLOSSOM

Benedict Arnold—nearly one hundred and seventy-five years after his death that name still stands as the most famous synonym for *traitor* in the English language.

Washington's most brilliant field general, Arnold was an officer of extraordinary bravery, military prowess, and personal magnetism. From Ticonderoga to Saratoga, in battle after battle, he led the attack, inspiring the ragged American troops with his own fierce courage. Twice he was wounded. The country rang with his praises; he was called the Hannibal of America.

There seemed no limits to the heights of success, happiness, and personal glory he might reach. He had a young wife of impressive family background, great beauty, and charm. They had a lovely child.

Then, when American fortunes were in doubt, he performed the one unforgivable act: he tried to deliver into the hands of the enemy his comrades, his commander in chief, and his struggling country. And he very nearly succeeded.

Benedict Arnold's treachery can probably never be fully explained or understood. To the extent that it can, here is the whole incredible tale, based on firsthand evidence and told with a compelling dramatic sweep.

Prologue

AFTER THE HARD WINTER which had nearly wiped out the remnant of the revolutionary army, spring returned to Valley Forge. In April 1778 came a promising report from abroad: France had agreed to send help to the long-oppressed colonies in America. At a time when the struggle for independence seemed doomed to defeat, the report came like a blessed reprieve, and General Washington was profoundly grateful. The camp at Valley Forge was stirring with hope again; it was swelling with men and officers, with hundreds, then thousands of volunteers.

On May 19, 1778, on a mild spring evening, a battered coach approached the ferry landing opposite Valley Forge. A young sentry stepped into the road. The Negro in the driver's box pulled on the reins, and the wheels came to a grinding halt.

"Well, what is it?" demanded a taut voice from inside the coach.

"Your pass," said the sentry, stepping closer.

The man inside pushed the curtains aside impatiently. "I'm Arnold," he said. "General Arnold. You've heard of me, eh?"

The young sentry swallowed. Everyone had heard of General Arnold, the Hannibal of the American army. From Quebec to Saratoga, his exploits had electrified the country. The sentry raised his lantern. He saw the stern hawklike features of the hero, the blue eyes curiously pale in the swarthy face. A short broad-shouldered man in his late thirties, Arnold was wearing gold epaulets on his blue and buff uniform; his bandaged leg lay stiffly on a pillow, his crutches propped against the window.

The sentry waved his lantern to the bargemen by the landing. "It's General Arnold!" he said, and the bargemen hurried to unhitch the horses. They pulled the coach onto the flatboat, lashed it down, and with their poles pushed the flatboat from the bank.

While the boat moved slowly across the black Schuylkill River, Arnold glanced out the coach window. On the far shore, to the north, rose the clustering hills of the camp at Valley Forge; to the south, some twenty miles below, lay Philadelphia, the largest city in America and for the past nine months the enemy-occupied capital. Tonight frequent bursts of fireworks could be seen over the city—the enemy appeared to be celebrating an important event.

Arnold's gaze returned and rested on his crippled leg. Since last October he'd spent most of his time in military hospitals flat on his back. Now, though his left leg was still festering at the kneecap and he couldn't get about without crutches, he wasn't altogether out of commission. The leg would mend, he'd always been strong as a bull, and he didn't intend to be put on the shelf, not after all he'd done to make a place for himself.

BEFORE THE WAR he had been in business. At twenty-one he had opened his own pharmacy and bookstore in New Haven. At twenty-six he left the store in his sister's charge and went into the West Indies trade. For half a dozen years he sailed his own sloops in the Caribbean, carrying horses from Canada to tropical ports, and returning home with cargoes of rum, molasses, and mahogany.

When he heard of the Boston Massacre he wrote home from Jamaica: "Good God! Are Americans all asleep and tamely giving up their glorious liberties?" He sailed for New Haven and threw all his driving energies into the revolutionary struggle. At last he had found a great cause in which to satisfy his hunger for heroic action, his craving for admiration and applause.

But almost as soon as he started to carve his public image, he found himself embroiled in a private warfare.

In the spring of 1775 he proposed the audacious attack on Fort Ticonderoga, the royal arsenal on the east shore of Lake Champlain. It meant the first open act of war against the mother country. He applied to the Massachusetts Assembly for a colonel's commission, but by the time he launched the expedition, his right to command was contested by Ethan Allen and the wild Green Mountain Boys from Vermont, who had set out on the mission just ahead of him. Arnold was forced to share the command with Allen, and nearly every step of the march on Ticonderoga was marked by bitter disputes between the two leaders. As they drew near the fort they broke into a race, each making a strenuous effort to be first to enter it. "Surrender!" Allen shouted to the sleeping garrison. "In the name of Jehovah and the Continental Congress!"

Even after they had taken the arsenal with its much needed guns, the dispute continued.

In May, when Arnold returned to New Haven, he learned that his wife had died during his absence, leaving him with three young sons; his spinster sister, Hannah, was taking care of the children.

In July of the same year, pursuing a new plan—a surprise attack on Canada—Arnold went to Cambridge and met with the recently appointed commander of the people's army, General George Washington. A cool and perceptive judge of men, Washington put Arnold in charge of the overland expedition against Quebec, while another force, under General Richard Montgomery, set out for Montreal by way of the Hudson River.

Leading eleven hundred men, Arnold left in September and made one of the hardest marches in the annals of war. For six weeks he and his volunteers fought their way through swamps, virgin forests, mountainous rocks, chasms, and raging torrents. They lugged two hundred boats, loaded with supplies, till the boats fell apart. Halfway through the march, a part of the troops deserted, taking most of the provisions; the rest staggered northward, with Arnold in the vanguard, beating their way through cold November rainstorms, through snow, half starving and half naked. For food they boiled their shoes and their leather breeches and chewed their cartridge pouches. After a march of nearly four hundred miles they emerged on the banks of the St. Lawrence, six hundred tattered rebel survivors Arnold had held together. In front of them, on the north side of the river, lay Quebec, a fortress with stone walls thirty feet high and a mile long, mounted with guns.

Arnold pitched camp and planned to lay siege to the fort. But when

Montgomery joined him from Montreal, he changed his plans. At midnight, on the last day in December, 1775, under cover of a blinding snowstorm, they attacked. Carrying scaling ladders, they climbed the stone walls and penetrated the town. Sir Guy Carleton and his French-Canadians gave them a furious reception: Montgomery was killed, Arnold wounded in the left leg by a musket ball, the invaders driven out or captured.

Arnold was carried back to camp, and there he rallied the survivors and prepared to lay siege. Through the bitter winter months he sent urgent pleas to Congress for supplies and reinforcements, but his pleas were largely ignored. The gentlemen were still divided as to the wisdom of breaking with the mother country; and meanwhile General John Burgoyne was on his way across the Atlantic with an army of ten thousand.

In June 1776, when Burgoyne was already sailing up the St. Lawrence River, Arnold, now a brigadier general, reluctantly prepared to retreat. Before he left he obtained supplies for his battered men. His rivals—Colonel Moses Hazen, Major John Brown, among others—accused him of plundering the merchants in Montreal; he had forced them to accept his worthless IOUs at the point of a bayonet, they charged. At St. Johns he put the last of his men into canoes; then, having stayed long enough to give a measured glance at the royal grenadiers emerging from the green forest, he shot his own horse and pushed off from the shore. The first rebel to enter Canada, he was the last one to leave it.

Some weeks later, while the gentlemen in Congress were debating whether to declare for independence, Arnold was on the lower end of Lake Champlain, building a flotilla against the pursuing enemy. In the Battle of Valcour Island in the fall of 1776 he engaged the forces of Carleton and Burgoyne with their huge reinforcements from overseas. Against hopeless odds he fought with daring and resourcefulness; and although in the end he was obliged to burn his own boats and escape on foot, he had delayed the enemy long enough to upset their campaign for the year—a reprieve for General Washington's hard-pressed army in New York.

Though half the country was singing his praises, not all in the army were impressed. Some of his fellow officers were annoyed by his acrobatic feats, his hairbreadth escapes, his ability to turn a bad situation to his own advantage. Others resented his growing fame. Major Brown pressed charges accusing Arnold of "great misconduct" in Canada, of disobeying his superiors, of having recklessly lost the fleet on Lake Champlain. Colonel Hazen demanded that Arnold be court-martialed.

When Arnold tried to collect from Congress the sums he claimed to have advanced to the army out of his own pocket, the Treasury Board held up settlement, on account of some missing vouchers. Missing vouchers! As if a commander of troops that endured such desperate trials could have kept track of every penny he spent for bread, shoes, medicine, arms, horses, and boats, for every pound of flour and every peck of nails!

When Congress promoted five of his juniors over his head, while delaying his own promotion to major general, Arnold tendered his resignation. Washington patiently asked him to reconsider for the good of the service, and Arnold was persuaded. "Although I sensibly feel the ingratitude of my countrymen," he wrote to Washington, "every interest shall be buried in my zeal for the safety and happiness of my country."

He soon had a fresh chance to prove his zeal. In April 1777 Connecticut was threatened by two thousand redcoats and Hessians landing along Long Island Sound. The moment the news reached Arnold he set out to defend his native shores. He rounded up some five hundred volunteers and with himself in front as the flying target hurled himself against the enemy. His example, his repeated exposure in the most dangerous spots, his coolness under fire encouraged the raw militiamen.

In one hotly contested action near Ridgefield his horse was shot from under him. Arnold tried to spring free, but his foot got caught in the stirrup. He fell, and a redcoat rushed up to him with pointed bayonet.

"You're my prisoner!" cried the redcoat.

"Not yet," said Arnold, and drew his pistol and shot the man. He rolled into the brush in a hail of musket fire, his hat full of bullet holes. Then he rose and rallied his scattered troops, and at Compo Point the British were driven back to their ships.

A few days later Congress commissioned Arnold as major general, but neglected to restore his seniority in rank.

Then came Saratoga. In the late summer of 1777 Arnold begged General Horatio Gates, commander of the northern army, to launch an offensive against Burgoyne. But Gates had made up his mind to take Burgoyne in a less costly way: by cutting off his supply lines. He refused to credit the alarming reports that Sir Henry Clinton was sailing up the Hudson to reinforce Burgoyne. If the two joined forces at Albany, some thirty miles below them, the country would be cut in two.

Arnold waited, then took things in his own hands. On September 19 he spearheaded an attack at Freeman's farm. Though Burgoyne's veterans were mauled and forced to fall back, Gates was furious. He forbade Arnold to plan another offensive. In councils of war he treated him "like a cipher." Arnold endured the treatment for a few days, then tendered his resignation, asking to go to Philadelphia to join General Washington. Gates jumped at the chance to get rid of the thorn in his side; he relieved Arnold of command and issued a pass for him and his aides.

Although burning with impatience, Arnold hung about camp; he didn't want to leave. On October 7, when Burgoyne was already advancing, Gates acted. But instead of a major attack, he indulged in cautious harassing operations. To Arnold the hour no longer seemed postponable.

"No man shall keep me to my tent today!" he cried, mounting his stallion and riding through camp. Without an official command or the right to give orders, he called to the men, summoning them like a trumpet of war, and many followed him gladly.

On a hilltop west of Bemis Heights stood Colonel Breymann's redoubt: its blazing guns protected Burgoyne's main column. That was the stronghold to be taken. "Victory or death!" cried Arnold, pointing his broadsword and riding toward it. The men pushed after him up the long unending slope that tilted skyward from the river. Gates sent out Major John Armstrong to recall the madman, but Arnold could not be overtaken. At times he was lost to view in clouds of smoke; at other times he could be glimpsed on the horizon, a swiftly moving bird of prey, plunging toward the far redoubt as if searching for death, as if blind to the unceasing crossfire.

Moving diagonally, Arnold led the way to the north of the redoubt, the open side, the side Burgoyne was sure the rebels could never reach. But they reached it. They entered the works. They stormed the guns. There in the hurly-burly it happened. Arnold was urging his horse through a sally port and as he dug his spurs into its flanks a fatal bullet pierced the beast. The big stallion reared, then crashed to the ground, and Arnold's left leg took a bone-smashing blow.

He remembered that hour when he lay helpless on the hilltop above Saratoga. The din and confusion in the gathering dusk when the armies mingled and boys with smoke-blackened faces came stumbling over the hill. He remembered their shouts and cries, the unearthly shrieks of the wounded horses, the shapes of the dying around him. And in the distance, drifting through the haze, the sounds of a retreating enemy.

On the walls of Quebec it had been young General Montgomery who had been killed; on the heights of Saratoga, where a thousand fell, Arnold was carried from the field alive. His time hadn't come, not yet.

WHEN THE FLATBOAT reached the far shore, the bargemen rolled out Arnold's coach and hitched up the horses. A party of officers had come down to the landing, among them Washington's aide, young Colonel Alexander Hamilton, to escort Arnold to the camp at Valley Forge. Behind them a fresh burst of fireworks lit up the skies over Philadelphia. "General Howe's farewell party," remarked Colonel Hamilton. "He's been recalled to England. Clinton is replacing him."

Early next morning Arnold left his quarters to pay his respects to General Washington. Limping through camp, he saw a number of familiar faces; when some of the men cheered him, Arnold smiled, with a hint of his old daredevil smile. As he hobbled into the small stone house which served as the general's headquarters, Washington stood up from his worktable to greet him with unusual warmth.

"I'm happy to have you with us." The majestically built farmer from Virginia took Arnold's free hand in both of his and pressed it. He helped him into a chair, his eyes resting on the short dark man with affection. The commander in chief considered Arnold one of his best officers and in reports to Congress had praised him repeatedly.

The general spoke of his immediate plans. "I wish you to attend our next council of war," he told Arnold. "I have an important post in mind for you, a post of high honor."

At the council Washington read the latest intelligence from Philadelphia. "No doubt remains," he said, "but that Clinton is ready to evacuate the city. He's packing, he may start for New York any day. And this should give us the opportunity to strike a blow."

The question was whether to risk a blow which might bring on a general action or to limit themselves to harassing operations. Some of the generals were in favor of a major stroke, but some were against even a partial blow.

"We mustn't take the offensive," General Charles Lee warned Washington in his emphatic manner. "We aren't strong enough to risk it! Let Clinton withdraw to New York. When the French alliance takes effect it will be more potent than anything we could do now!"

Arnold, unwilling to make combat plans for others, sat through the council, his game leg propped on a chair, without a word. After the meeting, Washington told him what he had in mind.

"When Clinton evacuates Philadelphia, I wish you to enter the city and serve as its military governor. It's a post of honor. An important and difficult post. The most important I can offer you." Arnold smiled, pleased. A post of honor, indeed!

A few days later Arnold drove out to the artillery park, a gun-ringed hilltop, and found Henry Knox. The stout young brigadier was sitting by a camp table surrounded by howitzers, his nose buried in a French artillery manual.

"I've come to renew my oath," Arnold informed him. Knox promptly produced the form. Leaning on a heavy cane to favor his leg, Arnold repeated the words after Knox:

"I, Benedict Arnold, Major General, do acknowledge the United States of America to be Free, Independent and Sovereign States, and declare that the people thereof owe no allegiance or obedience to George the Third, King of Great-Britain; and I renounce, refuse, and abjure any allegiance or obedience to him; and I do swear that I will, to the utmost of my power, support, maintain and defend the said United States . . . with fidelity, according to the best of my skill and understanding."

He signed the paper—a matter of form, of course; more than most, he had already demonstrated his loyalty.

With a glance to the south, toward the great city he was about to govern, Arnold left the hilltop.

CHAPTER 1

ARNOLD ENTERED Philadelphia on June 18, 1778, the day after the last of Sir Henry Clinton's troops had withdrawn. With a corps of Massachusetts men marching in front of him, he rode in an open coach. The air was torn with the sound of cheers, bells, drums, a booming thirteen-gun salute; thousands of his countrymen jammed the streets to catch a glimpse of him. But behind its show of welcome the capital was a hornet's nest buzzing with suspicion and ready to sting.

Though three thousand Tories had fled with the royal army, not all the twenty thousand citizens who stayed were happy with the latest change in government. Many of them had been enjoying a war boom. Although at Valley Forge the army was nearly starving, in Philadelphia the merchants and farmers had been eager to trade with the enemy. Some had made fortunes. And their daughters had entertained enemy officers in rounds of brilliant parties.

Now, with the return of the rebels, many were uneasy. The taverns were crawling with informers, the gentry afraid of reprisals, and the Sons of Liberty were rounding up suspected Tory sympathizers, denouncing them to the Committee of Safety.

Arnold was confident he could deal with the situation. He'd run the place efficiently, like an army camp. To give his office an air of authority, he set up his headquarters at Penn House, the great mansion that had served as the British headquarters. He posted sentries in front of it, hired liveried servants, and held formal receptions. One of his first official acts was to issue a proclamation suspending all trade and closing down all shops. He confiscated goods left behind by the enemy. He put the city under martial law.

The acts raised a storm of protest, and Arnold soon found himself the target of criticism. The measures had been approved by both the national Congress and the state council. The proclamation had been composed by Joseph Reed, who was a delegate to the Continental Congress and president of the Executive Council of Pennsylvania. But when the people's representatives heard the uproar which the emergency acts provoked, they were quick to shift all blame onto the military governor.

Arnold ignored the clamor. "I'll not be stung to death by insects!" He barely concealed his contempt for the politicians. The people, he thought, knew his record in the fight for independence. But he underestimated their fear and distrust of the military man in office, their anxiety to keep the military under strictest civilian control.

Reed, in particular, became his most persistent critic. A lean, puritanical politician, cautious but intensely ambitious, Reed had served on Washington's staff two years before; at the time when Washington was being forced to retreat from Long Island, Reed had tried to make terms with the enemy behind the general's back. Since then, he had grown zealous to prove himself the people's friend. He had become an almost fanatical crusader against Tories and Tory sympathizers. As president of the council, in effect the governor of Pennsylvania, he saw in Arnold a threat to his newly won power.

Line engraving of Benedict Arnold.

When Arnold issued a permit for the *Charming Nancy* to leave port, although its owners were suspected Tories, Reed accused Arnold of "usurpation of authority." A little later, when the ship had docked in Egg Harbor, New Jersey, and was threatened by enemy fire, Arnold sent army wagons from Philadelphia to remove its cargo to a safer place; Reed accused him of using public wagons for private profit.

As if deaf to the complaints, Arnold gave a big party on the Fourth of July to celebrate both the liberation of the city and the second anniversary of the Declaration of Independence.

It was a resplendent affair. Sitting in an alcove off the ballroom, his game leg propped on a hassock, Arnold watched the merrymakers with satisfaction. The musicians played the latest gavottes, and the sophisticated belles of Philadelphia whirled in the arms of glittering French officers. Liveried servants hurried through the crowded halls with silver trays of sweet cakes, fruits, liquid refreshment.

Though Joseph Reed and other members of the council looked

sourly at the display of extravagance and the guests whom they suspected of Tory sympathies, the best people in town came up to chat with Arnold, to compliment him, to cultivate his friendship.

The French ambassador informed Arnold confidentially: "Admiral d'Estaing may be expected to arrive soon, with a considerable fleet and troops." The French Alliance would help to translate the Declaration of Independence into a reality.

Robert Morris, the financier, held other views. He had signed the Declaration, he was still a member of Congress. "But believe me, General Arnold, I never considered it a practical measure. And now since the mother country is willing to grant us all we'd asked, I see little reason for prolonging a war which is ruining our economy." Privately he told his host, "We ought to think twice before rejecting the offers of the peace commissioners and allying ourselves with France, a power which has always been our greatest enemy in the past."

At intervals in the dance several of the young beauties left the ballroom to visit with their host.

Arnold observed them with interest. Some of the belles may have shown an unpatriotic hospitality to the late occupants of the city; some of them may even have attended the Mischianza, the farewell party with fireworks which Major John André had organized six weeks ago, in honor of Sir Henry Clinton, his departing chief. But Arnold wasn't one to make war on young ladies; he'd invited them to Penn House without investigating their politics.

Flushed from dancing and a little breathless, they came to take a peep at the wounded lion whom the newspapers described as the Hannibal of America. Sitting in his alcove, Arnold held court and looked with admiration at the charming girls. He saw curiosity and wonder in their shining eyes. In Peggy Shippen, youngest of three sisters, he saw something more.

A slim, blue-eyed beauty of eighteen, cool and poised, Peggy was the daughter of Judge Edward Shippen, a prominent Quaker attorney. During the occupation Peggy had been the toast of the king's officers. Major André, the most brilliant among them, had courted her, and Peggy's family wouldn't have been surprised if she married royalty. Other Philadelphia girls, less beautiful and less ambitious, had done so.

Peggy stepped up to General Arnold in a sudden rustle of silk and made a playful curtsy. Glancing up into his proud swarthy face, she smiled enchantingly. Arnold observed her, his pale eyes suddenly alert.

"You're a vision of delight, Miss Shippen," he remarked after a moment of silence. With a sigh he added, "I wish I could ask you for a dance."

Peggy smiled again. "Another time, perhaps?" She lowered her eyes demurely. Her first swift glance had been alive with recognition. She sensed the will to power in Arnold.

With a shock of surprise Arnold had caught that flash of recognition. Behind her grace and charm Peggy concealed an imperious drive of her own; she was determined to play a dazzling role in the world. Arnold sensed the similarity in their natures.

After the party he became a frequent visitor at the Shippens. His coach-and-four drew up almost daily in front of their place on Fourth Street, a red and black brick mansion with a walled garden that extended the whole block. And Punch, Arnold's faithful black servant from the West Indies, ambled in and out delivering bouquets for Miss Peggy and fine wines for Judge Shippen's table.

Practicing his most courtly manners, Arnold took special pains to cultivate Judge Shippen. The aristocratic old gentleman had been chief justice of Pennsylvania. Peggy was the apple of his eye and he considered Arnold unworthy of her little finger. But the judge had three expensive and marriageable daughters; a much-diminished income, with inflation threatening his security; and Arnold was military governor as well as a determined suitor.

On quiet evenings in the Shippen parlor Peggy would listen intently while Arnold spoke of his youth and his family. His father, a sea captain, had retired to Norwich, Connecticut, where Arnold was born; his mother had been "a pattern of piety, patience, virtue." His great-grandfather, the first Benedict Arnold, had served many years as governor of Rhode Island. As a boy Arnold had been the village daredevil, a leader in every prank. At ten he'd astonished his playmates by catching the arm of a turning mill wheel, holding on fast while the great wheel carried him high up in the air, then over and under the boiling stream, then up and around again. He was considered by many the best athlete in Connecticut; at sixteen the short broad-shouldered lad could jump over a loaded ammunition wagon without touching the bars. At school he had been outstanding in Latin and mathematics.

One evening Arnold ventured to ask Peggy about Major John André; he had heard remarks about the royal officer's playful pursuit of Peggy and he wondered how things stood. "He was a great admirer of yours, I understand?"

Peggy smiled faintly. "I found him amusing." She didn't mention that she wore a lock of André's hair as a keepsake in the little gold locket that hung from a necklace between her virginal breasts. The handsome royal officer had painted her portrait, composed sonnets to her eyebrows, designed her a fancy Turkish costume for the Mischianza.

Peggy showed Arnold the costume. "I never wore it," she explained. "Father was shocked at it." She made a woeful face, then suddenly laughed.

Peggy Shippen, from the drawing by Major André.

At least she didn't seem inconsolable because Major André had left. And she had a quality of nerve and cold passion, a love of splendor which matched his own. Together they could reach out for magnificence. Would she consent to become his bride?

He wrote his proposal to Peggy Shippen on September 25, 1778, having already asked Judge Shippen to sanction his suit. Unwilling to encourage it yet unable to prohibit it, Judge Shippen asked Peggy to defer her decision till spring. Peggy agreed.

IN THE MEANTIME, working behind the scenes, Joseph Reed and the council continued to fan public resentment against Arnold. The emergency was over, the enemy had left the city, was there any further need for a military governor?

General Arnold could be seen at the City Tavern, they said, in company of rich men who'd cornered stocks of flour, sugar, coffee, and were selling them at exorbitant prices. If Arnold wasn't also profiteering from the miseries of his country, how could he afford his extravagant way of life, his servants, parties, coach-and-four? They suspected him of trading on his official position to get a speculator's share in several privateering ventures; they suspected him of other shady financial schemes.

Unable to find evidence for their suspicions, the gentlemen seized on another inflammatory issue. On one occasion Major David Franks, Arnold's aide-de-camp, had ordered a sentry in front of Penn House to fetch a barber. The sentry had refused to do so, and Franks had cursed him roundly. The sentry's father happened to be Timothy Matlack, secretary of the council.

So a new complaint was brought against Arnold: he was trying to compel "the sons of freemen to perform menial duties." The indignant father threatened to withdraw his son from a service in which "commands are given him to obey which would lessen him in the esteem of the world."

Arnold said it was Sergeant Matlack's duty to obey an order. If Major Franks had been rude, he would apologize. "I trust I shall never countenance pride or insolence in any officer under my command," Arnold informed the secretary. At the same time he refused to be intimidated. "If the declaration that you will withdraw your son from the service and publish the reasons is intended as a threat, you have mistaken your object," he told Mr. Matlack.

Even his courtship of Peggy Shippen did not escape criticism. Mrs. Joseph Reed declared it disgraceful that a widower with three half-grown sons should be chasing after a girl twenty years younger than himself. Reed said it was a dangerous sign that Arnold should be intimate with the Shippens and their circle: Peggy's brother had been arrested as a Tory sympathizer; their rich friends were likely to be disloyal to America, in thought if not action; and Reed had reasons to believe that Arnold was becoming a "Tory-lover."

Post of honor, indeed! Arnold had had enough of it. Apart from political persecution, he was pestered by moneylenders, inflamed by his passion for Peggy, and irritated by his leg wound, which refused to mend. Before the end of the year he was ready to resign.

On the chance that he might secure a naval command, a service in which his crippled leg wouldn't be a handicap, he had written

Washington and offered to lead an expedition against the British ports in the West Indies. But nothing came of it. Arnold then asked Congress for command of a fleet of privateers. But the gentlemen turned him down.

If the country had no further use for his services, he would quit public life altogether. Veterans had been promised grants of land, and Arnold had his eye on a large tract in the Mohawk Valley in New York, not far from Saratoga.

He wrote to friends with influence in the New York assembly. They wrote back to say that they didn't expect the legislature to put any obstacles in his way: New York was well aware of the services General Arnold had rendered that state. On the strength of this, Arnold resigned his post in Philadelphia. Early in December 1778 he set out for Albany, where he expected to spend a month negotiating the land grant. But when he stopped en route at Morristown, New Jersey, where Washington now was—to pay his respects and ask the general's permission to resign from the army—he found a letter waiting for him which abruptly changed his plans.

As soon as Arnold had left Philadelphia, Reed had seized his chance and brought a series of eight charges against him. He published these in the newspapers, printed them as handbills, and laid them before Congress. He sent copies to governors in all thirteen states, with the request that they forward these to their legislatures. This included New York.

Arnold read the handbill—it was enclosed in the letter, from a well-wisher—and for a moment he was stunned. "A malicious fabrication," he said, showing it to Washington. "I'm returning to Philadelphia at once to demand a hearing." He would postpone his resignation from the army until his name was cleared.

Back in Philadelphia, he moved heaven and earth to get a prompt hearing. After three months Congress appointed a committee to investigate. When the committee found insufficient evidence and asked for proof, the council was unable to furnish any, so the committee submitted a report to Congress exonerating Arnold. The report raised a storm. Reed was unwilling to drop the charges, saying he needed more time to unearth the evidence. Congress, unwilling to antagonize the powerful council of Pennsylvania, agreed to postpone its decision.

Toward the end of March 1779, thinking that his fellow soldiers would be better judges of his conduct than civilians, Arnold petitioned for a hearing by court-martial. But Congress was unwilling to grant the army any jurisdiction in the case. Out of office, without a command, his name under a cloud, Arnold felt that he stood alone, surrounded by enemies.

CHAPTER 2

SURPRISING SOME of her friends among the belles of Philadelphia, Peggy Shippen retained her faith in Arnold's star. Her suitor was a man of destiny who would yet triumph over his persecutors. She was willing to share his fortune. Their wedding took place in a quiet ceremony in her father's house on April 8, 1779.

As a wedding gift Arnold presented his bride with an estate on Mount Pleasant—a big house with a hundred acres of orchards and gardens on the banks of the Schuylkill—and Peggy was radiant. To buy the place, Arnold had mortgaged himself to the hilt. He had made loans from moneylenders, signed IOUs, pledged his house in New Haven plus all his expectations from Congress. According to Arnold's computations Congress owed him the equivalent of twenty-five thousand dollars—sums he had advanced to the army out of his own pocket, commissions due on funds he had handled for the commissary, and his back salary.

From time to time Arnold tried to collect. Most of his claims dated from the first year of the war. He submitted his ledgers, made depositions, and appealed to Congress. The Treasury Board continued to delay the matter.

Meanwhile, with inflation reaching new heights, the money which Congress printed was becoming a currency of ridicule. More and more Arnold was inclined to share the confidential views of his guests at Mount Pleasant: the gentlemen in Congress were a plague of locusts worse than the country's former oppressors.

Most of the men who had debated and signed the Declaration of Independence were no longer members of Congress. Franklin, Jefferson, Hancock, and John Adams were serving abroad or in their home assemblies. Others were dead, on leave, in the army, or had failed to be reelected. The great senate was now reduced to twenty-odd members, most of them bickering newcomers; Arnold couldn't see a spark of genius in the whole lot.

Early in May a prisoner on parole called on him; Lieutenant Christopher Hele was a British officer who had been captured in a raid. Hele came to see Arnold on the pretext that he wished to join the American army. When Arnold informed him that, by Washington's orders, this was never done, Hele spoke in another vein.

"Both sides are weary of the war. You know this as well as I do, General Arnold." When Arnold remained silent the lieutenant went on to say, "There's need for a man of decision, someone with character to step forward and bring it to an end." Before he left, he placed a letter in a sealed envelope on Arnold's desk.

Arnold opened it. The letter was from Colonel Beverley Robinson, a rich Virginia planter and onetime friend of Washington's. Currently the colonel was raising battalions of loyalists in New York. He stood high in the councils of Sir Henry Clinton.

"Shall America continue to be but a theater of desolation?" asked Colonel Robinson. "Your lands lie fallow . . . your young men, dragged from their farms or useful trades, are harvested by war. And since your fatal alliance with France the quarrel is more envenomed than before. The exhausted colonies cannot much longer sustain the unequal contest. . . . We must seek a re-union without shedding any more blood. . . .

"One man alone can surmount the difficulties to reconciliation. Brave General Arnold: render your country this most important service! Put an end to all this misery. The American general who would reconcile His Majesty to his people, and them to him, will not only deserve the highest rewards and honors in life; he will also earn the immortal gratitude of a united people after his death!"

Arnold stared at the eloquent page. He knew that similar appeals were made from time to time to other American generals, yet now the words stood out like letters of fire. After the humiliations he had endured, the appeal made uncommon sense. The country did need a strong man, a soldier daring enough to step forward and risk the decisive step. He could see the widening prospect before him, the chance to enter a brilliant new arena, to refurbish his tarnished glory. In a single bold move he could solve a number of problems. And his fame as the champion of reunion could far outshine his past fame as a rebel.

When he showed Colonel Robinson's appeal to Peggy, she read it with quickening breath, then turned to him in a glow of admiration. "I see a great new part before you."

But he wasn't ready to act yet. Before he could make a decisive move his name must be cleared.

Again he petitioned Congress for a hearing by court-martial. Failing to get a response, he appealed to Washington. The general appointed a board, and a date was set. But the council objected: it needed more time to produce witnesses against Arnold. Another date was set, and again postponed. Arnold wrote once more to Washington and begged for a hearing without further delay.

Mount Pleasant, the Benedict Arnolds' house in Philadelphia.

A week of silence followed. No answer came. After another day of brooding he spoke to Peggy one evening in the privacy of their bedroom. "I intend to get in touch with Sir Henry Clinton."

Peggy was sitting in front of her dressing table in a pale blue negligee, brushing her hair. For a moment she paused. In the mirror, she searched the inscrutable eyes of her husband standing behind her. Was he ready to act at last, to play the strong man's part, as she hoped he would? A risky move, of course: correspondence with the enemy was a hanging matter. Yet nothing great was ever accomplished without an equally great risk.

She turned to Arnold with an encouraging smile. "We have a friend in New York, someone who may help."

"Who?"

"Major André. He wrote me from New York a few days ago." She took the note from her bureau and gave it to Arnold. Since General Howe's return to England, André had become General Clinton's favorite aide-de-camp. Arnold read the note, his face impassive.

"It would make me very happy to become useful to you here," the clever young man had written Peggy. "You know the Mischianza has made me the complete milliner." André would be glad to supply her with "capwire, needles, gauze, and other trifles, and render you service to the best of my abilities from which, I hope, you will infer a zeal to be further employed."

Arnold studied the last phrase: André was hinting at matters more important than needles or gauze.

"How did this reach you?"

"Mr. Stansbury brought it," Peggy said, locking the note in a drawer. "Our crockery man."

Joseph Stansbury ran a small shop. Occasionally the Sons of Liberty had smashed his wares, for Mr. Stansbury was suspected of Tory sympathies, but he had managed to stay in business. He had ways of slipping from town and making trips to New York, where he had useful contacts.

"I'd like to see this man," Arnold told Peggy.

The following morning Peggy sent Punch out with a shopping list, and a little later the crockery man called at General Arnold's residence. Peggy took him into the study, where Arnold sized him up. He appeared to be "a nimble, sugary, obliging little fellow," eager to be of service. With a show of frankness Arnold discussed the futility of continuing the war.

"Since Congress is blind to the country's real interest," he ended his preliminary remarks, "I now consider it my duty to take the first step." Pledging the crockery man to secrecy, Arnold told him what he had in mind. "I want you to go to New York with a message for Sir Henry Clinton. Let Sir Henry know that I am ready to offer him my services. To restore His Majesty's government and destroy the usurped authority of Congress, I am prepared to join his army at once."

For a moment Stansbury looked at the man of action with wonder. So this was the simple way in which great affairs were launched! He drew himself together. "You may count on me, General Arnold, I shall not fail you."

Arnold had put nothing in writing. If anything went wrong, who'd believe the crockery man's word against General Arnold's? But nothing would go wrong. Arnold felt sure that Clinton would welcome the offer from the hero of Saratoga. His change of sides would not only be a serious blow to rebel morale; it would bring to the enemy the services of an officer whom even the British considered among the most enterprising in Washington's army.

STANSBURY MADE THE TRIP to New York, where he met his contact, Reverend Jonathan Odell. The clergyman was on André's payroll. Among his numerous pursuits, André also directed Clinton's secret service and had dealings with an assortment of informers and double agents. As soon as Odell transmitted the surprising offer, André brought it to his chief's attention.

Clinton's headquarters were in a narrow red brick residence at No. 3 Broadway, near the Battery. There Sir Henry spent tedious hours in a high-ceilinged room he used for his private office. A stout, phlegmatic officer, forty years old, he had few friends or intimates. After four years of service in the colonies he was weary of the struggle; he wanted to return to England, to his wife and family, his fine country estate.

Lately Clinton had been delegating more and more authority to his aide-de-camp, the amiable young André. Sir Henry was fond of André and indulged him. André, for his part, was stimulated by the sense of power he derived from manipulating strings behind the scenes.

André was elated by Arnold's offer; it seemed plausible to him that his own artful note to Peggy had sparked the move. Sir Henry, however, was doubtful. He suspected a ruse on the part of the rebels. He knew that Arnold was under a cloud and without a command. "We'd best proceed with caution," he told his aide. But André was fertile with schemes. He urged Sir Henry to let him explore these. Sir Henry nodded skeptically, and André drafted a reply.

While Sir Henry was pleased to receive his offer, André indicated, he did not think that General Arnold should join the royal army at once. He could render more valuable service by remaining with the American army. He could obtain an important command and cooperate with Sir Henry. Until then, General Arnold might cooperate by furnishing Sir Henry with useful information. For example: the contents of dispatches from abroad; what reinforcements might be expected from France, and when; the number and position of the

American troops. For services rendered, Sir Henry could promise General Arnold rewards to exceed his expectations.

When Stansbury delivered this, Arnold was disappointed. He had offered his services as a soldier, but what Sir Henry proposed was a horse of another color. He considered Clinton's counterproposal, discussed it with Peggy; and they agreed that what Sir Henry suggested was not unreasonable: he wanted secret information as proof that his correspondent was really the celebrated General Arnold.

In the next three months a number of secret messages passed between Arnold and the enemy's headquarters, in a code designed by Major André. The code was in numbers, keyed to pages, lines, and words in Blackstone's *Commentaries* or Bailey's *Dictionary*; both parties had copies of the same edition of each book. Three numbers furnished the clue to each word: the first number indicated the page, the second the line, the third the word. When invisible ink was used, the method for uncovering the message was marked by the letter F for fire, A for acid. Arnold used the code names Monk or Gustavus, while André signed himself John Anderson. The agents who transmitted the messages remained Stansbury, the crockery man, and the Reverend Mr. Odell.

A nineteenth-century engraving of Major André.

Peggy helped Arnold to code and decode and, at times, to compose the notes. Raised in an attorney's household, the worldly young beauty had a quick, adroit intelligence, a flair for negotiation. She also had a natural talent for duplicity. She enjoyed her part in the dangerous game.

If Sir Henry had doubts as to Arnold's identity or good faith, Arnold on his part was also in need of more specific assurances. He was ready to risk his all; in return he wanted to be indemnified against his losses in property, both in Philadelphia and New Haven, and he wanted a reward equivalent to the risk and service involved. "I cannot promise success; I will try to deserve it." In proof of his good faith he sent Sir Henry various items of intelligence. But instead of specific guarantees he got only vague promises in answer. When he pressed for something more definite, André replied that Sir Henry "pledges himself [that your services] shall be rewarded beyond your warmest Expectations."

For Arnold this wasn't enough. "No assurance has been given me that my property in this country will be indemnified against any loss which might attend unfortunate discovery. I should hold myself unjust to my family were I to hazard all and part with a certainty for an uncertainty."

André had sent a concrete proposal. "Join the Army, accept a Command, be Surprized, be cut off—these things may happen in the Course of Manoeuvre" and no one would suspect. He sketched a plan involving Washington's army on the Hudson. "A Compleat Service of this Nature involving a Corps of 5 or 6000 Men would be rewarded with twice as many thousand Guineas."

Instead of answering in a coded note, Arnold summoned Stansbury and told him curtly, "You may inform Major André that his message isn't equal to Gustavus's expectations. Gustavus expects to be indemnified for any loss he may sustain in case of detection. Furthermore, whether this contest is finished by sword or treaty, he expects that ten thousand pounds will be assured him for his services."

When Stansbury delivered this, André again urged Arnold to act. "You must not suppose that in Case of detection or failure . . . you would be left a Victim," he wrote reassuringly. "But Services done are the terms on which we promise rewards. . . . As to an absolute promise of indemnification to the Amount of 10000 Pounds . . . whether Services are performed or not It can never be made."

Arnold dropped the correspondence for the time being. His negotiations had reached a stalemate. Hobbling about his house and garden, he spent the fall of the year at home, speculating on his next move. The gentlemen in New York had weighed his offer and found him wanting. "Join the Army, accept a Command," they said. They didn't consider a broken-kneed rebel too valuable a prize. Before he could bargain with Clinton, he must increase his value. And before he could obtain a command in Washington's army, he must clear his name of the council's charges.

His court-martial was still pending, and his situation was steadily deteriorating. Out of office, he was no longer sought after by business-men who wanted favors and could put him in the way of profitable ventures. His expenses were increasing. His sister, Hannah, and the boys had left New Haven to share his household. Peggy was pregnant. Though outwardly she tried to be gay and hopeful, she knew that his negotiations with Sir Henry were at a standstill. High-strung, tense, she was subject to fits of nerves; she wished her strong man would act decisively.

Near the end of the year, after Arnold had nearly given up hope, he received a notice. A new military court had been appointed by General Washington; the court was to convene on December 22, 1779, at Morristown, New Jersey—the army's winter quarters—to hear Major General Arnold's defense against the Pennsylvania council's charges.

At last! After all the damnable delays he had a chance to vindicate himself, and then—to obtain an important command.

WITH SOMETHING of his old zest for danger, Arnold set out for his trial at Morristown. He would act as his own attorney: no ordinary lawyer could prepare a better case for Arnold than Arnold himself.

The trial took place in the Norris Tavern, a big room with an open fireplace. It opened three days before Christmas and continued until January 26, 1780.

While the judge advocate general of the army reviewed the coun-cil's eight charges, Arnold sat stiffly, hands clasped on the knob of his heavy cane. Dressed in their regimentals, twelve of his fellow officers sat around a long table at the end of the room near the fireplace. Arnold observed the clerks, the secretaries, and the audience. He knew that the proceedings would be published and no doubt widely circulated. He intended to make the most of his opportunity.

When the judge advocate finished his review, Arnold came forward to present his defense. A lame veteran in blue and buff uniform, with the stern face of a much-injured party, he stood before the court, leaning on his cane.

Before answering the charges he asked the court's permission to read a few testimonials from Washington and the Congress as to his character and conduct. Then in the sessions that followed he took up the charges one after another.

First, that he had infringed on Washington's powers in issuing the permit for the *Charming Nancy* to leave Philadelphia. The charge was ridiculous, Arnold claimed. He had made no complaint, and did not "need the Council to defend his rights."

Second, that Arnold had closed down the shops and stores in Philadelphia, while he himself at the same time had bought up a quantity of goods for his own benefit.

Arnold's answer was emphatic. "In closing down the shops I was carrying out the instructions of both Congress and Council," he declared. "That I made any profit from this is a lie." Had the council found any evidence? His ledgers were always open to inspection, his aides could testify, they knew all his transactions. He looked at the gentlemen of the council challengingly. "Have my persecutors so little power of influence . . . as to be unable to furnish evidence of the truth?"

Reed stared at him uneasily. The council, after much investigation, had been unable to uncover any tangible evidence; yet Reed was certain that Arnold had been profiteering while in office; he suspected that Arnold had been shrewd enough to keep no records or to destroy any that had been kept.

Arnold took up the third accusation, Sergeant Matlack's objections to fetching a barber. It wasn't worth considering, in Arnold's opinion. But an order is an order, he said, and to assure the safety of the country the militia ought to be under the same discipline as the regular army.

The fourth charge, that he had taken a profiteer's share in the prize sloop, the *Active:* this had already been investigated by the grand jury of Philadelphia and had been dropped for lack of evidence. Arnold referred to it only briefly.

He came to the fifth charge, that he had used public wagons to transport private property. The wagons had been idle at the time, Arnold explained, the property in danger of destruction. He had felt it his duty to save it. He had been willing to pay for the use of the wagons, although since then the boss of the teamsters had doubled the price of hire—on advice of the council—and was currently suing Arnold for twice the original amount.

"Is it not very extraordinary," asked Arnold, "that I should be accused and tried before this honorable court for employing public wagons and, at the same time and by the same persons, be prosecuted in a civil court of Pennsylvania for employing the same wagons as private property?" The matter was ambiguous and Arnold's explanation did little to clarify it. Reed suspected that Arnold had been well paid by the owners for removing their property, but he was unable to produce any proof.

Arnold took up the last three complaints, one concerning the issuing of a travel permit, another alleging disrespect to the council, and finally his favoritism toward Tory sympathizers while neglecting the claims of patriots. Summing up his defense, he took pains to review his army record. A brilliant record, no one could deny. "I have ever obeyed the calls of my country, and stepped forth in her defense, in every hour of danger, when many were deserting her cause, which appeared desperate: I have often bled in it; the marks that I bear, are sufficient evidence of my conduct."

Before closing, he took a parting shot at the man whom he considered his chief persecutor, the president of the council. Everyone had heard of Joseph Reed's conduct when that gentleman was on Washington's staff in the summer of 1776. Arnold raised his voice to condemn his accuser.

"Conscious of my own innocence and of the unworthy methods taken to injure me, I can with boldness say to my persecutors in general and to the chief of them in particular"—he glanced at Reed sardonically—"that in the hour of danger when the affairs of America wore a gloomy aspect and our illustrious general was retreating through New Jersey with a handful of men, I did not propose . . . to quit the general and sacrifice the cause of my country to my personal safety by going over to the enemy! . . . This is more than a ruling member of the Council of the State of Pennsylvania can say, 'as it is alleged and believed!' "

A burst of coughing, a sudden shuffling of feet could be heard as Reed started to rise, face white with anger; Arnold turned away from him with a smile of contempt. He looked at his judges with resolution. He had confidence in "the judgment of my fellow soldiers. I shall (I doubt not) stand honorably acquitted of all the charges brought against me and again share with them the glory and danger of this just war."

So Major General Benedict Arnold ended his defense, and with a bow to the court he clomped back to his chair. The stern-faced veteran sat stiffly, as if indifferent to the nods and murmur of comment that eddied through the tavern.

ARNOLD RETURNED to Philadelphia toward the end of January, 1780. Before he left, the gentlemen had hinted that he could expect a favorable verdict at an early date, and Arnold was confident.

Week followed week, however, without any announcement. The court finally sent its report to Congress in the middle of March, and Congress made recommendations and forwarded them to the commander in chief. But Washington delayed announcing his decision. Arnold became increasingly restless. His position was not improving. The moneylenders refused to make further loans; he was in danger of losing his home; Peggy's baby was due.

On March 19 Peggy was in labor. Three women were with her in the bedroom on the second floor—her mother, her sister-in-law Hannah, and a midwife. The women were increasingly worried; Peggy was screaming with pain; her tense young body was violently resisting the delivery.

Arnold waited in the garden, listening to the ever-sharpening cries which came from behind the curtained windows. He felt utterly helpless. Peggy was his dearest treasure; nothing must happen to her. When her cries finally stopped, the stillness was terrifying.

Arnold hobbled into the house and upstairs. The bedroom door opened, and he saw the bed where Peggy lay motionless but breathing, her body covered with a sheet. A hard delivery. Then he heard a small sharp wail, and one of the women held up a small bundle to him. "A boy," she said; and, standing in the doorway, Benedict Arnold looked at his newborn son. Another spur, another hostage to fortune.

Three weeks later the verdict he had been waiting for was made public. He was cleared of all but two charges. On these two he was sentenced to a public reprimand.

Washington issued it in his General Orders of the day; it was read before the army on April 6, 1780:

"The Commander in Chief would have been much happier . . . bestowing commendations on an officer who has rendered such distinguished services to his Country as Major General Arnold; but in the present case a sense of duty and a regard to candor oblige him to declare, that he considers his conduct in the instance of the permit, as peculiarly reprehensible, both in a civil and military view, and in the affair of the waggons as 'Imprudent and improper.' "

Arnold could hardly believe it. A public reprimand! For what? For nothing. Was this a way to clear his name? By stamping his conduct as "peculiarly reprehensible . . . imprudent and improper"? The reprimand was another proof of injustice, an example of the treatment he could expect from his ungrateful country.

If he had had any doubts as to his decision to join the British, the reprimand had removed the last traces of them. The facts were plain: the country wasn't capable of independence. Its raw new politicians didn't know the art of government, nor how to treat its great men. A bold hand was needed to put an end to the revolution.

Always adroit in justifying his motives, Arnold didn't feel he was planning to betray his country; he was balancing the scales of justice. If the truth were known, he was the one betrayed—betrayed by his blundering countrymen, in whose service he had crippled himself, betrayed by his chief, whom he had served unstintingly.

He no longer saw the larger outline of the desperate struggle for independence. He was blind to the hopes and sacrifices of the people, to their faith in the future. And he was blind to the strength of its elected commander, the quiet farmer from Virginia who had endured tribulations as severe as Arnold's yet could never betray the cause. What Benedict Arnold saw was the way he could wield a master stroke to avenge his humiliations.

West Point was the key. Washington had turned it into the country's last great arsenal. The British commander was well aware of its importance; the control of West Point would decide the contest. To gain command of the citadel would not be easy. But the lame soldier was determined to obtain it.

On July 15, 1780—a year after he had made his first offer to Clinton —he sent Major André a note in code.

"If I point out a plan of cooperation by which Sir Henry shall possess himself of West Point, the Garrison, &. &. &. twenty thousand pounds Sterling I think will be a cheap purchase for an object of so much importance."

A cheap purchase, indeed!

CHAPTER 3

E VENTS WERE PLAYING into Arnold's hands in the summer of 1780. The long struggle for independence was entering its last most critical phase. Aided by Arnold's earlier reports, Sir Henry had captured Charleston, South Carolina, with its garrison of five thousand. Leaving Lord Cornwallis in charge in the South, he returned to New York, where he was expecting strong naval reinforcements. He was eager now to put an end to the rebellion as quickly as possible.

At the same time, the young Marquis de Lafayette had returned from Europe to report that the French fleet would be coming, with troops, to join the Americans; in anticipation of this, Washington began to make fresh preparations. He was badly in need of experienced officers.

In Philadelphia there were more than a few among Arnold's critics who, remembering his military services, now felt that he had been shabbily treated. Arnold was aware of the thaw in the cold war against him; he made the most of it.

"My wounds are mending," he advised the gentlemen in Congress. "I hope to rejoin the army very soon." To the delegates from New York, Arnold underscored the strategic importance of West Point. "Our forts on the Hudson are in increasing danger," he pointed out. "Now, more than ever, West Point needs the presence of an experienced commander. . . . Although the condition of my leg doesn't yet permit me to walk or ride with ease, my past experience may qualify me for the West Point command."

He hoped that his friends from New York would use their influence on his behalf. They did. Philip Schuyler paid a personal visit to Washington to recommend Arnold's appointment; Washington appeared to have no objections. "The general dwelt on your abilities, your merits, your sufferings," Schuyler reported to Arnold, "and the well-deserved claims you have on your country."

Arnold had reasons to think that he had paved the way to the command. Early in July he made further preparations. He left on a trip to New Haven, to sell his house and wind up his affairs there. When he returned to Philadelphia he found the place in considerable excitement. The most recent news was that a part of the French fleet, under Rochambeau, had arrived in Rhode Island and that Sir Henry was preparing to blockade it. Arnold also learned, from confidential sources, that General Washington was preparing a surprise attack on New York.

He informed Sir Henry of the latter plan, sending a message in code via Stansbury, along with the report that he, Arnold, expected to be appointed to the command of West Point within a short time. He then notified Congress that he was leaving for the Hudson to join Washington's army at Tappan. He needed funds to buy field equipment, he said, and again referred to his long overdue claims. This time Congress advanced him twenty-five thousand dollars, "subject to further accounting."

Then he said good-by to Peggy and his infant son; he would send for them soon. "Rest easy, my love," he told his beautiful young wife, "all will be well." She looked at him with pride and anxiety in her bright nervous eyes. The decisive event was near.

On the last day of July, 1780, Arnold reported to Washington on the west bank of the Hudson about ten miles below West Point. The general, on horseback, was observing his troops through his field glass from a rise of land above Stony Point. Though it was late in the afternoon the light was still strong, and the bronze-tinted waters of the river showed a line of flatboats and barges crowded with men and horses, the last of the detachments, crossing King's Ferry toward Verplanck's Point on the east side of the Hudson. In preparation for the march on New York nearly seven thousand troops had been ferried across the river.

Arnold rode up to the general. "I have come to report for duty, sir," he said.

Washington lowered his field glass and half turned in his saddle. "I am glad you are with us again, General Arnold." A smile of welcome warmed his craggy face. "We need you, more than ever."

"Have you thought of something for me, sir?" Arnold sat his horse stiff and erect, his heavy cane fastened to the pommel of his saddle.

"I have," said Washington. His eyes rested on the proud soldier whom he had been obliged to reprimand publicly. Arnold waited tensely, his face like a mask of stone.

"You shall have the command of honor," he heard Washington's encouraging words. "The left wing is yours." Arnold would have a chance to earn fresh laurels; he could spearhead the attack on the port of New York.

Not West Point, but the left wing! For a moment Arnold could hardly believe his ears. He tried to conceal his shock of disappointment. Had he made too much of his eagerness to serve his country and too little of his wounds which unfitted him for active service? With a bare nod he turned and rode from Stony Point.

River view from a blockhouse at West Point, early nineteenth century.

General Orders of the following day confirmed Washington's decision: "Major General Arnold will command the left wing."

The same morning Arnold rode into the village of Tappan and located the army's headquarters. Dismounting slowly, with deliberate effort, he hobbled in and found the general's busy young aides, colonels Alexander Hamilton and Tench Tilghman. The general himself had already crossed the Hudson.

"The general has offered me the left wing," Arnold explained to Colonel Hamilton. "I am honored, of course. . . . But I may have to decline such an active command. My wounds are still in a bad way." He shifted his cane. "I hoped the general might assign me to West Point." The lame hero of Saratoga looked at Hamilton earnestly; Hamilton's quick dark eyes glanced at Tilghman. It seemed out of character for fire-eating Arnold to solicit garrison duty, but his wounds were no doubt the explanation.

"I shall remind the general," Colonel Hamilton promised.

Two days later Washington was obliged to change his plans for the march on New York; Clinton had withdrawn his expedition to Rhode Island, the French had safely landed their troops at Newport, and Washington recrossed the Hudson with his army to set up camp at Tappan again. With an active campaign against New York no longer practicable, he made a change in Arnold's appointment. On August 3, 1780, a postscript to the General Orders of the day announced: "Major General Arnold will command at West Point."

Arnold promptly set up his headquarters at Robinson House, a private residence on the east bank of the Hudson opposite West Point—a part actually of the confiscated estate of Colonel Beverley Robinson, the same Colonel Robinson who had joined the British side and who had written the original letter to Arnold suggesting that he work with the British. Set on a high bluff, the two-story country house was perched among huge rocks and wooded ravines above the river in the wild and gloomy Hudson Highlands. It had no neighbor within a mile.

For his office Arnold used a part of the living room on the ground floor—a large square room with a fieldstone fireplace, oak ceiling beams, fine wainscoting, and doors opening to a terrace and garden. From the windows by his worktable Arnold could see the ramparts of West Point; through his field glass he could pick out the tiny figures of the sentries. Smaller adjoining rooms were used by Arnold's aides, Major David Franks and Colonel Richard Varick. A wide staircase on the south end led to the bedrooms upstairs.

Below Robinson House, at the foot of the bluff, stood a small dock, where Arnold kept a boat with a crew of six at his constant disposal. It was an old whaleboat which Arnold used on his trips up and down and across the river; it was known as "the General's Barge." The path from house to dock, winding among slabs of jagged rocks and clumps of stunted alders, was steep and usually half hidden by veils of mist from a falls nearby.

As commander of West Point, Arnold was in control over an area of some sixty square miles. The territory included half a dozen forts on both sides of the Hudson; outposts and dependencies in four counties; twelve miles of the river, from Constitution Island to King's Ferry—a vital part, for the crossing at King's Ferry was the last remaining passage open to the revolutionary army.

Much of the area was overhung with an air of desolation. After four years of war the once flourishing Hudson Valley had become a region of abandoned farms, burned-out houses with gaping windows and blackened chimneys. The wagon roads on both sides of the river were overgrown with weeds, the bordering fields and orchards fast turning back into wilderness. The thrifty Dutch and English farmers had been repeatedly pillaged by both the rebels and the king's men, and some had been murdered in their beds. The remaining country people, hostile and suspicious, barricaded their doors at night and kept their muskets handy. Parties of dangerous young men were prowling about the area on the east side of the river, in White Plains and the no-man's-land around Dobbs Ferry. They called themselves "skinners" if pro-American and "cowboys" if pro-British. They stole cattle and preyed on passersby; the lower Westchester County roads were no longer safe for unarmed travelers.

SIR HENRY CLINTON's reply reached Arnold after some delay. Coded by André, the message from New York stated that Sir Henry was eager to cooperate; he was willing to pay Arnold twenty thousand pounds sterling.

Before taking the final step Arnold wanted a personal meeting with Sir Henry's representative, one fully authorized to discuss terms— Major André, who had recently been made adjutant general to the British army, or possibly Colonel Beverley Robinson, his original contact. The interview would take place at Arnold's quarters, opposite West Point; it would have to be arranged discreetly.

Since he needed a more direct way of communicating with New York—Stansbury was no longer useful—Arnold searched for a new go-between. On August 5, two days after obtaining the command, he wrote audaciously to General Robert Howe, the commander whom he had relieved at West Point: "As the safety of this post and garrison in a great measure depends on having good intelligence of the movements and designs of the enemy, and as you have been fortunate in the agents you have employed for that purpose, I must request to be informed who they are, as I wish to employ them for the same purpose." General Howe gave Arnold the name of Joshua Hett Smith, Esquire.

Arnold was soon in touch with the gentleman. Smith lived near Haverstraw Bay, on the west side of the Hudson, some miles south of West Point, where he owned a big hilltop house and a farm. A plump, red-faced man of thirty, with a complacent smile, shrewd eyes, and a sly manner, Smith was anxious to retain his property. He played the patriot while keeping his eyes open to his own advantage.

At first, while sizing up the man, Arnold made use of Smith in smaller deals. To obtain better provisions for his larder, he traded flour and pork—which he had appropriated from the commissary—for more palatable items which Smith was able to procure from New York. Arnold's young aides, Franks and Varick, suspected the illegal barters; they despised Smith and tried to make allowances for their chief, whom both admired as a military hero. Neither of the young men had any inkling of the true direction of his activities.

Finally, on August 30, Arnold wrote to André, camouflaging his meaning by proposing a business interview with "John Anderson," a merchant in New York.

In anticipation of the rendezvous, Arnold notified Colonel Elisha Sheldon to be on the lookout for a young merchant from New York; Sheldon was in charge of the cavalry outpost at North Castle, some ten or twelve miles inland from Dobbs Ferry—he himself dealt with agents and he knew it was Arnold's duty to obtain enemy intelligence. If Mr. Anderson should come by way of Dobbs Ferry, which was in the British zone, and should reach North Castle, he was to be given safe-conduct to General Arnold.

Before the big changes took place Arnold wanted to have his family with him. He knew that after he had met with André and set the time and terms of the sale, events would move fast, and the possible fury of his countrymen was not left out of his calculations. So, at the same time as he made arrangements for the meeting with André, he sent Major Franks to Philadelphia to escort Peggy and the baby to Robinson House. A week should be sufficient for the journey. If all went according to plan, Peggy should be with him by September 10.

THE MILITARY SITUATION of the rebels was not improving. On September 6, Washington called an emergency council of war in Tappan. Gathered around a table behind closed doors, his key officers—including Knox, Lafayette, Nathanael Greene, Arnold, and others—heard Washington review the dismal state of affairs. For lack of provisions, the general had been obliged to dismiss half the militia; the starving men had been foraging the countryside. The regular troops were also disgruntled for lack of food or pay. The general had sent Congress a number of warnings: "The army must either disband, cease to exist, or live upon the plunder of the people. . . . To me it will appear miraculous if our affairs can maintain themselves much longer." But Congress was unable to help.

Only a part of the French fleet had arrived and landed troops, at Newport; its second division was missing. Meanwhile, fresh reinforcements from the royal navy had reached Clinton in New York, giving the enemy a decided advantage at sea.

The worst news was from South Carolina. "Gates has lost the battle at Camden," said Washington with a gray face. The officers had already heard the black report: Gates had fled before Cornwallis with disgraceful precipitation; the bulk of his army had surrendered; Virginia was open to invasion, the South as good as lost. "Gates," remarked Arnold with a scornful smile. "His name will live in infamy."

Washington was pinning his remaining hopes on the French. "The missing division should arrive any day," he said. "I expect to meet with Rochambeau shortly." In the meantime, since Clinton might decide on a move up the river, they must be on guard against any surprise attack. General Arnold must be particularly alert. "I want you to put West Point in the most defensible state possible," Washington told Arnold. The general had already ordered the transfer of the army's munitions to West Point.

"You may be sure I am doing all I can," Arnold assured his chief.

Arnold arrived back at West Point later the same afternoon. At the foot of the Point a number of men were at work on the dock, unloading barrels of precious powder, fieldpieces, and howitzers; flatboats and barges were still bringing these up the river from Tappan for safekeeping in the arsenal.

Arnold climbed the trail from the landing and made his way into the ramparts. In spite of the money and labor that had gone into strengthening the works, West Point was hardly in "the most defensible state possible." Some of the walls were broken, some were built of dry wood and could easily be set on fire. The approaches from the back-country roads were open, the walls in the rear of the fort, to the west, unfinished.

Colonel John Lamb, a grizzled, hard-bitten old veteran, was Arnold's second in command at the Point. Arnold located him now and asked for certain reports. "I must have an inventory of all the stores, with the total number of guns and the number of men in the garrison. Also, I want a copy of the plan for the disposition of the troops in case of alarm. Send these to me as soon as you can." Then Arnold asked whether the garrison had obtained its supply of winter fuel.

"Two hundred men are cutting wood at Fishkill."

"Send two hundred more," said Arnold.

"We can't spare so many. Not if the fort's to be safe from attack."

"Send them out," Arnold insisted. "You must have fuel to keep warm this winter."

A French map of West Point in 1780.

Before leaving, he looked up the French engineer who was working on a map of the fortifications. Arnold wanted a copy. "It must show the position of each new redoubt and battery," said Arnold. "It's important that I have it soon." The engineer promised to prepare it and then called Arnold's attention to the condition of the chain across the river.

The great iron chain stretched from West Point to Constitution Island to stop the passage of enemy ships. Buoyed by floating logs, each link in it weighed nearly two hundred pounds; one of its center links was reportedly damaged and coming apart.

"Have it removed," said Arnold. "It must be repaired or replaced." He knew that the blacksmith's work would take weeks. In the meantime the great chain, held together by a strand of rope, could easily be broken by a loaded ship—a matter which Sir Henry was bound to appreciate.

WHEN THREE MORE DAYS went by without a reply from André, Arnold became restless. Had his business letter to John Anderson been intercepted? The answer was brought unexpectedly by two young American officers who called at Robinson House on Sunday morning, September 10. They were from the outpost at North Castle: Lieutenant Colonel John Jameson had relieved Colonel Sheldon, who was ailing, while Major Benjamin Tallmadge commanded a detachment which patrolled the area between North Castle and Dobbs Ferry. Tallmadge was also in charge of Washington's secret service. The young men were puzzled by a letter which had been sent to Colonel Sheldon from New York.

"It reached us yesterday," said Jameson, showing Arnold the letter. "Colonel Sheldon's too ill to attend to it, and I myself don't know what to make of it."

Arnold scanned it with expressionless face.

"I am told that my name is known to you," André had written to Colonel Sheldon, "and that I may hope your indulgence in permitting me to meet a friend near your outpost. I will try to obtain permission to go out with a flag of truce which will be sent to Dobbs Ferry next Monday the eleventh at twelve o'clock noon when I shall be happy to meet Mr. Gustavus. . . . Let me entreat you, sir, to favor a matter so interesting to the parties concerned and which is of so private a nature that the public on neither side can be injured by it." The letter was signed "John Anderson, Merchant."

Arnold saw at once that the letter was dangerously indiscreet: André had set the time and place for their rendezvous, but he had also called attention to it by stating that he would "try to go out with a flag of truce." A flag of truce! What an extraordinary way of keeping their meeting a secret! Arnold glanced appraisingly at the two candid young officers in front of him.

"Thank you, gentlemen, for bringing the matter to my attention so promptly," he said in a tone of approval. "I am opening up a new line of intelligence from New York and am glad to hear from Mr. Anderson. . . . I've already mentioned the matter to Colonel Sheldon."

"Do you expect to meet this man yourself?" asked Major Tallmadge.

"I do," said Arnold casually. "The information he brings may be quite valuable."

The young men wondered about the name Gustavus.

"Oh yes," Arnold explained, "when I wrote to Mr. Anderson I signed myself Gustavus—as a precaution, you understand—to prevent any suspicion falling on him in case my note was intercepted."

Jameson was satisfied. "If it's in your hands, General Arnold, everything's in order, I'm sure." Tallmadge said nothing.

Arnold poured them drinks.

After the young men left, Arnold gave orders to get the barge ready for an overnight trip. He would spend the night at Smith's house, which was about halfway to Dobbs Ferry.

Next morning, after a quick breakfast with Smith, Arnold went to the boat dock below Smith's house. A thick fog shrouded the river; the autumn air was chilly. Wrapping his cloak around his shoulders, Arnold climbed into the barge and ordered the men to row downstream. While the men bent over their oars, he sat in the stern and kept a watchful eye.

Hidden by veils of mist, the barge moved down a ghostly river toward the enemy zone. When they passed Teller's Point on the east bank the morning sun broke through. Arnold raised his field glass from time to time—he was on the lookout for patrol boats, but saw none. Passing the western shore at Tappan near where Washington's army was camped, Arnold scanned the shore vigilantly. If a sentry should observe their passage, he would challenge the barge. But no one challenged them.

Toward noon, approaching Dobbs Ferry, Arnold caught sight of the *Vulture*, the enemy ship which had undoubtedly brought André to the rendezvous. She was anchored off the east shore with pennants flying, and her decks were lined with a dozen fat brass cannon. Three or four small gunboats were idling in the waters around her.

"Lay to!" said Arnold, pointing to the *Vulture*. Instead of waiting to meet André on shore, Arnold would visit him aboard ship. But not wanting to attract attention to his visit, Arnold did not display a flag of truce. As the barge drew near the warship one of the gunboats suddenly opened fire. The others followed suit, and all at once a deadly shower of bullets was hissing over Arnold and his crew.

Astonished, the bargemen stopped rowing, their oars frozen in midair. "Back, men, back!" Arnold shouted furiously. The men struggled to turn the heavy barge, while the gunboats continued to fire. One bullet struck an oar blade and shattered it, but the barge pulled out of range with no one hurt.

Arnold ordered the barge into a nearby cove. The sound of firing had attracted attention from the camp at Tappan; soldiers were already gathered on the bank, gaping at General Arnold's barge. A report of the incident would, no doubt, soon reach Washington.

Arnold climbed ashore grimly and called to one of the soldiers; a note was to be taken to General Washington's headquarters at once. Arnold rapidly wrote out his explanation: "Dear Sir: I came here this morning in order to establish signals to be observed in case the enemy came up the river . . . and to have a beacon fixed upon the mountain about five miles south of King's Ferry which will be necessary to alarm the country." He gave the note to the soldier, then climbed into the barge and ordered his crew to continue upstream, back to West Point. During the journey he sat and stared at the tide. His first attempt to meet with André had nearly cost him his life. They both had blundered. Arnold had failed to display a flag, André had failed to instruct the *Vulture*'s gunboats. Neither of them could afford to blunder again. Another meeting had to be arranged, but next time André must come to Arnold. Next time André must be the one to take the risk.

CHAPTER 4

UNLESS ARNOLD could close the deal quickly, he might find himself out on a limb. With the reinforcements from the royal navy Clinton might decide to sail up the Hudson and seize West Point—without Arnold's cooperation. There was also the danger that Washington might form a plan for joint action with the French fleet commander, Rochambeau, especially if the missing division of the fleet arrived, which again would change the balance of power.

To improve his bargaining position, Arnold collected the reports which he judged would be most valuable in negotiating with Sir Henry: the state of the defenses at West Point, the disposition of the troops and artillery, the matters discussed by Washington in the last council of war. He made copies of these on thin sheets of paper.

The rendezvous with Clinton's representative could not be delayed much longer while Arnold waited for his family. Although two weeks had elapsed since Major Franks had left to fetch her, Peggy still hadn't arrived. At last word came that Peggy and the baby had gotten as far as Haverstraw and had stopped at Smith's house. Arnold immediately summoned the bargemen and left to meet her. As soon as the barge had docked at Smith's landing, Arnold climbed out and started up the path. His heart beat faster when he caught sight of Peggy hurrying from the house to greet him. In his uneasy autumnal world she was a vision of spring, incredibly fair; after nearly two months' absence they met like bride and groom.

They stayed overnight at Smith's house. Before leaving there the next morning Arnold wrote to Major André to set the time and place of their meeting.

"I will send a person," he wrote, "in whom you may confide, by water, to meet you at Dobbs Ferry on Wednesday the 20th inst., between eleven and twelve o'clock at night, who will conduct you to a place of safety where I will meet you. It will be necessary for you to be disguised. . . ."

The person to meet André was to be Joshua Hett Smith. And Arnold sent the letter to André by Smith, in care of the Reverend Mr. Odell.

Having made these arrangements, Arnold escorted Peggy to Robinson House. A notice from General Washington had been delivered there during his absence. "I shall be . . . on my way to Hartford to meet the French admiral," wrote Washington from Tappan. "You will keep this to yourself as I want to make my journey a secret." The general's schedule favored his own plans, thought Arnold; while Washington was at Hartford conferring with the French, Arnold would be concluding his own transaction at West Point with the British commander's representative.

On Sunday evening Washington decided to stay overnight at Smith's house. After dinner Arnold excused himself and, leaving Peggy to entertain his military family, left for Haverstraw. After breakfast on the following morning, Monday, September 18, he accompanied Washington and his party to the ferry at Stony Point.

On the way across the river Washington stood on the starboard side of the flatboat, between Arnold and Lafayette, and through his field glass observed the *Vulture*. Anchored now off Teller's Point, the enemy warship was dangerously far up the Hudson. Since the Americans had no way of driving her back, her presence was an arrogant reminder of the enemy's superior strength at sea. A whole division of the French fleet, under Admiral de Guichen, was still missing. Without it the struggle was nearly hopeless. Young Lafayette, aware of Washington's anxiety, felt personally responsible. What could have happened to that part of the fleet? Turning to Arnold, the young marquis remarked: "You're in correspondence with the enemy, General Arnold—" For a moment Arnold stood electrified; had the young fool discovered his negotiations with Clinton? Arnold was on the verge of drawing his pistol, when Lafayette went on to inquire, "Perhaps you can tell us what's become of Guichen?"

Arnold shook his head. "I know nothing about it," he said brusquely, turning away.

When the flatboat reached Verplanck's Point the ferrymen led their horses ashore and Arnold prepared to part from the general. An escort of a captain and fifty dragoons was waiting to join the general's party. Washington mounted his horse. "My compliments to Mrs. Arnold," he said. "On my way back I intend to stop at your quarters."

"We shall be honored," said Arnold. "When does Your Excellency intend to return?"

"My conference will start Wednesday," said Washington. "I expect to be back by Saturday or Sunday. You will, of course, keep my schedule a secret."

Arnold nodded gravely; as Washington rode on he waved farewell to his commander in chief, a man he would never see again.

Back in Robinson House, Arnold told Peggy of Washington's impending visit. "He'll be here next Saturday?" she asked softly.

"Saturday or Sunday."

"Then the general will be a part of the prize?"

Arnold looked at her, then drew her into his arms. They shared the same vision of glory; they were ready to take the last dangerous leap. If the enemy were notified in time, Washington could be taken by surprise during his visit at Robinson House—a guard of fifty was no defense. With both West Point and the general captured, the rebellion would be doubly ended; and Arnold's services, crowned with triumph, even more richly deserving!

JOSHUA HETT SMITH called on Arnold the next morning. He reported that he had taken his wife to Fishkill for a visit, so that the Smith house at Haverstraw could be entirely at Arnold's disposal for his meeting. "Good," said Arnold. "Your services will not be forgotten." And he gave Smith safe-conduct passes to bring the visitor ashore from the *Vulture*.

In New York the same evening, Tuesday, September 19, Major André was preparing to leave for the rendezvous. To mark the occasion, Sir Henry was giving a banquet in his honor, a small but brilliant affair attended by Clinton's staff officers in full regalia. Many toasts were drunk to the accomplished young major—the paragon of the royal army, whose efforts had paved the way to a stroke which, if successful, would put an end to the rebellion in America, and for which he could probably count on a knighthood from his grateful sovereign, George III. Surrounded by admirers, his face glowing with wine and good fellowship, André was exuberant.

After the party Sir Henry spoke privately with André and again urged him to be cautious in dealing with Arnold. The rendezvous, though risky, was essential. "We must know for a certainty," Sir Henry repeated, "that the person who has been secretly corresponding with us, under an assumed name, is actually General Arnold in command at West Point. We must know the exact manner in which he means to surrender himself and the fort and troops, so that our men will be under no risk of surprise or counterattack. As for Arnold, he's anxious to meet with us for reasons of his own, which must be obvious." Sir Henry had already briefed André as to the amount and kinds of compensation he could offer Arnold.

In his last note to André, Arnold had written: "It will be necessary for you to be disguised." Sir Henry was firmly set against this. "Do not remove your uniform," he warned André. He also repeated his previous warnings, intended to prevent André from falling into the category of a spy. "Be sure to meet in a neutral zone. Do not enter the American lines. Wear your uniform at all times. Your agreement with Arnold is not to be put into writing. Carry no incriminating papers of any kind."

Sir Henry had already alerted the army and the fleet. As soon as André brought word that the terms were settled, Sir Henry would launch his force. With Arnold cooperating from within the fort, the attack on West Point should terminate in a quick and bloodless surrender. Sir Henry hoped that his confident young aide would be prudent.

André left New York and set out on horseback for Dobbs Ferry early Wednesday morning. Under his long blue cloak he wore the brilliant gold and scarlet uniform of a high-ranking British officer; his fine leather military boots were conspicuous. Reaching Dobbs Ferry, he learned that the *Vulture* had moved up to Teller's Point, ten or twelve miles beyond the British lines. Impatient to proceed with his mission, he made arrangements with a gunboat to take him up to the *Vulture*, and he reached the ship around seven o'clock in the evening.

But meanwhile, under Smith's charge, the plans were suffering a setback.

On board the *Vulture* André waited till midnight, increasingly expectant; Arnold's letter had specifically stated that he would send a person "between eleven and twelve o'clock at night." But midnight passed, and no one came. André paced the deck. The dawn hours of Thursday also dragged by; then noon, and afternoon; and still no word from Arnold.

André was puzzled. The rendezvous was as important to Arnold as to himself. What could have gone wrong?

The trouble was simple enough; Smith had been unable to procure a boat and boatmen. He had relied on two tenants, the Cahoon brothers, middle-aged farmers, to row him out to the enemy warship. The brothers had proved unwilling to do the job. When Arnold heard this, on Thursday, he could barely control his fury. He left for Smith's farm at once and personally confronted the Cahoons. Knowing nothing of Arnold's plot, they still felt that something was wrong and they did not want to be involved, but Arnold managed to bully them into undertaking the rowing. It was agreed that they would bring the visitor ashore from the *Vulture* Thursday night to the beach at the foot of Long Clove Mountain, and Arnold would be there at midnight to meet them.

At last, just twenty-fours hours late, with muffled oars the two Cahoon brothers, under Smith's direction, rowed cautiously through the dark moonless night of Thursday, September 21. When they left Stony Point the tide was on the last of the ebb; the black river was pulling them seaward.

Maneuvering their boat at an angle toward Teller's Point, they silently approached the hull of the *Vulture*. Smith displayed a white handkerchief and they were presumably under the protection of a flag. But it was too dark for any flag to be seen; moreover, the Cahoons had rowed so quietly that the lookouts aboard the warship had been unaware of their approach. All at once, startled by the clank of the oarlocks, a lookout came alive and the night air rang with a volley of oaths.

The watch officer on the quarterdeck ordered the intruders to draw alongside, else he'd blow them out of the water! "How dare you rascals sneak up on His Majesty's ship in the middle of the night?" he shouted.

While the Cahoons huddled in the boat Smith climbed the side of the hull by a rope. When he reached the deck he said his business was urgent, he had a letter for Colonel Robinson, but the watch officer wanted to put Smith in chains at once and investigate later. Smith then raised his voice indignantly, "The matter's important, I tell you, and if I'm delayed, you will be answerable!"

Roused by the commotion, Captain Andrew Sutherland sent a cabin boy up with the order, "Send the man below." After Smith showed the captain his safe-conduct, the captain took him to Colonel Robinson's cabin, and Smith delivered the letter. Robinson, a portly rubicund gentleman in his early fifties, glanced at Arnold's message with quick and observant eyes.

"This will be delivered to you by Mr. Smith, who will conduct you to a place of safety," wrote Arnold. "Neither Mr. Smith nor any other person shall be made acquainted with your proposals. If they are of such a nature, which I doubt not, that I can officially take notice of them, I shall do so with pleasure. I take it for granted that Colonel Robinson will not propose anything that is not for the interest of the United States as well as himself."

Colonel Robinson saw at once that Arnold's note was both clever and cautious: instead of André he was addressing Robinson, with whom he had already had official correspondence concerning a request Robinson had once made to discuss his confiscated estate. If the letter had been intercepted, it would not have incriminated Arnold. In addition, Arnold was asking Robinson to take the risk of going ashore.

"I am unable to go ashore with you," Robinson informed Smith immediately. "I am indisposed. Could General Arnold come aboard instead?" Before Smith could improvise an excuse, a half-dressed young gentleman entered the cabin and was introduced to him as Mr. Anderson.

When Colonel Robinson showed him Arnold's note, André turned to the go-between with an expectant smile. "I am ready to go with you, Mr. Smith."

The two older officers, Robinson and Sutherland, tried to dissuade him; it would be better, they said, if André waited till morning. But André was determined to leave on his mission at once. "The matter cannot be delayed any longer," he said, excusing himself, and went to his cabin to put on his uniform.

ARNOLD HAD LEFT Smith's house before midnight, taking with him a Negro servant of Smith's, with a spare horse, in case the visitor from the *Vulture* should have to ride to Smith's house to conclude their business. The place of their rendezvous was three or four miles south of the house, about halfway between Haverstraw and Tappan. At midnight Arnold was waiting at the foot of Long Clove Mountain, not far from the beach.

Hidden in a clump of firs, he waited for more than an hour. The Negro had tethered the horses and was lying on the ground fast asleep. Arnold moved from the thicket toward the beach. No moon or stars, not a glimmer of light—the whole countryside was shrouded in darkness. He stood on the edge of the thicket and listened, all his senses alert; except for the muted surge of the river not a sound could be heard.

Then, when he was about to turn back, he heard a faint rasping noise. There was a scraping of wood against stone, the splash of waders pulling a boat up on the sandy beach below.

Arnold waited. He sensed rather than saw the black forms moving toward him from the beach. Two figures were climbing over the wet rocks; when they reached the embankment near the thicket, Arnold whispered hoarsely, "Here I am, Smith. . . . This way . . ." He gave them an arm and led them through the brush. Fifty feet away they came to the clearing in the clump of firs where the Negro had tethered the horses.

Arnold picked up a hooded lantern and played a ray of light over his visitors. He caught Smith's sly familiar smile, then saw the stranger's face—a pale soft handsome young face like a girl's. Too soft, thought Arnold, too young for the hard business at hand.

He set the lantern on the ground, between himself and the visitor, and told Smith, "Wait by the boat till I call you." Smith had expected to be allowed to sit in on the important parley, but Arnold's tone was sharp. When the go-between had left, Arnold turned to André.

"Are you fully authorized to act?" he asked directly.

"I am." André threw open his long blue cloak and Arnold caught a flash of André's rich scarlet and gold uniform. Though it served to identify André as a royal officer, Arnold wasn't pleased. He had asked André to come in civilian clothes. Now, if anything unforeseen should happen, Arnold's position would be precarious; a secret interview with an enemy officer in the middle of the night would not be easy to explain.

"Along the lines I proposed?" Arnold continued.

"In general, yes. We assume that Gustavus is General Arnold, in command of West Point."

"Gustavus is Arnold, and I am he, in command at West Point." Arnold took an oilskin pouch from his tunic. "The papers I have should satisfy you." Taking several thin sheets of paper from the pouch, he handed them to André one by one. "A report on the garrison. Returns of ordnance. Battle orders in case of alarm. A report on the last council of war. A map of the fortifications . . ."

Squatting by the lantern, André looked at the reports. All in all, no one but the commander of the citadel was likely to have such a set of secret documents.

"The service you propose will be valuable," said André, returning the papers. "Sir Henry is ready to act. And you, of course, will be well rewarded."

"For the risk involved I need more specific assurances."

"You will have no cause to complain, believe me—"

"Twenty thousand pounds sterling. In addition to indemnification and equal rank in the army. A cheap purchase, I repeat, for an object of such importance."

"Sir Henry must be certain there won't be a counterattack."

"There won't be. Are my terms agreeable?"

"Yes. But in case of failure—"

"I don't intend to be left a victim."

"No. But services performed are the usual terms. Twenty thousand pounds, if West Point is taken."

"In case of failure, I will expect ten thousand pounds sterling, indemnification for my losses in property, and equal rank in the army."

"In case of failure, you will be indemnified for your actual losses and have corresponding rank in the army. Beyond this, I cannot make promises." André's tone was courteous but firm.

For a long moment the two men stood in silence. Time was running out for Arnold. "Very well," he said with decision. "I don't intend for our plan to fail."

They went into the specific details of the surrender. The day and hour for the attack, the system of signals by which they would keep in touch, the progression of incidents which would lead to a seemingly unavoidable surrender. Arnold expected to confuse his officers by giving them contradictory orders and to reduce the garrison by dispersing the men in small scattered detachments. He wanted the surrender to seem a military necessity, with no one to suspect the commander.

They were still talking when a thin gray light started to filter through the thicket. As it gradually revealed the scene around them, the two officers in the uniforms of opposing armies for the first time saw each other plain. André was surprised to see the proud, hawklike face of General Arnold; a corsair, he thought, hard and resourceful; dangerous as an enemy, more dangerous as a friend. They heard a rustling in the brush, and Arnold turned alertly; Smith was pushing his way toward them, his plump red face puffy and morose.

"It's nearly daylight," Smith complained. "The Cahoons want to get home." Wet and weary, they didn't intend to row back to the *Vulture*, not by daylight; patrol boats could already be seen on the river.

"Our business isn't finished." Arnold turned to André. "Smith's house is nearby, we can go there. You're safe under my protection and I'll see that you get aboard the *Vulture* tonight."

André was uncertain but had little choice. While Smith, the Cahoons, and the Negro left by boat, André followed Arnold on horseback. They rode inland along a wagon trail which soon turned north. As they entered the tiny village of Haverstraw a sentry with a musket challenged them. Arnold curtly gave the password, "Congress," and the man stepped aside. They rode on in silence, but André was thoughtful: for the first time he realized that he had entered the American lines.

They rode up the hill to Smith's house overlooking Haverstraw Bay. Arnold took André up to the big square room on the second floor. In the morning light André could see the *Vulture* at anchor on the far side of the river, waiting for his return. Arnold took a large rolled map of the area from a closet and spread it on the table, and the two sat to make their final plans. When Smith and his Negro servant arrived, Arnold called downstairs for breakfast. The Negro came up and set food on the table; then, after a wide-eyed glance at the stranger's uniform, he left the room.

The door had hardly closed behind him when a sudden boom of cannon shattered the morning stillness. Both André and Arnold went to the window; the *Vulture* was under fire from a hidden battery on Teller's Point!

Arnold was astonished and angry; through his field glass he tried to make out what was happening. Captain James Livingston, the young captain in charge of the blockhouse at Verplanck's Point, had apparently dragged out a pair of old howitzers and was attacking the twenty-gun warship. Some of his shots hit the ship's rigging and smashed a small boat; one shell struck the quarterdeck, another the main shrouds; a part of the ship was belching smoke as if on fire. The crew was frantically hoisting anchor, raising sail, trying to move the ship out of range. At first there was no wind. Then a breeze caught the sails. The *Vulture* began to move out of range and presently out of sight downriver.

Eyes drawn, Major André stood by the window for a moment. With his ship gone, he was now stranded behind enemy lines.

Smith came upstairs to the doorway. "The *Vulture*'s been driven off," he reported with a faintly superior air. The gentlemen had left him out of their parley, and now the gentlemen were left without their warship.

"She'll stop at Dobbs Ferry," Arnold told him. "You can take Mr. Anderson aboard tonight."

"The Cahoons won't row again!" Smith announced. Without waiting for Arnold's comment he scurried downstairs and back to bed.

"Never mind," said Arnold to André. He shot a glance at the pale young man; he could see he was disturbed. "I'll find a way. Shall we finish our business?"

In the next half hour they made the rest of the arrangements. Admiral Rodney was to command the fleet; General von Knyphausen, the army—five thousand troops, and as many in reserve. The attack was set for dawn on Monday, September 25, three days away; the surrender to take place before noon. Arnold explained that a link of the iron chain between West Point and Constitution Island had been removed, so the ships of the royal navy would find their passage unobstructed. He also pointed out how General Washington could be a part of the prize: the general expected to stay at Arnold's headquarters Sunday night; a picked party might capture the general before the attack on West Point.

Arnold prepared to leave Smith's house. "You must stay here till nightfall," he advised André. "Then leave for Dobbs Ferry. Smith will escort you that far, and from there on you will be safe. The *Vulture* will pick you up. By this time tomorrow you should be in New York."

He wrote out three safe-conduct passes. One for Smith and party to go with a boat and a flag; another, to go by way of White Plains; and a third for John Anderson alone: "A permit to pass the guards at White Plains or below if he chooses, he being on public business by my direction." Each pass was signed with a signature known in all the outposts along the Hudson: "Benedict Arnold, Major General."

He gave the last to André, along with the secret papers. "Take these, too," he said. The reports, on thin sheets of paper, were unsigned but in Arnold's handwriting. Though André was reluctant to take them, Arnold was firm. He considered them a part of their bargain. "Put them in your boots," he told the young man. He folded the papers to fit the shape of André's feet. "Better take off your stockings, too," said Arnold, "and hide them next to the soles of your feet." The men concealed a set of three folded reports in each stocking.

Then Arnold said, "If you return by land, as you may have to, you must change your uniform."

André shook his head. "I have strict orders not to remove my uniform under any condition."

"It's for your own safety, André. If you are seen within our lines wearing that uniform, you will be arrested or shot at once. Do you want to ruin our preparations?"

With heavy heart André realized his predicament.

Arnold hobbled to the door. "I must return to West Point before they miss me. I'll see Smith before I leave." At the door he turned back. "Remember, Smith knows little of our real business. Tell him nothing. A word too much could ruin the plans."

André stood, pale and thoughtful. They looked at one another. Chance and choice had thrown them together for a few short hours. Now the bond between them had grown as strong as life or death, and each held the other's fate in his hands; if either bungled, he stood in the shade of the scaffold.

"Good luck," said Arnold.

"Adieu," came André's farewell.

CHAPTER 5

MAJOR ANDRÉ spent the long day alone behind the closed door of the room upstairs. For hours he paced back and forth; he stood by the tall windows and searched the river for a sign of the *Vulture;* he sat by the round oak table, head resting on his arms, and tried to sleep but could not. Sir Henry, the army, the fleet were all expecting him; he had to get back to New York promptly; yet whether he could return at all had become uncertain.

Joshua Smith tried to be helpful. In the afternoon he searched his wardrobe and picked out a few odd garments he thought would do for a disguise. He took these up to Mr. Anderson. The young man glanced at the clothes and thanked Smith; but he was unwilling to change his uniform.

"I'd prefer to return the way I came," he said with a smile. "Is there any way you could row me down to the *Vulture,* Mr. Smith?" He looked at the agent hopefully.

Smith said he was sorry; the Cahoons had been badly alarmed by the cannon fire and they refused to row out to the *Vulture* again under any condition. Smith himself suffered from a touch of the ague, he said, and couldn't handle the oars. But he was willing to guide

Mr. Anderson through the lines by the land route, as far as Dobbs Ferry, if Mr. Anderson changed into civilian clothes.

Reluctantly André took off his officer's coat and put on the shabby purple jacket Smith had provided, along with a worn round beaver hat. André kept his breeches and his boots, and wrapped himself in his long cloak.

Between six and seven o'clock, Friday evening, they set out from the house, a party of three on horseback: Joshua Hett Smith, Esquire, escorting Mr. Anderson, a merchant from New York, followed by Smith's Negro servant. They rode along the dark wagon road toward Stony Point, where they expected to take the ferry. "I'll take you through," said Smith with growing confidence. "They know me in these outposts."

Muffled in his long cloak, André rode on in silence. He was riding northward, going deeper into the enemy coun-

The Joshua Hett Smith house above the Hudson River near Haverstraw, where Arnold and André met.

try. His mission could end in sudden failure, in utter disgrace, and through his own fault. Sir Henry had taken pains to warn him. André had rashly ignored his orders. He had left the neutral zone, had removed his uniform, had concealed a damning set of papers in his boots. If he were arrested now and searched, the rebels would have more than one reason to treat him like a common spy.

After nearly an hour's ride they came to an elevation just above the ferry landing. Below them lay the west end of King's Ferry. They could see a dim cluster of yellowish lights against the hazy black of the river. A string of smoky oil lanterns hung along the wharf, and they could hear the faint sound of soldiers singing in a nearby tavern.

While André and the Negro waited in the darkness above the landing, Smith rode to the blockhouse; dismounting, he went inside to visit with the guards. A man of property, Smith made frequent trips across the river; he was known to both men and officers. They offered him a bowl of punch; Smith drank; he became expansive. He was taking an important visitor to General Arnold's headquarters, he remarked, showing a lieutenant the safe-conduct Arnold had signed. "Better hurry," said the officer. "The boat is ready to leave."

Smith went to the ferrymaster's shack, paid eight dollars for the ferriage, then signaled to his party; they boarded the flatboat as she was about to pull out. About an hour later they reached Verplanck's Point on the east bank of the Hudson. Smith went into the blockhouse to see his friend, Captain Livingston.

André, waiting tensely in the shadows near the entrance, could hear their voices. The young captain was still elated by his morning's exploit. "With two little four-pounders we chased the *Vulture* away!" he was telling Smith jubilantly. "They anchored too close, you know, and they had no wind." Eager to tell more, he pressed a tumbler of rum on Smith and invited Smith's guest to step in and have a drink, too. But André politely said, "No, thank you," he'd wait outside.

Finishing another drink, Smith congratulated the captain, then hinted that he, too, was engaged in a mission of importance. He showed Livingston the safe-conduct. Since General Arnold was expecting Smith and his guest that night, they had better be going.

Outside, he rejoined André, and they resumed their journey. They came to a crossroad. The road to the south led to Dobbs Ferry, about twenty miles below. But Smith said it would not be safe if they headed south so soon after he had told Livingston he was going to Arnold's headquarters, which lay to the north. "Better if we ride inland a few miles, then go southward by another road. There's one at the junction by Crompond Corners." André said nothing. Smith seemed to know the countryside. Whatever André might think of his methods, without Smith he didn't have a chance.

The three silent travelers ambled inland along the hilly pitch-black country road until, four miles beyond Peekskill, they were halted by a sentry. Smith said he had a safe-conduct from General Arnold and must not be delayed. The officer in charge, Captain Ebenezer Boyd of the Westchester militia, came up. He held up his lantern to look over the party, then examined Smith's safe-conduct; he thought it unusual for civilians to be traveling at that late hour.

"The country isn't safe," said Captain Boyd. "Skinners and cowboys are abroad. Where do you intend to lodge tonight?"

Smith knew the names of certain officers in the Westchester militia. "We might stop with Colonel Drake," he improvised. "Or with Major Strong."

"I happen to know they're both absent from the county," said Captain Boyd. "Their houses are closed. It's dangerous for you to go any farther tonight. There's Miller's house up the lane; Miller will put you up."

Smith stepped aside to consult with his companion. André, with the plans of West Point burning in his boots, was anxious to move on, but Smith said the captain was suspicious, they'd better be cautious. So, following the captain's directions, they located the house in Hog Lane and roused the old farmer, Andreas Miller. Grumbling, he took the men to a shabby little room with a single bed.

Smith fell asleep almost at once, but André could not sleep. Without undressing, he lay on the bed. He did not remove his boots, not even the spurs. He spent the few remaining hours of the night tossing restlessly. Before dawn he shook his snoring guide awake. "Shouldn't we get started, Mr. Smith?" Without waking their host they left the house and, mounting their horses, continued their journey. A thick river fog hung over the unplowed fields and hills around them; in the dark they could hardly pick out the weedy, winding wagon road they were following.

They came to the junction at Crompond Corners an hour later. Strang's Tavern stood on one corner, a station with an armed sentry in front of it. When the sentry caught sight of the party he raised his musket and told them to stop. Then he rapped on the tavern window, and Captain Ebenezer Foote came out, took Smith's pass, then went back into the tavern to study it by better light. Through the small-paned windows they could see Foote carefully comparing the safe-conduct with another example of General Arnold's handwriting; he didn't seem satisfied. André was tempted to dig his spurs into the flanks of his horse and gallop southward into the unknown countryside. Then the tavern door opened again and Foote stepped out. He returned the pass to Smith. "You may proceed," was all he said.

Moving briskly from Crompond Corners, the travelers rode up a long hill. On the crest of it, coming toward them, they met an officer on horseback: Colonel Samuel Webb had been a military prisoner in New York until a few weeks ago; he had often seen Major André in

New York. André recognized him at once and felt sure he was lost. The hatchet-faced colonel glanced at the party, passed, turned for a second look at André, but failed to recognize him.

André became hopeful. He had a chance, he thought; his spirits lightened; he started to talk in an animated way. Smith was surprised. Riding through the drizzle in a dismal region of abandoned farms, the hitherto silent stranger entertained Smith with witty accounts of his life in London and Paris; the latest books and plays; the people he had known in the realms of art, music, and science.

When they came to Pine's Bridge on the Croton River, Smith stopped and said: "We may as well part here, Mr. Anderson. We're not far from Tarrytown; you'll be safe from here on." André looked at him questioningly; Smith was familiar with the roads, while André was a stranger and unarmed.

"I'll draw you a map," said Smith. He sketched a few lines on a scrap of paper. "Just follow this road and keep to the south and southwest, it will take you into Tarrytown. From there it's only a mile or two to Dobbs Ferry. You'll be among friends." He gave André the paper.

"I'm grateful to you, Mr. Smith." André drew a gold watch from his pocket and offered it to his guide. "Please take this," he said. "As a memento."

Smith looked at the handsome gift. He was tempted, but he shook his head. "You may need it."

"Please take it," André repeated. "I have two."

Smith took the watch. "You're generous, Mr. Anderson," he remarked with a somewhat puzzled expression. André smiled. They shook hands and parted.

André rode southward alone. When he reached the juncture at Chappaqua, he stopped to study the map his guide had sketched. The lines were confusing. He saw a boy in a farmyard and called to him, "Which is the road to Tarrytown?"

The boy, Jess Thorne, pointed to Hardscrabble Road; the stranger waved his thanks and galloped away.

Near Pleasantville he halted again. He watered his horse from a spring, then rode on a short way to Mekeel's Corners. Passing the Dutch miller's place, he saw two children playing by the sawmill pond and paused to ask them: "Is this the right road to Tarrytown?"

The road to Tarrytown lay west of Mekeel's Corners, a short way back, the boy told André and asked if he might hold the horse's bridle, while the girl ran to fetch a bowl of water. What charming little people, André thought. He gave the boy a sixpence for holding his horse, he gave the girl a sixpence for the drink of water; then, raising his hat to them with a flourish, he rode back to the crossroads.

An hour later, near ten o'clock Saturday morning, September 23, he reached the bridge over a brook near Tarrytown. Already he could see the spire of the Dutch church on the edge of the village; beyond it lay the wide Hudson River, where the *Vulture* was waiting. André smiled with relief as he started across the bridge. The worst is behind me, he thought. He felt proud and thankful.

MEANWHILE, AT ROBINSON HOUSE—some twenty miles to the north of Tarrytown—Arnold was waiting to hear from Smith. Unless André got back to New York in time, Sir Henry would delay the attack, and this would jeopardize the whole plan. A message from General Washington, delivered to Arnold Saturday morning, made the problem of timing most important. Washington had concluded his conference at Hartford. He was leaving for West Point and expected to arrive at Arnold's quarters Sunday night. If Sir Henry launched the attack early Monday, Arnold would be in command at West Point, and the surrender would take place as planned; if, however, the attack were postponed, Washington himself might take charge of West Point, and the results would be different.

When Smith reported to Robinson House, Arnold's aides glanced at the smiling civilian distrustfully. Arnold ignored them and took him by the arm and ushered him into a small office. "Well?" he said, closing the door. "Did you get him through?"

"Oh, yes, I got him through all right."

"When did you part from Mr. Anderson?"

"Early this morning. We had to stop over last night—"

"Did you take him to Dobbs Ferry?"

"Close enough to it. To the Tarrytown Road."

"What!"

"Oh, I drew him a map for the rest of the way. From Tarrytown to Dobbs Ferry it's only a couple of miles. I knew he'd be safe in the neutral zone."

"I see." Arnold looked at his complacent agent with an expressionless face. The fool had ignored his instructions. It was too late to make an issue of it.

During dinner, stimulated by Peggy's company and by liquor, Smith became more voluble. "I see big changes ahead," he predicted slyly. "The war can't go on much longer, everyone knows that. If Congress had any sense, this country could have made an honorable peace two years ago. The peace commissioners came with good offers—"

"They came with bait for gudgeons!" Major Franks told him sharply.

"Tut, tut, young man," Smith smiled. "I happen to know better." Franks found it hard to control his temper; the man was becoming unbearable.

When Punch served a platter of fish Peggy asked him to bring in more butter. "We've no more butter, ma'am," said the servant.

Arnold then told him, "Serve the oil I bought the other day. It will do with the fish." When Punch brought in the jug of oil Arnold remarked, "That oil cost me eighty dollars."

"Eighty cents, you mean!" said Smith. "A Continental dollar isn't worth more than a penny!"

"That isn't true," said Colonel Varick.

"Are you calling me a liar?"

"Yes!"

Face fiery red, Smith half rose. "I'll not be insulted—"

"Gentlemen, please!" cried Peggy.

Franks put in, "I suspect you're a scoundrel, Mr. Smith." Peggy left the table and went upstairs.

Smith glared at Franks. "Better hold your tongue, you dirty—"

As Franks seized a wine bottle Arnold struck his fist on the table so that the dishes danced. "That's enough! I'll not have such conduct at my table!"

After a moment's silence Franks rose. "Excuse me, sir," he said to Arnold. "I'll tender my resignation." He went to the door.

Arnold called after him, "I'm not releasing you, Major Franks!"

Franks left the house. (At West Point later that evening he told a friend, "There's something brewing that I don't understand and can't find out. All I can say is: Look out!")

Smith also left the table. He had to go on to Fishkill to fetch his wife, he explained, and Arnold didn't press him to stay. "I enjoyed the party," said Smith as he left.

Alone with his chief, Colonel Varick begged Arnold to have nothing more to do with Smith. "That man is dangerous, sir," said Varick. "Please be prudent. Believe me, your reputation will suffer if you continue your intimacy with Smith."

Arnold looked at Varick curiously. "Have you any reason for saying that?"

"I have." Varick took a letter from his coat. "I wrote to a friend in New York for information about Smith; today I got this reply." He showed Arnold the letter. It reported that Smith had been under surveillance for some time; suspected of being a double agent, he was probably selling information to both sides.

Arnold returned the letter to his troubled aide. "You were out of order in asking for such information behind my back," he remarked in an even tone. "But of course the information you got throws a different light on our friend. You may be sure that henceforth I'll not go to his house nor will he be invited here again."

As for the unhappy aides, both of whom wanted to resign, "I wish you and Major Franks to remain a part of my family." Arnold spoke softly. It didn't suit his plans to have either of them resign. Not for the next two days.

CHAPTER 6

WHEN MAJOR ANDRÉ started across the bridge into Tarrytown Saturday morning he was seen by the lookout for a party of skinners on the watch for loyalists who might pass that way with stolen cattle to sell in New York. Alerted by the sound of hoofs on the wooden bridge, the lookout, Isaac Van Wort, scrutinized the rider and then called to two of his mates who were nearby playing cards under a tree. "I see a stranger comin'. . . . He's wearin' good boots."

"We'd better stop him," said John Paulding, the leader of the party. Musket in hand, he scrambled out from under the tree, which was a huge wild tulip tree with many drooping branches. Paulding was twenty-one, and he had escaped from the Sugar House Jail in New

York only a few days before. He was still wearing the green jaeger coat of a Hessian; the coat had helped him in his escape.

When André reached the end of the bridge, Paulding stepped in front of him. "Stop!" he said, pointing his musket. Van Wort and Dave Williams, the third member of the party, reached for the horse's reins. André stared at the hard-bitten young men in surprise. Then his eyes lit on Paulding's green coat.

"I see you belong to our party!" he said.

"What party might that be?" inquired Paulding cagily.

"Why, the one below," André pointed southward.

"We do." Paulding nodded. "You can see by my coat—"

"Thank heavens!" André sighed with relief, then explained, "I am a British officer on a mission of greatest importance—you mustn't delay me." To identify himself as a British officer he produced a gold watch, held it in front of them, then made as if to ride on.

But Paulding stepped closer, musket in hand. "Wait!" he said. "I think you'd better get off that horse." And then he told him, "We're Americans!"

André thought fast. Instead of dismounting he glanced with admiration at the ragged young farmers. "Bless my soul! I was only testing you, friends! I have a safe-conduct from General Arnold himself! Look. Here it is!"

The only one among the skinners who could read, Paulding took the pass and studied it, scratching his chin.

André now spoke with authority. "You must let me go at once! I'm on General Arnold's business, as you can see. It's urgent, and if you delay me, you'll get yourselves into trouble!"

The skinners glanced at each other hesitantly; André watched their lean, hungry-looking faces; his fate hung in the balance.

Then Paulding said, "First you tell us you're a British officer and show us the watch to prove it. Now you show us a pass from General Arnold—"

"Keep the watch," said André, pressing it on Paulding. "I mustn't be delayed!" He spurred his horse, the animal reared, the men stepped back.

"Better let him go," said Williams. "He's got a pass—"

"Damn the pass," cried Paulding, catching the reins. "Dismount!" he told André. With a glance of exasperation, André dismounted.

"We don't mean to take anything from you," said Paulding, handing back the watch. "But we'd like to know more about you. What is your name?"

"John Anderson," said André after a pause.

Paulding nodded. "That's what it says on the pass," he remarked for the benefit of his comrades. "Well, Mr. Anderson, if you don't mind, we'd like to search you."

André started to protest, but Paulding pointed his musket. "There, under that tree . . ." They led him under the huge tulip tree with the drooping branches and forced him to remove his clothes. They searched his coat and breeches but found nothing except a handkerchief, a few coins, the watch, and the scrap of paper on which Smith had sketched his directions. André was traveling unarmed.

Currier & Ives depiction of the capture of André by Paulding, Williams and Van Wort, at Tarrytown.

"Mighty fine boots you're wearin'," Paulding remarked speculatively. "Would you mind takin' 'em off, Mr. Anderson?"

"Is all this necessary?" said André. "I'll have to report your conduct to General Arnold, I warn you—"

Paulding motioned to his fellows. "Give him a hand, boys."

They pulled off the boots and examined them, admiring the fine leather and workmanship. Finding nothing, they returned them regretfully to their owner.

"Wait a minute," said Paulding as André started to put on his boots. "Your stockin's are saggin'—they look padded to me." He gestured to his mates. "Pull 'em off!"

When they did so, the secret papers fell out. The three skinners stared at their unexpected find with a puzzled air. Paulding picked up the papers; he examined the reports on West Point, the battle orders, the council of war, the map. His companions watched his expression for a clue to the meaning of the mysterious documents.

"By gad!" Paulding exclaimed. "I do believe this man's a spy!"
They now looked at André as if he had turned into a two-headed
calf. Paulding approached him cautiously. "Where did you get these
papers, mister?"

André tried to improvise. "From a man at Pine's Bridge . . . a stranger . . ." They didn't believe him.

"Better get dressed," said Paulding. He folded the sheets of paper
and put them carefully inside his green coat. While André was
dressing, the skinners questioned him.

"What would you give us if we let you go?"

"Whatever you say."

"Your horse and saddle?" asked Williams.

"Yes . . ."

"A hundred guineas in gold?"

"Even more."

The skinners glanced at one another; none of them had ever seen
a hundred guineas in one lump.

"Would you give us a thousand guineas?" asked Paulding.

"Yes."

The men stared incredulously; the sum was fantastic; their captive
was obviously lying.

"Believe me," said André earnestly. "The money will be delivered
to you wherever you say. I am an officer of high rank and it's important that I get back to New York. You will get your reward. I will
write a note for one of you to take to the British lines, and you can
hold me until you get your reply."

The three skinners debated this. Should they take the chance?
What were the odds? The messenger would no doubt be arrested and
thrown in jail; a force would be sent out after the captive, and the
rest of them would be punished. If the young gentleman was so
important, perhaps they could collect a reward in a less risky way?

"Let's take him to General Washington," suggested Van Wort.
"He'll know what them papers mean."

"You're making a mistake," said André. "There is a good explanation for the papers. If anywhere, I advise you to take me to General
Arnold."

The men weighed the suggestion, then decided against it—Arnold's
quarters were too far up the river.

"If he's really a spy, we should take him to the nearest guard-house," said Paulding. The closest American outpost was at North Castle, ten or twelve miles northeast. They agreed to take André there.

With André on horseback, one of the skinners holding the bridle, the procession followed the winding roads of Westchester County away from Dobbs Ferry, moving inland in the direction André had ridden from so hopefully earlier in the morning.

"Would you try to get away if you could?" asked Van Wort.

"I would," said André simply.

"Don't try it," Paulding advised him, "for then we would have to shoot you."

André sighed. "I wish to God you'd blown my brains out when you stopped me."

When the party reached the cavalry outpost at North Castle, Lieutenant Colonel John Jameson heard Paulding's account. He looked at the papers, the safe-conduct, then questioned the prisoner.

André could see that Jameson was puzzled. "You will find it all a mistake," he assured the officer. "I am on a confidential mission. As you will note, sir, my safe-conduct is signed by General Arnold. I beg you not to delay me."

Jameson remembered that two weeks previously Arnold had asked him to be on the lookout for a Mr. Anderson and to send him to headquarters if he turned up. Now Mr. Anderson had turned up; his safe-conduct was undoubtedly in Arnold's handwriting; but so were the secret papers.

It didn't seem credible to Jameson that Arnold should have voluntarily given the stranger such important papers. Could Anderson have stolen them? In any case it appeared to be Jameson's duty to report the matter to Arnold.

"Suppose I send you to General Arnold?" Jameson said tentatively.

"As you wish, sir," said André. "I am sure he will clear up the matter to your satisfaction."

Jameson wrote a note to Arnold explaining the circumstances of Mr. Anderson's arrest. "He has a passport signed in your name and a parcel of papers taken from under his stockings which I think of a very dangerous tendency." He described the papers and said he was forwarding these to General Washington at Hartford.

He gave the note to Lieutenant Solomon Allen and asked the lieutenant to escort Mr. Anderson, with a guard of four dragoons, to General Arnold's headquarters. Between six and seven o'clock Saturday evening—about the time when Arnold was settling the dinner-table quarrel between Smith and his aides—André set out for Robinson House.

Less than an hour after the party had left, Major Tallmadge returned to the outpost from a scouting expedition in White Plains. Jameson told him about Anderson's arrest and showed him the papers.

"Sir, I think you ought to recall the guard," Tallmadge told his superior, "and have the prisoner brought back at once."

Jameson was unwilling. "I think it my duty to obey General Arnold's orders."

Tallmadge, sure that something was seriously wrong, argued and pleaded with him. "I beg you to recall the man!"

"It would show a great lack of confidence in Arnold," said Jameson. "He might well resent it."

"I'll take the responsibility," said Tallmadge. "Will you let me recall the man?"

Tallmadge was so insistent that at last Jameson, against his own inclination, wrote out a countermand to Lieutenant Allen to send his party back with Mr. Anderson, but to proceed to West Point to deliver the letter about the arrest to General Arnold.

Then Tallmadge immediately dispatched a fast rider; the prisoner was to be brought back to North Castle without fail. "The man is dangerous," Tallmadge warned the rider. "Keep him under close guard. If he tries to escape, shoot him."

The rider galloped along the dark roads toward the highlands; nearly two hours later he caught up with the party, a few miles from Robinson House, and the party turned back.

André, whose hopes had been high for a while, now saw his last chance slipping away; instead of going to Arnold, he was riding southward again, arms tightly bound behind him, retracing his path through the countryside.

By the time André was returned to North Castle, after midnight, Tallmadge had persuaded Jameson that for greater safety the prisoner ought to be transferred farther inland. In the dark rainy morning hours of Sunday, September 24, Tallmadge, the prisoner, and a guard of twenty dragoons reached the outpost at Salem. André had been in the saddle since four o'clock the previous morning; he hadn't slept a wink in the past three days. He was shabby in his borrowed clothes. Since leaving New York and Sir Henry's brilliant farewell party, the paragon of the royal army had become a sorry sight.

Toward noon on Sunday the messenger who was to deliver the secret papers to General Washington stopped at the Salem outpost on his way back from the north. The general had already left Hartford, the messenger reported, but he hoped to catch up with him before he reached West Point.

When André heard this he decided it was useless to continue his masquerade. While the messenger was still at the outpost, André asked permission to write a message to Washington.

Salem, 24 September, 1780

His Excellency
General Washington
   Sir: What I have as yet said concerning myself was in the justifiable attempt to be extricated; I am too little accustomed to duplicity to have succeeded. . . . No alteration in the temper of my mind, or apprehension for my safety, induces me to take the step of addressing you, but . . . to rescue myself from an imputation of having assumed a mean character for treacherous purposes of self-interest; a conduct incompatible with the principles that actuate me. . . . It is to vindicate my fame that I speak, and not to solicit security. The person in your possession is Major John André, adjutant-general to the British army. . . .

André then tried to justify his conduct. He had come ashore in a neutral zone

   . . . to meet a person who was to give me intelligence. . . . I was in my regimentals, and had fairly risked my person. . . . Against my intention and without my knowledge I was conducted within one of your posts. . . . I had to concert to escape; I quitted my uniform, and was passed another way in the night to neutral ground and . . . was left to press for New York. I was taken at Tarrytown by some volunteers. Thus was I betrayed into the vile condition of an enemy in disguise within your posts.

Major Tallmadge was astonished to learn that the prisoner (whom he had indeed suspected of being an important British agent) was no less than Clinton's adjutant general. Tallmadge noted that André had made no reference to General Arnold—the man who was probably most responsible for his predicament. Sealing the letter, Tallmadge gave it to the messenger, who then left the outpost in a fresh effort to locate General Washington.

Thirty hours had passed since André's arrest; but neither Washington nor Arnold had yet heard a word of it.

THE NEWS DID NOT REACH Arnold until early next morning, September 25, the Monday which had been set for the assault on West Point. The attack should have been launched at dawn. Momentarily expecting a signal, Arnold was breakfasting at Robinson House with Peggy, Franks, and three young officers from General Washington's party. Washington himself was due to arrive shortly; he had sent Colonel Hamilton ahead, with majors Shaw and McHenry, to apologize to Mrs. Arnold for the general's tardiness.

While Hamilton was paying his compliments to Peggy the delayed message from North Castle was delivered to Arnold. (For reasons unknown, Lieutenant Allen had spent Sunday at Peekskill.) "Excuse me," said Arnold to his guests. "This may be urgent." His guests continued to chat while Arnold glanced over Jameson's letter, a brief note big with disaster.

The words that spelled out the ruin of his plans leaped to his eye—André arrested; the papers "taken from under his stockings," forwarded to Washington! In split seconds Arnold considered his own remaining chances to escape. Washington hadn't yet received the incriminating papers, otherwise Arnold would already have been arrested. But the general was on his way and Arnold had not a moment to lose.

Without changing his expression he folded the note and put it carefully in the pocket of his uniform. He glanced at Peggy. She sensed at once that something had gone wrong.

Arnold apologized to his guests. "I'm afraid I will have to leave. An emergency calls me to West Point. Will you excuse me?" He left the table.

Hobbling into the courtyard, he called sharply to his servant

Punch, "Fetch me a horse! Signal to the bargemen I'm coming down. Be quick!"

He came back into the house and hurried upstairs into the bedroom. He buckled a brace of pistols under his coat, then took a last look at his sleeping son. Peggy went up after him. "What happened?" she asked breathlessly.

"André's been caught. I must fly for my life. I haven't a moment to lose." She heard the words, her eyes widening, her face pale as death. The bright world was collapsing about her.

He spoke rapidly. "You'll be safe here. You know nothing, nothing at all, you understand. They will not harm you." He looked at her for a moment longer, while she stared at him blankly. In the instant of their unexpected parting, his proud face was bitter with regret. She gave a cry of horror and started to fall. He caught her, set her on the bed, then hurried from the room.

Before leaving the house he told Hamilton, "Please make my apologies to the general. I expect to be back in an hour." When Franks followed him into the courtyard, Arnold told him, "Mrs. Arnold is ill, I'm afraid. Will you please get Dr. Eustis?" He glanced about the yard; Punch was only just coming from the stable, guards from Washington's party were now arriving from the north.

When an advance rider dismounted in front of Arnold to report, "His Excellency is approaching," Arnold pushed the rider aside and commandeered the horse. Hooking his cane on his wrist, and with Punch to give him a hand, he raised himself into the saddle, dug his spurs into the flanks of the horse and plunged forward, not toward the steep trail that led to the dock below, but straight forward, to the edge of the bluff, then over, then down.

He was crashing through the brush, hurdling sharp rocks, half sliding, half falling; he was racing wildly down the mountainside toward the torrent-whitened river below.

At the foot of the bluff he dropped from his horse and lurched toward the dock; he nearly fell into the barge. "Push off," he ordered, breathing heavily. "The general's coming." He pointed toward West Point. "Hurry! I must get back in time to meet him!" The bargemen swung their oars and the boat moved out into the river.

His dark face glistening with sweat, Arnold turned and craned his neck for a last glimpse of the house on the bluff. The blood was pounding in his head. Washington might have already arrived; any moment the hue and cry could break out. "Faster!" he urged the bargemen. "Two gallons of rum, if you hurry!" The bargemen strained at their oars.

Halfway across the river Arnold pointed his cane to the south. "Downstream!" he gave the new order. The men looked at him, puzzled; they thought they were trying to reach West Point. Arnold drew his pistols and cocked them. "Downstream!" he repeated grimly. The barge moved downstream. The sentries at Verplanck's Point recognized it and let it pass.

They passed from Haverstraw Bay, moved beyond Teller's Point, then approached Dobbs Ferry. Near noon on Monday, exactly two weeks after he had made his first attempt to board the *Vulture*, Arnold came in sight of the enemy warship. It was still waiting for André's return.

Arnold tied a white handkerchief to his cane as a flag of truce. He raised the cane high, his handkerchief fluttering, and the lookouts on board gave an answering sign. When the barge drew alongside, Arnold gripped the rope ladder and climbed up the side of the ship, followed by the bargemen. On deck he was met by Captain Sutherland, Colonel Robinson, and a row of British sailors.

"Colonel Robinson?" Arnold extended a hand. "I am Benedict Arnold."

Robinson looked in surprise at the fugitive. "Welcome, General Arnold." He glanced at the men behind Arnold, but failed to see the one face he was expecting. "Where is Major André?"

"André has been arrested," Arnold informed the colonel.

"But he left the ship under a flag," the colonel protested. "He was under your protection."

"Accidents intervened. He will not be held long. For the present it's important that I reach Sir Henry."

"I understand. The *Vulture* will take you to New York. But first I must send a protest to General Washington." The colonel went below to prepare it.

Arnold turned to the bargemen standing behind him. "You know who I am and you know my record," he addressed them brusquely. "The rebellion is hopeless, men. It's done for. I'm returning my allegiance to the king, and I want you to join with me." He looked at

West Point

Robinson House

N

Fort Montgomery

Fort Clinton

PEEKSKILL

Arnold flees to VULTURE, Sept. 25

VERPLANCK'S POINT

King's Ferry

Fort Lafayette

STONY POINT

HUDSON

CROTON RIVER

PINE'S BRIDGE

Smith's House

HAVERSTRAW BAY

HAVERSTRAW

VULTURE

Arnold and André confer, night of Sept. 21-22

Arnold sails for New York on VULTURE

TELLER'S POINT

RIVER

- - - → André's route

0   MILES   5'

André captured, Sept. 23

TAPPAN SEA

André hanged, Oct. 2

NEW YORK
NEW JERSEY

TAPPAN

X

TARRYTOWN

WHITE PLAINS

DOBBS FERRY

them appraisingly. "I can promise a reward for each of you—reward in cash and promotion in rank. What do you say?"

The men remained silent.

"Well? Speak up!" said Arnold. "Are you with me or not?"

One bargeman said, "One coat's enough for me at a time. I'll be damned if I serve on both sides!" The rest felt the same way.

Arnold turned to the crew of the *Vulture*. "Put these rebels in chains. In New York you can release them if you like." The sailors seized and overpowered the bargemen.

He now wished to write a few lines to General Washington, Arnold told the captain, and the captain took him to a cabin. Secure on the enemy warship, he wrote eloquently to his deserted chief, using noble words to justify his act.

> On board the *Vulture*, 25 September, 1780
>
> To His Excellency General Washington
>
> Sir: The heart which is conscious of its own rectitude, cannot attempt to palliate a step which the world may censure as wrong; I have ever acted from a principle of love to my country, since the commencement of the present unhappy contest between Great Britain and the Colonies; the same principle of love to my country actuates my present conduct, however it may appear inconsistent to the world, who very seldom judge right of any man's actions.
>
> I have no favor to ask for myself. I have too often experienced the ingratitude of my country to attempt it; but, from the known humanity of your Excellency, I am induced to ask your protection for Mrs. Arnold. . . . I beg she may be permitted to return to her friends in Philadelphia, or to come to me, as she may choose. . . .
>
> I . . . request that the enclosed letter may be delivered to Mrs. Arnold, and that she may be permitted to write to me. . . . I have the honor to be with great regard and esteem, your Excellency's most obedient humble servant.
>
> B. Arnold.

To remove suspicion from his associates Arnold added a postscript:

> In justice to the gentlemen of my family, Colonel Varick and Major Franks, I think myself in honor bound to declare, that they, as well as Joshua Smith, Esq., (who I know is suspected) are totally ignorant of any transactions of mine, that they had reason to believe were injurious to the public.

Enclosing a reassuring note to Peggy, he gave the letter to the captain, who sent it ashore under a flag with Colonel Robinson's note protesting the arrest of Major André. Then the *Vulture* set sail for New York.

WITHIN HALF AN HOUR after Arnold's flight Washington and his party arrived at Robinson House. Nervous young Major Franks apologized for the confusion: General Arnold had been called to West Point; Mrs. Arnold had been suddenly taken ill—Franks had already sent for the doctor, and Colonel Varick, also ill, was confined to his room with a fever.

After breakfast Washington and his staff, with the exception of Colonel Hamilton, left the house to inspect the fortifications at West Point. The general assumed that Arnold had gone ahead to make preparations. He was somewhat puzzled, when his boat reached Kosciusko's Landing, to hear no booming cannon salute from the hills above the river; nor was Arnold on hand to greet the visitors.

When Colonel Lamb—Arnold's second in command—appeared, he was surprised; he hadn't expected His Excellency.

"Isn't General Arnold here?" inquired Washington.

"No, sir," said Lamb. "We haven't seen him for the past two days."

Accompanied by his staff, Washington made the tour of inspection. He saw broken walls, unfinished battlements—how could' the commander of West Point have been so careless? Washington inquired after Arnold in several places, but no one had seen him. Toward three in the afternoon, with growing uneasiness, Washington started back for Robinson House.

He was met at the dock by Colonel Hamilton, whose expression was grim. During the general's absence the messenger from Salem had arrived and Hamilton had looked over his parcel. Escorting his chief to the house, Hamilton took him into a private room and showed him the papers in Arnold's handwriting, the safe-conduct, the note from North Castle, and André's letter confessing his true identity.

Washington was staggered. He called in his aides. "Arnold has betrayed us," he told them in a broken voice. "Whom can we trust now?" More than anyone, Washington had trusted the man who had dealt him this most piercing blow.

On the chance that Arnold had not yet reached safety, Hamilton left at once to alert the patrols. He learned from Captain Livingston at Verplanck's Point that Arnold's barge had passed downstream before noon. The captain gave Hamilton the letters which had been sent up from the warship; Hamilton looked at the one Arnold had written, "on board the *Vulture*," and saw with chagrin that the chief plotter had put himself out of reach. After sending a note of warning to General Greene at Tappan, Hamilton rode back to Robinson House.

Although not yet certain as to how many officers might be involved in the conspiracy and not wishing to alert them, Washington moved swiftly; throughout the night couriers from Robinson House were riding off in all directions.

He sent orders for the immediate arrest of Joshua Hett Smith; he sent a fast rider to Major Tallmadge at Salem with orders to bring André to Robinson House, under heavy guard; a rider to North Castle to summon Lieutenant Colonel John Jameson, whose "egregious folly" in writing to Arnold had tipped off the traitor and given him time to escape; he placed Major Franks and Colonel Varick under house arrest.

He relieved Colonel Lamb of command at West Point and put Colonel Nathaniel Wade in charge; Washington notified Wade: "General Arnold is gone to the enemy . . . and as the enemy may attempt some enterprise even tonight against these posts, I wish you to make immediately after the receipt of this the best disposition you can of your force."

He wrote to General Greene at Tappan: "I request that you will put the division on the left in motion as soon as possible, with orders to proceed to King's Ferry where they will be met with further orders. . . . Transactions of the most interesting nature and such as will astonish you have just been discovered."

Toward dawn on Tuesday, September 26, Smith was brought before General Washington. "All is known, Smith!" the general thundered. "You are charged with the blackest treason! By the powers granted me from Congress I am authorized to hang you—"

"But I'm innocent!" Smith cried out frantically.

"We want the names of your accomplices in the army and of anyone who was party to the scheme."

"I know nothing. Believe me!"

"You have until morning to make up your mind."

His legs buckling under him, Smith was taken from the room and locked up in another part of the house.

Then Major Tallmadge arrived with André. But Washington, not wishing to see the unfortunate prisoner, instructed Tallmadge to escort André to West Point. "The prisoner is to be well-treated, but he must be kept under strong guard at all times." André's fate would soon be determined by court-martial.

MEANWHILE, IN THE BEDROOM on the second floor, Peggy had been suffering fits of hysteria since the hour of Arnold's flight. The housekeeper had undressed her and put her to bed. Toward noon, distressed by her agitated cries, Colonel Varick left his own sickbed and went upstairs. Peggy was standing in her nightgown in front of her bedroom door, her hair disheveled, her eyes wild.

Seizing his hands, she fell on her knees. "Oh, Colonel Varick! Why have you ordered my child to be killed?" She begged him frantically to spare her and her child. Varick tried to lift her but was himself too weak with fever.

When Washington returned from West Point in the afternoon, Peggy kept calling for him from upstairs, "A hot iron is on my head! It's burning me! Help!"

"Here is General Washington," Varick told her. She stared without recognition at the tall figure who stood in the doorway.

"Oh no," she wailed suddenly, "that is not General Washington!" When the general stepped closer and gently tried to reassure her, "Yes, I am Washington," she shrank from him as if terror-stricken, and cried out, "No, you're not! You're the man who will help Colonel Varick kill my child!" And she hugged her baby to her breast as if to defend him.

With troubled face Washington stood by her bedside; Lafayette looked in on the scene, as did Colonel Hamilton, who had just returned from Verplanck's Point. The men were deeply moved. When they left the room they were certain that Peggy was an innocent victim who knew nothing of her husband's machinations. After Washington read Arnold's message from the *Vulture*, he sent the enclosure to Peggy with Colonel Hamilton. "Please tell Mrs. Arnold that although my duty requires that no means should be neglected to arrest

General Arnold, I take pleasure in acquainting her that he is safe on board a British vessel."

The next day, with Peggy recovering, Washington asked her whether she wished to join her husband in New York or return to Philadelphia. Peggy made her decision with misty eyes: "I wish to return to my father's house."

Escorted by Major Franks, she started back home the next morning. They stopped overnight at Paramus in the home of Peggy's friend, Theodosia Prevost. In the privacy of their bedroom Peggy described to Theodosia her dramatic performance at Robinson House two days before. "God, how tired I am of playing comedy!" she ended her recital. Of course, Arnold's failure was a bitter disappointment to Peggy; she was going home, and she didn't know if she'd ever care to join him again. "After all my efforts, he has ruined everything."

CHAPTER 7

MAJOR ANDRÉ'S TRIAL by court-martial was set to take place in Tappan on Saturday, September 30, 1780. In preparation for this he was transferred from the jail at West Point to Tappan, by boat, in Major Tallmadge's custody. During the few days of their acquaintance Tallmadge had found much to admire in his charge. Both the rebel and the royal officer were about the same age, under thirty. They shared a number of interests, and André, aware of the possible brevity of their acquaintance, revealed his thoughts on more than one subject.

On the way to the trial André wondered what his sentence might be; Tallmadge was reluctant to speculate on what he considered a certainty. But he did mention the name of his friend and former classmate at Yale; in New York, four years before, the British had hanged twenty-one-year-old Nathan Hale. "Surely our situation is different," said André hopefully. "I came within your lines at the request of your commanding officer." Tallmadge said nothing.

André's jail in Tappan was a room in Mabee's Tavern. The tavern was surrounded by an armed guard of forty men. Stationed inside were six sentries and two officers with swords drawn. They had orders to remain in the room with André at all times. Colonel Alexander Scammel, Washington's adjutant general, had warned them to be alert, the prisoner was not only a man of much importance to the enemy—"He is also a man of infinite artfulness who will leave no means unattempted to make his escape."

André's trial was brief. It took place in the old Dutch church across the street from Mabee's Tavern, a week after he had been captured. Washington had instructed the court to report, as speedily as possible, what penalty ought to be imposed. The generals had examined the papers; they interviewed the prisoner. André answered their questions candidly; he put the court to no burden of proof, nor would he incriminate anyone. Calm and composed, he admitted everything freely—except the intent to deceive.

"Did you come ashore under a flag of truce?" the judge advocate asked. This was a moot point, which the prisoner might have used to his own advantage.

"I did not see any flag," André answered truthfully. He added, "When I left the *Vulture* I did not consider myself under the protection of a flag." He signed a statement to the same effect.

André's composure, his frank manner and fine bearing had made a favorable impression on the court, but there seemed no way of saving the young man's life. The facts he had admitted so frankly put him in the category of a spy, and as such, Major André ought to suffer the punishment prescribed for spies. When General Washington received the court's verdict he issued an order the same Saturday afternoon: "The Commander in Chief approves the opinion of the Board of General Officers, respecting Major André, and orders that the execution of Major André take place tomorrow, at five o'clock p.m."

The harsh code of war left Washington with little choice. All the same, he intimated his private hopes to Colonel Hamilton, and Hamilton found a way of relaying these to Sir Henry Clinton. Though the hour for André's execution was set, Washington hoped that Sir Henry would propose an exchange whereby the man to hang would be Benedict Arnold.

As SOON AS Sir Henry learned that André had been sentenced he sent an appeal to General Washington for a postponement. To present the true facts in the case Sir Henry was sending three of his most prominent associates. "They will . . . wait near Dobbs Ferry for your permission and safe conduct." To explain other matters, including the threat of reprisals, Sir Henry instructed Arnold to prepare a strong letter to General Washington.

Washington agreed to postpone André's execution by one day; he sent General Greene to meet with Sir Henry's spokesmen. They met Sunday noon on the west bank of the Hudson less than three miles below Tappan. Only one of Sir Henry's men, Lieutenant General James Robertson, was permitted to come ashore; the other two were obliged to follow the conference through field glasses from aboard the *Greyhound*, the schooner in which they had come.

André's pen drawing of himself, sketched October 1, 1780, the day before his execution.

The lieutenant general in gold and scarlet regalia addressed General Greene in a long speech complimenting the rebels on the conduct of André's court-martial and the consideration which had been shown the prisoner. Green interrupted: "Please let us understand our position, sir. . . . Unless you can offer some new evidence, I cannot discuss Major André—the case of an acknowledged spy does not admit discussion."

Unwilling to admit that André might justly be considered a spy, Robertson said that the sanctity of the flag of truce, recognized by all civilized nations, was under question. "General Arnold states that Major André went ashore under the protection of a flag."

"We prefer to believe Major André," said Greene.

The British officer then showed him the letter which Arnold had written to General Washington. In it Arnold explained in detail the circumstances of his meeting with André. "As commanding officer in the department, I had an undoubted right to transact all these matters; which, if wrong, Major André ought by no means to suffer for them." Then Arnold warned Washington of the grim consequences. "I shall think myself bound by every tie of duty and honor to retaliate on such unhappy persons of your army as shall fall within my power." He referred to the forty important American prisoners in Charleston, who would also forfeit their lives. With the letter Arnold sent his formal resignation from the American army.

General Greene was nearly speechless with indignation. "I regard this as hypocritical, malignant, and impudent!" he exclaimed. When Robertson relayed Sir Henry's request that a new board be set up to review André's case—the board to include some Old World officers experienced in the laws of war and the usage of nations—Greene replied: "I will report your request to General Washington. Beyond that I cannot promise anything."

So the conference ended. After Robertson had returned to the schooner, it remained at Dobbs Ferry, for the delegates still hoped that André would be released and that they might return to New York with him on board. But Greene sent them a note the same afternoon saying that since no new evidence had been offered, neither he nor Washington saw reason for changing their opinion about the justice of André's sentence.

The execution would take place as scheduled.

EARLY MONDAY MORNING, October 2, in his office at No. 3 Broadway, Sir Henry was reading a farewell note from André: "The events . . . which led me to my present situation, were contrary to my own intentions, as they were to your orders. . . . I am perfectly tranquil in mind, and prepared for any fate. . . . With all the warmth of my heart, I give you thanks for your Excellency's profuse kindness toward me." André made a last request. "I have a mother and three sisters, to whom the value of my commission would be an object. . . . It is needless to be more explicit on this subject; I am persuaded of your Excellency's goodness."

Profoundly dejected, Sir Henry could see no way to save his protégé; there were rules in the bloody game of war and those who violated the rules did so at their own peril.

Then Arnold limped into the office. "There is only one way to save Major André," he told Sir Henry bluntly. "They want me. I am prepared to be exchanged."

Sir Henry looked up sharply. Was Arnold in earnest? Was he actually willing to return to the camp he had fled, where his name was now hated and reviled, to mount the scaffold that was waiting for him? Or was he making another dramatic gesture, a bid for the limelight? Was he taking a well-calculated risk, confident that his offer would be turned down?

Arnold silently awaited Sir Henry's decision. Sir Henry was tempted to accept the offer. The exchange would not only save André's life; it would remove from the royal army a difficult commander whose troops might well refuse to follow him. But Sir Henry was governed by larger considerations. His Majesty's fixed policy was to encourage desertions from the American army; rebels who wished to return their allegiance to His Majesty were assured protection; deserters were never given up. And Arnold *was* a deserter. . . . Sir Henry knew his duty.

"Your offer does you great honor, sir. But if André were my own brother, I could not accept it."

ON THE OUTSKIRTS of Tappan the carpenters had finished their work: two tall posts with a crossbeam stood on a knoll in an open pasture half a mile west of the village.

People gathered from all parts of the countryside to witness the promised spectacle. Among the sightseers who had arrived Sunday, the first date set for the execution, was Dr. James Thacher, an army surgeon. Thacher wrote in his diary on that October 1, 1780: "I went this afternoon to witness the execution. The crowd was assembled, the gallows was erected; but a flag of truce arrived from Sir Henry Clinton, and the execution is postponed until tomorrow at noon." Awaiting the event, many of the visitors camped overnight in the fields.

André spent Sunday afternoon and evening writing letters, farewell notes to his mother and sisters, to friends of his youth in England, to Sir Henry Clinton. He also wrote to General Washington requesting that he be granted a soldier's death in front of the firing squad. "Let me hope, sir, that I am not to die on a gibbet." With American officers who called on him, André chatted amicably; they admired his composure; he drew pen-and-ink sketches to present to them as souvenirs. According to the guard, who remained in André's cell all night, the prisoner was restless and spent the night pacing. "The agony of his mind as he walked the room was most distressing. It seemed to me that his very flesh crawled upon his bones."

Before breakfast Monday morning, October 2, Colonel Scammel visited the prisoner to inform him of the time of the execution— twelve noon—and to ask if he wished to have a chaplain. André smiled and said no, he was a freethinker, he did not feel in need of a chaplain.

After the colonel had left, André carefully shaved and prepared himself for the event of the day. He decked himself in his brilliant regimentals; his orderly, Laune, had been permitted to join him from New York and had brought André's clothes and personal belongings. When the orderly was unable to control his tears, André told him impatiently, "Please leave me, Laune, until you can show yourself more manly."

André slipped on his boots, the very fine boots which had proved so troublesome a possession; he put two large handkerchiefs in his coat pocket; he packed away his personal belongings. By this time the street in front of Mabee's Tavern was becoming crowded. Five hundred troops were assembling to escort the prisoner to his place of execution, and their movements and the clank of their arms could be heard distinctly in André's room. Ignoring the bustle, André completed his preparations. He locked his two small valises, then called Laune to give him precise instructions for their disposal. "I am counting on you to deliver my things in New York."

The two young officers who stood by the door with their swords drawn were watching his calm preparations with compassionate eyes; Major André might be getting ready for a ball at Windsor Castle. Toward eleven o'clock, when the muffled music of the band could be heard, André put on his laced hat and turned to them with a friendly nod. "I am ready, gentlemen, any time you are."

When the two officers seemed unwilling to move, André took a deep breath, then linked his arms in theirs and swung out through the door. The street was lined with troops in parade formation. Except for General Washington and his aides, most of the general officers were present, sitting on horseback, gentling their nervous mounts from time to time. Behind the assembled troops, on either side of the church, hundreds of spectators had gathered.

For a moment André stood in front of the tavern door and looked at the crowd: poorly dressed men and women from devastated farms, invalids from the garrison at West Point, dust-colored survivors in the long bitter struggle for independence. . . . They gazed back mutely at the pale young man in the laced hat and rich royal uniform.

The band struck up the "Dead March" and André stepped out into the street. A baggage wagon with a black pine coffin started to roll; the officers rode in front; an armed guard followed; then André on foot, flanked by his two escorts; then the rest of the troops, with the crowd behind.

The procession left the village and moved toward the open fields. West of Tappan it turned left from the road to enter a pasture. Here for the first time André caught sight of the gibbet. The high frame on the knoll stood out stark and plain against the gray sky. André halted in shocked surprise.

"What is it, sir?" asked one of his escorts.

André's eyes were fixed on the crude symbol of his degradation. "I am reconciled to my death," he said, "but I detest the mode of it." He turned to the officer with a pained expression. "Must I die in this manner?"

The officer looked away uncomfortably. "It is unavoidable, sir," he said. André had been sentenced as a spy; his mode of death was prescribed.

André sighed, then drew himself together. "It will be but a momentary pang." He resumed his walk toward the gallows.

After the armed guard had drawn up around the scaffold, the baggage wagon with the coffin was driven between the two posts by the hangman and his helper. The hangman was a Tory named Strickland who had been released from jail and promised his freedom for performing a task no one else was willing to perform. Strickland had smeared his face and hands with a mixture of grease and soot which gave him a hideous disguise.

André tried to mount the wagon by the tailgate but failed in his first attempt. When Laune stepped up to him to offer an arm, André spoke a few words and Laune stepped back. Then André seized the sideboards and jumped into the wagon. While Colonel Scammel was reading out the death warrant, André stood on top of his coffin and surveyed the scene around him.

To the southeast he could see the tall white steeple of the church at Tappan; farther south a solitary windmill was slowly revolving. Near at hand, around the baggage wagon, in all directions, hundreds of upturned faces were watching him.

Colonel Scammel finished reading the warrant, then addressed the prisoner. "Major André: if you have anything to say, you may speak now."

André bowed to him, then replied in a firm voice, "I have said all I have to say before. All I request of you now, gentlemen, is that you bear witness that I met my fate like a brave man."

The hangman climbed into the wagon. Standing behind André, he held the noose in his blackened hands. When he tried to slip it over André's head, André told him quickly, "You will keep your hands away from me." He removed his hat and, leaning from the wagon, gave it to Laune. He also handed Laune his gold watch. Then he opened his shirt and removed his white neckcloth. Taking the noose from Strickland, he put it around his neck and adjusted the slipknot. He took a handkerchief from his coat pocket and bandaged his eyes. Then he stood waiting.

When the colonel said that the prisoner's hands would have to be tied, André promptly pushed the bandage from his eyes and took a second handkerchief from his coat pocket; he passed it to the hangman, and pulled the bandage down over his eyes again. The hangman bound André's arms behind him with the handkerchief, and then fastened the end of the rope to the crossbeam.

The colonel raised his sword. The drums rolled. All eyes were fixed on the slight figure in the wagon who waited bareheaded, his gallant form clearly outlined against the autumnal sky.

The colonel dropped the point of his sword. The hangman's helper struck the horses, the wagon rolled forward, and André swung into the air. He did not struggle, his death was almost instantaneous; but due to the height of the crossbeam, his body continued to swing back and forth for nearly twenty minutes.

The crowd watched in hushed silence. When the body finally stopped swinging, the colonel himself cut the rope; two soldiers supported the body so it would not fall.

They carried André's body to a freshly dug grave, removed his uniform and boots and gave them to Laune, then wrapped the body in a shroud. A long line of spectators filed by for a last look and there was more than one tear-stained face in the company of his enemies. The body was placed in the coffin, the coffin lowered, the grave filled with earth. As the crowd slowly dwindled a woman came forward with a small peach tree in hand. She asked permission to plant it at the head of André's grave.

EPILOGUE

WHILE BOTH ARMIES lamented André's death, the whole country was shocked and horrified by Arnold's treachery. Had his plot succeeded, as it nearly did, the struggle for independence would have been crushed.

They hanged Arnold in effigy in New Haven, Boston, Philadelphia, and in many smaller towns and villages. In Norwich, Connecticut—Arnold's birthplace—his countrymen stormed the graveyard and demolished his father's tombstone because it carried the inscription, BENEDICT ARNOLD.

When one officer tried to assure General Washington that Arnold was suffering more severe punishment than André, since Arnold was "doomed to the permanent increasing torment of a mental hell," the general did not agree. "Arnold wants feeling," said Washington. "He seems to have been so hackneyed in villainy, so lost to all sense of honor, that while his faculties enable him to continue his sordid pursuits there will be no time for remorse."

The Executive Council of Pennsylvania confiscated Arnold's estate on Mount Pleasant. It sold his household goods in a public auction and ordered Mrs. Arnold to leave Philadelphia within two weeks. Peggy didn't want to go, and the Shippens fought the order bitterly. "We tried every means to prevail on the Council to permit her to stay with us and not compel her to go to that infernal villain, her husband, in New York." When the council remained unyielding, Judge Shippen was heartbroken. Peggy had little choice but to leave her father's house and rejoin Arnold in New York.

Another refugee, Joshua Hett Smith, arrived in New York soon afterward. Disguised in woman's clothing, Smith escaped from jail and made his way to New York; then he sailed for London. There he stayed for seventeen years, receiving a spy's pension of six shillings a day. Nearly twenty years after his escape, Smith returned home and converted his house above Haverstraw Bay into a school for boys.

The three skinners who had captured André became national heroes. Commending them to Congress, General Washington wrote: "They have prevented . . . our suffering one of the severest strokes that could have been meditated against us." Congress voted a silver medal for each of them, with pensions of two hundred dollars a year for life. When John Paulding died forty years later, a monument was raised to him near Peekskill.

Arnold spent the rest of the winter in New York; more isolated than he had been at Robinson House, he had no friends or confidants and revealed his thoughts to no one. Three weeks after André's execution, he pressed Sir Henry for his money claims. He expected ten thousand pounds sterling; he received six thousand.

When Peggy joined him in November, they lived in a house which Arnold had rented on lower Broadway, next to Sir Henry's headquarters. Outwardly she played her role as the general's dutiful lady, but something between them had changed.

Fretting with inaction, Arnold urged Sir Henry to let him lead an assault on West Point. But Sir Henry remained deaf to this as well as to his other proposals.

Finally, early in 1781 Sir Henry sent him on an expedition to help Lord Cornwallis in the South. Arnold made a series of savage raids along Chesapeake Bay, destroying much shipping, burning tobacco warehouses in Richmond, and capturing prize cargoes. He was aware that Governor Thomas Jefferson of Virginia was offering five thousand guineas for his head; Congress had already offered one hundred thousand dollars; attempts had been made to kidnap him. He kept a brace of loaded pistols at his side, ready for use day or night; his countrymen would never take him alive. When a captured American captain was brought before him, Arnold asked, "What would they do to me if *I* were caught?"

The captain told him, "They'd cut off that leg of yours that was wounded at Quebec and Saratoga and bury it with all the honors of war. The rest of you they'd hang on a gibbet."

In the fall of 1781 Arnold made his last and, for many, his most horrifying gesture of violence against his native land. Washington was making secret preparations to march his whole army southward against Cornwallis. When a hint of this reached Sir Henry he concluded that a threat against New England was most likely to keep Washington in the north. Arnold volunteered to lead an attack on the port of New London, Connecticut, and Sir Henry gave him the command. Arnold was familiar with the area; he had been born nearby, his childhood home still stood some miles inland from the port; among the defenders of New London were his former schoolmates and neighbors.

Landing his forces under cover of darkness, Arnold launched the surprise attack at daybreak. Accompanied by a heavy barrage from the warships, the troops seized Fort Trumbull, one of two small forts guarding New London, and then they swarmed into the astonished town. Firebrands in hand, the soldiers ran through the streets, spreading terror in every direction. They set fire to the courthouse, the church, the jail; they burned warehouses along the waterfront, set fire to dozens of fishing boats and privateering vessels, until the harbor became cloudy with huge coils of black smoke shot through with flames. Then a warehouse with a large store of gunpowder exploded and the whole town was showered with flaming debris. People ran screaming from their beds and blazing homes; fathers frantically packed their families, their half-dressed women and children, into wagons; they drove wildly out toward the open fields.

Toward evening on that day, September 6, 1781, Arnold observed from his post above the Thames River the results of the expedition. The harbor was still a small sea of fire and the roofs of the town he had known as a boy had fallen. Across the river Fort Griswold, the second of the forts guarding New London, had become the scene of a massacre, perhaps the most cruel and revolting in the entire struggle.

Apart from adding a shade of horror to his name, Arnold's assault on his birthplace did nothing to change the larger course of events. While Arnold had been trying to terrorize Connecticut, Washington had made the swift march to the south and trapped Cornwallis at Yorktown in Virginia. Blockaded by the French in the Chesapeake, unable to get help from Sir Henry in time, Cornwallis had no way out. On October 19, 1781, he was forced to lay down his arms, with an army of seven thousand veterans.

In effect, Cornwallis's surrender marked the end of the war. The rebellion in the New World had become a successful revolution; the colonies had won their independence; and the enemies of the new republic prepared to return to the Old World.

Less than two months later Arnold embarked for England on a warship, with a letter of recommendation from Sir Henry. Peggy, now with two babies—their second son not yet three months old—sailed on a merchant vessel with more comfortable accommodations.

Cartoon published in 1780 shows an effigy of a two-faced General Arnold being drawn to his execution. The Devil stands behind with a pitchfork ready to drive him into hell.

On December 15, 1781, the wintry morning of his departure, Arnold stood on deck and, with a freezing wind from the Hudson Valley blowing into his face, watched the fading landmarks of a country no longer his own. His ship was maneuvering toward the open sea, the misty air was loud with the sharp cries of gulls, and the gray, chilly waters were now carrying him toward an unknown horizon, away from the land which had crowned him with laurels and hanged him in effigy.

But Arnold did not intend to bid farewell to America.

Standing aboard the departing warship, the fallen hero—now forty years old—was designing a new plan to regain his lost glory. Despite the setback at Yorktown, he didn't believe that the army of the revolution had won a conclusive victory. When he reached England he would gain His Majesty's support and return to America to replace Sir Henry Clinton as commander in chief. The rebels could yet be crushed, Arnold was sure, and he was the man to lead the royal army to triumph.

Presented to George III at Windsor Castle, Arnold lost no time in broaching his plans, and His Majesty listened to his proposals with the sharpest interest. In the spring of the year they were seen walking arm in arm in the royal gardens at Windsor. The king of Great Britain and the limping renegade from America found much in common.

They shared similar obsessions—hunger for personal power and lust for glory. Now both burned to punish the ungrateful colonies.

But though the king favored Arnold's plans, Parliament held other views. The War Office turned down Arnold's proposals; it rejected his applications for service. Though London tolerated his residence, most Englishmen avoided his company. When he entered a theater, he was hissed; when he visited Parliament, the speaker refused to continue until Arnold had left.

A black aura enveloped him throughout the years that followed. Barred from the field of glory, Arnold threw his restless energy into speculative business. He sailed to Canada in 1787 and set up a trading post at St. John in New Brunswick. But after his warehouse burned down he was forced to return to England.

A few weeks after his return he fought a pistol duel with the Earl of Lauderdale. In the course of a debate in the House of Lords, Lauderdale had cited him as a notorious example of the traitor; Arnold demanded an apology; the earl refused. The duel took place in July 1792. Arnold fired, but missed. Lauderdale then refused to fire but told Arnold to take another shot. Arnold, furious, insisted that Lauderdale should fire or apologize. Lauderdale refused to do either, then, after consulting with his second, changed his mind and tendered his apology.

Like a hungry, aging, storm-battered hawk in search of prey, he repeatedly sought for a command, for a taste of fresh military glory, but all his offers were rejected by the War Office.

His ventures in privateering failed; he lost his ships and prize cargoes; he was defrauded by the captains he had been obliged to trust. His savings melted away. He fell increasingly in debt. Finally, near sixty, retired on a colonel's half pay, he was gnawed by a sharpening sense of failure. His swarthy face was deeply scored, his eyes had lost their magnetic fire; shoulders stooped and bony, he could not walk without a cane.

When Peggy saw Arnold's ventures failing, she urged him to provide for their children, who now numbered four sons and a daughter. She struggled to preserve their home, to secure scholarships for their education. Pinning her hopes on their careers, she warned her boys to avoid their father's propensity for impractical schemes. She warned them against early marriage. Peggy herself was now pitied for the man she had married. "If he were dead, she would be much noticed," one gentleman observed.

Twenty years older than his wife, Arnold continued to decline. Troubled by ailments he had picked up in his travels, he found it increasingly harder to breathe; he could not sleep at night. At the turn of the century the Connecticut boy who had caught the great mill wheel and held on as it rose above the raging stream had become a crippled old pensioner in the suburbs of London. For Arnold the wheel had turned a full circle, and stopped. The onetime Hannibal of America was ignored or forgotten. His state of mind may be gleaned from phrases in his last letters. "I am without rank or consequence, without friends or connections." But it was chance that had undone him, nothing more! His plan had been brilliant; he'd picked one or two faulty instruments; then fate tripped him up—So Arnold justified himself to the bitter end.

After three days' delirium he died, at last, at the age of sixty, on June 14, 1801. Peggy wrote to her father in Philadelphia: "The disappointments of all his expectations had broken his spirit and destroyed his nerves."

Buried in a crypt at Battersea on the south bank of the Thames, three thousand miles from his birthplace, Arnold had few obituaries. The London *Morning Post* reported: "Poor General Arnold has departed this world without notice. A sorry reflection this . . . for other turncoats."

Peggy died three years after Arnold, at the age of forty-four, afflicted with cancer of the womb. Buried behind the church at Battersea in August 1804, her bones share the same crypt with the traitor.

IN AMERICA, on a battlefield near Saratoga, a stone shaft was raised on Bemis Heights, a monument without a name:

> In memory of the most brilliant soldier of the Continental Army, who was desperately wounded on this spot . . . 7th October, 1777, winning for his countrymen the decisive battle of the American Revolution and for himself the rank of Major General.

BACKGROUND
TO DANGER

Background to Danger

A CONDENSATION OF THE BOOK BY
Eric Ambler

ILLUSTRATED BY CHARLES WILKINSON

Kenton was broke; worse even, he was hungry—a down-and-out journalist with nothing to write about. So when the odd-looking little man on the train offered him a sizable sum of money to carry a harmless-looking parcel of papers through the customs check at the border between Germany and Austria, he leaped at the chance. How could he know that the parcel contained political dynamite—enough to set off a worldwide conflagration, plunge him up to his neck in a deadly conspiracy, and make him personally the target of both Soviet and Nazi agents?

Here is the famous tale of terror and intrigue from that master of the spy thriller, Eric Ambler, author of such vintage classics as *Journey Into Fear* and *A Coffin for Dimitrios*.

PROLOGUE

ONE SUNNY MORNING in July, Mr. Joseph Balterghen's blue Rolls-Royce oozed silently away from the pavement in Berkeley Square, slid across Piccadilly into St. James's and sped softly eastward toward the City of London.

Mr. Balterghen's Rolls-Royce was a very large car while he, himself, was a very small man and anything but pleasing to the eye. But Mr. Balterghen was chairman of Pan-Eurasian Petroleum and of fifteen other companies, a director of thirty more and, in the words of those who write bank references, "highly respectable."

That the phrase had nothing to do with church attendances, ten-o'clock bedtimes and nicely rolled umbrellas was made obvious by his face. It was set in an impassive glare, and as his car glided down Northumberland Avenue, Mr. Balterghen gnawed thoughtfully at his black toothbrush mustache. The chauffeur, catching a glimpse of this in the rearview mirror, muttered, "The perisher's goin' to a board meetin'," and did not look in the mirror again.

Inside the new offices of the Pan-Eurasian Petroleum Company in Gracechurch Street, Mr. Balterghen was shot up to the sixth floor in a chromium-plated elevator. Then he went to his office, which his second secretary, Blundell, had once told his wife, "is more like a harlot's parlor than an office. He's got a red Turkey carpet and stippled green walls, a Second Empire desk, a neo-Byzantine bookcase and a Drage-Aztec cocktail cabinet that flies open when you press the button. Even if you didn't know from experience what a complete wart Balterghen is, that room would tell you."

The first thing Mr. Balterghen did on that sunny July morning was to operate his cocktail cabinet. From it he took a large bottle of stomach powder and mixed himself a draft. Then he lit a cigar to take the taste away and rang the fifth bell along on the Second Empire desk. After a short interval, Blundell came in.

"What time was the meeting called for, Blundell?"

"Eleven, Mr. Balterghen."

"It's five to, now; are the other directors here?"

"All except Lord Welterfield."

"We'll begin without his lordship. If a gentleman named Colonel Robinson calls for me about twelve forty-five, put him in a vacant office on the floor below to wait. I don't want him shown up here."

At 11:02 precisely, the board of directors of Pan-Eurasian Petroleum began their meeting. All knew that there was only one really interesting item on the agenda that day, but that tidbit had been placed last. When Lord Welterfield arrived at a quarter to twelve his profuse apologies were acknowledged hurriedly.

"I see," said Mr. Balterghen finally, "that the next item on the agenda concerns my Rumanian negotiations." The board settled itself in its chairs. "You will remember that in 1922 the company obtained a drilling concession from the Rumanian government, covering a tract of land east of Jassy which was believed at the time to be rich oil country. You will also remember that in the years 1923 and '24 only five thousand barrels were produced, and early in 1925 the most promising well ceased producing, and that finally, the concession was, to all intents and purposes, written off as a dead loss. At the time this did not matter very much, as our subsidiaries in Venezuela, Mexico and the Near East were producing profitably and, for that matter, still are."

There was a murmur of agreement.

"But," continued Mr. Balterghen, "political developments in Europe during 1935 and '36 have suggested that we should look once again in the direction of Rumania. At the moment Italy is taking large quantities of Rumanian oil. She will take more.

"I do not have to explain to you gentlemen that here is worthwhile business. Two months ago we made representations to the

Rumanian government, asking that the existing concessions be revised. We told them that we were ready to pay handsomely. All that we required was a fair share of the oil lands at present divided between our competitors. Our agents in Bucharest approached the right people. It was arranged that at the November session of the Rumanian Chamber of Deputies a responsible leader would present our proposals for concession revision as a necessary reform—as, of course, it is." The meeting signified its approval of this sentiment.

"Ten days ago," added Mr. Balterghen calmly, "I received news that at the November session concession reform would be defeated."

For a moment there was dead silence. Then everyone began to talk at once. The chairman held up his hand. "I can appreciate your feelings, gentlemen," he said amiably. "But allow me to give you the reasons for this setback. No blame attaches to our agents in Rumania. They have done their work admirably. The failure has resulted from one thing and one thing only—a scurrilous article published in Bucharest."

He produced a battered newspaper from the folder in front of him and held it up. "This is the sheet. It is published by the United Socialist Party of Rumania. I don't suppose any of you gentlemen read

Rumanian. I do; so I propose to read to you one or two extracts from the article. It is entitled, 'The Vultures Gather,' and after a rather wordy preamble on the subject of capitalist intrigue, it asks, 'Who are the directors of the Pan-Eurasian Petroleum Company?' and goes on to give our names, supplemented by a series of biographies which are such obvious lies that I will not trouble to translate them. Then it continues: 'There is a movement afoot to effect sweeping concession reforms. What exactly is meant by reform in this case? Simply, that the government is asked to break its contracts with existing oil concessionaires in order that the Pan-Eurasian Petroleum Company can have the lion's share of the increasing trade with Italy. Now there are three unsavory aspects of this business. First, there has evidently been wholesale bribery in governmental circles—there can be no other explanation of this sudden desire for revision. The second is the now familiar spectacle of foreign capitalist exploiters meddling with the destinies of the Rumanian people. The third is the obvious dangers of such a revision. The Pan-Eurasian Company probably has allies among the British and American interests already in our country; but what of the other nations? Our foreign alliances are too valuable to be jeopardized by corrupt officials and capitalist pawns. . . .' The article," continued Mr. Balterghen, "lapses here into mere abuse. The entire story is, of course, a flagrant distortion of the truth. We are businessmen and we are anxious to do business with the Rumanian government. We are not interested in politics."

There were several "Hear-hears."

"All the same," went on the chairman, "the article has caused us serious inconvenience. The paper was suppressed and its offices were destroyed by a band of youths armed with hand grenades, but too late to prevent wide distribution of the article. The public prosecutor has been compelled to charge several of our friends in the government with corrupt practices, public interest has been aroused, and concession reform will not be supported."

A stout man at the other end of the table cleared his throat. "Then we can't do anything so far as I can see."

"On the contrary, Sir James," said Mr. Balterghen, "we can do a great deal. I have, anticipating the confidence of the meeting, retained the services of a man with considerable experience in matters of this sort. He has worked for me before. His services will be expensive, but I think I can safely say that the results will warrant the expenditure. The man in question could, I suppose, best be described as a propagandist."

"As long as the fellow isn't a Red," said Lord Welterfield, "he can call himself anything he likes as far as I'm concerned."

"Then, gentlemen, I take it that I have your permission to deal with this man. I should like to make it clear, however, that for the moment I propose to keep the nature of the measures to be taken absolutely confidential."

The meeting declared that it had every confidence in the chairman's judgment and, after a few formalities, dispersed weightily to luncheon. Mr. Balterghen returned to his office.

Blundell followed him in. "Colonel Robinson is waiting in room five forty-two, Mr. Balterghen. Shall I show you the way?"

They went down in the elevator and walked along a corridor. As Mr. Balterghen opened the door and went in, Blundell heard his employer say, "Ah, Stefan!" He also noticed that Colonel Robinson's arm seemed to be a trifle stiff at the elbow as he shook hands, and when the two men began talking, it was in a language he did not recognize.

"Colonel Robinson my foot!" said Blundell to his wife that evening. "If that fellow's name is Robinson, then I'm Hitler. Salt, please."

CHAPTER 1

WITH HIS SHOULDERS hunched and his hands thrust deep in his overcoat pockets, Kenton waited at Nuremberg for the Frankfurt–Linz train. An icy November wind blustered through the almost deserted station, swinging the enamel reflectors and causing mad shadows to dance on the platform. He shivered and started to walk up and down. A thin, intelligent-looking man, Kenton appeared older than his thirty years. It was, perhaps, the pleasant quality of humor combined with discretion in the rather full lips. He looked more like an American than an Englishman.

As he paced the Nuremberg platform that night, his self-contempt increased with the numbness of his feet. It was not, he told himself, as if he enjoyed gambling. It bored him; but once he started to gamble, an unhappy quality of recklessness decreed that he go on until all the money in his pocket was gone. It had happened to Kenton before; but it had not mattered much. This time it was serious, for in his pocket that day he had been carrying his entire fortune, four-hundred-odd marks.

Kenton was accounted a good journalist. Most foreign news comes from the permanent correspondents of individual papers and the agency men. The free lance abroad does not, as a rule, stand a very great chance against them. Kenton, however, had three important assets: the ability to learn foreign idiom quickly and to speak it with an un-English accent, a very sound knowledge of European politics, and a quick and shrewd judgment of news values. The first was the most valuable. Kenton's ability to speak the language of a country as it should be spoken made the difference between getting and not getting an occasional crumb of exclusive news.

It had been in search of such a crumb that he had come to Nuremberg, lured by the rumor that high Nazi officials were gathered to make important decisions. The decisions were almost certain to be unpleasant, and, therefore, news.

Ninety percent of political reporting consists of waiting for conferences to end. The time is usually passed in a bar. When Kenton had arrived in Nuremberg several correspondents he knew were already installed at the Kaiserhof. It had been the Havas Agency man, a Pole, whom he liked, who had produced the poker dice. Kenton had lost steadily from the first.

By the time the conference adjourned, issuing no press communiqué, Kenton had just five pfennigs left in his pocket. He had explained the situation to the other three players over drinks, pointing out that the bankruptcy was merely temporary and that he possessed funds in Vienna. All that remained, he had added, was to get to Vienna. The Havas man had promptly volunteered a hundred marks. Kenton accepted it as gracefully as possible, and left soon after for the station. There he had found that he must resign himself to waiting for a slow train that went as far as Linz, in Upper Austria, where he could change for Vienna.

It would not have been so bad if his jaunty claim to funds in Vienna had been founded on fact; but it was not. He had no money whatever in Vienna. He was going there with nothing more than the faint hope that a Jewish instrument maker he knew would lend him some. Kenton had been able to help him get his family out of Munich in the bad days of 1934, and the instrument maker had been grateful. But, for all Kenton knew, his old friend might have left Vienna. Or he might have no money to lend. Still, it was his one chance.

He dug his fists deeper into his overcoat pockets. After all, he had been broke before, and invariably something had turned up to help him. Sometimes it had been an unexpected check from his New York agent for second rights on a long-forgotten article, sometimes a good news story. Perhaps Hitler would be on the Linz train on his way to meet the leader of the Austrian Social Democrats. The idea entertained him and he amused himself by sketching in the events that might render that fantastic encounter feasible. By the time the Linz train arrived he was feeling more optimistic. It was practically empty and he had a compartment to himself. He slung his suitcase onto the rack, wedged himself into a corner and went to sleep.

A stream of icy air woke him as the train was pulling out of Ratisbon. Another passenger had entered the compartment and opened the window an inch. Suddenly Kenton was wide awake—cold, stiff, hungry and wretched. All the artificial optimism had gone, and he was conscious of the true seriousness of his position. If Rosen wasn't in Vienna, what was his next move? He could wire home to a paper for money, but they would probably refuse him. His contributions were of necessity spasmodic, and since he preferred running around as a free lance abroad to a nice steady job doing police-court news in London, it was his own affair. Looking around for something else to think about, he glanced at his fellow passenger.

The author of this window-opening outrage was small, narrow-faced and very dark. He wore a dirty starched collar with a huge flowered tie and a crumpled dark-striped suit. On his knees rested an attaché case from which he was extracting paper bags containing sausage and bread. A bottle of Vichy water stood propped against the back of the seat beside him.

His eyes, dark brown and lustrous, met Kenton's. He waved a piece of sausage. "Please, you will accept some sausage?"

"It's very good of you. Thank you."

Kenton was passed a piece of garlic-impregnated sausage on a hunk of bread. He enjoyed it and accepted more gratefully. The brown-eyed man meanwhile finished his meal and announced that he would sleep.

"Please to wake me," he added, "when we approach the frontier." He curled up on the seat and seemed to go to sleep. Kenton went outside to smoke.

It was 10:30 by his watch; another hour should see him at Passau. As he crushed out his cigarette he noticed that he was no longer alone in the corridor. A few compartments down a man was leaning on the rail. He was gazing out at the distant lights of a Bavarian village, but Kenton had the impression that the man had been watching him. Then suddenly the man started walking toward him, glancing in each compartment as he passed it. He had small dull eyes set like pebbles in a puffy, unwholesome-looking face. As he came up, Kenton flattened himself against the window to allow him to pass, but the man did not do so. Glancing behind him, Kenton saw that he had stopped and was gazing into the compartment at Kenton's sleeping fellow traveler. With a muttered *"Verzeihung,"* he walked back and disappeared into the next coach. Kenton returned to the compartment.

The little man's eyes were closed. He looked sound asleep, but his forehead was shining with sweat. Then the brown eyes opened slowly and flickered toward Kenton.

"Has he gone—the man in the corridor?"

"Yes."

The other sat up and, after fumbling in his pocket, brought out a large, dirty handkerchief. He wiped his forehead and the palms of his hands. Then he looked at Kenton. "You are, perhaps, an American?"

"No, English."

"Ah, yes. Your clothes made me think . . ." His voice trailed off into inaudibility. Suddenly he leaped to the switch and plunged the compartment into darkness. The next moment Kenton's blood froze as he felt the man sit on the seat beside him. He could hear him breathing heavily.

"Please do not be alarmed, *mein Herr.*" The voice was strained, quick and breathless. "I am a German," he began.

Kenton said "Yes," but disbelieved him. He had been trying to place the man's accent.

"I am a Jew. They have ruined my business. I am a metallurgist. I had my own business, my own factory—small, you understand; but now that is over. I wish to leave Germany and start again a small business. I want to take the little money I have, but these Nazi brutes say no. I think perhaps I take it secretly across the frontier. All goes well. I meet a good English friend, we eat together as gentlemen. Then I see this Nazi spy and he recognizes me. You saw him stop and look at me. Now I know. They will search me at the frontier, strip me, send me to a concentration camp. In my pocket I have ten thousand marks in good German securities—all I have in the world. Unless you will consent to help me, they will take them from me at Passau." He paused, wiping his forehead again.

The man was lying; of that Kenton had no doubt. Metallurgist and Jew he might be. German he certainly was not. For one thing, his German was not as good as Kenton's own; for another, any German businessman would know that the only way to get money out of Germany was in hard cash. And the Nazis would not take the trouble to send spies to peep at non-Aryan metallurgists in third-class compartments. If they had wanted the man, he would not have been allowed to board the train at Ratisbon. All the same, the man in the corridor had certainly behaved oddly, and Brown-Eyes' fright was obviously linked in some way with his appearance. Kenton began to scent a story.

"I don't see how I can help you," he said.

The other leaned toward him. "You could take my securities past the frontier for me. You are an Englishman. They would not dare search you."

"I am afraid I cannot take the responsibility."

"But I will pay you, *mein Herr* . . ." He rummaged in his pocket and drew Kenton into the light from the corridor. He had a wallet in his hand. "Look! I will pay you one, two, three hundred marks to take my securities out of Germany for me."

Three hundred marks! A hundred owing to the Havas man left two hundred. Two hundred! Enough to get back to Berlin with plenty to spare. Kenton might be heading straight for a German prison, but it was worth the risk—for three hundred marks.

He hedged a little, then allowed the man finally to persuade him. Tears of emotion oozed from the brown eyes as he handed Kenton one hundred and fifty marks in advance. The balance was to be paid when the securities were handed back. They were, their owner hastened to explain, in his name, Herman Sachs, and of no value to anyone else. He laid his hand on Kenton's arm. "I am trusting you with my poor savings. You will not betray me?" His fingers gripped with surprising force.

Kenton protested his good faith, Herr Sachs's grip relaxed, and with a cautious glance at the corridor, he handed over a long, bulging envelope. Kenton could feel a bundle of stiff papers rolled up inside it. He put the envelope in his pocket. Sachs drew a deep breath and relapsed into his seat exhaling loudly.

Kenton found his exhibition of relief disconcerting. With a growing dislike, he watched the man open a large and battered composition suitcase which was stuffed with soiled linen. From one corner of the case Sachs withdrew a heavy-caliber automatic. He slipped it easily into a holster under his left arm.

There was, thought Kenton, more to Herr Sachs than met the eye.

THEY WENT THROUGH the customs formalities separately. Sachs hurried off first. Kenton, with a hollow feeling in the region of the solar plexus, the envelope lodged down his right sock and his German bank notes tucked in his left shoe, followed at a discreet distance.

Waiting his turn at the German control, Kenton saw his doubts of Sachs's story confirmed. Sachs was passed through with only the usual currency interrogation. He was neither searched nor detained. A little later Kenton also caught a glimpse of the "Nazi spy" crossing a lighted yard to the Austrian customs.

His own examination was casual enough, but he was profoundly relieved when it was over. Returning to the train, he found an anxious Sachs.

"Ah, here you are. You have it safely? Good. No, no, no, please!" as Kenton produced the envelope. "It is not yet safe. Put it in your pocket."

At that Kenton lost his temper. He was cold, depressed and disliking Herr Sachs intensely. Moreover, he had decided that the securities consisted of either (a) drugs, (b) stolen bearer bonds, (c) a report on white-slave traffic possibilities in Westphalia, or (d) something else equally incriminating. Whatever dingy game Sachs was up to, he, Kenton, was not going to be involved any longer.

"I must ask you to take your securities back," he said. "I contracted to bring them across the frontier. I have done so. And now, I think, you owe me one hundred and fifty marks."

Sachs, his brown eyes slightly opaque, leaned forward and touched the journalist on the knee. "Herr Kenton," he said quickly, "please put that envelope back in your pocket. I will increase my offer. Another three hundred marks if you will take my securities on to the Hotel Josef at Linz."

Kenton had opened his mouth to refuse. Then that same streak of recklessness that had already proved so expensive that day asserted itself again. Six hundred marks! Well, he might as well be hanged for a sheep as a lamb.

"All right," he said.

But even as he spoke the words, he knew that this time his weakness had led him into danger.

CHAPTER 2

THE ZURICH OFFICES of the firm of Kiessling und Pieper Maschinen, GmbH, are reached by walking along a narrow passage leading off a quiet street near the station, unlocking a battered but very sturdy door and climbing five flights of bare wooden stairs. At the top of these stairs is another door with the name of the firm painted on it. An arrow points to a bell marked *Bitte schellen*—Please ring— but this does not work. There is another bell which does work, but that is operated by inserting a key in the lock, and few know about it. The firm of Keissling and Pieper does not encourage business. Although the firm still retains its original name, Kiessling and Pieper themselves have long since severed their connection with it. The firm has not prospered since, chiefly because its subsequent proprietors have always had more important matters on their hands than the disposal for profit of vertical borers, milling machines and turret lathes, the trade it professes.

One afternoon in late November one of the proprietors, Andreas

Prokovitch Zaleshoff, sat at his desk staring thoughtfully at his office wall. The unofficial representative of the USSR in Switzerland was a broad-shouldered man of about thirty-eight, with brown, curly hair. His clean-shaven face was ugly, but not unpleasantly so, and he had a habit of shooting out his lower jaw when he wished to be emphatic. His eyes were blue and very shrewd. Now they moved to a sheet of paper on the desk, then glanced toward the door leading to the outer office.

"Tamara, come here," he called. A girl came into the room.

Tamara Prokovna Zaleshoff was not, by ordinary standards, beautiful. Her face was an idealized version of her brother's. The complexion was perfect and the proportions good, but the bone structure was a little too masculine. Her hands were exquisite.

"Have you decoded the letters?"

"Yes, Andreas. There were only two."

No correspondence came direct to Kiessling and Pieper. Those who had dealings with the firm at that time always addressed their communications to a Fräulein Rosa Neumann, care of general delivery. Twice a day Tamara became Rosa Neumann and went to collect them. It was then her business to translate into sense the jumbled strings of letters and numbers before passing them on to her brother. Most of the messages were dull and the routine bored her exceedingly.

She took off her coat and hung it behind the door. Then she looked at her brother curiously. "What is it, Andreas?"

"While you were out collecting the letters, Petroff telephoned from Berlin. He was notified by Moscow last night that Borovansky has turned traitor. They found out at headquarters that he'd taken photographs of all B2 mobilization instructions and was on his way to Germany. Petroff says that Borovansky took the train to Ratisbon this afternoon and that he bought a through ticket to Linz. It looks as though he'll deliver the photographs there. Petroff has put Ortega on the job."

"Ortega?"

"That Spaniard of Petroff's who uses a knife. Petroff admits that the man is an obscenity, but says that he is very useful."

"Can he be trusted?"

"That is one of his virtues in Petroff's eyes. Ortega is wanted for murder—he slit a woman's throat in Lisbon two years ago—and Petroff would put the police on to him if necessary."

Tamara looked thoughtful. "I never liked Borovansky very much."

Zaleshoff shook his head. "Neither did I. But they said he was useful because he had worked for years in German factories and knew the Germans well. Silly nonsense! Borovansky could work all his life in a country and not even learn to speak the language like a native, much less think like one. Besides, I'd sooner be served by a fool I could trust than an expert who might betray me."

Zaleshoff picked up a large pipe, tapped the stem against his strong white teeth, then put it down. His attention seemed suddenly to have wandered. The girl watched him for a minute.

"Just how serious is this affair, Andreas?" she said at last.

He shrugged. "Nobody quite knows—yet. We have so little to work on. If we knew even who was paying Borovansky, we could move. You see, Tamara, those B2 mobilization instructions aren't just ordinary military information. If it were gunnery reports or fortification details, we should know where we stood. But it isn't. I feel in my bones that there is a political end to this business, and I don't like it. If Borovansky wanted something to sell, there are so many more marketable things he could have stolen. Why, Tamara, must he photograph these specific instructions?"

"Either because he hadn't time to get anything else or because someone had offered him money for them."

"Exactly! Now, if he was merely going to steal and photograph anything of value he could find, he would realize that the B2 papers were, for his purpose, valueless. Would he risk his life getting away with something that he knew to have no market value? No. Someone wanted the B2 stuff and Borovansky is being paid to get it. The worst of it is that nothing can be done to stop him until he gets into Austria. Berlin wants an excuse for another anti-Soviet drive and we don't want to provide it. We must hope that he does not deliver the goods before he leaves Germany."

"Why in heaven's name wasn't he stopped before he left Soviet territory?"

"They didn't know anything was wrong. Borovansky was acting as liaison between Moscow and our people in Riga. He might have remained unsuspected for several extra days if he'd had the sense to report at Riga before he made for Germany." He rose abruptly, walked to a cupboard in a corner of the room, took a bulky file from it and started turning the pages.

"A report came in from the Geneva agent this afternoon," said Tamara. "He says that the Pan-Eurasian Petroleum Company of London has failed to obtain a revision of their oil concession by the Rumanian government. Pan-Eurasian Petroleum is, he reminds us, an English company under the control of Joseph Balterghen of Gracechurch Street, London, who also has interests in Cator and Bliss Limited and other English munitions firms."

Zaleshoff, immersed in the file, grunted.

"I have turned up Balterghen's record," Tamara went on. "He is an Armenian by birth, was naturalized English in 1914, and had his fingers in the oil business as early as 1907. In 1917 he endeavored to negotiate a concession for the Baku fields with the Russian Provisional Government immediately before Kerenski's fall. In 1918 he arrived in Odessa and again tried to negotiate for the Baku fields, this time with General Almazoff, a White Army commander in the sector. He worked through an agent named Talbot. He—"

But Zaleshoff had leaped across the room and was shaking her by the arm. "What name did you say, Tamara?"

"Talbot."

"And Odessa in 1918? Balterghen was there?"

"Yes."

"Then look, Tamara. Look at this!"

Zaleshoff thrust the file he had been reading into her arms and dashed into the outer office. A second or two later the girl heard the hook of the telephone rattling furiously. She sat down, lit a cigarette slowly, then, nursing the file in her lap, began to read from the strips of typewriting pasted to thick yellow paper.

DOSSIER S8439 Copy 31 Zurich

Name. Stefan Saridza.

Place of birth. Adrianople (believed).

Date of birth. 1869 (about).

Parents. Not known.

Political sympathies. Not known.

Remarks. No useful photograph obtainable. This man has been known since 1904. See below.

Following details from Ochrana archives (Kiev): Court-martial of General Stësel 1906 for failure to hold fortress of Port Arthur against forces of Japanese. Stësel pleaded betrayal of fortress. Accused Bulgarian named Saridza. Failed to secure Saridza for examination.

Trial of Captain Bertrand Stewart (British) in Berlin 1911 for espionage. Stewart victim of agent provocateur employed at instance of German counterespionage bureau by R. H. Larsen, alias Muller, alias Schmidt, alias Talbot. Believed Saridza.

Following details supplied by Commissariat for Interior: Odessa. December 1918. Reported (K19) that agent named Talbot (see above) attempted negotiations with General Almazoff for petroleum concession at Baku. Believed acting for English oil interests.

Following details supplied by Commissariat for Foreign Affairs: March 1925. Reported (V37 Barcelona) that agent named Luis Gomez (identified as Saridza 1929) engaged in anti-Soviet propaganda particularly with reference to Soviet petroleum imports in Spain. Believed acting for English oil interests.

February 1930. Case heard before Judge Mahoina in New York City. Cator and Bliss (New York) Inc. (defendant) versus Joshua L. Curtice (plaintiff). Curtice alleged nonpayment of $100,000 expenses in connection with counterdisarmament propaganda work done at second disarmament conference Geneva. Curtice employed by London directors of Cator and Bliss Limited. Agreement reached between litigants. Curtice claimed Swiss citizenship. Identified as Saridza by B71.

Remarks. Saridza is understood to possess large organization, principally in Europe and Near East. Activities now mainly political propaganda on behalf of industrial and banking groups. Excellent organizer. Unscrupulous. Speaks English (slight accent), French (bad accent), German, Russian and Slovene.

Appearance. Height, average. Thin build. Gray hair, nearly bald, sallow complexion. Small gray clipped mustache stained with nicotine. Has been known to carry firearms.

Important Note. On every occasion on which Saridza has been identified it has been through the fact that his left arm is incapable of full articulation at the elbow. This disability produces an unmistakable awkwardness in the use of the arm.

Tamara closed the file and crushed out her cigarette. Through the open door she could hear her brother speaking rapidly.

"The Pan-Eurasian Petroleum Company, there is not a doubt of it, Petroff. The affair becomes a little clearer. You have heard of Balterghen's failure in Rumania? . . . Yes, yes, that is so. . . . But I will leave you to notify Moscow. . . . No . . . Yes . . . I shall go straightaway to Linz. . . . Yes . . . I shall take Tamara. I will recall J12 from Berne to take charge here. Please be good enough to warn Vienna."

There was a long pause. Tamara could feel her heart beating.

"Ortega?" Zaleshoff went on. "Yes, I remember his face. Who could forget it? *Au 'voir.*"

There was a clatter as he hung up. When he came bustling back into his office, Tamara was looking at the file again. "You have read it? You heard me speaking to Petroff?" He was looking excited.

"Yes. But why do we go to Linz?"

"It was I who identified Saridza in New York. I know his face well. Our people in Vienna do not. Saridza is an important enemy. It will be a great coup for us. Now, please, Tamara, get me Berne on the telephone."

Waiting in the dark little outer office for the call, she heard him rummaging furiously in his desk. She called to ask him if he wanted anything, but it was only ammunition for his revolver and he had found it.

"Andreas! We are going back to Moscow next month?" she asked.

"Yes, Tamara, next month."

"For three months?"

"Perhaps."

She was silent for a moment. When she spoke again, her voice had dropped slightly. "Andreas, shall we always do this work?"

"I hope so. We are good at it."

The telephone pressed to her ear, she stared at the clumsy, old-fashioned typewriter as she went on. "I suppose Borovansky will be dead by the time we reach Linz?"

"Ortega has instructions not to kill, but to get the photographs at all costs; do not let your imagination dwell on it."

She pressed the shift key on the typewriter thoughtfully. "Do you remember Borovansky's eyes, Andreas? One would not think that anyone with such soft brown eyes could be treacherous."

"A man's eyes, a man's nose, his forehead, his ears—none of those things, Tamara, has anything to do with the mind behind them.

There were never two people in the world who understood each other's minds by looking at each other's faces." There was a pause and she heard him open a cupboard. "We are a long time getting through to Berne. There is a train in twenty minutes."

"You must take a thick scarf, Andreas. It will be cold."

Zaleshoff came through the door. Around his neck was a wool muffler. He leaned forward and kissed her lightly on the cheek.

The telephone crackled suddenly.

"The Berne agent," said Tamara.

CHAPTER 3

FOR MOST OF the three and a half hours it took to get from the frontier to Linz, Herr Sachs talked incessantly. Herr Kenton, he said, was a person on whom a man could rely. Why should an honest man not receive payment for his honesty? He was satisfied to pay. He started picking his teeth.

Kenton fidgeted. Why should Herr Sachs be prepared to pay six hundred marks to a perfect stranger to carry the envelope to a hotel in Linz? One thing, and one thing only, was clear. All this talk of securities, Jewish suspects and Nazi spies was sheer nonsense. Kenton had, in his time, interviewed some of the most agile liars in Europe. Herr Sachs was wretchedly unconvincing by comparison. The whole business was very puzzling.

As the train approached Linz, Herr Sachs put on his hat, buttoned up his overcoat collar to conceal his mouth and nose, and hauled his case from the rack. "The Hotel Josef," he said, "is near the river, beyond the Weinzinger in the old town. You will find it. But please to delay half an hour before you come. I have business to attend to before that."

Kenton nodded.

"Good. I trust you, Herr Kenton, as I would my own mother. You will be there and I will give you the money I have promised. I, too, am to be trusted. You shall see. Please," he added, "to see if the corridor is empty."

When, some three minutes later, the train drew into Linz, Herr Sachs was out and away before it had come to a standstill, picking his way around some piles of packing cases until the shadows hid him. Then Kenton, from the compartment, saw another figure move into the light for a moment and disappear after Sachs. He shrugged. Nazi spy or no, the man with the small eyes and unwholesome face had to leave the station with the rest of the passengers. The fact that he was following Sachs meant nothing. He picked up his suitcase and left the train.

Few things are more dispiriting than the railway station of a strange town in the early hours of the morning. As Kenton walked along the platform, he vowed that, whether he could afford it or not, he would spend the night in a comfortable bed. The sky was starry and it was horribly cold. He found an open café—the Café Schwan—near the station, went inside and ordered coffee.

It was after two o'clock in the morning, when man's vitality is said to be at its lowest ebb. For Kenton the minutes that passed while his coffee grew cold enough to drink were among the most dismal he had ever spent. Here was he, thirty years of age, a comparatively responsible member of a dignified profession, throwing his money away like an undergraduate and having to accept dubious commissions from unknown men with firearms in their pockets. Well, it had to stop. He would discharge his end of the bargain, collect his money, go straight back to Berlin and get down to some real work. Meanwhile, there was the envelope. He took it from his pocket and examined it.

It was made of cheap gray paper and was stuck down firmly. There was no writing on it, and holding the envelope against the light revealed nothing.

He put the envelope back in his pocket and drank his coffee. Then, having left his suitcase with the café proprietor, he set out for the Hotel Josef. After crossing a narrow steel bridge over the river, he made his way toward the old town. A policeman of whom he inquired the way looked suspicious and directed him down a series of dark and deserted alleyways. He came at last to a short street of old houses. About halfway down it, a dimly lit box sign announced the Hotel Josef.

The entrance was not imposing. Two worn stone steps led up to a door. Kenton pushed it open and walked into a narrow passage. On the left was a small counter labeled INFORMATION. On the right a letter and key rack hung on the wall. Most of the keys were in their places.

There was no one behind the counter, but Kenton heard the sound of snoring coming from along the passage. He moved forward, a little uncertainly, to a half-open door and looked in. A candle cast a flickering light on a man wearing an apron and carpet slippers, stretched full-length on a red plush sofa. This, he assumed, was the night porter. The man woke as Kenton rapped on the door.

"Herr Sachs?" asked Kenton.

The man rose unsteadily to his feet and moved toward Kenton. Reaching the door, he leaned heavily against the wall. He smelled strongly of stale wine. *"Was ist's?"* he demanded thickly.

"Herr Sachs, *bitte.*"

The man breathed heavily for a moment or two and moistened his lips. "Whom shall I announce?"

"Herr Kenton."

"Herr Kenton! *Ach ja!*" The porter prepared to return to his sofa. Kenton, it seemed, was expected to guess the room number.

"Auf Zimmer Nummer . . . ?" he said encouragingly.

"Zimmer fünfundzwanzig, dritter Stock," the man said and, with a heavy sigh, lay back on the sofa. As Kenton started to climb the stairs, he heard the snoring begin again.

Once out of range of the passage light, the stairs were in pitch darkness and, having failed to find any switches, Kenton had to keep striking matches to light his way. When he reached the third floor it took him several minutes and many matches to find room 25. He knocked and the door swung ajar.

Except for a shaft of light from a source he could not see, the place was in darkness. It appeared to be a small sitting room. He called Sachs's name softly, but there was no response. Then he pushed the door open and stepped inside.

The light was coming through a communicating door from a single naked lamp in the bedroom, where he could see the bedclothes turned back ready for the occupant. But of Herr Sachs there was no sign.

The Hotel Josef was getting on his nerves. He called again without result and went to the bedroom door. The next instant he stood stock-still. Protruding into view beyond the bed was a man's foot.

His spine crawled. With an effort he remained motionless. Then, edging forward, he stepped into the bedroom. The man was half lying, half kneeling in a pool of blood. The knees were drawn up. The hands were clasped tightly on the handle of the knife that had been driven hard into the right side just below the rib cage. On the bed near him his jacket lay with the lining ripped out.

Kenton glanced quickly around the room. On the floor on the other side of the bed were the remains of the composition suitcase,

ransacked and slashed all over with a knife. Then his eyes returned to the body. He took one step forward. The slight movement was enough. With scarcely a sound it rolled over onto its back.

The brown eyes were no longer luminous.

THERE ARE PERSONS who can, like undertakers, adopt a matter-of-fact attitude toward dead bodies; who can touch and move them, close the eyes. Kenton was not one of those. He found that he wanted to be sick.

But he knew he ought to find out if Sachs were still alive, and if he were, to go for a doctor. Carefully avoiding the blood, he went down on his knees beside the body. He had always found it extremely difficult to locate even his own pulse. Perhaps he should undo Sachs's grimy shirt and rest his hand over the heart. He gritted his teeth and started on the waistcoat. Then he noticed that his fingers were slipping on the buttons and realized that he had gotten blood on them. He stood up quickly. The perspiration was running from his forehead. He stumbled over Sachs's torn suitcase to the washbasin, poured some water and rinsed his hands. He looked once again at the body. Suddenly he felt himself losing control. He must give the alarm, call the police, anything. This was no affair of his. He must get out as quickly as possible. He walked rapidly through the sitting room into the darkness of the corridor.

Outside the door, he stopped and began to think. What exactly was he going to do? The night porter was asleep and drunk. It was no use attempting to explain things to him. The nearest policeman was probably streets away. The thing to do was to telephone to the police from the desk downstairs.

He was about to carry out this intention when another aspect of the situation occurred to him. How was he to account for his own presence on the scene? The Austrian police would demand an explanation. They would ask certain questions.

What was his profession?
Journalist.
Ah, yes, and of what journal?
No particular paper—a free-lance.
Indeed! And where had he come from?
Nuremberg.
And for what purpose?
To borrow money in Vienna.
Then he was short of money?
Yes.
And why had he not gone on to Vienna?
He had met the deceased on the train and the deceased had requested him to carry an envelope containing documents of value to the Hotel Josef.
But the deceased was himself going to the Hotel Josef; why should he wish documents of value taken where he himself was going?
He did not know.
Did Herr Kenton expect payment for his service?

Yes. Six hundred marks.

Kenton imagined the incredulity with which that statement would be received.

How did Herr Kenton know that the deceased possessed that sum?

Herr Sachs had shown him on the train.

Ah, then he had had an opportunity to inspect the wallet of the deceased?

Yes, but—

And so Herr Kenton decided to save himself the trouble of going to Vienna to borrow money? Instead, Herr Kenton followed the deceased to the Hotel Josef?

Yes, but—

And there Herr Kenton stabbed the deceased? Then, horrified at his deed and thinking to put the police off the scent, he telephones for their aid. Is it not so?

Absurd!

The night porter deposes that Herr Kenton asked for Herr Sachs soon after that gentleman arrived.

Yes, and Herr Sachs had left word that he was expecting him.

Indeed? The night porter has no recollection of it.

The night porter was drunk.

Perhaps; but not too drunk to identify Herr Kenton.

He went back into the sitting room. It was, he decided, out of the question to allow himself to be identified with the affair. The only thing was to go while the going was good. But first there was some thinking to be done.

He hesitated, then walked into the bedroom and took a small shaving mirror off a nail in the wall. Turning it glass downward, he went over to the body and, bending down, held the mirror against Sachs's mouth. There was no trace of moisture on the glass when he looked.

Satisfied that there was nothing a doctor could do for the man, he replaced the mirror and returned once more to the sitting room. There, he seated himself in a chair facing the bedroom door and lit a cigarette.

One thing was evident. Whoever had murdered Sachs had wanted the envelope that was now in his, Kenton's, pocket. Point two: the murderer had not got it. That meant that he might still be in the immediate neighborhood. Dismissing a strong desire to look under the bed, Kenton took the envelope from his pocket and ripped it open.

Carefully placed between folds of blank paper were a series of glossy photographs. There were fifteen prints in all. Two were of large-scale sectional maps, heavily marked with crosses and numbers; the remaining thirteen were miniature reproductions of closely type-written sheets. The language was Russian, his knowledge of which was sketchy, but he knew enough to decipher the heading on the title page.

COMMISSARIAT FOR WAR
Standing orders (B2, 1925) for operations contra Bessarabia. To be observed only in the event of attack by Rumania or Rumanian allies on Ukraine along front Lutsk–Kamenets.

There followed twelve and a half pages of telegraphic but highly complicated instructions concerning bridgeheads, stores, communications, water supply, railway rolling stock and engines, fuel, roads and all the other essential details of organization attendant upon a modern army on the move.

Kenton glanced through it all hurriedly. Then he stuffed the photographs into his pocket. He was, he felt, getting into deep waters. The only proper place for the photographs was the British consulate. Meanwhile, however, both he and the photographs were in the Hotel Josef with a murdered man.

He went to the window. By drawing aside the curtains and pressing his face against the pane, he found that he could see the length of the street in front of the hotel. In a shadowed doorway on the other side of the road stood two motionless figures. A little farther down, drawn up facing his way, was a big black sedan. The way out of the hotel was closed.

He let the curtains fall and stood there for a moment. The men outside might owe their allegiance to either of two parties: the owners of the photographs which were now in his pocket, or to those who wanted the photographs. On which side had Sachs been? Probably the latter. But as he, Kenton, had the photographs, he was an object of interest to both parties. Did Sachs's friends know that he had them? Sachs had said that he had business to attend to before going to the Hotel Josef. He might have told them then. At all events, one of the parties was now waiting outside in force. The other was—where?

If he were to escape from his present predicament unscathed, Kenton had to think fast. He went into the bedroom, put on his gloves, and with his handkerchief wiped everything he could remember touching. He had no desire to leave his fingerprints for the police. Then he buttoned his coat and, after a last look around, prepared to go.

As he moved away from the bed, he felt something soft beneath his foot. Looking down, he saw Sachs's wallet. He picked it up. Just then, through the bedroom door, he heard the faint creak of a floorboard in the corridor. Slipping the wallet into his overcoat pocket, he tiptoed into the dark sitting room and stood by the door.

There was silence for a moment, then the door handle turned slowly and, as the door creaked open, Kenton pressed himself against the wall behind it. A man stepped into the room and closed the door carefully behind him. The man's back was toward him, but Kenton saw that he was short and thickset and wore a woolen muffler wound twice around his neck.

The man walked into the bedroom and glanced, without evident surprise, at Sachs's body. Then he moved out of sight, and Kenton heard sounds that suggested that the room was being searched. Now was the time to go.

He edged carefully toward the door handle and turned it. The lock made no sound. He reached the corridor, closed the door carefully and moved to the head of the stairs. He remembered vaguely having felt the draft from a window as he had climbed, but he could not recollect on which floor. He felt for his matches and found that he had now two left—one for each landing. But they burned too quickly, and by the time he had looked around the first landing and felt his way down to the second, he was depending upon touch to find the window.

Keeping the fingers of one hand brushing lightly against the wall and the other arm stretched out in front of him, he moved carefully down the corridor. After about six paces he felt the corridor turn half left. The next moment he was pulled up by a bedroom door. He was in a cul-de-sac. Retracing his steps, he followed the wall too far and failed to regain the head of the stairs. Another few paces brought him up against a blank wall. He had begun to grow desperate when he felt a slight but very cold breeze on his face. He rounded a corner and saw the window in an alcove facing him.

He leaned out. About ten feet below, he could discern the dim shape of a small outbuilding. He climbed out onto the ledge and lowered himself carefully until he was hanging in midair. Then he shut his eyes and let go.

The impact took his breath away, and he had to clutch at the tiles to prevent himself rolling off the sloped roof to the ground below. The noise he made seemed appalling, and he clung there waiting for the alarm to be raised. But nothing happened, and shortly he clambered from the roof to the ground.

He found himself in a small and very dark courtyard, and he made for a pool of shadows which might mark a way out. He was feeling his way along a concrete wall when he heard a slight sound somewhere ahead of him.

With a sinking heart he stood still and listened. The noise came again—the scratch of shoe leather on a gritty surface. There came a soft whisper from the darkness ahead.

"Is that you, Andreas?" The voice was a woman's and she spoke in Russian.

He held his breath. Then a little gasp of terror came from the darkness. The next instant a blinding light shone full in his face for a second and went out again. He ducked sideways and ran forward blindly. Another concrete wall brought him to a sharp halt. He stood where he was and stared helplessly into the darkness. Then he began to work his way along the wall.

He had moved about four yards when his fingers felt the latch of a wooden door. In a single movement he opened the door, slid through it and shut it again. Then he saw that he was in a back street and waited no longer. He ran.

HE WAS SOON LOST in a network of streets and slowed down to a sharp walk. Once or twice he looked back, but no one was following him. His idea was to make for the river, and then get back to the station. He would spend what remained of the night in a hotel, then see the British consul and hand over the photographs just before he left for Berlin. The first thing was to collect his suitcase from the café.

When he reached the river the sky was already beginning to lighten and the stones were white with frost. He was feeling very tired, but it was purely physical fatigue. Questions were jostling each other in his brain. What was the significance of the photographs in his pocket? For whom had Sachs been working? Who had killed him? Who were the sinister-looking gentry outside the Hotel Josef? Who was the thickset man with the muffler? And who was the woman who had mistaken him for someone else in the courtyard?

He could, he thought, answer the first of those questions. The trade in military secrets was, he knew, a very busy one now that nations were arming as fast as they could. He supposed that the Russian plans for military organization in the event of war with Rumania would be welcomed at Bucharest.

He had an uncomfortable feeling, however, that this answer was not quite right. The question of Bessarabia's incorporation into Rumanian territory had, he knew, been a bone of contention between Bucharest and Moscow ever since the Rumanians, driven back by the Germans, had established themselves there early in 1918. As Rumania's ally, nominally at all events, Russia had not objected. Then, following the war, Russia was preoccupied with more immediate troubles and had allowed Rumanian dominion over Bessarabia to go unchallenged until the fait accompli was generally recognized abroad and it was too late for anything but protests. Surely Rumania must have allowed for the fact that, in the event of a general European conflict, Russia might attempt to assert her undoubted legal rights by annexing Bessarabia. Besides, the orders were dated 1925. If Rumania had been able to do without the information they contained for so long, they couldn't be so very valuable. Very odd.

As for Herr Sachs, Kenton now knew what he had suspected all along; namely, that the man had not been what he claimed. The fact that he had been carrying military secrets of a somewhat unsensational nature instead of dangerous drugs or stolen bank notes merely confused the issue.

The credit for the murder of Sachs might, he decided, be awarded to the "Nazi spy," who had looked quite capable of it. Having failed to find the photographs, the murderer could have summoned his friends to await the arrival or departure of an accomplice with the photographs. In that case the man with the muffler might have been an ally of Sachs.

That explanation, however, would not do. The man with the muffler had behaved as though he already knew of Sachs's murder. Then there was the woman. Judging by her voice, she was young, and since she had spoken in Russian, probably interested in the destination of the photographs. She had addressed him as Andreas. Who was Andreas?

He gave it up; but, rather to his surprise, he found himself speculating as to the girl's appearance. Her voice had possessed an oddly attractive quality. The chances of his ever meeting her face to face were, he thought, remote. A dark courtyard, a single whispered sentence, the momentary glare of a flashlight—and that was all. How curious it was! Until the end of his life, probably, he would remember and wonder at odd moments what the owner of the voice had looked like.

He had crossed the river and was within a few minutes of the station when his thoughts were interrupted by the squeal of brakes. He looked around quickly, but he could see no sign of a car. He walked on a little way and looked around again.

The road was fairly broad and well lighted, but deserted. Suddenly there was the whine of a car being driven hard in reverse gear and a big sedan backed out of a side street he had just passed. It pulled up with a jerk, then shot forward in the direction from which he had come. It was the car that he had last seen waiting outside the Hotel Josef.

He watched it disappear around a corner with relief. Evidently they had not spotted him. Then he mentally kicked himself. How could they spot him? They did not, could not, know of his existence. He walked on, cursing himself for a nervous fool. When, turning the next corner, he glanced back and thought he saw a figure dissolve quickly into the shadows by the wall, he decided that the sooner he got some sleep the better.

He was still considering the dangers of an overwrought imagination when he arrived at the Café Schwan. Having reclaimed his suitcase and learned that the Hotel Werner, two streets away, was both good and cheap, he decided that after the excitements of the past hour, a cup of hot chocolate would be a good introduction to sleep.

While it was being prepared, and he was feeling in his pocket for his cigarettes, his fingers met the wallet he had picked up in Sachs's room. He fingered it a trifle unhappily. He had slipped it into his pocket without thinking. He should have left it for the police to find. However, now that he *had* it, he might as well learn what there was to be learned from it. He took it out.

It was of imitation leather with the initial B in one corner and had obviously cost very little. Inside, however, were over eight hundred marks in notes, four hundred and fifty of which belonged by rights to him. The only other thing in the wallet was a small green notebook with all but two of its pages blank. The two pages contained addresses, but the writing was so bad that Kenton postponed the task of deciphering them. He tore them out and stuffed them into his overcoat pocket.

There remained the money. After a good deal of quibbling with himself, he decided that he had a legitimate claim against the estate of Herr Sachs. Accordingly, he transferred four hundred and fifty marks to his own wallet.

He finished his chocolate and then asked the man behind the counter for envelopes and stamps. In the first he placed the balance of the money and addressed it to Herr Sachs at the Hotel Josef. The police would take charge of it. In the second he put one hundred marks with a note of thanks to the Havas man. In the third he put the photographs.

The first two envelopes he stamped. The third he marked with his own name and handed it over, accompanied by five marks and a circumstantial story, to the man behind the counter for safekeeping. With something approaching a light heart, he posted his letters and made his way to the Hotel Werner. The sky was graying by the time he got to his room.

He flung his suitcase on the bed, drew the curtains and sank into a chair. His eyes were aching and, leaning over to the bedside lamp, he switched the light off. He sat still for a minute, then started to take off his tie. But even as he fumbled with the knot he felt sleep pressing on his eyelids. His fingers relaxed and his head fell slowly forward. It must have been about twenty minutes later that he was disturbed by a knock at the door. He rose wearily to his feet and walked to the door. "What is it?"

"Service, *mein Herr*," said a voice. "The gentleman may be cold. I have brought extra blankets."

Kenton unlocked the door, and turning away, started once more to remove his tie.

The door opened. There was a quick movement behind him. The next instant he felt a terrific blow on the back of the neck. For a split second an agonizing pain shot through his head. Then he lost consciousness.

CHAPTER 4

ZALESHOFF AND TAMARA arrived in Linz at ten o'clock in the evening and drove from the station in a taxi to an address on the other side of the town.

Kölnerstrasse 11 was a grocer's shop in a quiet residential quarter. Leaving his sister to pay off the taxi, Zaleshoff rang a bell at a side door. After several minutes' waiting, the door opened an inch and a woman's voice demanded hoarsely who it was who rang.

"Rashenko?" said Zaleshoff.

The woman opened the door and grunted that Rashenko was on the top floor. Tamara and Zaleshoff went up five flights of bare wooden stairs to a landing with only one door. Zaleshoff turned to his sister.

"You must not be surprised at Rashenko. He was taken by some czarist officers and badly treated. As a result he is, among other things, dumb."

The girl nodded and he rapped loudly on the door.

The man who opened it was tall, white-haired and stooping. He was incredibly thin and his eyes, set deep in his head, gleamed like two pinpoints of light from the dark hollows. His thin lips stretched tightly in a smile of welcome when he saw Zaleshoff, and he stood aside to let them in.

The room was so full of furniture that it was almost impossible to move. An unmade bed was in one corner, and a wood fire burning in a small stove in another made the place insufferably hot. Rashenko waved them to chairs, then sat down himself and looked at them expectantly.

Zaleshoff took off his coat, folded it carefully over the back of his chair and sat down. Then he leaned forward and laid his hand gently on the other's arm. "How are you, my friend?"

The dumb man picked up a newspaper from the floor, produced a pencil from his pocket, wrote in the margin and displayed it.

"Better?" said Zaleshoff. "Good. This is my sister, Tamara."

Rashenko wrote again and held the paper up.

"He says," said Zaleshoff, turning with a smile to Tamara, "that you are very beautiful. Rashenko was always considered an expert in these matters."

The girl smiled. She found it extraordinarily difficult to say anything to the dumb man.

"Have you heard from Vienna that I am taking charge of this business here?" asked Zaleshoff.

Rashenko nodded and wrote on the paper, "Ortega will come here when he has interviewed Borovansky."

Zaleshoff nodded approval. "Did you ever hear of a man called Saridza?" he said. "He was with Almazoff's army."

The dumb man looked quickly from brother to sister. A guttural noise came from his throat. Then he snatched at the newspaper and started scribbling furiously. Tears were streaming down his face. Suddenly he was still and the lids drooped over his burning eyes.

Zaleshoff stood up and looked over Rashenko's shoulder, then turned to the girl. "It was Almazoff's men who tortured him," he said. "It was over eighteen years ago, but they did their work well."

Rashenko's eyes were now open and he smiled apologetically at them. Tamara looked away. The heat of the room was making her head ache.

A telephone bell shrilled suddenly.

Rashenko rose painfully to his feet and, going to a wall cupboard, lifted the instrument from a hook inside and put it to his ear. Then he pressed a small Morse key and signaled three sharp buzzes into the transmitter. For a moment he listened, then he signaled again and replaced the telephone.

He reached for his pencil, wrote a message and passed it to Zaleshoff, who turned to Tamara. "Vienna says that Ortega telephoned twenty minutes ago from Passau. He and Borovansky arrive at two thirty."

For the girl the next hundred and fifty minutes were unbearably slow. Eventually, murmuring that she was going to smoke a cigarette, she put on her coat and went out to the landing. After the heat of the sick man's room, the cold air was immediately refreshing. Through a sloping skylight just above her head she could see the stars dimmed by a rising moon. The sound of the wind was curiously soothing, and she was still there some time later when the sharp rattle of a bell far below told her that Ortega had at last arrived.

The moment the Spaniard came into the room it was obvious that something was wrong. He was out of breath from running, and the gray, puffy cheeks were flecked grotesquely with two patches of color. His dull, pebblelike eyes, blinking in the light, darted suspiciously around the room. One corner of his mouth twitched slightly.

Zaleshoff shut the door behind him and said in German, "You have what you were sent for?"

Ortega shook his head. "They were not there."

Zaleshoff gripped the sleeve of the man's coat. "No lies, my friend," he said grimly. Then he let go of the coat and held up his hand. It was smeared with blood.

"What happened?" he added threateningly.

The Spaniard, recovering his breath, assumed a jaunty air. "I kill him perhaps, eh?" He snickered. "He saw me on the train and tried to escape me at the station; but I was too quick for him perhaps. I follow him to the Hotel Josef. I wait outside the door and hear the porter give him the number. He named himself Sachs. It was room twenty-five on the third floor. Then I hear him tell to expect a Herr Kenton who would call."

"Kenton? That is an English name."

"Perhaps. On the train with him from Ratisbon there is an American or perhaps he may have been English. Perhaps this American has the photographs."

Zaleshoff made a gesture of impatience. "Quick, what did you do?"

"I go to his room by the back way so that no one sees me and I knock at his door. He says to come in, Herr Kenton, and although my name is not Kenton, I go in. When he sees me he cried out and go for the gun he had. But I reach him first and get him."

The veins stood out on Zaleshoff's forehead. "You fool!" he

shouted. "You were ordered not to kill. You kill. You were ordered to get the photographs from Borovansky. You do not get them. There is only one place for you, my friend." His voice dropped suddenly. "Lisbon. Or perhaps you would prefer the Austrian police to the Portuguese. The telephone, please, Rashenko."

"*Madre de Dios*," screamed the Spaniard, "I tell you that there were no photographs."

Zaleshoff sneered. "So you say. But I do not believe you. There was no doubt a wealthier bidder for your services. How much did they offer you, Ortega, to turn traitor?"

"Mother of God, I swear that's not so!" Sweat was pouring from his face.

"Where did you look?"

"His coat, his luggage, everything. There is nothing."

"He had hidden it in the room."

"He had no time."

"Did you look?"

"It was necessary that I go perhaps."

"And this Herr Kenton, did he arrive?"

"I do not know. I go."

"What did this American on the train look like?"

"Tall, thin, a soft hat, young perhaps."

Zaleshoff turned to the others. "It is necessary that we search that room immediately. You and I will go, Tamara. You have a pistol, Rashenko?"

Rashenko nodded.

"Good. Ortega will remain with you. If he tries to go, shoot him."

ANDREAS PROKOVITCH ZALESHOFF was, as many could have testified, a deceptive character. For one thing, he gave the impression of being almost childishly naïve; for another, he possessed a subtle sense of the value of histrionics. Violent displays of emotion, if well timed, distract the shrewdest observer and hamper his judgment. Zaleshoff's timing was invariably perfect. He rarely said what he actually thought without making it sound like a clumsy attempt to dissemble. For Tamara, who understood him better than he supposed, he was a constant source of entertainment.

As she kept watch in the darkness behind the Hotel Josef she was, however, worried. His anger with Ortega had been genuine. That could mean only one thing: that he was badly puzzled.

She was turning this over in her mind when she was startled by the noise of Kenton's arrival on the roof of the outbuilding. Wondering why her brother had not returned the way he had gone (by the tradesmen's door), she moved away from the wall to meet him.

Fortunately for Kenton, Tamara was not used to automatics. But for that fact, the career of a little-known but promising journalist might have been cut short by death in, as the newspapers say, mysterious circumstances. As the glare from her flashlight showed for a split second that the man before her was not her brother, her forefinger jerked involuntarily at the trigger of the gun Zaleshoff had slipped into her hand before he had gone inside. If the safety catch had been disengaged, not even Kenton's leap for the wall would have saved him.

Zaleshoff joined her some five minutes later with the expected news that the photographs were missing. Hurriedly she told him of her encounter. "He might easily," she concluded, "have been an American or possibly English."

Zaleshoff was silent for a moment or two. Finally, he led the way into the street again. "Go back to the Kölnerstrasse and wait there until I telephone you," he said.

He watched her out of sight, then turned and made his way by a circuitous route to the street in front of the Hotel Josef. There, keeping in the shadows, he could see four men in a sedan near the entrance, and two more gazing up at the hotel windows from farther up the street.

For a quarter of an hour they were motionless. He began to get stiff with cold. Suddenly two men got out of the car and entered the hotel. As they disappeared through the frosted glass door, the leading man raised his left hand with an awkward gesture to the inside breast pocket of his coat. His arm seemed slightly stiff at the elbow. Andreas Prokovitch, noting that fact, was feeling quite pleased with himself.

After about three minutes the two men came hurrying out of the hotel and gave a sharp order in German to the driver of the car. Zaleshoff caught only two words—"der Engländer"—then the door slammed and the car roared away.

Zaleshoff went in search of a telephone booth. Five minutes later he was giving certain instructions to Tamara. An hour later he stepped out of another telephone booth near the station and asked a man hosing the roadway how to get to the Hotel Werner.

But as he turned the corner of the street in which it lay, he saw by the cold gray light of early morning that he was too late. Two men were carrying between them what looked at first like a large limp sack from the hotel entrance to the waiting car. *Der Engländer* had been found.

CHAPTER 5

WHEN CONSCIOUSNESS BEGAN to return to Kenton's brain it brought immediate awareness of the horrible ache in his head, and of a sharp edge crushing the back of his left hand. He opened his eyes, saw a fawn-colored trouser leg, then saw its owner's foot pinning his left hand to a fiber mat. He now realized that he was lying on the floor of a car moving fast over rough ground. Striving to keep his head from contact with the vibrating floor, he lay still and closed his eyes. For a time he slipped into semiconsciousness, and heard only the steady whine of the car climbing fast in lower gear. Then the car slowed down, turned a sharp corner, rolled smoothly over concrete for a few yards and stopped.

The door opened and two men clambered over his legs to get out. There was the sound of receding footsteps. Raising his head slightly, he looked out through the open door of the car. The back of a man wearing a chauffeur's uniform partly obscured the opening, but what he could see through the gap was sufficiently astonishing. He was looking at a ridge of snowcapped hills, their summits radiant with the halation of the rising sun behind them.

For a moment Kenton forgot his aching head and cramped legs. He began to think again, to remember. He had had a room in the Hotel Werner. It had been getting light when he had arrived there. If the sun were only just rising, he must be somewhere in the hills very near Linz. What on earth had happened?

His mind was still searching feverishly among a jumble of impressions when someone shouted in the distance and the chauffeur turned and tapped him smartly on the leg with the barrel of a revolver. Kenton slid forward until his feet touched the ground, hauled himself gingerly upright and looked around. He was standing near a garage surrounded by tall fir trees. Through them he could see the top of a white house set in a niche in the hillside.

He shivered. The air was clean and exhilarating, but very cold, and he had no overcoat. The chauffeur prodded his arm with the gun.

"*Los! Vorwärts!*"

Obeying the man's order, Kenton started along a path sloping up through the firs to a flagged courtyard in front of the house. Waiting for them at the door was the owner of the fawn trousers.

He was a tall, lean, middle-aged man with a hard, stupid, rather handsome face. He wore a belted raincoat and carried what looked like a short thick stick in one hand. He gripped Kenton's arm and then, to the journalist's surprise, addressed him in English.

"Feeling a bit ill, are you, old man?" He grinned. "Well, well! Better pull yourself together, the chief wants to see you."

"Look here—" began Kenton angrily.

"Shut up and come on." Suddenly he tightened his grip on the muscles in Kenton's upper arm. The journalist cried out in pain.

The other laughed. "Good trick that, isn't it, eh?" He jerked Kenton forward through the door.

There are houses which can give the impression of wealth and luxury without the aid of soft carpets and splendid furniture. This was one of them. With the exception of two or three fine rugs, there was no covering on the waxed pine floor of the spacious entrance hall. On the far side a broad staircase curved up to a small gallery. A pair of exquisite cinquecento candlesticks stood on a narrow table against the wall, and a pinecone fire roared in a massive grate.

The Englishman led Kenton across the hall to a small door below the gallery, opened it and pushed him in. The first thing he noticed was a very pleasant smell of freshly made coffee. Then the door closed behind him and he heard from the other end of the room the clink of a cup being placed in a saucer. He looked around. Sitting behind a large desk with the sunlight now streaming through the tall windows glinting on his gray hair, was a man eating breakfast from a tray. He looked up. "Good morning, Mr. Kenton. I think you could probably do with a cup of coffee."

An impressive-looking man in his sixties, with a smart gray cavalry mustache and a monocle, he looked at first sight like a *Punch* drawing of a retired English general. He spoke, however, with a pronounced Russian accent, and the skin of his face was stretched like creased yellow parchment over a bone structure which was certainly not English. The mouth below the gray mustache was loose and curiously cruel, and the monocle did nothing to hide a pair of pale, calculating and very dangerous eyes. Kenton experi-

enced an immediate, powerful sense of dislike. He came to the point.

"I should like to know by what right—" he began angrily.

The other held up his hand. "Mr. Kenton, please! I have not been to sleep all night. I must ask you to spare me your outraged feelings. We are all feeling outraged this morning, aren't we, Mailler?" He addressed the last words over Kenton's shoulder.

"My God, yes," said Kenton's escort.

"All the same," continued the man at the desk, "I understand your indignation. What right have I, a perfect stranger, to tell my men to club you and to carry you off in so high-handed and uncomfortable a manner—you, an English journalist, if the press card in your pocket does not lie? What right, I say?" He thumped the desk with his fist.

"Exactly," said Kenton, a little bewildered by this vigorous presentation of his case.

"The answer is none! No right at all except my own wishes."

"And those are?"

"Surely," the man said, "you are in no doubt about that?"

"I'm afraid I am," said Kenton with rising irritation. "I can only conclude that you have mistaken me for someone else. I don't know who you are or what your game is, but you have placed yourself in a very awkward position. The British consul in Linz will not, I should think, be disposed to intercede with the police on your behalf and, unless I am immediately released and taken back to Linz, nor shall I. Now, if you please, I wish to go."

The man at the desk smiled broadly. "Excellent, Mr. Kenton, excellent. Mailler is appreciating your performance, too. You and he would, I feel sure, grow to like each other very much. Captain Mailler was in the Black and Tans, and was also, at one time, the only professional strikebreaker in America with an English public school education. At the moment, of course, he is hoping that you will attempt to leave this room."

Kenton studied an inkwell on the desk. He had an uncomfortable feeling that no mistake had been made and that he could guess only too well what was wanted. He looked up.

The man behind the desk was lighting a cigarette rather awkwardly, as though his arm were very stiff at the elbow. He blew a long, thin jet of smoke into the air, then turned to Kenton again. "Sit down, Mr. Kenton. You, too, Captain."

Kenton sat down.

"Why did you kill Borovansky, Mr. Kenton?"

"Who?"

"Borovansky. You may have known him as Sachs."

"Never heard of him."

The man behind the desk sighed wearily. "It may be," he said with an air of great patience, "that you doubt my motives. Borovansky, personally, was not of the slightest interest to me. He was, however, carrying certain property of mine. I wish you to restore that property to me. If you have examined it, you know that the photographs are of no monetary value to you. You will also realize that anyone being so foolhardy as to interfere in such affairs places

419

himself in a very delicate position. Borovansky's wallet with all his money in it is, I find, in your pocket. You see, Mr. Kenton, it was hardly tactful of you to mention the police, even in fun."

"You're talking nonsense. I did not kill Sachs."

"Ah, then you did know him?"

Kenton stirred in his chair. He did not seem to be doing very well. He changed his tactics. "You can hardly expect me to treat you with great confidence. Quite apart from the fact that your thug here has assaulted me and that you are holding me prisoner, I have no idea who you are."

"I fail to see that it can be of any help to you to know my name, Mr. Kenton. It is, however, Robinson—Colonel Robinson."

"English?"

Colonel Robinson smiled. "No, Mr. Kenton. Why should I bother to deceive you? My accent, as you know, is not quite perfect." He leaned forward. "Now, my friend, where are the photographs? I know they are not on your person."

Kenton hesitated. His first impulse was to supply the information and get out. He glanced at the two men. The ex-Black and Tan captain was lounging in his chair, absently biting his nails. Across his knees lay the short, shiny black stick. Colonel Robinson was leaning forward in his chair, a cigarette smoldering between his lips. In their eyes, watching him intently, there was a hint of amused expectation. Rather to his surprise, he became conscious of a new and unfamiliar sensation. For the first time in his adult life someone was trying to coerce him with threats into making a decision, and his mind was reacting with cold, angry, obstinate refusal. There was an edge to his voice when at last he answered.

"I am afraid I have no intention of telling you any such thing. Certain property was entrusted to my care. The man who entrusted it to me is now dead. He was no friend of mine. I met him on the train coming to Linz. But he paid me well for safeguarding his property and I accepted the responsibility. That he was subsequently stabbed to death does not seem to me to affect that responsibility in the slightest."

"Then how, may I inquire, do you intend to relieve yourself of the responsibility?"

"The photographs," Kenton replied cautiously, "would seem to be the property of the Russian government. If you can show me credentials authorizing you to act on their behalf, I shall be pleased to hand over the photographs when I am released."

There was dead silence for a moment or two. Then the captain rose slowly to his feet. "Now," he began, "you're going to get—"

The man at the desk waved him into silence and turned to Kenton. "I don't think you quite understand the position, Mr. Kenton. Borovansky, or, if you prefer it, Sachs, was working for me. It was to me that he was delivering the photographs."

"Then why did he hand them over to me?"

"He was afraid that he would be attacked and the photographs stolen from him before I could provide him with protection."

"And yet he was murdered."

"Shortly after you appeared, Mr. Kenton," said the colonel pointedly. "When he arrived at the Hotel Josef, Borovansky telephoned to say that you were carrying the photographs. My men were on the spot in time to see you go in. They did not see you leave."

"Sachs was already dead when I arrived. I left by the back entrance."

"With the photographs?"

"Certainly."

"Don't you think you are being rather foolish, Mr. Kenton?"

"Why?"

Colonel Robinson's yellow skin tightened suddenly. "Because, Mr. Kenton, whatever your prim notions of responsibility may be, I want those photographs and intend to have them. Furthermore," he added slowly, "I am prepared to take any steps necessary to overcome your scruples."

"Such as?"

The colonel's face relaxed. "What paper do you work for, Mr. Kenton?"

"I am a free lance."

"Indeed? Dear me, that makes it very easy. Do you know that I could, through my principals in London, have your name blacklisted by the proprietors of every important group of newspapers in England?"

Kenton smiled. "I'm afraid I can't take that very seriously, Colonel. You see, quite apart from the fact that many editors make a point of circumventing that sort of order from a proprietor, I use at least six pseudonyms in my work, none of which is anything like Kenton. Under the circumstances, your principals might find you a little tiresome."

The moment he finished, he knew his flippancy had been a mistake. The man behind the desk was silent, not a muscle of his face moved, but in some subtle fashion the mask changed from one of watchful geniality to one of malignant fury. He fingered his lower lip and gazed at Kenton thoughtfully.

"The art of persuasion," he said, "has always interested me, Mr. Kenton. The days of the rack, the wheel and the thumbscrew are past. Today we look toward new horizons. To Fascist Italy must go the credit of the discovery of the *bastonatura in stile*, a process that consists of treating the lower part of the face with rubber truncheons, such as the one Captain Mailler is holding, until the jaw is shattered. Oddly enough, the subject frequently dies of lung congestion some few months later. The American police have given us, beautiful in its simplicity, the dentists' burr drill to grind the teeth of reluctant mouths. Rubber hoses, blinding arc lamps, lighted cigarettes and well-placed kicks all have their advocates. You see what is in my mind, Mr. Kenton?"

The journalist was silent.

Colonel Robinson smiled slightly. "I think you do. But I am going to place you in a room by yourself for twelve hours. If at the end of that time you have not decided to be frank with me, then I shall hand you over to Captain Mailler and his assistants for interrogation." He nodded to the captain. "All right, Mailler, put him in the top room."

"Get up," said Mailler.

Kenton got up. His face was white with fatigue, his swollen eyelids were twitching with the pain in his head, but his mouth had set in an obstinate line. "Your name might actually be Colonel Robinson," he said. "I doubt it. But whatever your name is, you are, in my opinion, a nitwit. At one stage in this conversation I was willing to wash my hands of the entire business and hand over the photographs to you. You made the mistake of supposing that I could be intimidated. It is a mistake that quite a number of persons of your stupid, brutish kind are making in Europe today."

Mailler's fist with the truncheon in it dashed into his face. He reeled backward, caught his foot in the chair and went down, blood trickling from the corner of his mouth.

Mailler went to the door and called two men in. He gave them a sharp order in bad German, and Kenton was dragged to his feet and taken out. He was carried to a room at the top of the house, where he was dumped on the floor. The shutters were pulled to and fastened with a padlock and chain. Then the door slammed and a key was turned in the lock.

For a time Kenton remained where he had been dropped. At last he raised his head painfully and looked around. The sun was sending long, slanting bars of light through the shutters. By its reflection, Kenton could see that there was no furniture in the room. For a moment he contemplated the pattern of sunlight on the floor thoughtfully. Then, resting his head in the crook of his arm, he lay back and closed his eyes. A minute or two later he was asleep, and on his lips was the slight, contented smile of the man who remembers work well done.

CHAPTER 6

WHEN KENTON AWOKE the room was in almost complete darkness, and for some seconds he did not realize where he was. Then he remembered and got stiffly to his feet. His face felt badly bruised, and his lower lip was swollen. His head, however, was no longer aching. He went to the window and, by crouching down, he could see a black sky through the slats. It was evidently quite late. Colonel Robinson's ultimatum must expire very soon.

Nearly twelve hours of sleep had left Kenton wondering why on earth he had made such a fuss. His reaction to the methods employed by Colonel Robinson and his aide to secure the Sachs photographs had been emotional. All that absurd fit of heroics had produced was a swollen lip and a bruised face. The best thing he could do was to hand over the photographs and get back to Berlin.

He sat on the floor with his back to the wall and considered his plight. He did not feel very hungry; but that was probably because he was so thirsty. His last meal had been off Sachs's garlic sausage in the train. That seemed a long time ago. He found it a little difficult to get the events of the past twenty-four hours into perspective. What curious business had he become involved in? Had Sachs, or rather Borovansky, been working against the Russian government? And the colonel's "principals in London"—who were they? Principals in London in a position to influence newspaper proprietors sounded suspiciously like big business.

Kenton had often observed, in his study of foreign politics, that it was the power of business that shaped the destinies of nations. The foreign ministers of the great powers might make the actual declarations of their governments' policies; but it was the big businessmen —the bankers and their dependents, the arms manufacturers, the oil companies, the big industrialists—who determined what those policies should be.

Kenton found a cigarette in his pocket and lit up. It looked as if big business was, in this case, interested in either Bessarabia or Rumania. He drew at his cigarette and the end glowed in the darkness. He watched it thoughtfully. He had recently heard something about Rumania that had interested him. Ah yes! That business about concession reform. A newspaper that had printed an article against it had been wrecked. Well, there didn't seem to be much to be gotten out of that; though, of course, you never could tell. One end of the game was played in the rarefied atmosphere of boardrooms and weekend shooting parties; the other was played, with persons like Sachs as agents, in trains and cheap hotels. Someone spoke in an office in Birmingham or Pittsburgh, or maybe on board a yacht off Cannes, and a few weeks later a bomb burst in a newspaper office in Bucharest. Between those two events, unknown both to the man who had spoken and to the man who had pulled the pin from the bomb, was a misty hinterland in which the Colonel Robinsons of the earth moved silently about their business. Yes, he would certainly give up the photographs. His role had always before been that of spectator; let it remain so.

He crushed his cigarette out on the floor and rose to his feet. As he did so he heard the sound of approaching footsteps, a pause, then the rattle of a key in the lock. The door opened, the beam of a flashlight cut across the room, then swung around and shone straight into his eyes.

"Well, old man," said the voice of Captain Mailler, "are you going to be sensible or do I have to knock hell out of you first?"

For about five seconds Kenton did not speak. In those five seconds all his sane reflections on the desirability of giving in gracefully and keeping out of trouble were swept away by just two things—Captain Mailler's voice and Captain Mailler's words. The entire structure of anger and defiance that reason had so completely demolished was once more reerected. And this time it was supported by a body no longer tired, a brain no longer distracted by the aftereffects of concussion.

"You can do exactly what you like," he said at last. "But if you think you can bully me into doing anything, you've made a mistake."

"Don't be silly, old man," said the captain evenly. "The chief wants to see you. He's not feeling very pleased with you."

"I'm not feeling very pleased with him," retorted Kenton.

Mailler grinned unpleasantly. *"Vorwärts!"* he said.

Two men appeared from the passage outside and seized Kenton's arms. He shook them off and received a kick on the ankle, the pain of which took his breath away. Then he was hauled downstairs to the colonel's room.

The colonel, wearing a suit of tweeds, was standing in front of a fire, looking a picture of landed respectability. "Are you ready to be sensible yet?" he asked Kenton coldly.

"If by that," replied Kenton promptly, "you mean am I prepared to hand over to you what is obviously somebody else's property, the answer is no."

The colonel's arm shot out; he caught hold of Kenton's jacket and jerked him forward. "Listen, my friend," he said quietly, "I am in no mood for drawing-room pleasantries. I need those photographs and I am going to get them. What did you do with them?" He struck the journalist across the face with the back of his hand.

Kenton's hand went to his face. Then he looked at his fingers. The colonel wore a ring and it had opened his cheek. He decided on revenge.

"I—I don't remember," he stammered weakly.

The colonel shook him violently and struck him again.

"Perhaps that'll help you."

Kenton cringed. "Yes, yes," he babbled, "I will tell you. I put them in an envelope and gave it to the *patron* of the Café Schwan to be called for."

The colonel drew a deep breath and turned to Mailler. "Quickly now. Take the car and one man with you and get to the Café Schwan immediately."

The captain started for the door.

"Just a minute," said Kenton loudly. "I am sorry to dash your hopes so soon," he went on smoothly, "but I forgot to add that when I gave the photographs to the *patron*, I said that on no account was he to give the envelope up to anyone but me in person. I hinted that it was an affair of the heart, and you know what a reputation for discretion these café proprietors have. The *patron* would, I am afraid, regard Captain Mailler as the villain of the piece if he tried to get that envelope." He smiled reproachfully at Mailler.

There was not a sound in the room except the ticking of a clock. Then the colonel cleared his throat. "It seems, Mr. Kenton, that we shall have to insist upon your cooperation."

"You won't get it."

"I think so."

"My God, yes," said Mailler. "Leave the little swine to me."

The colonel caressed his lower lip. "Yes," he said thoughtfully, "I shall leave him to you. Only don't take too long about it, Mailler. Bastaki is expecting me in Prague tomorrow. And don't forget that this man's face must not be damaged and that he must be able to walk." He turned to Kenton. "In view of your claim, Mr. Kenton, that your possession of the photographs is purely accidental, I find your attitude completely incomprehensible."

"You would," retorted Kenton rudely. "But your treatment of me leaves me no alternative. Anything I can do to cause you and your charming principals inconvenience gives me the liveliest satisfaction."

Colonel Robinson warmed his hands at the fire and shook his head sorrowfully. "Believe me, Mr. Kenton," he said slowly, "my treatment of you until now will seem like a mother's caress compared with what you will experience in the next few hours." He nodded to Mailler. "All right, take him away and get on with it."

Kenton was marched across the hall to a door under the stairs, then down a flight of narrow stone steps. Mailler went ahead, switching on lights. The two men held Kenton by the wrists and drew him after them. At the bottom of the stairs was a long stone-flagged corridor which led through an archway into an old wine cellar. Mailler pressed a switch, and a naked lamp bulb glowed yellowly on a dusty collection of broken furniture, rusting ironwork and old curtains. The four walls were lined with empty wine bins.

Mailler extracted a chair with sound legs from the rubbish and dumped it in the middle of the floor. "Tie him up," he ordered in German.

The two men pushed Kenton into the chair, produced a hank of thick cord and proceeded to lash his legs to the frame. He glanced at Mailler.

The captain seemed very excited. He had taken the rubber truncheon from his pocket and was weighing it in his hand and flicking it viciously against the side of the arch. An unpleasant change had come over his face. The jaw had dropped slightly, his cheeks were sunken, he was breathing quickly and his eyes had become curiously glazed. Already frightened, Kenton began to feel an almost hysterical terror stealing over him.

The two men tested their knots carefully and stood up. Mailler walked over and stood in front of Kenton. Suddenly he lifted the truncheon high into the air and went up on his toes. Kenton clenched his teeth. The truncheon came down with lightning speed and stopped an inch from his cheek.

Kenton broke out into a cold sweat. The two Germans laughed. Mailler's lips smiled and he tapped the side of Kenton's head playfully with the truncheon. The next moment Mailler's smile changed to a glare of animal ferocity and he brought the truncheon around in a vicious arc. Again it stopped just short of Kenton's face. Again Mailler smiled.

"Enjoying yourself, Kenton?"

Kenton said nothing.

Still smiling, Mailler flicked him lightly across the face with the truncheon. For a moment Kenton thought that his jaw had been shattered by the blow. The pain was agonizing.

Mailler stood back. "Going to be sensible, old man?" he said. "Or do I have to make a real start on you?"

Kenton did not answer. His silence seemed to madden the captain, for suddenly he stepped forward and lashed furiously at Kenton's knees and legs. When at last the rain of blows ceased, the journalist, almost fainting from the pain, felt his willpower going. If Mailler repeated his attack, principles or no principles, he would agree to anything.

"Had enough yet?"

Kenton wanted to shriek, to scream that they could have their photographs. But his conscious brain had lost control of his body. He gasped out a single syllable, "No."

He saw Mailler raise the truncheon again, his face contorted with vindictive fury. Kenton shut his eyes and his body stiffened to receive the blow.

But no blow came. An uncanny quiet seemed to have fallen. Slowly he opened his eyes.

Mailler was still standing in front of him, but the truncheon had fallen to the floor and his hands were raised high above his head. Beyond him the two Germans stood in similar postures. Kenton turned his head. In the entrance to the cellar stood a stocky little man with a dark pugnacious face. Wound twice around his neck was a thick woolen muffler. In his hand was a large blue revolver with the hammer cocked.

"The first one that moves," said Zaleshoff in German, "I will kill."

ZALESHOFF STEPPED FORWARD a pace or two and his eyes met Kenton's for a second. "Mr. Kenton?" He spoke English with an American accent.

Kenton nodded.

"Are there any more upstairs?"

"There's a man who calls himself Colonel Robinson."

"Has he a stiff arm?"

"Yes."

Zaleshoff jerked the barrel of the revolver toward one of the rather bewildered Germans. *"Lass ihn los!* Let him go!"

Under the Russian's watchful eye, the man produced a large clasp knife and hacked at the cords which bound Kenton. The journalist eased his muscles and tried to get up, but the battering Mailler had given his legs made this process painful.

"Can you stand?" asked Zaleshoff anxiously.

"I'll be all right in a minute."

"Okay. Be as quick as you can."

"My God, you'll get hell for this," the captain burst out.

Zaleshoff bent down, picked up the rubber truncheon and, keeping his eyes on the three men in front of him, held it out to Kenton.

"Here you are. Do you want to try it on him?"

"Very much; but at the moment I should prefer to get away from here."

"Good. Take that rope he's cut off you, tie their hands behind them, put them against the wall and tie them to the bins. Then gag them. I'll keep watch."

Kenton did as he was told, but when he came to the gagging process he was at a loss.

"Tear pieces off those old curtains," directed Zaleshoff, pointing to the corner of the cellar. "Screw them up, stuff them in their mouths, then tie them in with the mouth open."

Kenton followed instructions. Mailler swore and then refused to open his mouth, but Zaleshoff tapped his jaw with the truncheon and the captain gave no more trouble.

"Now," said Zaleshoff, "if you're ready, we'll go."

Kenton followed him down the corridor, along a narrow boarded passage and out into the open air. The sky was black with cloud. There was no wind, but Kenton's teeth started to chatter with the cold. Then he felt something warm and soft being pushed into his hand and found that his companion was giving him his muffler. Murmuring his thanks, he put it on and felt better. The other's hand pressed his arm, enjoining silence, and drew him forward along a loose stone path and through a fringe of bushes. Kenton realized that they had reached the fir trees near the garage. Suddenly Zaleshoff gripped Kenton's arm tightly. They stood still. Out of the darkness came the sound of a man whistling a German love song.

"We must pass the garage to get to the road," Zaleshoff whispered. "The way through the forest would take too long."

"The chauffeur's got a gun," returned Kenton.

Zaleshoff was silent for a moment, then, whispering to Kenton to stay where he was, he crept forward to the edge of the garage clearing. Kenton leaned against a tree and waited.

Left to himself, he began to ponder the question of his companion's identity. There was no mistaking that stocky figure with the large muffler. This was Andreas, the man who had searched Sachs's room at the Hotel Josef, and for whom he had been mistaken in the courtyard. So he might be Sachs's murderer. Not a very comforting possibility! However, the man knew his name and seemed to be on his side—whatever that might be—and had so far exhibited no homicidal tendencies.

Zaleshoff returned. "The chauffeur's doing something to the car, but we must get past without his seeing. We can't stay here. If Saridza goes to see how those men in the cellar are progressing, we shall be caught."

"Saridza?"

"Colonel Robinson. His name's Saridza."

Kenton decided that that matter could wait. "All right. What's your plan?"

"I have a car, but it is about two kilometers down the road to the valley. We must get there before they can get after us."

"Where do we start?"

"The drive to the garage is cut through a rise in the ground. It is narrowest at the top of the rise, but there the sides of the cutting are too high. We must cross nearer and choose a moment when the chauffeur is looking the other way."

"All right."

They began to work their way carefully to the left. There were places where the bushes were close together and they had to worm their way below the branches to avoid the rustling leaves. At last the garage light showed through the bushes to the right and Zaleshoff halted.

"We are near the edge of the cutting," he whispered. "There's a drop of about two meters to the drive."

They went forward. Suddenly Kenton saw a patch of brightly lit concrete six feet below him. He leaned forward to get a better view. About fifteen yards away stood the black sedan. The hood was up, and the chauffeur was working on the engine.

Zaleshoff gripped an overhanging branch and began to lower himself down to the edge of the concrete. Kenton followed, and they were soon crouching in the shelter of a bush at a point from which they could see both the chauffeur and the bank on the opposite side of the drive.

For several minutes they stayed there, until finally the chauffeur went into the garage.

"Now," whispered Zaleshoff, and the next moment he was walking calmly across the drive toward the bushes on the other side. Kenton followed, and was soon blundering through the dark trees again after his companion.

A short time later Zaleshoff gave vent to a Russian crow of self-congratulation. "Now we make for the car," he added. "We shall

have to get straight down to the lower bend in the road. It will be tough going and I dare not use a light. Someone might see it."

The descent was, for Kenton, the worst sort of nightmare. His experiences of the past twenty-four hours, his weakness resulting from lack of food, the bruises on his legs, had left him in no condition for traveling long distances by foot, but Zaleshoff urged him on ruthlessly. The face of the hill was covered with deep hollows and the forest was pitch-black. He kept missing his footing and slithering down wildly, only to be brought up with sickening force by the trees. The steep slope of the ground made it necessary to go on all fours in places. One trouser leg was ripped by a dead branch. His face and hands were badly grazed and he wrenched a wrist. By the time he reached the road at the bottom, he was in a state of collapse.

Zaleshoff took his arm and hurried him along the road. It seemed to Kenton that they kept going for hours. At last Zaleshoff slackened his pace and Kenton saw, through half-closed eyes, the shape of a large touring car with no lights. By the driver's door stood a girl. She started forward to meet them.

"What is it, Andreas?" said a familiar voice.

Kenton began to laugh hysterically. "Andreas," he panted, "there's no need to introduce me. We've met before." He withdrew his arm from Zaleshoff's, took a step forward and stood still. His knees seemed to give way and there was a rushing noise in his head. For the first time in his life, he fainted.

CHAPTER 7

KENTON BECAME CONSCIOUS of a pleasant burning sensation in the pit of his stomach and a taste of something like a mixture of turpentine and olive oil in his mouth. A man's voice said something in Russian that he did not understand and a glass clinked against his teeth. The next moment he sat up choking and coughing, and opened his eyes. He was on a red plush sofa in what, at first sight, looked like a secondhand furniture shop. Bending over him was an elderly man with cadaverous cheeks and sunken eyes, who held a small glass half filled with a colorless liquid. Kenton realized the reason for the warm glow inside him and the curious taste in his mouth. He had been drinking vodka.

Seated at a table, watching him gravely, was the man he knew as Andreas.

"You are feeling better?" said Zaleshoff.

Kenton nodded a little uncertainly and raised his hand to wipe the remains of the vodka from his chin. The hand was stained with iodine. Kenton looked inquiringly toward Zaleshoff and opened his mouth to speak. The Russian forestalled him.

"You are in a house in Kölnerstrasse in Linz," Zaleshoff said. "My sister and I brought you here. She has gone out to buy some food. Our host here, Rashenko, does not understand English, and he is, poor fellow, dumb."

Kenton nodded his thanks to Rashenko, then turned again to Zaleshoff. "I'm sorry to be a nuisance," he said. "But do you mind telling me who you are and why I am here? I should also like to know how you knew my name, why you rescued me from that house, and whether you were responsible for the death of a man called Sachs or Borovansky, whose room you searched. I am curious, too, about the man calling himself Colonel Robinson. Why do you call him Saridza? There are other things that are puzzling me, but I'm sure you will see the general idea. Incidentally, what time is it?"

"Just after midnight," said Zaleshoff. He pursed his lips. "As for the rest of your questions, Mr. Kenton, I suggest we wait until after we have refreshed ourselves with food before we start on the explanations. Tamara and Rashenko shall cook for us."

Kenton smiled. "I like you, Andreas," he said. "You know perfectly well that I have something that you want; you hear with well-concealed surprise that I saw you search Sachs's room, and yet you propose that we eat before we talk! Why, I haven't even thanked you for rescuing me!"

Zaleshoff shook his head gravely. "You mistake my motives, Mr. Kenton. Try to stand up."

Kenton obeyed. His head swam and a wave of nausea swept over him. He sat down again quickly.

"You see, Mr. Kenton, it would be a waste of time to start talking just at the moment. Rashenko used to be a doctor. He reports that you are in a state of extreme nervous and physical exhaustion. You are suffering from the aftereffects of concussion and lack of food. The wild elation you are experiencing at the moment is produced by the vodka. You had better have some more."

Rashenko was now busy at the stove. Zaleshoff reached for the bottle, poured out two large tots and handed one to Kenton. "Vodka," he said, "should be poured straight down the throat. I will show you. *Pros't!*"

He raised the glass to his lips, jerked his head back and swallowed once. Then he set down the empty glass.

Kenton followed suit and felt the liquid burn in his stomach.

"All the same," he resumed obstinately, "I should like to know who you—"

A knock at the door interrupted him. Zaleshoff turned in his chair, and Kenton saw that the blue revolver was in the Russian's hand. The door was opened, and Tamara came into the room carrying a bulky string bag.

"Mr. Kenton," said Zaleshoff, flourishing the revolver in a grand gesture, "this is my sister, Tamara. Tamara, this is Mr. Kenton."

The girl nodded gravely to Kenton. "Please, Andreas," she said, "do not wave that pistol about so. It is dangerous."

Her brother took no notice and turned to Kenton. "What do you think of her, my friend?"

"She is remarkably beautiful," said Kenton. "As beautiful as her voice."

Zaleshoff slapped his knee delightedly. "You see, Tamara, what vodka will do even to a cold-blooded Englishman."

"You will embarrass him," said the girl calmly, and emptied the string bag onto a chair. "Be careful, Mr. Kenton," she added over her shoulder. "My brother is endeavoring to lull you into a sense of false security in the hope that you will take him into your confidence."

Zaleshoff bounded to his feet and pointed a denunciatory finger at his sister. "Look," he roared at Kenton. "Hampered and thwarted at every turn by my own mother's daughter! I soothe you, I give you vodka to drink, we become friendly, then—*piff*—Tamara breaks the spell with her foolishness." He sank back into the chair and buried his head in his hands.

"Very amusing," said Kenton evenly. "Do you think I might have a glass of water?"

Zaleshoff raised his head slowly and stared sullenly at Kenton. Suddenly he brought the flat of his hand down on the table with a crash and started to roar with laughter.

"There, Tamara," he gasped at last. "We do not deceive him, you see. He is unmoved. He sees through our little tricks to gain his confidence." He turned, beaming, to Kenton. "My apologies, Mr. Kenton. One should have realized that such foolish histrionics were an insult to your intelligence. We have your forgiveness?"

"Naturally," said Kenton uncomfortably.

The Russian sighed with relief.

"That is good to know," he said fervently. "If only," he went on dreamily, "we knew a little more of Mr. Kenton's thoughts." He leaned forward suddenly. "Why, for instance, is he prepared to go to such lengths to preserve the property of the Soviet government?"

The suddenness of the attack took the journalist completely by surprise. He was silent for a moment. Zaleshoff, no longer benignly theatrical, was watching him intently with blue eyes that had become extraordinarily shrewd and calculating.

All this Kenton saw in the fraction of a second. Then he smiled easily. "I thought we had postponed business until after we had eaten. Still, if you wish . . ."

Instantly Zaleshoff was all apologies. Yes, yes, of course, Mr. Kenton was right. Meanwhile, some more vodka. No? Zaleshoff then began to give the girl a wildly exaggerated account of their escape from the house on the hill.

The meal came at last. It consisted of borscht with sour cream, and little pasties filled with chopped vegetables and, except for a paean of congratulation directed by Zaleshoff at Rashenko, it was eaten in silence. The moment they were finished Rashenko began to clear the dishes from the table. Kenton accepted a cigarette from Zaleshoff. He was feeling better.

Zaleshoff turned to the girl. "Where did you put that paper, Tamara?" She went to the cupboard and returned with a sheet of gray paper covered with small writing. Her brother took it, pressed Kenton into a seat on the sofa and sat on a chair facing him. The girl sat behind the table with a pencil in her hand and a notebook in front of her.

"A court of inquiry?" said Kenton. He saw a look of faint amusement flicker across the girl's face.

"Not at all," Zaleshoff replied, a little too emphatically. He held out the gray paper for Kenton to take.

It was headed "Dossier K4596" and began: "Desmond d'Esterre Kenton, journalist, born Carlisle 1906." It went on to describe, in German, his parents and their histories, his appearance, his character, his career, his political leanings and his work for various papers, with an accuracy and insight that he found very disconcerting. He read it through twice and handed it back.

"I showed this to you," Zaleshoff said, "more to make my position clear than to impress you. It is unimportant." He threw it on the table. "Tamara, you may tear it up."

Kenton noticed, however, that the girl put the paper carefully in the back of the notebook.

"And now to business," Zaleshoff went on affably. "How, Mr. Kenton, did you come to be in the Hotel Josef the other night?"

Kenton examined his cigarette. "I shall be glad to tell you," he murmured, "but I want to know first to whom I am talking."

Zaleshoff frowned fiercely. "My name will convey nothing to you. However"—he shrugged—"it is Andreas Prokovitch Zaleshoff."

"Zaleshoff?" Kenton leaned back on the sofa thoughtfully. Then he snapped his fingers. "Got it! Weren't you deported from the United States for Communist agitation in 1922? Pittsburgh, I fancy, though it may have been Detroit."

He expected an outburst of theatrical indignation, but to his intense surprise he saw a deep blush creeping over the Russian's face.

"Chicago," muttered Zaleshoff almost sheepishly.

The girl began to laugh. It was, thought Kenton, a very pleasant sound, but her brother rounded on her angrily and pounded the table with his fist. "Stop, Tamara, stop at once!" He turned to Kenton. "You are right," he said with a comical attempt at jauntiness. "I was very young at the time. A boyish escapade, nothing more. But it was 1925, my friend, and in Chicago." He laughed rather unconvincingly. "It was good of you to remember the name, but your facts were quite wrong."

"That," said Kenton, "is hardly to be wondered at. When you were being deported from Chicago I was a rather pimply adolescent. Until just now I had never heard your name before in my life."

Zaleshoff leaned back in his chair, breathing noisily through his nose. It was the girl who spoke first.

"Do you mean, Mr. Kenton," she said, her voice broken with suppressed laughter, "that you made up that story about my brother?"

Kenton nodded. "Yes, I made it up. You both speak English fluently with an American accent. You must have spent a number of years in America. I had every reason to believe that your brother was employed by the Soviet government. I wanted to annoy him into showing his hand. The deportation business had the right circumstantial feeling about it."

"Well, I'll be—" began Andreas Prokovitch Zaleshoff, but the girl interrupted him.

"Our father was killed secretly by the Ochrana in 1910. Our mother escaped from Baku with Andreas to America, through Mexico, where I was born. But she never took out the proper papers, and when Andreas got into trouble with the police for his propaganda they found out about us and we were deported. Our mother was dead; we spoke Russian better than English, so we claimed Soviet citizenship. It is quite simple."

"If, Tamara, you have quite finished these domestic revelations," snarled her brother, "I wish to talk to Mr. Kenton myself." He turned to the journalist. "Now, Mr. Kenton, you know who I am. Supposing you tell me how you came to be at the Hotel Josef?"

"Very well, there seems to be no harm in that."

Zaleshoff listened intently while Kenton described his meeting with Sachs, his reason for accepting Sachs's offer and his visit to the Hotel Josef. When he came to his interview with Colonel Robinson, however, the Russian began to interrupt with questions. What exactly had been said? Had the subject of oil been mentioned? When Kenton spoke of the colonel's principals in London, Zaleshoff rapped out an excited comment in Russian to his sister. The colonel's intention of going to Prague was noted carefully.

"And then," Kenton concluded, "you appeared on the scene—how, I cannot imagine."

"That is easily explained. I saw Saridza's men carry you out of the Hotel Werner. Later, I searched your room. I found a small piece of paper torn from a notebook in one of your overcoat pockets. It had two addresses on it. One was the Hotel Josef, the other was the Villa Peschik. That was the name of the house in which I found you."

"But how did you know of my existence?" A thought struck him. "I suppose that pasty-faced specimen that Sachs told me was a Nazi spy wasn't one of your little friends?"

Zaleshoff looked mystified.

"Who murdered Sachs?" persisted Kenton.

Zaleshoff shrugged. "Who can say?"

"All right," said Kenton irritably, "let it go. Is there any further information I can give you?" he added ironically. His head had begun to ache.

"There are two things more," purred Zaleshoff. "I heard the end of your conversation with Saridza from outside the window before you were taken to the cellar. Why did you not surrender the photographs and save yourself that rather painful interlude with Captain Mailler?"

Kenton laughed shortly. "Zaleshoff," he said, "my father was Irish, my mother was French. Rather to my surprise, I find that I have inherited from them two curious qualities—obstinacy and the faculty of resentment."

The Russian glanced at his sister. "Does that make sense to you, Tamara?"

The girl nodded. Her brother turned again to Kenton. "One other thing," he said. "Where can I find those photographs?"

Kenton thought swiftly. Zaleshoff had obviously not heard enough of his interview with the colonel to know about the café. "If you really don't know," he said, "I'm going to bargain with you."

"Indeed?"

"Yes. During the past twenty-four hours quite a lot of unpleasant things have happened to me. I demand compensation."

The Russian's lips tightened. "How much?" he said quietly.

Kenton registered horror. "Dear me, not money! That makes the third time I have been offered bribes in connection with this bunch of rather uninteresting photographs. I didn't think it of you," he added reproachfully.

Zaleshoff's face darkened. "Come to the point, please."

"Certainly. I am a reporter. I want to know who Saridza's principals in London are, and why they're so interested in Bessarabia and Rumania. I want to know what oil has to do with it and where you come in. I want the works, in exchange for the photographs."

Zaleshoff looked grim. "I'm afraid, Mr. Kenton, that I am not empowered to make statements to the press. In any case, the affair is purely commercial, of no political significance. No paper would publish anything so unimportant."

"I'll tell you about that when I've heard the facts."

There was a long pause, then the girl spoke. "I think, Andreas," she said, "that we shall have to compromise with Mr. Kenton."

The Russian glanced at the journalist for a moment or two. Then he shrugged. "Very well. I suppose it makes no difference. One can only regret," he added viciously, "that one did not leave Mr. Kenton to the excellent Captain Mailler for just a little longer."

Rashenko brought them tea in glasses. Zaleshoff crushed a slice of lemon into his glass and stirred the contents moodily. At last he looked up. "You must understand, Mr. Kenton," he said with an air of brisk candor, "that my connection with this affair is purely accidental. I am a private Soviet citizen with business interests in Switzerland—the importation of machinery, to be precise." He paused.

"However," he went on, sipping at his tea, "the Soviet citizen is, in common with other nationals abroad, always ready to place his country's interest before his private business affairs. When, therefore, I was requested to assist in a rather unusual matter of government business, I had no alternative but to agree. That, Mr. Kenton, explains my position in this affair."

Kenton, secretly amused at this naïve evasion, nodded solemnly and lit a cigarette. "And Borovansky's murder?" he said.

Zaleshoff waved the question aside. "An insignificant incident. We will talk about it another time."

"In that event, I feel sure you will excuse me if I return to my hotel and get some sleep. It is late and I am tired." Kenton stood up and started toward the door.

"Just a minute, Mr. Kenton."

He turned. Zaleshoff was standing behind the table. In his hand was the blue revolver.

The journalist shrugged. "I am getting a little bored with all this melodrama," he said acidly. "What is it?"

"The photographs, Mr. Kenton."

"I have already made you an offer."

Zaleshoff's jaw shot forward angrily. "What you ask is absurd. Be sensible, Mr. Kenton."

"Colonel Robinson was anxious, too, that I should be sensible."

"I am not interested in Colonel Robinson's anxieties."

"Nor I in yours. I am going to be sensible from my own point of view. I am interesting myself professionally in this affair."

For a moment the two men glared at each other in angry silence.

"I think," said Tamara, "that it would be better and more comfortable if we all sat down again."

"You keep out of this."

The girl flushed slightly. "I will not keep out of it, Andreas. You persist in treating this man as if he were a cretin like Ortega, but I think that you will have to accept his terms."

Kenton expected an outburst from the Russian, but it did not come. Zaleshoff dropped the revolver into his pocket, sat down and began pouring himself some fresh tea. Kenton glanced at the girl uncertainly. She motioned him back to the sofa.

"So," Zaleshoff said sardonically, "you are feeling sure of yourself, eh? Andreas Prokovitch is forced to give way to the demands of the gutter press."

"A question of *quid pro quo*, surely?"

"*Quid pro quo!*" repeated Zaleshoff with deep contempt. "There is a great deal too much *quid* and not enough *quo* about this business."

"He will stop talking nonsense in a minute," said the girl calmly.

"Quiet!" snarled her brother. "This interfering busybody of a reporter pays you a stupid compliment and you lose your senses completely." He turned to Kenton suddenly. "Why, my interfering friend, do you suppose I wish you to give me those photographs?"

"Because the documents are important," said Kenton promptly.

"Very clever of you. The photographs were taken illegally by a man in a government department in Moscow."

"Borovansky?"

"Yes. The man who told you his name was Sachs."

"And where does Colonel Robinson come in?"

"Saridza was the man who bribed Borovansky to take the photographs."

"Then he was speaking the truth when he said that Sachs was on his way to deliver them?"

"Yes."

"Who was the man in the train of whom Sachs was afraid?"

"I know of no man in the train," said Zaleshoff shortly.

Kenton decided to shelve the point for the moment.

"Who is Saridza?"

Zaleshoff looked thoughtfully at the glass in his hand, and it seemed to Kenton that the Russian was talking to himself. "They say that persons like Al Capone and John Dillinger are products of America's corrupt administration and clumsy lawmaking. Saridza and his kind must be the products of the world business system. The difference between Al Capone and Stefan Saridza is that Capone worked to increase his own income. When Saridza ordered that captain to beat you with a cudgel until you gave him some photographs, it was to increase the income of what he called his principals in London—gentlemen who would, in all probability, hesitate before they swatted a fly. You see, your businessman desires the end, but dislikes the means. He is a kindhearted man. He likes an easy conscience. He likes to sit in his office and deal honestly with other businessmen. That is why Saridza is necessary. For at some point or other in the amazingly complicated business structure of the world, there is always dirty work to be done. It may be simple bribery, it may be the manipulation of public opinion by means of incidents, rumors or scandals, it may even be an affair of assassination—but whatever it is, Saridza and his kind are there to do it, with large fees in their pockets and the most evasive instructions imaginable.

"Saridza started his career in Bulgaria in the early 1900s, by intimidating shopkeepers—the protection racket, as it is called in America. But he has progressed. Today his specialty is molding public opinion, and he is a person of curious importance. He has been decorated by most European governments. Those same governments also have his dossier in their files of dangerous foreign agents. He calls himself a propagandist. A better description would be political saboteur."

Kenton fidgeted. "But what would he want with those photographs?"

Zaleshoff wagged an expressive finger. "Ah! There you have it. What indeed? As soon as I had positively identified Saridza with this affair, we set ourselves to examine the problem."

"We?"

"Tamara and me," said Zaleshoff blandly. "We concluded that the key to the situation was in Rumania. Saridza had some years previously been in touch with the Pan-Eurasian Petroleum Company, and he had been employed, apart from that, by the present chairman of the company, Mr. Balterghen. It is the Pan-Eurasian Company that has been behind the agitation for oil-concession reform in Rumania."

"Wait a minute. There was some business about a newspaper being wrecked for printing an article about that, wasn't there?"

"There was, and we have learned that the orders to wreck the newspaper offices originated with the agent of the Pan-Eurasian Company in Bucharest. The idea was, apparently, to kill the issue in which the article appeared, but the paper was already distributed before the thing happened. It wasn't a very good article, but it upset the concession reform proposals and resulted in an official inquiry."

"You mean that Saridza's principals in London are the Pan-Eurasian Petroleum Company?"

"It seems likely."

"But I still don't see where Sachs and his photographs come in."

Zaleshoff lit a cigarette. "Have you studied Rumanian politics recently, Mr. Kenton?"

"Consistently."

But the question had evidently been rhetorical, for Zaleshoff went on as if the journalist had not spoken. "Until 1936," he said, "Rumania's foreign policy was based on friendship with Russia. But there is reaction in the air of Rumania. With Fascism in Italy, National Socialism in Germany and the Falange in Spain, it was hardly likely that Rumania would escape the contagion. Rumania's little Hitler is Cornelius Codreanu, a lawyer who formed a party called the Iron Guard. Its policy is a familiar one—anti-Semitism, a corporate state and an alliance with Germany. But Antonescu, who is now foreign minister, has formed an alliance with Poland, aiming at strict neutrality toward *both* Germany and Russia. This means that unless something serious happens, Codreanu cannot achieve personal power and the German alliance. Now do you see where Saridza stands, Mr. Kenton?"

"You mean that he has been employed to provide that 'something serious'?"

"Exactly. You are familiar with the old Bessarabian quarrel between Russia and Rumania. The Iron Guard is out to drive Rumania into the bosom of Germany by inflaming public opinion against Russia. The Soviets, they will declare, are planning to attack and seize Bessarabia. They will create a scare; then, suddenly, dramatically, they will produce the evidence—those photographs—as proof of Russia's intentions. It is merely a question of skillful timing. Mass hysteria will do the rest."

"Would it? I wonder."

Zaleshoff snorted irritably. "My dear Mr. Kenton, there is probably in the British War Office a complete plan of attack by England against France. It is part of the business of war offices to evolve such things. Nobody in England dreams of attacking France. The two countries are allies. But supposing you published that plan in France, and swore that England was greedy for French Morocco—what sort of effect do you suppose it would have on public opinion there? A disposition to distrust England's motives in the future would be the least of the damage done. Yet England and France are as friendly now as two nations can be in this world. Imagine, then, the damage to the relations between two countries in the position of Russia and Rumania. Wars have been fought over less."

"But where does Pan-Eurasian Petroleum come in?"

"The price of Saridza's assistance to Codreanu in gaining power is the immediate use of that power to revise the oil concessions in Pan-Eurasian's favor. It's an old game. The big oil interests played it in Mexico for years. That's why there used to be so many revolutions."

Kenton was thoughtful for a moment. "What makes you so sure," he said at last, "that what you have told me will not prevent me from giving up the photographs? For all you know, I might be a diehard Tory with a nice holding of Pan-Eurasian shares."

Zaleshoff smiled grimly. "Please give me credit for a little sense. If you had held any shares of any value at all, you would not have needed money in Nuremberg so badly. And your dossier credits you with a sort of modest radicalism, very common among English journalists."

Kenton yawned. "Well, you needn't worry. I'll let you have the photographs. You were right, of course, about there being nothing in it from my point of view. Something that nearly happened isn't news." He stood up. "The photographs are with the *patron* at the Café Schwan. I arranged with him that he was to hand them over to nobody except me in person. He's open all night, so we'll go now if you like."

Zaleshoff looked inquiringly at the girl.

"We cannot risk it," she said.

Zaleshoff nodded and turned again to Kenton. "I regret," he said, "that you will have to spend what remains of the night here. In the morning we will consider what to do."

Kenton looked grimly from one to the other. "I don't quite understand," he said.

"It will be more comfortable—" began Zaleshoff in a conciliatory tone.

But the girl interrupted him. "He had better know the truth," she said. "Mr. Kenton, it is quite impossible for you to claim that packet at the Café Schwan. It would even be dangerous for you to be seen in the street."

"Why?"

"Because there is not a newspaper in Austria tonight that does not carry your name, description, and a large reproduction of a fingerprint found on the washbasin in room twenty-five at the Hotel Josef. Every policeman is on the lookout for you. There is a price on your head of one thousand schillings. You are wanted for the murder of Herman Sachs."

AT A QUARTER PAST TWO that morning the proprietor of the Café Schwan telephoned the police with news that, ten minutes earlier, three masked men had driven up in a black closed car, menaced his customers with revolvers and ransacked his premises. One of the two men present at the time, a railway official from the station, had attempted to resist the bandits and had been shot in the foot. No money had been taken, but a small packet, left by a young American, had been removed. The man who had shot the railway official was tall and thin. The other two were of medium height. The arm of one of them, the left arm, he thought, had appeared to be rather stiff at the elbow. No, he could not remember the name of the American—it might have been Krause.

The police promised to investigate the affair.

CHAPTER 8

IN THE COMPLEX ANATOMY of cause and effect, in that crazy pastiche of history which some dismiss as "the blind workings of fate," there is often to be observed a certain artistry.

In 1885 there lived in Salzburg a young married couple named Hoesch. Karl, the husband, was employed in the office of one Buscher, a maker of glass beads. Early in 1886 Herr Buscher died. In his will, among other bequests to his employees, he left his clerk Hoesch a German translation of the *Iliad* "for the nourishment and improvement of his mind and that of his good wife." From then on Karl read the *Iliad* assiduously, both to himself and to Frau Hoesch. When, in 1887, it was known that their first child would soon be born, the pair decided immediately that if it were a boy he should be called Achilles. In August of that year, Achilles Karl Hoesch was baptized.

The young Achilles was a lusty and pugnacious lad, who, on leaving school, entered the service of the State Railways. After twenty-six years he was made a subinspector of freight traffic at Linz; and it was about two years later that he formed the habit of dropping into the Café Schwan when he was on night shift, to drink a *Kaffee* and eat a piece of *Kuchen*.

He had been thus occupied when Colonel Robinson and his assistants had appeared on that November night with pistols in their hands and threats on their lips. Quivering with a rage worthy of his namesake, Achilles, on being invited to put up his hands, had grabbed a chair and hurled it at Captain Mailler's head. The captain ducked, fired at Achilles' legs and hit him in the foot. At the hospital it was found that the bullet had passed through the fleshy part of the heel.

Almost every town of any size has its nightly quota of violence. Unless the case possesses that mysterious quality called news value, little is heard of it. The wounding in the heel of an unknown Linz railway official would have possessed no news value. Nor would the wounding in some unspecified part of the body of Achilles Hoesch. But the wounding in the heel of a man named Achilles *did* possess news value—it was a good joke.

Half an hour after Achilles was carried into the hospital, an agency message was being ticked out by tape machines in the offices of every Vienna morning paper, and was promptly squeezed onto the front page of all late editons. It was headed ACHILLES' HEEL.

SHORTLY AFTER HALF PAST SEVEN that morning Zaleshoff rose stiffly from a chair beside the stove in Rashenko's room in Kölnerstrasse 11, felt his way in the semidarkness to the washstand and sluiced his face with cold water. This done, he peered at his sister curled up in an armchair.

"Tamara," he whispered softly, "I'm going out to get some air." He listened for a moment to the faint snores coming from the sofa and to Rashenko's heavy breathing from the bed. "Don't wake them," he added.

The door squeaked slightly and he was gone.

The girl gazed for a moment at the dull glow of the dying fire, then shut her eyes again. It seemed to her that she had scarcely done so before her brother was by her side, shaking her arm and whispering to her to get up and put on her coat. In his hand was a newspaper.

When, two hours later, Kenton awoke, Zaleshoff and Tamara had gone. A shaft of pale sunlight filtering through the gap between the curtains was shining in his eyes. He sat up on the sofa and something fell to the floor beside him. It was a piece of paper folded in three. He opened it.

Dear Mr. Kenton,

On the table in the middle of the room there is today's newspaper. Two news items on the front page will interest you. The one which concerns yourself should not, I think, be taken too seriously. The police are always expected to make an arrest within the next few hours. The other item will explain itself and our absence. The race is to the swift. Do not attempt to communicate with anyone. Remain here with Rashenko until I am able to arrange for you to be moved out of Austria. My sister, whose maternal instincts are clearly aroused, sends her best wishes.

The note was unsigned. Zaleshoff was nothing if not careful.

Kenton looked for the news items to which the note referred, and a short paragraph recording the incident at Café Schwan the night before caught his eye. So Saridza had got his photographs after all! That was that.

He moved the curtains aside and gazed out of the window, down at the pavement far below. There were a few children playing, an old woman, one or two hurrying men. He experienced a sudden desire to get out of Rashenko's cramped, stuffy room and walk in the open air. And why not? He had done nothing criminal. It was absurd that they should suspect him. Absurd that . . . but they didn't *suspect* him. This was Austria, not England. Until he should prove his innocence, he was not merely suspect—he was guilty!

He let the curtains fall and stood up. The bottom half of his body ached badly. This was due partly to the stiffness of his joints and partly to a colorful display of bruises. However, a small mirror on the wall showed that, except for an unsavory growth of beard, his face had returned to its normal proportions. His clothes had fared badly—a huge rent in his trouser leg and minor tears on the sleeves and back of the jacket. A bath was badly needed. He stripped and, going to the washstand, did what he could with the small handbasin and a jug of cold water. He dried himself and put on his shirt and trousers again. Then he lit a cigarette, sat down and began to read more carefully the account of police activity in connection with the murder.

Fingerprints! He had thought he had wiped everything he had touched. He must have forgotten the basin where he had washed his hands of Sachs's blood. The night porter's description was fairly good, though the name was spelled Kent*en*. The man could not have been as drunk as he had looked. There was money missing. Sachs had paid in advance for his room and the porter had seen the wallet. There was no mention of the money he had posted to the hotel, but the police were no doubt keeping the handwriting on the envelope as a conclusive tidbit for the trial. What a fool he had been to send it! The Hotel Werner had contributed handsomely to the evidence. The murderer, stated the manager, had arrived in the early hours of the morning looking very disheveled, as if he had been struggling with someone. When his flight had been discovered later that day, the room had been in great confusion. This, Kenton concluded, was not unlikely in view of the fact that both Saridza and Zaleshoff had searched his things. It was a watertight circumstantial case. His only defense could be the rather feeble assertion that Sachs had been already dead when he, Kenton, had arrived. The story of the photographs would do more harm than good; it could only serve to provide the prosecution with an additional motive for the crime. His one chance lay in finding the real murderer and bringing him to book.

He paced the room distractedly. If only Zaleshoff had not slipped away. He would have forced the Russian to tell the truth about the murder. He remembered the blank looks and cold denials that had met his inquiries. Either the "Nazi spy" or Zaleshoff himself had stabbed Sachs, of that he was convinced. Zaleshoff, acting, no doubt, on the information he had given him the previous night, was on his way to Prague. The pasty-faced thug of the Nuremberg–Linz train was doubtless hundreds of miles away. To Zaleshoff, as long as his government's aims were achieved, the fate of an obscure English journalist was a matter of minor importance. He should have wrung the truth out of the man the previous night. But Zaleshoff and his sister had been clever. They had found out what he had done with the photographs before they told him about the police. The haggling had been playacting. How relieved they must have been that he had not insisted on the name of Sachs's murderer!

Kenton raged at their perfidy. The girl, at least, might have had a little more consideration for him. He smiled dryly. Consideration! What a prim, respectable word to use in connection with so grotesque a business! He was, he decided, losing his sense of proportion. The point was, what was he to do now?

Zaleshoff badly wanted those photographs. He, Kenton, had surrendered them for a news story that he couldn't use. They had been his only bargaining weapon. Supposing, by some means or other, he could regain possession of that weapon. Then . . .

It was crazy, hopeless. How could he possibly get hold of the photographs? Saridza was probably already in Prague. Zaleshoff was by now speeding after him. Moodily Kenton crushed his cigarette out and rested his head in his hands. A psychiatrist would have observed the journalist's behavior during the succeeding two minutes with professional interest. The expression of utter dejection on the face changed suddenly. The lower jaw drooped, the eyes opened wide, the forehead creased thoughtfully. Then the forehead returned to normal and the mouth spread slightly in the beginning of a grin. Kenton stood up, snapped his fingers, said, "Ha!" and whistled softly. For he had remembered something—something all-important—the fact that Colonel Robinson was going to Prague *to meet someone named Bastaki.*

In his hurry to tell Zaleshoff his story, he had forgotten all about the name. He had not, indeed, regarded Saridza's destination as being of importance. Now, however, the knowledge of Saridza's destination *had* become important. It might make it possible for him to regain possession of the photographs before the Russian could do so, in spite of the latter's head start. Prague was a large place. With nothing at all on which to work, Zaleshoff's task was a formidable one. On the other hand the name Bastaki might prove to be an invaluable lead. At all events, he told himself, he had nothing to lose. If he failed to find Saridza or if, having found Saridza, he failed to get the photographs, he could still try to get to England through Poland.

The feeling of having a definite object in view cheered him enormously. The first necessity was clothes. His hat and overcoat were at the Hotel Werner or had been removed to the police station. His trousers were useless if he wanted to get anywhere without attracting attention. The next essential was money. He counted the contents of his wallet. He had four hundred and sixty-five reichsmarks and a little loose change. If he spent the sixty-five on clothes, that should leave enough to last a week or two and, if necessary, buy passage home on a boat.

He walked over to the bed where Rashenko was lying on his back. "Rashenko," Kenton said. The eyes opened. "You know," he went on in German, "that Zaleshoff and his sister have gone?"

Rashenko nodded. Then he clambered slowly out of bed and wrapped an old dressing gown around his shoulders. The journalist watched him go to a table and scribble rapidly on a piece of paper. At last he held it up for Kenton's inspection.

"You have made up your mind to go," Kenton read, "but I beg that you remain here. It is safer. Andreas Prokovitch will not fail you."

"How did you know that I was going?"

Rashenko scribbled again. "I have been watching your face. I saw you make up your mind. You will be caught. It is our wish to help you; but if you leave this house we can do nothing."

"I must take my chance."

"Where do you go?"

"To England. Then I am safe from arrest."

"You will be caught at the German frontier, if not before."

"I shall go via Czechoslovakia."

For a second, suspicion gleamed in the Russian's sunken eyes, then he shrugged his shoulders slightly and, turning to the stove, began to make coffee and heat some rolls that he took from the cupboard. Over the coffee and rolls Kenton stated his wants—a razor, some Austrian money in exchange for his German notes and some clothes. Rashenko nodded gloomily, took one of Kenton's hundred-mark notes and showed him where the razor was. Then he went out.

Wondering whether the Russian intended doing his shopping in a dressing gown, Kenton started on his beard. He decided to leave himself a mustache. When, however, he came to the point of shaping it he was in a difficulty. He had never before attempted to wear a mustache and was uncertain of the technique. A toothbrush effect would look too English. He decided finally to let the stubble finish at the corners of his mouth. The result, he was interested to note, made him look extremely bad-tempered. He was examining the work critically when Rashenko reappeared with a large bundle of clothes.

Kenton took it eagerly. On the top was a little pile of Austrian money. The clothes consisted of a gray soft hat with a round, flat, continental brim, a pair of thick brown trousers and a voluminous dark gray overcoat. They were obviously not new.

"Where did you get them?" he asked.

Rashenko smiled, but made no attempt to answer.

Kenton put on the hat and looked at himself in the mirror. There was something curiously familiar about the way the crown was pinched in that he could not identify. He shrugged. There must be hats like it all over Europe.

Ten minutes later he buttoned up the overcoat, shook hands with Rashenko and left Kölnerstrasse 11. On the pavement outside he stopped for an instant, took a deep breath of fresh, cold air and turned to the left.

CHAPTER 9

TAKING A ROUTE described by Rashenko, Kenton made for a travel agency in the center of town. To his relief, the place was far from empty. At a long counter a Swiss couple were asking about trains to Basel. A little farther on, a chattering group laden with cameras and binoculars sat beside a large notice which announced in German, French and English that at twelve o'clock a conducted party would leave by luxury motor coach for a tour of the Bohemian Forest country.

He had decided to go by train to some point near the Czech frontier, wait for nightfall and strike off cross-country, trusting to luck and the darkness to get him past any frontier guards who might be patrolling the unfrequented stretches. He could then rejoin the road on the Czech side, walk to a town and board a train for Prague.

On one wall he found a map of Austria. It revealed two routes, neither of which seemed promising. Then he noticed that due west of Freistadt a single road was shown crossing the frontier into Czechoslovakia. He looked again and saw that across the empty area surrounding it was the word Böhmerwald.

Böhmerwald—the Bohemian Forest! And just behind him, sitting waiting, was a party going that way by motor coach. He glanced at the clock. It was twenty to twelve. He returned to the map. His road went through a place called Neukirchen. He went up to the counter and a man hurried forward.

"I have only a few hours to spare in Linz. Is there perhaps a drive, a tour that one could make?"

Certainly, there were many. There was an afternoon drive to the Hallstätter excavations. Or, if *mein Herr* wished, there were trips to the Pöstlingberg and Steyr with many places of educational and artistic interest.

Kenton nodded carelessly in the direction of the motor coach group. "This excursion here, for instance. It is good?"

Yes, yes; a beautiful drive; through Neukirchen up into the woodlands to the highest point, one thousand meters, from which one could see into the heart of old Bohemia. Unfortunately, if *mein Herr* had only a little time it was not possible. The return was not until evening.

Kenton explained hurriedly that he did not leave until late that evening, bought a ticket, sat down as quickly and unobtrusively as he could with the rest of the group, and broke out into a nervous sweat. "Highest point one thousand meters," "see into the heart of old Bohemia"—the two phrases were ringing in his head. He forced himself to breathe easily and regularly, and took stock of his traveling companions. He counted nineteen and, as far as he could see, they were mostly Austrians. In front of him, however, was a rather severe-looking young Frenchman talking in a passionate undertone to a woman next to him. Next to them was a man immersed in a newspaper. His back was to Kenton, but the journalist saw, with a pang of fear, that he was reading about the Hotel Josef murder. Kenton stared at the floor and wished he had thought to buy a book or a newspaper behind which to hide his face.

After a few moments his eyes wandered furtively toward a small table about six feet away from him. On it were arranged neat piles of travel booklets. He gazed at them longingly. With one of those to look at he would not look so conspicuous. At last he stood up and walked to the table. In his overwrought imagination everyone in the room promptly stopped what he or she was doing and stared at him. Unnerved, he grabbed a booklet from the nearest pile and turned quickly to get back to his seat. The metal buckle on the belt of his overcoat hanging loose at his side promptly swung around and hit the table with a loud report.

Crimson in the face, Kenton blundered back to his seat and buried his face in the booklet. It proved to be a list of December sailings from Genoa. Two minutes later, to his profound relief, it was announced that their motor coach had arrived and they might now take their places.

Kenton, who had maneuvered himself to the tail of the procession, found when he climbed inside the coach that there was only one seat left. It was beside the newspaper reader, a thin-faced little man with rimless spectacles and a pair of very sharp blue eyes. He sat down and looked out of the nearside window. The next instant his heart nearly stopped beating, for he was staring straight into the eyes of a policeman standing on the pavement. His first impulse was to scramble out through the offside door and run. Then he saw that, owing to the reflection on the window glass, the policeman could not see him. He relaxed, wiped his forehead furtively with the back of his hand, and prayed silently that the driver would get a move on.

"Funny outfits, aren't they?" It was the thin-faced little man and he was talking English with the unmistakable accent of the inner London suburbs.

Forcing himself to keep calm, Kenton turned to the speaker. "Bitte?"

The sharp blue eyes gleamed with amusement through the spectacles. "Go on! You're not going to tell me you're not a Britisher?"

Kenton laughed feebly. "I'm sorry. One gets so used to speaking German." He felt himself blushing. "Yes, they do look a little odd," he added hastily.

"Efficient lot, though, the Austrian police," pursued the other. "I've been in and out of the country for years now and I reckon they're one of the smartest lots in Europe. Get their man every time."

Desperately Kenton changed the subject. "How did you know I was English?"

The other winked heavily. "Spotted you right away. You'd never guess how."

"The clothes?" said Kenton cunningly.

"Yes and no." He fingered Kenton's overcoat contemptuously. "That's continental stuff. The hat's German. No, it was your jacket lapel, showing under your overcoat collar. Your jacket's English."

Kenton remembered that he had bought the jacket in London. "I don't see how you can tell. I might have got it in Paris, Berlin, anywhere."

The little man shook his head triumphantly. "No, you couldn't, friend. The only stitch of that worsted on the Continent is in a bag of samples at my hotel. I'm the continental rep for the firm that makes it—Stockfield, Hatley and Sons of Bradford. It's my day off. Hodgkin's the name."

"You're very observant," said Kenton, who was beginning to feel slightly hysterical.

"Get used to looking at stuffs if you're in the trade," said Mr. Hodgkin.

To the journalist's relief the coach started, and for a few minutes Mr. Hodgkin stared out of the window. Kenton made up his mind to change his seat at the first stop they made. If he were to carry out his intention of slipping away from the party near the frontier it was essential to disengage himself from Mr. Hodgkin. The man was obviously the sort who would cling like a leech, given the slightest encouragement.

"I've never heard such talkers as the Austrians," resumed Mr. Hodgkin suddenly. "They'd make a mother's meeting look like a party of deaf-mutes. The Czechs now are different. Businesslike. No nonsense. The Czech police are pretty hot, too," he added inconsequently.

Kenton began to find these references to police efficiency a little disquieting. "Business good?" he said.

Mr. Hodgkin laughed bitterly. "I ask you, friend, with labor the price it is in Czecho and Hungary? The old buyers know me and take my stuff because they like the quality of it. But they won't sell it, and they know it. Too pricey. But I expect you've got troubles enough of your own without mine. May I ask what your line is?"

"Oh, I'm more or less holiday-making."

"You don't say!" Mr. Hodgkin produced a pipe and started to fill it from an oilskin pouch. "You know, until I saw that jacket of yours, I should have put you down as a German. You spoke German as good as a native when you were talking over the counter. That overcoat, too—" He broke off suddenly and pointed with his pipe-stem out the window. "See that? That means snow tonight."

Kenton followed the other's gaze. The coach was running smoothly down a long treelined slope. The sun was shining, but far away to the northeast there was a curious leaden look about the sky.

"I shan't mind bed tonight," said Mr. Hodgkin cheerfully. "Where are you stopping at Linz?"

Kenton remembered just in time that the representative of Stock-field, Hatley and Sons might have overheard his conversation with the agency clerk. "I'm leaving for Vienna tonight."

"Ten o'clock train?"

"Yes."

"It's the best." Mr. Hodgkin lit his pipe, and there was silence for a time.

His companion, the journalist decided, was typical of that strange species of Englishman—the export travelers. They spoke foreign languages, drank foreign drinks, ate foreign foods, listened to foreign points of view and remained indomitably English.

A few minutes later, as the coach approached Neukirchen, Mr. Hodgkin nudged Kenton sharply with his elbow. "We're stopping for lunch. They'll probably try and scoop us into one of these tourist restaurants off the square. You and I'll slip off on our own, friend. I always do this trip when I'm in Linz, and I know where we can get better grub, and a darn sight cheaper."

"That'll be fine," Kenton replied weakly, and soon found himself following his companion down a side street to an unpretentious eating house behind a church.

Over a meal of stuffed cabbage and beer, Mr. Hodgkin told several old and salacious anecdotes, all concerned with the amorous adventures of commercial travelers. "It's a treat," he said, "to swop yarns with a Britisher. These foreigners' funny stories are always about politics or suchlike."

Kenton agreed a little absently and got on with his food. It might be many hours before he could safely eat again. It occurred to him, however, that there was a possibility that Mr. Hodgkin might solve one very important problem. Over the brandy he asked if Mr. Hodgkin knew Prague.

"Like the back of my hand," was the prompt reply. "It's quite a nice city. The lavatories are as clean as the German, which is more than you can say for Italy, even if they do have German plumbing."

"I've always liked Prague, too," said Kenton. "I wonder if you know a man named Bastaki."

Mr. Hodgkin shook his head slowly. "Name seems familiar somehow, but I can't place it. What does he do?"

"I don't know. A friend of mine mentioned him."

Mr. Hodgkin screwed up his eyes, raised his right hand and snapped his fingers several times as if to summon divine assistance.

"What nationality?" he said suddenly.

Kenton, convinced that Mr. Hodgkin could not help him, took a long shot. "Rumanian."

Mr. Hodgkin tapped the table triumphantly with his forefinger. "Got it! I knew I'd heard the name somewhere. Bastaki! He's in Prague. I suppose your friend isn't Eccles, of Parker, Sons and Kelsey, of Oldham?"

"I'm afraid not."

"Well, that's a pity. You'd like Eccles. Parker, Sons and Kelsey do a bit of business over here."

"He knows Bastaki?"

"Of course, that's what I'm telling you. Bastaki's one of his customers in the electrical trade. Eccles is in cotton, of course."

"But you said Bastaki is in the electrical trade."

"Yes, that's right—cable making. Use hundreds of miles of yarn a year for insulation. Braiding, that's what they call it. Eccles sells him the stuff in bobbins—hundreds of miles of it. He's got a factory outside Prague."

"Who? Eccles?" Kenton was getting confused.

"No, Bastaki. Pots of money, of course. Eccles says Bastaki's father owns pretty near half Rumania—industry, not land, of course. His wife's a Czech or something."

"Bastaki's wife?"

"That's right. It's a pity you don't know Eccles. He's a nice chap. Well," he continued, "I suppose we ought to be getting back now. Not that they'll be ready to start."

HALF AN HOUR LATER the coach left Neukirchen and ran once more into the open country. Mr. Hodgkin, silent for the moment, stared gloomily out the window. Kenton, who had plenty to think about, pretended to doze.

Bastaki was a Rumanian. His father was an important Rumanian industrialist. Saridza was meeting him. In association those facts told their own story. And it was a familiar story. What the Thyssens and Krupps did for Hitler, the Bastakis and Balterghens could do for Codreanu. Although Kenton had not the remotest idea what to do with his knowledge, he was enjoying a sense of quiet elation. Then he reminded himself that he was still well inside Austria, that he had a frontier to cross without showing a passport, and that he had acquired, with his information about Bastaki, the leechlike representative of Stockfield, Hatley and Sons of Bradford. He decided that elation was a trifle premature. He must devise some plan of action, but it was warm and comfortable in the coach. He had arrears of sleep to make up. Unaccountably, he found himself thinking of Zaleshoff's sister. In his note, Zaleshoff had declared caustically that her maternal instincts had been aroused. He smiled to himself. It was pleasant to think of her. Her hands were lovely. Maternal? That was what Zaleshoff *would* say, of course. A lovely mouth.

A minute later his head nodded forward onto his chest and he was asleep.

He awoke with a start, Mr. Hodgkin's elbow at work on his ribs.

"We're there, friend."

"Ah yes! I must have dropped off to sleep for a moment."

"Best part of an hour," said Mr. Hodgkin.

Kenton looked out of the window. The coach was grinding slowly over the crest of a steep hill. Trees grew almost to the edges of the road. A little way ahead was a small highly colored timber inn set back from the road in a clearing. The coach stopped and they got out, shivering. Mr. Hodgkin peered at Kenton over his misted spectacles. "Do you want to follow the others to look at the view, or shall I show you a better spot? I found it two years ago."

Kenton glanced uncertainly at the rest of the passengers being marshaled by the conductor for the walk to the heights. "Won't the conductor think we're lost?"

"Fat lot he cares. They've had our money."

"All right."

Mr. Hodgkin led the way down a path beside the inn. For a hundred yards or so the way was clearly defined, then the path lost itself among the trees. The inn was soon completely out of sight, and they were threading their way among the trunks of tall firs growing so closely together that the foliage overhead almost shut out the sunlight. It was very cold and quiet. Except for the faint stirring of the branches above, there was no sound but the crunching of pinecones under their feet. After a little the ground sloped sharply upward and there was a gleam of light between the trees. A minute later they had left the forest and were standing in a rocky clearing a few yards wide. On three sides of it the firs rose like stockades. On the fourth there was nothing but the wooded hills of Bohemia rolling away into the distance.

"There!" said Mr. Hodgkin, drawing a deep breath and gazing out solemnly toward the gray, misty horizon.

"It's a splendid view." Kenton was racking his brains for an idea. What could he do now? Run? The ground sloping away from the promontory was not very steep and the trees started again a short way down. Even if Hodgkin ran after him, he would lose him among the trees. Then he saw that the little man's shrewd eyes were watching him. He smiled. "The air's good," he said.

Mr. Hodgkin looked away. "The frontier is four miles from here," he said slowly. "If you start now, you'll reach it by dusk, Mr. Kenten."

For a moment Kenton felt as if a bomb had exploded under him. He knew that there was something he should say, but his brain had gone numb. It seemed to him that he had stood there for hours before he uttered a sound. At last he spoke.

"Kenton, not Kenten," he said. It was the best he could do.

There was the suspicion of a grin on Mr. Hodgkin's thin lips. "Sorry, friend, they've got Kenten in the papers."

"A small point," said Kenton evenly. He was beginning to recover himself. "When did you spot me?"

"As soon as you walked into that agency." He looked grave. "I tell you, friend, you've had some pretty good luck today. You walk into a travel agency two minutes after the police have been in making inquiries about you there, peek right and left like a villain, and start glaring at a map. You've got a bit of scrub on your upper lip that looks about a day old and an English tweed jacket showing under an overcoat that doesn't fit you. Then you march up to the counter and say you've only got an hour or two to spare, but you'll take a trip that lasts eight. Then you grab a Genoa sailing list as though you're pinching the till. You see a policeman and look as if you're going to have a heart attack, tell me you're leaving for Vienna by a train that doesn't run, and start asking questions about one of the biggest twisters from here to Shanghai. And if you'll pardon my mentioning it, there's a stain the size of Lake Geneva on the back of your right sleeve that looks like blood. Yes, friend, you've been pretty lucky."

Kenton laughed rather shakily.

"It's no laughing matter," said Mr. Hodgkin severely, "and you aren't clear yet. The frontier's four miles ahead and you have to veer slightly to your right, because the road bends to the right toward the frontier. And when you're crossing it, look out for alarm bells. If you get through, you can pick up a bus at one of the villages on the other side that'll take you to Budweis. There you'll be okay for a train. But for goodness' sake get rid of that coat and hat. They're poison."

Mr. Hodgkin turned away and began to fill his pipe. There was a pause. "Have you gone yet?" he asked over his shoulder.

"No," said Kenton. "I was waiting to thank you, to say good-by and to shake hands."

Mr. Hodgkin turned back grimly. "Listen, friend," he said, "I've done a lot for you today. I don't say it's been a hardship, because I've enjoyed having one of my own countrymen to talk to. But if you think I'm going to shake hands with a cold-blooded murderer, you've got another think coming."

"If you believe I'm a cold-blooded murderer," said Kenton angrily, "why aren't you giving me up and collecting the reward?"

A curious expression crossed Mr. Hodgkin's sharp pinched face. "Why?" he echoed derisively. "I'll tell you why, friend. Listen. If this was England I'd hand you over to the nearest copper I could see because that'd be the proper thing to do, guilty or not guilty. Why don't I hand you over now? The answer is, friend, because I'm getting a bit of my own back. Fifteen years I've been trailing about this blasted Continent now, and I've hated every minute of it. I hate their way of going on, and I hate them. I was in sunny Florence when the Fascisti went for the Freemasons in '25. Night after night of it with shooting and beating and screams, till you felt like vomiting. I was in Vienna in '34 when they turned the guns on the municipal flats with the women and children inside them. I saw the Nazis in Frankfurt kick a man to death in his front garden. In Spain, they tell me, they doused men with petrol and set light to them.

"Nice chaps, aren't they? Picturesque, gay, cleverer, more logical than silly us. Good businessmen they are, too. They take no pride in the stuff they produce. They're out to make money. I don't blame them for that. We all are. But they don't want to give value for money. Business for them isn't honest trading. It's just another sort of politics and nearly as crooked. Because I hate them, and because you're a Britisher, I'm telling you to get out now while the getting's good. Now for God's sake leave me."

His thin face was flushed, he was breathing quickly, there were tears glistening behind his spectacles. He looked away.

The journalist watched him for a moment, then turned on his heel and started down the slope toward the trees. When he reached them he stopped and looked back up the hill, but Mr. Hodgkin had gone.

Sick at heart, Kenton walked on among the trees. The sun filtering through obliquely from the west made patterns of light on the soft brown surface of the hillside. It was, he thought, better than the view from Mr. Hodgkin's promontory.

CHAPTER 10

BY NIGHTFALL KENTON was within a few yards of the frontier. It had taken longer than he had expected. With vague memories of reading that persons unused to forests lost their sense of direction and walked in circles, he had made repeated detours to reestablish contact with the road. In this way the four miles had become more like six. The sun had gone down when at last he saw, from the edge of the road about a quarter of a mile away, a small white guardhouse and the striped barrier of the frontier post.

He retreated into the forest until he had put about half a mile between himself and the road, and then began to work his way forward in darkness, with only the upward slope of the ground to guide him. After about twenty minutes the ground became level, the pines thinned, and, putting out his hand to feel for obstacles ahead, he touched the smooth, cold surface of a sawed-off tree stump. He halted, then moved forward and came up against another tree stump. He was in the frontier clearing.

He remained still for a moment. There was no sound, but far away on his left a pinpoint of light appeared, bobbing jerkily from side to side. Someone was coming, and whoever it was, was flashing a lantern among the bushes. He stepped back hastily into the shadow of the trees and crouched down.

The light came nearer, and Kenton could hear the crunch of a man's feet on what was evidently a path. The footsteps grew louder and the man drew level. He was humming softly. The light swept across the ground once and he was past. Kenton stood up quickly and peered after him. The man was in uniform and had a rifle slung over his left shoulder. Of more immediate interest to Kenton was what he could see by the light of the lantern. It depressed him profoundly.

He was about thirty yards from the actual frontier line. From where he stood on the edge of the forest to the path there was roughly twenty yards of half-cleared ground, dotted with tree stumps and squat, scrubby bushes. The path itself was about six feet wide and covered with large gray stone chips. Beyond the path the ground sloped up sharply to the most formidable-looking fence Kenton had ever seen—eight feet high and composed of barbed wire stretched tightly between heavy steel stanchions, grounded into concrete bases at intervals of ten feet. The wires were so close together and the horizontal strands had been festooned with so many additional coils of wire that it looked more like a bramble thicket than a fence.

Kenton sat on a tree stump to think things over.

One thing was clear. There could be no crawling through the fence. He considered putting his overcoat on top of the fence and endeavoring to climb over. But he would need several thicknesses of blanket to muffle the wire sufficiently; and, even if he could get across that way, it would be difficult to retrieve his coat once it was entangled in the wire. He wanted to leave no trace of his passage across the frontier which would put Czech authorities on the lookout for him.

The wind was blowing harder, and he shivered miserably, remembering Mr. Hodgkin's prophecy of snow. Should he return to Linz? No. Even if he could find some means of getting back, there was the risk of capture. Mr. Hodgkin's catalogue of his blunders had shaken his confidence in his ability to avoid arrest. There was nothing for it but to get across the frontier—somehow.

He glanced in the direction in which the guard had gone, saw that the coast was clear and crossed the path to the fence. If he could not go through it or over it, he must go *under* it. He knelt down and found, to his joy, that the ground at the foot of the fence consisted for the most part of large stones piled up to form a small embankment. He began to pull them away and, after about five minutes' work, was able to push his hand under the bottom wire. Suddenly he stood up and scurried back to the trees. The guard with the light was returning.

Kenton crouched behind a tree until the man had passed. Then he went back to the fence and worked away furiously at the stones and earth. Speed was essential, for as the gap under the wire grew wider and deeper, the risk of its being seen by passing guards increased. Twenty minutes later he was experimenting with getting his head and shoulders through the gap when he had to dash once more for cover.

This time Kenton was thoroughly frightened. The guard would surely see the breach in the embankment, now about a yard wide and surrounded by loose stones and earth. The man came on steadily, then suddenly stopped. Kenton crouched down, his heart thumping painfully. In the silence, he heard footsteps approaching from the right. A second or two later someone coughed and said, *"Guten Abend."*

" 'n Abend," answered the man on the path.

While the two men gossiped for a few moments, Kenton cautiously raised himself to see them. The Austrian guard was standing on the path, his lantern shining through the fence onto the feet of a man in the uniform of a Czech infantryman. To Kenton's horror, they were no more than six feet from the gap. Fortunately the Czech guard had extinguished the small flashlight he carried.

"We have been told," the Austrian was saying, "to keep a special lookout for the Englishman, Kenten, who murdered that German in Linz."

"He has been seen?"

"A woman reported that there were two Englishmen on a tourist bus who got out at the inn, and one of them did not return. She has been questioned by the police, and says that she thinks that the one who returned is the murderer. She says he scowled a lot at her and smoked a pipe, but it appears his papers are in order. For the other, we must keep a lookout."

He gestured with the hand holding the lantern, and the beam danced across the ground near the gap. Kenton waited breathlessly for discovery, but the guard went on talking, until at last the Czech announced that he had to report at the guardhouse, and they moved off in opposite directions.

The moment they were out of earshot, Kenton went back to work. Below the stones he struck solid earth and progress was slower; but after another quarter of an hour, he found that by wriggling forward

on his back and holding the bottom wire away from his face and clothes, he could squeeze through. Having carefully piled the stones by the edge of the hole so that he could refill the breach from the other side, he prepared to go. Two minutes later, disheveled and very dirty, he crawled into Czechoslovakia.

He had just crammed the loose stones back into place when he heard footsteps approaching and saw the intermittent flashing of the light. He turned and dashed for cover, but he had gone no more than a dozen paces when his foot caught in a tree stump and he went down flat on his face. The next instant his outstretched fingers touched a thick strand of rusty wire. In a flash, he remembered Mr. Hodgkin's warning about alarm bells.

He lay still, paralyzed with fright. A few yards away the footsteps almost stopped, and the flashlight flickered among the tree stumps. Then the man started to cough, a heavy bronchial cough and painful, for Kenton heard the man gasp out an oath as the paroxysm subsided. The light went out and the heavy boots grated once more on the stones. The man went by and his footsteps died away.

Kenton took a deep breath and stood up. Then, holding the rusty wire carefully between his thumb and forefinger, he stepped over it and went on slowly.

Once in the forest again he pushed on steadily, setting a course which he judged would bring him to the road about a mile from the frontier. After an hour's walking he came out on the road. It was deserted. A clock somewhere was striking eight when, having dusted himself off and straightened his tie, he walked into the village of Manfurth.

In the tiny square a ramshackle bus was standing outside the post office with lights on and engine running. Inside sat a peasant woman with a crate of live chickens. According to the destination board the bus was bound, via Hohenfurth, Silberberg and Kaplitz, for Budweis.

AT A QUARTER TO twelve that night the train from Budweis steamed slowly into Prague.

Kenton, with his left hand deep in his pocket so that the sleeve of his overcoat was hidden, got off, walked along the platform and crossed to the nearest exit.

The station was crowded, and he did not notice the two men until they were level with him. Suddenly his arms were linked forcibly with those on either side of him and he felt the hard ring of a gun barrel pressed under his rib cage. His heart sank.

"Herr Kenton?"

He hesitated, then shrugged his shoulders. They had got him. How, he couldn't think; but it was not much use trying to brazen things out.

"Ja."

They led him through the exit and down the steps to a large closed Mercedes with a uniformed chauffeur. Under their prodding he got into the back of the car and sat in the middle. The blinds were pulled down and the engine started. The men—nondescript, clean-shaven, with black mackintoshes and gray felt hats—looked like typical continental plainclothes police. But there was an unusual informality about their behavior. He turned suddenly to the man on his left.

"Where are you taking me?" he said in German.

"Be silent!"

The revolver was rammed into his side to enforce the instruction, and Kenton sat back in his seat thinking furiously. If they were not the police, then who on earth were they and where were they taking him?

The car, after ten minutes of twisting, turning and hooting, settled down to a straight run on a road which Kenton judged to be a main road out of the city. A few minutes later the car swung to the left and dropped downhill, then slowed to a stop.

Kenton, flanked by his escorts, climbed out and mounted a broad flight of steps leading to an imposing pair of doors. He was ushered into a long, narrow and brilliantly lighted hall. A door at the far end opened, and a man came out and hurried forward, beaming. For a moment, Kenton was too surprised to speak. Then he nodded slowly.

"I might have known it," he said grimly.

"You might indeed," chuckled Zaleshoff. "But I expected you by an earlier train. You must be tired. Come on in and have a drink. Tamara's looking forward to seeing you again," he added.

CHAPTER 11

KENTON GLANCED AROUND the room into which he had been led and nodded appreciatively. "Nice place you have here."

"The man who owns it is a secret admirer of the late-lamented Empress Eugénie," Zaleshoff said. "That explains the decorations." He handed Kenton a whiskey and soda.

The journalist held it up to the light. "No knockout drops, no little-known vegetable poisons, no dopes?"

Zaleshoff frowned. "You have an irritating habit of facetiousness, Kenton. If you don't want the drink, say so before I pour another for myself."

Kenton put the glass down. "Sorry, Andreas, but you really can't blame me. You push off and leave me with a murder charge; I ask your henchman, Rashenko, for help in getting away, and he gives me an overcoat stained with blood, which, I can't help feeling, once belonged to Borovansky—the blood, I mean; then you send along a couple of thugs, disguised as detectives, to kidnap me. Now you offer me a drink. Why, in heaven's name, *shouldn't* it be doped?"

The door of the room opened and Tamara came in. Her face lit up when she saw Kenton. "I'm glad you got here safely," she said.

"Mr. Kenton was just explaining," put in Zaleshoff, "that he suspects me of poisoning his whiskey and soda."

"What nonsense!"

"Then for God's sake!" exploded Kenton angrily. "Why the devil have you brought me here?"

"Now, now," said Zaleshoff soothingly, "let's sit down and talk things over. Take your coat off."

Kenton mastered his rising temper. He must, he told himself, keep cool. He took off the overcoat. Zaleshoff took it from him and held out the sleeve for the girl's inspection.

"You see," he said, "it doesn't show unless you're behind a man wearing it. Rashenko could not have seen it."

"Of course," put in Kenton sarcastically.

Zaleshoff patted him on the arm. "Now listen, Mr. Kenton. When I left Linz this morning I wrote you a note asking you to wait at Rashenko's room until I could fix things for you. Why didn't you?"

"Because I don't trust you. Why should I? You have your job to do. It's probably very convenient for you to have me accused of murder instead of that nasty-looking employee of yours on the train."

"Employee? Train?"

"Certainly. When Rashenko gave me this hat it seemed vaguely familiar. On the train tonight I remembered where I'd seen it—on the head of the man Sachs told me was a Nazi spy. I didn't remember the coat well enough to identify that as well; but putting two and two together it seemed that the owner of the hat was probably the owner of the coat too, and a friend of yours. The coat had a bloodstain on the sleeve; Sachs had been scared out of his wits by the man wearing it; I had found Sachs stabbed. Well, how would that have looked to you?"

Zaleshoff pursed his lips. "You said, 'putting two and two to-gether,' Mr. Kenton. What did you mean by that?"

"Rashenko got that hat and coat from somewhere in his house. He didn't go out, because he was in a dressing gown."

"And so you decided to come to Prague. How did you get here?"

"I sneaked across the frontier at Manfurth."

Zaleshoff whistled. "You don't mean to say you climbed over it?"

"To be precise, I crawled underneath it." He explained what he had done.

"There's resource for you," said Zaleshoff delightedly. "You know, Tamara, I like this guy Kenton."

"Let's get back to the point," said Kenton grimly. "I came to Prague to steal those photographs back from Saridza and make a deal with you. My price for the photographs was going to be your friend with the nasty face, complete with evidence ready for the police."

"A little optimistic, weren't you, Mr. Kenton?" the girl said.

"Not necessarily. This morning I remembered a piece of informa-tion I'd forgotten to give Andreas. Something Saridza said to Mailler that seemed unimportant at the time."

"What was it?" snapped Zaleshoff.

Kenton shook his head. "Nothing doing, Andreas. Being wanted for a murder you didn't commit has a curious effect. You become strangely secretive."

There was a pause.

"Supposing," said Zaleshoff at last, "that I were able to tell you that I knew who murdered Borovansky. Supposing I told you that I had intended from the start to use that knowledge to free you from suspicion. Supposing I told you that, in view of your pigheadedness, I had decided to hand you over to the police forthwith. What would you say?"

"I'd say you were being silly, because I know it's far more impor-tant to you that you have a line on Saridza than that you shield the real murderer or score off me."

The girl laughed. "Very good, Mr. Kenton! Very good indeed! Now do drink your whiskey and soda. It really is quite harmless."

"And sit down," added Zaleshoff irritably. "It's quite impossible to think with you standing about."

Kenton sat down beside the girl and sipped at his drink cautiously.

"You really have very little to think about, Andreas," he said. "Are you going to talk business with me or aren't you?"

Zaleshoff looked at him thoughtfully. "You know, Kenton," he said, "the trouble with you is that you were born a member of one of the ruling races. Your sense of danger is deficient, your conceit is monumental. Or is it, I wonder, that you lack imagination?"

"You mean I'm in no position to dictate terms?"

"Exactly. Those men who brought you here are both good shots, and what is more, they have no inhibitions. You could not leave this house without my express permission."

"I can't think why you got me here."

"Probably not. Would you be very surprised if I told you that it was largely for your own good?"

"Very surprised, and rather skeptical."

The Russian rose and walked the length of the room and back. He stopped in front of the journalist's chair. "Listen," he said, "I think you're bluffing, but I can't call your bluff. Frankly, I want those photographs badly. If I don't get them there'll be trouble, and it won't be only in Rumania. I can't risk ignoring a speck of information. So I'm going to tell you who murdered Borovansky and how you're going to get out of the spot you're in. But you're not going to do anything about it until I say so. You'll see why. Then you can tell me what you know—if anything."

He poured himself another drink and sat down. "When Borovansky left Berlin a friend of mine there instructed a man named Ramon Ortega, a Spaniard, to follow him and recover the photographs in Austria."

"Ortega being the owner of my hat and coat," Kenton put in.

"If you're going to interrupt . . ." Zaleshoff snarled, then continued. "Ortega exceeded his instructions. When he got to the Hotel Josef he stabbed Borovansky. He said Borovansky pulled a gun, but he was probably lying. Ortega, you see, *likes* stabbing people."

"Sachs did have a gun in a holster under his arm. It was gone when I found him."

"Ortega took it. What he didn't take was the photographs. You had them. Anyhow, Ortega got out by the back entrance and went to Kölnerstrasse 11. Rashenko arranged to hide him in an empty room on the floor below. Then the police got on to you. Now I'm no sentimentalist, but I didn't like the idea of a man being charged for a killing he didn't do. So I persuaded Master Ortega to write and sign a confession."

"Just asked him kindly if he'd mind signing a life sentence for himself in an Austrian prison?" said Kenton unpleasantly.

Zaleshoff bounded to his feet with a roar of anger. "Listen to me," he said violently. "Ortega confessed because he's wanted for murder in Lisbon anyway, and I threatened to turn him in for extradition unless he confessed to killing Borovansky. He thought we wanted another screw to turn on him in the future. Besides, what's one conviction more or less to a guy like that? Both Portugal and Austria have abolished the death sentence for murder and he couldn't be in two prisons at once, so what the hell? Anyhow, I'd got his confession ready to use if things got hot for you. If you were arrested you'd certainly tell your little story and that might be inconvenient at present. If I'd fixed it for Ortega to be taken he'd have spilled *his* story too with a bit added on. When Rashenko telephoned that you were coming to Prague he said he'd given you Ortega's things to wear. He hadn't spotted the bloodstain on that sleeve, and when I told him about it he nearly threw a fit. I must say I was a little anxious until you arrived. I suppose you realize it was that stain that enabled those two men to pick you up at the station?"

"How does Rashenko talk on the telephone if he's dumb?"

"He's got a special signaling arrangement hooked up."

"Hm! I still don't see why he had to give me Ortega's things."

Zaleshoff sighed noisily. "Because, my dear Mr. Kenton, it would have been too dangerous to buy them in a shop in a town the size of Linz. The police, you know, are not complete fools."

"So now I'm expected to hang about here until you're ready to tell the Austrian police that I'm innocent."

"That's right," said Zaleshoff blandly, "though it's not that simple. Ortega must be discovered in suitable circumstances—circumstances that do not involve Rashenko or myself."

"You're a cold-blooded devil, aren't you, Andreas? This man Ortega may be a lousy cutthroat, but I don't like handing him over to the police with a confession he wrote to save himself."

"Very fussy all of a sudden, aren't you, Mr. Kenton? A little while ago you were cracking on about the injustice of their accusing you. Now that there's a fair prospect of your seeing justice done, you don't like it." He turned to the girl. "That, Tamara, is a typical piece of Anglo-Saxon thinking."

The girl was about to answer when there was a sharp knock at the door. Zaleshoff excused himself and went out of the room, closing the door behind him.

"What's happening?" asked Kenton.

"I don't know," answered Tamara.

Kenton let this obvious untruth pass. "I have been puzzled," he said. "Do you mind explaining how you came to be mixed up in this business?"

"It is a question I constantly ask myself. I never get any reply. One day, soon I hope, for the first time in years my brother and I will take a holiday. For a little while, perhaps, we shall live as normal people away from this imbecile game."

"That sounds as if you don't like it."

Before she could reply, the door burst open and Zaleshoff came back into the room. His manner had changed. "Sorry to have been so long," he said with an elaborate air of carelessness. "I had a little matter of business to attend to."

Behind the Russian's ease and indifference there was, Kenton felt, something very much akin to a boiler a few seconds before it is to burst. Clearly, something important had happened while he had been alone with Tamara.

Zaleshoff sat down on the edge of a chair. "Now, Mr. Kenton," he said genially, "I've set your mind at rest on the unfortunate subject of Borovansky's killing. Supposing you give me that precious piece of information you talked about?"

Kenton nodded. "All right, here it is." He leaned forward impressively. "When I told you that Sarizda said he was going to Prague, I forgot one thing—that he said he was going to meet a man named Bastaki. In the coach to the frontier I met an English commercial traveler named Hodgkin. I found out from him that not only is Bastaki a Rumanian but also that his father is one of the biggest industrialists in Rumania. Bastaki himself has an electric-cable works just outside Prague and this man Hodgkin described him as one of the biggest cable twisters from here to Shanghai."

Zaleshoff rose slowly to his feet and walked to the window. For a moment or two he stood looking at the pattern on the heavy curtains. Then he turned around.

"Mr. Kenton," he said solemnly, "words fail me. I should, without a doubt, have handed you over to the police in Linz. I have expended a considerable amount of both time and breath on you in the hope that you had the merest scrap of information to give me, and what do I get?"

"Don't you believe me?"

Zaleshoff clapped his hands to his forehead and closed his eyes as if praying for strength. "Certainly I believe you, Mr. Kenton. Certainly!" His voice rose. "I believe you, my dear friend, because I was given exactly the same information over the telephone three minutes ago. I can even add something. Saridza met Bastaki at the cable-works office exactly one hour ago. With Saridza were the photographs. Half an hour later, while you were trying to decide whether I was doping your drink or not, Bastaki left for the station and caught the twelve-twenty train. Saridza has gone with Mailler to Bastaki's house on the other side of Prague. Half an hour ago, Mr. Kenton, those photographs were within reach. Thanks to you, they are now on their way to Bucharest." He paused and drew a deep breath. "Well, what have you to say to that?"

Kenton looked at the carpet. "Nothing much."

Zaleshoff laughed unpleasantly. "Nothing! That's splendid."

"I said nothing *much*."

Zaleshoff snorted impatiently and started pacing the room. "Tamara," he said suddenly, "telephone the police and tell them that you have had a diamond necklace stolen by a man who held up your car in the Altstadt. Give Bastaki's description. Say that your chauffeur chased the man into the station and that he caught the twelve twenty going to Bucharest. Tell them to hold him at Brünn. No, that won't do. Make up your own story, but arrange it so that Bastaki is held at the frontier long enough for us to get at him. Tell Serge to get the small car ready and to put on his uniform. Grigori will get out the Mercedes for me. Whatever you do, hurry!"

The girl started for the door.

"Wait," said Kenton. "I shouldn't bother about Bastaki. He hasn't got the photographs."

"What?" snapped Zaleshoff.

Kenton leaned back in his chair. "You know, Mr. Zaleshoff," he said in malicious parody of the Russian's manner, "your great weakness is that you jump to conclusions. Bastaki meets Saridza who has the photographs. Bastaki afterward leaves for the station and catches a train. You're so obsessed by the bogey of those photographs getting to Bucharest that you immediately assume that Bastaki must be taking them there. He's not."

"How do you know?"

"Because I've frequently caught the twelve twenty from Prague myself. It's a very convenient train, but it doesn't go to Bucharest. It goes to Berlin."

"Berlin?"

"Exactly. And why is Bastaki going to Berlin after meeting Saridza? You should know. In that very clear exposition you gave me of Saridza's relations with the Rumanian Fascists, you will remember pointing out that one of Codreanu's principal aims was a German alliance."

Zaleshoff nodded.

"The fact that Bastaki's father is a big Rumanian industrialist is misleading. Why doesn't Saridza deal with the father, who is, presumably, a financially interested party? Where does Bastaki junior come in? Those, Andreas, were the questions I asked myself while I was waiting at Budweis for a train this evening. Accordingly, as I had time to spare, I called a Prague news agency, pretending I was their Vienna correspondent, who happens to be a friend of mine, and made a few inquiries about the Bastakis. I learned that Bastaki's wife is a Czech—that's why he works here—but she is a German Czech, and her brother is Schirmer, the Nazi under secretary at the German Foreign Ministry. Now do you see why Bastaki goes to Berlin after seeing Saridza? Bastaki's job was to inspect the photographs, assure himself of their authenticity and run off to brother-in-law Schirmer to tell him the glad news. Codreanu is no fool. He's making sure of his support before he makes a move. Meanwhile Saridza sits tight until Bastaki returns with the official blessing. Balterghen is no fool, either. He's not moving to help Codreanu until he's quite sure he's going to get his money's worth. I should say you could rely on Saridza's sitting on the photographs in Bastaki's house a clear thirty-six hours—that is, until Bastaki returns."

Kenton squirted some soda water into a glass and drank it. Suddenly he felt the Russian's hand on his shoulder.

"I think, Mr. Kenton," said Zaleshoff, "that I must be getting old. Or perhaps it is that I haven't been to sleep these three nights. I am sorry, my friend, that I insulted you."

"That's all right."

"Thirty-six hours is your estimate?"

"Perhaps a little longer. I was allowing reasonable time for him to get to Berlin, see Schirmer and get back again to Prague."

Deep in thought, Zaleshoff walked to the door. Then he turned around. "Is there any way I can reward you, my friend? That is," he added hastily, "apart from the matter of Ortega."

"Yes, there is," said Kenton promptly. "I should like a hot bath and a comfortable bed."

The Russian turned to his sister. "You know, Tamara," he said, "I like this guy Kenton. He's reasonable."

FORTY MINUTES LATER, for the first time in three days, Kenton went to bed. For a minute or two he lay relaxing his muscles and enjoying the soothing ache of his tired body. Then he reached out and switched off the light. As he did so there was a slight creak from the passage outside and a soft *click* as his door was carefully locked. Grinning to himself in the darkness, he turned over on his side. As the warmth of sleep began to steal over him, he heard the faint sound of a car starting. Then he slept.

FRAU BASTAKI, a silent, middle-aged woman with untidy, graying hair and an unhealthy complexion, sat stiffly in a high-backed chair and stared at her clasped hands. It was obvious that she found her husband's guests uncongenial. Seeing that they had both finished their brandies, she rose and suggested that she should show them to their rooms.

The man who called himself Colonel Robinson stood up and bowed slightly. "Come, Mailler," he said in English, "the woman is anxious to get rid of us."

Captain Mailler set his glass down and followed them. A few minutes later the two men nodded a casual good-night to one another and went into their adjoining rooms.

Saridza went to a suitcase, got out a box of capsules, swallowed one, half filled a tumbler with water and drank it. In an hour's time he would be able to sleep. He switched out the light and sat down by the window.

For half an hour he sat there motionless in the darkness. Outside, wind-driven clouds raced across the risen moon. Then came a gap in the clouds and for a few seconds the moonlight shone clearly on the gardens. Suddenly he leaned forward in his chair and wiped the slight mist from the window. Then he got up and went to the communicating door.

Captain Mailler was already in bed when Saridza entered.

"Hallo, chief, not in bed yet?"

"Go down quietly to the room next to the one in which we were sitting and switch on the lights. Look as though you've come down for a cigarette. That's all. There is someone outside on the terrace. I wish to see who it is. No, don't take a gun; just do as I tell you."

He went back to the window and stood looking down. A minute later, light flooded suddenly across the terrace and a short, thickset figure moved quickly into the shadows. When Captain Mailler returned he found Saridza getting undressed for bed.

"Spot him, chief?"

"Yes, it is Zaleshoff, the man who took the journalist. Now get to bed, Mailler."

At the door the captain paused. "I'd like to get my fingers on that little swine."

Saridza smiled faintly. "I think you will have an opportunity of doing so. Good night, Mailler."

CHAPTER 12

KENTON WAS AWAKENED by the unlocking of his bedroom door. There was a pause, then a discreet knock. He said, "Come in!" and a man entered carrying a tray. Kenton recognized the leader of the previous night's kidnapping party.

The man put the tray on a table by the bed, drew back the curtains, went into the bathroom and turned on the water, then withdrew with a friendly nod.

Kenton ate his breakfast and went into the bathroom. A razor, a toothbrush, a comb and towels were laid out ready for use.

When he returned to the bedroom he found that in his absence a suit of clothes together with clean underwear and a shirt had been left for him on the bed. The suit, a rather Alpinesque green tweed, proved a reasonably good fit. He dressed and made his way down to the room into which he had been led the night before.

There he found Zaleshoff sitting in front of a roaring fire, drinking tea and reading a newspaper.

As he entered, the Russian put down the paper and surveyed him critically. "Quite good," he said at last. "I'm glad you kept the mustache. You'll find a pair of clear glass spectacles in one of the pockets. Put them on."

Kenton did so and examined the result in a large gilt mirror on the wall.

"A little theatrical perhaps?" he suggested.

"That's only because you're not used to yourself that way. You ask Tamara; she'll be down in a minute. Have a good night?"

"Very good, thanks. Your chief kidnapper is an excellent valet."

"Grigori is a mechanic in Prague when he isn't working for the man who owns this house—or me."

"I still say he's a good valet. I hope you feel better after your night's rest."

Zaleshoff chuckled. "You heard me go out then? I went to reconnoiter Bastaki's house. You see, I take your deductions seriously. It's about six kilometers from here and stands in its own grounds." He poured himself out some more tea. "How would you like to assist in the recovery of those photographs? I shall want more men than I have here even if Tamara drives the car. You could carry an unloaded automatic and come with me."

"That doesn't sound very useful."

"It will be. You see, we don't know whether Saridza carries the photographs on him or has them hidden in his room. We must be free to search." Zaleshoff produced a rough sketch map of a house from his pocket. "All you have to do is to follow instructions. Serge will take the garage, Peter will keep a lookout at the gate, Grigori, you and I will go inside. There are only Saridza and Mailler there, apart from three maidservants and Frau Bastaki. Grigori will look after the women. And you and I will attend to the real business."

"I don't see how I can attend to anything with an unloaded automatic."

"There must be no shooting. You are already wanted by the Austrian police for murder. It would be unfortunate if you really did kill somebody. Automatics are tricky things, and an unloaded one looks just as dangerous as a loaded one."

"All right, when do we start?"

"About ten o'clock tonight, I think. I don't want to wait till they're in bed."

At that moment Tamara came in.

"I was just explaining tonight's program to Mr. Kenton," said Zaleshoff. "He is disappointed because I say his automatic must not be loaded. I tell him he might kill somebody."

"Mr. Kenton looks quite capable of it in that outfit," said Tamara. She herself, Kenton noted, was looking extremely attractive in a blouse and skirt.

"Your brother said that you would approve of the disguise."

She smiled. "If Saridza's wearing dark glasses he may have to look twice before he recognizes you."

"That doesn't sound so good."

"You needn't worry," said Zaleshoff. "Saridza won't get in touch with the police. He'd have too much explaining to do."

Kenton was silent for a moment. "I wonder," he said at last, "what Saridza will say when he loses his photographs."

Zaleshoff looked at his watch. "Nine hours from now," he remarked, "we should be hearing the answer to that question. Come, Tamara, we have work to do."

Left to himself, Kenton wandered over to the fire and stood watching the flames. If only, he thought, Herr Sachs had chosen a different compartment.

A LITTLE AFTER 9:30 that evening, Zaleshoff inspected a large Luger automatic, made sure the breech was empty and handed it to Kenton.

The journalist slipped it into the pocket of the leather raincoat with which he had been provided. They might, it seemed to him, have been setting out on a picnic. Tamara produced a thermos flask full of hot coffee; Zaleshoff could not make up his mind whether he should wear a scarf or not; Serge and Grigori wrangled over their places in the car. Kenton, whose nerves were by this time thoroughly on edge, was on the point of losing his temper with all of them when Zaleshoff, looking at his watch, announced that they would leave immediately.

Any hopes that Kenton had entertained of surveying the neighborhood in which Zaleshoff's headquarters were situated, were dashed. The girl climbed into the driver's seat and drew the blinds over the partition behind her. Grigori repeated the process with the remaining windows. Kenton was placed beside Zaleshoff in the back seat facing Grigori and Serge. The third man, Peter, sat in front with the girl. The car turned to the right onto the main road, but after running for a short distance along it, swung left onto a secondary road with a poor surface. For fifteen minutes more the Mercedes leaped and slithered among the potholes; then it slowed down and stopped. The engine was switched off, and the men got out, leaving Tamara to wait for them in the car. By the faint light from the sky, Kenton could see that they were at the entrance to a small, dark lane. There were trees all around them. It was very cold.

"*Vorwärts*," said Zaleshoff. They moved into the blackness of the lane. The trees shut out the sky, and they were walking forward blindly. Then the ground rose sharply and Kenton heard a faint ripple of water. The next moment they were crossing an iron bridge over a stream. A dark mass loomed up.

"These are the gates. Peter stays here," Zaleshoff whispered. "In a moment we will see the house, but we must give Serge time to reach the garage. He's gone ahead."

For five minutes they stood there motionless. Then Zaleshoff signaled to Kenton and Grigori, and a second or two later they emerged from the trees.

The house was built on rising ground and the garden was terraced up to a long stone balcony onto which three pairs of French windows opened from the ground-floor rooms. With the exception of the light showing through chinks in the curtains of the two balcony rooms farthest from the main entrance, the house was in darkness.

Zaleshoff murmured something in Russian to Grigori, who moved silently away. "He's gone round the back to deal with the kitchen. We'll give him a minute, then go for the balcony."

They waited, then started to move up under cover of a neatly pruned hedge. A minute or two later they stood on a stone path in front of and slightly below the balcony. Another five seconds and they were in the shadow of the wall. Zaleshoff began to edge slowly toward the first of the lighted windows. His heart beating wildly, Kenton followed.

A foot from the window, Zaleshoff stopped. Kenton leaned forward. The faint murmur of a man's voice came through the window.

Zaleshoff listened intently. "Polish," he muttered over his shoulder.

He listened for a moment longer, then turned around and gently propelled Kenton back along the wall. "It's too muffled to hear what he's saying," he whispered. "Saridza doesn't speak Polish, but I suppose he must be there. This way."

He moved along the balcony to the unlighted window, and Kenton saw him take something that looked like an engraver's tool from his pocket. He inserted the tool carefully in the jamb of the window and pressed. Immediately the window swung open.

Zaleshoff stood back quickly. "They weren't fastened," he said. "I don't like the look of that." Then he shrugged his shoulders. "Come along."

They stepped into the dark room. Kenton felt a thick carpet beneath his feet, and his outstretched hand touched a small table. He experienced a sudden desire to retreat. "Zaleshoff . . ." he whispered.

The Russian gripped his arm. "Mind that chair. Have you got your gun ready?"

Kenton's hand went to his side pocket. The gun caught in the lining as he pulled it out. He fumbled with the smooth, cold metal and cursed under his breath. Zaleshoff already had the door open and was peering into the dark hall. Kenton followed him.

Zaleshoff shut the door carefully behind them and moved to the left toward a door with a thin strip of light showing beneath it. Again they could hear the murmur of a man's voice. Kenton saw Zaleshoff lean against the doorpost and turn the handle of the door slowly. Suddenly, Zaleshoff's arm moved. The door flew open and the light from a chandelier flooded into the hall. A split second later Zaleshoff was in the room.

A fire blazed merrily in the grate. The scent of a cigar hung in the air. On one side of the room was a large radio. As Kenton entered, the voice speaking in Polish ceased and a faint hum came from the loudspeaker. But the journalist barely noticed these things, for he was staring stupidly at the sole occupant of the room. It was the man Serge. He was lying on the floor, his mouth open and his eyes glazed. Sticking from his back between the shoulder blades was the handle of a knife.

Zaleshoff was the first to move. He stooped quickly and gripped the dead man's wrist. Just as suddenly, he let it go and stood up. "Quick," he muttered huskily, "something has gone wrong. We must get out of here."

He started for the window. Kenton put one foot forward to follow him. He got no farther.

"Keep perfectly still and drop your guns."

There was a second's icy silence. Then Kenton loosened his grip on the automatic, and it thudded to the carpet. The blood had drained from his head and there was a singing in his ears. He saw Zaleshoff's revolver fall to the floor, but did not hear it.

"Turn round."

He turned slowly. In the doorway, a smile on his lips and a heavy revolver in his hand, stood Saridza.

CHAPTER 13

SARIDZA MOTIONED THEM away from the windows. "Put your hands behind your heads," he ordered. "That's better." He leaned across the back of a chair. "This is a pleasant reunion, Comrade Zaleshoff. I hope you won't spoil it by making any foolish attempt to escape."

Zaleshoff shook his head. "No. Saridza has a reputation for accurate revolver shooting," he added to Kenton.

Saridza beamed. "What a memory you have, Zaleshoff! I wonder if you remember our last meeting in New York? It was New York, wasn't it?"

"That's right, in 1930."

Kenton listened as if in a dream. The two might have been business acquaintances talking over old times.

Saridza's eyes flickered toward the journalist. "And Mr. Kenton, I am surprised to see you here. I really believed your story about meeting Borovansky on the train—a cruel deceit. However, Mailler will be glad to see you again, and you too, Comrade Zaleshoff. You must excuse him for a moment. He is attending to a friend of yours whom he found wandering in the servants' quarters. A lot of people seem to be wandering about Frau Bastaki's house tonight. This poor fellow here on the floor Mailler found tampering with the cars in the garage. The body was brought here by way of a little surprise for you. Mailler's idea. A trifle macabre perhaps, but then Mailler's tastes incline that way."

"You still talk as much as ever," said Zaleshoff.

The smile on Saridza's lips faded a little.

"Yes, Zaleshoff, I still talk. I still act also. That fact has probably not escaped you."

"It has not. I am curious to know how you knew I was calling."

"I have insomnia to thank for that."

"You mean you saw me last night. That was when Mailler switched on the light, I suppose. I thought I was quick enough."

"Not quite. I could have shot you easily, but I thought you might come again and bring your friends. I took the precaution of installing a small garrison and of sending Frau Bastaki and the maids into

Prague. I was right, although I did not count on this young man's presence. You seem strangely silent, Mr. Kenton. Is it the mustache or the glasses that worry you? The last time we met you had quite a lot to say for yourself."

At that moment there was a crackle of speech from the radio, and a second or two later an orchestra burst into a noisy rendering of "The Blue Danube" waltz.

Saridza backed to the instrument, touched a switch and the noise ceased abruptly. "A curious touch of the grotesque," he commented seriously. "A dead man on the floor, two condemned men with their hands behind their heads and a Strauss waltz for a funeral march—what could be more entertaining? By the way, our little jest with the loudspeaker was my idea. It is a pity, however, that you had to come so early. That lecture from Cracow about the folk dances of Galicia was the best we could do. Half an hour later you would have had Dr. Goebbels."

Kenton barely heard what was being said. Serge was dead. The mechanic, Grigori, might be dead too. What had happened to Peter at the gate, and to Tamara? Even as these thoughts flashed through his mind there came the distant sound of three shots fired in quick succession.

He glanced at the others. Zaleshoff's face was quite expressionless. But Saridza had a tautness in his expression; he was listening intently. There was dead silence for a moment. Then Zaleshoff cleared his throat. "How unfortunate if Captain Mailler has been shot," he remarked.

"Unlikely, I think."

"Don't be too sure, Saridza. My sister shoots well and, with the man I left at the gate, Mailler and his party may have been outflanked."

But at that moment there was the sound of footsteps in the hall and Mailler walked into the room. "Well, chief," he said, "you've got the swine all right. There's another wired up in the kitchen. I had to bash him a bit."

"What was that shooting?"

"There were a couple more of them with a car. They took a few potshots at the sky and cleared off in a hurry."

Saridza grunted angrily. "You ought to have stopped them, Mailler. They may come back. We shall have to get these men away. Hold them here. I will make arrangements."

Saridza went out of the room. Mailler surveyed Kenton and Zaleshoff through narrowed eyes. "Quite a nice little bag," said Mailler softly. He raised his voice. *"Heinrichs, komm her."*

A tall thin man with a disfiguring birthmark down one side of his face came into the room. He stumbled over the legs of the dead Serge and kicked them viciously out of the way.

"Keep them covered with your gun and see that they don't move," ordered Mailler in German.

"Jawohl, Herr Kapitän." The man took up his position and thumbed back the hammer of his revolver.

Mailler stared at the prisoners for a moment, then raised his revolver and walked toward Zaleshoff. "So you're the dirty little Red, are you?"

Zaleshoff looked at him steadily. "I'm pleased to meet you again, Captain. You see, I've found out a little about you. Your real name is Hollinder. What is more, you are wanted in New Orleans for the murder of a woman named Robbins."

Mailler drove his gloved fist straight into the Russian's face. Zaleshoff staggered back. Mailler's revolver crashed across the side of the Russian's head. Zaleshoff pitched forward on his face and lay still.

Mailler fumbled in his pocket, produced a length of thick copper wire and a pair of pliers and proceeded to lash Zaleshoff's wrists together behind his back. He tightened the wire with a violent twist of the pliers.

He turned next to Kenton. "Now you get yours. Lower your hands —slowly—and put them behind you." Kenton obeyed, and the wire bit into his flesh. He flinched.

Mailler laughed. "Bit tight, old man? That's all right; your wrists'll go numb in a minute. Sit down." He pushed Kenton backward and put out his foot. Kenton tripped over it and fell heavily. His ankles were lashed together with the wire, and Mailler was giving it a final twist when Saridza returned. He glanced at the insensible Zaleshoff.

"What is this, Mailler?"

"The swine got cheeky."

Saridza turned to Kenton. "I regret that we must soon part company again, but you are going for a little ride. Mailler, get them in the car. We shall take them to the cable works. The man in the kitchen may as well go with them." He looked thoughtfully at the corpse on the floor. "This prank of yours, Mailler, has made rather a mess on the carpet. That must be put right before Bastaki returns in the morning. The lake at the back of the house and plenty of weights will take care of this offal. Hurry now."

Mailler went out of the room and returned shortly with a pale-faced, vicious-looking young man whom he addressed as Berg. Under Mailler's directions Heinrichs and the newcomer carried out the body of Serge.

When they had gone, Saridza walked across the room and looked down at the journalist. "You, my friend," he said, "are a fool."

"For the first time, I find myself agreeing with you," retorted Kenton.

"And yet," went on the other, "I am not entirely satisfied to see you die. Within limits you appear to be intelligent. You are a capable journalist. You possess a quality which, as a businessman, I value highly—a sense of loyalty. I could use your services, Mr. Kenton."

"Are you offering me a job?"

"I am. I offer you an alternative to death. If you agree to my proposition, you will remain here instead of going with these other two."

"What is your proposition?"

"A simple one. You would continue in your work as before, but under my direction. From time to time you would be given special items of news to be reported. That is all. In return I would pay you a retaining fee of fifty thousand French francs a year. But please don't think that by agreeing to my suggestion you could interfere any further in this present affair. Your liberty would not be restored to you for several weeks."

"Until Codreanu is in control, the German alliance cemented and the oil concessions revised in favor of Pan-Eurasian Petroleum?"

"You are even more intelligent than I had hoped. Yes."

"And is that all?"

"Not quite. You see, you might also be thinking that if you agree now, you may save your skin and be able to retract later. That would not do. I shall require proof of your intentions."

"What sort of proof?"

"In the kitchen is the man captured by Mailler. On the floor beside you is Zaleshoff. By this time tomorrow, both these men will most certainly be dead. Supposing, therefore, that we were to ask you to shoot them for us? Just two shots, with Mailler's assistants as witnesses. You would merely be anticipating the inevitable."

It is difficult to be dignified when one is lying on the floor trussed like a hen, but Kenton managed it somehow. "I'd say," he said deliberately, "that you ought to be in a home for homicidal maniacs."

Saridza's lips tightened. "You don't think, Mr. Kenton, that anything might cause you to change your mind?"

"No, I don't."

Saridza sighed. "That is the first time," he said, "that I have seen a man commit suicide by saying three words." He turned to Mailler, who had just come back. "Get these two into the car."

Kenton was carried across the hall and put on the floor in the back of a car which was standing in the drive. A few minutes later, Zaleshoff, still unconscious, was tumbled onto the floor beside him. Then Mailler and Berg reappeared carrying Grigori. The mechanic's face was covered with blood, and he groaned faintly as he was dumped on the seat. His breathing was stertorous.

A minute later Saridza came out. "Take Berg with you," Kenton heard him say. "Heinrichs and I will follow in the other car. I will leave you two to deal with the watchman."

Mailler grunted acknowledgment, the door on the driver's side slammed and they jerked forward. The car roared along at breakneck speed. Bound and helpless, Kenton was buffeted about unmercifully. It was all he could do to prevent Grigori's limp body from sliding off the seat on top of himself and Zaleshoff.

At last the car pulled up and the two men in front got out. Kenton heard their footsteps and then a murmur of voices ahead. An instant later there was a strangled cry and the sound of a scuffle. A moment or two more and Kenton heard the creak and clang of heavy gates being opened. They must, he decided, be at the cable works. The cry had come from the watchman. Presently Mailler and Berg returned to the car, climbed in and sat in silence. Then another car sounded on the road behind them, and they jerked forward once more. A few yards farther on they stopped. There was a slamming of doors, and footsteps died away. A few minutes later Berg and Heinrichs came back, lifted him out and carried him down a concrete path to a wooden door set in a brick wall. Berg held it open while Heinrichs dragged the journalist through.

In spite of the dim light, Kenton could see that he was in a long narrow factory building. There was a strong smell of raw rubber and asphalt. He made out the shapes of a row of curious machines looking in the gloom like huge crouching insects. In the far corner of the shop, light was coming from a small bay partly separated from the main shop by a corrugated iron partition. It was toward this bay that he was carried, and he saw that Saridza and Mailler were waiting there. Kenton's bearers dropped him on the concrete floor.

"Go back for the other two men," ordered Saridza. Then he and Mailler started talking in low tones. Kenton rolled over to his left side and looked around him. The bay was about eight yards wide and twice as long. It was devoid of machinery. Two narrow-gauge rail tracks, about three yards apart, ran the length of the shop. At one end they stopped below an overhead traveling crane mounted on a gantry. At the other end of the bay they ran right up to two round convex iron doors, each about six feet in diameter and hung on massive hinges. On one of the tracks stood three squat trolleys. Two of them carried large metal drums of cable.

Mailler disappeared into the darkness of the main shop and Saridza walked over to Kenton. "Puzzled, Mr. Kenton?"

"Very."

"Let me explain. I did intend to bring you here, shoot you and leave you. But you will be spared that unpleasantness. Do you know what today is?"

"No."

"It is Saturday; or rather, it was Saturday until a short while ago. Nobody will come here again until Monday morning. The watchman lives on the premises, but he will not intrude until someone arrives to release him. By that time I shall be many hundreds of miles away. Convenient as it is for shooting, this factory offers other amenities." He indicated the two iron doors. "Do you know what those are?"

"They look like a pair of safe-deposits."

"They are vulcanizing tanks. The drums of rubber-covered cable are pushed inside on those trucks two at a time, the steam is turned on, and an hour or so later the trucks are pulled out with the cable on them all ready for braiding. It is an interesting process."

"I take it that you intend to roast us to death."

"Dear me, no. There is no steam available just now. No, you will just be left there to think. The doors seal almost hermetically."

"You mean you're going to shut us up to suffocate?"

"Believe me, Mr. Kenton, I regret the necessity, but you have heard and seen too much. Men like Zaleshoff know what risks they run. You, so to speak, are a civilian casualty. However, there are worse ways of dying than by asphyxia. A little hardship at first, perhaps; but in the later stages everything becomes quite peaceful."

Suddenly Kenton lost his head. He knew that he was shouting at the top of his voice at Saridza, but he did not know what he was saying. He realized dimly that Zaleshoff had been put on the floor beside him. Feet grated on the floor and somebody laughed. Then he saw that Mailler had undone the wheel nut that fastened one of the doors and was opening the tank. The heavy iron door opened slowly, revealing the black interior. Mailler walked toward him.

Kenton was dragged across the concrete, and a moment later was lying across the rails inside the tank. The dead body of Grigori was thrust in. It crouched grotesquely against the tank's curved wall. Zaleshoff came last. Then the door began to close.

Kenton watched the shrinking crescent of light in silence and without emotion. He was feeling sick. The light narrowed to a thread, then disappeared. In the darkness, Kenton listened to the faint squeak of the wheel nut being tightened from the other side of the door.

CHAPTER 14

FOR A TIME KENTON kept his eyes open, but soon the absolute darkness seemed to press unbearably on his pupils. He shut his eyes and lay listening to Zaleshoff's breathing.

The tank was still warm from its use earlier that day. The atmosphere reeked of hot rubber. It would not, he thought, be long before unconsciousness put an end to his fear and misery. Meanwhile there was time to be endured—seconds, minutes, perhaps hours of it—time in which his brain would go on working and his body feeling. It was that, he decided, which he feared. The actual business of dying seemed, by comparison, unimportant. To distract his mind he began to repeat to himself some odd scraps of verse of which he was fond— a sonnet of Donne's, part of *Kubla Khan,* a speech from Marlowe's *Tamburlaine*—but after a time he found himself repeating the same line over and over again and gave it up. It was curious, he reflected, how little comfort poetry brought to physical adversity. Perhaps . . .

"Kenton!"

The word was spoken in a whisper, but it rang in the confined space.

"Is that you, Zaleshoff?"

"Yes."

"Have you just woken up?"

"I came round as they picked me out of the car. You were yelling at Saridza like a crazy man when I arrived."

Kenton was silent for a moment. Then, "You know where we are?"

"Yes. I'm sorry. It was my fault."

"How do you feel?"

"Not so good. I've been trying to persuade a pneumatic drill in my head to lay off; but it just keeps on drilling."

"Did you hear Saridza tell me that this vulcanizing tank is pretty well airtight?"

"I guessed that. What's the diameter of the door?"

"I don't know. About two meters, I suppose."

"And how far back does this go?"

"Saridza said it took two trucks of cable. About four meters, I should say. Why?"

Zaleshoff muttered to himself for a moment. "That means," he went on, "that we've got about twelve and a half cubic meters of air in here. Allowing for the volume of our bodies, say eleven. Is Grigori alive?"

"I don't think so."

"That gives us five and a half cubic meters each. With a bit of luck and if this tank cools fairly quickly that might keep us alive for as long as seven hours, if we keep still. The workers should be here by then."

"Is there any chance," Kenton said, "of Tamara looking for us here?"

"No. She's got her work to do. Those three shots you heard were Tamara's getaway signal. She'll be keeping tabs on Saridza and getting in touch with our people in Prague. What puzzles me is why Saridza didn't shoot us. He must be getting tenderhearted."

Kenton took a deep breath. "I wish he had shot us. You see, Andreas, no workers will be here for another thirty hours. It's Sunday."

For a minute there was no sound but the ticking of the watch on Zaleshoff's wrist. Then the Russian laughed softly. "I see," he said. "That means we shall have to do some thinking."

For a long time neither spoke. Kenton began to sweat profusely and found that he was breathing a little faster than usual. He guessed that the amount of oxygen in the tank had begun to diminish.

"We must do something," said Zaleshoff after a time. "Isn't there a watchman?"

"Slugged by Mailler."

"Have you got anything we can knock on that door with? If the watchman got free, we might be able to attract attention."

A slender chance, Kenton felt, but something to think about. "I haven't anything. What about Grigori?"

"They might have left his gun. Have you any matches?"

"In my pocket, but I can't get at them."

"Roll over beside me."

Kenton did as he was told. He felt Zaleshoff's manacled hands fumbling at his coat pocket. A moment or two later, Zaleshoff grunted that he had the box. "We can't afford to waste oxygen on matches," he said. "I'm going to strike one and put it out after three seconds. In that time you must see where Grigori is lying and where his right side pocket is. He kept his gun there."

The match flared, lit up the black side of the tank and went out. Kenton began to wriggle his way toward the body. The exertion made him pant for breath and the sweat ran into his eyes, but at last he rolled over and his knuckles pressed against the dead man's coat. The pocket was empty.

"No gun," he said. "But I can tell you why the air's going quickly. There's a truck with a drum of cable on it in with us."

"That will take up nearly a third of the volume," Zaleshoff said after a pause. "We've only got about four and a half hours to go now."

"Four and a half too many."

"Maybe you're right."

They lay silent. Kenton's head was beginning to ache. He tried to sleep but in spite of the lassitude he could feel stealing over his body, sleep would not come. It seemed to him that he lay there weeks and years. He wished that his heart would not pump so rapidly in his head. Perhaps if he raised himself to a sitting position on the rails and leaned against the curved side of the tank the blood would drain from his head. But he found that he could not summon sufficient energy to make this move. Suddenly he gave a convulsive start. He had been dozing. He knew now that he must keep awake at all costs. Someone might come. No sooner had the thought crossed his mind than, following it, came the bitter reflection that of all human follies the most pitiful was the hope that sprang eternal, the refusal to accept the inevitable, even when the footsteps of the executioner were ringing in the corridor outside. Someone might come. His eyes filled with tears. Something, the impossible, might happen.

"Zaleshoff," he said at last, "do you think we could untie each other's hands?"

There was no reply.

"Zaleshoff!" he cried sharply.

"All right, I was thinking. A little while ago we were looking for something to bang on the door with. We've got it. That truck of cable. It's on rails. If we get behind the truck, we'll have about a six-foot run to the door. If we could get a bit of momentum on it, it would give the door a bad shaking."

"And make plenty of noise. Yes, I see."

"It might do more than make a noise. I've been feeling the surface of that door. It's made of cast iron, and cast iron is brittle."

Kenton's heart missed a beat. For the first time there was a minute scrap of justification for hoping. He repressed his rising spirits firmly. "But we can't do anything with our hands and feet tied."

"No, that's the first thing to tackle. We could try undoing each other's hands, but my fingers are paralyzed."

"So are mine. There's not a scrap of feeling in them."

"The only thing we can do then," said Zaleshoff, "is to file a wire through on the edge of one of the rails we're lying on. The inside edge is quite sharp."

"We'll never do it."

"We've got to try."

Kenton heaved himself into a sitting position, but found that it was impossible, in that position, to get any pressure on the rail. He was forced to lie alongside it on the steel crosspieces that functioned as sleepers. He started on the strand nearest his hands.

The two men worked in silence. Eventually the rail edge made a nick in the copper of the inch of wire between Kenton's wrists, and he found the going easier. But even so, the exertion in the rapidly fouling air and the cramped position soon left him gasping for breath. He rested his aching head against the warm side of the tank.

"Keep at it," panted Zaleshoff.

Setting his teeth, Kenton attacked the wire again. Bruising his wrists and arms and cutting his fingers, he hacked away desperately. He was nearly sobbing with exhaustion when, suddenly, Zaleshoff let out a hoarse cry of triumph. "Made it!"

Kenton put out his last ounce of strength; the wire gave, and the tension on his wrists slackened. He rolled onto his back and began massaging his fingers to restore the circulation. They started to ache. The ache became excruciating pins and needles as the blood flowed back into his hands. He reached down, freed his ankles and then, very gingerly, stood up.

"Okay?" said Zaleshoff.

"More or less."

"What about Grigori?"

"We'll have to get him out of the way."

"There's a space below the rail sleepers."

They felt their way to the body and dragged it to the center of the track. Then they slid it downward, feet first, between two of the crosspieces. As they eased the head down Zaleshoff murmured some words in Russian.

"He was a good Soviet citizen," he added, "and also of the Greek Church." He was silent for a moment. "Come on," he said at last.

They squeezed their way past the truck. There was a foot to spare between the cable drum and the end of the tank.

"Now," panted Zaleshoff, "we push together." They heaved at the truck. It squeaked forward a few inches.

"Again!"

The truck gathered speed. The next moment there was a loud crash as it hit the door. They stumbled after it and tried the door, but it was firm.

"Back with it."

They lugged the truck back into position and tried again, but still the door held. After the eighth attempt Kenton sank to his knees exhausted. By this time the air had become almost insufferably hot and foul. Kenton wanted to retch, and his arms and legs felt as if they did not belong to his body. "It's no use," he gasped. "We're finished."

A stinging slap on the face brought him around with a jerk. "Kenton! Get up."

He crawled slowly to his feet and lurched against the truck.

"Back with it, Kenton . . . For God's sake, push!"

Scarcely knowing what he was doing, the journalist stumbled forward. The truck rolled ponderously to the end of the tank. Fighting for breath, Kenton dragged himself around the side.

"Quick . . ." Zaleshoff gasped. "Last chance . . . then sleep . . ."

Through the roaring of the blood in his head, Kenton heard the other's voice. With a tremendous effort, he straightened himself and gripped the end of the truck. He felt the Russian's body slide against his.

"Now!"

The truck began to move. A sob broke from Zaleshoff's lips. Kenton flung himself forward. The truck screeched over the rails and smashed into the door. There was a sound like the crack of a whip. Zaleshoff cried out. Dimly, Kenton heard him scrambling toward the door. Then he was being dragged forward over the rails and out into the bay. A moment later he realized that he was breathing cold air.

THE SKY OUTSIDE was beginning to lighten and the glass in the roof had become dark blue. Zaleshoff struck a match and looked at his watch. "It says ten to five," he said. "We must have been in that filthy hole over four hours. How do you feel?"

"Apart from a head that feels as if it's falling in half and a pulse that's still working overtime, not too bad. I've got you to thank for that."

"For what?"

"For saving my life. I couldn't have done anything without you."

"You wouldn't have been in there if I hadn't been so dumb. How do your legs feel?"

"A bit wobbly."

"Good enough to get going on? We've got to get out of here. I still have to get those photographs, and Bastaki is due in an hour or two."

"All right."

They went into the main shop. The door through which they had been carried in was locked, and there were no windows.

"There must be some form of ventilation in the place," said Kenton.

"Probably windows in the roof."

"Can we go out that way?"

"I noticed an overhead crane at the end of that vulcanizing room. They must be able to get up to do things to it, if it goes wrong."

"That's an idea."

Zaleshoff would not allow the lights to be switched on, and Kenton used up the best part of a box of matches before they found a steel ladder, bracketed against one of the stanchions supporting the gantry. Telling Kenton to stay where he was, Zaleshoff climbed up to the top of the ladder and crawled along the gantry. The journalist watched him moving among the girders, a vague black shape against the smoky blue of the lightening sky. A minute later he called out that he was coming down.

"There is a window," he reported. "It's opened from down here. We shall have to move the crane along until it's just below the window."

Further search revealed an ironclad switchboard. Adjacent to it was the crane control box. Zaleshoff lit one of their few remaining matches and Kenton explored the board.

"Here we are!" he said at last.

He pulled down a switch and went to the control box. A second later there was a whirring noise from overhead and the rumble of wheels.

"Hold on," said Zaleshoff. "I'll tell you when it's below the window."

After a considerable amount of maneuvering, Zaleshoff called out that the crane was in position, and Kenton switched off the current. He found the Russian working at the winding gear that opened the skylight. "It only opens about eighteen inches," he reported. "It'll be a tight fit."

Zaleshoff led the way back to the steel ladder and started to climb.

Kenton followed him up and moved out onto the top of the gantry.

"Be careful," said Zaleshoff. "It's greasy."

It was about eight inches wide. Kenton edged forward cautiously to where Zaleshoff was standing by the hoist platform. Together they clambered on top of the hoisting gear and stood up. About eight feet above their heads was the open skylight.

"You go first," said Zaleshoff. "You can take off from that joist there."

Kenton grasped the joist, jumped, and hauled himself up. For a moment he hung suspended in midair, then he got his foot in the crutch of two intersecting steel angles and shifted his hold to the window frame. A few seconds later he was lying face downward on a sloping galvanized-iron roof. A cold drizzle of rain caressed the back of his head. There was a scuffling noise from below, and then Zaleshoff was lying beside him.

The sky was now gray and Kenton could see the jagged outlines of the chimneys and roofs of the rest of the cable works.

Zaleshoff's voice, when he spoke, sounded curiously remote in the open air. "Let yourself slide down. There's a ridge you can catch your foot in."

Kenton did as he was told, and they commenced to work their way along the ridge to the end of the roof. A few minutes later they lowered themselves down a drainpipe to a cinder path running between the walls of two factory buildings.

They walked to one end of the path and found themselves in a large yard. Facing them were the main gates—steel frames filled in with rusty plating and surmounted by spikes. They crept forward. The gates were locked.

They retraced their steps to the point at which they had descended from the roof, and then continued on toward the other end of the cinder path. But beyond a narrow door in the left wall it was overgrown with grass and weeds; the end of it was heavily shadowed, and for a minute Kenton thought they were in a cul-de-sac. Then Zaleshoff gave a sudden crow of delight and ran forward. "A private railroad siding. Look! It has got to leave the factory somewhere."

Kenton followed him up the embankment and, in the lightening gloom, he could see wet rails curving away from the factory buildings toward a high corrugated-iron fence.

"There must be a gate that shuts across the track," said Zaleshoff.

They started toward the fence across what was evidently the works refuse dump. Loose coils of wire caught around their feet; they sank ankle-deep into ash and cinders. Suddenly, from ahead, came the creak of rusty hinges. The two stopped dead.

"Stay here," muttered Zaleshoff. The Russian picked up a short length of lead-covered cable from the refuse heaps, weighed it ominously in his hand and dissolved into the shadows by the fence. For a minute or two Kenton could see nothing. Suddenly he heard a cry. He dashed forward and saw two figures locked together swaying from side to side.

One of them was Zaleshoff. The other was Tamara.

CHAPTER 15

WHEN THE MAN PETER had come running out of the darkness with Mailler, Heinrichs and Berg at his heels, Tamara had very nearly lost her head. But her right foot was resting on the electric starter of the Mercedes. In her agitation she pressed it. The roar of the engine startled her. Thereafter she acted with decision. Almost before Peter was on the running board she had the car in gear. As she accelerated, she drew the automatic from a pocket in the door and fired the three signal shots out of the window of the car. Mailler's answering shot smacked into the rear offside door panel by Peter's legs.

Half a mile down the road she switched on the lights and stopped the car. Peter climbed in beside her.

"What happened?" she asked.

"They came upon me in the dark. I heard their footsteps and thought it was Andreas Prokovitch and the Englishman returned. Then, a few paces from me, two of them spoke, and I knew that they were enemies. They did not see me, but in the darkness I stumbled and they heard."

Tamara tapped the steering wheel thoughtfully with the automatic. "You, Peter," she said at last, "must go back and keep watch from the road to see if they leave. I will come back as soon as I can."

The man got out. "You will not be long, Tamara Prokovna?"

"I will not be long."

Tamara drove to her brother's headquarters, dialed a Prague number and had a short telephone conversation. As a result, two nondescript-looking men, each with a photograph of Petre Bastaki in his pocket and very precise instructions concerning the original of it, spent the night near the Berlin arrival platform in the station at Prague. Afterward she went to the cupboard, got out a pair of Colt revolvers and a box of ammunition, then went back to the car. Five minutes after she had rejoined Peter near the end of the lane, she saw the two cars leave for the cable works. She followed at a discreet distance and waited for half an hour a short way beyond the works entrance. When the four men left, she trailed them back to the Bastakis' house. There Peter had been joined by the reinforcements from Prague she had asked for—a small man with a very large motor-cycle who announced that he was from Comrade Smedoff. To this man she gave careful instructions, then headed once more for the cable works.

She spent an hour trying unsuccessfully to find some way of get-ting inside. Finally she drove toward the city until she found a tele-phone booth. She talked and listened for five minutes, after which she drove back to a quiet road near the cable works. There she sat, drinking coffee from the thermos flask and smoking, until the first pale streaks of dawn appeared in the sky. Then she started out once more to reach her brother.

THE REUNION of Zaleshoff and Tamara was affectionate but hurried. Zaleshoff gave a brief and, Kenton thought, grossly understated ac-count of their adventure and asked anxiously what she had been doing.

"Saridza went back to the Bastakis' place after leaving you here," said Tamara. "I put one of Smedoff's men on him after that. A short while later, Saridza and Mailler left by themselves for the Hotel Amerika in Prague. I also put two of Smedoff's men at the station to pick up Bastaki if he came back before we were ready."

"Good," said Zaleshoff. "But we must get Smedoff to countermand those instructions now. I don't want to interfere with Bastaki if I can help it. How do we get out of this place?"

"At the back. I would have gotten to you before, but it was too dark to see anything. Where are Grigori and Serge?"

She was silent when Zaleshoff told her. The stony look which Kenton had seen before in her brother's face came into hers. Then she said, "Your wrists and hands are bleeding, Andreas, and so are Mr. Kenton's."

"We can see to them as we go."

She led them through the gates over the siding, across a desolate, muddy patch of ground to a narrow, rutted road.

"Where to now?" said Kenton when they reached the car.

"First to a telephone and then home," replied Zaleshoff.

He spent about thirty seconds in the telephone booth. "Our plans are changed," he said abruptly as he got in the car again. "We will go to Smedoff's. Mr. Kenton," he added as the car started, "please exercise the greatest discretion over anything you may see or hear during the next hour or so."

"What has happened, Andreas?" said the girl over her shoulder.

"Bastaki arrived at the Hotel Amerika ten minutes ago."

"But the men at the station . . . ?"

"He came by air."

It was daylight when the Mercedes swung into the deserted streets of Prague at racing speed. In the Altstadt, Tamara slowed and stopped outside a narrow building belonging, ostensibly, to a firm of wood veneer manufacturers.

They alighted from the car and went through the door along a stone corridor to an elevator, and Zaleshoff pressed the button marked BASEMENT. To Kenton's surprise the elevator rose slowly to the sixth floor and stopped. Zaleshoff went to a door set in the wall at one end of the bare landing, pushed it open and waved them inside. Kenton found himself in a small carpeted hall with three doors facing him.

"Bedroom, parlor, bathroom," said Zaleshoff, pointing to each in turn. "Tamara, you can have the bedroom and make do with a wash. Mr. Kenton and I need baths. You take the bathroom first, Kenton, and be quick. The coffee will be ready in a minute."

Kenton went into the bathroom. The first thing he saw on the wall over the bath was a large papier-mâché plaque of Lenin's head in bas-relief. One corner of the bathroom was filled with bottles and tins of bath salts. An overhead shelf was loaded with face creams, skin foods, lotions, astringents and cosmetics. The owner of the apartment was clearly a woman. He gave up his inspection and got on with his bathing.

The vulcanizing tank had covered his body with rust. The crane had added a thick coating of black grease to his face and hands. By the time he had removed the worst of the dirt, Zaleshoff was banging at the door.

He dressed hurriedly and went into the parlor. It was a small room furnished with red-seated steel chairs, a glass-topped steel table and a black divan. A faded brown photograph of Rosa Luxemburg in a rococo gilt frame hung on one wall. Seated at the table drinking coffee were Zaleshoff and Tamara. Facing them was one of the fattest women Kenton had ever seen. She was talking in Russian to Tamara.

Zaleshoff waved to him to sit down. "Have some coffee. This"—
he indicated the fat woman—"is Smedoff."

The woman glanced at him, nodded and resumed her conversation with Tamara. Zaleshoff went into the bathroom. The journalist
sipped his coffee and stared, fascinated, at Madame Smedoff.

She might have been anywhere from sixty to ninety years old. The
flesh of her face, which quivered as she talked, was a mass of tiny
wrinkles. Her hair was short, hennaed and dressed in innumerable
curls. Her mouth was very carefully painted to correct an obtrusive
lower lip. A thick coating of white powder, two feverish dabs of
rouge high on the cheeks, plucked and penciled eyebrows and dark
blue eye shadow completed the work. There was not a vestige of
character left in the features. She wore a black silk dress and around
her shoulders was, of all things, a red tartan shawl. She adjusted it
repeatedly as she talked.

Suddenly she turned and fixed Kenton with a piercing stare. To
his amazement, the blue eyelids fluttered coquettishly and an arch
smile twisted her lips. "I have heard of you, Mr. Kenton," she said
in English. "You remind me very much of de Maupassant. You have
the same mouth."

"It is impossible that you should remember, Madame Smedoff.
You can have been no more than a young child when he died."

Madame Smedoff looked surprised, then preened herself and gig-
gled. "You say he is an Englishman, Tamara Prokovna? I cannot believe it. He is as insincere as a Frenchman, and as grave as a German.
It is droll."

Feeling rather foolish, Kenton buttered a piece of bread. The fat
woman resumed her conversation with Tamara; but now from time
to time she cast roguish glances in his direction, and after a while he
kept his eyes on the tray in front of him.

In spite, however, of Madame Smedoff's distracting presence he
did a certain amount of thinking. Almost imperceptibly, he realized,
he had come to regard himself as an ally of Zaleshoff and an opponent of Saridza. The fact that this had been brought about largely
by Saridza's brutal tactics was beside the point. Where exactly did
he stand? He was wanted by the Austrian police for the murder of
Sachs. His presence in Czechoslovakia was both illegal and precarious. This Russian, Zaleshoff, had it in his power to put him out of

danger so far as the Austrian police were concerned. He, Kenton, was virtually a prisoner awaiting the pleasure, through their representative, of the Soviet government. The thought irritated him, and he munched his breakfast gloomily. The sight of Zaleshoff, coming in pink and businesslike from the bath, intensified his sense of frustration. The fellow wasn't even good at his job! Here was that thug Saridza making ready to leave for Bucharest at any moment while the champion of the forces of democracy was taking baths and drinking coffee with a preposterous old harridan who ought to be . . .

"Well, Andreas," he said, "what do we do now?"

Zaleshoff lit a cigarette. "I haven't decided."

The fat woman snorted and turned to Kenton. "You, young man. You appear to have some sense. What do you think?"

"I think you're wasting time. Saridza may be getting away."

"There's no train to Bucharest until four this afternoon," said Madame Smedoff. "There's no plane to Bucharest until tomorrow morning. There is one man watching Saridza's car and another on the second floor of the hotel watching his room. Didn't you hear what we were talking about?"

"He doesn't speak Russian," said Tamara.

Madame Smedoff emitted a little screech of laughter. "Then the poor boy doesn't know what a wicked old woman I am!" She wriggled her huge body kittenishly.

"Olga!" snapped Zaleshoff.

She waved the interruption aside. "Listen, Mr. Kenton," she said, "this man Zaleshoff is all very good in his way, but he has no sense of strategy, as distinct from tactics. Your attempt, Andreas Prokovitch, on the Bastaki house was doomed to failure. The strategy was crude. Now again you make the same mistake. You would go to the Hotel Amerika and wave pistols at these men, club them, bind them, search for the photographs. I tell you, my friend, that even if you are successful in your violence, you will not find the photographs."

"Why not?"

Madame Smedoff rearranged her shawl. "Because they are not there. Saridza's no fool. The night he saw you, he knew what you wanted. It is obvious that he would put the photographs in a place of safety. But where? That we must find out and quickly. I think Saridza will travel by car this morning."

"Why?"

"The four o'clock train is a bad one. It is necessary to change at Budapest, and there is a long wait. Also Saridza rarely travels by train. So we must wait for him to leave and follow him. You ought to be able to do something between here and the Hungarian frontier."

"It's absurd, Olga, and you know it. Saridza might have left the photographs in the hotel safe, or at the luggage office at the station—anywhere."

"If I might make a suggestion?" put in Kenton apologetically.

"Well, young man?"

"If I were in Saridza's place, knowing that further attempts might be made to recover the photographs, I should have copies made by rephotographing the original prints and put them somewhere safe."

Madame Smedoff heaved herself out of her chair, went over and patted Kenton on the head. "There, Andreas Prokovitch, you see he has intelligence. Copies, of course." She beamed at Kenton. "And how do we find which photographer he went to?"

"He wouldn't go to an ordinary photographer. To safeguard himself he'd go somewhere where he had a pull with the operator. My bet is that those photographs and a duplicate set of prints are now waiting somewhere in a newspaper office. When Saridza's ready, he'll collect one set, of course, and leave the other in the safe. It's easy."

"But why a newspaper office?"

"It's got a photographic studio. It's well protected. There are people there day and night. It's the ideal place."

"So," said Zaleshoff ironically, "that is a great help. There can't be more than fifty newspaper offices in Prague."

Madame Smedoff grunted. "Use your brains, Andreas Prokovitch. Saridza would not leave them with just *any* paper. I have an idea." She flung an arch look at Kenton and waddled out of the room.

Zaleshoff made a gesture of despair. "Always," he said, "that old woman makes me feel like ten cents."

"How old is she?"

"God knows! She knew Lenin in London. Once she mentioned casually that she'd met Marx. Marx died in the early '80s, so that must make Olga well over seventy. She never forgets a fact or a face, and speaks nine languages."

"What does she do her face up like that for?"

"She used to have looks. Then while she was organizing a strike somewhere in Galicia, a woman threw vitriol in her face and scarred her. That's why she puts so much makeup on."

Madame Smedoff came back into the room with a grin of triumph on her lips. "The *Prager Morgenblatt* is the paper. I looked through the lists of shareholders of the German language papers—twenty-five percent of the shares of the *Prager Morgenblatt* are in the name of Elsa Schirmer, who is Frau Bastaki. She would have quite a lot of influence in the *Morgenblatt* offices, and Saridza would know it."

Zaleshoff got to his feet. "Tamara, we go immediately. Kenton, you may come if you wish. Olga, please see that Saridza does not get away without our knowing."

As they hurried out, Kenton glanced back. Madame Smedoff's eyes met his and she chuckled. Then, very deliberately, she winked.

CHAPTER 16

AMARA PULLED THE Mercedes up outside the offices of the *Prager Morgenblatt*. From the windows above came the clatter of Linotype machines. Zaleshoff and Kenton got out and walked to the main entrance. It had been arranged that Kenton, knowing something of newspaper offices, was to make the first move.

Inside, a doorkeeper sat in a small glass office. Followed by Zaleshoff, Kenton approached him. "A packet for Colonel Robinson was to be ready for him this morning. I have come to collect it on the colonel's behalf."

The man shook his head slowly. "I know nothing of it."

"It is curious," persisted Kenton. "The matter was arranged." His hand opened slightly and a bank note rustled.

"If you could perhaps tell me with whom the matter was arranged, *mein Herr*?"

Kenton took a chance. "With the *Herr Redakteur*."

"Ah! One moment, *mein Herr*." The man picked up a telephone and pressed a switch. "*Entschuldigen, Herr Direktor.* Two gentlemen have called on behalf of Colonel Robinson. They desire a packet as was arranged." There was a pause. "*Ja, Herr Direktor.*" He hung up the receiver and turned to them. "Please to wait a few minutes, the packet will be ready."

"*Danke.*" Kenton opened his hand and the note fluttered to the doorkeeper's table.

"*Danke schön, mein Herr.*"

"Well," murmured Kenton triumphantly, "what do you know about that? A managing editor isn't in his office at nine o'clock on a Sunday morning for nothing."

"I don't like it," replied the Russian. "It's too easy."

In about ten minutes the doorkeeper's telephone buzzed and the man picked up the receiver and listened. Kenton saw a curious expression cross the man's face and his eyes flickered toward them as he hung up.

"The *Herr Redakteur* will see you. This way."

The man led the way up a flight of narrow stone stairs and along a glass-partitioned corridor into a small outer office with a secretary's desk in it. On the far side was an imposing pair of mahogany double doors. Their guide threw them open and the two walked in.

It was a large cedar-paneled room with a window occupying nearly the whole of one wall. To the right was a smaller door. The man who sat behind the massive desk was a large, square-headed young German with thick glasses which magnified grotesquely his pale blue eyes.

"Be seated, gentlemen."

They remained standing. "We have very little time," said Zaleshoff. "We understand that the photographs are now ready. We may add that the colonel has instructed us to take the copy prints also."

The pale blue eyes moved from one to the other. "That is understood. Everything will be ready for you in a short time now."

There was silence in the room. The German sat motionless behind his desk. Kenton wandered across to the window and looked down into the street below. He could see the Mercedes. Suddenly a closed car dashed around the corner and pulled up in front of the building with a squeal of brakes. A second later uniformed figures got out and ran along the pavement. Kenton turned with a start. "Zaleshoff! Here, quick! It's the police!"

The Russian dashed to the window, looked down and swore.

They swung around. The German was pointing a small revolver

at them. "Put your hands up and don't move. I took the precaution," he said, his pale eyes gleaming, "of telephoning Colonel Robinson before inviting you in here. He advised me to call the police. The doorkeeper will show them up in a moment. The evidence of Soviet perfidy is now on its way by special messenger. Rumania will soon be convinced, in common with the rest of the world, of the reality of the Soviet menace."

"And the copies of the evidence?"

"They are in the safe in the wall behind me. When the time comes the evidence will be given to the German nation."

Kenton glanced at Zaleshoff. The Russian was standing slightly in front of him, his arms half raised above his head, his attitude that of a man who recognizes defeat when he sees it.

"Stop, Kenton!" he suddenly shouted warningly in German.

The trick succeeded. The German jerked the gun in Kenton's direction and Zaleshoff sprang. The revolver went off, and plaster showered from the ceiling as the two rolled to the floor.

"Lock the door, quick!" gasped Zaleshoff.

Kenton dashed to the double doors and slammed them. There was a sound of hurrying footsteps in the outer office. He swung around in time to see Zaleshoff bring the butt of the revolver down hard on the German's head. The man fell forward on his face. Outside the door, pandemonium had broken loose. Orders were being shouted. Then a bullet crashed through the woodwork by the lock.

The Russian rummaged in the German's pockets, then rose to his feet with a bunch of keys in his hand. He went to the small wall safe and began to try the keys one by one. He glanced around as another shot rang out. "See where that other door leads to."

Kenton was already opening the small door. Inside was a lavatory and above the washbasin was a narrow frosted-glass window. He flung it open and looked out. A few feet below was a flat roof. He dashed back into the room. "There's a window we can get through onto the roof."

"Good."

A volley of shots tore through the lock. Then shoulders were put to the door. It shook violently and there was a loud splitting noise. By this time Zaleshoff had the safe open and was scattering the contents right and left. Then there was a tinkle of breaking glass and

Kenton saw that Zaleshoff had thrown a packet of negative plates onto the carpet and was pounding them to dust with his heel. At the same instant there was a crash from the door.

"Look out!"

They dashed into the lavatory. Quickly Kenton slammed the door and put the catch up. "Have you got the prints?"

Zaleshoff held up a large paper envelope, tore it in half and crammed the pieces in his pocket. "Through the window with you!"

Already the lavatory door was being subjected to a furious battering, and a bullet tore through the thin woodwork.

Kenton landed on the roof on all fours. A second later Zaleshoff dropped beside him. Keeping close to the brickwork they followed the wall along, rounded a corner and faced a door set in the brickwork. There was a shout and Kenton saw that they had been seen from a window on the far side of the roof. As they leaped for cover a volley of shots spattered the wall beside them.

Zaleshoff tried the door. It was locked. He jumped forward and rammed his foot square on the lock. The door flew open and they tumbled down a flight of iron stairs. Before them was a pair of swinging doors from which came the clatter of Linotype machines. "Through here," snapped Zaleshoff. "Don't run, walk quickly."

They pushed through the swinging doors and marched in. The machines had evidently drowned the noise of the shots, for the men were working as if nothing had happened. It was a long narrow room, and they had to pass down its entire length to reach the door on the far side. They were about halfway through when a man, who looked like the foreman, looked up from a table piled with galley proof, frowned and moved to intercept them. Zaleshoff made for him instantly.

"Have you seen two men run through here?"

"*Nein.*" The man looked at them suspiciously.

"We are police. Two escaped criminals are in the building. If you see them, stop them at once. Is there any way they can get out except by the main entrance?"

"*Jawohl, Herr Kapitän.* There is the fire escape between this room and the engraving section."

"A man must be posted there immediately," said Zaleshoff brusquely. "Keep alert and report instantly if you see these men."

"Jawohl, Herr Kapitän."

The man hurried off importantly to tell his subordinates. As he did so the police burst through the swinging doors and shouted something. The foreman looked around uncertainly.

"Run for it," snapped Zaleshoff.

They dashed through the door leading to the fire exit, and the next moment the two were clattering down the fire escape. A bullet rang on the steel stairs above their heads, but by then they were well under cover.

At the foot of the stairs they found themselves in a concrete yard at the back of the *Prager Morgenblatt* building. Kenton glanced up and saw that three of the policemen were halfway down the fire escape.

"Run for the car," shouted Zaleshoff.

A few yards up the street was the Mercedes. As they sprinted toward it, Tamara opened the door and they tumbled in. A bullet zipped through the windshield and buried itself in the upholstery of the front seat.

"Keep down," cried Zaleshoff.

The Mercedes shot forward and swung around, its tires slithering over the wet asphalt. Tamara changed into second gear, rammed the accelerator down and cut in the supercharger. There was a whining roar from the exhaust and the big sedan flew up the street like a shot from a gun.

"To the Hotel Amerika, quickly!" said Zaleshoff.

The girl made a skid turn into the main road and they roared across the bridge over the Moldau. Zaleshoff drew the two halves of the envelope of prints from his pocket and tore them into minute pieces, which he scattered out of the window as they went.

Kenton began to get his breath back. "Not a bad guess of mine, was it?" he said.

Zaleshoff allowed the last of the fragments to trickle through his fingers. "No," he said grimly, "it wasn't. But now it is all the more necessary to get the original prints. You heard what that German said? The Nazis are going to use those photographs as a jumping-off spot for another anti-Soviet drive. Strategy or no strategy, I'm going to bust Saridza wide open."

Kenton laughed. He was feeling a little shaky.

"What's the matter?"

"I wonder what Saridza will say when he sees us."

"You'll soon find out." Zaleshoff leaned over to the girl. "Turn down a quiet street and run slowly for a minute." Then he pulled back the carpet and pried up one of the floorboards. The car slowed. Kenton saw the Russian catch hold of a mud-caked wire running beneath the floorboards and give it a sharp pull. Something clattered to the road and the car accelerated again.

"What on earth is that?"

Zaleshoff replaced the floorboard.

"It's an old Chicago custom. I've shed the Austrian license plates. There's a Belgian registration showing now. Have you got the Belgian papers, Tamara?"

"Yes, Andreas."

"Throw the others down a drain when we stop. Here, Kenton, you'd better have this with you if you want to hear what Saridza's got to say." He pulled a revolver, similar to the one he himself carried, from a pocket in the door and handed it to the journalist. "Take care. This one's loaded."

Kenton took the gun gingerly.

"That is, of course," added Zaleshoff with a faint smile, "if your professional instincts are still functioning."

Kenton slipped the revolver into his pocket. "Andreas Prokovitch," he said wearily, "you are one of the three most infuriating men I have ever met."

"Who are the other two?"

"Saridza and Captain Mailler."

Two minutes later they drew up in front of the Hotel Amerika garage. A man came out of a doorway opposite the entrance and walked to the car. Zaleshoff leaned out of the window. There was a quick muttered conversation, then Zaleshoff sat back, a grim look on his face.

"The map, Tamara." The girl passed a thick folded map over in silence.

"What is it?" said Kenton.

"Saridza and Mailler left in their car five minutes ago. They've taken the road due east to the German frontier. They aim to get out of Czechoslovakia as quickly as they can and go down through Poland to Bucharest." For a minute or two he pored over the map, then folded it up. "Make for Nimburg, Tamara. Smedoff is getting a check there. We shall have to try and catch them between Nimburg and the frontier. Have you plenty of gas?"

"Plenty."

"Then let's go."

<h2 style="text-align:center">CHAPTER 17</h2>

TAMARA DROVE WITH skill and assurance, and the Mercedes flew up and down the hills, the speedometer needle edging past the sixty-mile mark. Yet every time they slowed for a corner Kenton's right foot moved, pressing down an imaginary accelerator to drive the car on faster and faster.

It was more than the excitement of the chase. Separated by miles of road were two cars. In the first one were fifteen pieces of chemically coated paper with a message of fear, suspicion and hatred more dangerous than the deadliest poison gas. If the first car reached its destination, that message would be delivered. All that stood in the way of its doing so was a pitiful band of three—two worried Russians and a tired journalist with a gun he didn't know how to use.

It took the Mercedes forty minutes to reach Nimburg. Tamara slowed as they entered the town. Zaleshoff leaned forward. "Stop outside the *Spielhaus*."

When Tamara pulled up, Zaleshoff got out and walked over to a man with a piece of red ribbon in his buttonhole, who was standing on the pavement. Zaleshoff raised his hat politely, like a motorist asking a bystander for directions. The man said something and pointed in the direction in which the car was facing. Zaleshoff raised his hat again and walked back to the car.

"Quick, Tamara," he said as he got in. "They passed through here eight minutes ago. It's only two hours from here to the frontier. We shall have to go fast."

The car shot forward again. As they left the town behind them, Kenton saw the speedometer needle creep around to the ninety-mile mark and stay there. There was little traffic on the road and for this mercy he was thankful. The road, though straight and good, was narrow and slippery from the rain. The girl seemed unaware of these limitations.

"Have you been in many smashes with your sister driving?" Kenton asked after one specially hair-raising moment.

"She's never had an accident in her life," said Zaleshoff. But Kenton thought the tone of the assurance a little too emphatic.

Twice they were held up at road crossings. Once, on the outskirts of a small town, they were stopped by a police patrol. Zaleshoff showed the Belgian registration papers, and the man waved the car on with apologies and the information that he had been told to stop all cars with foreign registrations, as a gang of international thieves had that morning broken into a newspaper office in Prague. Somewhat overwhelmed by the narrowness of their escape, they drove on.

The clouds were very low and the car kept running into patches of thin, drenching mist. The girl was forced to slow down a little. Then, on a clear straight stretch of road, about a quarter of a mile ahead, they saw the black sedan. Almost immediately it ran into mist, but a thrill of excitement went surging through Kenton's veins.

"Wait until you're round the corner, then pass them and get about a hundred meters ahead," ordered Zaleshoff. "Get down, Kenton. We can't afford to be seen."

The two crouched on the floor, and Kenton's heart was thumping against his ribs.

Suddenly Tamara spoke. "They're accelerating."

"Crowd them in on the next corner."

Kenton heard the supercharger whine and felt the car leap forward. A moment later it swerved violently. There was a sharp crash and the Mercedes rocked and swerved again.

"Caught them with a fender," said Tamara.

"Pull up quickly and back across the road."

There was a shriek of brakes, and Kenton was hurled forward against the back of the driver's seat. He felt the car skidding wildly. Then gears crunched and the Mercedes lurched backward. The motor stalled. There was a moment's silence, then Kenton heard the roar of an exhaust.

"They're turning round," cried Tamara.

"Quick, Kenton! Out!"

Zaleshoff scrambled onto the road. Twenty-five yards away the black car was reversing to turn around. There was a spit of flame from one of the side windows and a bullet hit the body of the Mercedes a foot from Kenton's head. Out of the corner of his eye he saw Zaleshoff raise his gun deliberately. The Russian fired. The next instant there was a stream of flame from the gas tank in the rear of the black car.

"Quick!" cried Zaleshoff. "Off the road!"

The road was built on a low embankment fringed on either side

with birch trees. The two jumped down the side of the embankment and, keeping their heads low, ran along the gully at the bottom toward the blazing car. Already flames were leaping into the air, and blazing gasoline was pouring all over the road. Zaleshoff stopped and raised his head cautiously. A shot rang out above the roar of the flames and a bullet hit the edge of the road two feet away. Zaleshoff ducked down again.

"They've taken cover down off the other side of the road. Get back to the car and stay behind it. Take potshots at them from there. You won't hit them at that distance—but I want to keep them busy so that I can get at them from this side."

"All right." Kenton ran back along the gully and got behind the car. Through the space between the spare wheel and the car's body he could see Mailler and Saridza crouching beside a pile of stones below the road level. Tamara got out of the driver's seat and stood beside him. He rested his revolver on the spare-wheel casing, squinted along the barrel and squeezed the trigger. The gun kicked, and he saw Mailler duck.

"Have you ever fired a revolver before?" said the girl.

"No, why?"

"You nearly hit your man."

The next moment the girl gave a little cry. "Look!"

Then he saw that Zaleshoff had left the shelter of the embankment and was crawling across the road.

"He's crazy! He'll get killed!" As Kenton spoke he saw the Russian's arm shoot out and a stab of flame from his gun. Mailler's hands went to his head. Almost at the same moment Saridza fired and Zaleshoff fell forward. The next instant Saridza turned and vanished among the trees.

Kenton dashed along the road. When he got to Zaleshoff, the Russian was trying to get to his feet, his hand clasped to his side, his face contorted with pain. The wounded man waved him away. "Saridza," he gasped. "He's got away."

Revolver in hand, Kenton plunged down the embankment and threaded his way among the trees. Then he stopped and listened. For a moment there was not a sound but the dripping of water from the branches. Then he heard a slight movement ahead to the left, and moved carefully in that direction. Suddenly a twig snapped beneath his foot. A second afterward a bullet whipped through the undergrowth. He bent double and crept forward. The man ahead fired again. Kenton halted. Then, through a gap between the trees, he saw Saridza. The man was peering about him like a hunted animal. Kenton raised his gun. At that moment Saridza saw him. His arm jerked up. The revolver in his hand clicked twice, but no shot came. He had run out of ammunition. Kenton saw panic seize him. Saridza dropped the revolver and put his hands up.

"I surrender," he said quickly.

His finger quivering on the trigger, the journalist walked forward into the clearing. His eyes met those of the other man and he knew that he could not shoot.

Saridza licked his lips. "What are you going to do?"

"I haven't decided," he said, knowing that he would have to bluff. "I'm trying to think of a single reason why I shouldn't shoot you as dead as you would have shot me a minute ago."

"You were armed."

"If our positions were reversed, you would tell me that to run out of ammunition was part of the fortune of war—that is, if you bothered to do any explaining."

Saridza regarded him warily. "I know you want the photographs. Let me go free and you shall have them. That is a fair bargain."

"You are not in a position to bargain. I could take the photographs off your dead body. I know what you are thinking at the moment. You are thinking that the longer you can keep me talking the less likely I am to shoot you down in cold blood." Kenton raised his revolver until it was pointed at the man's chest. "I don't think we need prolong this interview."

Saridza's face went a yellow gray.

"I'll give you half a minute to get those photographs from your pocket," said Kenton, "and throw them on the ground where I can pick them up. Put one hand in slowly and take them out. Keep the other hand up. I hope your nerves are good, because if your hand jerks a fraction of an inch I shall fire."

Saridza obeyed. A packet fell at Kenton's feet. Keeping his eyes fixed on the man in front of him, Kenton stooped and picked it up. He eased the prints out of the packet and counted them.

"There are only ten here. Where are the other five?"

Saridza hesitated. Kenton thumbed back the hammer of the revolver.

"In the other pocket."

A few seconds later another envelope was lying on the ground. Kenton counted the remaining prints carefully and put them all in his pocket.

"All right, walk back four paces."

Saridza did so. Kenton stepped forward and picked up the revolver the man had dropped. They faced each other.

"May I ask you a question, Mr. Kenton?"

"Yes?"

"Who released you from that tank?"

"No one. We released ourselves."

"I bow to your ingenuity. May one ask how?"

"I'm afraid I haven't got time to go into that now. Turn round."

The other obeyed. Kenton reversed the revolver he had picked up and held it by the barrel like a club. He walked up behind Saridza.

"Just a moment, Mr. Kenton."

"What is it?"

"Before you knock me insensible I should like to remind you of an offer I made to you last night. That offer is still open, but I would, if you reconsidered your decision, double the retaining fee. A letter addressed to me care of Mr. Balterghen of the Pan-Eurasian Petroleum Company, London, will always find me. That's all."

"Turn round, Saridza."

The man turned. Kenton stood back. "The Anglo-Saxon sense of humor, Saridza, is one of the most emasculating influences known to mankind. I am the unfortunate possessor of such a sense of humor. You can go. Go on. Clear out. But I warn you. If you show your face within the next twenty-four hours, I shall shoot you on sight."

Saridza turned without a word and walked off among the trees. Kenton made his way back to the road.

Zaleshoff had crawled to the side of the road and was attempting to stanch his wound with a blood-soaked handkerchief. His eyes searched the journalist's face anxiously as Kenton clambered up the embankment.

"You failed?" Zaleshoff asked.

Kenton took the two envelopes from his pocket and scattered the contents on the ground by the wounded man. Zaleshoff examined them feverishly. Then he looked up. "I heard shots. You killed him?"

Kenton shook his head.

The Russian was silent for a moment. "It is a pity," he said at last, "but I am glad you did not. It would have worried you."

Kenton glanced at the body of Mailler lying at the bottom of the embankment. "What about him?"

"Dead. Have you got a match?"

Kenton went down on one knee, crumpled the photographs together and set light to them. When they were burned, he scattered the ashes with his foot.

IT WAS LATE IN THE AFTERNOON when Madame Smedoff waddled into her parlor. Kenton sat up on the divan on which he had been dozing. "How is he?"

Madame Smedoff rolled down the sleeves of her black silk dress. "He has a little fever, but the wound is not dangerous. The bullet passed through the side, just below the rib cage. In a fortnight he will be up."

"Oughtn't we to get a doctor?"

She fluttered her eyelids at him and smiled impishly. "I am a doctor, Mr. Kenton. I was trained at the Sorbonne."

"I beg your pardon."

"Don't be a silly boy. Go in and see Andreas Prokovitch. He needs sleep badly, but says he must see you." She looked at him solemnly. "He is embarrassed. He asked me to thank you for what you did for him today."

Kenton smiled and went into the bedroom.

Tamara was sitting beside the bed. Her eyes were shining in a way Kenton had not seen before.

Zaleshoff greeted him weakly. "Look at Tamara," he added. "She is happy. For years I have not seen her look so happy. And all because I say we will go to Moscow for a holiday."

Kenton saw that there were tears in the girl's eyes. She smiled.

"Did she tell you, Kenton," muttered Zaleshoff, "that Ortega was apprehended this morning?"

"Yes, how did you work it?"

"He was found by the railway track, dead."

"Dead!"

"He died the night after he killed Borovansky. The confession was found by his body with the gun that killed him. He committed suicide."

"I'm ready to make allowances for a sick man, Andreas, but you don't expect me to believe that, do you?"

"He committed suicide just as surely as if he had fired the gun himself. Just before we got you back to Kölnerstrasse, he tried to escape from Rashenko. That *is* suicide."

"Then where had he been all this time?"

"In the empty room below Rashenko. Rashenko owns the whole of that house. The woman who lives downstairs is his cousin."

"And you let the police go on hunting me all this time?"

"I told you to stay with Rashenko. When you turned up in Prague I was told to keep you with me in case you communicated with the newspapers or the English authorities. I did so."

Kenton swallowed hard. "Well, Zaleshoff," he said at last, "when I classed you with Saridza and Mailler as my pet banes, I did them a gross injustice. You beat them with plenty to spare."

Zaleshoff's gaze flickered from Kenton to his sister. Then a slow smile spread over his face, and he closed his eyes again.

"You know, Tamara," he murmured drowsily, "I like this guy Kenton. He amuses me."

Two DAYS LATER Kenton boarded the Berlin train at Prague.

A lot of sleep, numerous baths and new clothes (supplied by an adamantly insistent Zaleshoff) had done much toward repairing the ravages of the previous few days. An invitation, issued by Zaleshoff through Tamara, to visit Moscow in two months' time had induced an optimistic outlook. He was feeling good.

The train was fairly crowded. He shared a compartment with three men. One of them he judged to be Hungarian. The other two were Czechs. From their conversation, Kenton gathered that all three were commercial travelers. He began to read the newspaper he had bought at a kiosk.

As the train drew slowly out of the station, he put the paper down and felt in his pocket for a cigarette. The Hungarian caught his eye. "Pardon, *mein Herr*," he said, "we are about to play a game of poker dice—one pfennig is the maximum stake. Would you care to play also?"

Kenton hesitated. Then he smiled regretfully and shook his head. "Thank you, *mein Herr*. It is good of you. I am afraid I don't play."

KLAUS FUCHS

Klaus Fuchs

A CONDENSATION FROM
THE TRAITORS

by Alan Moorehead

The extraordinary story of Klaus Fuchs, who
betrayed British and American atomic secrets to
the Russians, is a classic study of the type of
traitor whom the author describes as "the man
who is not a professional spy, nor a turncoat
politician, nor a man out essentially for personal
gain, but a self-appointed idealist."

Fuchs was such a man—a brilliant atomic
scientist, a shy, self-effacing man burningly
convinced of the purity of his own motives.
Alan Moorehead's portrait of Fuchs, coupled with
the exciting story of how British intelligence
slowly drew its net about him, makes for
fascinating and illuminating reading.

Mr. Moorehead, an Australian who became a
famous British journalist, is the author of many
distinguished books on subjects of contemporary
and historical interest, among them *Gallipoli*,
The Blue Nile and *Darwin and the Beagle*.

CHAPTER 1

I N 1949 KLAUS FUCHS was a senior man at the Atomic Energy Research Establishment at Harwell, England. He was head of one of the most important departments, a respected scientist of international standing.

In manner Fuchs was serious, shy, and self-effacing. He had a bulging forehead, a set mouth, and a slightly weak chin. He was woefully shortsighted and wore horn-rimmed glasses with thick lenses. His sensitive, inquiring face and mildly lost air made a great appeal, especially to women. His thin body was stronger and more resilient than it looked. He never played games (because he believed he could never play them well), but he was an exceptionally good dancer, a mountaineer of more than average tenacity, and a skier.

He had very few close friends, and outside these he was not notably well liked at Harwell by his department or his acquaintances. He was too difficult to know. Despite his long years in England, he seemed to have had no success in adopting British manners or a British cast of thinking; he remained German, and there were times when his subordinates felt this keenly. But Harwell is a small community, brought together by the brains and not by the social graces of its inmates. By 1949 Dr. Fuchs was established there in the same way as an officer is established on a ship or a resident doctor in a hospital. He was known, and he was a fixture. He was a strange man in many ways, but there were other strange men in Harwell too, and his strangeness, his eccentricities, became the accepted and familiar pattern by which he was known.

When he sat down, for example, he had a nervous trick of crossing his knees and constantly turning one of his feet around and around. He was a chain smoker of cigarettes, and a fabulous drinker. He drank, not persistently, but on special occasions, and with a sort of undergraduate bravado. He drank tumblers of neat gin. He consumed neat whisky by the bottle, and never turned a hair. At one party he took a gargantuan draft of spirits, and led the guests on a conga around the house. Then he summoned up his decorum again; and there he was, Dr. Fuchs, head of the department of theoretical physics, poised and in command, equally ready to drive the guests home or launch into a discussion of isotopes. There were great stories of his drinking prowess. At a celebration in Los Alamos it was Dr. Fuchs who, having filled his own glass all evening, finally put the barman to bed. He was not a drunkard, nobody suggested that. But he was a mighty drinker when he chose.

The one thing that sent him into rages was inefficiency. There was, for the doctor, a right way of doing things, and to ignore it was nothing less than sheer idleness and silliness. This rule applied to physics, love affairs, domestic life, and, in the end, to politics. He was the sort of man who can look through a railway timetable in a moment and make clear, exact arrangements for a rendezvous, and he was never late. In his exasperation at some muddle he would exclaim, "I'll handle it"—and he usually did, extremely well.

Fuchs was an erratic driver. He adored speed—or rather the risks attendant on speed, not the speed itself. One of his friends recalls driving home with him one night through a drenching storm when the car skidded badly. Fuchs pulled it back onto the proper side of the road again. "I love skids," he said. "They give you the opportunity of controlling them."

He had no hobbies and took no regular exercise. There were times when he played chess, and, very occasionally, cards. He was the chairman of a civil servants' committee at Harwell which settled the domestic affairs of the community, dealing with complaints and the water rates and so on—and he was a balanced and excellent chairman. Though he prepared innumerable reports, he never wrote a book, and he was not a reader outside his own studies. Apart from a slight interest in music, he cared nothing for the arts. On sight-seeing tours his friends would implore him, "But you must look at it, Klaus. It's one of the most beautiful pictures [or sculptures, or buildings] in the world." He remained unmoved, detached, and unimpressed.

He would go to the movies as everybody else did at Harwell, but it was impossible to obtain any real reaction from him after the show. He had liked it. He liked them all.

In the society of women he relaxed. He was the kind of man who needs women, and that need naturally evoked a response; from his student days onward there was always some woman with whom he was intimate, with whom he would be at ease and talk as he seldom did in the company of men. He was not lively, but he was devoted. And on the woman's side, there was usually a motherly desire to comfort this sincere and introspective man, to draw him out and nurture him.

He was not an untidy man, but there were days when he did not shave and his dark blue beard sprouted in an ugly mat through his pale skin. In all else he was precise.

He was almost a fanatic about security. He was the one who, at declassification conferences, was often opposed to the release of information to the public. He was forever going to the security officer to give him his keys for safekeeping, and he was meticulous in locking up his documents and guarding his speech among nonofficial people. No one ever accused Klaus Fuchs of careless talk; his was the type of bureaucratic mind which is always on the safe side, which keeps secrets when it is quite unnecessary, purely out of ingrained habit and an absurd feeling for the mystique of the official word. He liked affairs to be either black or white; and a genial compromise was, to him, always a mistake. He never mastered the art of talking easily to strangers. He had a sense of humor, but he lacked warmth. He ate sparingly, often without appetite, and he was extravagant in nothing except those endless cigarettes and the occasional showy bouts of drinking.

In the late 1940s a spot developed on his lung, and he handled this illness in a curious way. There were times when he looked haggard and ghastly white, but he persisted in going on with his work and he never complained. No one could induce him to see a doctor and go to bed. One of his friends recalls a drive along the Riviera during their summer holidays. The heat was excessive, and the twisting road was full of traffic. Fuchs drove all day with a morose and frantic determination, and he looked as though he would faint at any moment. In the morning, when he was obviously better, he said to his friends, "I took my temperature last night. It was a hundred and four."

Then, on other occasions, he would give way—and more than give way—to his illness. He would lie for hours, even days on end, with his face turned to the wall, eating next to nothing, saying nothing, reading nothing, abandoning himself to a trance of physical grief. Sometimes these morbid fits went far beyond anything created by his illness, for that was finally looked after by a doctor and he had been cured. Once one of his women friends went to him and said, "Look, Klaus, why don't you get up? You are not really ill any longer."

He turned around and answered, in a normal voice, "All right. I'll get up if you think so." Then he calmly dressed himself and went out to his office to work.

This queerness was by no means a regular thing with him—it is remembered because it was exceptional. But those friends who had known him best over a long period noted something else which they regarded as much more interesting. This was the great change that came over Fuchs at Harwell. In his early student days in the English universities he had been oblivious to what was going on around him, to the little, ordinary things of life. He was not gauche or unwilling, but it would simply never occur to him that he might open a door for a woman or give a present on a birthday or make a gesture of any kind. A perfect specimen of an abstracted professor in the making, he worked as though driven by demons. It was the work that mattered. All the rest was a killing of time.

One of Fuchs's colleagues during World War II has described his first impression of him. "I thought him," he said, "a colorless, disembodied, and methodical brain."

Now at Harwell in the late 1940s he still worked with the same utter concentration, but in his relationship to the people around him he had developed into a paragon of thoughtfulness and kindness. He was the one who quietly went out to the kitchen and did the washing up after dinner. He remembered on his trips to London to buy cream puffs for a friend who had a passion for them. He would go out at any time of night to meet someone at the station, to run an errand, or sit with a sick friend.

Consequently there were people at Harwell who grew to like Fuchs very much indeed, and he was much more to them than a brilliant, disembodied mind. He had come to England sixteen years before, penniless, unable to speak the language, a refugee from the Nazis in Germany. In those sixteen years he had never been involved in a scandal, had never come to the notice of the police in any way except insofar as he was an alien when war broke out. And now, entirely through his own devoted work with the British, he had risen to the top in the most elect and difficult of all sciences, the theory of nuclear physics, and they were proud of him in a way.

The Atomic Energy Research Establishment at Harwell, Berkshire, England

He was one of the first to arrive at Harwell in 1946, when it was just a bleak encampment on a deserted airfield in Berkshire. He had seen it grow up from next to nothing, and he had helped in all the planning. If there was one thing about Fuchs that was entirely apparent, it was his devotion to Harwell. It was his home and the center of his work, and he loved the place.

His friends knew this. They knew his house, his habits, his work, his oddities, his income, and his fixed loyalty to his colleagues. And they had known these things over a long period of time.

WHAT THEY DID NOT know, what they did not conceive by the barest inkling, was that all this was a façade and a lie. It was a lie when they first met him and it had developed now into a lie of such stupendous size that very few of them were going to recover entirely from its consequences. For Klaus Fuchs, during a period of some seven years, had secretly been passing information to the Russians about the atomic bomb. It was not only the betrayal of secrets; others had done that too, and the Russians could never have made a bomb at that time out of Fuchs's information alone. Nor was it merely the fact that, in a peculiarly horrible and deceitful way, he had evoked in his colleagues' minds a deep distrust of one another, for who could be above suspicion after this?

The real issue went much further. They were confronted in Fuchs by a man who was prepared to betray all people anywhere at any time, according to the dictates of his own conscience. The rules of society, built up through a long and painful history, meant nothing to him. The undermining of trust, and physical suffering, meant nothing. Only the conscience counted. That was the one thing, in Fuchs's code, that could not be betrayed, and he saw himself as a martyr to it. The conscience was divine, unquestioned, and inexplicable; it simply gave forth its inevitable light, and one obeyed. There have been anarchists before in the world, but Fuchs was a peculiar kind of anarchist, for he loved not chaos but order. He liked skidding on a wet road, not because of the skidding itself, but because it enabled him to put the car to rights again.

It is probably true that most men love power, even though they hate responsibility, and they will use power whenever they can get it. Fuchs found himself in possession of great power, and he at once went trotting to his divine conscience for instructions as to what he should do with it. He did not pause to ask society for its advice. His conscience was above society. This is the peculiar menace of Fuchs, for if he were to propagate himself, if thousands of Fuchses and their consciences were let loose on the world, they would be almost as deadly as the worst atomic bomb invented yet. Split atoms follow at least predictable courses, and the Fuchses do not.

It is useful, then, to turn back through Fuchs's life, and see if we can discover where his conscience came from, who made it, and who twisted it to these perverse and unpredictable ends.

CHAPTER 2

ONE OF THE THINGS that must be put down against the Nazis is that they probably did more toward the corruption of Klaus Fuchs's mind than anything the Communists ever achieved. They ruined the Fuchs family just as effectively as some contagious plague might have done.

The Fuchses were not Jews, and in the beginning they were not Communist, so they were not natural targets for the Nazis. They were a Protestant family and lived in rather poor but respectable circumstances in the industrial west of Germany. Dr. Emil Fuchs, the father, was a Lutheran pastor of immense religious faith, and he brought up his family in the belief that they must always do what they felt to be right whatever the consequences. It was not sufficient merely to know what was right; you had to act upon it. This was the center of his creed: a positive and active Christianity, supported by the love of God and a firm belief that every man knew within himself what was right and what was wrong. He became a Quaker, an active pacifist, and as a member of a group known as the Religious Socialists, he was the first Lutheran pastor to join the Social Democratic party after World War I, an action which for a pastor was something of a scandal.

Dr. Fuchs enjoyed forty years of life in a settled community in Germany before the 1914 war broke out. He could not foresee the effect of his teachings on children who never knew his stability in their daily lives, who were born and brought up in wars and their aftermath, when all the old values and loyalties were breaking up around them. Life for them became a frantic struggle for existence, before they had fairly gotten their roots into the ground. The love of God was not as apparent to them as it was to Dr. Fuchs, and consequently there was a great danger in his teaching, for there was always the possibility that his children would absorb one part and forget the rest—would lose their faith in God, and yet still believe in their absolute right and their duty to take decisions into their own hands, to act as they themselves thought best. This was a dangerous proposition, a demand for positive individual action which was not based on faith but on personal judgment, and it is precisely what destroyed the younger son.

Klaus was born in the village of Rüsselsheim, not far from Darmstadt and Frankfurt am Main, on December 29, 1911, and christened Emil Julius Klaus. His first memories were of life in provincial towns in the industrial belt, where his father traveled from one poor parish to another. He seems to have been happy enough as a small child, but later on he particularly remembered his first act of public defiance, soon after World War I was over. This happened one day when there was a celebration for the Weimar Republic, which had succeeded the Kaiser's government. Not all Germans were ready to accept their defeat and the tame compromise of a Socialist republic. They were willing to erect the Weimar flags on the public buildings, but in privacy they had other views. The flags went up on Klaus's school building, but once the pupils got inside, many of them took off their republican badges and put up the imperial colors instead. At home, no doubt, Klaus had heard a great deal about his father's fervent hopes for the new constitution. So he stuck to his Weimar colors, and the other pupils tore them off him. That was his first ostracism, his first effort at doing what he thought right no matter what the consequences might be.

In 1925, when Klaus was thirteen, his father joined the Society of Friends, and the background of his schooldays is that of a poor, pious, and strictly Quaker home. Klaus then moved on to the University of Leipzig and was gathered at once into those tortuous and futile undergraduate intrigues which bedeviled university life all over Germany at that time.

First, like his father, he joined the Social Democrats. Next, he joined the Reichsbanner as well. This was already a contradiction of his pacifism, for the Reichsbanner was a semimilitary organization designed to defend the democrats in case of violence. It was his first break with his father's philosophy, the first stage of the long downhill ride that would take him into either Communism or Fascism.

In 1931 Fuchs's father was given a professorship of religious science at a teachers' training college at Kiel, and the whole family moved to the north. Fuchs continued studying for his degree in physics and mathematics, and at once picked up the political lines he had left behind at Leipzig. He made his first decisive move to the left when he joined an unwholesome new organization composed partly of Social Democrats and partly of Communists—although, since it was persistent Communist policy to attack the Social Democrats, no genuine Social Democrat could have joined.

Fuchs became chairman of this group. It sought to infiltrate the Nazi party, to gain the confidence of Nazi members—drawing them into illegal adventures and then double-crossing them by exposing them at the last minute. He soon found an admirable occasion for a maneuver of this kind. The Nazis were agitating for a reduction of the university fees. Very well, Fuchs proposed to them, let us jointly organize a strike of the students. The Nazis agreed to discuss the matter. Fuchs waited until the negotiations were well advanced, and then, without warning the Nazis, he issued a public pamphlet making it clear just what had been going on. As a method of making enemies, it would be hard to find an improvement on this, and indeed the Nazis did not forget.

Long after, Fuchs said he had some misgivings. He had violated some standard of decent behavior, and for a long time he could not straighten out the incident in his mind to his own satisfaction. Finally he accomplished it by saying that in a struggle of this kind any such regrets were simply weakness.

Meanwhile he was moving farther to the left, and with the Reichstag elections, beginning in July 1932, he went the whole way. Hindenburg had been proposed by the right for Reich president, and the Social Democrats decided not to oppose him with a candidate of their own, lest they should split the vote and let Hitler in. Fuchs argued that you could not stop Hitler by combining with the right. The only way to do it was through a united working-class party. He offered himself as a speaker for the Communists at the election, and the Social Democrats expelled him.

When Hindenburg was elected, and von Papen as Reichschancellor dismissed the democratic Prussian government, it was painfully clear to Fuchs that he had been right. The Social Democrats were moribund and finished. The only place for him now was with the full-blooded, fighting Communists.

From a practical democrat of Christian principles and a firm believer in the freedom of the individual, he had developed into a militant Communist, an atheist who had handed over his free will to the Party, and he convinced himself that it had all happened logically, step by step.

It did not occur to him that he and the Communists had played their part in destroying the Social Democrats and the last hope of liberal democracy in Germany.

He joined the Communists outright, and in his first glow of enthusiasm for the one true party, felt called upon for some act of heroism. Presently he found occasion for that too.

On January 30, 1933, Hitler became Reichschancellor, and soon afterward the Nazis in Kiel decided to hold a students' strike at the university. The brownshirts paraded before the classrooms, and Fuchs, who had something of his father's courage, deliberately showed himself among them. They caught him one day, manhandled him, and threw him in the river. If there was one thing needed to confirm Fuchs in his Communism it was that. He had suffered for the cause. From now on he was prepared to accept the Party line, whatever it might be.

He was chosen to attend a Communist students' congress in Berlin, and very early on the morning of February 28, 1933, he got up and took a train for the capital. He bought a newspaper and saw that the Reichstag in Berlin had been burned down the night before. The debacle had begun. "I immediately realized the significance," he said later, "and I knew that the underground struggle had started. I took the badge of the hammer and sickle from my lapel which I had carried until that time." And on arrival in Berlin he went into hiding.

There are not now many people in Berlin who survived unscathed the terror that broke out that summer and ultimately spread over the whole world. Hundreds of thousands of Germans were killed, arrested, put into concentration camps, or they fled across the borders. Klaus's mother had committed suicide the previous year, but his father was still in Kiel, and holding to his Socialist views. They put him in prison for several months before he was brought before a People's Court. He stood up, unrepentant, before the judges, declaring that nothing would make him alter his views or prevent him from speaking openly about what he believed to be right. The Nazis were not yet prepared to obliterate a well-known Quaker minister, and there had been an outcry at Dr. Fuchs's imprisonment. He was released, and the Gestapo contented itself by keeping an eye on him from then on. At the same time they noted in their books at Kiel that Klaus Fuchs, the doctor's younger son, was a Communist Party member, and that his present whereabouts was unknown.

The other three children—Gerhardt, the elder brother, and the two girls, Kristel and Elisabeth—had by this time also gone over to Communism. Gerhardt managed to avoid arrest, and for a time he and his father ran a car-rental business for getting anti-Nazi refugees out of the country. Eventually he escaped to Switzerland, where he obtained treatment for a tubercular infection. Kristel managed to get to America later, and settled down with her husband at Cambridge, Massachusetts. Elisabeth had a tragic fate. She was an artist and she married a Communist sympathizer named Kittowski. They had one child. The family was arrested and put into prison. From prison Elisabeth managed to help in organizing her husband's escape to Czechoslovakia. For months she heard nothing from him, but she and the baby were released from prison, and eventually she got word through underground channels that he was in Prague. The strain of this separation, and the danger in which they were all living, began to unhinge Elisabeth's mind, and when in March 1939 the Nazis marched into Prague, she became frantic with grief and worry. Her father was traveling with her one day on a Berlin train. He held her hand, knowing that she might do something desperate, since she was convinced that her husband had been caught in Prague and tortured by the Nazis. He let go her hand for a moment while he took the train tickets out of his pocket, and in that instant she threw herself out on the track and was killed.

The fate of Klaus had been a good deal easier. The Gestapo never found him in Berlin. He attended the students' secret conference and received much praise for his work at Kiel. He was advised then by the Party to make his way out of the country so that he could complete his studies abroad and then return one day and help in the building of the new Germany when Hitler's regime had collapsed. As a first step he was asked to attend a United Front rally to be held in Paris in August.

After five months in hiding, Fuchs clandestinely crossed the frontier into France in July and made his way to Paris. He was now twenty-one. He had no funds, no friends other than acquaintances in the French Communist Party, and he spoke nothing but German. It happened that about this time a friend of his, a German girl who was engaged to one of his cousins, was living with an English Quaker family in Somerset, England. Fuchs wrote to her from Paris, where he was by now destitute. The Quaker family sent a generous invitation to Fuchs to come to them in England so that he could complete his studies. He arrived there, white-faced, half starved, with a bundle of dirty linen in a canvas bag, on September 24, 1933.

He told the immigration officer he had come to England to study physics at the University of Bristol, and he gave as a reference the name of the Quaker family in Somerset, saying that they were friends of his father. He was registered on the official records of the aliens department of the Home Office as a refugee; a steady stream of refugees was arriving at this time, and he was given leave to land. Fuchs said nothing about his Communist connections. He went at once to his Quaker friends and remained with them for the next two years.

Already, in 1933, Klaus Fuchs was an interesting study in loyalties. Already he had abandoned not one, but several causes. He had walked out on the Social Democratic party. He had turned his back on both his pacifism and his Christianity. And now he was about to adopt an entirely new nationality. He had been submitted to frightening experiences—his father later said he had been sentenced by the Nazis to be lynched—and they had very nearly finished him.

For his father, who had remained in Germany, the issues were not the same, for Dr. Fuchs had his faith in God, and that was absolute.

The spring and summer of 1933 [Dr. Fuchs wrote] were good to look upon. But my children were scattered, my life's work broken. My friends were in danger; some had fled; others had been imprisoned; many had been killed. And around me was the success of what I knew was the power of destruction and injustice. I hated the beauty of that spring, and I fled the sight of families and the sounds of music. Hiding its terrors behind sparkling life made fate seem doubly cruel. But then came the experience of Christ's presence, and it became stronger and stronger in my being.

Klaus had none of this faith. He was hungry, threadbare, and bitter. It was probably out of nothing more nor less than a natural instinct for self-preservation that he turned toward the only two things that had any appearance of solidity in his life. One was his study of physics, and the other was Communism.

CHAPTER 3

THE COMMUNIST PARTY WAS busy among the refugees from Nazi Germany. German Communism gave them a link with their homes, and there was always the prospect that, through Communism, they would return to Germany once Hitler was ousted. In all the

Western democracies new cells of refugee Communists were set up. They profited by the current left-wing liberalism and anti-Fascism of the West, especially on the outbreak of the Spanish Civil War. They became active in all refugee organizations, in charitable and religious groups, in working-class movements, and in the universities. These societies were obvious points of gravitation for every refugee as soon as he arrived—there he could find friends, financial help, and people who could speak his own language—and the Communists at once set about drawing him into the Party.

The Nazis were well aware of all this. From the moment they seized power their embassies and consulates abroad were supplied by the Gestapo with lists of Germans who had escaped. And they never ceased warning the democracies against these dangerous Reds. At times they demanded their extradition.

In November 1934 the German consul at Bristol reported unofficially to the chief constable of the city that Klaus Fuchs was a Communist. This piece of gratuitous information was hardly likely to make any great stir in the chief constable's office. In the first place, the German consul was the representative of the Nazi government; secondly, he admitted that the source of his information was a Gestapo report from Kiel, and already in the early 1930s the Gestapo was regarded with horror. In any case it was not illegal in England for a man to be a Communist; indeed, it was a guarantee that he was not a Nazi. Moreover, there were no means of checking Fuchs's past record except from the Germans themselves, and they were scarcely unprejudiced—automatically they branded a man as a Jew or a criminal or a Red if he dared to escape from the fatherland.

This 1934 report from the German consul in Bristol was the only definite evidence of Fuchs's Communism that was ever presented, right up to the time of his arrest. It was known among his friends that he had left-wing views; in Bristol he never made any secret of it. He associated with other German refugees who were known to be strongly anti-Nazi. But he never committed any public act that indicated his allegiance to Communism. He never joined the British Communist Party. He never told the police or any official body, then or later, that he was a Communist. And he never took an active part in any Communist meeting or demonstration—unless you count the fact that he was on the committee of a Spanish relief organization which was largely concerned with assistance to Spanish refugees.

In forwarding the Gestapo report to the authorities in London, the chief constable commented that Fuchs was not known to have taken part in any Communist activities in Bristol, nor had he in any way come to the unfavorable notice of the police. As an alien, whose permit to stay and work in England had to be extended from time to time, he was checked on three separate occasions by the Bristol police—each time with the same negative result. It is of course true that, had the police cared to inquire among Fuchs's friends and neighbors, they would have turned up the fact that privately he held strong left-wing views—which was nothing more than they might have suspected already. The Quaker family with which he stayed used to make Intourist trips to Russia, and were, at that time, enthusiastic about what they saw there. But friends and neighbors were hardly likely to know anything about the boy's political background in Germany. In any case there were hundreds of Fuchses running around in England in the 1930s; and provided they did not break the peace or make a nuisance of themselves, the police had neither the means nor the desire to pry very deeply into their private lives.

The New York Times, March 2, 1933

Fuchs, in fact, was living a very quiet life. It was as though his recent experiences in Germany had exhausted him and drained him of all desire for action.

For a year he stayed in the country with his Quaker friends, eating very little, learning English, reading his books, seeing very few people. He was a shy and unobtrusive visitor in the house. Those who knew Fuchs then describe him as an exceptionally gentle young man; he would never have hurt a fly. And he was grateful for what was being done for him. Soon after his arrival he was taken down to the University of Bristol, and there he met Professor Nevill Mott of the physics department, who spoke fluent German. Mott heard the story of how Fuchs had all but completed his degree in physics in Kiel when he was forced to go into hiding, and it was arranged that he should attend the university free of charge. In October 1934 he entered as Mott's first research student. About the same time his Quaker friends moved into the city, and Fuchs moved with them. Later, when a little money reached him through charitable institutions, he moved into rooms of his own in the suburb of Redlands.

The physics laboratories of the University of Bristol have had few students with the ability of Klaus Fuchs. He worked with a persistent, methodical concentration, and there was very little in his life but his work. In 1937 he was awarded his doctorate of philosophy in mathematical physics, and was given a research scholarship to continue his studies under Professor Max Born at Edinburgh. He did well there, and began to contribute accounts of his original research to scientific journals. Within two years he got his doctorate in theoretical physics. He was then awarded a Carnegie Research Fellowship, and continued to work at Edinburgh.

Meanwhile, Fuchs was studying the philosophy of Karl Marx in the privacy of his bedroom. He described this later in his confession:

> The idea which gripped me most was the belief that in the past man has been unable to understand his own history and the forces which lead to the further development of human society; that now, for the first time, man understands the historical forces and he is able to control them, and . . . he will be really free. I carried this idea over into the personal sphere and believed that I could understand myself and that I could make myself into what I should be.

In Germany events had happened so rapidly and so violently; the struggle had been so immediate and so personal. For Fuchs, here was the philosophy behind it, the explanation and the justification, the indication of the way ahead. *Das Kapital* captivated him, just as it was captivating so many others in the universities just then. But Fuchs's faith was doubly strong. Having been brought up in the habit of religion, yet having abandoned Christianity, he was desperately in need of something to replace it.

All this he wrestled with quite alone. He never tried to convert anybody else; indeed, in a political conversation he tended to keep silent. Equally, there is no ground for believing that at this time in England he was acting as an agent for either the German or the Russian Communists.

It has been suggested by one of the scientists who knew Fuchs well that Communism was for him a kind of Sunday observance. Like a businessman who is involved in his affairs all the week, he kept his religion in a separate compartment of his mind, and for the most part it did not impinge on his work in the laboratory. It may have been that by the outbreak of war in 1939 there was a certain weakening of his Communism. Certainly, he confessed later, he received a jolt when Molotov and Ribbentrop signed the Russo-German Non-aggression Pact. Up to that time he had automatically accepted the idea that most of the things you heard about Soviet Russia were deliberate lies. But here was a solid, indigestible fact: the Russians had gone over to the Nazis, the people he most loathed in all the world. He explained this away by reassuring himself that Russia had signed the pact simply to gain time so that she could expand her influence against Germany in the Balkans. And then, when Hitler *did* attack Russia in 1941, he observed with delight that it was precisely as he had thought. For a time also he found Russia's attack on Finland in 1940 a difficult pill to swallow. But this, too, was susceptible to logic: Russia was simply preparing her defenses against *all* imperialistic powers.

He succeeded, then, in resolving his doubts—but at least he did have doubts. He was now twenty-seven, and beginning to think again for himself. He spoke English with a German accent, but fluently, and he had made English and Scottish friends. He was beginning to accept the English way of life. On July 17, 1939, he applied for British naturalization.

On the face of it there was no reason why he should not have been naturalized then. He was supported by the Quakers and the universities. For six years he had been a loyal citizen, and his postgraduate work in the British laboratories had been remarkably good. But by July it was too late. The war began before his application could go forward, and from September 1939 all such naturalizations of enemy aliens were put aside.

In November, when the country had already been at war with Germany for two months, Fuchs was summoned before the Enemy Aliens Tribunal at Edinburgh. He had been classified by the Home Office as a refugee from Nazi oppression, and there was now an investigation into his record.

The tribunal had before it a letter from Professor Max Born of the University of Edinburgh saying that Fuchs had been a member of the Social Democratic party in Germany between 1930 and 1932. In view of his excellent record in Britain, the tribunal exempted him from the special restrictions which were then applicable to enemy aliens. He had to report to the police, but that was all. Fuchs went back to his work at the university.

This was the so-called phony-war period, when there was as yet no bombing of civilian towns and no real activity on the Western Front. But with Hitler's attack on France and the Low Countries in the following spring, this picture altered entirely. Britain was now faced with an acute national emergency, and the prospect of invasion. There were obvious reasons for keeping the closest check upon all German nationals. Quite apart from the question of their loyalty—and there was no time to investigate it then—refugees from Germany were likely to be one of the first targets of the Gestapo if Britain were to be invaded. In addition, the food shortage was starting, and no adequate staff or accommodation was available for the internees. There was therefore an urgent need to get them out of the country. Fuchs was interned under the Defense Act in May 1940.

He was sent first to the Isle of Man in the Irish Sea, and then transported across the Atlantic to the Sherbrooke camp in Quebec, Canada. All this was done in some haste and confusion, for the country was absorbed in fighting for its own existence at the time. Without doubt some of the internees were compelled to live under harsh conditions during the early stages of the evacuation. Fuchs was bundled unceremoniously aboard a ship where some of the prisoners felt they were treated more as criminals than ordinary human beings.

The ship was the *Ettrick*, and the journey from Liverpool to Quebec took a fortnight. A strict discipline was enforced, and in his daily inspection tours the captain had his presence announced by a hunting horn, so that the prisoners were warned in advance to spring to attention. On their arrival in Canada they often were greeted with jeers of "How's Hitler?" On one occasion a hearty British major assembled the prisoners before him. Most of their families had been murdered, imprisoned, or ruined by Hitler, and many of them had barely escaped the Nazis with their own lives. Consequently they were astonished when the major declared, "I'm British and I am loyal to my king. You are Germans, and you think you have got to be loyal to Hitler. As long as that's clear and we understand one another we will get along together all right." On still another occasion, when the prisoners were making a minor protest of some kind, the guards turned their rifles on them. Since men probably resent indignity more than anything else, especially indignity founded upon misunderstanding and injustice, it seems possible that Fuchs began then to harbor a resentment against the democracies.

The confusion still persisted in Canada, for there had been no time to sort out the prisoners properly in England before their embarkation. Fuchs, now wearing a prisoner's uniform with a large, colored patch on the back, was placed in a camp designed to accommodate avowed and unrepentant Nazis.

Fuchs made no complaint later about his internment beyond saying that he realized that, at the time, Britain "could not spare good people to look after the internees" and that being deprived of newspapers he was prevented from knowing how the British were getting on in the war and from learning more about the real character of the British people.

Cut off from his work, in the idleness of camp life he turned to the other and secret passion of his life—the study of Russian Communism. And he made one friend, Hans Kahle, a case-hardened Communist who was a much older man than Fuchs and highly persuasive. He was born in Berlin in 1899, and is reported to have been an officer in the Reichswehr before he became a Communist adventurer. He was in the Soviet Union in 1935 and 1936, and subsequently commanded a unit of the Republican Army in the Spanish Civil War.

In 1939 Kahle came to England, where he wrote a book on the civil war, and quickly fell in with well-known British Communists. He was also active in working among organizations for the relief of refugees from Germany and Spain until war broke out, when he was interned and sent to Canada. Later he was released and throughout the rest of the war he was a Communist organizer and a member of the executive council of the German Communist Party in Britain. Soon after the war he went to the Soviet zone in Germany, was given an important police post, and died there in 1947.

This man was the close friend and companion of Fuchs during the six-odd months they were together in Canada. It is still a matter for speculation as to just how much Fuchs was affected by his meeting with Kahle.

A docile prisoner, Fuchs took only a normal part in the camp politics. Once he joined a protest against the appointment of the son of the former German crown prince as camp leader. (The young man had been studying in England when war broke out, and was regarded as a Nazi sympathizer.) On another occasion he protested a report that Jewish internees were to be exchanged for Canadian prisoners in Germany. But he was not obstreperous on these issues. There was, however, one other interesting fact which indicates how devious are the threads that pass through an espionage pattern. While in camp Fuchs used to receive papers and magazines from Israel Halperin, a professor of mathematics at Queen's University, Kingston, Ontario. Halperin, who was born of Russian parents in Canada, was closely questioned by the Canadian Royal Commission in 1946, and finally acquitted. Fuchs says he never met Halperin, and does not know why Halperin sent him the magazines. Halperin crops up again in another way in the Fuchs case; when the Canadian police raided Halperin's home they found an address book, and in that book was the name of Fuchs. This information was available to the authorities in 1946—a good three years before Fuchs was arrested—and the connection has never been satisfactorily explained.

Fuchs remained under internment in Canada for the rest of 1940, but Professor Born and other scientists who valued his work were pressing for his release. And by now the authorities in England had had an opportunity to check on the men who had been so hurriedly sent away in the crisis. In January 1941 Fuchs was released. He returned at once to his research work at the University of Edinburgh.

CHAPTER 4

I N THE SPRING OF 1941 Professor Rudolf Peierls of the University of Birmingham wrote to Fuchs, asking him if he would be interested in undertaking some work of a special nature. He suggested that Fuchs come down to Birmingham to discuss the matter.

Peierls was already working secretly on the atomic bomb, and he needed an assistant who was competent to make elaborate mathematical calculations. Most of the abler English physicists had already been pressed into essential wartime research, and it was necessary to look now among the enemy aliens. Peierls had read some of Fuchs's research papers, and he knew that Professor Mott of Bristol, Professor Born, and other scientists thought highly of his abilities.

The interview took place in Birmingham and was satisfactory. Fuchs was not told the full nature of the work; he was simply informed that it was urgent, it was secret, and it was connected with the war. He accepted the job. Peierls now had to get the appointment approved by the authorities in London.

The security services were consulted. There was, they said, the report from the German consul at Bristol, which had to be regarded as a tainted source. There was nothing else against Fuchs; in the seven years since he had come to England he had given no grounds for suspicion. However, since he was an enemy alien, it was reasonable for the time being to put him on a low security rating—he should not be given access to more classified work than was strictly necessary. And it had to be estimated that, if he did give any information, he was more likely to give it to the Russians than the German enemy.

In England the function of the security services is simply advisory. It is the responsibility of the government department concerned to decide whether it shall employ the man. In this case the department concerned was the Ministry of Aircraft Production, which had been given responsibility for the work on atomic energy. The ministry just then was engaged in producing aircraft to fight the Battle of Britain, and pronounced views were held by Mr. Churchill and his cabinet; anyone, they argued, who was able to help Britain win the war ought to be pressed into service at once. Fuchs was employed. And since it was manifestly absurd to ask him to engage in the work without telling him what it was about, he was later given access to classified material in Birmingham. He began work in May 1941 and signed a declaration accepting terms of the Official Secrets Act.

Since he was poor and alone, the Peierls family found room for him in their house in Birmingham, and he continued living with them, as an intimate member of their household, until 1943, when he moved to quarters of his own. Through all this time he never indicated, by anything he said or was observed to do, that he was in touch with the Russians. The university staff and his friends were entirely without suspicion. They found him shy, rather silent, and abstracted. He was quite hopeless at the business of looking after himself; unless someone in the Peierls household had sewn on his buttons, helped him buy his Christmas presents, and occasionally taken him out to social gatherings, none of these things would have

Professor Rudolf Peierls, Fuchs's mentor

been done. He returned from his work each evening, and if nobody prevented him he simply went to his room and continued to work. He liked children, he was fond of dogs, and in a mild, unworldly fashion he attended family and university gatherings. He made occasional trips up to London, sometimes in connection with his work, but otherwise Fuchs seldom went outside Birmingham.

There was just one incident that might have indicated to the scientists in Birmingham that they had a strange man among them. It was a New Year's Eve party. They were singing Russian songs and Fuchs was observed standing a little apart from the others, with a look of transcendental exultation on his face—a look of such rapture that the woman who saw it imagined that he must suddenly have fallen in love.

Six months after Fuchs arrived in Birmingham the organization known as "Tube Alloys" was set up to coordinate the work of the atomic scientists in the various universities. It was a small and very secret affair, with unobtrusive offices in Old Queen Street, Westminster. It had a miniature staff directly responsible to the lord president of the council (Sir John Anderson) and the prime minister. One of their duties was to act as a clearinghouse for information as the work on atomic energy progressed. The scientists engaged on the project in Oxford, Cambridge, Birmingham, and elsewhere were asked to send in monthly reports which could be disseminated among themselves so that redundancies could be avoided and the work would march forward evenly. The man who never failed to bring in his reports on time—who never pleaded that he was too busy, or that he was occupied with an experiment that could not wait—was Klaus Fuchs. And his reports were lucid, well-written, and precise. When asked to interpret them for scientists in other fields, he also had a flair for reducing their technicalities to simple, effective language.

Very soon Professor Peierls realized he had acquired in Fuchs something of inestimable value—a perfectly methodical, calculating brain. Fuchs learned astonishingly fast, could be asked to tackle any calculation, and one could rely entirely upon his results.

The work at Birmingham was mainly concerned with the gas-diffusion process of separating the uranium isotopes, still in the experimental stage both in Britain and the United States. Professor Peierls was a gas-diffusion enthusiast, and Fuchs soon became an enthusiast as well.

In 1942 Fuchs again applied for naturalization, with the strong backing of the Tube Alloys directorate. The reason given was that Fuchs was engaged on work of national importance. He had to become a British citizen in order to be given access to certain prohibited places in connection with his work.

There was a police investigation. The eight-year-old report of the German consul was again brought up, and it was still the only evidence against him. Fuchs himself was examined at an open hearing, and on August 7, 1942, on being naturalized, he took the following oath of allegiance:

> I, Emil Julius Klaus Fuchs, swear by Almighty God that I will be faithful and bear true allegiance to His Majesty, King George the Sixth, His Heirs and Successors, according to law.

WHEN HE TOOK that oath Fuchs was in active and regular contact with a Russian agent. He established that contact very soon after he arrived in Birmingham in 1941, and it was not the Russians who had come to him—he himself had approached them first and had offered to pass information.

Through the refugee organizations and the universities Fuchs knew a number of Communists who had reached England from Germany since 1933, and it was one of these who passed him on to Simon Kremer, the secretary to the Soviet military attaché in London.

Throughout his association with Kremer, Fuchs knew him only by the name of "Alexander," but Kremer was quite a familiar figure to diplomats and military people in London during the war. His full name was Simon Davidovich Kremer and he was a Russian, born in Gomel in 1900. He arrived in England to take up his post at the Russian embassy two years before the war, and his job was, without doubt, a cover for more important activities. He left England long before Fuchs's arrest.

What made Fuchs suddenly decide to turn active traitor in 1941? We have his own version of the matter:

> Shortly after my release [from internment] I was asked to help Professor Peierls in Birmingham on some war work. I accepted it, and I started work without knowing at first what the work was. . . . When I learned about the purpose of the work I decided to inform Russia, and I established contact through another member of the Communist Party. Since that time I have had continuous contact with persons who were completely unknown to me, except that I knew they would hand over whatever information I gave them to the Russian authorities. At this time I had complete confidence in Russian policy, and I believed that the Western Allies deliberately allowed Russia and Germany to fight each other to the death. I therefore had no hesitation in giving all the information I had, even though occasionally I tried to concentrate mainly on giving information about the results of my own work.

The phrase "another member of the Communist Party" is interesting, for it indicates that, even though he had no contact with the Party in England, he still regarded himself as a member.

Certainly the timing was important. In June 1941, when Fuchs began to work on the atomic bomb, the Nazis attacked Russia, and then all those anxious doubts about the Russo-German pact and the invasion of Finland were swept out of Fuchs's mind. There followed Stalin's persistent demand for a "second front"—an invasion by the Western Allies of western Europe so that the strain on Russia would be relieved. When time went on and that demand was not answered, when Moscow nearly fell, when the battle for Stalingrad was fought and the losses of the Russians were frightful, it might indeed have seemed to Klaus Fuchs that his chosen people were being left to bear the brunt. He felt an ardent burning to do something for the cause.

There were many other people who felt the same way; Mrs. Churchill was organizing her Russian relief committee, and an intensely pro-Russian feeling spread over Britain. Workers redoubled their labors in the factories, and there was great enthusiasm when the first British arms were sent off to heroic Russia on the Murmansk run. Klaus Fuchs took copies of the monthly reports of his work on atomic energy to Simon Kremer in London. That was his contribution to the heroes of Stalingrad.

He had at least four meetings with Kremer between the end of 1941 and the end of 1942. Since it was not always easy for him to get away from Birmingham during the working week, the meetings were fixed at weekends and in the evening. The first was at a private house not far from the Russian embassy in Kensington Palace Gardens. Here he met just one man, the Russian who spoke English and called himself Alexander. Fuchs, a meticulous man, may have had some doubts as to whether his contact was genuine, and whether the information was actually getting through to the Russians, because, soon after this first meeting, he went openly to the Russian embassy to make inquiries, a thing that was absolutely forbidden to agents. He was reassured, however, for he took up his appointments with Kremer again—usually in quiet residential streets or at crowded bus stops.

The Russian embassy, Kensington Palace Gardens, London

The technique of spying is capable of infinite variation, but certain basic rules exist, such as the obvious one that forbids the spy to do anything as foolhardy as paying a visit to a Soviet consulate or embassy. Some time before the war the Russian intelligence service was reorganized and spies were also forbidden to have any connection with the local Communist Party. These local parties were still used as a recruiting ground for spies, but immediately a man was chosen he was obliged to break off all association with known Communists. Under the new arrangements the Russians found it much more profitable to work through traitors—ideological foreigners like Fuchs—

than through their own nationals. The Russians themselves supplied the director of each net; he was usually placed in a country outside the one his net was spying on.

The employment of traitors also called for a new kind of dealing since few of them entered the service for money. Nevertheless, it was necessary to make sure they would not weaken or turn again, and so the Russian intelligence service forced money, however small in amount, on their agents, and obtained receipts—which were useful for blackmail in case of necessity.

Russian agents are trained in the double life, and by the use of cover names and other devices they were all kept in separate compartments. The object here, of course, was to ensure that if a man was discovered he could give only limited information about his actual contacts. The main channels of communication were normally through Russian embassies and legations. They, in turn, used diplomatic couriers, who passed regularly to Moscow. Alternately, coded messages were sent by illegal radio stations.

Crowded streets and underground stations were favored meeting places for spies and couriers, since for the most part the contact lasted just long enough to pass a document in a folded newspaper or a piece of microfilm in a cigarette. As a rule spies made no signal of recognition when they met, but moved off to another place where the information was handed over, and arrangements were then made for the next meeting. As a precaution a third man, unknown to the other two, sometimes stood by to make sure that the meeting was not observed.

All these matters are fairly common knowledge now, but in 1941 and 1942 they were far from commonplace. Fuchs had to learn the new conspiratorial technique from the beginning, and he showed a remarkable aptitude for it: the Russians could have had few agents as precise as he was, few men as exact in their memory, as clear in exposition, as punctual and as eager.

It was in October 1941 that Fuchs began passing carbon copies of his reports, which he had typed himself, or manuscript in his own handwriting. At this stage all the information came from his own brain and was the result of his own work.

At the end of 1942 Alexander disappeared, and Fuchs was told that from then on he would be dealing with a new contact, a woman.

The rendezvous was changed from London to Banbury, a market town some forty miles from Birmingham. The new series of meetings occurred at intervals of two or three months. On each occasion Fuchs took an afternoon train down from Birmingham during the weekend, and then walked along a country road just outside the town. The woman waited for him there. She did not live in Banbury; she came there specially for these meetings. Just once they had a rendezvous in a café in Birmingham.

There have been many assessments of what Fuchs may have given the Russians through 1943. But it is known that he gave them the results of his own calculations on the theory of the gas-diffusion process for separating the isotopes of uranium, and the fact that U-235 produced in that way might be used in an atomic bomb.

Dr. Karl Cohen, of Columbia University, has commented, in a letter to the Joint Committee on Atomic Energy in Washington, on the state of Fuchs's knowledge at that time. He wrote:

> Fuchs' name appeared on theoretical papers on the gaseous diffusion process to my certain knowledge in 1942, and I believe as early as 1941. Because of visits to this country of Peierls and others in early 1942, when the relative merits of the Birmingham and Columbia versions of the diffusion process were discussed at length . . . it is clear that before Fuchs' arrival he had good knowledge of the American plans for the gaseous diffusion plant. It is important to bear in mind that because of Fuchs' grasp of the theoretical principles involved, which interrelate the process variables so that the choice of a few determines the remainder within narrow limits, he would be able to reconstitute our whole program from only scattered pieces of information. Thus . . . he could have transmitted a very good outline of the American gaseous diffusion project.

Dr. Cohen added, "Compared to these consequences, Fuchs's betrayal of the personal integrity of scientists is of minor importance. Nevertheless it was a blow which all scientists bitterly resent." This was a point that had not yet occurred to Fuchs himself in 1943, though it was going to overtake him with some force later on. Meanwhile he continued meeting his woman contact, and toward the end of 1943 he told her that he had been selected to go to the United States as a member of the British team which was to continue work on the gas-diffusion process in New York.

Precise instructions were then given him by the woman for making contact with the Russians in New York. He was to go to a street corner on the Lower East Side on a Saturday, carrying a tennis ball in his hand. There he would see a man carrying a book with a green binding, and wearing gloves, with an additional pair of gloves in his hand. This man would be known to him as "Raymond." The two men would then take a taxi to a restaurant on lower Third Avenue, where Fuchs would hand over his information and arrangements would be made for their future meetings.

In November 1943 Professor Peierls, Fuchs, and others embarked at Liverpool on the troopship *Andes* for the United States.

CHAPTER 5

AFTER HIS TWO crossings of the Atlantic as an internee the voyage in the troopship *Andes* seemed a great luxury to Fuchs. He was lively and—for him—in high spirits. He was traveling with friends, and as a representative of the British government. He was going to work that he loved, and now, at the approach of his thirty-second birthday, he had an established reputation. His conspiratorial life was untroubled by any misgivings or hesitations, and his conscience had arrived, no doubt, at some sort of a mystical peace with itself.

He landed with the Peierls in early December, and they proceeded at once to Washington to sign the usual security undertaking with the United States government. There was no further investigation into Fuchs's credentials—he had been cleared by the British authorities—and in the ensuing two-and-a-half years while he was in the United States no other check was made on him.

From Washington he went to the Taft Hotel in New York. Subsequently he moved to the Barbizon-Plaza and then to an apartment of his own at 128 West Seventy-seventh Street. He visited his sister Kristel in Cambridge, Massachusetts, within a few days of his arrival —she had now settled permanently with her husband and children in the United States—and he continued to keep in touch with them throughout his stay in the country. There was indeed a plan at one time for the family to come and live with him in New York, but it fell through when, the following year, he was posted to Los Alamos.

Starting on December 7, 1943, Fuchs attended a series of meetings which enabled the American and British teams to clear their ideas about the gas-diffusion process with one another, and to plan their future operations together. The scientists working on this part of the atomic energy project were divided into two groups: those at Columbia University, who were mainly engaged on research, and those at the Kellex Corporation, where the large-scale gas-diffusion plant was designed.

It was soon realized that the best contribution the British could make would be to help on the theory of the control of the gas-diffusion plant, and Fuchs was specifically asked to make numerical calculations for its design. At the conclusion of the December meetings part of the British team went home, while Peierls, Fuchs, and some others remained to cooperate with the Americans. From this time forward Fuchs was intimately connected with the work, both at Columbia University and at the Kellex Corporation. He had an office at the British center in Wall Street and he was a frequent visitor to both laboratories.

He did little else but work; it filled all his days. One can imagine that he was content, for after so much experiment and theorizing, the moment of definite decisions was approaching. The first chain reaction had been achieved in Chicago on December 2, 1942, and it was now to be used to produce a nuclear explosion. Fuchs's contribution was substantial. He decided to make that contribution, and much else besides, available to the Russians. From this time forward he gave them everything he could, whether it was his own work or not. Fuchs then knew little of the United States plans; but he knew nearly all there was to be known about the gas-diffusion plant in the Manhattan Engineering District, and that information the Russians got from him.

Throughout his stay in America his only contact was Harry Gold, alias Raymond, a biochemist who was born in Switzerland and had become a naturalized American. What he did not know was that, through Gold, he was drawn into an elaborate espionage network which had been working in the United States for some time. Fuchs and the American traitors between them made a nonsense of the security regulations, showing that all the paraphernalia of barbed wire and policemen, unless carried to a stultifying extreme, is a useless barrier in the affairs of the mind. When the atomic bomb came to be exploded, not only was Fuchs standing inside the barbed wire at Los Alamos, but an American traitor was there as well, with free access to their courier outside, Harry Gold.

FUCHS PROCEEDED WITH his tennis ball to the first rendezvous with Gold, on the Lower East Side in New York, early in 1944. They met, they proceeded by taxi to a restaurant, and they arranged to meet again. It was Fuchs's practice from this time on to warn Gold in advance of what he proposed to give him at their next meeting; normally it would be a package of papers which he had typed or written himself. He was also prepared to answer questions. Gold, on his side, adopted a system by which, immediately he left Fuchs, he handed over the package to his superior in the network, the Russian vice-consul in New York, Anatoli A. Yakovlev, who would often be waiting around the corner of the next street—unknown, of course, to Fuchs. Gold then went home—he had a tortuous procedure of jumping on and off trains at the last minute to make sure he was not being followed—and wrote out a report on his conversation with Fuchs. This report would be given to Yakovlev at a later meeting. In the course of these proceedings Fuchs was once offered fifteen hundred dollars. He turned it down flat.

There were five meetings between Fuchs and Gold in New York, possibly more. In March 1944 they met on Madison Avenue, when they were together just long enough for Fuchs to hand over his papers. They met again in the middle of June at Woodside, Queens, and Fuchs promised to bring information of the actual plans for the design of the uranium bomb. At the end of that month, when they met near the Brooklyn Borough Hall, he did, in fact, deliver those plans. In mid-July they were together again, at Ninety-sixth Street and Central Park West, and strolled for an hour and a half through the park.

Years afterward, when he was questioned, Fuchs could only remember that Raymond was a man who understood something of the technicalities they discussed. Possibly, he thought, he might have been a chemist. For the most part at this time he passed over his own original manuscripts—which his office supposed he had destroyed after official copies had been made.

The main value of the information supplied was that it gave the principles and some details of the gas-diffusion production plant at Oak Ridge, Tennessee. It also indicated the scale and timing of the American program. From Fuchs's notes the Russians could have deduced the principles of one of the methods chosen for separating uranium isotopes.

At the Central Park meeting they fixed the next rendezvous at the Brooklyn Museum, and as an alternative in case either of them failed to keep the first appointment, they were to meet again at Central Park West.

But Fuchs failed to keep either of these appointments. It was a matter of concern for the net when an agent vanished in this way, for there was always the possibility that he had been arrested or had decided to cease his activities and had turned traitor to the traitors. Gold's movements then were like those of some agitated insect that has suddenly lost its way. He waited fruitlessly at the meeting place. He went to Fuchs's apartment on Seventy-seventh Street, but the doorman there could tell him nothing except that Fuchs had gone away. Yakovlev hunted up the address of Fuchs's sister Kristel, and Gold was posted off to Cambridge to see her. Gold explained to her that he was a friend of Fuchs's, and wanted rather urgently to see him. Kristel could remember only that Fuchs had gone off "somewhere in the Southwest." He had promised to spend the coming Christmas with her if he could. Then, Gold said, would she ask him to telephone when he arrived? He left her a New York number. Then he went away to report to Yakovlev, and to wait.

What had happened was that Fuchs had been sent to Los Alamos in New Mexico. Professor Peierls and his family had gone there some time before, leaving Fuchs in charge of the New York office, and now Fuchs himself was wanted to help on the work for the actual construction of the bomb. It was one of the quirks of Fuchs's pedantic mind that security should always be observed—at any rate until he chose to break it, in a way and at a time of his own choosing. Los Alamos was a great secret. The director, Dr. J. Robert Oppenheimer, was assembling there a group of perhaps the most distinguished scientific minds ever gathered together. Fuchs decided not to pass on this information to the Russians, nor even the news of his own departure. It was, for the moment, too secret.

At Los Alamos he was given a room in the bachelors' dormitory, and there began for him perhaps the happiest time of his life. Living there, high among the pines, in the clear, dry air of the desert, he developed a new physical well-being. On his days off he went mountain climbing. In the winter he went skiing. The photographs taken at this time of Fuchs in his skiing clothes show that the change in him was remarkable. He appeared lithe and assured and good-looking. There was much casual entertaining among the families at Los Alamos, and Fuchs frequently went out dining and dancing. He had more money, and although money was never a major interest for him, he knew how to spend it generously and well. Since he loved motoring, Mrs. Peierls persuaded him to go down to the town of Sante Fe and buy a car—a second-hand Buick. In every way he seemed more relaxed and at ease than his friends had ever before known him to be.

Fuchs's American accomplice, Harry Gold

Los Alamos was ringed with barbed wire; there was one pass to get into the residential camp, and another to visit the laboratories and offices. The guards at the gate were punctilious. Once inside the camp, conversation among the scientists and their families was free and easy, but the pass system was formidable, and the townspeople down at Santa Fe had no notion of what was going on up there on the bare heights above. They believed, as Harry Gold put it in court much later, that it was a "sort of boondoggling outfit." Still, the scientists could and did go to Santa Fe, and it was always possible for them to get passes for leave.

Early in 1945, after six months of this work, Fuchs went to Cambridge to spend a short holiday with his sister, and there the faithful Harry Gold appeared. He came to the apartment and asked Fuchs about his work at Los Alamos. Fuchs agreed to put down all he knew in writing, and this material was handed over to Gold at a second meeting in a Boston street a few days later.

By now Fuchs was able to reveal a great deal. In his notes he gave details of the plutonium bomb, its design, the method of construction, and the fact that the plutonium was produced in atomic piles at Hanford, Washington. In particular, he gave a description of an implosion lens which was to be used in detonating the bomb. Later Gold succeeded in getting actual drawings of the lens from the American traitor David Greenglass, who was also working in Los Alamos.

Before Fuchs and Gold parted in Boston it was agreed that they should meet again at the Castillo Street Bridge in Santa Fe. The time was to be 4:00 p.m. on June 2, 1945.

Looking back now, Fuchs's friends can remember that he returned from Boston at the end of February, after ten days' absence, looking harassed and depressed. He offered no explanation beyond saying that he was worried about his sister.

The June meeting took place precisely as arranged. Gold came from New York by train. Wary as ever, he bought a map of Santa Fe so that he could find his way to the Castillo Street Bridge without inquiring of anyone, and a few minutes after four Fuchs appeared in his Buick. They were together barely half an hour. Fuchs handed over another batch of papers. He said that there had been tremendous progress and that the first atomic explosion would take place in the Alamogordo desert in July. They fixed the next meeting at 6:00 p.m. on September 19, near a church on a road leading out of Santa Fe, and Fuchs drove off to Los Alamos. Gold then took a bus to Albuquerque, sixty miles away, and there had an interview with his other contact at Los Alamos, David Greenglass. It was then that Greenglass gave him the drawings of the implosion lens. It must have been one of the most profitable journeys Gold or any other Russian agent ever made.

When President Truman met Stalin at Potsdam the following month, and told him that the American and British scientists had developed a new kind of bomb far more destructive than anything known before and that it would be dropped on Japan unless she surrendered, Stalin manifested nothing more than polite interest. He made no attempt to inquire further, or follow up on the conversation in any way. No doubt he was aware that his director of intelligence in Moscow had already a full account of the making of the bomb, based on the information of Fuchs, Greenglass, and others.

The first atomic bomb was exploded in the Alamogordo desert on July 16, 1945. For Fuchs and all at Los Alamos who had worked upon this single project for so many years, there was an excitement and a tension that was almost past bearing.

On the previous day Peierls and Fuchs were assigned to a military bus, and drove off to the scene. Being theorists who were not concerned with the actual work of exploding the bomb, their party was directed to a position on rising ground some twenty miles away from the tower on which the bomb was erected. They were on the spot before midnight, and the bomb was timed to go off in the early hours of the morning, so that there would be the advantage of photographing the explosive light against darkness. Each man was given dark glasses and instructed to lie down when he saw the flash.

Shortly before zero hour, word came through on the field telephones that a technical hitch had occurred and there would be a delay.

It was on the point of getting light, and they were about to accept a postponement until the following night, when an enormous flash filled the sky. Its form and coloring they had anticipated—the white column rising to an orange ball, and the purple shade created by the ozone above—but it was far brighter than anything they had expected. Some flung themselves on the ground. Fuchs and others remained standing. This was the end of their years of work.

There was no wind and no sound, and this absence of sound seemed unnatural and frightening. They remained fixed in their positions until at last there was a little crack—rather like a distant rifle shot. It was so mild a thing, compared to the awesome and expanding light, that one of the party who was not a scientist asked incredulously, "What was that?"

The party got back into the bus and drove toward Albuquerque, two hours away. They were exhausted, and their one thought was breakfast. At Albuquerque, however, they were told that orders had been issued that they were not to stop, lest the townspeople should see the elation in their faces. Glumly the party continued for another three hours to Los Alamos, where their families appeared to be fully informed about what had happened. One scientist who was ill declared he saw the flash from his bed in the camp hospital. Alamogordo was a hundred and fifty miles away.

THE ALAMOGORDO EXPLOSION WAS THE beginning of the end of Anglo-American association in atomic-bomb research. The bomb was dropped on Hiroshima by the American air force August 6, 1945, and on Nagasaki August 9; six days later the war against Japan was over.

The British scientists began winding up their affairs in the United States, and in September a farewell party of more than normal scope was arranged. Fuchs went down to Santa Fe to buy the supplies. He was hours late in returning—so late that his friends thought he must have had an accident. When he finally arrived he merely said that he had been delayed. He had indeed "been delayed," for this was September 19, and in addition to buying the liquor he had been talking to Harry Gold.

They had met, as they had arranged, by the church on the road leading out of Santa Fe, and this, their last, was a long meeting. Fuchs had written down the size of the bomb, what it contained, how it was constructed, and how it was detonated. He gave his own calculations of the actual dimensions of the parts. And he handed all this over to Gold. He also talked. He spoke with awe of the explosion and the excitement it had caused. Its flash had been visible two hundred miles away, and now that the secret of the Los Alamos camp was out, the local townspeople regarded the scientists as heroes. But there was no longer, he said, the same free and easy cooperation between the Americans and the British. New security regulations had come into force, and a number of the departments were closed to him. He had been told that he would soon have to return to England.

He said he was troubled about his return. There was a possibility that his father, who had survived the war in Germany, might visit him in England, and the old man might talk about his son's connection with the Communist Party in Germany in his student days. Furthermore, it was worrisome that the British and not the Russians had captured Kiel. There was a Gestapo dossier on him at Kiel, and it would be awkward if it fell into the hands of British intelligence, for that dossier would reveal that he had been a leader of the Communist student group.

But he was prepared to continue his espionage for Russia, and arrangements were made with Gold for making contact again on his return to England.

On the first Saturday of every month Fuchs was to be at the street

The first atomic bomb, Alamogordo, New Mexico, July 16, 1945

entrance of a particular underground railway station in London at 8:00 p.m. He was to be carrying five books, bound with string and supported by two fingers of one hand; in the other hand he was to be holding two more books. His contact was to be carrying a book by Bennett Cerf, *Try and Stop Me.*

Fuchs was one of the last of the British scientists to leave Los Alamos. Long after Professor Peierls had gone, he continued as chief of the dwindling British team to write his reports on the work of the previous two years in America. Before this he had already been offered the post of head of the theoretical physics division at the new British atomic energy center at Harwell, in Berkshire. He was commended everywhere for his work in the United States, and security in particular was full of praise for his caution.

During his last eight months in Santa Fe, Fuchs made no attempt to get in touch with the Russians, or they with him. It seems likely that traitors as well as everybody else suffered from the general feeling of inertia that succeeded the war; there was no longer the same urgency. Nor were there as many secrets.

Toward the end of November 1945 Fuchs made a brief visit to Montreal and Chicago on official business—it was on this trip that he was interviewed for his Harwell appointment. In the following month he went with the Peierls on a holiday to Mexico. It seems possible that in Mexico—one of the regular staging posts for Communist agents—he may have contemplated continuing on to Russia. But he came back to the United States with the Peierls, and then, on June 16 of the next year, he left Los Alamos for the last time. He traveled first to Washington, and then continued north for a final visit with his sister in Cambridge. On June 28 he left Montreal by air for England.

CHAPTER 6

WHEN FUCHS ARRIVED at Harwell in July 1946, it was still mainly an airfield on a windy hilltop, with the Atomic Energy Research Establishment still under construction. He was now helping to start something from the beginning. He staffed his own division of theoretical physicists. He gave the orders for their work, and to

Ground zero at Hiroshima, August 6, 1945

some extent he fixed the program. In the end a part of Harwell was his own creation.

He lived at first in the staff club. When he heard that there was a feeling in Harwell that the club should be reserved for junior members of the staff, he moved to a boardinghouse at Abingdon, five or six miles away. He was eventually given one of the prefabricated houses in the encampment, and in 1948 he moved into number seventeen. He got rid of his dilapidated eight-horsepower Morris, and bought from a colleague a gray MG sedan; he was now making a good salary and could live more expansively. He began to make friends, notably Professor and Mrs. W. H. B. Skinner, and the senior security officer, Wing Commander Henry Arnold, and his wife.

He took one holiday with the Peierls in Switzerland, and another in the south of France with Professor and Mrs. Skinner. On the Swiss holiday he went to Saas-Fee, near Zermatt, where the Peierls had taken an apartment; and it was here that he met Gerhardt, his elder brother, who came over from Davos for a couple of days. They had not met since before the war. Gerhardt had grown very fat and feeble, and life was ebbing away from him. The two brothers spent a long time talking together alone.

In November 1947, when Klaus had been at Harwell nearly eighteen months, he flew to Washington for a declassification conference. This was attended by representatives of the United States, Canada, and Britain, and the object of the meeting was to examine the atomic knowledge shared by the three countries in the war, in order to decide what should or should not be published. No knowledge which the three countries had acquired independently since the war was discussed. Fuchs was a member of a subcommittee which specifically considered the Los Alamos period, and he is remembered as being generally conservative on the release of information.

While in America he paid a short visit to the Argonne Laboratory in Chicago to discuss neutron spectroscopy, but on the instructions of United States security, he saw nothing secret.

In England, Fuchs often went up to London for conferences at the Ministry of Supply. It was sometimes the practice of the Harwell scientists who attended these meetings to stay on in London for a few hours to shop or go to the theater. Fuchs never accompanied them. He returned alone and late, often bringing with him some small present for the wives of his friends. His consideration for his friends at this time, his many kindnesses, did not seem to them then to be anything else than the expression of a genuine affection. Nor have they altered their opinion since. During these years Fuchs was not perhaps a companionable man, but he developed a warmth and an ease of manner that was something new. He did not entertain very much; after his arrest his charwoman remarked that he ate his meals at the staff club, and the prefab was nothing much more than a bachelor's bungalow. But she found him a pleasant man.

He still showed no signs whatever of getting married, but he discussed with the scientists' wives his arrangements for bringing the son of his dead sister, Elisabeth, to live with him and attend school in England. In 1947 he gave Mrs. Peierls a blank check so that she could buy clothes for his father on his first visit to England. Then again in 1949 he helped Dr. Fuchs with his expenses on a visit to the United States, and entertained him on his return. His Quaker friends remember meeting Klaus about this time and asking him if he still held to his left-wing views. He replied that he had given them up entirely. The Russians were intractable. The only hope now was to form a close alliance of the Western democracies.

Among the scientists at Harwell he never talked politics. In committee meetings he sat silently through most of the discussions, and when he was asked for his opinion he gave it precisely and clearly, in the manner of someone who has already delved deep into the matter and has firmly made up his mind. He had his occasional fits of illness, his drinking, his incessant smoking of cigarettes, but all the rest was work. He presided like a housemaster over the Harwell welfare committee, and he had a housemaster's pride in the affairs of the whole establishment.

That was his outward life. During these three years—from 1946 to 1949—his secret life was performing new and unpredictable evolutions of its own. He did not keep the rendezvous at the underground station as he had agreed, nor any of the alternative appointments. On their side the Russians made no attempt to approach him. So he continued for a year in England, without making a move. Then early in 1947, like a drug addict who had mastered his mania for a time and suddenly succumbs again, Fuchs went in search of the Communist who had originally put him in touch with Simon Kremer six years before. He failed to find him, but in the course of his inquiries he found a woman Party member who was willing to help.

The woman introduced him to the Russians in London, and the drug began to work again. Soon Fuchs received instructions to go to a public house in north London. He was to carry a copy of the weekly paper *Tribune* and take a seat on a certain bench. His contact would carry a red book.

Fuchs went and found his man. The meeting opened unfavorably; Fuchs was berated for reestablishing contact through a known member of the Communist Party. Henceforth he was to steer entirely clear of all known Communists. This scolding may have added to his feeling of guilt at having deserted the Russians for so long, and may explain what he did next. He accepted a gift of a hundred pounds in bank notes. Up to this time he had rejected any payment, except small sums to cover his expenses in getting to and from his places of rendezvous. But this hundred pounds was far too much for such expenses, and not nearly enough to make espionage a really profitable undertaking. Fuchs himself says that he took the money as a symbol, as a formal act to bind himself to the cause. He took no more money from the Russians after this.

There began now a series of meetings, always with the same man. The meetings were in London, and in one of two public houses—the Spotted Horse in High Street, Putney, or the Nag's Head at Wood Green. If one of the two conspirators failed to appear, it was understood they should meet precisely a week later at the same place. Should the rendezvous fail a second time, they would meet at the alternative public house a month later. If this failed, they would come back again to this second public house the following week.

In 1948 they made further arrangements in case all these appointments should go wrong: Fuchs would go to a private house in Richmond which was pointed out to him on one of his London trips and there throw a periodical over the fence. He was to write a message on the tenth page. One other arrangement was that if either of them wished to indicate in advance that he could not keep an appointment he would chalk a cross at an agreed spot near the Kew Gardens railway station.

However, the meetings seem to have succeeded admirably. Fuchs came up from Harwell (possibly on those days when he had official committees to attend at the Ministry of Supply) and slipped off to his appointment in the early evening. He and his contact never made a signal of recognition when they met in the saloon bar. Instead they would walk out into the street independently, and then stroll along together while Fuchs handed over his information. Sometimes the contact would leave Fuchs standing in the street for ten minutes or so, and then come back and resume his questioning; clearly another man (who kept out of Fuchs's sight) was being consulted.

There cannot have been a great deal that Fuchs gave the Russians during this period. He was cut off from nearly all the secret American research that had been continued after the war, and Harwell was still in its early stages. But he gave them various details of the British plutonium piles at Windscale, in Cumberland, and he gave figures of American production up to the time he left Los Alamos.

Now that they were making their own bombs, the Russians were avid for anything they could get; once they even urged Fuchs to go to Paris and make contact there at a certain address with other agents who had a technical knowledge of his work. But this he refused to do. It was by now late in 1948, and Fuchs was beginning to have doubts about the Russians. Worse still, he began to detect a new weakness in himself: an attachment to Harwell, an unwillingness to go on cheating his friends there indefinitely. In this twilight stage, when for once his conscience did not point the right way ahead with a clear, burning light, he found himself drifting into a compromise, a thing he would never have done in the bright, certain days of Los Alamos, when the double life was so easy to live and everything was either black or white. He decided not to break with the Russians altogether, but gradually to give them less and less while his conscience wrestled with the problem, until it gave him a new lead one way or the other.

Fuchs has himself explained the process:

In the course of this work I began naturally to form bonds of personal friendship, and I had to conceal them from my inner thoughts. I used my Marxist philosophy to establish in my mind two separate compartments: one compartment in which I allowed myself to make friendships, to have personal relations, to help people, and to be in all personal ways the kind of man I wanted to be, and the kind of man, which, in a personal way, I had been before with my friends in or near the Communist Party. I could be free and easy and happy with other people without fear of disclosing myself, because I knew that the other compartment would step in if I approached the danger point. I could forget the other compartment and still rely upon it. It appeared to me at the time that I had become a "free man," because I had succeeded in the other compartment in establishing myself completely independent of the surrounding forces of society. Looking back on it now, the best way of expressing it seems to be to call it a controlled schizophrenia.

In the postwar period I began again to have my doubts about the Russian policy. It is impossible to give definite incidents, because now the control mechanism acted against me also, in keeping away from me facts which I could not look in the face; but they did penetrate, and eventually I came to the point where I knew I disapproved of many actions of the Russian Government and of the Communist Party, but I still believed that they would build a new world and that one day I would take part in it, and that on that day I would also have to stand up and say to them that there are things which they are doing wrongly. During this time I was not sure that I could give all the information that I had. However, it became more and more evident that the time when Russia would expand her influence over Europe was far away, and that therefore I had to decide for myself whether I could go on for many years to continue handing over information without being sure in my own mind whether I was doing right. I decided that I could not do so. I did not go to one rendezvous because I was ill at the time. I decided not to go to the following one.

There have been evidences of insanity in all the members of Fuchs's family except his father and mother. This passage quoted from his confession is not insanity, but there is a megalomania in it. He is not only deciding for himself but for society as well; he is the judge, the prosecution, the witness, and the executioner all rolled into one. And then there is the glory of being the "free man"—the superman who is above the normal rules of the community, who has perfectly pigeonholed his emotions and his duties. He did not acknowledge the existence of any controlling force outside himself. *He* decided. Not even Marx and the Russians were infallible, or competent to control him, for now he says he will have to stand up to the Russians and tell them they were wrong.

There may be features of this mentality which are common to most men at some time in their lives: that desire for rightness, the adolescent dream of a world that is perfectly pure and good, and oneself a shining hero in it. Equally, in moments of frustration or bravado, few men have not felt the craving to heave a brick through a window just to establish that they are not people to be lightly neglected. It is the peculiarity of Fuchs that he carried these adolescent emotions on into adult life, and by the accident of his splendid mathematical mind there was put into his hand an enormous brick, with the possibility of his heaving it through an enormous window. His knowledge of the atomic bomb made him a king for a moment, with the fate of mankind in his hand. And all the conspiratorial business of tennis balls and chalk crosses and meetings in pubs must have given the drama a certain schoolboy relish.

Now, IN 1948, THE THING that Fuchs had not bargained for begins to happen. He begins to feel the stirrings of attachment to the ordinary, fallible human beings around him. There are his friends at Harwell: the Skinners, the Arnolds, Professor Peierls and his wife. He begins to think that he might owe them a duty, too, even though that duty may conflict with his larger design of creating a perfect world. He begins to feel he needs their affection. There is his department at Harwell, all the work that has yet to be done. Perhaps there might be claims on him there, too. And, finally, it is even possible that something is due to England itself, since he has accepted its hospitality for so long and has grown to depend on it.

The business of growing up when one is already an adult is never easy, and for Fuchs it was a torment. An incident occurred about this time—August 1948—when Fuchs was tapering off the information he was giving the Russians, and it reveals something of the strain under which he lived. Nothing was thought of this incident at the time, but it was remembered later with interest.

A Mr. S. M. Duke of Harwell had been attending a meeting at the General Electric Company at Wembley, outside London, with Fuchs and one or two other colleagues. When the meeting was over Duke gave Fuchs a lift back to Harwell in his car. Fuchs sat next to Duke on the front seat. They had reached a spot on the Oxford Road between Gerrards Cross and Beaconsfield when some object struck the windshield with a sharp report. The glass cracked into tiny pieces and became opaque. The car was traveling about forty miles an hour, and Duke, unable to see where he was going, knocked out the windshield with his hand while he braked as hard as he could. Fuchs slid off the seat onto the floor under the dashboard, and there was a look of extreme fear in his face.

When they came to a standstill Fuchs remained in the car. Duke got out and began picking out the remaining bits of broken glass, remarking that a stone must have flown up from the roadway. Fuchs pointed out that the road surface was clean, smooth tarmac, and that no other car could have thrown up a stone since there was no other traffic on the road. He spoke excitedly, and was badly shaken. He would not get out of the car until an Automobile Association patrol and others arrived.

It was then discovered that some of the pieces of broken glass showed traces of lead streaks, which could have come from an uncoated bullet fired from a .22 rifle or revolver. Since he had heard no bang, Duke was inclined to think that it was a bullet fired from some distance off—possibly a ricochet from the rifle of somebody who was out after rabbits. Fuchs was not reassured, and they completed the journey home in great discomfort.

It seems inconceivable that anyone tried to murder Fuchs that day, for he was not traveling in his own car, he had accepted the lift with Duke quite by chance, and this was not the only route between Wembley and Harwell. But clearly, for a moment, he thought he had been shot at, and the self-control on which he had prided himself for so long deserted him.

Then an illness intervened. He went down to the Mediterranean on holiday with the Skinners in the spring of 1949, and he was not very well on the journey. When he got back, it developed that he had a spot on one lung, which—he says—made him miss one of his London appointments. Mrs. Skinner nursed him in her own house at Harwell. This was one of the times when he lay staring at the wall without eating or speaking; he persisted in remaining in bed after his illness had gone and it was no longer necessary. These unrecorded hours, when he struggled with his perplexed loyalties, when he hunted and hunted through his mind for some clear answer, were probably the crisis of Fuchs's existence—the death throes, as it were, of his private life. When he got up at last, he had resolved to break with the Russians. He would not confess; that opened up possibilities that were too frightful. But from now on he would live one life instead of two: he would give his allegiance to Harwell, his work, and his friends. He could not repent: he had done all he had done with a clear moral conscience. But in the future he would live the easier life, where what he said and did openly would be at one with his thoughts.

But it was too late. In the summer of 1949 an investigation had already begun. And on September 1 President Truman made an announcement in Washington which meant that neither traitors nor anyone else were going to sleep quite securely in their beds for some time to come, if ever at all. Russia had exploded her first atomic bomb.

CHAPTER 7

WHEN THE HARWELL Atomic Energy Research Establishment was set up in 1946, it was decided that in addition to its police a special security officer should be appointed. The officer, Wing Commander Henry Arnold, arrived at Harwell a few weeks after Fuchs had come from America. In one of his reports to MI-5 Arnold drew attention to the presence of Fuchs on the staff, and to the fact that he was a German who had become naturalized during the war.

A check was begun at once. It continued (without Fuchs's knowledge) for five months. There was nothing to go on beyond the report —now twelve years old—of the German consul in Bristol, which said that this distinguished and respected scientist had once in his youth been a Communist. The investigation was made simply as a precautionary measure, and it turned up nothing. No meeting he had, no word he uttered, and no journey he took revealed the slightest grounds for suspicion. Ironically, of course, the investigation happened to coincide with just that period, on his return from the United States, when Fuchs was dormant. It was not until after the investigation had finished that he took up again his contacts with the Russians.

Then, in the summer of 1949, just before the explosion of the first Russian bomb, it developed from some chance evidence in the

United States that the Russians had been getting information about the atomic bomb. The evidence was not very precise, and it did not go very far, but the indications were that it was not an American but a British scientist who had been in touch with the Russians. This information was passed on to London by the FBI. Fuchs was not the only British scientist who had been in the United States, but he did in some ways fit the case. His investigation was taken up once again.

Henry Arnold, security officer at Harwell

There was no question of confronting Fuchs with a charge directly; if he denied it, as most certainly he would, then he would have been alerted, and security would in no way be improved. There was also the possibility that he might warn his contacts and leave the country, and under English law he could not have been stopped, since there was no direct evidence against him. Every precaution had to be taken to avoid arousing his suspicions while he was under observation. At the same time it was necessary to question him. This unexpectedly was made possible by an act of his own.

During October he came to Wing Commander Arnold and said that he wanted some advice on a personal matter that was worrying him: he had received word from Germany that his father, who was then living at Frankfurt am Main, in the American zone, had accepted an appointment as professor of theology at the University of Leipzig, in the Russian zone. A question of security was involved. He was concerned, Fuchs said, about his own position as a senior scientist at Harwell if his father should ever get into difficulties with the Russians. Ought he to resign from Harwell? Arnold replied that he was not competent to advise Fuchs on whether he should resign—that was something for the administrative authorities. Arnold said that the question, however, was this: what would Fuchs do if the Russians were to put pressure on him through his father? Fuchs answered that he did not know; he might do different things in different circumstances. The two men met again a few days later, and Fuchs repeated that he was in some doubt as to what he should do if the Russians were to arrest his father.

There were several curious aspects about this business. Dr. Fuchs had been visiting his son in England very recently. He was remembered as a lively septuagenarian, with a ruddy face and white hair, and there had been no talk then of his going into the Russian zone. His Christian faith and his charity appeared to be remarkable (though some people thought him a garrulous old man and had doubts about his sincerity). He had brought up his dead daughter's child—the boy Fuchs was to educate in England—and he had just returned from a long stay in the United States, where he had spoken widely among the Quakers.

Was it possible that the Russians were deliberately luring the old man into their zone in order to put pressure on the son? Or was this some device of Klaus's own?

Even later on, when most of the truth came out, these points were never entirely cleared up. If the Russians had intended to blackmail Fuchs through his father, they never did so. From the time Fuchs broke contact with them early in 1949 to the moment of his arrest he was never approached by any agent. Nevertheless, Fuchs may have been deliberately trying to maneuver himself into a position where he could confess by drawing the attention of security to himself. Or he might have made up his mind to get out of Harwell before he was discovered.

These are his own words on the matter, when he confessed later:

Shortly afterwards [after his last contact with the Russians] my father told me that he might be going into the Eastern Zone of Germany. At that time my own mind was closer to his than it had ever been before, because he also believed that they are at least trying to build a new world. He disapproved of many things and he had always done so; but he knew that when he went there he would say so, and he thought that in doing so he might help to make them realise that you cannot build a new world if you destroy some fundamental decencies in personal behaviour.

I could not bring myself to stop my father from going there. However, it made me face at least some of the facts about myself. I felt that my father's going to the Eastern Zone, that his letters, would touch me somewhere and that I was not sure whether I would not go back [presumably to Germany]. I suppose I did not have the courage to fight it out for myself, and therefore I invoked an outside influence by informing security that my father· was going to the Eastern Zone. A few months passed and I became more and more convinced that I had to leave Harwell.

This is the language of Othello, a man who has loved his conscience not wisely but too well, and now he is perplexed in the extreme. Yet he still clings to some vestige of logic. As a youth of twenty-one, Fuchs had left Germany with the avowed object of getting himself educated abroad so that he could return once Hitler had been destroyed and help to rebuild a Communist fatherland. Hitler has now been destroyed. If his father writes to him, giving glowing accounts of affairs in the Soviet zone, will he not be tempted to go back to Germany? And how can he stay at Harwell in those circumstances?

Up to this point Fuchs has never had any qualms about betraying Harwell, but now this duality has become intolerable.

To Arnold and his superiors it was clear that Fuchs could not be left with access to secret work while he was under investigation. Already a difficulty had come up. As soon as the news of the first Russian bomb was announced it was naturally presumed at Harwell that Fuchs would be consulted about it. He was invited to attend preliminary meetings on the matter, but it was obvious that he could not be told vital secrets and that the sooner he left Harwell the better.

No one envisaged that this was going to be particularly easy, since by now Fuchs regarded himself as the hub of Harwell, but various proposals were considered for finding him a university post. While this matter was going forward, further information had arrived from the United States which made it much more likely that Fuchs was the man they were after.

Various other slight clues were beginning to appear. Sometime previously, for example, when Dr. Fuchs was visiting his son, they had been invited to dinner by a colleague. Arnold had been one of the party. Now, months later, it came to Arnold's knowledge that Fuchs had been furious that Arnold had been invited. Evidently Fuchs feared that his father would blurt out something about his Communist days at the University of Kiel.

In the second half of December it was decided that Fuchs should be questioned outright, using as a pretext for the interrogation the fact that Fuchs himself had sought advice about his father's appointment to Leipzig. The man chosen to carry out the investigation was William James Skardon.

Skardon was one of the most able and experienced investigators in England. He was a man with a quiet, self-effacing manner. He had patience and tact and considerable tenacity, and it was apparent that all these qualities were going to be needed in the handling of Klaus Fuchs.

On December 21, 1949, Skardon went down to Harwell, and by appointment met Fuchs in Henry Arnold's office. Outwardly it was a routine meeting on a security problem, between a senior Harwell executive and a security officer. After making the introduction, Arnold withdrew. Skardon opened by referring to the information Fuchs had given about his father. Was there something more that Fuchs could tell them?

For the next hour and a quarter Fuchs discussed his background with great frankness. He confirmed that he had a sister living in Cambridge, Massachusetts, and a brother at Davos in Switzerland. He revealed that in Kiel, in 1932, at the Social Democrat party election for a vice-president, he had supported the Communist candidate in the absence of a Socialist. For that, Fuchs said, he was expelled from the Socialist party, and had drifted into the Communist camp. He remembered the name and address of the Quaker family who had befriended him when he first came to England in 1933.

Then there were his years with Professor Born in Edinburgh; his six months as an internee in Quebec, where he had met Hans Kahle —he had seen Kahle only once after that, at a Free German Youth Organization meeting in London. He spoke of his work for Tube Alloys in Birmingham, of his trip to the United States in 1943, and of how he had twice visited his sister in Massachusetts.

All this was given by Fuchs quite calmly and readily. And then Skardon said to him, "Were you not in touch with a Soviet representative while you were in New York? And did you not pass on information to that person about your work?"

Fuchs opened his mouth in surprise and then smiled slightly. "I don't think so," he said.

Skardon went on. "I am in possession of precise information which shows that you have been guilty of espionage on behalf of the Soviet

Union; that when you were in New York you passed to them information concerning your work."

When Fuchs again shook his head, saying that he did not think so, Skardon suggested that, in view of the seriousness of the matter, this was rather an ambiguous reply.

Fuchs answered, "I don't understand; perhaps you will tell me what the evidence is. I have not done any such thing." He continued then to deny any knowledge of the matter, and added that in his opinion it had been wise to exclude Soviet Russia from information about the atomic bomb. Skardon then went on to other questions. Had Fuchs ever heard of Professor Halperin? Yes, Halperin used to send him periodicals while he was interned in Canada, but he had never met him.

At 1:30 p.m. there was a break in the interview. Fuchs went off and lunched alone. When they resumed a little after 2:00 p.m., Skardon again confronted Fuchs with the charge of espionage, and Fuchs again denied it, saying there was no evidence. But in view of the suspicions about him, he said he felt he ought to resign from Harwell. The meeting ended with another discussion about his father's movements in Germany. The two men had been together for four hours in all, and Fuchs had shown no signs of breaking. Skardon went back to London.

Something had been gained, but not much. There had been an admission of Fuchs's activities in his youth, and there had been that inadequate phrase, "I don't think so." He had given a few details of his movements and his acquaintances. But that was all, and it was not enough. On this evidence he could not be arrested. There was always the possibility of mistaken identity.

Now that Fuchs had been alerted, there was the question of what to do next. If he was guilty, he might try to escape from England. It was even conceivable that he would commit suicide. There were those who favored the idea of getting him into custody at once. But Skardon was for waiting and taking a chance; he was not yet persuaded that Fuchs was in fact the guilty man. Still, he had come away from Harwell convinced that Fuchs was wrestling with a moral problem of his own. If he were handled carefully, there was a very good chance that in the end he would break down of his own free will. In any event, without his confession they could not proceed against him. Skardon did not believe that Fuchs would make any desperate move. This was just a hunch, but in the end he had his way.

It was not until December 30, on the day after Fuchs's thirty-eighth birthday, that Skardon went down to Harwell again. He found Fuchs calm and unhurried. He again denied the charges, and said that he could not help. There was a detailed discussion of his movements in the United States in 1944, but this led to nothing new.

On January 10, 1950, the director of the Atomic Energy Research Establishment, Sir John Cockcroft, sent for Fuchs and told him that in view of his father's departure for Leipzig it would be best for all concerned if Fuchs resigned from Harwell and went to some university post instead.

On January 13 Skardon came down to Harwell for a third meeting. Did Fuchs remember the exact address of his apartment in New York in 1944? Nearly six years had gone by, and he was not quite certain of it. However, with the aid of a map he identified the place as West Seventy-seventh Street, in the middle of a block between Columbus Avenue and Amsterdam Avenue. When Skardon told him that security was pressing inquiries about this apartment and other matters in New York, Fuchs appeared unconcerned. He still denied all the charges. He said he knew now, however, that he would have to leave Harwell. It should not be difficult, he said, for him to find a university post. But first he would take a holiday.

All along Skardon had urged upon Fuchs that security was not trying to ruin him. If some slip had been made in New York during the war, then it was much better to have the thing out in the open. Fuchs was a valuable man at Harwell. It was always possible that once this business was thrashed out some arrangement could be made to enable him to continue with his work. But the present strain was intolerable for everybody.

Fuchs was well aware that security had no inkling of the extent or duration of his treason. Through this fortnight in January he was asking himself, Shall I admit the lesser crime if they will let me stay on at Harwell? But if I remain, can I trust myself not to turn traitor again? He revealed all this in his confession when he said:

> I was then confronted with the fact that there was evidence that I had given away information in New York. I was given the chance of admitting it and staying at Harwell or clearing out. I was not sure

enough of myself to stay at Harwell, and therefore I denied the allegation and decided that I would have to leave Harwell.

However, it became clear to me that in leaving Harwell in these circumstances I would do two things. I would deal a grave blow to Harwell, to all the work which I have loved; and furthermore that I would leave suspicions against people whom I had loved, who were my friends and who believed that I was their friend.

I had to face the fact that it had been possible for me in one half of my mind to be friends with people, to be close friends, and at the same time to deceive them and to endanger them. I had to realise that the control mechanism had warned me of danger to myself, but that it had also prevented me from realising what I was doing to people close to me.

I then realised that the combination of the three ideas which had made me what I was, was wrong: in fact every single one of them was wrong: that there are certain standards of moral behaviour which are in you and that you cannot disregard. That in your actions you must be clear in your own mind whether they are right or wrong. That you must be able, before accepting somebody else's authority, to state your doubts and try and resolve them. And I found that at least I myself was made by circumstances.

This is very complicated. But several clear things come out of it. He still regards himself as essential to Harwell. But now at last he is aware that suspicion might fall on his friends. They might be hurt. He had never thought of this before because the "control mechanism" had prevented him from taking account of anything as minor as the human beings around him whom he had betrayed. They were the casual victims of his grand design for the perfection of the world. But now he realized he had no right to hurt them. This was a considerable advance, but Fuchs was still a long way from realizing the real enormity of what he had done; he still could not see that what mattered was not his friends' feelings, but the fact that they and everybody else on this earth might be blown to smithereens as a consequence of his treason. This point never seems to have entered his mind, then or since. He was obsessed throughout by his own personal moral position.

After the January 13 meeting, Skardon was on slightly firmer ground. An atmosphere of confidence had been created, and he felt sure that Fuchs would make no move without consulting him. The two men, the hunter and the quarry, were entering now into that strange, intensely intimate world of criminal investigation where each man trusts the other, even though they know that before the end one of them has got to be destroyed. There is an insect quality about this business—the slow, inevitable waiting of the spider for the fly. The fly has to be caught, and the spider has to pounce, and there is nothing either of them can do about it.

Outwardly Fuchs remained perfectly calm. He went about his work in the normal way, and his friends at Harwell knew nothing of what was going on, and they noticed nothing peculiar about him. There was just one incident.

A scandal broke out among the members of Fuchs's own staff. It was nothing more than an untidy love affair gone wrong, an incident of the kind that happens in every garrison, but which seems outrageous because of the special intimacy of garrison life. Fuchs

William Skardon, Fuchs's Inquisitor

made a point of visiting the distracted woman in the hospital—he might have felt that this was one more sign that the life at Harwell he knew and liked so well was breaking up around him. At all events, the incident seems to have brought him to a decision. On Sunday, January 22, he phoned Arnold and said he wanted a private talk. They arranged to lunch at the old Railway House Hotel at Steventon on Monday. At that luncheon Fuchs said he was opposed to Communism as practiced in Russia now—and he also said he should like to see Skardon again; he had something more to tell him. It was agreed that the meeting should take place at Fuchs's prefab at 11:00 a.m. next day, Tuesday, January 24.

Arnold met Skardon at Didcot railway station and drove him to Harwell. Skardon walked down to prefab number seventeen alone. It was ten days or more since the two men had met, and the change in Fuchs was remarkable. He looked unusually pale, and he seemed to Skardon to be in a state of some agitation. When Skardon said,

"You asked to see me, and here I am," Fuchs answered at once, "Yes. It's rather up to me now."

But then he stopped—as though overtaken by some sudden misgiving about what he had to say. While Skardon waited he went wandering off into a long dissertation about his life, going over and over again the details they had discussed so much before. He told nothing new, but talked with his head in his hands and his face haggard.

After two hours of this Skardon said, "You have told me a long story providing the motives for actions, but nothing about the actions themselves." He suggested they have some lunch.

There was a luncheon van that went around Harwell selling snacks. Skardon indicated this van, which was passing the house just then, and said, "Will we have some fish and chips?"

Fuchs answered, "No. Let's go into Abingdon."

They got into Fuchs's car, and on the five-mile run into Abingdon, Fuchs drove with a reckless speed that bordered on insanity. He cut corners on the wrong side of the road, he passed all other traffic with inches to spare; and they raced at last to the door of Abingdon's principal hotel.

An English pub on a wet winter's afternoon is not a place that lends itself easily to high drama. There were other guests in the dining room. Skardon and Fuchs ate their way through a prosaic meal, talking about the gossip of Harwell, about anything but treason. It was a strained and desultory conversation.

Then they went into the lounge for coffee. Skardon spoke of Professor Skinner's departure from Harwell and asked who was going to take his place. Fuchs said he did not know.

"You are number three, aren't you?" Skardon said. "Might you not have got the job?"

"Possibly," Fuchs said, and Skardon shook his head. There was no likelihood of that now—not at any rate until Fuchs had confessed. Suddenly Fuchs jumped up and said, "Let's go back."

They returned to Harwell with excruciating slowness. For a great part of the way they drove behind a lorry traveling at barely ten miles an hour, and Fuchs would not pass it. They got out in silence at the prefab, and as soon as they were inside Fuchs made his announcement. He had decided to confess, he said. His conscience was clear, but he was worried about his friends and what they might think.

"When did it start?" Skardon asked.

"About the middle of 1942," Fuchs answered, "and it has continued until about a year ago."

That was seven years. That covered the whole period of the bomb, its conception, its construction, and its explosion. It covered the years in England, as well as those in New York and Los Alamos. This was the first shock Skardon had that afternoon. It was the first intimation that he or anybody else had had that they were dealing here, not with leakage of a few facts and figures, but with treason on an immense scale and for a very long time.

Now that he was beginning to feel the relief of confession, Fuchs ran on quickly, recounting unbelievable facts. There had been frequent but irregular meetings, he said. He had taken the initiative. At first he had told the Russians merely the products of his own brain, but as time went on he had given them everything he knew. His contacts were sometimes Russians, sometimes people of other nationalities. He realized that he was carrying his life in his hands, but he had learned to do that in his underground days in Germany.

He spoke in a rapid voice, and it was no moment for Skardon to take notes or to interrupt. As soon as he could, he asked Fuchs what he had actually given the Russians—and he received then his second shock that afternoon.

He supposed, Fuchs said, that the worst thing he had done was to tell the Russians the method of making the atomic bomb.

Now finally the truth was out, and it could not have been worse. Any possibility of Fuchs's remaining at Harwell or anywhere else except inside a prison was out of the question. All that could be done now was to so manage him that he would continue to talk until he had nothing left to say. Now that the break had come, Skardon was anxious to end the interview as soon as possible so that he could take advice and get the full confession down in writing.

But Fuchs wanted to go on. He explained carefully that it was impossible for him, of course, to do more than tell the Russians the principle on which the bomb was made. It was up to the Russians to produce their own industrial equipment, and he had been astonished when they had succeeded in making and detonating a bomb as soon as the previous August. He had not supposed that commercially and industrially they were so far developed.

As for his own information, he had been gradually diminishing it over the past two years. That was because he began to have doubts about what he was doing. He still believed in Communism, he said, but not as now practiced by Russia. He had decided that the only place for him to live was in England, and he returned again to the subject of his friends. What were they going to think about his behavior—especially Henry Arnold, whom he had deceived most of all? He insisted that his sister Kristel in the United States knew nothing of his contact with the Russians.

By the time Skardon brought the interview to an end, Fuchs was calmer and more self-possessed. He agreed that, since they both were tired, it would be best to break off and meet another time. He recalled that he had a committee meeting the following day, but the day after that, January 26, he would be free.

Skardon drove back to London with his sinister report. What gave the affair a special sense of unreality was that Fuchs still believed that all would be well—they would still continue to employ him at Harwell. Indeed, in the course of the interview he had made it clear that this was the reason why he had invited Skardon to Harwell and had confessed. He had been a Russian agent. That was a mistake, and now he had admitted it. But he had ceased to be a Russian agent. Now it was up to Skardon to explain all this to the authorities and wind up any tiresome official formalities as quickly as possible so that Fuchs could get on with his work.

Fuchs, in other words, was still a thousand miles away from any understanding of the real issues at stake. Yet there were certain advantages for security in his absurd illusions. So long as he was thinking along these lines, it was not likely that he would bolt or commit suicide. Moreover, he would help in every way he could. More than ever now, it was necessary not to alarm him, not to surround him with police, not to drag him down from the dreamworld in which he was still living.

The next meeting, on January 26, again took place at Harwell. Fuchs was ready with a mass of details about his meetings with his contacts in London, Boston, New York, and Santa Fe. He had been to see Arnold in the interval, and at that painful meeting had said he was a little worried lest Skardon had not appreciated the significance of the whole affair. In particular he was concerned about the forthcoming declassification meeting with the Americans. Did Skardon appreciate that it was essential for Fuchs to be there? If he were not, people would notice his absence. Suspicions would be aroused. And this would be a very bad thing for Harwell. Arnold had reassured Fuchs, and suggested he might raise the matter at his next meeting with Skardon. And now, on January 26, Fuchs urged Skardon to move quickly, as he was anxious to have his position clarified.

Skardon put forward three choices: Fuchs could write out a confession himself, he could dictate it to a secretary, or he could dictate it to Skardon himself. Fuchs at once chose the last course, and it was arranged that they should meet the following day in a room at the War Office in London. The understanding between the two men was now complete. The fly was in the web, but he was held there by nothing visible. They were on a first-name basis, they had a certain respect for one another, and to Fuchs at least it seemed that they were acting out their parts merely as instruments of some sort of inevitable fate that was larger than themselves. After the drama was over they could go away and take up their normal lives again.

Certainly after nearly eight years of silence and of living the double life, it must have been an immense relief for Fuchs to tell the whole story to someone who would understand. That was the important thing—to be understood. To make oneself perfectly and precisely clear. As soon as Skardon had left, Fuchs had a talk with Arnold, and readily answered questions on what kind of information he had passed on to the Russians.

The following day, still in this mood of confession, Fuchs came up to London without police supervision of any kind. Skardon met him at Paddington Station and drove him to the War Office. They sat down, and when Skardon gave him the usual official caution and asked if he were ready to make a statement, Fuchs answered, "Yes, I quite understand. I would like you to carry on."

Skardon took the confession down by hand.

I am deputy Chief Scientific Officer (acting rank) at Atomic Energy Research Establishment, Harwell. I was born in Russelsheim on December 29, 1911. My father was a parson and I had a very happy childhood. I think that the one thing that stands out is that my father always did what he believed to be the right thing to do, and he always told us that we had to go our own way even if he disagreed. He himself had many fights because he did what his conscience decreed, even if this meant that he was at variance with accepted conventions. For example, he was the first parson to join the social democratic party.

So it went on through the whole involved story. It was when they were drawing to the end of it that Fuchs for the first time had something to say of his contrition.

I know that I cannot go back on that [on what had happened] and I know that all I can do now is to try and repair the damage I have done. The first thing is to make sure that Harwell will suffer as little as possible and that I have to save for my friends as much as possible of that part that was good in my relations with them. This thought is at present uppermost in my mind, and I find it difficult to concentrate on any other points.

However, I realise that I will have to state the extent of the information I have given and that I shall have to help as far as my conscience allows me in stopping other people who are still doing what I have done. There is nobody I know by name who is concerned with collecting information for the Russian authorities. There are people whom I know by sight whom I trusted with my life and who trusted me with theirs, and I do not know that I shall be able to do anything that might in the end give them away. They are not inside the project, but they are intermediaries between myself and the Russian Government.

At first I thought that all I would do would be to inform the Russian authorities that work on the atomic bomb was going on. I concentrated at first mainly on the product of my own work, but in particular at Los Alamos I did what I consider to be the worst I have done, namely to give information about the principle of the design of the plutonium bomb.

Later on at Harwell I began to be concerned about the information I was giving, and I began to sift it, but it is difficult to say exactly when and how I did it because it was a process which went up and down with my inner struggles. The last time when I handed over information was in February or March 1949.

Before I joined the project most of the English people with whom I made personal contacts were left wing, and affected in some degree or other by the same kind of philosophy. Since coming to Harwell I have met English people of all kinds, and I have come to see in many of them a deep-rooted firmness which enables them to lead a decent way of life. I do not know where this springs from and I don't think they do, but it is there.

I have read this statement and to the best of my knowledge it is true.

Then he signed "Klaus Fuchs," and Skardon made a note at the bottom that Fuchs had read the statement through, made such alterations as he wished, and had initialed each page.

Fuchs had one more reservation, however, and that in itself was part of the moral wonderland in which he was still drifting: he would not tell Skardon the technical details of the construction of the atomic bomb that he had passed on to the Russians, because Skardon had not been cleared for access to such information.

He agreed to confide in a qualified person, Mr. Michael Perrin, whom he had known since 1942 in Birmingham, and who was now with the atomic energy division in the Ministry of Supply. An appointment was fixed for January 30 in London; Fuchs said he would like a rest over the weekend to gather his thoughts. He again repeated that he was anxious about his future, and did not want to waste time in getting it settled. He then returned alone to Harwell by train.

That same night a strange thing happened. Arnold got word that there was a light burning in Fuchs's office. He went at once to the administrative block and quietly let himself in. A light was indeed burning in Fuchs's room, and there were sounds that indicated that there was someone inside.

Arnold used his passkey to get into a room which was directly opposite across a corridor. The partitions between these offices in the administrative block have glass panes let into them about eight feet from the floor, close to the ceiling. By getting up on a cupboard Arnold found he could look across the corridor and through a glass pane into Fuchs's room. Fuchs was sitting there at his desk, going through his papers. His file cabinet was open, and as he read he smoked. The rest of the building was in darkness and silence.

For a long time Arnold watched him. Many things were possible. It could have been that Fuchs was intending to commit suicide after all. He might also have been planning to escape from England in the night, taking his papers with him. Again, he might merely have come there to destroy those papers.

Arnold watched and waited. But Fuchs continued quietly reading, pausing occasionally to take other documents from the cabinet and sort them out in piles on the desk. Then, toward 11:00 p.m., he got up, left his papers on the desk and the light burning, locked the door behind him, and went out. Arnold calculated that Fuchs was bound to come back, if only to put out the light, and he remained standing on the cupboard in the darkness.

It was an hour, however, before Fuchs returned. Then he sat down and began reading again. This continued for another half hour or more, while still Arnold watched and waited. Then at last, about 12:30 a.m., Fuchs got up, locked his office door, put out the light, got into his car, and drove home. Arnold then entered the room and found that the papers which Fuchs had been reading dealt only with unimportant routine matters. The room, with the papers still spread out on the desk, remained untouched until it was officially searched after Fuchs's arrest.

Attorney General Sir Hartley Shawcross

Fuchs took a morning train up to London on Monday, January 30. He arrived at Paddington at 10:45 a.m., and then Skardon brought him to the War Office, where Perrin was waiting.

Skardon opened the proceedings by saying that Fuchs had decided to reveal everything. Perrin replied that he had plenty of notepaper, and they set to work. They went through the seven years of meetings chronologically, noting just what Fuchs had given to the Russians at each time and place.

After an hour or two the three men broke off for lunch. They went to a hotel behind the War Office, and finding all the tables occupied, perched themselves at the snack bar, as strange a luncheon party as any in London that day. Then they went back to work again.

It was 4:00 p.m. when the statement was finished. Fuchs then went off alone to Harwell, while Perrin got his notes typed; it was a long document of many pages. Now at last the authorities had enough to make the arrest.

The legal formalities were complicated. First, the prime minister,

Mr. Clement Attlee, had to be acquainted with the confession. Then the attorney general, Sir Hartley Shawcross, had to be found—he was somewhere in the north of England. Shawcross returned to London, reading through the case in the train, and in London the Special Branch at Scotland Yard and others worked on the precise wording of the charge. These matters occupied the whole of January 31 and February 1. By February 2 they were ready to move.

Security preferred not to make the arrest inside Harwell, where nothing was yet known of the investigation. They decided to get Fuchs quietly to London, and the best way of doing this was for Perrin to telephone Fuchs and ask him to come up for a further interview. The arrest would take place at Perrin's office at Shell-Mex House. Perrin agreed to do this—though as a layman he lacked some of security's enthusiasm for the idea. His only stipulation was that if Fuchs was to be arrested in his office, he, Perrin, should not be present. He got through to Fuchs by phone on the morning of February 2 and said, "Can you come up again this afternoon?" Fuchs agreed, and suggested a train which would get into Paddington around 2:30 p.m.

It was arranged then that Commander Leonard Burt of Scotland Yard should be present in Perrin's room at 2:30 p.m., with the charge and a warrant for Fuchs's arrest. Perrin, somewhat restlessly, took up a position in his office at 2:30; and then for half an hour nothing whatever happened. Perrin telephoned security, and was assured that Burt was on his way. At 3:00 p.m. Perrin's secretary telephoned to say that Fuchs had arrived. Perrin gave instructions that Fuchs should be kept in his outer office until Burt appeared, and in some agitation he telephoned security once again.

Finally, at 3:20 p.m., Burt arrived with a police inspector, and they were shown at once into Perrin's room. The delay had been caused by last-minute arrangements over the wording of the charge. They then sent for Fuchs, who had been waiting all this time in the adjoining room. Perrin introduced him quickly to Burt, and then slipped away into another room. Burt read out the charge at once and told Fuchs he was under arrest. Fuchs made no comment. He sat down in Perrin's chair, and then asked if he could see Perrin himself.

Burt agreed, and brought Perrin back into the room again. Fuchs's face had suddenly gone gray. Now at last the whole elaborate dream edifice had collapsed, and looking directly at Perrin, he made his final absurd and touching *cri de coeur:*

"You realize what this will mean at Harwell?"

The officers noted that down and took him away to Bow Street Police Station, and then to Brixton Prison.

CHAPTER 8

FUCHS'S THREE APPEARANCES in court are remarkable for their brevity, for what was not said or given in evidence, and for the dispatch with which they were managed. He was never allowed bail, and within a month of his arrest he had been arraigned, tried, and sentenced. He himself spoke only once or twice, and very briefly, and he uttered nothing in his own defense.

His first appearance was before the chief magistrate, Sir Laurence Dunne, at Bow Street, on February 3, and this was a purely formal proceeding. Commander Burt, as witness, related the circumstances of the arrest. Fuchs said he had no questions to ask of Burt, and the magistrate said to him, "Is there anything you want me to do for you in the way of legal representation?"

Fuchs answered, "I don't know of anybody."

The magistrate asked if he was a man of means, and the prosecutor, Mr. T. Christmas Humphreys, replied, "Yes, there is no reason to think he cannot afford to pay for legal representation. He has a substantial salary." The magistrate ordered that the prisoner's spectacles and other articles which were taken from him at the time of his arrest should be returned to him, and the case was then remanded for a week, while Fuchs obtained lawyers and the prosecution prepared their brief. Fuchs remained at Brixton Prison.

At the second hearing, on February 10, Arnold, Skardon, and Perrin all gave evidence, but the confession was not given in court. The prosecutor, Mr. Humphreys, said this:

"The mind of Fuchs may possibly be unique, and create a new precedent in the world of psychology. It is clear from his statement that he had half of his mind beyond the reach of reason and the impact of facts. The other half lived in a world of normal relationships and friendship with his colleagues and human loyalty. This dual personality has been consciously and deliberately produced. He broke his mind in two, describing it as controlled schizophrenia. He has produced in himself a classic example of the immortal duality in English literature, Jekyll and Hyde."

Fuchs again had nothing to say, and he was committed for trial at the Old Bailey.

Three weeks later, on March 1, he appeared in court before the lord chief justice, Lord Goddard. The case had now attracted very wide attention in the newspapers. They recorded the appearances of the lord chief justice, with his scarlet and ermine, coming into court behind the sword-bearer and the mace-bearer in their medieval costumes, and the hush in the crowded room as he settled into his chair under the sword of justice. They recorded the presence of the duchess of Kent, and other notables, and that a Miss Giesler Wagner, a cousin of the prisoner and his only relative in England, was there too. They noted that Fuchs was attended by a doctor, that he looked pale, that throughout the hearing his eyes remained fixed on the bench, and that he made no sign of any kind.

But there was no great drama in court that day. The case was over in an hour and a half, and Skardon was the only witness. Yet those ninety minutes must have been for Fuchs one of the strangest anti-climaxes any man has ever experienced, for he had just heard, as he came into the court, that he was not going to die. His senior counsel, Mr. Derek Curtis-Bennett, had seen him in the cells immediately before the hearing and had told him that counsel would do their best, but there was no hope of an acquittal; he had to expect the maximum penalty.

Fuchs had answered, "Yes. I understand."

"You know what the maximum penalty is?" Curtis-Bennett asked.

And Fuchs replied, "Yes, I know. It's death." He had apparently believed all this time that he was about to die.

"No," said Curtis-Bennett. "No. It is fourteen years."

Upon this Fuchs made no sign of relief or surprise; he went on calmly into court, followed the proceedings closely, and spoke up clearly and firmly at the end. He was charged with having communicated to unknown persons information which might be useful to an enemy on four separate occasions: in Birmingham, in 1943; in New York, between December 1943 and August 1944; in Boston, in

February 1945; and in Berkshire, England, in 1947. Fuchs pleaded guilty to all four counts.

The attorney general, Sir Hartley Shawcross, opened for the Crown:

"The prisoner is a Communist, and that is at once the explanation and indeed the tragedy of this case. Quite apart from the great harm the prisoner has done the country that he adopted and which adopted him, it is a tragedy that one of such high intellectual attainments as the prisoner possesses, should have allowed his mental processes to have become so warped by his devotion to communism, that, as he himself expresses it, he became a kind of controlled schizophrenic, the dominant half of his mind leading him to do things which the other part of his mind recognized quite clearly were wrong. . . ."

Sir Hartley then made a statement on the nature of Communism and gave an account of Fuchs's career, quoting largely from the confession. He made the point that the confession was not obtained by any sinister pressure, nor after any "long period of secret incarceration incommunicado." Skardon supported this in the witness box, and added that since his arrest Fuchs had done all he could to help the authorities.

Curtis-Bennett at the outset based his case for the defense on the intense political pressure which had been put upon Fuchs in his youth in Germany. He said:

"Then the struggle burst into flames in February 1933, when somebody set the Reichstag on fire. . . . There was a screech throughout Germany against the Communists. This scientist, this scholarly man, read that news in the newspaper on the train the morning after it happened. He went underground, scarcely saving his own life, and came to this country in 1933 for the purpose of conducting his scientific studies in order to fit himself out to be a scientist to help in the rebuilding of a Communist Germany, not to throw atom bombs at anybody, but to study physics. . . . He pursued his peaceful studies, and had not the War come he might have been a candidate for a Nobel Peace Prize or a membership of the Royal Society rather than for gaol."

"In England," Mr. Curtis-Bennett said, "Fuchs never pretended to be anything but a Communist."

Lord Goddard: "I don't suppose he proclaimed himself as a Communist when naturalized or when taken into Harwell or when he went to the U.S.A."

Curtis-Bennett: "It was on his records in this country at the Home Office that he was a member of the German Communist Party."

Sir Hartley Shawcross: "It was realized when he was examined by the Enemy Aliens Tribunal at the beginning of the war that he was a refugee from Nazi persecution, because in Germany he had been a Communist. All the investigations at that time and since have not shown that he had any association whatever with British members of the Communist Party."

All he wished to say, Curtis-Bennett replied, was this: ". . . anybody who has read anything of Marxist theory must know that any man who is a Communist, whether in Germany or Timbuctoo, will react in exactly the same way when he comes into possession of information. He will almost automatically, unhappily, put his allegiance to the Communist ideology first."

Lord Goddard: "I have read [his] statement with very great care more than once. I cannot understand this metaphysical philosophy, or whatever you like to call it. I am not concerned with it. I am concerned that this man gave away secrets of vital importance to this country."

Curtis-Bennett: "If Your Lordship does not think that the state of mind a man acts under is relative to sentence—"

Curtis-Bennett, Fuchs's senior counsel

Lord Goddard: "A man in that state of mind is one of the most dangerous that this country could have within its shores."

Curtis-Bennett: "I have to endeavour to put before Your Lordship this man as he is, knowing that Your Lordship is not going to visit him savagely, but justly, both in the interests of the state and the interests of this man. . . . He is a scientist, a pencil-and-paper man, and . . . A scientist is in this position: he is taught, or teaches himself, or learns, that A plus B equals C. If he is told tomorrow that it is A minus B that equals C, he does not believe it. But your sensible citizen or politician, moving in the affairs of the world, told that, would agree with both. He has to. But the change of political alignments is not the business of scientists, for scientists are not always politically wise. Their minds move along straight lines, without the flexibility that some others have."

Finally, Curtis-Bennett said, Fuchs had recanted. "There you have this man being logical . . . having decided to tell everything, [he] tells everything, makes it about as bad for himself as he can, and provides the whole of the case against him in this court. There is not one piece of evidence produced in the case which is not the result of the written and oral statements he made to Mr. Skardon in December and January of this year."

No further evidence was produced. Lord Goddard told Fuchs he was convicted, and asked him if he had anything to say. Fuchs then gave the only public statement he had made since his arrest:

"My Lord, I have committed certain crimes, for which I am charged, and I expect sentence. I have also committed some other crimes, which are not crimes in the eyes of the law—crimes against my friends; and when I asked my counsel to put certain facts before you, I did not do it because I wanted to lighten my sentence. I did it in order to atone for those other crimes.

I have had a fair trial, and I wish to thank you and my counsel and my solicitors. I also wish to thank the Governor and his staff of Brixton Prison for the considerate treatment they have given me."

This was Lord Goddard's summing up:

"In 1933, fleeing from political persecution in Germany, you took advantage of the right of asylum, or the privilege of asylum, which has always been the boast of this country to people persecuted in their own country for their political opinions. You betrayed the hospitality and protection given you by the grossest treachery.

In 1942, in return for your offer to put at the service of this country the great gifts Providence has bestowed upon you in scientific matters, you were granted British nationality. From that moment, regardless of your oath, you started to betray secrets of vital importance for the purpose of furthering a political creed held in abhorrence by the vast majority in this country, your object being to strengthen that creed which was then known to be inimical to all freedom-loving countries.

There are four matters which seem to me to be the gravest aspects of your crime. In the first, by your conduct you have imperilled the right of asylum which this country has hitherto extended. Dare we now give shelter to political refugees who may be followers of this pernicious creed, and disguise themselves and then treacherously bite the hand that feeds them?

Secondly, you have betrayed not only the projects and inventions of your own brain for which this country was paying you and enabling you to live in comfort in return for your promises of secrecy. You have also betrayed the secrets of other workers in this field of science, not only in this country, but in the United States, and thereby you might have caused the gravest suspicions to fall on those you falsely treated as friends and who were misled into trusting you.

Thirdly, you might have imperilled the good relations between this country and the great American republic with which His Majesty is aligned.

And fourthly, you have done irreparable and incalculable harm both to this land and to the United States, and you did it, as your statement shows, merely for the purpose of furthering your political creed, for I am willing to assume you have not done it for gain.

Your statement, which has been read, shows to me the depth of self-deception into which people like yourself can fall. Your crime to me is only thinly differentiated from high treason. In this country we observe rigidly the rule of law, and as technically it is not high treason, so you are not tried for that offence.*

I have now to assess the penalty which it is right I should impose. It is not so much for punishment that I impose it, for punishment can mean nothing to a man of your mentality.

My duty is to safeguard this country; and how can I be sure that a man, whose mentality is shown in that statement you have made, may not, at any other minute, allow some curious working of your mind to lead you further to betray secrets of the greatest possible value and importance to this land?

The maximum sentence which Parliament has ordained for this crime is fourteen years' imprisonment, and that is the sentence I pass upon you."

Without any visible display of emotion, Fuchs left the dock.

---

* In England the charge of high treason, for which the penalty is death, can be made only against a traitor who assists an enemy. Fuchs gave information to an ally.

NO ONE CAME FORWARD to protest against the sentence. Instead there was a very sober feeling that something had happened here which was beyond the power of any court to punish or correct. It was not just a question of the prisoner Fuchs, or the intriguing quality of his mind. The whole question of British security was involved. How far had security slipped? How many other Fuchses were running around in the British and American laboratories? How was it possible that a traitor could walk through all the security barriers in England and America, and for years, without anyone's being the wiser?

The lord chief justice, Lord Goddard

Several events followed rapidly. On March 3, 1950, the prime minister, Mr. Attlee, saw Sir Percy Sillitoe, the head of MI-5, in Downing Street, and the documents in the case were sent to Mr. Truman and the FBI in the United States. Mr. Truman had already announced in February that the United States would press on with the manufacture of the hydrogen bomb. But this was to be purely an American effort; the exchange of atomic weapons information with England had already ceased since the war.

On March 6 Mr. Attlee made a statement on Fuchs to the House of Commons.

On March 7 the Tass agency published a statement that the Soviet government had no knowledge of Fuchs and that no agent of theirs had been in contact with him.

On March 10 the Joint Congressional Committee on Atomic Energy met in Washington, and it had before it the two vital documents: the first confession to Skardon and the second, technical, confession to Perrin. The committee was, in the word of its chairman, Senator McMahon, "shocked." A hunt to track down Fuchs's contacts was begun on both sides of the Atlantic.

Fuchs in prison was repeatedly questioned and shown hundreds of photographs. He had known none of his contacts by their real names, and in the intervening years he had forgotten very largely what they looked like. He actually passed over a photograph of Harry Gold, saying he had never seen him before.

The FBI concentrated on Gold. They sent two men to question Fuchs in England, they made minute inquiries of hundreds of possible suspects in the United States, they questioned Fuchs's sister Kristel; and finally, on May 22, when they were convinced that Gold must be their man, they got him to confess. It was the map of Santa Fe which Gold had bought so that he could find his way to his rendezvous with Fuchs in 1945 that was his undoing. When the FBI searched his apartment and discovered this map, Gold was so utterly taken aback that he broke down. And it happened that within an hour of his arrest word came from England that Fuchs had at last identified Gold from some motion pictures of him which had been taken a short time before.

From Gold the trail led to David Greenglass, to the Rosenbergs, and to others in the American spy ring. In England it was found that most of Fuchs's contacts had already decamped to Soviet Germany. About this time also, Fuchs's elder brother, Gerhardt, was expelled from Switzerland. He went to the Soviet zone and died there.

On June 27 Fuchs himself was sent to Stafford jail in Staffordshire. He never exercised his right of appeal, and he made no effort to have his case reviewed. After this brief passage through the courts —and as a compact and rapid process of law, the case was something of a model of its kind—he vanished almost before the public was aware of him, though he left behind an enormous field of misgiving and speculation.

Probably not even Fuchs himself could describe the processes of his mind on his arrest, when at least some of his illusions were broken at last. Those who saw him in prison immediately afterward were struck by the improvement in his appearance. He had no resentment at his arrest, and, in fact, more than once while he was awaiting trial he sent for Skardon to give him further information. He was still not quite sure that he could give away his contacts in the Russian intelligence service, and he was not particularly good at remembering faces and dates and places; still, within these limits he was ready to help as much as he could.

It is doubtful if Fuchs ever admitted to himself the full extent of the harm he had done society. But of his private treason, his betrayal of his immediate friends, he was acutely conscious. He wrote to them at length. Prisoners in British jails are not allowed fountain pens, but he did the best he could with a scratchy prison nib and the unglazed prison notepaper that blotted badly at times. He wrote in a small, neat hand, and the grammar and phrasing were precise.

He said he had begun at last—too late—to understand affection. As a boy in Germany he had always joined himself to other students because their political beliefs were the same as his own—not because he liked them or admired them for their own sakes. Friends, then, had always been a means to an end; now he was beginning to see that that was false and inhuman, and it was not easy for him in his thirties to learn what most others knew when they were sixteen. He said he realized that his friends would never want to hear from him again.

His friends, however, did not desert him. Their first reaction to the news of the arrest was utter stupefaction. Those whom he had particularly harmed were people like Professor Peierls, who were themselves originally refugees from Nazi Germany and who, after a long struggle, had established themselves in England and were known as men of great integrity and intelligence. Scientists of the distinction of Professor Peierls were unlikely to be much affected, but it was impossible to avoid feeling that Fuchs had cast suspicion upon them all.

Peierls, however, went to Fuchs in prison as soon as he heard the news, to see how he could help to straighten out the mess—for Harwell, for the scientists, for the British, for Fuchs, and for everybody else. There were other visitors, too, all of whom had been undermined in some way by this treachery, and perhaps these painful meetings were the most salutary things that could have happened to Fuchs. For they must have revealed to him that there are people in the world who are always moved by distress, and who still regard friendship as a tie, even when it has been rejected and betrayed.

They found him humble, and ready to be reviled. He was not demoralized, but he had no defenses left. He expected only punishment. One of his women friends saw him in Brixton before the trial, when he was still entitled to wear his own clothes, and could buy cigarettes and receive gifts, but she was appalled that he should be in prison at all. She asked him, "Where are you sleeping, what are you getting to eat, what is it like?"

He answered, "It's not bad. Old [here he named an acquaintance who had luxurious tastes] would have died a thousand deaths. But it's not bad."

After the trial, when he saw that his friends had not deserted him, he continued to write to them. He said that Curtis-Bennett and others had spoken to him a great deal about arrogance. But was there nothing between abasement and arrogance? Was there no sort of self-respect that he could hope for now, after what had happened? Any schoolboy might have told Klaus Fuchs a great deal about self-respect and arrogance, but this is not a subject that is easy to learn—as Fuchs himself saw—at the age of thirty-eight. It is even impossible to learn if one remains fixed in the belief that the individual will is a law to itself and that one's conscience must be one's guide no matter what harm one does to anybody else. In Fuchs's book there had been no allowance for the fact that one's conscience may be shining bright while his ignorance of what is right and wrong may be appalling. Truth had fallen down a deep well between the two selves he had created for himself, and it is still to be wondered whether Fuchs has yet succeeded in dredging it up again.

In the gloom of prison, Fuchs began to compose poetry, in English, and with a Tennysonian flavor. He wrote much and posted the results off to his friends. Of his own case he wrote less and less. What else was there to say?

To Henry Arnold, the security officer at Harwell, his attitude was: "Don't blame yourself that I deceived you. Blame Stalin, Lenin, Marx, and all the other Communists. I was learning affection at Harwell. I was already changing. I was beginning to see the deep-rooted firmness of the English, and their decent way of life. I would have come to you in the end, whatever happened, and I would have told you what I had done."

Fuchs had a deep regard for Arnold. The relationship between the two men is, indeed, an interesting study in the field of counterespionage. Arnold from the first had had a general reservation in his mind about Fuchs. It hardly amounted to a suspicion; he simply felt that if anyone at Harwell was betraying secrets, then it was more likely to be Fuchs than anybody else. So, from 1946 onward, he deliberately cultivated Fuchs's friendship. At first Fuchs did not respond very eagerly, and it was Arnold who had to make all the approaches.

Then, little by little, Fuchs began to come around, and by 1949 a genuine intimacy had grown up between them.

By then Fuchs wanted to accept Arnold's friendship *in toto* and come over to his side. But he could not bring himself to make an open avowal to his friend of the appalling things he had done. This was the point where Arnold handed him over to Skardon; and Fuchs, no doubt, found it a good deal easier to confess to a stranger whom he had not personally betrayed.

Now that it was all over, Fuchs began to discover that Arnold had no personal bitterness against him. It was Arnold who wound up Fuchs's estate at Harwell. He sold the gray MG sedan. He disposed of the furniture, the clothes, and the books in prefab number seventeen; he settled Fuchs's debts and deposited for him the three or four hundred pounds that were left. One thing, however, Arnold could not bring himself to sell or keep was a prisoner's uniform with a patch on the back that Fuchs had worn as an internee in Canada. He had kept it all these years in a trunk under his bed. Arnold wrote to Fuchs in prison and told him he proposed to burn it. Fuchs indifferently agreed, and that was one more bit of the past that was gone for good.

The Fuchs case was considered just once again at a public hearing in December 1950, when the Deprivation of Citizenship Committee debated on whether Fuchs should be deprived of his British citizenship. Fuchs did not exercise his right to appear before the committee, nor was he represented. But he presented a letter in which he argued that there could be little doubt as to where his loyalties now lay. If his citizenship was to be taken away from him as a punishment, then he had nothing to say, even though he was already serving the maximum sentence. But he did suggest that the opinion of MI-5 and the director of public prosecutions should be obtained. He had made his confession, he said, of his own free will. He had cooperated loyally with MI-5 and the FBI since his arrest, and he had done this without any threat or promise having been made to him.

Fuchs very much wanted to retain his citizenship. It was clear that he felt that here in England his loyalties had become fixed at last. When he heard that the authorities were bound by the law, and that they were determined on taking his nationality away, he did not press the matter, but he was much distressed. The order went through and was published in the London *Gazette* in February 1951.

These were among the last contacts Fuchs had from prison with the outside world. He remained at Stafford jail, something of a celebrity among the other prisoners, but with no substantial differences in privileges or treatment. He corresponded less and less with his friends as he sank back into a world where there is no free will, and where the conscience is supplanted by steel bars. He was liked by the other prisoners. Those who emerged from jail spoke of his quietness, and of his generosity in sharing his cigarettes.

It is a remarkable thing that nearly all the people who came into contact with Fuchs for the first time during the period of his arrest and his trial thought him very reasonable. Those who knew nothing of his work as a physicist still respected him for his serious intelligence in other matters, and some of them grew to like him very much. It is perhaps all too easy to find virtues in a broken man, for no one need be jealous of him any longer. Napoleon on Elba is a much more sympathetic figure than Napoleon at Austerlitz.

Klaus Fuchs leaving for East Germany, June 1959

But at the time of the trial, and for long afterward, it seemed to many ordinary people that treason had come much closer to their lives than it had ever done before. In the phrase of Rebecca West, "a vast gap had been knocked in the hedge," and who among us was going to be able to trust anyone else, entirely, ever again? In other words, Fuchs had committed the crime society is least able to forgive: he had made society distrust itself. And for that he was hated.

AFTERWORD

Fuchs got a remission of his prison sentence for good behavior. He emerged from Stafford jail in June 1959, after serving only nine years, and at once flew to East Germany. Here he was met by his eighty-five-year-old father, with whom he went to live in Leipzig. To journalists who questioned him, he said he was still a Marxist, and that he was in the process of becoming an East German citizen. In September 1959 it was announced that he had been appointed deputy director of the East German Central Institute for Nuclear Research near Dresden, where a research reactor was being built with Soviet assistance. At the same time he revealed that he had married Frau Greta Keilson, the widow of the former head of the East German Foreign Ministry Press Department. They had first met in Paris when they were both refugees from Nazi Germany.

In 1960 Fuchs was visited by an American journalist in his comfortable villa which overlooks the city of Dresden. He was wearing the East German Communist Party badge in his lapel, and said that he had never left the Party but had simply lost touch with it during the war.

Looking back on his espionage, he said that he "would do it again." He appeared to be engrossed in his work, which was concerned mostly with the development of industrial atomic energy, and he deplored the fact that there was not a fuller exchange of information in this field, especially with America.

It may be, of course, that Fuchs was bound to reaffirm his loyalty to Communism in order to obtain and continue with his job, and that secretly he has a nostalgia for the West. Perhaps he dreams of the day when the West will join hands with Russia to form a common front against China, and thus his private ambivalence will be forgotten and forgiven. But who knows? Perhaps the safest guess is that for the time being he has had enough commotion in his life and now only wishes to continue with his chosen work as a private citizen.

THE SPY WHO CAME
IN FROM THE COLD

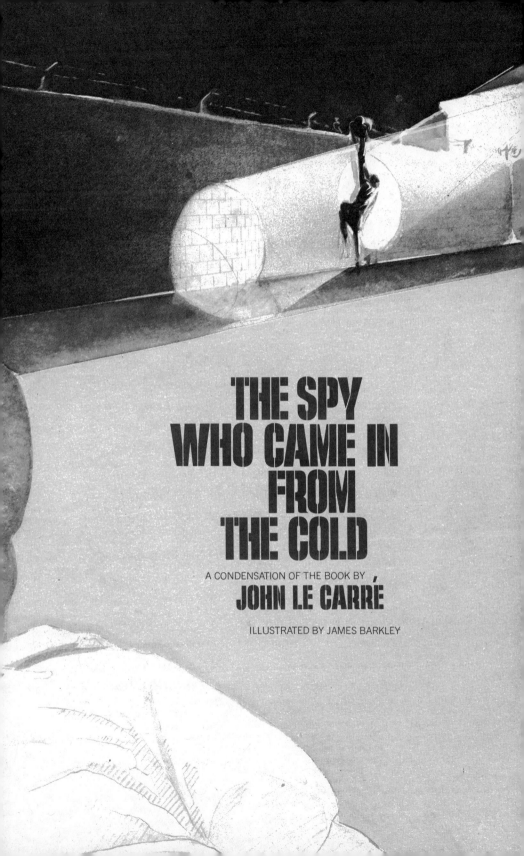

THE SPY WHO CAME IN FROM THE COLD

A CONDENSATION OF THE BOOK BY

JOHN LE CARRÉ

ILLUSTRATED BY JAMES BARKLEY

"We do disagreeable things so that ordinary people can sleep safely in their beds at night," says the head of British Intelligence in *The Spy Who Came In From the Cold*—for in the field of espionage, the cold war ceases to be cold and is fought remorselessly by both sides. In this case the "disagreeable thing" is a fiendishly subtle murder plan, the unfolding of which will keep the reader rapt and guessing until the very end.

John le Carré's masterly novel was a publishing sensation—that almost unheard-of thing, a suspense story that became a number one best seller. A onetime British diplomat as well as an intelligence officer in Austria, the author tells his story with gripping realism and authority. Mr. le Carré is also the author of such books as *The Looking Glass War* and *A Small Town in Germany*.

1

THE AMERICAN HANDED Leamas another cup of coffee and said, "Why don't you go back and sleep? We can ring you if he shows up."

Leamas said nothing, just stared through the window of the Western checkpoint, along the empty street toward the East German sector of Berlin.

"You can't wait forever, sir. Maybe he'll come some other time. We can have the *Polizei* contact you; you can be back here in twenty minutes."

"No," said Leamas, "it's nearly dark now."

"But he's nine hours over schedule."

"If you want to go, go. You've been very good."

"But how long will you wait?"

"Until he comes." Leamas walked to the observation window and stood between the two motionless policemen. Their binoculars were trained on the Eastern checkpoint. "He's waiting for the dark," Leamas muttered. "I know he is."

"This morning you said he'd come across with the workmen," the American, a CIA man, said.

Leamas turned on him. "Agents aren't airplanes. They don't have schedules. Someone's blown him. He's on the run, he's frightened. Mundt's after him, now, at this moment. He's got only one chance. Let him choose his time."

The younger man hesitated, wanting to go and not finding the moment.

A warning bell rang inside the hut. They waited, suddenly alert. One of the watching policemen said in German, "Black Opel Rekord, Federal registration." Then he left the hut and walked to the sandbag emplacement two feet short of the white boundary demarcation which lay across the road like the base line of a tennis court.

The other policeman waited until his companion was crouched behind the telescope in the emplacement, then put down his binoculars and carefully adjusted his black helmet on his head. Somewhere high above the checkpoint the arc lights sprang to life, casting theatrical beams onto the road through the Wall.

The policeman began his commentary in German: "Car halts at the first control. Only one occupant, a woman. Escorted to the Vopo hut for document check."

"What's he saying?" said the American. Leamas didn't reply. Picking up a spare pair of binoculars, he gazed fixedly toward the East German controls.

"Document check completed. Admitted to the second control."

"Is that your man?" the American asked Leamas. "I ought to ring the agency."

"Wait."

"Where's the car now? What's it doing?"

"Currency check, customs," Leamas snapped.

Leamas watched the car. There were two Vopos—*Volkspolizei,* or People's Police—at the driver's door, one doing the talking. A third was sauntering around the car. He stopped at the trunk, then walked back to the driver. He wanted the key. He opened the trunk, looked inside, closed it, returned the key and walked thirty yards up the road to where, midway between the two opposing checkpoints, a solitary East German sentry was standing, a squat silhouette in boots and baggy trousers. The two stood together talking, self-conscious in the glare of the arc light.

With a perfunctory gesture the Vopos waved the car on. It reached the two men in the middle of the road and stopped again. They walked around the car, stood off and talked; finally, almost unwillingly, they let it continue across the line to the Western sector.

Pushing up the collar of his jacket, Leamas stepped outside into the icy wind. He saw the usual small crowd of onlookers on the West Berlin side. It was something you forgot inside the hut, this group of puzzled faces. The people changed but the expressions were the same. It was like the helpless crowd that gathers around a traffic accident, no one knowing whether you should move the body.

Leamas walked over to the car and said to the woman in it, "Where is he?"

"They came for him and he ran. He took the bicycle. They can't have known about me."

"Where did he go?"

"We had a room near the Brandenburg Gate. I think he'll have gone there. Then he'll come over."

"Tonight?"

"He said he'd come tonight. The others have all been caught— Paul, Viereck, Ländser. He hasn't got long."

Leamas stared at her. "Ländser too?"

"Last night."

One of the policemen from the hut came up to Leamas. "You'll have to move away from here," he said. "It's forbidden to obstruct the crossing point."

Leamas half turned. "Go to hell," he snapped.

The German stiffened, but the woman said, "Get in. We'll drive down to the corner."

He got in beside her and they drove slowly until they reached a side road.

"I didn't know you had a car," he said.

"It's my husband's," she replied indifferently. "Karl never told you I was married, did he?" Leamas was silent. "My husband and I work for an optical firm. They let us through the Wall to do business. Karl only told you my maiden name. He didn't want me to be mixed up with . . . you."

Leamas took a key from his pocket. "You'll want somewhere to stay," he said. His voice sounded flat. "There's an apartment in the Albrecht-Dürer-Strasse. Number twenty-eight A. You'll find everything you want. I'll telephone you when he comes."

"I'll stay here with you."

"I'm not staying here. There's no point in waiting now."

"But he's coming to this crossing point."

Leamas looked at her in surprise. "He told you that?"

"Yes. He knows one of the Vopos here, the son of his landlord. It may help. That's why he chose this route."

"And he told *you* that?"

"He trusts me. He told me everything."

"Good God!"

He gave her the key and went back to the hut, out of the cold. The policemen were muttering to each other as he entered; the older one scowled at him.

"I'm sorry I bawled you out," said Leamas. He rummaged in a tattered briefcase and produced a half bottle of whisky. With a nod the policeman accepted it, half filled three coffee mugs and topped them off with black coffee. The CIA man had gone.

Leamas asked, "What are your rules for shooting to protect a man coming over? A man on the run."

The younger policeman answered. "We can only give covering fire if the Vopos shoot into our sector."

The older man said, "We can't *really* give covering fire, Mr. . . ."

"Thomas," Leamas replied.

". . . Mr. Thomas. They tell us there'd be war if we did."

"It's nonsense," said the younger policeman, emboldened by the whisky. "If the Allies weren't here the Wall would be gone by now."

"So would Berlin," muttered the older man.

"I've got a man coming over tonight," said Leamas.

"Here? At this crossing point?"

"It's worth a lot to get him out. Mundt's men are looking for him."

"There are still places where you can climb," said the younger policeman.

"He's not that kind. He'll bluff his way through; he's got papers, if they are still good. He's got a bicycle."

There was only one light in the hut—a reading lamp with a green shade; but the glow of the arc lights, like artificial moonlight, filled the cabin. Darkness had fallen. Leamas went to the window and waited. In front was the road, and to either side the Wall, a dirty, ugly thing of cinder block and strands of barbed wire, lit with cheap yellow light, like the backdrop for a concentration camp. Both east and west of the Wall lay the unrestored part of Berlin, a half-world of ruin.

That damned woman, thought Leamas, and that fool Karl, who'd lied about her. Lied by omission, as agents do the world over. You teach them to cheat, to cover their tracks, and they cheat you as well. He'd only produced her once, after that dinner last spring. Karl had just had his big scoop, and the head man from London—"Operational Control," whom they called simply Control—had wanted to meet him. Control always came in on success. They'd had dinner together—Leamas, Control and Karl. Karl had turned up looking like a Sunday-school boy, scrubbed and shining, doffing his hat and all respectful.

Control had shaken his hand for five minutes and said, "I want you to know how pleased we are, Karl. Damn pleased."

When they'd finished dinner Control pumped their hands again and, implying that he had to go off and risk his life somewhere else, got back into his chauffeur-driven car. Then Karl had laughed, and Leamas had laughed with him, and they'd finished the champagne, still laughing. Later they'd gone to the Alter Fass; Karl had insisted on it, and there Elvira was waiting for them, a forty-year-old blonde, tough as nails.

"This is my best-kept secret, Alec," Karl had said, and Leamas was furious. Afterward they'd had a row.

"How much does she know? Who is she? How did you meet her?"

Karl had sulked and refused to answer. "If you don't trust her, it's too late anyway," he'd said, and Leamas took the hint and shut up. But he went carefully after that, told Karl much less, used more of the hocus-pocus of espionage technique. And there she was, out there in her car, knowing everything, the whole network, the safe house, everything; and Leamas swore, not for the first time, never to trust an agent again.

"Look, Herr Thomas!" the young policeman whispered. "A man with a bicycle."

Leamas picked up the binoculars.

It was Karl—the figure was unmistakable even at that distance—shrouded in an old Wehrmacht mackintosh, pushing his bicycle. He's made it, thought Leamas. He's through the document check; only currency and customs to go.

Leamas watched Karl lean his bicycle against the railing, walk casually to the customs hut. Don't overdo it, he thought. At last

Karl came out, waved cheerfully to the man on the barrier, and the red-and-white pole swung slowly upward. He was through, he was coming toward them, he had made it. Only the Vopo in the middle of the road, the zone line—and safety.

At that moment Karl seemed to hear some sound, sense some danger; he glanced over his shoulder and began to pedal furiously, bending low over the handlebars. There was still the lonely sentry on the road; he had turned and was watching Karl. Then, totally unex-

pected, the searchlights went on, white and brilliant, catching Karl and holding him in their beam like a rabbit in the headlights of a car. There was the seesaw wail of a siren, the sound of orders wildly shouted. In front of Leamas the two policemen dropped to their knees, peering through the sandbagged slits, deftly flicking the rapid load on their automatic rifles.

The East German sentry fired, quite carefully, away from them, into his own sector. The first shot seemed to thrust Karl forward, the second to pull him back. Somehow he was still moving, still on the bicycle, passing the sentry, and the sentry was still shooting at him. Then he sagged, rolled to the ground, and they heard the clatter of the bike as it fell. Leamas hoped to God he was dead.

EAMAS WAS A SHORT man with close-cropped, iron-gray hair, and the physique of a swimmer. His great strength was discernible in his shoulders, in his neck, in the stubby hands and fingers. He had an attractive muscular face, with brown eyes and a stubborn line to his mouth. He was Irish, some said, but it was hard to place Leamas. If he were to walk into a London club, the porter would certainly not mistake him for a member, but in a Berlin nightclub they usually gave him the best table. Now, in his plane seat, watching the Tempelhof runway sink beneath him, he looked like a man who could make trouble.

The stewardess thought he was interesting. She guessed that he was fifty, which was about right, and rich, which he was not. She guessed he was single, which was half true. Somewhere long ago there had been a divorce; somewhere there were children, now in their teens.

Leamas was not a reflective man. He knew he was written off by his superiors—it was a fact of life with which he must now live, as a man lives with cancer or imprisonment. He met failure as one day he would probably meet death, with cynical resentment and the courage of a solitary. He'd lasted longer than most; now he was beaten, and it was Mundt who had beaten him.

Ten years ago he could have taken the other path—a desk job in that anonymous government building in Cambridge Circus; but he wasn't made that way. You might as well have asked a jockey to become a betting clerk as expect Leamas to abandon operational life for the offices of what they called simply the Circus. He had stayed on in Berlin, conscious that Personnel had marked his file for review at the end of every year: stubborn, willful, contemptuous of instruction. Intelligence work has one moral law—it is justified by results. Leamas got results. Until Mundt came.

It was odd how soon Leamas had realized that Mundt was the writing on the wall.

Hans-Dieter Mundt, born forty-two years ago in Leipzig. Leamas knew his dossier, knew the photograph on the inside of the cover, the blank, hard face beneath the flaxen hair; knew by heart the story of Mundt's rise to power as deputy director and effective head of operations of the East German Intelligence Department, known to agents simply as the department—the Abteilung.

Until 1959 Mundt had been a minor functionary of the Abteilung, operating in London under the cover of the East German Steel Mission. He returned to Germany in a hurry after murdering two of his own agents to save his skin and was not heard of for more than a year. Quite suddenly he reappeared at the Abteilung's headquarters in Leipzig as head of the Ways and Means Department—responsible for allocating currency, equipment and personnel for special tasks. At the end of that year came the big struggle for power within the Abteilung. The number and influence of Soviet liaison officers were reduced, and two men emerged: Fiedler as head of counterintelligence, and Mundt as deputy director of the entire Abteilung.

Then the new style began. The first agent Leamas lost was a girl who had been used for courier jobs. Mundt's men shot her dead in the street as she left a West Berlin cinema. The police never found the murderer.

A month later a railroad porter in Dresden, a discarded agent in Peter Guillam's network, was found dead beside a railroad track. Soon after that, two members of another network under Leamas' control were arrested in the East Zone and summarily sentenced to death. So it went on: remorseless and unnerving.

And now they had Karl Riemeck, and Leamas was leaving Berlin without a single agent worth a farthing. Mundt had won.

FAWLEY, FROM PERSONNEL, met him at the airport and drove him to London. "Control's pretty cross about Karl," he said, looking sideways at Leamas.

Leamas nodded.

"How did it happen?" asked Fawley.

"He was shot. Mundt got him."

"Dead?"

"I should think so, by now. He should never have hurried; they couldn't have been sure. The Abteilung got to the checkpoint just after he'd been let through. They started the siren, and a Vopo shot him twenty yards short of the line."

"Poor devil."

"Precisely," said Leamas.

Fawley thought Leamas suspect, but if Leamas knew, he didn't care. Fawley was a man who belonged to clubs and wore their ties, and used his service rank in office correspondence. Leamas thought him a fool.

"Where do I go now?" Leamas asked. "On ice?"

"Better let Control tell you, old boy."

"Do you know?"

"Of course."

"Then why the hell don't you tell me?"

"Sorry, old man," Fawley replied.

Leamas very nearly lost his temper. Then he reflected that Fawley was probably lying anyway. "Well, tell me one thing. Have I got to look for a bloody flat in London?"

Fawley scratched his ear. "I don't think so, old man, no."

CONTROL SHOOK HIS HAND carefully, like a doctor feeling the bones. "You must be awfully tired," he said apologetically. "Do sit down." That same dreary, donnish voice.

Leamas sat down in a chair facing an electric heater with a bowl of water balanced on top of it.

"Do you find it cold?" Control asked, stooping over the heater, rubbing his hands together. He wore a cardigan under his black jacket, a shabby brown one. Leamas supposed Control's wife had knitted it; he remembered her, a stupid little woman called Mandy who seemed to think her husband was on the Coal Board.

"It's so dry, that's the trouble," Control continued. "Beat the cold and you parch the atmosphere. Just as dangerous." He went to the desk and pressed a button. "We'll try and get some coffee," he said. "My girl's on leave, that's the trouble. They've given me some new girl. It really is too bad."

He was shorter than Leamas remembered him, but otherwise just the same. The same affected detachment, the same horror of drafts, the same milk-and-water smile, the same elaborate diffidence and courtesy, the same adherence to a conventional code of behavior which he pretended to find ridiculous.

Control sat down, and there was a pause. Finally Leamas said, "Karl Riemeck's dead."

"Yes, indeed," Control declared, as if Leamas had made a good point. "It is very unfortunate. Most. I suppose that girl blew him—Elvira?"

"I suppose so." Leamas wasn't going to ask him how he knew about Elvira.

"How did you feel? When Riemeck was shot, I mean?"

Leamas shrugged. "I was bloody annoyed," he said.

Control put his head to one side and half closed his eyes. "Surely you felt more than that? Surely you were upset? That would be more natural."

"I was upset. Who wouldn't be?"

"Did you like Riemeck—as a man?"

"I suppose so," said Leamas helplessly. "There doesn't seem much point in going into it," he added.

"How did you spend the night, what was left of it, after Riemeck had been shot?"

"What are you getting at?" Leamas asked hotly.

"Riemeck was the last," Control reflected, "the last of a series of deaths. If my memory is right, it began with the girl they shot outside the cinema. Then there was the Dresden man, and the arrests at Jena. Now Paul, Viereck and Ländser—and finally Riemeck." He smiled deprecatingly. "That is quite a heavy rate of expenditure. I wondered if you'd had enough."

"What do you mean—enough?"

"I wondered whether you were tired. Burned out." There was a long silence.

"That's up to you," Leamas said at last.

"We try to live without sympathy, don't we? That's impossible of course. We act it to one another, all this hardness, but we aren't like that really. I mean, one can't be out in the cold all the time. One has to come in from the cold. Do you see what I mean?"

Leamas saw. "I can't talk like this, Control," he said at last. "What do you want me to do?"

"I want you to stay out in the cold a little longer." Leamas said nothing, so Control went on. "The ethic of our work is based on the assumption that we are never going to be aggressors. Do you think that's fair?"

Leamas nodded.

"Thus we do disagreeable things, but we are *defensive*. We do disagreeable things so that ordinary people can sleep safely in their beds at night. Is that too romantic? Of course, we occasionally do very wicked things." He grinned like a schoolboy. "But you can't be less ruthless than the opposition simply because your government's *policy* is benevolent, can you now?" He laughed quietly to himself. "That would *never* do."

Leamas was lost. This was like working for a bloody clergyman. He'd never heard anything like this from Control before. What *was* he up to?

"That is why," Control went on, "I think we ought to try and get rid of Mundt. . . . Oh really," he said, turning irritably toward the door, "where is that damned coffee?" He crossed to the door, opened it and talked to some unseen girl in the outer room. As he returned to his chair he said, "I really think we *ought* to get rid of him if we can manage it."

"Why? We've got nothing left in East Germany. Karl Riemeck was the last. We've nothing left to protect."

Control looked at his hands. "That is not altogether true," he said, "but I don't think I need to bore you with the details."

Leamas shrugged.

"Tell me," Control continued, "are you tired of spying? Forgive me if I repeat the question. We understand this here. You know, like aircraft—metal fatigue, I think the term is. If you are, we will have to find some other way of taking care of Mundt. What I have in mind is a little out of the ordinary."

The girl came in with the coffee and poured out two cups. Control waited till she had left the room. "Such a *silly* girl," he said, almost to himself. "It seems extraordinary they can't find good ones anymore." He stirred his coffee disconsolately for a while. "We really must discredit Mundt," he said. "Tell me, do you drink a lot? Whisky and that kind of thing?"

Leamas had thought he was used to Control. "I drink a bit," he said. "More than most."

Control nodded understandingly. "What do you know about Mundt?"

"I know he's a killer; that when he was here with the East German Steel Mission he was in charge of an agent, the wife of that Foreign Office man—Fennan. He killed her."

"And he tried to kill George Smiley. And of course he shot Fennan too. He is an ex-Nazi; very distasteful man. Now George Smiley knew the Fennan Case well. He isn't with us anymore, but I think you ought to ferret him out. He lives in Chelsea. Bywater Street, do you know it?"

"Yes."

"And Peter Guillam was on the case as well. He's in Satellites Four, on the first floor now. Spend a day or two with them; they know what I have in mind. Then I wondered if you'd care to stay with me for the weekend. My wife," he added hastily, "is looking after her mother, I'm afraid. It will be just you and I."

"Thanks. I'd like to."

"We can talk about things in comfort then. It would be very nice. I think you might make a lot of money out of it. You can have whatever you make."

"Thanks."

"That is, of course, if you're *sure you want to*. No metal fatigue or anything?"

"If it's a question of killing Mundt, I'm game."

"Do you really feel that?" Control inquired politely. And then, having looked at Leamas thoughtfully, he observed, "Yes, I really think you do. But you mustn't feel you *have* to say it. I mean, in our world we pass so quickly out of hate or love. All that's left in the end is a kind of nausea; you never want to cause suffering again. Forgive me, but isn't that rather what you felt when Karl Riemeck was shot? Not hate for Mundt, nor love for Karl, but a sickening jolt like a blow on a numb body? They tell me you walked all night—just walked through the streets of Berlin. Is that right?"

"It's right that I went for a walk."

"All night?"

"Yes."

"What happened to Elvira?"

"God knows. I'd like to take a swing at Mundt," he said.

"Good . . . good. Incidentally, if you should meet any old friends in the meantime, I don't think there's any point in discussing this with them. In fact," Control added, "I should be rather short with them. Let them think we've treated you badly. It's as well to begin as one intends to continue, isn't it?"

IT SURPRISED NO ONE very much when they put Leamas on the shelf. Berlin had been a failure for years, they said, and someone had to take the rap. Besides, he was old for operational work, where your reflexes often had to be as quick as a professional tennis player's. Leamas had done good work in Norway and Holland in the war, everyone knew that. And at the end of it they gave him a medal and let him go. Later, of course, they got him to come back.

It was bad luck about his pension. Elsie in Accounts section had let it out. She said in the canteen that poor Alec Leamas would only have four hundred pounds a year to live on, because of his interrupted service. Elsie felt the rule ought to be changed; after all, Mr. Leamas had *done* the service, hadn't he?

Leamas' contract had a few months to run, and they put him in Banking to do his time. Banking section was different from Accounts; it dealt with overseas payments, financing agents and operations. Most of the jobs could have been done by an office boy were it not for the high degree of secrecy involved. Banking was regarded as a laying-out place for officers shortly to be buried.

Leamas went to seed. In the full view of his colleagues he was transformed into a resentful, drunken wreck—and all within a few months. There is a kind of stupidity among drunks, particularly when they are sober—a kind of disconnection which the unobservant interpret as vagueness and which Leamas seemed to acquire with unnatural speed. He developed small dishonesties, borrowed insignificant sums from secretaries and neglected to return them, arrived late or left early under some mumbled pretext. At first his colleagues treated him with indulgence; perhaps his decline scared them in the same way as we are scared by cripples because we fear we could ourselves become like them. But in the end his neglect, his brutal, unreasoning malice, isolated him.

To people's surprise, Leamas didn't seem to mind being put on the shelf. His will seemed suddenly to have collapsed. The young secretaries, reluctant to believe that intelligence services are peopled by ordinary mortals, were alarmed to notice that Leamas had become definitely seedy. He lunched in the canteen which was normally the preserve of junior staff, and it was obvious that he was drinking. He became a solitary, belonging to that tragic class of active men prematurely deprived of activity—swimmers barred from the water or actors banished from the stage.

Some said he had made a mistake in Berlin, and that was why his network had been rolled up; no one quite knew. All agreed that he had been treated with unusual harshness, even by a personnel department not famed for its philanthropy. They would point to him covertly as he went by, as men will point to an athlete of the past, and say, "That's Leamas. He made a mistake in Berlin. Pathetic, the way he's let himself go."

And then one day, before the termination of his contract, he vanished. He said good-by to no one, not even, apparently, Control. In itself that was not surprising; the nature of the service precluded elaborate farewells and the presentation of gold watches. But even by these standards Leamas' departure seemed abrupt. Elsie, of Accounts, offered two crumbs of information: Leamas had drawn the balance of his pay in cash, which, if Elsie knew anything, meant he was having trouble with his bank. And his severance pay was to be paid at the turn of the month. She couldn't say how much, but it wasn't four figures, poor lamb.

Then there was the story about the money. It leaked out—no one, as usual, knew from where—that Leamas' sudden departure was connected with irregularities in the accounts of Banking section. A largish sum was missing, and they'd gotten back nearly all of it and stuck a lien on his pension. Some didn't believe it. If Alec had wanted to rob the till, they said, he'd know better ways of doing it than fiddling with those accounts. But others pointed at his large consumption of alcohol, at the expense of maintaining a separate household, and above all at the temptations put in the way of a man handling large sums of hot money when he knew that his days in the service were numbered. All agreed that if Alec Leamas had dipped his hands in the till he was finished for all time. Personnel would give him no reference, or one so icy that any employer would shiver at the sight of it.

For a week or two after his departure a few people wondered what had become of him. But his former friends had already learned to keep clear of him. He had become a resentful bore, constantly attacking the service and its administration. He never missed an opportunity of railing at the Americans and their intelligence agencies. He seemed to hate them more than the Abteilung, and he would hint that it was they who had compromised his network. This seemed to be an obsession with him, and it was poor reward for attempts to console him; it made him bad company, so that those who had known and even liked him, wrote him off. Leamas' departure caused only a ripple on the water, and was soon forgotten.

HIS FLAT WAS SMALL AND SQUALID, done in brown paint, and looked directly onto the gray back of a stone warehouse. Above the warehouse lived an Italian family, quarreling at night and beating carpets in the morning. Leamas had few possessions with which to brighten his rooms. He bought a shade for the lamp, and two pairs of sheets to replace the coarse cotton squares provided by the landlord. The rest he tolerated: the threadbare curtains, the fraying carpet, like something from a seaman's hotel.

He needed a job. He had no money at all, so perhaps the stories of embezzlement were true. A firm of adhesive manufacturers seemed unconcerned by the inadequate reference with which the service provided him, and offered him the post of personnel officer. He stayed for a week, by which time the foul stench of decaying fish oil had so permeated his clothes and hair that he had to throw away two suits and have his hair cut short to the scalp. He spent another week trying to sell encyclopedias to suburban housewives, but he was not a man whom housewives liked or understood. Night after night he returned wearily to his flat, his ridiculous sample under his arm.

At the end of a week he telephoned the company and told them he had sold nothing. Expressing no surprise, they reminded him of his obligation to return the sample. He stalked out of the telephone booth in a fury, leaving the sample behind, went to a pub in Bayswater and got drunk. They threw him out for shouting at a woman who tried to pick him up. They were beginning to know him there.

They were beginning to know his gray, shambling figure everywhere in Bayswater. Not a wasted word did he speak, not a friend did he have. They guessed he was in trouble—run away from his wife, like as not. He never knew the price of anything, never remembered it when he was told. He patted all his pockets whenever he looked for change; he never remembered to bring a basket, always buying shopping bags. They didn't like him, though they were almost sorry for him; he was dirty, the way he didn't shave weekends and his shirts all grubby. A Mrs. McCaird cleaned for him for a time, but having never received a civil word from him withdrew her labor.

She was an important source of information for the tradesmen, who told one another what they needed to know in case he asked for credit. Mrs. McCaird's advice was against credit. Leamas was known to drink like a fish. He never had a letter, she said, and they agreed that that was serious. It was her opinion he had a bit to live on, and that that bit was running out. She knew he drew his unemployment benefit on Thursdays. Bayswater was warned and needed no second warning.

4

FINALLY HE TOOK the job in the library. The Labour Exchange put him on to it each Thursday morning as he drew his benefit. He'd always turned it down. "It's not really your cup of tea," Mr. Pitt said, "but the pay's fair and the work's easy for an educated man."

"What sort of library?" Leamas asked.

"It's the Bayswater Library for Psychic Research. An endowment. They've got thousands of volumes, all sorts, and they've been left a whole lot more. They want another helper," Mr. Pitt said. "They're an odd lot, but I think it's time you gave them a try, don't you?"

It was odd about Pitt. Leamas was certain he'd seen him before. At the Circus, during the war.

The library was like a church hall, and very cold. The oil stoves at either end made it smell of kerosene. In the middle, in a cubicle like a witness box, sat Miss Crail, the librarian.

"I'm the new assistant," he told her. "My name's Leamas." He pushed a form across the counter, with his particulars on it. She picked it up and studied it.

"You are Mr. Leamas." This was not a question, but the first stage of a laborious fact-finding investigation. "And you are from the Labour Exchange."

"Yes. They told me you needed an assistant."

"I see." A wooden smile.

At that moment the telephone rang; she lifted the receiver and began arguing with somebody, fiercely. Leamas drifted toward the bookshelves. He noticed a girl in one of the alcoves, standing on a ladder sorting large volumes. "I'm the new man," he said. "My name's Leamas."

She came down from the ladder and shook his hand a little formally. "I'm Liz Gold. Have you met Miss Crail?"

"Yes, but she's on the phone at the moment."

"Arguing with her mother, I expect. What will you do?"

"I don't know. I haven't done this kind of thing before."

"We're marking just now; Miss Crail's started a new index."

She was a tall girl, with a long waist and long legs. She wore flat shoes to reduce her height, and her face, like her body, had large components which seemed to hesitate between plainness and beauty. Leamas guessed she was twenty-two or -three, and Jewish.

"It's just a question of checking that all the books are on the shelves," she said. "When you've checked, you pencil in the new reference and mark it off on the index."

"What happens then?"

"Only Miss Crail's allowed to ink in the reference. It's the rule."

"Whose rule?"

"Miss Crail's. Why don't you start on the archaeology?"

Leamas nodded, and they walked to the next alcove, where a shoe box full of cards lay on the floor. She left him there, and after a moment's hesitation he took out a book. It was called *Archaeological Discoveries in Asia Minor. Volume Four.* They seemed to have only volume four.

By one o'clock Leamas was very hungry. He walked over to Liz Gold and said, "What happens about lunch?"

"Oh, I bring sandwiches." She looked a little embarrassed. "You can have some of mine. There's no café for miles."

Leamas shook his head. "I'll go out, thanks."

It was half past two when he came back. He smelled of whisky. He put two shopping bags in a corner of the alcove and wearily began marking the archaeology books. About ten minutes later he became aware that Miss Crail was watching him.

"*Mister* Leamas."

He was halfway up the ladder, so he looked down over his shoulder and said, "Yes?"

"Do you know where these shopping bags come from?"

"They're mine."

"They are yours." Leamas waited. "I regret," she said at last, "that we do not allow shopping bags in the library."

"There's nowhere else I can put them."

"If you took the normal lunch break, you would not have time to shop. Neither Miss Gold nor I do."

"Why don't you two take an extra half hour?" Leamas asked. "You could work another half hour in the evening."

She watched him for some moments, obviously thinking of something to say. Finally she announced, "I shall discuss it with Mr. Ironside," and went away.

At exactly half past five Miss Crail put on her coat and, with a pointed "Good night, Miss Gold," left. Leamas went into the next alcove, where Liz was sitting on the bottom rung of her ladder reading what looked like a tract. When she saw Leamas she dropped it guiltily into her handbag and stood up.

"Who's Mr. Ironside?" Leamas asked.

"He's her big gun when she's stuck for an answer. I asked her once who he was. She went mysterious and said, 'Never mind.' I don't think he exists."

"I'm not sure Miss Crail does," said Leamas, and Liz Gold smiled.

At six o'clock she locked up. It was cold outside.

"Got far to go?" asked Leamas.

"Twenty-minute walk. I always walk. Do you?"

"I'm not far off," said Leamas. "Good night."

He walked slowly back to the flat, let himself in and turned the light switch. Nothing happened. On the doormat was a letter. He picked it up and took it out into the pale yellow light of the staircase.

It was the electricity company, regretting that it had no alternative but to cut off the electricity until the outstanding account had been settled.

By the next day Miss Crail had developed such an intense hatred for Leamas that she found it impossible to communicate with him. Either she scowled at him or she ignored him, and when he came close she began to tremble, looking to left and right, either for something with which to defend herself or perhaps for a line of escape.

Occasionally she would take immense umbrage, such as when he hung his mackintosh on *her* peg. She quivered all that day, and conducted a telephone call in a stage whisper for half the morning. "She's telling her mother," said Liz. "She always tells her mother. She tells her about me too."

On paydays he would come back from lunch and find an envelope on the third rung of his ladder with his name misspelled on the outside. The first time it happened he took the money over to her with the envelope. "It's L-e-a, Miss Crail," he said, "and only one s." Whereupon she was seized with a veritable palsy, rolling her eyes and fumbling erratically with her pencil until Leamas went away. She conspired into the telephone for hours after that.

About three weeks after Leamas began work at the library Liz asked him to supper. She pretended it was an idea that had come to her quite suddenly, at five o'clock that evening; she seemed to realize that if she were to ask him for tomorrow or the next day he would forget or just not come. Leamas seemed reluctant to accept, but in the end he did.

They walked to her flat through the rain, and they might have been anywhere—Berlin, London, any town where paving stones turn to lakes of light in the evening rain and the traffic shuffles despondently through wet streets.

Her flat was a bed-sitting-room and kitchen. This was the first of many meals that Leamas had there. When she discovered he would come, she asked him often. She took to setting the table in the morning before leaving for the library, even putting the candles on the table, for she loved candlelight. Leamas never spoke much, and she always knew that there was something deeply wrong with him; that one day, for some reason she could not understand, he might break, and she would never see him again. She tried to tell him she knew this. She said, "You must go when you want. I'll never follow you, Alec."

His brown eyes rested on her for a moment. "I'll tell you when," he replied.

After supper he would lie on the sofa. She would kneel there, holding his hand against her cheek, talking. One evening she said, "Alec, what do you believe in? Don't laugh—tell me."

She waited and at last he said, "I believe a number-eleven bus will take me to Hammersmith. I don't believe it's driven by Father Christmas."

"You must believe in something," she persisted. "Something like God. I know you do, Alec; you've got that look sometimes, as if you'd got something special to do, like a priest. Alec, don't smile, it's true."

He shook his head, not smiling. "Sorry, Liz. I don't like conversations about life."

"But, Alec—"

"And I should have added," Leamas interrupted, "that I don't like people who tell me what I ought to think." She knew he was getting angry but she couldn't stop herself anymore.

"That's because you don't *want* to think. You don't dare! There's some poison in your mind, some hate. You're like a man who's . . . sworn vengeance or something."

The brown eyes rested on her again. When he spoke she was frightened by the menace in his voice. "If I were you," he said roughly, "I'd mind my own business." And then he smiled, a roguish Irish smile. Liz knew he was putting on the charm. "What does Liz believe in?" he asked.

"I can't be had that easy, Alec," she replied.

Later Leamas himself brought it up again. He asked whether she was religious.

"You've got me wrong," she said. "I don't believe in God."

"Then what do you believe in?"

"History."

He looked at her in astonishment, then laughed.

"Oh, Liz—oh, *no! You're not a bloody Communist?"

She nodded, blushing like a small girl at his laughter, angry but relieved that he didn't care.

That night they became lovers. She couldn't understand it; she was so proud and he seemed ashamed.

When he left her flat it was foggy. Twenty yards down the road stood a man in a raincoat, short and rather plump. He was leaning against the park railings, silhouetted in the shifting mist. As Leamas approached, the mist seemed to thicken, closing in around the figure, and when it parted the man was gone.

ONE DAY, about a week later, Leamas didn't come to the library. Miss Crail was delighted; she stood in front of the archaeology shelves where he had been working and stared with theatrical concentration at the rows of books. Liz knew she was pretending to work out whether Leamas had stolen anything.

Liz entirely ignored her for the rest of that day, and worked assiduously. When the evening came she walked home and cried herself to sleep.

The next morning she arrived early at the library. She somehow felt that the sooner she got there the sooner Leamas might come; but as the morning dragged on, her hopes faded, and she knew he would never come. She had forgotten to make sandwiches for herself, and she felt sick and empty, but not hungry. Should she go and find him? She had promised never to follow him, but he had promised to tell her before he left. At lunchtime she hailed a taxi and gave his address.

She made her way up the dingy staircase and pressed the bell of his door. The bell seemed to be broken; she heard nothing. There were three bottles of milk on the mat and a letter from the electricity company. She hesitated a moment, then banged on the door, and she heard a faint groan. She rushed downstairs and through a door, into the back room of a grocer's shop. An old woman sat in a corner, rocking back and forth.

"The upstairs flat," Liz almost shouted. "Somebody's very ill. Who's got a key?"

The old woman looked at her a moment, then called toward the shop. "Arthur, come in here. There's a girl here!"

A man in brown coveralls and a gray felt hat looked around the door and said, "Girl?"

"There's someone seriously ill in the upstairs flat," said Liz. "He can't get to his door. Have you a key?"

"No," replied the grocer, "but I've got a hammer." He fetched it, and they hurried up the stairs together. The grocer knocked on the door sharply. There was no answer.

"I know I heard a groan before," Liz said.

"Will you pay for this door if I bust it?"

"Yes. I promise."

The hammer made a terrible noise. With three blows he wrenched out a piece of the frame, and the lock came with it. Liz went in first and the grocer followed. It was bitterly cold in the room and dark, but on the bed in the corner they could make out the figure of a man.

Oh God, thought Liz, if he's dead I don't think I can touch him. Drawing the curtains, she knelt beside the bed. He was alive. "I'll call you if I need you, thank you," she said without looking back, and the grocer went downstairs.

"Alec, what's making you ill? What is it, Alec?"

Leamas moved his head. His sunken eyes were closed. The dark beard stood out against the pallor of his face.

"Alec, you must tell me. Please!" Tears were running down her cheeks. Desperately she wondered what to do; then, getting up, she ran to the tiny kitchen and put on a kettle. She wasn't quite clear what she would make, but it comforted her to do something. Leaving the kettle on the gas, she picked up her handbag and ran downstairs and out to the shops. She bought calf's-foot jelly, breast of chicken, beef extract, rusks and a bottle of aspirin. Altogether it cost her sixteen shillings, which left four shillings in her handbag and eleven pounds in her post-office savings. By the time she returned to his flat the kettle was boiling.

She made beef tea as her mother used to, in a glass with a teaspoon in it to stop its cracking; and all the time she glanced toward him as if she were afraid he was dead.

She had to prop him up to make him drink the tea. It frightened her to touch him; he was so drenched in sweat that his short gray hair was damp and slippery when she held his head. After he had taken a few spoonfuls of tea, she crushed two aspirins and gave them to him in the spoon. She talked to him as if he were a child, sitting by the bed, letting her fingers run over his head and face, whispering his

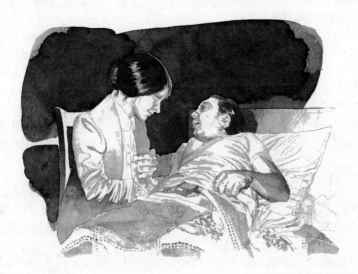

name over and over again. Gradually his breathing became more regular, his body more relaxed, as he drifted from the taut pain of fever to the calm of sleep. Liz sensed that the worst was over, and suddenly she realized it was almost dark.

Then she felt ashamed because she hadn't cleaned and tidied. Jumping up, she fetched the carpet sweeper and a dustcloth from the kitchen and set to work with feverish energy. She washed up the odd cups and saucers that lay around the kitchen. When everything was done she looked at her watch and it was half past eight. She put the kettle on again and went back to the bed. Leamas was looking at her.

"Alec, don't be cross!" she said. "I promise I'll go, but let me make you a proper meal. You're ill, you can't go on like this, you're— Oh, Alec!" and she broke down and wept, holding both hands over her face, the tears running between her fingers like a child's.

He let her cry, watching her with his brown eyes, his hands holding the sheet.

She helped him wash and shave, and found some clean bedclothes. She gave him some calf's-foot jelly and some breast of chicken from the jar she'd bought. She watched him eat, and she thought she had never been so happy before. Soon he fell asleep, and she drew the blanket over his shoulders.

Liz slept in the armchair and did not wake until it was nearly light, feeling stiff and cold. When she went to the bed, Leamas stirred as she looked at him, and she touched his lips with the tip of her finger. He did not open his eyes but gently took her arm and drew her down onto the bed, and then nothing else mattered, and she kissed him again and again and when she looked at him he seemed to be smiling.

SHE CAME EVERY DAY for six days. He never spoke to her much, and once, when she asked if he loved her, he said he didn't believe in fairy tales. She would lie on the bed, her head against his chest, and sometimes he would put his fingers in her hair, holding it quite tight, and Liz laughed and said it hurt.

On Friday evening she found him dressed but not shaved, and she wondered why he hadn't shaved. For some imperceptible reason she was alarmed. Little things were missing from the room—his clock and the cheap portable radio. She wanted to ask and did not dare.

She had bought eggs and ham, and she cooked them while Leamas sat on the bed and smoked one cigarette after another. When supper was ready Leamas went to the kitchen and came back with a bottle of red wine.

He hardly spoke at the table, and her fear grew until she could bear it no more and she cried out suddenly, "Alec . . . oh, Alec . . . what is it? Is it good-by?"

He got up, took her hands and kissed her in a way he'd never done before, and spoke to her softly for a long time, told her things she only dimly understood, only half heard, because all the time she knew it was the end and nothing mattered anymore.

"Good-by, Liz," he said. "Good-by," and then, "Don't follow me. Not again."

Liz nodded. She was thankful for the biting cold of the street and for the dark which hid her tears.

IT WAS THE NEXT MORNING, a Saturday, that Leamas asked at the grocer's for credit. He did it in a way not calculated to ensure him success. He ordered half a dozen items—they didn't cost more than a pound—and when they had been wrapped and put into a bag he said, "You'd better send me that account."

The grocer, remembering Mrs. McCaird's warning, smiled a difficult smile and said, "I'm afraid I can't do that." The "sir" was definitely missing.

"Why the hell not?" asked Leamas, and the line behind him stirred uneasily.

"Don't know you," replied the grocer.

"Don't be bloody silly," said Leamas. "I've been coming here for months."

The grocer colored. "We always ask for a banker's reference before giving credit," he said, and Leamas lost his temper.

"Don't talk bloody tripe!" he shouted. "Half your customers have never seen the inside of a bank and never will." This was heresy beyond bearing, since it was true.

"I don't know you," the grocer repeated thickly, "and I don't like you. Now get out of my shop!" And he tried to recover the bag which, unfortunately, Leamas was already holding.

Opinions later differed as to what happened next. Some said the grocer, in trying to recover the bag, pushed Leamas; others that he did not. Whether he did or not, Leamas hit him—most people think twice—without disengaging his right hand, which still held the bag. He seemed to deliver the blow not with his fist but with the side of his left hand, and then, as part of the same phenomenally rapid movement, with the left elbow; and the grocer fell straight over and lay as still as a rock.

It was said in court, and not contested by the defense, that the man had two injuries—a fractured cheekbone from the first blow and a dislocated jaw from the second. The coverage in the daily press was adequate, but it was not overelaborate.

5

A T NIGHT HE LAY on his bunk listening to the prisoners. There was a boy who sobbed and an old jailbird who sang "On Ilkla Moor," beating out the time on his food tin. There was a guard who shouted, "Shut up, George," after each verse, but no one took any notice.

Leamas exercised as much as he could during the day in the hope that he would sleep at night, but it was no good. At night you knew you were in prison; nothing could keep out the taste of prison, the smell of prison uniform, the stench of prison sanitation heavily disinfected, the noises of captive men. It was at night that the indignity of captivity became insufferable and that Leamas had to force back the urge to fall upon the bars with his bare fists, to split the skulls of his guards and burst into the free, free space of London. Sometimes he thought of Liz. He would recall for a moment the soft-hard touch of her long body, then put her from his memory. Leamas was not accustomed to living on dreams.

He was contemptuous of his cellmates, and they hated him because he succeeded in being what each in his heart longed to be: a mystery. New prisoners are largely of two kinds—those who for shame, fear or shock wait in fascinated horror to be initiated into the lore of prison life, and those who trade on their novelty to endear themselves to the community. Leamas did neither, and they hated him because, like the world outside, he did not need them.

After about ten days they had had enough, so they crowded him in the dinner lineup. Crowding is a prison ritual; it has the virtue of an apparent accident, in which the prisoner's mess tin is upturned and its contents spilled on his uniform. Leamas was pushed from one side while from the other a hand descended on his forearm, and the thing was done. Leamas said nothing, looked thoughtfully at the two men on either side of him, and accepted in silence the filthy rebuke of a guard who knew quite well what had happened.

Four days later, while working with a hoe on the prison flower bed, he seemed to stumble. He was holding the hoe with both hands across his body, the end of the handle protruding about six inches from his right fist. As he strove to recover his balance, the prisoner to his right doubled up with a grunt of agony, his arms across his stomach. There was no more crowding after that.

Perhaps the strangest thing of all about prison was the brown paper parcel when he left. They handed it to him and made him sign for it, and it contained all he had in the world. Leamas felt it the most dehumanizing moment of the prison term, and he determined to throw the parcel away as soon as he got outside.

"What are you going to do when you leave here?" the warden asked. Leamas replied, without a ghost of a smile, that he thought he would make a new start, and the warden said that was an excellent thing to do.

The probation officer wanted Leamas to become a male nurse at a mental home, and Leamas agreed to apply. He even took down the address.

So they gave him the parcel and he left. He took a bus to Marble Arch and walked through Hyde Park. He had a bit of money in his pocket, and he intended to give himself a decent meal.

London was beautiful that day. Spring was late, and the park was filled with crocuses. A cool, cleaning wind was blowing from the south; he could have walked all day. But he still had the parcel, and he had to get rid of it. The litter baskets were too small. He sat down on a bench and put the parcel beside him, not too close, and moved a little away from it. After a couple of minutes he walked back toward the footpath, leaving the parcel. He had just reached the path when he heard a shout; he turned, a little sharply perhaps, and saw a man in a raincoat, holding the brown paper parcel and beckoning to him.

Hands in his pockets, Leamas stood looking back over his shoulder. The man hesitated, evidently expecting Leamas to give some sign of interest, but Leamas gave none. Instead, he shrugged and continued along the footpath. He heard another shout and ignored it, and he knew the man was coming after him. There were footsteps on the gravel, half running, and then a voice, a little breathless, a little aggravated, "Here, you—I say!"

Leamas stopped, turned and looked at him. "Yes?"

"This is your parcel, isn't it? You left it on the bench. Why didn't you stop when I called you?"

Tall, with rather curly brown hair; orange tie and pale green shirt;

a little bit petulant, a bit effeminate, thought Leamas. Could be a schoolmaster. Weak-eyed.

"You can put it back," said Leamas. "I don't want it."

The man colored. "You can't just leave it there," he said. "It's litter."

"I bloody well can," Leamas replied. "Somebody will find a use for it." He was going to move on, but the stranger was standing in front of him. "Get out of the light," said Leamas. "Do you mind?"

"Look here," said the stranger, and his voice had risen a key, "I was trying to do you a favor; why do you have to be so damned rude?"

"If you're so anxious to do me a favor," Leamas replied, "why have you been following me for the last half hour?"

He's pretty good, thought Leamas. He hasn't flinched but he must be shaken rigid.

"I thought you were somebody I once knew in Berlin, if you must know."

"So you followed me for half an hour?" Leamas' voice was heavy with sarcasm; his brown eyes never left the other's face.

"Nothing like half an hour. I caught sight of you in Marble Arch and thought you were Alec Leamas, a man I borrowed some money from when I was with the BBC in Berlin. I've had a bad conscience about it ever since. That's why I followed you. I wanted to be sure."

Leamas went on looking at him and thought he wasn't all that good, but he was good enough. His story was scarcely plausible, but that didn't matter. The point was that he'd produced a new one and stuck to it after Leamas had wrecked what promised to be a classic approach.

"I'm Leamas," he said at last. "Who the hell are you?"

He said his name was Ashe, with an e, he added quickly, and Leamas knew he was lying. They went to Soho for lunch. Ashe pretended not to be quite sure that Leamas really was Leamas, so over drinks they opened the parcel and looked at his National Insurance card, like, thought Leamas, a couple of schoolboys looking at a dirty postcard. Ashe ordered lunch with just a fraction too little regard for expense, and they drank some Frankenwein to remind them of the old days in Berlin.

Leamas began by insisting he couldn't remember Ashe, and Ashe, in a hurt tone, said he was surprised. They met at a party Derek Williams gave in his flat off the Kurfürstendamm (he got that right), and all the press boys had been there; surely Alec remembered that? No, he did not. . . . Well, surely he remembered Derek Williams from the *Observer?* Leamas had a lousy memory for names, after all they were talking about '54. . . . Ashe (his Christian name was William, by the by, most people called him Bill) remembered *vividly.* They were all rather tiddly, and Derek had provided some really gorgeous girls, half the cabaret from the Malkasten, *surely* Alec remembered now? Leamas thought it was coming back to him, if Bill would go on a bit.

Bill did go on, ad lib no doubt, but he did it well, about how they'd finished up in a nightclub with three of these girls, and Bill had been so embarrassed because he hadn't any money on him and Alec had paid, and—

"Heavens!" said Leamas. "I remember now, of course I do."

"I *knew* you would," said Ashe happily, nodding at Leamas over his glass. "Look, do let's have the other half bottle, this is *such* fun."

Ashe conducted his human relationships according to a principle of challenge and response. Where there was softness, he would advance; where he found resistance, retreat. Having no particular opinions or tastes, he relied upon whatever conformed with those of his companion. To Leamas this passivity was repellent; it brought out the bully in him, and he would lead Ashe into a position where he was committed, and then himself withdraw, so that Ashe was constantly scampering back from some cul-de-sac into which Leamas had enticed him.

There were moments when Leamas was so brazenly perverse that Ashe would have been justified in terminating their conversation— especially since he was paying; but he did not. The little sad man with spectacles who sat alone at the neighboring table, deep in a book on the manufacture of ball bearings, might have deduced, had he been listening, that Leamas was indulging a sadistic nature; or perhaps, if he was a man of subtlety, that Leamas was proving to his own satisfaction that only a man with a strong ulterior motive would put up with that kind of treatment.

It was nearly four o'clock before they ordered the bill. Ashe paid it and took out his checkbook in order to settle his debt to Leamas.

"Twenty of the best," he said, and filled in the date on the check form. Then he looked up at Leamas, wide-eyed and accommodating. "I say, a check is all right with you, isn't it?"

Coloring a little, Leamas replied, "I haven't got a bank at the moment—only just back from abroad. But give me the check and I'll cash it at your bank."

"My dear chap, I wouldn't *dream* of putting you to that trouble!" Leamas shrugged, and they agreed to meet at the same place on the following day at one o'clock, when Ashe would have the cash.

Ashe took a cab at the corner of Old Compton Street. When the cab was out of sight Leamas looked at his watch. It was now four o'clock. He guessed he was still being followed, so he walked down to Fleet Street and had a cup of coffee in a café. He looked at bookshops, read the evening papers displayed in the show windows of newspaper offices and then quite suddenly, as if the thought had just occurred to him, he jumped on a bus. When the bus was held up in a traffic jam near a subway station, he dismounted and caught a train. He stood in the end car and got off at the next stop. He caught another train to Euston, trekked back to Charing Cross. It was dark when he reached the station. There was a van waiting in the forecourt; the driver was fast asleep. Leamas glanced at the number, went over and called through the window, "Are you from Clements?"

The driver woke up with a start and asked, "Mr. Thomas?"

"No," replied Leamas. "Thomas couldn't come. I'm Amies from Hounslow."

"Hop in, Mr. Amies," the driver replied, and opened the door. They drove west, toward Chelsea. The driver knew the way.

CONTROL OPENED the door. "George Smiley's out," he said. "I've borrowed his house. Come in." Not until the door was closed again did Control put on the hall light.

They went into the little drawing room. It was a pretty room; tall, with eighteenth-century moldings, long windows and a good fireplace. There were books everywhere. "They picked me up this morning," Leamas said. "A man who calls himself Ashe. We're meeting again tomorrow."

Control listened carefully to Leamas' story, from the day he hit the grocer to his encounter that morning with Ashe. "How did you find prison?" he inquired. He might have been asking whether Leamas had enjoyed his holiday. "I am sorry we couldn't improve conditions for you, provide little extra comforts, but that would never have done."

"Of course not."

"One must be consistent at every turn. Besides, it would be wrong to break the spell. I understand you were ill. I am sorry. What was the trouble?"

"Just fever. I was in bed about a week."

"How very distressing; and nobody to look after you, of course."

There was a very long silence.

"You know she's in the Party, don't you?" Control asked quietly.

"Yes," Leamas replied. Another silence. "I don't want her brought into this."

"Why should she be?" Control asked sharply, and for a moment—just for a moment—Leamas thought he had penetrated the veneer of academic detachment. "Who suggested she should be?"

"No one," Leamas replied. "But I know how all these offensive operations go. They take sudden turns in unexpected directions. You think you've caught one fish and you find you've caught another. I want her kept clear of it."

"Oh quite, quite."

"Who's that man in the Labour Exchange—Pitt? Wasn't he in the Circus during the war?"

"I know no one of that name. Pitt, did you say?"

"Yes."

"No, the name means nothing to me. In the Labour Exchange?"

"Oh, for God's sake," Leamas muttered audibly.

"I'm sorry," said Control, getting up. "I'm neglecting my duties as deputy host. Would you care for a drink?"

"No. I want to get away tonight, Control. Go down to the country and get some exercise. Is the house open?"

"I've arranged a car. I'll ring Haldane and tell him you want to play some squash tomorrow morning." Control gave himself a whisky and began looking idly at the books in Smiley's shelf.

"Why isn't Smiley here?" Leamas asked.

"He finds the operation distasteful," Control replied indifferently. "He sees the necessity, but he wants no part in it."

"He didn't exactly receive me with open arms."

"Quite. But he told you about Mundt; gave you the background?"

"Yes."

"Mundt is a very *hard* man," Control reflected. "We should never forget that. And a good intelligence officer."

"Does Smiley know the reason for the operation? The special interest?"

Control nodded and took a sip of whisky.

"And he still doesn't like it?"

"He is like the surgeon who has grown tired of blood. He is content that others should operate."

"Tell me," Leamas continued, "how are you so certain this will get us where we want? How do you know the East Germans are on to it—not the Czechs or the Russians?"

"Rest assured," Control said a little pompously, "that that has been taken care of."

As they got to the door, Control put his hand lightly on Leamas' shoulder. "This is your last job," he said. "Then you can come in from the cold. About that girl—do you want anything done about her, money or anything?"

"When it's over. I'll take care of it myself then."

"Quite. It would be very insecure to do anything now."

"I want her left alone," Leamas repeated with emphasis. "I don't want you even to have a file on her. I want her forgotten." He nodded to Control and slipped out into the night air. Into the cold.

6

ON THE FOLLOWING DAY Leamas arrived twenty minutes late for his lunch with Ashe, and smelled of whisky. He hadn't shaved and his collar was filthy. Ashe's pleasure on catching sight of him was, however, undiminished. He claimed that he had himself only that moment arrived. He handed Leamas an envelope. "Singles," he said. "I hope that's all right?"

"Thanks," Leamas replied. "Let's have a drink."

They lunched well, with a lot to drink, and Ashe did most of the work. As Leamas had expected he first talked about himself, an old trick but not a bad one.

"I've got on to rather a good thing recently," said Ashe. "Free-lancing newspaper features for the foreign press. After Berlin I made rather a mess of things at first—the BBC didn't renew my contract. Then I got a letter from an old friend, Sam Kiever, who was starting up a new agency for small features on English life especially slanted for foreign papers. You know the sort of thing—six hundred words on morris dancing. Sam had a new gimmick, though; he sold the stuff already translated. If an editor's looking for a half-column feature, he doesn't *want* to waste time and money on translation. And it's paid damn well."

Ashe paused, waiting for Leamas to speak about himself. But Leamas just nodded dully and said, "Bloody good." He'd had four large whiskies, and he seemed to be in bad shape; he had the drunkard's habit of ducking his mouth toward the rim of his glass just before he drank, as if his hand might fail him and the drink escape.

"You don't know Sam, do you?" Ashe asked.

"Sam?"

A note of irritation entered Ashe's voice. "Sam Kiever, my boss. The chap I was telling you about. He did some free-lance stuff in Germany. You might have met him."

"Don't think so." A pause.

"What do *you* do these days, old chap?" asked Ashe.

Leamas shrugged. "I'm on the shelf," he replied.

"I forget what you were doing in Berlin," Ashe said. "Weren't you one of the mysterious cold warriors?"

Leamas thought, You *are* stepping things up. He hesitated, then said savagely, "Office boy for the bloody Yanks, like the rest of them."

"You know," said Ashe, as if he had been turning the idea over for some time, "you ought to meet Sam. You'd like him." And then, all of a bother, "I say, Alec—I don't even know where to get hold of you!"

"You can't," Leamas replied listlessly.

"I don't get you, old chap. Where are you staying?"

"Around the place. Roughing it a bit. I haven't got a job, and they wouldn't give me a proper pension."

Ashe looked horrified. "But Alec, that's awful, why didn't you *tell* me? Look, why not come and stay at my place? It's only tiny, but there's room if you don't mind a camp bed."

"I'm all right for a bit." Leamas tapped the pocket which contained the envelope. "I'm going to get a job." He nodded with determination. "Get one in a week or two. Then I'll be all right."

"What sort of job?"

"Oh, I don't know. Anything. I've done all sorts of things. Selling encyclopedias for some bloody American firm, punching work tickets in a stinking glue factory. What the hell *can* I do?" He wasn't looking at Ashe but at the table before him, his agitated lips moving quickly.

Ashe responded with emphasis, almost triumph. "But Alec, you speak German like a native; I remember you do. All you need is *contacts*. I know what it's like; I've been on the breadline myself. I don't know what you were doing in Berlin, but it wasn't the sort of job where you could meet people who matter, was it? If I hadn't met Sam five years ago I'd *still* be on the breadline. Look, Alec, come and stay with me for a week or so. We'll ask Sam around and perhaps one or two of the old press boys from Berlin."

ASHE HAD A FLAT in Dolphin Square. It was just what Leamas had expected—small and anonymous, with a few, no doubt hastily assembled, curios from Germany: beer mugs, a peasant's pipe and a few pieces of second-rate Nymphenburg china. They fixed the camp bed up in the tiny drawing room. It was about four thirty.

"How long have you been here?" asked Leamas.

"Oh—about a year or more. I spend weekends with my mother in Cheltenham; I just use this place midweek. It's pretty handy," he added deprecatingly.

He made tea and they drank it, Leamas sullenly, like a man not used to comfort. Afterward Ashe said, "I'll go out and do a spot of shopping before the shops close, then we'll decide what to do about everything. I might give Sam a tinkle later this evening—I think the sooner you two get together the better. Why don't you get some sleep? You look all in."

Leamas nodded. "It's bloody good of you"—he made an awkward gesture with his hand—"all this." Ashe gave him a pat on the shoulder and left.

As soon as Ashe was safely out of the building Leamas left the front door of the flat slightly ajar and went down to the center hall, where there were two telephone booths. He dialed a number and asked for

Mr. Thomas' secretary. Immediately a girl's voice said, "Mr. Thomas' secretary speaking."

"I'm ringing on behalf of Mr. Sam Kiever," Leamas said. "He has accepted the invitation and hopes to contact Mr. Thomas personally this evening."

"I'll pass that on to Mr. Thomas. Does he know where to get in touch with you?"

"Dolphin Square," Leamas replied, and gave the address.

After making some inquiries at the reception desk he returned to the flat and lay down on the camp bed. He decided to accept Ashe's advice and get some rest. As he closed his eyes he remembered Liz, and he wondered what had become of her.

He was wakened by Ashe, accompanied by a small, rather plump man with long, graying hair. He spoke with a slight Central European accent, German perhaps. He said his name was Sam Kiever.

They had a gin and tonic, Ashe doing most of the talking. It was just like old times, he said, in Berlin: the boys together and the night their oyster. They agreed to eat at a Chinese restaurant that Ashe knew of, where you brought your own wine. Oddly enough, Ashe had two bottles of Burgundy in the kitchen, and they took them along in the taxi.

They drank both bottles with their dinner. Kiever opened up a little on the second; he'd just come back from a tour of West Germany and France. France was in a mess, and God alone knew what would happen next. Perhaps Fascism.

"What about Germany?" asked Ashe, prompting him.

"It's just a question of whether the Yanks can hold them." Kiever looked invitingly at Leamas.

"What do you mean?" asked Leamas.

"What I say. The Yanks give them a foreign policy one minute, then take it away the next. The Germans are getting waspish."

Leamas nodded abruptly and said, "Bloody typical Yanks."

"Alec doesn't like our American cousins," said Ashe, stepping in heavily, and Kiever, with complete disinterest, said, "Oh really?"

Kiever played it, Leamas reflected, very long. Like someone used to horses, he let you come to him. He conveyed to perfection a man who suspected that he was about to be asked a favor, and was not easily won.

After dinner Ashe said, "I know a place in Wardour Street—you've been there, Sam. Why don't we get a cab and go along?"

"Just a minute," said Leamas. "Tell me something, will you? Who's paying for this jolly?"

"I am," said Ashe quickly.

"Because I haven't got any bloody money; you know that, don't you? None to throw about, anyway."

"Of course, Alec. I've looked after you so far, haven't I?"

"Yes," Leamas replied. "Yes, you have."

He seemed to be going to say something else, and then to change his mind. Ashe looked worried, not offended, and Kiever as inscrutable as before.

They took a taxi to Wardour Street, and Ashe led them down a narrow alley, at the far end of which shone a tawdry neon sign: PUSSYWILLOW CLUB—MEMBERS ONLY. On either side of the door were photographs of girls, and pinned across each was a thin, hand-printed strip of paper which read *Nature Study. Members Only.*

Ashe pressed the bell. The door was at once opened by a very large man in a white shirt and black trousers. "I'm a member," Ashe said. "These two gentlemen are with me."

"See your card?"

Ashe took a buff colored card from his wallet and handed it over. "Your guests pay a quid a head, temporary membership." The man held out the card, and as he did so, Leamas stretched past Ashe and took it. He looked at it, then handed it back to Ashe.

Taking two pounds from his pocket, Leamas put them into the waiting hand of the doorman. "Two quid," said Leamas, "for the guests," and ignoring the astonished protests of Ashe, he led them through the curtained doorway into the dim hallway of the club. He turned back to the doorman. "Find us a table and a bottle of Scotch. And see we're left alone."

The doorman hesitated for a moment, then escorted them downstairs. As they descended they heard the subdued moan of unintelligible music. They got a table at the back of the room. A two-piece band was playing and girls sat around in twos and threes. Two got up as they came in, but the big doorman shook his head.

Ashe glanced at Leamas uneasily while they waited for the whisky. Kiever seemed slightly bored. The waiter brought a bottle and three tumblers, and they watched in silence as he poured a little whisky into each glass.

Leamas took the bottle and added as much again to each. Then he leaned across the table and said to Ashe, "Now perhaps you'll tell me what the bloody hell's going on."

"What do you mean, Alec?" Ashe sounded uncertain.

"You followed me from prison," he began quietly, "with some bloody silly story of meeting me in Berlin. You gave me money you didn't owe me. You've bought me expensive meals, and you're putting me up in your flat."

Ashe colored and said, "If that's the—"

"Don't interrupt," said Leamas. "Your membership card for this place is made out for someone called Murphy. Is that your name?"

"No, it is not."

"I suppose a friend called Murphy lent you his card?"

"No. If you must know, I used a phony name to join the club."

"Then why," Leamas persisted ruthlessly, "is Murphy registered as the tenant of your flat?"

It was Kiever who finally spoke. "You run along home," he said to Ashe. "I'll look after this."

A GIRL PERFORMED A STRIPTEASE—a young, drab girl with a pitiful, spindly nakedness. Leamas and Kiever watched her in silence.

"I suppose you're going to tell me that we've seen better in Berlin," Leamas suggested at last, and Kiever saw that he was still very angry.

"I expect *you* have," Kiever replied pleasantly. "I have often been to Berlin, but I am afraid I dislike nightclubs."

Leamas might not have been listening. "Perhaps you'll tell me why that sissy picked me up," he suggested.

Kiever nodded. "By all means. I told him to."

"Why?"

"I am interested in you. I want to make you a proposition, a journalistic proposition."

"Journalistic," Leamas said. "I see."

"I run an international feature service. It pays very well for interesting material."

"Who publishes the material?"

"It pays so well, in fact, that a man with your kind of experience of . . . the international scene, a man with your background, you understand, who provided convincing, factual material, could free himself in a comparatively short time from further financial worry."

"Who publishes the material, Kiever?" There was a threatening edge to Leamas' voice, and for a moment a look of apprehension passed across Kiever's smooth face.

"International clients. I have a correspondent in Paris who disposes of a good deal of my stuff. Often I don't even know who *does* publish. I confess," he added with a disarming smile, "that I don't awfully care. They pay and they ask for more. They're the kind of people, you see, Leamas, who don't fuss about awkward details; they pay promptly, and they're happy to pay into foreign banks, where no one bothers about things like taxes."

They're rushing their fences, Leamas thought; it's almost indecent. He remembered some silly music-hall joke: "This is an offer no respectable girl could accept—and besides, I don't know what it's worth." Tactically, he reflected, they're right to rush it. I'm down and out, prison experience still fresh, social resentment strong. I'm an old horse, I don't need breaking in; I don't have to pretend they've offended my honor as an English gentleman. On the other hand, they will expect *practical* objections. They will expect me to be afraid, for the service pursues traitors as the eye of God followed Cain across the desert.

"They have to pay a hell of a lot," Leamas muttered at last. Kiever gave him some more whisky.

"They are offering a down payment of fifteen thousand pounds. The money is already lodged at the Banque Cantonale in Bern. My clients will provide identification so you can draw the money. And they reserve the right to put questions to you over the period of one year on payment of another five thousand pounds. They will assist you with any . . . resettlement problems that may arise."

"How soon do you want an answer?"

"Now. You are not expected to commit all your reminiscences to paper. You will meet my client and he will have the material . . . ghostwritten."

"Where am I supposed to meet him?"

"We felt for everybody's sake it would be simplest to meet outside the United Kingdom. My client suggested Holland."

"I haven't got my passport," Leamas said.

"I took the liberty of obtaining one for you," Kiever replied suavely; nothing in his voice or his manner indicated that he had done other than negotiate a business arrangement. "We're flying to Rotterdam tomorrow morning at nine forty-five. Shall we go back to my flat and discuss any other details?"

KIEVER'S FLAT was luxurious and expensive, but its contents also gave the impression of having been hastily assembled.

As Kiever showed him to his room Leamas asked him, "How long have you been here?"

"Oh, not long," Kiever replied lightly. "A few months."

There was a bottle of Scotch in Leamas' room and a siphon of soda on a silver-plated tray. A doorway at the end of the room led to a bathroom. "Quite a little love nest. All paid for by the great Worker State?"

"Shut up," said Kiever savagely. Then he added, "You'd better look through this." He pulled out a British passport. It was made out in Leamas' name, with his own photograph embossed by a deep-press Foreign Office seal. It described Leamas as a clerk and gave his status as single. Holding it in his hand for the first time, Leamas was a little nervous. It was like getting married: whatever happened, things would never be the same again.

"What about money?" he asked.

"You don't need any. It's on the firm. I shall be awake tonight. If you want me, there's an intercom telephone to my room."

"I think I can manage my buttons now," Leamas retorted.

"Then good night," said Kiever shortly, and left the room.

He's on edge too, thought Leamas.

7

IT WAS COLD next morning at the airport. The light mist was damp and gray, pricking the skin. Kiever had provided Leamas with luggage. It was a nice detail; Leamas admired it. Passengers without luggage attract attention, and it was not part of Kiever's plan to do that. They checked in at the airline desk and followed the signs to passport control. There was a ludicrous moment when they lost the way and Kiever was rude to a porter. Leamas supposed Kiever was worried about the passport. He needn't be, thought Leamas, there's nothing wrong with it.

"Going to be away for a long time, sir?" the passport officer asked Leamas.

"A couple of weeks," Leamas replied.

"You'll want to watch it, sir. Your passport's due for renewal the end of the month."

"I know," said Leamas.

They walked side by side into the passengers' waiting room. On the way Leamas said, "You're a suspicious devil, aren't you, Kiever?" and the other laughed quietly.

"Can't have you on the loose, can we? Not part of the contract," he replied.

THE FORMALITIES AT the airport in Rotterdam provided no problem. Kiever seemed to have recovered from his anxieties. He became jaunty and talkative as they walked the short distance from the plane to the customs sheds. The young Dutch officer gave a perfunctory glance at their luggage and passports, and announced in awkward, throaty English, "I hope you have a pleasant stay in the Netherlands."

"Thanks," said Kiever, almost too gratefully. "Thanks very much."

They walked to the main exit between kiosks displaying perfume, cameras and fruit. As they pushed through the revolving glass door Leamas looked back. Standing at the newspaper kiosk, deep in a copy of the *Continental Daily Mail*, stood a small, froglike figure wearing glasses, an earnest, worried little man. He looked like a civil servant. Something like that.

A Volkswagen with a Dutch registration, driven by a woman, was waiting for them in the parking lot. She ignored them, driving slowly, always stopping if the lights were amber, and Leamas supposed she had been briefed to drive that way and that they were being followed by another car. He knew Holland quite well and guessed that they were traveling northwest toward the coast. He was right; in less than two hours they came to a colony of villas bordering the dunes along the seafront.

Here they stopped. The woman got out and rang the doorbell of a cream-colored bungalow. A wrought-iron sign hung on the porch, with the words LE MIRAGE in Gothic script. There was a notice in the window proclaiming that all the rooms were taken.

The door was opened by a plump, kindly-looking woman, who came down the drive, smiling with pleasure. "How nice that you have come," she declared; "we are so *pleased* that you have come!"

They followed her into the bungalow. The driver got back into the car. Leamas glanced down the road which they had just traveled; a hundred yards away a small black car had parked. A man in a raincoat was getting out.

In the hall the woman shook Leamas warmly by the hand. "Welcome, welcome to Le Mirage. Did you have a good journey?"

"Fine," Leamas replied.

"I'll fix your lunch," she said. "A special lunch, something especially good. What shall I bring you?"

Leamas swore under his breath, and the doorbell rang. The woman went quickly into the kitchen; Kiever opened the front door.

THE MAN IN the raincoat was about Leamas' height, but older. Leamas put him at fifty-five. His face had a hard, gray hue and sharp furrows; he might have been a soldier. He held out his hand. "My name is Peters," he said. The fingers were slim and polished. "Did you have a good journey?"

"Yes," said Kiever quickly, "quite uneventful."

"Mr. Leamas and I have a lot to discuss; I do not think we need to keep you, Sam. You could take the Volkswagen back."

Leamas saw relief in Kiever's smile. "Good-by, Leamas," he said, his voice jocular. "Good luck, old man."

Leamas nodded, ignoring Kiever's hand. "Good-by," Kiever repeated, and let himself quietly out the front door.

Leamas followed Peters into a back room with thick lace curtains at the window. The furniture was heavy, pseudoantique. In the center of the room was a table with two carved chairs; before each chair was a pad of paper and a pencil. On a sideboard there was whisky and soda. Peters went over to it and mixed them both a drink.

"Look," said Leamas suddenly, "from now on I can do without the goodwill, do you follow me? We both know what we're about; both professionals. You've got a paid defector—good luck to you. But don't pretend you've fallen in love with me." He sounded on edge, uncertain of himself.

Peters nodded. "Kiever told me you were a proud man," he observed. Then he added without smiling, "After all, why else does a man attack a tradesman?"

Leamas guessed Peters was Russian, but he wasn't sure. His English was nearly perfect; he had the ease and habits of a man long used to civilized comforts.

They sat at the table. "Kiever told you what I am going to pay you?" Peters inquired.

"Yes. Fifteen thousand pounds. He said you would pay another five thousand if I kept myself available for follow-up questions for one more year." Peters nodded. "I don't accept that condition," Leamas continued. "You know as well as I do, it wouldn't work. I want to draw the fifteen thousand and get clear. Your people have a rough way with defected agents; so have mine. I'm not going to sit still in some place like Saint Moritz while you roll up every network I've given you. My people aren't fools; they'd know who to look for. For all you and I know, they're on to us now."

Peters nodded. "You could, of course, come somewhere . . . safer, couldn't you?"

"Behind the Curtain?"

"Yes."

Leamas just shook his head and continued. "I reckon you'll need about three days for a preliminary interrogation. Then you'll want to refer back to headquarters for a detailed briefing after they've had your report."

"Not necessarily," Peters replied.

Leamas looked at him with interest. "I see," he said. "They've sent the expert. Or isn't Moscow Center in on this?"

Peters was silent; he was just looking at Leamas, taking him in. At last he picked up his pencil and said, "We'll begin with your war service. Just talk."

"I ENLISTED IN the Engineers in 1939. I was finishing my training when a notice came around inviting linguists to apply for specialist service abroad. I had Dutch and German and a good deal of French, so I applied. I already knew Holland. My father had a machine-tool agency at Leiden, and I'd lived there for nine years. I had the usual interviews and went off to a school near Oxford, where they taught me the usual monkey tricks.

"In '41 they dropped me into Holland, and I stayed there nearly two years. It was murder. Holland's a wicked country for our kind of work—it's got no real rough country, no out-of-the-way place to keep a headquarters or a radio set. Always on the move, always running away. We lost agents quicker than we could find them. I got out in '43. Then I had a go at Norway—that was a picnic by comparison.

"In '45 they paid me off, and I came over to Holland to try my father's old business. That was no good, so I joined up with a friend who was running a travel agency in Bristol. That lasted eighteen months, then we went bankrupt. Then out of the blue I got a letter from the department: would I like to go back? By late '49 I was back on the payroll. Broken service, of course—reduction of pension rights. Am I going too fast?"

"Not for the moment," Peters replied. "We'll discuss it again of course, with names and dates."

There was a knock at the door, and the woman came in with lunch, an enormous meal of cold meats and soup. Peters pushed his notes aside, and they ate in silence.

"So you went back to the Circus," said Peters when lunch was cleared away.

"Yes. For a while they gave me a desk job, processing reports, making assessments of military strengths in Iron Curtain countries, tracing units and that kind of thing."

"Which section?"

"Satellites Four. I was there from February '50 to May of '51."

"Who were your colleagues?"

"Peter Guillam, Brian de Grey and George Smiley. Smiley went over to counterintelligence in early '51, and in May I was posted to Berlin as DCA—Deputy Controller of Area. That meant all the operational work."

"Who did you have under you?" Peters was writing swiftly. Leamas guessed he had some homemade shorthand.

"Hackett, Sarrow and de Jong. They all ran networks and I was in charge. It was late '54 when we landed our first big fish in Berlin: Fritz Feger, second man in the East German Defense Ministry. Up till then it had been heavy going. Fritz lasted about two years, then suddenly we heard no more of him. I hear he died in prison. It was another three years before we found anyone to touch him. Then, in 1959, Karl Riemeck turned up. Karl was on the presidium of the East German Communist Party. He was the best agent I ever knew."

"He is now dead," Peters observed.

A look of something like shame passed across Leamas' face. "I was there when he was shot," he muttered.

Leamas was sweating. Peters appraised him like a professional gambler across the table. What would break Leamas, what attract or frighten him? Above all, what did he know? Would he keep his best card to the end and sell it dear? Peters didn't think so; Leamas was too much off-balance to monkey about. He was a man at odds with himself, a man who knew only one life and had betrayed it.

Peters had seen it before, even in men who had found a new creed, undergone a complete ideological reversal. Even they, filled as they were with new zeal and new hope, had to struggle against the stigma of treachery, against the almost physical anguish of saying that which they had been trained never to reveal. This was why Leamas had fiercely rejected a human relationship with Peters; his pride precluded it.

Peters knew, too, that the very fact that Leamas was a professional agent could make the interrogation difficult, for Leamas would select information where Peters wanted no selection. Leamas would anticipate the type of intelligence Peters required—and in doing so he might pass by some casual scrap which could be of vital interest to the evaluators. To all that, Peters must add the capricious vanity of an alcoholic wreck.

"I think," he said, "we will now take your Berlin service in some detail. That would be from May 1951 to March 1961."

Leamas watched him light a cigarette, and noticed that Peters had put the cigarette in his mouth with the brand name away from him, so that it burned first. It was a gesture Leamas liked; it indicated that Peters, like himself, had been on the run. Leamas wondered vaguely what Peters' real name was. There was something very orthodox about him which Leamas liked. It was the orthodoxy of strength, of confidence. If Peters lied, there would be a reason. The lie would be a calculated, necessary lie, far removed from the fumbling dishonesty of Ashe.

Ashe, Kiever, Peters; this was a progression in quality, in authority. It was also, Leamas suspected, a progression in ideology: Ashe, the mercenary; Kiever, the fellow traveler; and now Peters, for whom the end and the means were identical.

Leamas began to talk about Berlin. It had taken a long time, he explained, to build a decent East Zone network from Berlin. In the earlier days the city had been thronging with second-rate agents; intelligence was discredited and so much a part of the daily life of Berlin that you could recruit a man at a cocktail party, brief him over dinner and he would be blown by breakfast. For a professional it was a nightmare. They had their break with Feger in 1954, true enough. But by '56, when every service department was screaming for high-grade intelligence, they were becalmed. Feger had spoiled them for second-rate stuff that was only one jump ahead of the news. They needed the real thing—and they had to wait another three years before they got it.

Then one day one of the three network heads, de Jong, took his family for a picnic in the woods on the edge of East Berlin. He had a British military license plate on his car, which he parked, locked, on a gravel road beside the canal.

After the picnic his children ran on ahead, carrying the basket. When they reached the car they hesitated, dropped the basket and ran back. Somebody had forced the car door—the handle was broken and the door slightly open. De Jong swore, remembering that he had left his camera in the glove compartment. He examined the car. The camera was still there, and on the driver's seat was a tobacco tin containing a small nickel film cartridge from a subminiature camera, probably a Minox.

De Jong drove home and developed the film. It contained the minutes of the last meeting of the presidium of the East German Communist Party, the SED. By an odd coincidence there was collateral evidence from another source; the photographs were genuine.

Leamas had taken the case over then. He was badly in need of a success. He'd produced virtually nothing since arriving in Berlin, and he was getting past the usual age limit for full-time operational work. Exactly a week later he took de Jong's car to the same place and went for a walk.

It was a desolate spot: a strip of canal bordered by a gravel road, some parched, sandy fields, and on the eastern side a sparse pinewood. But it had the virtue of solitude—something that was hard to find in Berlin—and surveillance was impossible. Leamas walked in the woods, making no attempt to watch the car because he did not know from which direction the approach might be made, and if he were seen watching the car, the chances of retaining his informant's confidence were ruined.

He need not have worried. When he returned, there was nothing in the car, and he drove back to West Berlin, kicking himself for being a damned fool; the presidium was not due to meet for another fortnight. Three weeks later he borrowed de Jong's car and took a thousand dollars in twenties in a picnic case. He left the car unlocked for two hours, and when he returned there was a tobacco tin in the glove compartment. The picnic case was gone.

The films were packed with first-grade documentary stuff. In the next six weeks he did it twice more, and the same thing happened.

Leamas knew he had hit a gold mine. He gave the source the cover name of Mayfair and sent a pessimistic letter to London. He knew that if he gave the Circus half an opening they would control the case direct, which he was desperately anxious to avoid. The Circus would have theories, make suggestions, urge caution, demand action. They would want him to give only new dollar bills in the hope of tracing them; they would plan clumsy tailing operations and tell other departments.

Leamas worked like a madman for three weeks. He combed the personality files of each member of the presidium. From the distribution list on the last page of the facsimiles, he extended the total of possible informants to thirty-one, including the secretarial staff.

Confronted with the almost impossible task of identifying an informant from the incomplete records of thirty-one candidates, Leamas returned to the original material. It puzzled him that in none of the photostated minutes were the pages numbered, that none was stamped with a security classification, and that here and there words were crossed out. He finally concluded that the photocopies were not of the minutes themselves, but of the *draft* minutes. This placed the source in the secretariat itself and the secretariat was very small.

Leamas returned to the personality index. There was a man called Karl Riemeck in the secretariat, a former corporal in the medical corps, who had served three years as a prisoner of war in England. His sister had been living in Pomerania when the Russians overran it, and he had never heard of her since. He had once been married and had a daughter named Carla.

Leamas decided to take a chance. He found out, from London, Riemeck's prisoner-of-war number, which was 29012, and the date of his release, which was December 10, 1945. He bought an East German children's book of science fiction and wrote on the flyleaf in German in an adolescent hand: *This book belongs to Carla Riemeck, born December 10, 1945, in Bideford, North Devon. Signed Moonspacewoman 29012.* Underneath he added: *Applicants wishing to make space flights should write to the usual address stating when and where they wish to be met. Applications will be considered in seven days. Long Live the People's Republic of Democratic Space!*

He drove to the usual place, still in de Jong's car, and left the book on the passenger seat, with five used one-hundred-dollar bills inside the cover. When Leamas returned, the book was gone, and there was a tobacco tin on the seat instead. It contained three rolls of film.

Leamas developed them that night. One contained as usual the minutes of the presidium's last meeting. The second showed a draft revision of the East German relationship to COMECON—Council for Mutual Economic Assistance, the Communist equivalent of Western Europe's Common Market. The third was a breakdown of the East German Intelligence Department, complete with functions of departments and details of personalities.

Peters interrupted. "Just a minute," he said. "Do you mean to say all this intelligence came from Riemeck?"

"Why not? You know how much he saw."

"It's scarcely possible," Peters observed, almost to himself. "He must have had help."

"He did have, later on; I'm coming to that."

"I know what you are going to tell me. But did you never have the feeling he got assistance from *above* as well as from the agents he afterward acquired?"

"No. No, I never did. It never occurred to me."

"When you sent all this material back to the Circus, they never suggested that even for a man in Riemeck's position the intelligence was phenomenally comprehensive?"

"No."

"Did they ever ask where Riemeck got his camera from, or who instructed him in document photography?"

Leamas hesitated. "No . . . I'm sure they never asked."

"Remarkable," Peters observed dryly.

Exactly a week later, Leamas continued, he drove to the canal, and this time he felt nervous. As he turned into the gravel road he saw three bicycles lying in the grass and three men fishing. He got out of the car and began walking toward the pinewood. He had gone about twenty yards when he heard a shout. He looked around and saw one of the men beckoning to him. The other two were looking at him also.

Leamas had his hands in his mackintosh pockets, and it was too late to take them out. He knew that the men on either side were covering the man in the middle and that if he took his hands out of his pockets they would probably shoot him, thinking he was holding a revolver. Leamas stopped ten yards from the center man.

"You want something?" Leamas asked.

"Are you Leamas?" He was a small, plump man, very steady. He spoke English.

"Yes."

"What is your British national identity number?"

"PRT stroke L five-eight-oh-oh-three stroke one."

"Where did you spend V-J night?"

"At Leiden in Holland, in my father's workshop, with some Dutch friends."

"Let's go for a walk, Mr. Leamas. You won't need your mackintosh. Leave it on the ground where you are standing. My friends will look after it."

Leamas hesitated, shrugged and took off his mackintosh. Then they walked together briskly toward the wood.

"You know as well as I do who he was," said Leamas wearily, "third man in the Ministry of the Interior, secretary to the presidium, head of the Coordinating Committee for the Protection of the People. I suppose that was how he knew about de Jong and me: he'd seen our counterintelligence files in the Abteilung. He had three things to offer: his position with the presidium, some internal political and economic reporting, and access to the files of the East German Intelligence Department."

"But only *limited* access. They'd never give an outsider the run of all their files," Peters insisted.

Leamas shrugged. "They did," he said.

"How much did you tell London?"

"Everything, after that. I had to; then the Circus took over and told the other departments. After that," Leamas added venomously, "it was only a matter of time before it fell apart. With the departments at their backs, the Circus got greedy. They began pressing us for more. Finally Karl had to recruit other agents, and we took them on to form a network. It was bloody stupid; it put a strain on Karl, endangered him, undermined his confidence in us. It was the beginning of the end."

"How much did you get out of him?"

Piece by piece, Leamas recounted the full extent of all Karl Riemeck's work. His memory was, Peters noted approvingly, remarkably precise, considering the amount he drank. He could give dates and names, he could remember the reaction from London, sums of money demanded and paid, the dates of the conscription of other agents into the network.

"I'm sorry," said Peters at last, "but I do not believe that one man, however well placed, however industrious, could have acquired such a range of detailed knowledge. Even if he had, he would never have been able to photograph it."

"He *was* able," Leamas persisted, suddenly angry. "He bloody well did and that's all there is to it."

"And the Circus never told you to go into it with him, exactly how and when he saw all this stuff?"

"No," snapped Leamas. "Riemeck was touchy about that, and London was content to let it go."

"Well, well," Peters mused. After a moment he said, "You heard about that woman, incidentally?"

"What woman?" Leamas asked sharply.

"Elvira. Karl Riemeck's mistress. She was murdered. Shot from a car as she left her flat."

"It used to be my flat," said Leamas mechanically.

"Perhaps," Peters suggested, "she knew more about Riemeck's network than you did."

"What the hell do you mean?" Leamas demanded.

Peters shrugged. "It's all very strange," he observed. "I wonder who killed her."

They talked long into the night and throughout the next day, of less spectacular agents, of the procedures in Leamas' Berlin office—its secret flats, transport, recording, photographic equipment; and when at last Leamas stumbled into bed the following night, he had betrayed all that he knew of Allied intelligence in Berlin.

One thing puzzled him: Peters' insistence that Karl Riemeck must have had a high-level collaborator. How could he be so sure Karl hadn't managed alone? But Peters, after all, would know precisely how much Karl had been able to get his hands on. Control had asked him the same question—he remembered now—about Riemeck's access. On this point, Peters and Control were evidently agreed.

Perhaps there *was* somebody else. Perhaps this was the special interest whom Control was so anxious to protect from Mundt. Perhaps that was what Control had spoken to Karl about, alone, that evening in Leamas' flat in Berlin.

Anyway, tomorrow would tell. Tomorrow he would play his hand.

He wondered who had killed Elvira, and *why*. Of course, Elvira, knowing the identity of Riemeck's special collaborator, might have been murdered *by* that collaborator. . . . No, that was too farfetched. Elvira had, after all, been murdered in *West* Berlin.

As he fell asleep he muttered, "Karl was a damned fool. That woman did for him, I'm sure she did."

So Elvira was dead. . . . He remembered Liz.

8

PETERS ARRIVED at eight o'clock the next morning, and without ceremony they sat down at the table and began. "So you came back to London. What did you do there?"

"I had to go straight to Control and report about Karl. Then they put me on the shelf, in Banking section. Supervision of agents' salaries, overseas payments for clandestine purposes—a child could have managed it. I can't remember much about that part—I began hitting the bottle a bit. That was why they gave me the push, really."

"What *do* you remember about Banking section?"

Leamas shrugged. "Sat on my behind in the same room as a couple of women. Thursby and Larrett. I called them Thursday and Friday." Peters looked uncomprehending. "We just pushed paper. A letter would come down from Finance: 'The payment of seven hundred dollars to so-and-so is authorized as of such and such a date.' Thursday and Friday would kick it about a bit, file it, stamp it, and I'd sign a check or get the bank to make a transfer."

"In fact, then, you knew the names of agents all over the world?"

"Not necessarily. In most cases we had the money transferred to a foreign bank. Then our local man—our resident in that particular country—could draw it himself and hand it to the agent."

Peters looked disappointed. "You mean you had no way of knowing the names of the payees?"

"Not usually, no."

"But occasionally?"

"Well, all the fiddling about between Banking, Finance and Special Dispatch led to mix-ups, of course. Too elaborate. Then occasionally we came in on special stuff which brightened our life a bit." Leamas got up. "I've made a list," he said, "of all the payments I can remember. It's in my room. I'll get it." He walked out of the room, the rather shuffling walk he had affected since arriving in Holland, and returned with a couple of sheets of paper from a notebook.

"I wrote these down last night," he said, sitting down again at the table. "I thought it would save time."

Peters read the notes slowly and carefully. He seemed impressed. "Good," he said, "very good."

"I remember best a thing called Rolling Stone. I got a couple of trips out of it. One to Denmark and one to Finland. Just dumping money at banks."

"How much?"

"Ten thousand dollars in Copenhagen, forty thousand marks in Helsinki."

Peters put down his pencil. "Who for?" he asked.

"God knows. We worked Rolling Stone on a system of savings accounts. The service gave me a phony British passport; I went to the Royal Scandinavian Bank in Copenhagen and the National Bank of Finland in Helsinki, deposited the money and drew a passbook on a joint account: for me, under my alias, and for someone else—the agent, I suppose—under *his* alias. I gave the banks samples of the co-holder's signature I'd gotten from Head Office.

"Later, the agent was given the passbook and a false passport, which he showed at the bank when he drew the money. All I knew was the alias." He heard himself talking, and it all sounded so ludicrously improbable.

"Was this procedure common?"

"No. It was a special payment. It had a subscription list."

"What's that?"

"It means the file was circulated to very few people. It covered payments of ten thousand dollars in different currencies and different capitals."

"Always in capital towns?"

"Far as I know. I read in the file that there had been two other Rolling Stone payments before I came to the section, but in those cases they got the local resident to do it."

"These other payments that took place before you came: where were they made?"

"One in Oslo. I can't remember where the other was."

"Was the alias of the agent always the same?"

"No. That was an added security precaution. I heard later we pinched the whole technique from the Russians. It was the most elaborate scheme I'd met. In the same way I used a different alias and of course a different passport for each trip." That would please him, and help him to fill in the gaps.

"Do you know why earlier payments were made by the local residents, and later ones by someone traveling out from London?"

"Control was anxious that—"

"*Control?* Do you mean to say Control himself was running this?"

"Yes, he was running it. He was afraid the local residents might be recognized at the bank. So he used a postman—me."

"When did you make your journeys?"

"Copenhagen, the fifteenth of June. I flew back the same night. Helsinki at the end of September. I stayed two nights there, flew back around the twenty-eighth."

"And the other payments—when were they made?"

"I can't remember the dates. Sorry."

"Was it your impression that the agent had been operating for some time before the first payment was made?"

"No idea. The file simply covered actual payments. With a limited subscription, different files handle different bits of a single case. Only someone with the master file could put it all together."

Peters was writing all the time now. Leamas assumed there was a tape recorder hidden in the room, but the subsequent transcription would take time. What Peters wrote down now would provide the background for this evening's telegram to Moscow, while at the Soviet embassy in The Hague the girls would sit up all night telegraphing the verbatim transcript on hourly schedules.

"Tell me," said Peters, "these are large sums of money. The arrangements for paying them were elaborate and very expensive. What did you make of it yourself?"

Leamas shrugged. "I thought Control must have a bloody good source. But I didn't like the way it was done—it was too complicated, too high-powered. Why couldn't they just meet him and give him the money in cash? Did they really let him cross borders on his own passport, with a forged one in his pocket to use at the bank? I doubt it." It was time he clouded the issue. Let Peters chase a hare.

"What do you mean?"

"I mean that for all I know the money was never drawn from the bank. Suppose he was a highly placed agent behind the Curtain—the money would be on deposit for him when he could get at it later. That was what I reckoned, anyway. I didn't think about it all that much. It's part of our work only to know pieces of the whole setup. You know that. If you're curious, God help you."

Peters thought for a moment. Then he asked, "What names did you use in Copenhagen and Helsinki?"

"In Copenhagen, Robert Lang, electrical engineer from Derby."

"When exactly were you in Copenhagen?" Peters asked.

"I told you, June the fifteenth."

"Which bank did you use?"

"Oh come on, Peters," said Leamas, suddenly angry, "the Royal Scandinavian. You've got it written down."

"I just wanted to be sure," the other replied evenly, and continued writing. "And at Helsinki, what name?"

"Stephen Bennett, marine engineer from Plymouth. I was there," he added sarcastically, "at the end of September."

"Did you take the money with you from England?"

"Of course not. We just transferred it to the local resident's account. He drew it, met me at the airport with the money in a suitcase, and I took it to the bank."

"Who's the resident in Copenhagen?"

"Peter Jensen, a bookseller in the university bookshop."

"And what were the names which would be used by the agent?"

"In Copenhagen, Horst Karlsdorf. I remember I kept wanting to say Karlshorst. From Klagenfurt, in Austria."

"And in Helsinki?"

"He would call himself Adolf Fechtmann, from Saint Gallen, Switzerland. With a title—yes, that's right: Dr. Fechtmann, archivist."

"I see. Both German-speaking."

"Yes, I noticed that. But this agent can't be a German."

"Why not?"

"I was head of the Berlin setup, wasn't I? A high-level agent in East Germany would have to be run from Berlin. I'd have known." Leamas got up, went to the sideboard and poured himself some whisky.

"You said yourself there were special precautions in this case. Perhaps they didn't think you needed to know."

"Don't be bloody silly," Leamas rejoined shortly. "Of course I'd have known." This was the point he would stick to through thick and thin. It made them feel they knew better, gave credence to the rest of his information. "They will want to deduce *in spite of you*," Control had said. "We must give them the material and remain skeptical of their conclusions. Rely on their intelligence and conceit, on their

suspicion of one another—that's what we must do."

Peters nodded as if he were confirming a melancholy truth. "You are a very proud man, Leamas," he observed once more. He left soon after that. It was lunchtime.

PETERS DIDN'T APPEAR that afternoon, nor the next morning.

Leamas stayed in, waiting with growing irritation for some message, but none came. He asked the housekeeper, but she just smiled and shrugged her heavy shoulders. At about eleven o'clock he went out for a walk by the seafront.

There was a girl standing on the beach throwing bread to the sea gulls. Her back was turned to him. The sea wind played with her long black hair and pulled at her coat, making an arc of her body, like a bow strung toward the sea. He knew then what it was that Liz had given him; the thing that he would have to go back and find if ever he got home to England: it was the caring about little things—the simple faith in ordinary life that made you break up a bit of bread into a paper bag, walk down to the beach and throw it to the gulls. It was this caring that he had never been allowed to possess; whether it was bread, or love, whatever it was, he would go back and make Liz find it for him. A week, two weeks perhaps, and he would be home. Control had said he could keep whatever they paid—and that would be enough. With fifteen thousand pounds and a pension from the Circus, a man—as Control would say—can afford to come in from the cold.

He made a detour and returned to the bungalow at a quarter to twelve. The woman let him in without a word, but when he had gone into the back room he heard her dial a number and speak for a few seconds.

At half past twelve the woman brought his lunch and, to his pleasure, some English newspapers. Leamas, who normally read nothing, read newspapers slowly and with concentration. He remembered details, like the names and addresses of people in small news items. He did it almost unconsciously as a kind of mental exercise.

At three o'clock Peters arrived, and as soon as Leamas saw him he knew that something was up.

"I've got bad news for you," Peters said. "They're looking for you in England. I heard this morning. They're watching the ports."

Leamas replied impassively, "On what charge?"

"Nominally for failing to report to a police station within the statutory period after release from prison."

"And in fact?"

"The word is going around that you're wanted for an offense under the Official Secrets Act. Your photograph's in all the London evening papers. The captions are very vague."

Leamas was standing very still. Control had done it. Control had started the hue and cry. There was no other explanation. "A couple of weeks," he'd said. "I expect they'll take you off somewhere for the interrogation—it may even be abroad. After that, the thing should run itself. A couple of weeks should see you through. But I've agreed to keep you on operational subsistence until Mundt is eliminated; that seemed the fairest way."

And now this.

This wasn't part of the bargain. What the hell was he supposed to do? By pulling out now he could wreck the operation. It was possible that Peters was lying, that this was a test—all the more reason he should agree to go. But if he went, if he agreed to go east, to Poland, Czechoslovakia, God knows where, there was no reason why they should ever let him out.

Yes, Control had done it—he was sure. The terms had been too generous, he'd known that all along. They didn't throw money about like that unless they thought they might lose you. Money like that was a warning. Leamas had not heeded the warning.

"Now how the devil," he asked Peters quietly, "could they get on to this?" A thought seemed to cross his mind and he said, "Your friend Ashe could have told them, of course, or Kiever."

"Such things are always possible in our job," Peters replied. "The fact is," he added with something like impatience, "that by now every country in Western Europe will be looking for you."

Leamas might not have heard. "You've got me on the hook now, haven't you?" he said. "Your people must be laughing themselves sick. Unless they gave the tip-off themselves."

"You overrate your own importance," Peters said sourly. "Now let us stick to what we know. How your own authorities have got on to you does not at the moment concern us; the fact is, they have. You know the alternatives: you let us take care of you, or you fend for yourself—with the certainty of eventual capture. You've no false papers, no money, nothing. Your British passport will expire in less than a fortnight."

"There's a third possibility. Give me a Swiss passport and some money and let me run. I can look after myself."

"I am afraid that is not considered desirable."

"You mean you haven't finished the interrogation. Until you have, I am not expendable?"

"That is roughly the position."

"When you have completed the interrogation, what will you do with me?"

Peters shrugged. "What do you suggest?"

"A new identity. Scandinavian passport perhaps. Money."

"It's very academic," Peters replied, "but I will suggest it to my superiors. Are you coming with me?"

Leamas smiled a little uncertainly. "If I didn't, what would you do? After all, I've quite a story to tell, haven't I?"

"Stories of that kind are hard to substantiate."

Leamas went to the window. A storm was gathering over the gray North Sea. He watched the gulls wheeling against the dark clouds. The girl had gone.

"All right," he said at last, "fix it up."

"There's no plane east until tomorrow. There's a flight to Hamburg in an hour. We'll take that. It will be very close."

LEAMAS ADMIRED the efficiency of Peters' arrangements. The passport must have been put together long ago. It was made out in the name of Alexander Thwaite, travel agent, and filled with visas and frontier stamps. The Dutch frontier guard at the airport just nodded and stamped it. Peters was three or four behind Leamas in the line and took no interest in the formalities.

As he entered the passengers-only enclosure Leamas caught sight of a bookstall showing a selection of international newspapers. A girl came around to the front of the kiosk and pushed a London *Evening Standard* into the rack. Leamas hurried across and took the paper. "How much?" he asked. Thrusting his hand into his trouser pocket, he suddenly realized that he had no Dutch currency.

"Thirty cents," the girl replied. She was pretty—dark and jolly.

"I've only got two English shillings. That's a guilder. Will you take them?"

"Yes, please," she replied, and Leamas gave her the coins. He looked back. Peters was still at the passport desk, his back turned. Without hesitation Leamas made straight for the men's lavatory. There he glanced rapidly at each page, then shoved the paper in the litter basket and emerged. It was true. There was his photograph with a vague little passage underneath. He wondered if Liz had seen it. He made his way thoughtfully to the passengers' lounge.

Ten minutes later they boarded the plane for Hamburg and ultimately Berlin. For the first time since it all began, Leamas was frightened.

THE MEN CALLED on Liz in her flat at the northern end of Bayswater the same evening.

She was afraid to think of Leamas too much now, because she had forgotten what he looked like. So she let her mind think of him for brief moments, like running her eyes across a faint horizon; and then she would remember some small thing he had said or done, some way he had looked at her, or more often, ignored her. The terrible thing was that she had nothing to remember him by—no photograph, no souvenir, nothing.

She had been around to his room. It had been rented, but she had talked to the landlord. He had been very kind about Alec; Mr. Leamas had paid his rent like a gentleman, right till the end. Then there'd been a week or two owing, and a chum of Mr. Leamas'—a funny little shy chap with specs—had dropped in and paid up handsome. He'd always said it of Mr. Leamas, he was a gent. Of course he drank more than was good for him, but he never acted tight when he came home, and he only did to Ford the grocer what a good many had been wanting to do.

She went on working at the library—because there, at least, Leamas still existed. The shelves, the books, the card index, were things he had known and touched, and one day he might come back to them. He had said he would never come back, but she didn't believe it.

Miss Crail thought he would come back; she had discovered she owed him some wages, and it infuriated her that her monster had been so unmonstrous as not to collect them.

After Leamas had gone, Liz often asked herself the same question: Why had he hit Mr. Ford? He must have intended to do it right from the start. Why else had he said good-by to her the night before? He knew that he would hit that man the next day. And she knew—she had always known—that there was something else Alec had to do. He'd told her that himself. What it was she could not guess.

They'd talked about Alec in the meeting of her Party branch. George Hanby, the branch treasurer, had actually been passing the grocer's as it happened. He hadn't seen much because of the crowd, but he'd talked to a bloke who'd seen the whole thing. It was just a case of hatred against the boss class. This bloke that Hanby spoke to (he was just an ordinary little chap with specs, white-collar type) said it had been so sudden—spontaneous protest was what he meant.

Liz had kept very quiet while Hanby talked; none of them knew, of course, about her and Leamas. She realized that she hated George Hanby; he was a pompous, dirty-minded little man, always leering at her and trying to touch her.

Then the men called. They said they came from Scotland Yard, and they had printed cards with photographs in cellophane cases; but she thought they were a little too smart for policemen. The one who did most of the talking was short and rather plump. He had glasses and wore odd, expensive clothes. He was a kindly, worried little man, and Liz trusted him somehow without knowing why.

"I believe you were friendly with Alec Leamas," the man in glasses began.

She was prepared to be angry, but he was so earnest that it seemed silly. "Yes," she answered. "How did you know?"

"We found out quite by chance. When you go to . . . prison, you have to give next of kin. They asked Leamas whom they should inform if anything happened to him in prison. He said you."

"I see."

"Does anyone else know you were friendly with him?"

"No. No one else knew. Not even my parents. And I don't think it would occur to Miss Crail, at the library, that there was anything between Alec and me."

The little man peered very seriously at her for a moment. Then he asked, "Did it surprise you when Leamas beat up Mr. Ford?"

"Yes, of course."

"Why do you think he did it?"

"I don't know. Because Ford wouldn't give him credit, I suppose. But I think he always meant to." She wondered if she was saying too much, but she longed to talk to somebody about it and there didn't seem any harm. "That night, the night before it happened, we had supper, a sort of special one with wine. Alec said we should, and I knew that it was our last night. I asked him, 'Is this good-by?' "

"What did he say?"

"He said there was a job he had to do. Someone to pay off for something they'd done to a friend of his. I didn't really understand it all."

There was a very long silence, and the little man looked more worried than ever. Finally he asked her, "Do you believe that?"

"I don't know." She was suddenly terrified for Alec, and she didn't know why.

Then the man said, "Leamas has two children by his marriage. Yet he gave your name as next of kin. Why do you think he did that?" The little man seemed embarrassed by his own question.

Liz blushed. "I was in love with him," she replied.

"Was he in love with you?"

"Perhaps. I don't know."

"Are you still in love with him?"

"Yes."

"Did he say he would come back?" asked the other man.

"No."

"But he did say good-by to you?" he asked quickly.

"Did he say good-by to you?" The man in glasses repeated the question slowly, kindly. "Nothing more can happen to him, I promise you. But we want to help him, and if you have any idea why he hit Ford—the slightest notion, from something he said, perhaps casually, or something he did—then tell us for Alec's sake."

Liz shook her head. "Please don't ask any more questions. Please go now," she said.

As he got to the door the plump man took a card from his wallet and put it on the table gingerly, as if it might make a noise. Liz thought he was a very shy little man.

"If you ever want any help—if anything happens about Leamas, ring me up," he said. "Do you understand?"

"Who are you?"

"I'm a friend of Alec Leamas'." He hesitated. "One last question. Did Alec know you were . . . Did he know about the Party?"

"Yes," she replied hopelessly. "I told him."

"Does the Party know about you and Alec?"

"I've told you. No one knew." Then, white-faced, she cried out suddenly, "Where is he? Tell me where he is. I can help him. I'll look after him . . . even if he's gone mad. I don't care, I swear I don't. I wrote to him in prison; I said he could come back anytime, I'd wait for him always. . . ." She couldn't speak anymore. She sobbed and sobbed, her face buried in her hands.

The man in glasses watched her. "Alec's gone abroad," he said gently. "We don't quite know where he is. He isn't mad, but he shouldn't have said all that to you. It was a pity."

The other man said, "We'll see you're looked after. For money and that kind of thing."

"Who are you?" Liz asked again.

"Friends of Alec's," the man in glasses repeated. "Good friends."

She heard them go downstairs and into the street. From her window she watched them drive away in a small black car.

Then she remembered the card. She picked it up and held it to the light. It was engraved; more than a policeman could afford, she thought. No rank, no police station. And whoever heard of a policeman living in Chelsea?

MR. GEORGE SMILEY, 9 BYWATER STREET, CHELSEA. Then the telephone number underneath.

It was very strange.

10

LEAMAS UNFASTENED his seat belt. It is said that men condemned to death are subject to sudden moments of elation. After making his decision, Leamas was aware of a comparable sensation; relief, short-lived but consoling, sustained him for a time. It was followed by fear and hunger.

He was slowing down. Control was right. He'd noticed it first early last year. Karl Riemeck had gotten something special for Leamas and was making one of his rare visits to West Germany under the cover of some legal conference at Karlsruhe. He'd sent a message asking Leamas to meet him.

Leamas had flown to Cologne and picked up a car at the airport. It was quite early in the morning, and he'd hoped to miss most of the autobahn traffic to Karlsruhe, but the heavy trucks were already on the move. He was weaving between the traffic, taking risks to beat the clock, when a small car nosed its way out into the fast lane just ahead of him. Leamas stamped on the brake, turning his headlights full on and sounding his horn, and by the grace of God he missed it. As he passed the car he saw four children in the back, waving and laughing, and the stupid, frightened face of their father at the wheel. He drove on, cursing, and suddenly his hands were shaking feverishly, his face was burning hot, his heart palpitating wildly.

He had managed to pull off the road, then had scrambled out of the car and stood, breathing heavily, staring at the hurtling stream of giant trucks. He had a vision of the little car caught among them, pounded and smashed, and the bodies of the children torn, like refugees he had seen in the war on the road across the dunes in Holland. He drove very slowly the rest of the way and missed his meeting with Karl.

He never drove again without some corner of his memory recalling the tousled children waving to him from that car, and their father grasping the wheel. Control would call it "fever."

Now he sat dully in his seat over the wing. There was an American woman next to him, wearing high-heeled shoes in plastic boots. He had a momentary notion of passing her some note for the people in Berlin, but he discarded it at once. She'd think he was making a pass at her. Besides, what was the point? Control had made all this happen. There was nothing to say.

He wondered what would become of him. Control hadn't talked about that—only about the technique: "Don't give it to them all at once. Make them work for it. Confuse them with detail, leave things out, go back on your tracks. Be testy, cussed, difficult. Drink like a fish. Don't give way on the ideology, they won't trust that. They want to deal with a professional they've bought, not some fuzzy-minded convert. Above all, they want to *deduce*. The ground's prepared; we did it long ago, little things, difficult clues. You're the last stage in the treasure hunt. One thing I can promise you: it's worth it. For our special interest, Alec. Keep that man alive and we've won a great victory."

He'd had to agree to do it; you can't back out of the big fight when all the preliminary ones have been fought for you. But he didn't think he could stand torture.

It was nearly dark when they landed at Tempelhof. Leamas watched the lights of West Berlin rise to meet them, felt the thud as the plane touched down. For a moment he was anxious lest some former acquaintance recognize him at the airport. But as Peters and he went through the customs and immigration check, and no familiar face turned to greet him, he realized that his anxiety had in reality been hope; hope that somehow his decision to go east would be revoked by circumstance.

They were walking toward the main entrance when Peters abruptly changed direction and led Leamas to a side entrance which opened onto a parking lot. Peters hesitated beneath the light over the door, then put down his suitcase, deliberately removed his newspaper from under his arm, folded it, pushed it into the left pocket of his raincoat and picked up his suitcase again. Immediately a pair of headlights in the parking lot sprang to life, were dipped and then extinguished.

"Come on," said Peters, and they started to walk briskly across the lot. As they reached the first row of cars the rear door of a Mercedes was opened from the inside, and the courtesy light went on. Peters went quickly to the car, spoke softly to the driver, then called to Leamas, a few yards behind, "Here's the car. Be quick."

Leamas sat beside Peters in the back. As the car pulled out it overtook a small DKW with two men in the front. Twenty yards down the road a man was talking in a telephone booth, and he watched them go by, talking all the time. Leamas looked back and saw the DKW following them. Quite a reception, he thought.

They drove very slowly. Leamas sat with his hands on his knees, looking straight in front of him. This was his last chance, he knew. The way he was sitting now, he could drive the side of his right hand into Peters' throat, smashing the promontory of the thorax. He could get out and run, weaving to avoid the bullets from the car behind. There were people in Berlin who would take care of him—he could get away.

He did nothing.

Crossing the sector border was easier than Leamas had expected. For about ten minutes they dawdled, and he guessed that they had to cross at a prearranged time. Then, as they approached the West German checkpoint, the DKW overtook them with an ostentatious roar and stopped at the police hut. The Mercedes waited several yards behind. Two minutes later the red-and-white pole lifted to let through the DKW, and as it did so, both cars drove over together, the Mercedes' engine screaming in second gear, the driver pressing himself back against his seat, holding the wheel at arm's length.

The booms at the eastern side of the checkpoint were already lifted, and they drove straight through, past the Vopos. A few minutes later the DKW disappeared, but soon Leamas sighted it again behind them. They began driving fast.

"Where are we going?" Leamas asked Peters.

"We are there. The German Democratic Republic."

"I thought we'd be going further east."

"We are, but we are spending a day or two here first. We thought the Germans ought to have a talk with you. After all, most of your work has been on the German side. I sent them details from your statement."

"And they asked to see me?"

"They've never had anything quite like you. Nothing quite so . . . near the source. My people agreed that they should have the chance to meet you."

"Whom will I see on the German side?"

"Does it matter?"

"Not particularly. I know most of the Abteilung people by name, that's all. I just wondered."

"Whom would you expect to meet?"

"Jens Fiedler," Leamas replied promptly, "head of counterintelligence. Mundt's man. I've heard about him. He does all the big interrogations. He caught an agent of Peter Guillam's and bloody nearly killed him."

"Espionage is not a cricket game," Peters observed sourly. So it *is* Fiedler, Leamas thought.

Leamas knew Fiedler, all right. He knew him from the photographs in the file and from Karl's accounts of him. A slim, neat man, quite young, with dark hair and bright brown eyes; intelligent and savage. A lithe, quick body and a patient, retentive mind; a man seemingly without ambition for himself but remorseless in the destruction of others. Fiedler was a rarity in the Abteilung—he took no part in its intrigues, belonged to no clique, seemed content to live in Mundt's shadow without prospect of promotion. He was a solitary; feared, disliked and mistrusted. Whatever motives he had were concealed beneath a cloak of destructive sarcasm.

"Fiedler is our best bet," Control had explained. They'd been sitting together over dinner—Leamas, Control and Peter Guillam—in

Control's dreary little house in Surrey. "Fiedler is the acolyte who one day will stab the high priest in the back. He's the only man who's a match for Mundt"—here Guillam had nodded agreement—"and he hates his guts. Fiedler's a Jew, and Mundt is still, at heart, a Nazi. Not at all a good mixture. It has been our job," he declared, indicating Guillam and himself, "to give Fiedler the weapon with which to destroy Mundt. It will be yours, my dear Leamas, to encourage him to use it. Indirectly, of course, because you'll never meet Fiedler. At least I certainly hope you won't." It had seemed a good joke at the time, at least by Control's standards, and they'd all laughed.

It MUST BE after midnight, Leamas thought. For some time they had been traveling an unpaved road, partly through a wood and partly across open country. Now they stopped, and a moment later the DKW drew up beside them.

As he and Peters got out Leamas noticed that there were now three men in the second car. Two were already getting out. The third was sitting in the back seat looking at some papers by the light from the car roof, a slight figure half in shadow.

They had parked by a low farmhouse with walls of timber and whitewashed brick; a sort of shoddy barrack hut was attached to the back of the building. The moon was up, and shone so brightly that the wooded hills behind were sharply defined against the pale night sky. They walked to the house, Peters and Leamas leading and the two men behind. The third man in the DKW still had not moved.

They reached the door, and while one of the men fiddled with a bunch of keys the other stood off, his hands in his pockets, covering him. "They're taking no chances," Leamas observed to Peters. "What do they think I am?"

"They are not paid to think," Peters replied, and turning to one of them, he asked in German, "Is he coming?"

The German shrugged and looked back toward the car. "He'll come," he said. "He likes to come alone."

The house, which was furnished like a hunting lodge, had a neglected, musty air as if it had been opened for the occasion. There were little touches of officialdom here and there—a notice of what to do in case of fire, institutional green paint on the doors; and in the drawing room, which was quite comfortably done, dark, heavy furniture and the inevitable photographs of Soviet leaders.

For about ten minutes Peters and Leamas sat and waited, then Peters spoke to one of the two men standing awkwardly at the other end of the room. "Go and tell him we're waiting. And find us some food, we're hungry." As the man moved, Peters called, "And tell them to bring whisky and some glasses." The man gave an uncooperative shrug of his heavy shoulders and went out, leaving the door open.

"Have you been here before?" asked Leamas.

"Yes," Peters replied, "several times, for this kind of thing."

"With Fiedler?"

"Yes."

"Is he good at this?"

Peters shrugged. "For a German, he's not bad," he replied, and Leamas, hearing a sound, turned and saw Fiedler standing in the doorway.

He held a bottle of whisky in one hand and glasses in the other. He couldn't have been more than five feet six. He wore a dark blue single-breasted suit; the jacket was cut too long. He was sleek and slightly animal.

He was not looking at them but at the guard beside the door. "Go away," he said, "and tell the other one to bring us food."

"I've told him," Peters called. "But he brought nothing."

"They are great snobs," Fiedler observed dryly in English. "They think we should have servants for the food."

Fiedler had spent the war in Canada. Leamas remembered that, now that he detected the accent. His parents had been German-Jewish refugees and Marxists, and it was not until 1946 that they had returned home, anxious to take part in the construction of Stalin's Germany.

"Hello," Fiedler said to Leamas, almost by the way. "Glad to see you."

"Hello, Fiedler."

"You've reached the end of the road."

"What the hell do you mean?" asked Leamas quickly.

"I mean that contrary to anything Peters told you, you are not going farther east. Sorry." He sounded amused.

Leamas turned to Peters. "Is this true?" His voice was shaking with rage. "Tell me!"

Peters nodded. "Yes. I am the go-between. We had to do it that way. I'm sorry," he added.

"Why?"

"*Force majeure*," Fiedler put in. "Your initial interrogation took place in the West, where only an embassy could provide the communications facilities we needed. The German Democratic Republic has no embassies in the West. Not yet."

"You swine," hissed Leamas. "You knew I wouldn't trust myself to your rotten department; that was the reason, wasn't it? That was why you used a Russian."

"We used the Soviet embassy at The Hague, but aside from that, it was our operation. Neither we nor anyone else could have known that your own people in England would get on to you so quickly."

"No? Not even when you put them on to me yourselves? Isn't that what happened, Fiedler? You knew damn well I'd never come here unless I had to." Always remember to dislike them, Control had said. Then they will treasure what they get out of you.

"That is an absurd suggestion," Fiedler replied shortly. Glancing toward Peters, he added something in Russian.

Peters nodded and stood up. "Good-by," he said to Leamas. "Good luck." He smiled wearily, nodded to Fiedler, then walked to the door. There he turned and called to Leamas again: "Good luck." But Leamas might not have heard. He had grown very pale, he held his hands loosely across his body, the thumbs upward as if he were going to fight. Peters remained at the door.

"I should have known," said Leamas, and his voice had the odd, faulty note of a very angry man. "You'd never have the guts to do your own dirty work, Fiedler. It's typical of your rotten little half-country and your squalid little department that you get Big Uncle to do your dirty work for you. You're not a country at all, you're not a government, you're a fifth-rate dictatorship of political neurotics." Jabbing his finger at Fiedler, he shouted, "I know you, you bloody sadist! You were in Canada in the war, weren't you? A good safe place to be, wasn't it? And what are you now? A creeping little acolyte to Mundt, with twenty-two Russian divisions to protect you. Well, I pity you, Fiedler, the day you wake up and find them gone. There'll be a killing then, and Big Uncle won't save you from getting what you deserve."

Fiedler looked at his thin, strong fingers. "I find it slightly ridiculous that you should be so indignant. After all," he added silkily, "your own behavior has not, from the purist's point of view, been irreproachable."

Leamas was watching Fiedler with an expression of disgust. "They say you want Mundt's job. I suppose you'll get it now. It's time the Mundt dynasty ended; perhaps this is it."

"I don't understand," Fiedler replied.

"I'm your big success, aren't I?" Leamas sneered.

Fiedler seemed to reflect for a moment, then he shrugged and said, "The operation was successful. Whether you were worth it is questionable. We shall see. But the operation satisfied the only requirement of our profession: it worked."

"I suppose you take the credit?" Leamas persisted, with a glance at Peters, still standing by the door.

"There is no question of credit," Fiedler replied crisply. He sat down on the arm of the sofa and looked at Leamas thoughtfully. "You are right to be indignant about one thing. Who told your people we had picked you up? You may not believe me, but we didn't.

And surely not Ashe or Kiever, since they would not both be under arrest if—"

"Under arrest?"

"So it appears. Not specifically for their work on your case, but there were other things. . . ."

"Well, well."

"It is true, what I said just now. We would have been content with Peters' report from Holland. But you hadn't told us everything; and I want to know everything."

There was a silence, during which Peters, with an abrupt and by no means friendly nod in Fiedler's direction, quietly let himself out of the room.

Fiedler picked up the bottle of whisky and poured a little into each glass. "We have no soda, I'm afraid," he said. "Do you like water?"

"Oh, go to hell," said Leamas. He suddenly felt very tired.

Fiedler shook his head. "You are a very proud man," he observed, "but never mind. Eat your supper and go to bed."

One of the guards had come in with a tray of food—black bread, sausage and a green salad. "It is a little crude," said Fiedler, "but quite satisfying. No potato, I'm afraid. There is a temporary shortage of potatoes."

They ate in silence. Afterward the guards showed Leamas to his bedroom. Carrying his own luggage, he walked between them along the wide central corridor of the house. They came to a door, and one of the guards unlocked it and beckoned to Leamas to go first. He pushed open the door and found himself in a small barrack bedroom with two bunk beds, like something in a prison camp. There were pictures of girls on the walls, and the windows were shuttered. At the far end of the room was another door. They signaled him forward again. Putting down his baggage, he went and opened the door. The second room was identical to the first, even to the door at the far end, but there was one bed and the walls were bare.

"You bring those cases," he said. "I'm tired." He lay down on the bed, fully dressed, and within a few minutes he was fast asleep.

A SENTRY WOKE HIM with breakfast: black bread and ersatz coffee. He got out of bed and went to the window.

The house stood on a high hill. Beneath his window a pine forest fell steeply to the valley. Beyond, spectacular in their symmetry, unending hills, heavy with beech and pine, stretched into the distance. Here and there a log skid or firebreak formed a thin brown divide between the pines. There was no sign of man; not a house or church —only the road, a yellow dirt road, a crayon line across the basin of the valley. There was no sound. It seemed incredible that anything so vast could be so still. The day was cold but clear, and the whole landscape was so sharply defined against the white sky that Leamas could distinguish even single trees on the farthest hills.

He dressed slowly, drinking the sour coffee meanwhile. He was about to start eating the bread when Fiedler came in.

"Good morning," he said cheerfully. "Don't let me keep you from your breakfast." He sat down on the bed. "You have presented us with an intriguing problem."

"I've told you all I know."

"Oh no." Fiedler smiled. "You have told us all you are *conscious* of knowing."

"Bloody clever," Leamas muttered, pushing his food aside and lighting a cigarette.

"Let me ask you a question," Fiedler suggested, with the exaggerated bonhomie of a man proposing a party game. "As an experienced intelligence officer, what would *you* do with the information you have given us?"

"Which part of the information?"

"My dear Leamas, you have only given us one piece of real intelligence. You have told us about Riemeck: we knew about him. You have told us about your Berlin organization, about its personalities and its agents. That, if I may say so, is old hat. Accurate—yes. Good collateral material; here and there a little fish which we shall take out of the pool. But not—if I may be crude—not worth fifteen thousand pounds."

"Listen," said Leamas, "I didn't propose this deal—you did. You named the price and took the risk. So don't blame me if the operation's a flop." Always make them come to you, Leamas thought.

"It isn't a flop," Fiedler replied. "I said you had given us one piece of intelligence. I'm talking about Rolling Stone. What would *you* do if I, or Peters, had told *you* a similar story?"

Leamas shrugged. "I'd feel uneasy," he said. "It's happened before.

You get an indication, several perhaps, that there's a spy in some department or at a certain level. So what? You can't arrest the whole government service or lay traps for a whole department. You just sit tight and hope for more. In Rolling Stone you can't even tell what country this agent is working in."

"You are an operator, Leamas," Fiedler observed with a laugh, "not an evaluator. That is clear. Let me ask you some elementary questions." Leamas said nothing. "The file—the actual file on operation Rolling Stone. What color was it?"

"Gray with a red cross on it—that means limited subscription, a small circulation."

"Was anything attatched to the outside?"

"Yes, the caveat: a label with a legend saying that any person not named on the label who found the file in his possession must at once return it unopened to Banking section."

"Who was on the list for Rolling Stone?"

"Control's personal assistant, Control, Control's secretary, myself in Banking, Miss Bream of Special Registry, and Satellites Four. That's all, I think."

"Satellites Four? What do they do?"

"Iron Curtain countries, excluding the Soviet Union and China. That includes the Zone."

"You mean the German Democratic Republic?"

"I mean what we call the Zone."

"Isn't it unusual for a whole section to be on such a list?"

"I wouldn't know—I'd never handled limited-subscription stuff before. Except in Berlin, of course. But it was all different there."

"Who was in Satellites Four at that time?"

"Oh, hell. Guillam . . . Haverlake. De Jong, I think. De Jong was just back from Berlin."

"Were they *all* allowed to see this file?"

"I don't know, Fiedler," Leamas retorted irritably.

"Isn't it odd that one whole section—Satellites Four—was on the subscription list, while all the rest of the subscribers are individuals?"

"I tell you I don't know—how could I know? I was just a clerk in all this."

"Who carried the file from one subscriber to another?"

"Secretaries, I suppose—I can't remember. It's months since—"

"Then why weren't the secretaries on the list? Control's secretary was." There was a moment's silence.

"No, you're right; I remember now," Leamas said, a note of surprise in his voice. "We passed it by hand. One of the women in Banking had done it before, but when I came I took it over."

"Then you alone in your section passed the file by hand to the next reader?"

"Yes—yes, I suppose I did."

"To whom did you pass it?"

"I . . . I can't remember."

"*Think!*" Fiedler had not raised his voice, but it contained a sudden urgency which took Leamas by surprise.

"To Control's personal assistant, I think, to show what action we had taken or recommended."

"Who brought the file to *you* to read?"

Leamas' fingers touched his cheek in an involuntary nervous gesture. "It's difficult to remember, Fiedler. I was putting back a lot of drink in those days." His tone was oddly conciliatory.

"I ask you again. Think. Who brought you the file?"

Leamas sat down at the desk and shook his head.

"I can't remember, really I can't. It may come back to me. It's no good chasing it."

"It can't have been Control's girl, can it? You always handed the file *back* to Control's assistant. You said so. So those on the list must all have seen it *before* Control."

"Yes. I suppose they must."

"Then there is Special Registry. Miss Bream."

"She was just the woman who kept the safe where the files were stored when they weren't in action."

"Then," said Fiedler silkily, "it must have been Satellites Four who brought it, mustn't it?"

"Yes, I suppose it must," said Leamas helplessly, as if he were not quite up to Fiedler's brilliance.

"Do you remember *who* brought it from Satellites Four? Or do you remember ever going to collect the file from them?"

In despair Leamas shook his head. Then suddenly he cried, "Yes. Yes, I do! I got it from Peter!" Leamas seemed to have waked up; his face was flushed, excited. "That's it, I once collected the file from

Peter in his own room. We chatted together about Norway. We'd served there together, you see."

"Peter Guillam?"

"Yes, Peter—I'd forgotten that. He was on the list! It was Satellites Four, and P. G. in brackets, Peter's initials."

"What territory did Guillam cover?"

"The Zone—East Germany. Economic stuff. He headed a small research and evaluation section. A sort of backwater. He didn't run agents at that time, so I don't quite know how he came into it."

"Didn't you discuss it with him?"

"No, that's taboo with those files. No discussion; no questions."

"But taking into account the elaborate security precautions surrounding Rolling Stone, isn't it possible that Guillam's so-called research job might have involved the partial running of this agent they called Rolling Stone?"

"I've told Peters," Leamas almost shouted, banging his fist on the desk, "it's just bloody silly to imagine that any operation could have been run against East Germany without my knowledge—without the knowledge of the Berlin organization. How many times do I have to say that? I would have known!"

"Quite so," said Fiedler softly, "of course you would." He stood up and went to the window. "You should see it in the autumn," he said, looking out. "It's magnificent when the beech leaves are turning."

11

FIEDLER AND LEAMAS went for a walk that afternoon, following a gravel road down into the valley, then branching into the forest along a broad track lined with felled timber. All the time Fiedler asked questions. About the building in Cambridge Circus and the people who worked there. What social class did they come from? In what parts of London did they live? He asked about their pay, their morale, their love life, their gossip, their philosophy. Most of all he asked about their philosophy.

To Leamas that was the most difficult question of all. "What do you mean, philosophy?" he replied. "We're not Marxists. We're nothing. Just people."

"What makes them do it, then?" Fiedler persisted. "They must have a philosophy."

"Why must they? Not everyone has a philosophy," Leamas answered a little helplessly.

"But what is the justification for their work then? For us, it is easy. The Abteilung is to the Communist Party what the Party is to socialism: we are its vanguard in the fight for peace and progress. Stalin said—" he smiled dryly, "it is not fashionable to quote Stalin—but he said once, 'Half a million liquidated is a statistic, and one man killed in a traffic accident is a national tragedy.' He was laughing, you see, at bourgeois sensitivities. He was a great cynic. But what he meant is true: a movement which protects itself against counterrevolution can hardly stop at the elimination of a few individuals. All our work—yours and mine—is rooted in the theory that the whole is more important than the individual. Some Roman said it, didn't he, in the Christian Bible—it is expedient that one man should die for the benefit of many?"

"I expect so," Leamas replied wearily.

"Then what do you think? What is your philosophy?"

"I just think the whole lot of you are scum," said Leamas savagely.

Fiedler nodded. "That is a viewpoint I understand. It is primitive, negative and very stupid, but it is a viewpoint. It exists. What about the rest of the Circus?"

"I don't know." He hesitated, then added vaguely, "I suppose they don't like communism."

"That justified your write-off rate of agents and so on?"

Leamas shrugged. "I suppose so. We've got to defend ourselves, haven't we?"

"But you people believe in the sanctity of human life. You believe every man has a soul which can be saved. You believe in sacrifice. Well—" Fiedler smiled. "I like the English," he said, almost to himself. "My father did too. He was very fond of the English."

"That gives me a nice, warm feeling," Leamas retorted and lapsed into silence.

They were in the woods, climbing steeply now. Leamas liked the exercise, walking ahead with long strides, his shoulders thrust forward. Fiedler followed, slight and agile as a terrier. They must have been walking for an hour or more when suddenly the trees broke above them and the sky appeared. They had reached the top of a small hill and could look down on a solid mass of pine and beech. Across the valley Leamas glimpsed the house and barrack, perched on the opposite hill.

In the middle of the clearing was a rough bench beside a pile of logs and the damp remnants of a charcoal fire. "We'll sit down for a moment," said Fiedler, "then we must go back." He paused. "Tell me: this money, these large sums in foreign banks—what did you think they were for?"

"I've told you. I thought they were payments to an agent from behind the Iron Curtain."

"Why did you think so?"

"First, it was a hell of a lot of money. Then the special security. And, of course, Control being mixed up in it."

"What do you think the agent did with the money?"

"Look, I've told you—I don't even know if he collected it."

"What did you do with the passbooks for the accounts?"

"I handed them in as soon as I got back to London."

"Did the Copenhagen or Helsinki bank ever write to you in London—to your alias, I mean?"

"I don't know. I suppose any letters would have been passed straight to Control."

"The false signatures you used to open the accounts—Control had a sample of them?"

"Yes. I practiced them a lot and Control's office had samples."

"I see. Then letters could have gone to the banks after you had opened the accounts. You need not have known. The signatures could have been forged."

"Yes. That's right. I suppose that's what happened. I signed a lot of blank sheets too."

"But you didn't actually *know* of such correspondence?"

Leamas shook his head. "You've got it all out of proportion. I've been in on things all my life where I'd only know a little and someone else would know the rest. There were lots of papers going around; I didn't sit at my desk all day wondering about Rolling Stone. Besides," he added a little shamefacedly, "I was hitting the bottle a bit."

"So you said. It occurred to me," Fiedler continued, "that you could still help us to establish whether any of that money was ever drawn, by writing to each bank and asking for a current statement. We could say you were staying in Switzerland, use an accommodation address. Do you see any objection to that?"

"It might work. It depends on whether Control has been corresponding with the bank independently, over my forged signature. It might not fit in with what he's written."

"I don't see that we have much to lose."

"What have you got to win?"

"If the money *has* been drawn, we will know where the agent was on a certain day. That seems a useful thing to know."

"You're dreaming. How are you any the wiser? You don't even know whether the man is East German."

Fiedler gazed across the valley. "You said you are accustomed to knowing only a little, and I cannot answer your question without telling you what you should not know." He hesitated. "But Rolling Stone was an operation against us, I can assure you."

"Us?"

"The German Democratic Republic." He smiled. "The Zone, if you prefer. I am not really so sensitive."

Leamas was watching Fiedler now, his brown eyes resting on him reflectively. "But what about me?" he asked. "Suppose I don't write the letters?" His voice was rising. "Isn't it time to talk about me, Fiedler?"

Fiedler nodded. "Why not?" he replied agreeably.

There was a moment's silence, then Leamas said, "I've done my bit, Fiedler. You and Peters between you have got all I know. I never agreed to write letters to banks—it could be bloody dangerous. That doesn't worry you, I know. As far as you're concerned I'm expendable."

"Now let me be frank," Fiedler replied. "There are, as you know, two stages in the interrogation of a defector. The first stage in your case is nearly complete: you have given us what you think important. You have not told us whether your service prefers pins or paper clips because we haven't asked you, and because you did not consider the information worth volunteering. There is a process on both sides of unconscious selection. Now it is always possible—and this is the worrying thing, Leamas—that in a month or two we shall unexpectedly and desperately need to know about the little things that apparently don't matter—pins and paper clips. That is normally taken care of in the second stage—that part of the bargain which you refused to accept in Holland."

"You mean you're going to keep me on ice?"

"The profession of defector," Fiedler observed with a smile, "demands great patience."

"How long?" Leamas insisted. Fiedler was silent. "Well?"

Fiedler spoke with sudden urgency. "I give you my word that as soon as I possibly can I will answer your question. Look—I could lie to you: I could say one month or less, just to keep you happy. But I am telling you I don't know because that is the truth. You have given us some clues to pursue; until we have run them to earth I cannot let you go. But afterward, if things are as I think they are, you will need a friend, and that friend will be me. I give you my word as a German."

Leamas was so taken aback that for a moment he was silent. "All right," he said finally, "I'll play, Fiedler, but if you are stringing me along, somehow I'll break your neck."

"That may not be necessary," Fiedler replied evenly.

A MAN WHO lives a part, not only to others but when alone, is exposed to obvious dangers and temptations. In itself, the practice of deception is not particularly exacting; it is a matter of experience, of professional skill. But while a confidence man, an actor or a gambler can relax after his performance, the secret agent cannot. He must protect himself not only from without but from within, and against the most natural of his impulses. Though he earn a fortune, his role may forbid him to buy a razor; though he be an affectionate husband and father, he must withhold himself from those in whom he would naturally confide.

Thus, even when he was alone, Leamas compelled himself to live with the personality he had assumed. The qualities he exhibited to Fiedler—the restless uncertainty, the arrogance concealing shame—he remained faithful to when alone; also the slight dragging of the feet, the personal neglect, the indifference to food and reliance on alcohol. He would even exaggerate these habits a little, mumbling to himself about the iniquities of his service. Only very rarely, as now, going to bed that evening, did he allow himself the dangerous luxury of admitting the great lie he lived.

Control had been phenomenally right. Fiedler was walking, like a man led in his sleep, into the net that Control had spread for him. It was uncanny to observe the growing identity of interest between Fiedler and Control: it was as if they had agreed on the same plan, and Leamas had been dispatched to help them fulfill it.

Perhaps that was the answer. Perhaps Fiedler was the special interest that Control was fighting so desperately to preserve. Leamas hoped to God it was true. It was possible, just possible in that case, that he would get home.

12

LEAMAS WAS STILL in bed the next morning when Fiedler brought him the letters to sign. One was on the thin blue writing paper of the Seiler Hotel Alpenblick, Lake Spiez, Switzerland, the other from the Palace Hotel, Gstaad. The first was to the manager of the Royal Scandinavian Bank, Copenhagen.

> Dear Sir,
> I have been traveling for some weeks and have not received any mail from England. Accordingly I have not had your reply to my letter of March 3rd requesting a current statement of the savings account of which I am a joint signatory with Herr Karlsdorf. To avoid further delay, would you be good enough to forward a duplicate statement to me at 13 Avenue des Colombes, Paris XII, France, where I shall be staying for two weeks.
> I apologize for this confusion.
>
> Yours faithfully,
(Robert Lang)

"What's all this about a letter of March third?" Leamas asked. "I didn't write them any letter."

"No, you didn't. That will worry the bank. If there is any inconsistency between the letter we are sending them now and letters they have had from Control, they will assume the solution is to be found in the *missing* letter of March third. Their reaction will be to send you the statement as you ask, regretting that they have not received your letter of the third."

The second letter was the same as the first; only the names were different. The address in Paris was the same. Leamas took a blank piece of paper and his fountain pen, and wrote half a dozen times in a fluent hand, "Robert Lang," then signed the first letter. Sloping his pen backward, he practiced the second signature, then wrote "Stephen Bennett" under the second letter.

"Admirable," Fiedler observed, "quite admirable."

"What do we do now?"

"They will be posted in Switzerland tomorrow. Our people in Paris will telegraph the replies to me as soon as they arrive. We should have the answer in a week."

"And until then?"

"We shall be constantly in one another's company. I know that is distasteful to you, and I apologize. I thought we could go for walks, drive around in the hills a bit. I want you to relax and talk about Cambridge Circus. Tell me the gossip, talk about the pay, the leave, the rooms, the people. The pins and the paper clips. Incidentally"—a change of tone—"we have facilities here for . . . for diversion and so on."

"Are you offering me a woman?" Leamas asked. "If so, no thank you."

Fiedler went on quickly. "But you had a woman in England, didn't you—the girl in the library?"

Leamas turned on him, his hands open at his sides. "Don't ever mention that again," he shouted. "Not as a joke, not as a threat, not even to turn the screws, Fiedler, because it won't work. You'd never get another bloody word from me as long as I lived. Tell that to Mundt or whichever little alley cat told you to say it—tell them what I said."

"I'll tell them," Fiedler replied. "I'll tell them. But it may be too late."

IN THE AFTERNOON they went walking again. The sky was dark and heavy, and the air warm.

"I've only been to England once," Fiedler observed casually. "That was on my way to Canada, with my parents before the war. I nearly went there again a few years back. I was going to replace Mundt on the steel mission. I always wondered what that job would have been like."

"Usual game of mixing with the other Communist bloc missions, I suppose. Certain amount of contact with British business—not much of that." Leamas sounded bored.

"But Mundt got about all right; he found it quite easy."

"So I hear," said Leamas. "He even managed to kill a couple of people."

"So you heard about that too?"

"From Peter Guillam. He was in on it with George Smiley. Mundt bloody nearly killed George as well."

"The Fennan Case," Fiedler mused. "It was amazing that Mundt managed to escape at all, wasn't it?"

"I suppose it was."

"You wouldn't think that a man whose photograph and personal particulars were filed at the Foreign Office as a member of a foreign mission would have a chance against the whole of British Intelligence."

"From what I hear, they weren't too keen to catch him anyway."

Fiedler stopped abruptly. "What did you say?"

"Peter Guillam told me he didn't reckon they wanted to catch Mundt, that's all I said. We had a different setup then—an adviser instead of an operational control. A man called Maston. Maston made a mess of the Fennan Case from the start. Guillam reckoned that if they'd caught Mundt they'd have tried him and probably hanged him, and the dirt that came out in the process would have finished Maston's career. Peter never knew quite what happened, but he was sure there was no full-scale search for Mundt."

"You are sure Guillam told you that in so many words? No full-scale search?"

"Of course I am sure."

"Guillam never suggested any other reason why they might have let Mundt go?"

"What do you mean?"

Fiedler shook his head and they walked on along the path.

"Tell me something about Karl Riemeck," Fiedler said. "He met Control once, didn't he?"

"Yes, in my flat in Berlin about a year ago."

"Why?"

"Control loved to come in on success. We'd got a lot of good stuff from Karl, so Control came to Berlin and asked me to fix it up for them to meet."

"Were you all three together, all the time?"

"Not quite. I left them alone for a quarter of an hour or so—not more. Control wanted a few minutes alone with Karl, God knows why, so I left the flat on some excuse."

"Do you know what passed between them while you were out?"

"How could I? I wasn't that interested, anyway."

"Didn't Karl tell you afterward?"

"I didn't ask him. Karl was a cheeky sort in some ways, always pretending he had something over me. I didn't like the way he sniggered about Control. Mind you, he had every right to snigger—it was a pretty ridiculous performance. We laughed about it together, as a matter of fact, since I didn't want to prick Karl's vanity by backing Control. The whole meeting was supposed to give Karl a shot in the arm."

"Was Karl depressed then?"

"No, far from it. He was spoiled already. He was paid too much, loved too much, trusted too much. If we hadn't spoiled him, he wouldn't have told that bloody Elvira woman about his network."

They walked on in silence for a while, until Fiedler observed, "I'm beginning to like you. But there's one thing that puzzles me. It's odd—it didn't worry me before I met you."

"What's that?"

"Why you ever came over. Why you defected." Leamas was going to say something when Fiedler laughed. "I'm afraid that wasn't very tactful, was it?" he said.

THEY SPENT that week walking in the hills. In the evenings they would return to the lodge, eat a bad meal washed down with a bottle of rank white wine, then sit endlessly over their Steinhäger in front of the fire. Leamas didn't mind those evenings. What with the fresh air all day, the fire and the schnapps, he would talk unprompted, rambling on about his service. He supposed it was recorded, but he didn't care.

As each day passed in this way, Leamas was aware of an increasing tension in his companion. Once they went out in the DKW—it was late in the evening—and stopped at a telephone booth, where Fiedler made a long phone call.

When he came back Leamas said, "Why didn't you ring from the house?"

Fiedler shook his head. "We must take care," he replied. "You too, you must take care."

"Why? What's going on?"

"The money you paid into the Copenhagen bank—we wrote, you remember?"

"Of course I remember."

Fiedler wouldn't say any more, but drove on in silence into the hills. There they stopped. Beneath them, half screened by the ghostly patchwork of tall pine trees, lay the meeting point of two great valleys. The steep wooded hills on either side gradually yielded their colors to the gathering dusk until they stood gray and lifeless in the twilight.

"Whatever happens," Fiedler said, "don't worry. It will be all right." His voice was heavy with emphasis, his slim hand rested on

Leamas' arm. "You may have to look after yourself a little, but it won't last long. Do you understand?"

"No. And since you won't tell me, I shall have to wait and see. Don't worry too much for my skin, Fiedler." He moved his arm—he hated being touched—but Fiedler's hand still held him.

"We've talked about Mundt," Fiedler said. "He shoots first and asks questions afterward. It's an odd system in a profession where the questions are supposed to be more important than the shooting." Leamas knew then what Fiedler wanted to tell him. "It's an odd system unless you're frightened of the answers," Fiedler continued under his breath.

Leamas waited. After a moment Fiedler said, "He's never taken on an interrogation before. He's left it to me, always. He used to say to me, 'I'll catch them and you make them sing, Jens; no one can do it like you.' Then he began to kill them before they sang; one here, another there. I begged him, 'Why not let me have them for a month or two? What good to you are they when they are dead?' I had the feeling that he'd prepared the answer before I ever asked the question. He said that counterintelligence people are like wolves chewing the dry bones of an old kill. You have to take away the bones and make them find new quarry. I can see that.

"Mundt's a good operator, very good. He's done wonders with the Abteilung—you know that. But he's gone too far now. Why did he kill Viereck? Why did he take him away from me? Viereck was fresh quarry; he had much more to tell us. So why did Mundt kill him, Leamas? Why?" The hand clasped Leamas' arm tightly; in the total darkness of the car Leamas was aware of the frightening intensity of Fiedler's emotion.

"I've thought about it night and day," Fiedler went on. "Ever since Viereck was shot, I've asked for a reason. At first it seemed fantastic. I told myself I was jealous, that the work was getting to me—that I was seeing agents behind every tree. We people get like that. But I couldn't help myself, I had to work it out. There'd been other things before. Leamas, he was afraid—afraid we would catch an agent who would talk too much!"

"What are you saying? You're out of your mind!" said Leamas, and his voice held the trace of fear.

"It all held together, you see. Mundt escaped so easily from England; you told me so yourself. And Guillam said they didn't *want* to catch him! Why not? I'll tell you why—he was their man; they turned him. They caught him, don't you see, and to come over to you was the price of his freedom."

"I tell you you're out of your mind!" Leamas hissed. "He'll kill you if he ever thinks you make up this kind of stuff, Fiedler. Shut up and drive us home."

At last the hot grip on Leamas' arm relaxed. Fiedler said, "You provided the answer yourself, Leamas. That's why we need one another."

"It's not true!" Leamas shouted. "I've told you again and again, the Circus couldn't have run him against the Zone without my knowing! It just wasn't an administrative possibility. You're trying to tell me Control was personally directing the deputy head of the Abteilung without the knowledge of the Berlin station. You're just bloody well off your head!"

For a moment neither spoke.

"That money," Fiedler said, "in Copenhagen. The bank replied to your letter. The manager is very worried lest there has been a mistake. The money was drawn by your cosignatory exactly one week after you paid it in. The date it was drawn coincides with a two-day visit which Mundt paid to Denmark."

13

LIZ LOOKED AT the letter from the Communist Party Center and found it a little puzzling. She had to admit she was pleased, but why hadn't they consulted her first?

Had the district committee put up her name, or was it Center's own choice? No one in Center knew her, so far as she was aware, but she'd met occasional speakers at her branch. Perhaps the man from cultural relations had remembered her—that fair, rather effeminate man. Ashe, that was his name. He'd taken her out for coffee after the meeting and asked her masses of questions about herself. How long had she been in the Party? Did she get homesick living away from her parents? Had she lots of boy friends or was there a special one?

She hadn't cared for Ashe much, but his talk at the meeting had gone down quite well. It was about the worker state in the German Democratic Republic. He knew all about East Germany; he seemed to have traveled a lot.

That was it, she was sure now; it must have been Ashe who'd remembered her and handed her name on. It still seemed a funny way to go about things, but then the Party always was secretive. The secrecy seemed dishonest to Liz, but she supposed it was part of being a revolutionary party.

She read the letter again. It began, "Dear Comrade." Liz hated that "Comrade," too; it sounded so military.

Dear Comrade,

We have recently discussed with our comrades in the German Democratic Republic the possibility of rank-and-file exchanges between members of our two parties. They have generously invited us to send five branch secretaries with a good record of stimulating mass action at street level. We therefore asked London district to name the young Party workers who might get the biggest advantage from the trip, and your name has been put forward. We want you to go if you possibly can.

Each comrade will spend three weeks attending meetings, studying Socialist progress, and seeing at firsthand the evidence of Fascist provocation by the West. This will also be a grand opportunity for our comrades to establish contact with German Party branches whose members have the same kinds of problems as their own. Bayswater branch has been paired with Neuenhagen, a suburb of Leipzig, which is preparing a big welcome.

We are sure you realize what an honor this is, and are confident you will not allow personal considerations to prevent your accepting. The visits are all to take place within a few weeks, but the selected comrades will travel separately as their invitations are not concurrent.

Will you please let us know immediately whether you can accept?

The more she read the letter, the odder it seemed. Such short notice for a start—how could they know she could get away from the library? Then she recalled that Ashe had asked her whether she had taken her vacation this year, and whether she had to give a lot of notice before she did so. Why hadn't they told her who the other nominees were? There was no particular reason why they should, perhaps, but it somehow looked odd when they didn't.

It was quite a long letter too. They were so hard up for secretarial help at Center that they usually kept their letters short or asked comrades to telephone. This was so efficient, so well typed—it might not have been done at Center at all. But it *was* signed by the cultural organizer; she'd seen his signature at the bottom of many notices. And the letter had that awkward, semibureaucratic, semimessianic style she had grown accustomed to without ever liking.

It was stupid to say she had "a good record of stimulating mass action at street level." She hadn't. She hated that side of Party work —the loudspeakers at the factory gates, selling the *Daily Worker* at the street corner, going from door to door during the local elections. Helping the Party fight for peace did mean something to her: then she knew that the Party leaders were good, good people. You could look at the kids in the street as you went by, at the mothers pushing carriages, at the old people, and you could say, "I'm doing this for *them*." But fighting for votes and for sales of the *Daily Worker* somehow cut the Party down to size. It was easy when there were a dozen or so at a branch meeting to rebuild the world and feel that you marched at the vanguard of socialism. But afterward she'd go out into the streets with an armful of *Daily Worker*s and wait an hour, two hours, to sell a copy.

Sometimes she'd cheat, as the others cheated, and pay for a dozen herself just to get out of it and go home. At the next meeting they'd boast about it—forgetting they'd bought the papers themselves: "Comrade Gold sold eighteen copies on Saturday night—*eighteen!*" It would go into the minutes then, and the branch bulletin as well. Theirs was such a little world; she wished they could be more honest. But she lied to herself about it all, too. Perhaps they all did. Or perhaps the others understood more *why* you had to lie so much.

It seemed so odd that they'd made her branch secretary. She supposed they'd voted for her because she could type, because she'd do the work and not make them go canvassing on weekends. Not too often anyway. . . . It was all such a fraud. Alec had understood that; he just hadn't taken it seriously. "Some people keep canaries, some join the Party," he'd said, and, at least in Bayswater, it was true. District headquarters knew that perfectly well. That's why it was so peculiar that she had been nominated. Perhaps Ashe had a crush on her?

Liz gave a rather exaggerated shrug, the kind of overstressed gesture people make when they are excited and alone. It was abroad anyway, it was free and it sounded interesting. She had never been
abroad; it would be rather fun.

She went to the desk and opened the drawer where she kept the
branch stationery. Putting a sheet of paper into her old Underwood
typewriter, she wrote a neat, grateful letter of acceptance. As she
closed the drawer again she caught sight of Smiley's card.

She remembered that little spectacled man with the earnest, puck-
ered face, standing at the doorway and saying, "Does the Party know
about you and Alec?" How silly she had been. Well, this would take
her mind off it.

14

FIEDLER AND LEAMAS drove back the rest of the way in silence. In
the dusk the hills were black and cavernous, the pinpoint lights
struggling against the gathering darkness like the lights of distant
ships at sea.

Fiedler parked the car in a shed at the side of the house and they
walked together to the front door. They were about to enter when
they heard someone calling Fiedler's name. They turned, and in the
twilight Leamas distinguished three men standing twenty yards
away, apparently waiting for Fiedler.

"What do you want?" Fiedler called.

"We want to talk to you. We're from Berlin."

Fiedler hesitated. "Where's that damn guard?" he asked Leamas.
"There should be a guard on the front door. And why aren't the
lights on in the hall?" But he began walking slowly toward the men.

Leamas waited a moment, then, hearing nothing, made his way
through the unlit house to the shoddy barrack hut at the back, with
its three connecting bedrooms. Leamas had never known who occupied the room beyond his—the door between it and his own room
was kept locked—but he had supposed that someone watched him
from there. He had only discovered it was a bedroom by peering
through a narrow gap in the curtains early one morning as he went
for a walk. The two guards who followed him everywhere at fifty

yards' distance had not yet rounded the corner of the hut, and he had looked in at the window. The room contained a single bed, made, and a small desk with papers on it. Now, as he walked through the doorway from the house into the hut and stood in the guards' bedroom, he had the distinct feeling that something was wrong.

All the lights in the hut were controlled from a central point; they were turned on and off by some unseen hand. Usually they stayed on till eleven, but now, although it was only nine o'clock, the lights were out and the shutters had been closed. He had left the connecting door from the house open, so that a little pale twilight from the hallway reached the guards' bedroom, and by it he could see the two beds. As he stood there, surprised to find the room empty, the door behind him closed. Perhaps by itself, but Leamas made no attempt to open it. It was pitch-dark. No sound accompanied the closing of the door, no click or footstep. To Leamas, his instinct suddenly alert, it was as if a sound track had stopped. Then he smelled the cigar smoke. It must have been hanging in the air, but he had not noticed it till now. His senses of touch and smell, like a blind man's, were sharpened by the darkness.

There could only be one explanation for the silence—they were waiting for him to pass from the guards' room to his own. Therefore he determined to remain where he was. He took one pace sideways, pressed his back against the wall and remained motionless. Then from the direction of the main building he clearly heard a footstep. The door which had just closed was tested, the lock turned. Leamas was a prisoner in the hut.

Very slowly he lowered himself to a crouching position, putting his hand in the pocket of his jacket as he did so. He was quite calm, almost relieved at the prospect of action, but memories were racing through his mind. "You've nearly always got a weapon: an ashtray, a couple of coins, a fountain pen—anything that will gouge or cut." It was the favorite dictum of the mild little Welsh sergeant at that house near Oxford where he had trained in the war. "If you can't find anything to hit with, keep the hands open and the thumbs stiff," the sergeant would add.

Leamas took a box of matches from his pocket and crushed it, so that the small jagged edges of boxwood protruded from between the fingers of his right hand. Then he edged along the wall until he came to a chair which he knew was in the corner. Indifferent now to the noise he made, he shoved the chair into the center of the floor. Counting his footsteps as he moved back from the chair, he positioned himself in the angle of the two walls. As he did so, he heard the door of his own bedroom flung open. Vainly he tried to discern the figure that must be standing in the doorway, but there was no light from his own room either. He dared not move forward to attack, for the chair was now in the middle of the room; it was his tactical advantage, for he knew where it was and they did not. He must make them come for him before their helper outside had reached the master switch and put on the lights.

"Come on, you swine," he hissed in German. "I'm here, in the corner. Come and get me, can't you?" Not a move, not a sound. "I'm here. Can't you see me? What's the matter then? What's the matter, children, come on, can't you?"

He heard one stepping forward, and another following; and then the oath of a man as he stumbled against the chair. That was the sign Leamas was waiting for. Tossing away the matchbox, he slowly, cautiously crept forward, his left arm extended in the attitude of a man warding off twigs in a wood until, quite gently, he had touched an arm and felt the warm prickly cloth of a military uniform. Still with his left hand, Leamas deliberately tapped the arm twice and heard a frightened voice whisper in German, "Hans, is it you?"

"Shut up, you fool," Leamas whispered in reply, and in that same moment reached out and grasped the man's hair, pulling his head forward and down; next, with a terrible cutting blow he drove the side of his right hand into the nape of the man's neck, pulled him up again by the arm, hit him in the throat with an upward thrust of his open hand, then let him fall. As the man's body hit the ground the lights went on.

In the bedroom doorway stood a young captain of the People's Police holding a pistol, and behind him two men, one of them in uniform. They were all looking at the man on the floor. Somebody unlocked the other door, and Leamas turned to see who it was, but the captain shouted at him to stand still. Slowly he turned back and faced the three men.

His hands were still at his sides when the blow came. It seemed to crush his skull as he fell, drifting warmly into unconsciousness.

LEAMAS OPENED HIS EYES, AND like a brilliant light the pain burst upon his brain. He lay quite still on his back, refusing to close his eyes, watching the sharp, colored fragments race across his vision. His feet were icy cold, and he was aware of a sour prison stench. He tried to raise his hand and touch the blood that was caked on his cheek, but his hands were locked behind him. His feet too must be bound; the blood had left them, that was why they were cold. Painfully he looked about him, trying to lift his head an inch or two from the floor. To his surprise he saw his own knees in front of him. Instinctively he tried to stretch his legs, and as he did so his whole body was seized with a pain so sudden and terrible that he screamed out a sobbing, agonized cry.

He lay panting, attempting to master the pain; then through the sheer perversity of his nature he tried again, quite slowly, to straighten his legs. At once the agony returned, but Leamas had found the cause: his hands and feet were chained together behind his back. When he attempted to stretch his legs the chain tightened, forcing his shoulders down and his damaged head onto the stone floor. They must have beaten him up while he was unconscious; his whole body was stiff and bruised. He wondered if he'd killed the guard. He hoped so.

Above him shone the light, large, clinical and fierce. No furniture; just whitewashed walls, quite close all around, and a gray steel door. There was nothing else. Nothing to think about, just the savage pain.

He must have lain there for hours before they came. It grew hot from the light; he was thirsty but he refused to call out. At last the door opened and Mundt stood there. He knew it was Mundt from the eyes. Smiley had told him about them.

15

GUARDS UNTIED HIM and carried him to a small comfortable room, furnished with a desk and armchairs. Venetian blinds half covered the barred windows. Mundt sat at the desk and Leamas in an armchair, his eyes half closed. The guards stood at the door.

"Give me a drink," said Leamas.

"Whisky?"

"Water."

Mundt filled a carafe at a washstand in the corner and put it with a glass on the table beside Leamas. "Bring him something to eat," Mundt ordered, and one of the guards left the room, returning with a mug of soup and some sliced sausage. Leamas drank and ate, and they watched him in silence.

"Where's Fiedler?" Leamas asked finally.

"Under arrest," Mundt replied curtly.

"What for?"

"Conspiring to sabotage the security of the people."

Leamas nodded slowly. "So you won," he said. He waited a moment, trying to focus on Mundt. "When did you arrest him?"

"Last night."

"What about me?" Leamas asked.

"You're a material witness. You will of course stand trial yourself later."

"So I'm part of a put-up job by London to frame Mundt, am I?"

"That's right," Mundt said.

"A pretty elaborate operation," Leamas observed.

Mundt said nothing. Leamas became used to his silences as the interview progressed. Mundt had rather a pleasant voice—which Leamas hadn't expected—but he seldom spoke. It was part of Mundt's extraordinary self-confidence, perhaps, that he allowed long silences to intervene rather than exchange pointless words. Most interrogators set store by initiative, by the evocation of atmosphere and the psychological dependence of a prisoner upon his inquisitor. Mundt despised technique; he was a man of fact and action. Leamas preferred that.

Mundt looked like an athlete. His fair hair was cut short. His face had a hard, clean line, and a frightening directness; it was barren of humor. He looked young but not youthful; older men would take him seriously. Leamas found no difficulty in recalling that Mundt was a killer. There was a coldness about him, a self-sufficiency which perfectly equipped him for the business of murder.

"The other charge on which you will stand trial, if necessary," Mundt added quietly, "is murder."

"The sentry died, did he?" Leamas replied. A wave of intense pain passed through his head.

Mundt nodded. "So your trial for espionage is somewhat academic.

I propose that the case against Fiedler should be publicly heard. That is also the wish of the presidium."

"And you want my confession?"

"Yes."

"In other words you haven't any proof."

"We shall have proof. We shall have your confession." There was no menace in Mundt's voice, no theatrical twist. "On the other hand, there could be mitigation in your case. You were blackmailed by British Intelligence; they accused you of stealing money and then coerced you into a plot against myself. The court would have sympathy for such a plea."

Leamas seemed to be taken off his guard. "How did you know they accused me of stealing money?"

Mundt did not reply to this. "Fiedler has been very stupid," he observed. "As soon as I read Peters' report I knew why you had been sent, and I knew that Fiedler would fall into the trap. Fiedler hates me so much." He nodded, as if to emphasize the point. "Your people knew that, of course. It was a very clever operation. Who prepared it, tell me? Was it Smiley?"

Leamas said nothing.

"I told Fiedler to send me his report of his own interrogation of you. When he procrastinated I knew I was right. Then yesterday he circulated it among the presidium and did not send me a copy. Someone in London has been very clever."

Leamas said nothing.

"When did you last see Smiley?" Mundt asked casually.

Leamas hesitated, uncertain of himself. His head was aching terribly. "I don't remember," he said at last. "He isn't really in the outfit anymore."

"He is a great friend of Peter Guillam, is he not?"

"I think so, yes."

"Guillam, you thought, studied the economic situation in the German Democratic Republic. Some odd little section in your service; you weren't quite sure what it did."

"Yes." Sound and sight were becoming confused in the mad throbbing of his brain. His eyes were painful. He felt sick.

"Well, when did you last see Smiley?"

"I don't remember . . . I don't remember."

Mundt shook his head. "You have a very good memory—for anything that incriminates me. We can all remember when we *last* saw somebody. Did you, for instance, see him after you returned from Berlin?"

"Yes, I think so. I bumped into him . . . in the Circus once." Leamas had closed his eyes; he was sweating. "I can't go on, Mundt . . . I'm sick," he said.

"After Ashe had picked you up, after he had walked into the trap that had been set for him, you had lunch together, didn't you?"

"Yes. Lunch together."

"Lunch ended at about four o'clock. Where did you go then?"

"I went down to the City, I think. For God's sake, Mundt," he said, holding his head with his hand, "I can't go on. My bloody head's . . ."

"And after that where did you go? Why were you so keen to shake off your followers?"

Leamas said nothing; he was breathing in sharp gasps, his head buried in his hands.

"Answer this one question, then you can go. You shall have a bed. Otherwise you must go back to your cell, do you understand? You will be tied up again and fed on the floor like an animal. Tell me where you went."

The wild pulsation of his brain suddenly increased, the room was dancing; he heard voices around him and footsteps; someone was shouting, but not at him. The room was full of people, all shouting now, and then they were marching away; the stamping of their feet was like the throbbing of his head. Then, like the touch of mercy itself, a cool cloth was laid across his forehead, and kindly hands carried him away.

He woke on a hospital bed, and standing at the foot of it was Fiedler, smoking a cigarette.

16

LEAMAS TOOK STOCK. A bed with sheets. A room with no bars in the windows, just curtains and frosted glass. Pale green walls, dark green linoleum; and Fiedler watching him.

A nurse brought him food: an egg, some thin soup and fruit. He felt like death, but he supposed he'd better eat it. So he did, and Fiedler watched.

"How do you feel?" Fiedler asked.

"Bloody awful," Leamas replied.

"But better?"

"I suppose so." He hesitated. "Those swine beat me up."

"You killed a sentry, you know that?"

"I guessed I had. . . . What do they expect, with such a damn stupid operation? Why didn't they pull us both in at once? Why put all the lights out? If anything was overorganized, that was."

"I am afraid that as a nation we tend to overorganize. Abroad that passes for efficiency."

There was a pause.

"What happened to you?" Leamas asked.

"Oh, I too was softened for interrogation by Mundt's men. *And* Mundt. He had a special interest in beating me up."

"Because you dreamed up that story about—"

"Because I am a Jew."

"Oh God," said Leamas softly.

"That's why I got special treatment. But now that's all over."

"Why? What's happened?"

"The day we were arrested I had applied to the presidium for a civil warrant to arrest Mundt as an enemy of the people."

"You're mad—I told you, you're raving mad! He'll never—"

"There was other evidence against him apart from yours. Evidence I have been accumulating, piece by piece, over the last three years. Yours provided the proof we needed; that's all. As soon as that was clear I prepared a report and sent it to every member of the presidium except Mundt. They received it on the same day that I made my application for a warrant."

"The day we were pulled in."

"Yes. I knew Mundt would fight. I knew he had friends on the presidium, or yes-men at least, people who were sufficiently frightened to go running to him as soon as they got my report. And I knew he would lose in the end. The presidium had the weapon it needed to destroy him; they had the report, and while you and I were being questioned they read it and reread it until they knew it was true, and each knew the others knew. In the end they acted. They turned against him and ordered a tribunal. A secret one, of course. Mundt is under arrest."

"How is this tribunal conducted?" Leamas asked.

"That is up to the president. This will not be a people's court—it is more in the nature of a committee of inquiry, appointed by the presidium to investigate and report upon a certain . . . subject. Its report will contain a recommendation. In a case like this the recommendation is tantamount to a verdict, but remains secret, as a part of the proceedings of the presidium."

"How does it work? Are there counsel and judges?"

"There are three judges," Fiedler said; "and in effect, there are counsel. I myself shall put the case against Mundt. Karden will defend him."

"Who's Karden?"

"A very tough man. Looks like a country doctor, small and benevolent. He was at Buchenwald."

"Why can't Mundt defend himself?"

"It was Mundt's wish. It is said that Karden will call a witness."

Leamas shrugged. "That's your affair," he said.

Fiedler was silent for a time, then said reflectively, "Special treatment . . . That long, long pain and all the time you say to yourself, 'Either I shall faint or I shall grow to bear the pain,' and the pain just increases like a violinist going up the E string. You think it can't get any higher, but it rises and rises. I wouldn't have minded so much if Mundt had hurt me for hate or jealousy, or for the Party. But all the time he was whispering '*Jew . . . Jew*'—"

"All right," said Leamas, "you should know. He's a swine."

"Yes," said Fiedler. He seemed excited. He wants to boast to somebody, thought Leamas.

"I thought a lot about you," Fiedler added. "You remember that talk we had about philosophy?" He smiled. "The thing that embarrasses you . . . I'll put it another way. Suppose Mundt is right? He asked me to confess that I was in league with British spies—that the whole operation was mounted by British Intelligence in order to entice us—me, if you like—into liquidating the best man in the Abteilung."

"He tried that on me," said Leamas indifferently. And he added, "As if I'd cooked up the whole bloody story."

"But what I mean is this: suppose you had done that, suppose it were true—would you kill a man, an innocent man—"

"Mundt's a killer himself."

"Suppose he wasn't. Suppose it were me they wanted to kill: would London do it?"

"It depends on the need. . . ."

"Ah," said Fiedler contentedly, "it depends on the need. As we said, the traffic accident and the statistics. That is a great relief."

"Why?"

"You must get some sleep," said Fiedler. "Order what food you want. Tomorrow you can talk."

Soon Leamas was asleep, content in the knowledge that Fiedler was his ally and that they would shortly send Mundt to his death. That was something he had looked forward to for a very long time.

17

LIZ WAS HAPPY in Leipzig. Austerity pleased her—it gave her the comfort of sacrifice. The little house she stayed in was dark and meager; the food was poor, and most of it had to go to the children. They talked politics at every meal, she and Frau Lüman, secretary of the Neuenhagen branch, a small gray woman whose husband managed a gravel quarry.

It was like living in a religious community, Liz thought; a convent or an Israeli kibbutz or something. You felt the world was better for your empty stomach. Liz knew a little German, and she was surprised how quickly she was able to use it. She tried it on the children first, and they grinned and helped her.

In the evenings there was Party work. They distributed literature, visited branch members who were in arrears on their dues or lagged behind in their attendance at meetings, called in at the district office for a discussion on "Problems Connected with the Centralized Distribution of Agricultural Produce," and attended a meeting of the workers' consultative council of a machine-tool factory on the outskirts of the town.

At last, on the fourth day, came their own branch meeting. Liz expected this to be the most exhilarating experience of all; it would be an example of all that her own branch in Bayswater could one day be.

They had chosen a wonderful title for the evening's discussions— "Coexistence After Two Wars"—and they expected a record attendance. The whole ward had been circularized, and they had taken care to see that there was no rival meeting in the neighborhood that evening; it was not a late shopping day.

Seven people came.

Seven people and Liz and the branch secretary and the man from the district office. Liz put a brave face on it, but she was terribly upset. She could scarcely concentrate on the speaker. It was like the meetings in Bayswater—the same dutiful little group of lost faces, the same fussy self-consciousness, the same feeling of a great idea in the hands of little people. She almost wished no one would turn up, because that was absolute and it suggested persecution—it was something you could react to.

But seven people were nothing; they were worse than nothing, because they were evidence of the inertia of the uncapturable mass. They broke your heart.

The room was better than the schoolroom in Bayswater, but even that was no comfort. In Bayswater it had been fun trying to *find* a room. In the early days they'd taken back rooms in pubs or met secretly in one another's houses. Then Bill Hazel from the secondary school had joined and they'd used his classroom—the headmaster thought Bill ran a drama group. Even that was a risk, and they might still be chucked out. Somehow it all fitted better than this Peace Hall in precast concrete with the cracks in the corners and the picture of Lenin. Why did they have that silly frame all around the picture— bundles of what looked like organ pipes sprouting from its corners and the bunting all dusty? It was like something from a Fascist funeral.

Sometimes she thought Alec was right—you believed in things because you needed to. No, Alec was wrong—it was a wicked thing to say. Peace and freedom and equality—they were facts. Of course they were. And what about history—all those laws the Party proved? The Party was the vanguard of history, the spearpoint in the fight for peace. . . .

She went over the phrases a little uncertainly. She wished more people had come. Seven was so few. They looked so cross; cross and hungry.

The meeting over, Liz waited for Frau Lüman to collect the unsold literature from the table by the door, fill in her attendance book and put on her coat, for it was cold that evening.

The speaker had left. Frau Lüman was standing at the door with her hand on the light switch when a man appeared out of the darkness, framed in the doorway.

"Comrade Lüman?" he inquired.

"Yes?"

"I am looking for an English comrade, Gold. She is staying with you?"

"I'm Elizabeth Gold," Liz put in, and the man came into the hall, closing the door behind him.

"I am Halten, from the district," he said.

He showed some paper to Frau Lüman, who was still standing at the door, and she nodded and glanced a little anxiously toward Liz.

"I have been asked to give a message to Comrade Gold from the presidium," he said. "It concerns an alteration in your program, an invitation to attend a special meeting."

"Oh," said Liz rather stupidly. It seemed fantastic that the presidium should even have heard of her.

"It is a gesture," Halten said. "A gesture of goodwill."

"But I . . . but Frau Lüman—" Liz began helplessly.

"Comrade Lüman, I am sure, will forgive you under the circumstances."

"Of course," said Frau Lüman quickly.

"Where is the meeting to be held?"

"It will necessitate your leaving tonight," Halten replied. "We have a long way to go. Nearly to Görlitz."

"To Görlitz. . . . Where is that?"

"East," said Frau Lüman quickly. "On the Polish border."

"We will drive you home now. You can collect your things and we will continue the journey at once."

"Tonight? Now?"

"Yes." Halten didn't seem to consider Liz had much choice.

A large black car was waiting for them. There was a driver in the front and a flag post on the hood. It looked like a military car.

18

THE COURT WAS no larger than a schoolroom. On one side, on the few rows of benches which were provided, sat guards and warders, members of the presidium and selected officials. At the other side of the room the three members of the tribunal sat on tall-backed chairs at an unpolished oak table. Above them, suspended from the ceiling, was a large red star made of plywood.

On either side of the table, their desks a little forward of it and facing one another, sat two men. One was about sixty and wore a gray tie and a black suit, the kind of suit they wear in church in German country districts. The other was Fiedler.

Leamas sat at the back, a guard on either side of him. Between the heads of the spectators he could see Mundt, himself surrounded by police, his fair hair cut even shorter, his broad shoulders covered in the familiar gray of prison uniform.

The president of the tribunal, sitting at the center of the table, rang a bell, and a shiver passed over Leamas as he noted that the president was a woman. She was fiftyish, small-eyed and dark. Her hair was cut short like a man's, and she wore a kind of functional dark suit. She looked sharply around the room, nodded to a sentry to close the door, and began at once to address the court.

"All of you know why we are here. This is a tribunal convened expressly by the presidium, and it is to the presidium alone that we are responsible. The proceedings are secret, remember that. We shall hear evidence as we think fit." She pointed perfunctorily toward Fiedler. "Comrade Fiedler, you had better begin."

Fiedler stood up. Nodding briefly toward the table, he drew a sheaf of papers from the briefcase beside him and began. He talked quietly and easily, with a diffidence which Leamas had never seen in him before. Leamas considered it a good performance, well adjusted to the role of a man regretfully hanging his superior.

"You should know first, if you do not know already," Fiedler began, "that on the day the presidium received my report on the activities of Comrade Mundt I was arrested, together with the defector Leamas. Both of us were imprisoned and . . . invited, under extreme duress, to confess that this whole terrible charge was a Fascist plot against a loyal comrade.

"You have before you the written record of this case and know how it was that Leamas came to our notice; we ourselves sought him out, induced him to defect and finally brought him to Democratic Germany. Nothing could more clearly demonstrate the impartiality of Leamas than that he still refuses, for reasons I will explain, to believe that Mundt was a British agent. It is therefore grotesque to suggest that Leamas is a plant: the initiative was ours, and Leamas' evidence provides only the final proof in a long chain of indications reaching back over the last three years.

"The charge against Comrade Mundt is that he is the agent of an imperialist power. The penalty for this crime is death. There is no crime more serious in our penal code, none which exposes our state to greater danger nor demands more vigilance from our Party." Here he put the papers down.

"Let me tell you some details of Comrade Mundt's career. He was recruited into the Abteilung at the age of twenty-eight and underwent the customary instruction. Having completed his probationary period, he undertook special tasks in the Scandinavian countries, where he succeeded in establishing an intelligence network. He performed this task well, and there is no reason to suppose that at that time he was other than a diligent member of his department.

"But, Comrades, you should not forget this early connection with Scandinavia. The networks established by Comrade Mundt soon after the war provided the excuse, many years later, for him to travel to Finland and Norway, where he drew thousands of dollars from foreign banks in return for his treacherous conduct. For make no mistake: Comrade Mundt did not fall victim to bourgeois capitalist thinking. First cowardice, then greed, were the motives for his treachery. The acquirement of great wealth was his dream. Ironically, it was the elaborate system by which his lust for money was satisfied that brought the forces of justice on his trail."

Fiedler paused, and looked around the room, his eyes suddenly alight with fervor.

Leamas watched, fascinated.

"Let that be a lesson," Fiedler shouted, "to those other enemies of the state, whose crime is so foul that they must plot in the secret hours of the night!" A dutiful murmur rose from the spectators in the back of the room.

"They will not escape the vigilance of those whose blood they seek to sell!" Fiedler might have been addressing a large crowd rather than the handful of officials and guards assembled in the room.

Leamas realized that Fiedler was taking no chances: the deportment of the tribunal, prosecutors and witnesses must be politically impeccable. Fiedler, knowing no doubt that the danger of a subsequent countercharge was inherent in such cases, was protecting his own back; the polemic would go down in the record, and it would be a brave man who set himself to refute it.

Fiedler now opened the file that lay on the desk before him. "At the end of 1956 Mundt was posted to London as a member of the East German Steel Mission. He had the additional special task of undertaking countersubversionary measures against émigré groups, and he obtained valuable results."

Leamas looked again at the three figures at the center table. To the president's left was a dark, youngish man, with lank, unruly hair and the gray complexion of an ascetic. His slim hands were restlessly toying with the papers which lay before him. Leamas guessed he was Mundt's man; he found it hard to say why.

On the other side of the president sat a slightly older man, balding, with an open face. Leamas thought he looked rather an ass. He guessed that if Mundt's fate hung in the balance, the young man would defend him and the woman president condemn. He thought the second man would be embarrassed by the difference of opinion and side with the president.

Fiedler was speaking again. "When Comrade Mundt began to recruit agents he exposed himself to great danger, and eventually he fell foul of the British secret police; they issued a warrant for his arrest. Mundt went into hiding. Ports were watched; his photograph and description were distributed throughout the British Isles. Yet after two days in hiding, Comrade Mundt took a taxi to London airport and flew to Berlin.

" 'Brilliant,' you will say, and so it was. With the whole of Britain's police force alerted—her roads, railways, shipping and airports under constant surveillance—Comrade Mundt takes a plane from London airport. Brilliant indeed. Or perhaps you may feel, Comrades, that

Mundt's escape from England was a little *too* brilliant, a little *too* easy, that without the connivance of the British authorities it would never have been possible at all!" Another murmur, more spontaneous than the first, rose from the back of the room.

"The truth is this: Mundt *was* taken prisoner by the British and they offered him the classic alternative. Was it to be years in an imperialist prison, or was Mundt to make a dramatic return to his home country, against all expectation, and fulfill the brilliant promise he

had shown? The British, of course, made it a condition of his return that he should provide them with information, and said they would pay him large sums of money. With the carrot in front and the stick behind, Mundt was recruited.

"It was now in the British interest to promote Mundt's career. We cannot yet prove that Mundt's success in liquidating minor Western intelligence agents was the work of his imperialist masters betraying their own collaborators—those who were expendable—in order that Mundt's prestige should be enhanced. But it is an assumption which the evidence permits.

"Ever since 1960—the year Comrade Mundt became deputy director of the Abteilung—indications have reached us from all over the world that there was a highly placed spy in our ranks. You all know Karl Riemeck was a spy; we thought when he was eliminated that the evil had been stamped out. But we continued to lose collaborators abroad at an alarming rate.

"In late 1960 a former collaborator of ours approached an Englishman in Lebanon known to be in contact with their intelligence service. He offered him—we found out soon afterward—a complete breakdown of the two sections of the Abteilung for which he had formerly worked. His offer was transmitted to London, and rejected. That could only mean that the British already possessed the intelligence; *and that it was up-to-date.*

"And then in early 1961 we had a stroke of luck. We obtained, by means I will not describe, a summary of the information which British Intelligence held about the Abteilung. It was complete, it was accurate and it was astonishingly up-to-date. I showed it to Mundt, of course—he was my superior. He told me it came as no surprise to him; he had certain inquiries in hand and I should take no action for fear of prejudicing them. And I confess that at that moment the thought crossed my mind, remote and fantastic as it was, that Mundt himself could have provided the information. For there were other indications too. . . .

"I need hardly tell you that the last, the very last person to be suspected of espionage is the operational head of the Abteilung. The notion is so appalling, so melodramatic, that few would entertain it, let alone give expression to it! I confess that I myself have been guilty of excessive reluctance to do so. That was an error on my part.

"But, Comrades, the final evidence has been delivered into our hands." He turned to the other side of the room. "Bring Leamas forward."

The guards on either side of him stood up, and Leamas made his way to the front and stood facing the table. First, the president addressed him.

"Witness, what is your name?" she asked.

"Alec Leamas."

"What is your age?"

"Fifty."

"What is your profession?"

"Assistant librarian."

Fiedler angrily intervened. "You were formerly employed by British Intelligence, were you not?" he snapped.

"That's right. Till a year ago."

"The tribunal has read the reports of your interrogation," Fiedler continued. "I want you to tell them again about the conversation you had with Peter Guillam in May last year."

"You mean when we talked about Mundt?"

"Yes."

"It was at our Cambridge Circus headquarters in London. I bumped into Peter in the corridor. I knew he was involved in the Fennan Case and I asked him what had become of George Smiley. Then we got to talking about Mundt, who was mixed up in the thing too. Peter said he thought that Maston—he was in charge of the case then—had not wanted Mundt to be caught."

"How did you interpret that?" asked Fiedler.

"I knew Maston had made a mess of the Fennan Case. I supposed he didn't want any mud raked up, as it might have been if Mundt had appeared in court."

"So if Mundt had been caught, he would have been legally charged?" the president put in.

"It would depend on who caught him. If the police got him, they'd report it to the Home Office. After that no power on earth could stop him from being charged."

"And what if your service had caught him?" Fiedler inquired.

"Oh, that's a different matter. I supposed they would have interrogated him and then tried to exchange him for one of our own people in prison over here."

"Might they not have tried to recruit him as their agent?"

"Yes, but they didn't succeed."

"How do you know that?"

"Oh, for God's sake, I've told you over and over again. I was head of the Berlin command. If Mundt had been one of our people, I would have known. I couldn't have helped knowing."

"Quite."

Fiedler seemed content with that answer, confident perhaps that the tribunal was not. He now turned his attention to operation Rolling Stone, took Leamas once again through the special security governing the circulation of the file, the letters to the Copenhagen and

Helsinki banks and the one reply which Leamas had so far received. Addressing himself to the tribunal, Fiedler commented:

"Leamas deposited money at Copenhagen on June fifteenth. Among the papers before you, there is the facsimile of a letter from the Royal Scandinavian Bank addressed to Robert Lang—the name Leamas used to open the Copenhagen savings account. From it you will see that the entire sum—ten thousand dollars—was drawn by the cosignatory of the account one week later.

"I imagine," Fiedler continued, indicating the motionless figure of Mundt in the front row, "that it is not disputed by the defendant that he was in Copenhagen on June twenty-first, nominally on work for the Abteilung."

He paused and then continued: "Leamas' visit to Helsinki took place on about September twenty-fourth." Raising his voice, he turned and looked directly at Mundt. "On the third of October, Comrade Mundt made a clandestine journey to Finland—once more allegedly in the interests of the Abteilung."

There was silence. Fiedler addressed himself again to the tribunal. In a voice at once subdued and threatening he asked, "Are you complaining that the evidence is circumstantial? Let me remind you of something more." He turned to Leamas. "Witness, during your activities in Berlin you became associated with Karl Riemeck, formerly secretary to the presidium. What was the nature of that association?"

"He was my agent until he was shot by Mundt's men."

"Quite so. He was shot by Mundt's men. One of several spies who were summarily liquidated by Comrade Mundt before they could be questioned. Will you describe Riemeck's meeting with your head man—the one you call Control?"

"Control came over to Berlin from London to see Karl. I fixed it for Karl to come to my flat, and the three of us dined together. Control had asked me beforehand to see that he had a quarter of an hour alone with Karl, so during the evening I left the flat on some excuse and then came back."

"Were Control and Riemeck still talking? If so, what were they talking about?"

"They weren't talking at all when I came back."

"Thank you. You may sit down."

Leamas returned to his seat at the back of the room. Fiedler turned to the three members of the tribunal. "I want to talk first about the spy Karl Riemeck, who was shot. You have before you a list of all the information which Riemeck passed to Alec Leamas in Berlin, so far as Leamas can recall it. It is a formidable record of treachery. As you can see, Riemeck gave his British masters a detailed breakdown of the work and personalities of the whole Abteilung and described its most secret sessions. He also handed over minutes of the most secret proceedings of the presidium.

"The second part was easy for him: he himself, as secretary, compiled the record of every meeting. But Riemeck's *access* to the secret affairs of the Abteilung is a different matter. Who, at the end of 1959, got Riemeck onto the Committee for the Protection of the People, which coordinates the affairs of our security organs? Who proposed that he should have access to the files of the Abteilung? Who at every stage singled him out for posts of exceptional responsibility?

"I will tell you," Fiedler proclaimed. "The same man who was uniquely placed to shield him in his espionage activities: Hans-Dieter Mundt. Let us recall how Riemeck contacted the British—how he sought out de Jong's car and put the film inside it. Are you not amazed at Riemeck's foreknowledge? How could he have known where to find that car on that very day? Only through our own security police, who reported de Jong's presence as a matter of routine as soon as the car passed the inter-sector checkpoint. That knowledge was available to Mundt, and Mundt made it available to Riemeck. I tell you, Riemeck was his creature, the link between Mundt and his imperialist masters!"

Fiedler paused, then added quietly, "Mundt—Riemeck—Leamas, that was the chain of command, and it is axiomatic of intelligence technique the whole world over that each link of the chain be kept, as far as possible, in ignorance of the others. Thus it is *right* that Leamas knows nothing to the detriment of Mundt; that is no more than the proof of good security by his masters in London.

"You have also been told how the whole case known as Rolling Stone was conducted under conditions of special secrecy, how Leamas knew in vague terms of a section under Peter Guillam which was supposedly concerned with economic conditions in our republic—a section which surprisingly was on the distribution list of Rolling Stone. Let me remind you that that same Peter Guillam was one of several British intelligence officers involved in the investigation of Mundt's activities in England."

The dark, youngish man to the president's left lifted his pencil. Looking at Fiedler with hard, cold eyes, he asked, "But why did Mundt liquidate Riemeck, if Riemeck was his agent?"

"He had no alternative. Riemeck was under suspicion. His mistress had betrayed him by boastful indiscretion. Mundt gave the order that he be shot on sight, got word to Riemeck to run, and the danger of betrayal was eliminated. Later, Mundt assassinated the woman.

"I want to speculate for a moment on Mundt's technique. When he returned to Germany in 1959 he was not a senior functionary of our service, but he saw a good deal, and what he saw he began to report. He was, of course, communicating with his masters unaided. We must suppose that he was met in West Berlin, that on his short journeys to Scandinavia and elsewhere he was contacted and interrogated. The British would have weighed what he gave them with painful care against what they already knew, fearing that he would play a double game. But gradually they must have realized they had hit a gold mine—Mundt took to his treacherous work with the systematic efficiency for which he is renowned. So they established in London, under Guillam, a tiny undercover section, and paid Mundt by a special system which they called Rolling Stone.

"This is consistent with Leamas' protestations that Mundt was unknown to him although Leamas not only paid him but in the end *actually received from Riemeck and passed to London the intelligence which Mundt himself obtained.*

"It was toward the end of 1959 that Mundt found within the presidium the man he needed as intermediary: Karl Riemeck.

"How did Mundt dare to establish Riemeck's willingness to cooperate? You must remember Mundt's exceptional position: he had access to all the security files, could tap telephones, open letters, employ watchers; he could interrogate anyone with undisputed right, and had before him the detailed picture of their private life. Above all he could silence suspicion in a moment by turning against the people the very police power"—Fiedler's voice was trembling with fury—"which was designed for their protection." Returning effortlessly to his former rational style, he continued:

"You can see now what London did. Still keeping Mundt's identity a close secret, they connived at Riemeck's enlistment and enabled indirect contact to be established between Mundt and the Berlin command. That is the significance of Riemeck's contact with Leamas. *That* is how you should interpret Leamas' evidence. *That* is how you should measure Mundt's treachery."

He turned and, looking Mundt full in the face, he shouted, "There is your saboteur, terrorist! There is the man who has sold the people's right!

"I have nearly finished. Mundt gained a reputation as a loyal and astute protector of the people, and he silenced forever those tongues that could betray his secret. Thus he killed in the name of the people to protect his Fascist treachery and advance his own career within our service. When you come to give your judgment to the presidium, do not shrink from recognizing the full bestiality of this man's crime. For Hans-Dieter Mundt, death is a judgment of mercy."

19

THE PRESIDENT TURNED to the little man in the black suit sitting directly opposite Fiedler. "Comrade Karden, you are speaking for Comrade Mundt. Do you wish to examine the witness?"

"Yes, yes, I should like to," he replied, getting laboriously to his feet and pulling the ends of his gold-rimmed spectacles over his ears. He was a benign figure, a little rustic, and his hair was white.

"The contention of Comrade Mundt," he began in his mild voice, "is that Leamas is lying, and that Comrade Fiedler, either by design or ill chance, has been drawn into a monstrous plot to disrupt the Abteilung. We do not dispute that Karl Riemeck was a British spy—there is evidence for that. But we deny that Mundt was in league with him, or accepted money for betraying our Party. We say there is no objective evidence for this charge, that Comrade Fiedler is intoxicated by dreams of power and blinded to rational thought. We maintain that from the moment Leamas returned from Berlin to London he lived a part; that he simulated a swift decline into degeneracy, drunkenness and debt; that he assaulted a tradesman in full public view and affected anti-American sentiments—all solely in order to attract the attention of the Abteilung.

"We believe that British Intelligence has deliberately spun around Comrade Mundt a mesh of circumstantial evidence—the payment of money to foreign banks, its withdrawal to coincide with Mundt's presence in this or that country, the casual hearsay evidence from Peter Guillam, the secret discussion between Control and Riemeck—these all provided a spurious chain of evidence, and Comrade Fiedler, on whose ambitions the British so accurately counted, accepted it. At best he is guilty of a most serious error; at worst of conniving with imperialist spies to undermine the security of the worker state and to murder—for Comrade Mundt now stands to lose his life—one of its most vigilant defenders.

"We also have a witness." Karden nodded benignly at the court. "Yes. We too have a witness. For do you really suppose that all this time Comrade Mundt has been ignorant of Fiedler's fevered plotting? For months he has been aware of the sickness in Fiedler's mind. It was Comrade Mundt himself who authorized the approach that was made to Leamas in England; would he have taken such an insane risk if he himself might be implicated?

"When the reports of Leamas' first interrogation in Holland reached the presidium, Comrade Mundt had only to look at the dates of Leamas' visits to Copenhagen and Helsinki to realize that the whole thing was a plant—a plant to discredit Comrade Mundt himself. Those dates did indeed coincide with Mundt's visits to Denmark and Finland; they were chosen by London for that very reason. Mundt had known of those earlier 'indications' as well as Fiedler—remember that. Mundt too was looking for a spy within the ranks of the Abteilung. . . .

"When, after Leamas arrived in our country and Fiedler embarked on his own interrogation, no further reports came from him, Comrade Mundt knew what Fiedler was hatching. He could guess how Leamas was nourishing Fiedler's suspicions with hints and oblique indications—never overdone, you understand, but subtly dropped here and there.

"By then the ground had been prepared—the man in Lebanon, our discovery of how much British Intelligence knew about the department, both seeming to confirm the presence of a highly placed spy within the Abteilung. . . .

"It was wonderfully well done. It could have turned—it could still turn—the defeat which the British suffered through the loss of Karl Riemeck into a remarkable victory.

"But Comrade Mundt took one precaution while the British, with Fiedler's aid, planned his murder. He caused scrupulous inquiries to be made in London. He examined every tiny detail of that double life which Leamas led. He was looking, you see, for some human error in a scheme of almost superhuman subtlety. Somewhere, he thought, in Leamas' long sojourn in the wilderness he would have to break his oath of poverty, degeneracy, above all of solitude. He would need a companion; he would long for the warmth of human contact, long to reveal a part of his other self.

"Mundt was right. Leamas, that skilled, experienced operator, made a mistake so elementary, so human that—" He smiled. "The witness is here; procured by Comrade Mundt. Later I shall call—that witness." He looked a trifle arch, as if to say he must be allowed his little joke. "Meanwhile I should like to put one or two questions to Mr. Alec Leamas."

"TELL ME," Karden began, "are you a man of means?"

"Don't be bloody silly," said Leamas shortly. "You know how I was picked up."

"Yes, indeed," Karden declared. "It was masterly. I may take it, then, that you have no money at all?"

"You may."

"Have you friends who would lend you money, give it to you perhaps? Pay your debts?"

"If I had, I wouldn't be here now."

"You cannot imagine that some kindly benefactor would ever concern himself with putting you on your feet . . . settling with creditors and that kind of thing?"

"No."

"Thank you. Do you know George Smiley?"

"Of course I do. He was in the Circus."

"He has now left British Intelligence?"

"He quit after the Fennan Case."

"Ah yes—the case in which Comrade Mundt was involved. Have you ever seen him since?"

"Once or twice."

"Have you seen him since *you* left the Circus?"

Leamas hesitated. "No," he said.

"After you left prison—the day of your release, in fact—you were picked up by a man called Ashe?"

"Yes."

"You had lunch with him in Soho. After the two of you had parted, where did you go?"

"I don't remember. Probably to a pub. No idea."

"Let me help you. You went first to Fleet Street. From there you seem to have zigzagged by bus, subway and private vehicle—rather inexpertly for a man of your experience—to Chelsea. Your van turned into Bywater Street, and our agent reported you were dropped at number nine. That happens to be George Smiley's house."

"That's drivel," Leamas declared. "I should think I went to the Eight Bells; it's a favorite pub of mine."

"By van?"

"That's nonsense too. I went by taxi, I expect."

"But why all the running about beforehand?"

"That's just tripe. They were probably following the wrong man. That would be bloody typical."

"Going back to my original question," Karden said, "you cannot imagine that Smiley would have taken any interest in your welfare after you went to prison, or that he would have spent money on your dependents?"

"No. I haven't the least idea what you're trying to say, Karden, but the answer's no. If you'd ever met Smiley, you wouldn't ask. We're about as different as we could be."

Karden seemed rather pleased with this, smiling and nodding to himself as he referred elaborately to his file. "Oh yes," he said, as if he had forgotten something, "when you asked the grocer for credit, how much money had you?"

"Nothing," said Leamas carelessly. "I'd been broke for a week."

"What had you lived on?"

"Bits and pieces. And I'd been ill—some fever. I'd hardly eaten anything. I suppose that made me nervous too—helped make me hit the grocer."

"You were, of course, still owed money at the library, weren't you?"

"How did you know that?" asked Leamas sharply.

"Why didn't you go and collect it? Then you wouldn't have had to ask for credit, would you, Leamas?"

He shugged. "I forgot. Probably because the library was closed on Saturday mornings."

"I see. Are you sure it was closed on Saturday mornings?"

"No. It's just a guess."

"Thank you. That is all I have to ask."

Leamas was sitting down as the door opened and a woman came in. She was large and ugly, wearing a gray coverall with chevrons on one sleeve. Behind her stood Liz.

20

S HE ENTERED THE COURT slowly, looking around her, wide-eyed, like a half-awakened child entering a brightly lit room. Leamas had forgotten how young she was. When she saw him sitting between two guards, she stopped. "Alec."

A guard guided her forward to the spot where Leamas had stood. It was very quiet in the courtroom.

"What is your name, child?" the president asked abruptly.

Liz's long hands hung at her sides, the fingers straight.

"What is your name?" the president repeated loudly.

"Elizabeth Gold."

"You are a member of the British Communist Party?"

"Yes."

"And you have been staying in Leipzig?"

"Yes."

"When did you join the Party?"

"Nineteen fifty-eight. No—'57, I think—"

She was interrupted by the screech of furniture forced aside, and Leamas' voice, hoarse, high-pitched, ugly, filling the room. "You swine! Leave her alone!"

Liz turned in terror and saw a guard hit him with his fist, so that he half fell, his white face bleeding and his clothes awry. Then both guards were upon him, had lifted him up, thrusting his arms high behind his back. His head fell forward on his chest, then jerked sideways in pain. They released him.

"If he moves again, take him out," the president ordered. She nodded to Leamas in warning, adding, "You can speak again later if you want. Wait." Then, leaning forward and staring at Liz intently, she said, "Elizabeth, have you been told in your Party about the need for secrecy?"

Liz nodded.

"And you have been told never, never to ask questions of another comrade on the organization and plans of the Party?"

Liz nodded again. "Yes," she said, "of course."

"Today you will be severely tested in that rule. It is far better for you that you should know nothing. Nothing," she added with sudden emphasis. "Let this be enough: we three at this table hold very high rank in the Party. We are acting with the knowledge of our presidium, in the interests of Party security. We have to ask you some questions, and your answers are of the greatest importance. By replying truthfully and bravely you will help the cause of socialism."

"But *who* is on trial?" Liz whispered. "What's Alec done?"

The president looked at Mundt and said, "Perhaps no one is on trial. Or perhaps only the accusers. It can make no difference *who* is accused," she added. "It is a guarantee of your impartiality that you cannot know."

Silence descended for a moment on the room; and then, in a voice so quiet that the president instinctively turned her head to catch her words, Liz asked, "Is it Alec?"

The president again leaned forward and said, with great intensity, "Listen, child, do you want to go home? Do as I tell you and you shall. But if you—" She broke off, indicated Karden and added, "This comrade wants to ask you some questions. Then you shall go. Tell the truth."

Karden stood again, and smiled his kindly, churchwarden smile. "Elizabeth," he inquired, "Alec Leamas was your lover, wasn't he?"

She nodded.

"You first met at the library where you work."

"Yes."

"Have you had many lovers, Elizabeth?"

Whatever she said was lost as Leamas shouted again, "Karden, you swine," but as she heard him she turned and said, quite loudly, "Alec, don't. They'll take you away."

"Yes," observed the president dryly. "They will."

"Tell me," Karden resumed smoothly, "did Alec know you were a Communist?"

"Yes. I told him."

"What did he say when you told him?"

She didn't know whether to lie, that was the terrible thing. The questions came so quickly she had no chance to think. All the time they were listening, watching, waiting for a word, a gesture perhaps, that could do terrible harm to Alec, for there was no doubt in her mind that he was in danger.

"What did he say?" Karden repeated.

"He laughed. He was above all that kind of thing."

"Tell me, was he a *happy* person, always laughing?"

"No. He didn't often laugh."

"But he laughed when you told him you were in the Party. Do you know why?"

"I think he despised the Party."

"Do you think he *hated* it?" Karden asked casually.

"I don't know," Liz replied pathetically.

"Was he a man of strong likes and dislikes?"

"No . . . no; he wasn't."

"But he assaulted a grocer. Now why did he do that?"

Liz suddenly didn't trust Karden—the caressing voice, the good-fairy face.

"I don't know."

"But you thought about it?"

"Yes."

"Well, what conclusion did you come to?"

"None," she said flatly.

Karden looked at her thoughtfully, a little disappointed perhaps, as if she had forgotten her catechism.

"Did you," he asked—it might have been the most obvious of questions—"did you *know* that Leamas was going to hit the grocer?"

"No," Liz replied, perhaps too quickly, so that, in the pause that followed, Karden's smile gave way to a look of amused curiosity.

"Until now, until today," he asked finally, "when had you last seen Leamas?" The voice was kind but persistent.

Liz wished she could turn and see Leamas, read in his face some sign telling how to answer. She was becoming frightened for herself, frightened of these questions which proceeded from charges and suspicions of which she knew nothing.

"Elizabeth, when was your last meeting with Leamas until today?"

Oh, how she hated that silken voice! "The night before it happened, the night before he had the fight with Mr. Ford."

"The fight? It wasn't a fight, Elizabeth. The grocer never had a chance. Very unsporting!" Karden laughed, and it was all the more terrible because no one laughed with him. "Tell me, where did you meet Leamas that last night?"

"At his flat. He'd been ill, not working. He'd been in bed, and I'd been coming in and cooking for him."

"And buying the food? Shopping for him?"

"Yes."

"How kind. It must have cost you a lot of money," Karden observed sympathetically. "Could you afford to keep him?"

"I didn't keep him. I got it from Alec. He—"

"Oh," said Karden sharply, "so he *did* have some money?"

Oh dear God, thought Liz, what have I said?

"Not much," she said quickly. "A pound, two pounds, not more. He didn't have more than that. He couldn't pay his bills—his electric light and his rent—they were all paid afterward, you see, after he'd gone, by a friend."

"Of course," said Karden quietly, "a friend paid. Came specially and paid all his bills. Some old friend, someone he knew before he came to Bayswater, perhaps. Did you ever meet this friend, Elizabeth?"

She shook her head.

"What other bills did this good friend pay, do you know?"

"No . . . no."

"Why do you hesitate?"

"I said I don't know," Liz retorted fiercely.

"Did Leamas ever speak of this friend? A friend with money who knew where Leamas lived?"

"He never mentioned a friend at all. I didn't think he had any friends."

"Ah."

There was a terrible silence in the courtroom, more terrible to Liz because like a blind child among the seeing she was cut off from all those around her; they could measure her answers against some secret standard, and she could not know what they had found.

"How much money do you earn, Elizabeth?"

"Six pounds a week."

"Have you any savings?"

"A little. A few pounds."

"How much is the rent of your flat?"

"Fifty shillings a week."

"That's quite a lot, isn't it, Elizabeth? Have you paid your rent recently?"

She shook her head helplessly.

"Why not?" Karden continued. "Have you no money?"

In a whisper she replied, "I've got a paid lease. Someone paid the whole lease and sent me the receipt."

"Who?"

"I don't know." Tears were running down her face. "I don't know who it was. . . . A month ago they sent it, a bank in the City. I swear I don't know who . . . A gift from a charity, they said. You know everything. . . . You tell me who—"

Burying her face in her hands she wept, her shoulders shaking. No one moved, and at length she lowered her hands but did not look up.

"Why didn't you inquire?" Karden asked simply. "Or are you used to receiving anonymous gifts of that size?" She said nothing, and Karden continued. "You didn't inquire because you guessed. Isn't that right?"

Raising her hand to her face again, she nodded.

"You guessed it came from Leamas' friend, didn't you?"

"Yes," she managed to say. "I heard that the grocer had got a lot of money from somewhere after the trial, and I knew it must be Alec's friend. . . ."

"How very strange," said Karden, almost to himself. And then: "Tell me, Elizabeth, did anyone get in touch with you after Leamas went to prison?"

"No," she lied. She knew now that they wanted to prove something against Alec, something about the money or his friends.

"Are you sure?" Karden asked, his eyebrows raised above the gold rims of his spectacles.

"Yes."

"But your neighbor," Karden objected patiently, "says that two men called soon after Leamas had been sentenced. Who were they?"

She did not reply. Then Karden shouted suddenly; it was the first time he had raised his voice. "*Who?*"

"I don't know. Friends of Alec's."

"More friends? What did they want?"

"I don't know. They kept asking me what he had told me. They told me to get in touch with them if—"

"*How? How* get in touch with them?"

At last she replied, "He lived in Chelsea. His name was Smiley . . . George Smiley . . . I was to ring him."

"And did you?"

"No!"

A deathly silence had descended on the court. Pointing toward Leamas, Karden said, in a voice more impressive because it was perfectly under control, "Smiley wanted to know whether Leamas had told her too much. Leamas had done the one thing British Intelligence had never expected him to do; he had taken a girl and wept on her shoulder." Then Karden laughed quietly, as if it were all such a neat joke. "Just as Karl Riemeck did. He made the same mistake."

"Did Leamas ever talk about himself?" he said.

"No."

"You know nothing about his past?"

"No. I knew he'd done something in Berlin. Something for the government."

"Then he did talk about his past, didn't he? Did he tell you he had been married?"

There was a long silence. Liz nodded.

"Why didn't you see him after he went to prison? You could have visited him."

"I didn't think he'd want me to."

"And when he had served his time in prison, you didn't try to get in touch with him?"

"No."

"In fact, you were finished with him, weren't you?" Karden asked with a sneer. "Had you found another lover?"

"No! I waited for him . . . I'll always wait for him." She checked herself. "I wanted him to come back."

"Then why didn't you try to find out where he was?"

"He didn't want me to, don't you see! He made me promise . . . never to follow him . . . never to . . ."

"*So he expected to go to prison, did he?*" Karden demanded triumphantly.

"No—I don't know. How can I tell you what I don't know?"

"And on that last evening," Karden persisted, "on the evening before he hit the grocer, did he make you renew your promise?"

With infinite weariness she nodded in a pathetic gesture of capitulation. "Yes."

"And you said good-by?"

"We said good-by."

"What reason did he give for breaking off your relationship?"

"He didn't break it off," she said. "Never. He just said there was something he had to do; someone he had to get even with, whatever it cost, and afterward, one day perhaps . . . he would . . . come back, if I was still there and . . ."

"And you said," Karden suggested with irony, "that you would always wait for him, no doubt? That you would always love him?"

"Yes," Liz replied simply.

"Did he say he would send you money?"

"He said . . . he said things weren't as bad as they seemed. That I would be . . . looked after."

"And that was why you didn't inquire when some charity in the City casually made you a large present?"

"Yes! Yes, that's right! Now you know everything—you knew it all already. Why did you send for me if you knew?"

Imperturbably Karden waited for her sobbing to stop. "That," he observed finally to the tribunal, "is the evidence of the defense. I am sorry that a girl whose perception is clouded by sentiment should be considered by our British comrades a suitable person for Party office."

Looking first at Leamas and then at Fiedler he added brutally, "She is a fool. It is fortunate, nevertheless, that Leamas met her. This is not the first time that a reactionary plot has been uncovered through the decadence of its architects."

With a precise little bow to the tribunal Karden sat down.

As he did so Leamas rose to his feet, and this time the guards let him alone.

London, he was thinking, must have gone raving mad. He'd *told* them to leave her alone. And now it was clear that from the moment he left England—before that even, as soon as he went to prison— some bloody fool had gone around tidying up—paying the bills, settling with the grocer, the landlord; above all, Liz. It was insane. What were they trying to do—kill Fiedler, kill their agent? Sabotage their own operation? Or was it just Smiley? Had his wretched little conscience driven him to this?

There was only one thing to do—get Liz and Fiedler out of it and carry the burden himself. He was probably written off anyway. If he could save Fiedler's skin, perhaps there was a chance that Liz would get away.

How the hell did they know so much? He was sure he hadn't been followed to Smiley's house that afternoon. And how had Mundt picked up the story about his stealing money from the Circus? That was designed for internal consumption only . . . Then how? For God's sake, how?

Bewildered, angry and bitterly ashamed, he took his place before the tribunal again, stiffly, like a man facing the scaffold.

21

"ALL RIGHT, Karden." His face was white and hard as stone, his head tilted in the attitude of a man listening to some distant sound. There was a frightful stillness about him; his whole body seemed to be in the iron grip of his will. "All right, Karden, let her go."

"No, Alec." Liz was staring at him, her face crumpled and ugly, her dark eyes filled with tears. There was no one else in the room for her—just Leamas straight as a soldier.

"Don't tell them," she said, her voice rising, "whatever it is, don't tell them just because of me. . . . I don't mind anymore, Alec. I promise I don't."

Leamas turned to the president. "She knows nothing. Nothing at all. Get her out of here and send her home. I'll tell you the rest."

The president glanced at the men on either side of her. Then she said, "The witness may leave the court, but she cannot go home until the hearing is finished. Then we shall see."

"She knows nothing, I tell you!" Leamas shouted. "Karden's right. It was a planned operation. How could she know that? She's just a frustrated little girl from a crackpot library—she's no good to you!"

"She is a witness," replied the president shortly. "Fiedler may want to question her." It wasn't Comrade Fiedler anymore.

At the mention of his name Fiedler seemed to wake from a reverie. His deep brown eyes rested on Liz for a moment, and he smiled very slightly. He was a small, forlorn figure, oddly relaxed.

"She knows nothing," he said. "Leamas is right, let her go." His voice was tired.

"You realize what you are saying?" the president asked. "What this means? Have you *no* questions to put to her?"

"She has said what she had to say." Fiedler studied his hands as if they interested him more than the proceedings of the court. "It was all most cleverly done." He nodded. "Let her go. She cannot tell us what she does not know." With a certain mock formality he added, "I have no questions for the witness."

A guard unlocked the door and called into the passage outside. In the total silence of the court they heard a woman's answering voice, and her ponderous footsteps approaching. Fiedler abruptly stood up, and taking Liz by the arm, he guided her to the door. There she turned and looked back toward Leamas, but he was staring away from her like a man who cannot bear the sight of blood.

"Go back to England," Fiedler said to her, and suddenly Liz began to sob uncontrollably. The wardress put an arm around her shoulder, more for support than comfort, and led her from the room. The guard closed the door. The sound of her crying faded gradually to nothing.

"THERE ISN'T MUCH to say," Leamas began. "Karden's right. It was a put-up job. When we lost Karl Riemeck we lost our only decent agent in the Zone. We couldn't understand it—Mundt seemed to pick them up almost before we'd recruited them. I came back to London and saw Control. Peter Guillam was there and George Smiley, though George was in retirement really. We knew we had our backs to the wall: we'd failed against Mundt, and now we were going to try to kill him. We all hated Mundt, I think, although we didn't say it; we planned the thing as if it were all a bit of a game. . . .

"Anyway, they'd dreamed up a way to get Mundt to trap himself. Then we worked it out backward, so to speak. If Mundt *were* our agent, how would we have paid him? How would the files look? And so on. Peter remembered that some Arab had tried to sell us a breakdown of the Abteilung a year or two back and we'd sent him packing. Afterward we found out we'd made a mistake. Peter had the idea of fitting that in—as if we'd turned it down because we already knew everything. That was clever.

"You can imagine the rest. The pretense of going to pieces; drink, money troubles, the rumors that I had robbed the till. We got Elsie in Accounts to help with the gossip, and one or two others. They did it bloody well," he added with a touch of pride. "Then I chose a morning—a Saturday morning, lots of people about—to assault the grocer. It made the local press and you people picked it up. From then on," he added with contempt, "you dug your own graves."

"Your grave," said Mundt, looking at Leamas with his pale, pale eyes. "And perhaps Comrade Fiedler's."

"You can hardly blame Fiedler," said Leamas. "He happened to be the man on the spot; he's not the only man in the Abteilung who'd willingly hang you, Mundt."

"We shall hang *you*, anyway," said Mundt reassuringly. "You murdered a guard. You tried to murder me."

"Smiley always said it could go wrong. He said it might start a reaction we couldn't stop. His nerve's gone—you know that. He's never been the same since the Fennan Case—since the Mundt affair in London. What I can't make out is why they paid off the bills, the girl and all that. It *must* have been Smiley, wrecking the operation on purpose. He must have had a crisis of conscience, thought it was wrong to kill or something."

Turning to the tribunal he said, "You're wrong about Fiedler; he's not ours. Why would London take this kind of risk with a man in Fiedler's position? They counted on him, I admit. They knew he hated Mundt—why shouldn't he? Fiedler's a Jew, isn't he? You know, you must know, all of you, what Mundt thinks about Jews.

"I'll tell you something—no one else will. Mundt had Fiedler beaten up, and all the time, while it was going on, Mundt baited him and jeered at him for being a Jew. You all know what kind of man Mundt is, and you put up with him because he's good at his job. But"—he faltered for a second—"but for God's sake . . . enough people have got mixed up in all this without Fiedler's head going into the basket. Fiedler's all right—ideologically sound, that's the expression, isn't it?"

He looked at the tribunal. They watched him impassively, curiously almost, their eyes steady and cold.

Fiedler, who was listening with rather studied detachment, looked at Leamas blankly for a moment. "And you messed it all up, Leamas, is that it?" he asked. "An old dog like Leamas, engaged in the crowning operation of his career, falls for a . . . what did you call her? . . . 'a frustrated little girl from a crackpot library'? London must have known; Smiley couldn't have done it alone." Fiedler turned to Mundt. "Here's an odd thing, Mundt; they must have known you'd check up on every part of his story. That was why Leamas lived the role so carefully. Yet afterward they sent money to the grocer, paid up Leamas' rent, paid a long lease for the girl. Of all the extraordinary things for them to do—to pay a thousand pounds to a girl, *to a member of the Party*, who was supposed to believe he was broke. Don't tell me Smiley's conscience goes that far. Control must have done it. What a risk!"

Leamas shrugged. "Well, Smiley was right. We couldn't stop the reaction. We never expected you to bring me here—Holland, yes—but not here. And I never thought you'd bring the girl. I've been a bloody fool."

"But Mundt hasn't," Fiedler put in quickly. "Mundt knew what to look for. He knew the girl would provide the proof. Very clever, I must say! He even knew about that lease—amazing really. I mean, how *could* he have found out? She wouldn't have told anyone." He glanced toward Mundt. "Perhaps Mundt can tell us *how* he knew?"

Mundt hesitated, a second too long, Leamas thought. "It was her subscription," he said. "A month ago she increased her Party contribution by ten shillings a month. I tried to establish how she could afford it. I succeeded."

"A masterly explanation," Fiedler replied coolly.

"I think," said the president, glancing at her two colleagues, "that the tribunal is now in a position to make its report to the presidium. That is," she added, turning her small, cruel eyes on Fiedler, "unless you have anything more to say."

Fiedler shook his head. Something seemed to amuse him.

"In that case," the president continued, "my colleagues are agreed that Comrade Fiedler should be relieved of his duties until the disciplinary committee of the presidium has considered his position.

"Leamas is already under arrest. The people's prosecutor, in collaboration with Comrade Mundt, will no doubt consider what action is to be taken against a British *agent provocateur* and murderer."

She glanced at Mundt. But Mundt was looking at Fiedler with the dispassionate regard of a hangman measuring his subject for the rope.

And suddenly, with the terrible clarity of a man too long deceived, Leamas understood the whole ghastly trick.

22

LIZ STOOD at the window, her back to the wardress, and stared blankly into the tiny prison yard outside. She was in somebody's office; there was food on the desk, but she couldn't touch it. She felt sick and terribly tired; her face felt stiff and raw from weeping.

"Why don't you eat?" the woman asked. "It's all over now." She said this without compassion, as if the girl were a fool not to eat when the food was there.

"I'm not hungry."

The wardress shrugged. "You may have a long journey," she observed, "and not much at the other end."

"What do you mean?"

"The workers are starving in England," she declared complacently. "The capitalists let them starve."

"Who told you that?"

The woman smiled and said nothing. She seemed pleased with herself.

"What is this place?" Liz asked.

"Don't you know?" The wardress laughed. "You should ask them over there." She nodded toward the window. "They can tell you what it is."

"Who are they?"

"Enemies of the state," she replied. "Spies, agitators."

"How do you know they are enemies?"

"The Party knows. The Party knows more about people than they know themselves. Haven't you been told that? This is a prison for all who fail to recognize socialist reality, who think they have the right to err, who slow down the march. Traitors," she concluded briefly.

Liz asked, "What do you do here?"

"I am commissar here," the woman said proudly.

"You must be very clever," Liz observed, approaching her.

"I am a worker," the woman replied acidly. "The concept of brain workers as a higher category must be destroyed. There are no categories, only workers. Haven't you read Lenin?"

"Then the people in this prison are intellectuals?"

The woman smiled. "Yes," she said, "they are reactionaries who defend the individual against the state. Do you know what Khrushchev said about the counterrevolution in Hungary?"

Liz shook her head. She must show interest, make this woman talk.

"He said it would never have happened if a couple of writers had been shot in time."

"Whom will they shoot now?" Liz asked quickly. "After this trial?"

"Leamas," she replied indifferently, "and Fiedler."

Liz thought she was going to fall, but her hand found the back of a chair and she managed to sit down. "What has Leamas done?" she whispered.

The woman looked at her with her small, cunning eyes. She was very large; her scant hair was stretched back to a bun at the nape of her thick neck. Her face was heavy, her complexion flaccid and watery.

"He killed a guard," she said.

"Why?"

The woman shrugged. "As for the Jew, it is said that he plotted with Leamas against Comrade Mundt. Comrade Mundt knows what to do with Jews. Are you going to eat that?" she inquired, indicating the food on the desk. Liz shook her head. "Then I must," she declared, with a grotesque attempt at reluctance. "They have given you a potato. You must have a lover in the kitchen." The humor of this observation sustained her until she had finished Liz's meal.

LIZ WENT BACK to the window. In the confusion of her mind, there predominated the appalling memory of Leamas as she had last seen him in the courtroom, his body stiff, his eyes averted from her own. She had failed him and he dared not look at her before he died; would not let her see the contempt, the fear perhaps, that was written on his face.

But how could she have done otherwise? If Leamas had only told her what he had to do—even now, it wasn't clear to her—she would have lied and cheated for him, anything! Surely he understood that; surely he realized she would take on his pain, if she could, that she prayed for nothing more than the chance to do so. But how could she have known how to answer those veiled, insidious questions? There seemed no end to the destruction she had caused. She remembered how, as a child, she had been horrified to learn that with every step she made, thousands of minute creatures were destroyed beneath her foot; and now she had been forced to destroy a human being; perhaps two, for was there not also Fiedler, who had been gentle with her, taken her arm and told her to go back to England?

Why did it have to be Fiedler—why not the fair one who smiled all the time? Whenever she turned around she had caught sight of his smooth, blond head and his smooth, cruel face smiling as if it were all a great joke. It comforted her that Leamas and Fiedler were on the same side. She turned to the woman and asked, "Why are we waiting here?"

The wardress pushed the plate aside.

"For instructions," she replied. "They are deciding whether you must stay."

"Stay?" repeated Liz blankly.

"It is a question of evidence. Fiedler may be tried. I told you, they suspect conspiracy between Fiedler and Leamas."

The telephone rang. The woman lifted the receiver.

"Yes, Comrade. At once," she said, and put down the receiver. "You are to stay here," she said shortly. "That is the wish of Comrade Mundt."

"Who is Mundt?"

The woman looked cunning. "It is the wish of the presidium that you stay," she said.

"I don't want to stay," Liz cried, but the woman did not reply.

Slowly Liz followed her along endless corridors, through barred gates manned by sentries, past iron doors from which no sound came, down endless stairs, across whole courtyards far beneath the ground, until she thought she had descended to the bowels of hell itself, and no one would even tell her when Leamas was dead.

SHE HAD NO IDEA what time it was when she heard the footsteps outside her cell. It could have been five in the evening—it could have been midnight. She had been awake—staring blankly into the pitch-darkness, longing for a sound. She had never imagined that silence could be so terrible. Once she had cried out, and there had been no echo, nothing. Just the memory of her own voice. She had visualized the sound breaking against the solid darkness like a fist against a rock. She had moved her hands about her as she sat on the bed, and it seemed to her that the darkness made them heavy, as if she were groping in water.

She knew the cell was small, that it contained the bed on which she sat, and a crude table; she had seen them when she first entered. Then the light had gone out, and she had run wildly to where she knew the bed stood, had struck it with her shins, and then sat there, shivering with fright. Until she heard the footsteps, and the door of her cell was opened abruptly.

She knew at once that it was the blond, smiling man she had seen in the courtroom, although she could only discern the smooth line of the cheek and the short fair hair against the light in the corridor.

"It's Mundt," the man said. "Come with me, at once." His voice was contemptuous yet subdued, as if he were anxious not to be overheard.

Liz was suddenly terrified. She remembered the wardress: "Comrade Mundt knows what to do with Jews." She stood by the bed, staring at him, not knowing what to do.

"Hurry, you fool." Mundt seized her wrist and drew her into the corridor. Bewildered, she watched him quietly relock the door of her cell. Roughly he took her arm and forced her quickly along the corridor, half running, half walking. Now and then she heard other footsteps in passages branching from their own. She noticed that Mundt hesitated, drew back even, until he had confirmed that no one was coming, then signaled her forward. He seemed to assume that she would follow, that she knew the reason. It was almost as if he were treating her as an accomplice.

And suddenly he had stopped, was thrusting a key into a dingy metal door. She waited, panic-stricken. He pushed the door savagely outward, and the sweet, cool evening air blew against her face. He beckoned to her with the same urgency, and she followed him down two steps onto a gravel path. They followed the path to an elaborate Gothic gateway which gave onto the road beyond. Parked in the gateway was a car. Standing beside it was Alec Leamas.

"Wait here," Mundt warned her. He went forward alone and for what seemed an age the two men stood together, talking quietly. Her heart was beating madly, and she shivered with cold and fear.

Finally Mundt returned and led her to where Leamas stood. The two men looked at one another for a moment.

"Good-by," said Mundt indifferently. "You're a fool, Leamas. She's trash, like Fiedler." He turned and walked quickly away into the twilight.

She put her hand out and touched Leamas, and he half turned from her, brushing her hand away as he opened the car door. He nodded to her to get in, but she hesitated.

"Alec," she whispered, "Alec, what are you doing? Why is he letting you go?"

"Shut up!" Leamas hissed. "Don't even think about it, do you hear? Get in."

"What was it he said about Fiedler? Alec, why is he letting us go?"

"He's letting us go because we've done our job. Get into the car. Quick!"

Under the compulsion of his extraordinary will she got into the car. Leamas got in beside her.

"What bargain have you struck with him?" she persisted, suspicion

and fear rising in her voice. "They said you had conspired against him, you and Fiedler. Then why is he letting you go?"

Leamas had started the car and was driving fast along the narrow road. On either side were bare fields; in the distance, dark monotonous hills mingling with the gathering darkness.

Leamas looked at his watch. "We're one hundred and thirty miles from Berlin," he said. "We've got to meet a contact, in Cöpenick, outside Berlin, after midnight, by quarter to one. We should do it easily."

For a time Liz said nothing; she stared through the windshield down the empty road, confused and lost in a labyrinth of half-formed thoughts. They turned onto an autobahn.

"Was I on your conscience, Alec?" she said at last. "Is that why you made Mundt let me go?"

Leamas said nothing.

"You and Mundt are enemies, aren't you?"

Still he said nothing. He was driving faster now, the speedometer showed 120 kilometers; the autobahn was pitted and bumpy. He had his headlights on full, and didn't bother to dip them for oncoming traffic. He drove roughly, leaning forward, his elbows almost on the wheel.

"What will happen to Fiedler?" Liz asked suddenly, and this time Leamas answered.

"He'll be shot."

"Then why didn't they shoot you?" Liz continued quickly. "You conspired with Fiedler against Mundt, that's what the commissar said. And you killed a guard. Why has Mundt let you go?"

"All right!" Leamas shouted suddenly. "I'll tell you. I'll tell you what you were never, never to know—neither you nor I. Listen: Mundt is London's man, their agent; they bought him when he was in England. We are witnessing the lousy end to a filthy, lousy operation to save Mundt's skin. To save him from a clever little Jew in his own department who had begun to suspect the truth. They made us kill Fiedler, do you see? Now you know, and God help us both."

23

"IF THAT IS SO, Alec," she said at last, "what was my part in all this?" Her voice was calm, almost matter-of-fact.

"I can only guess, Liz, from what I know and what Mundt told me outside the prison just now. Fiedler had suspected Mundt ever since Mundt came back from England; he thought Mundt was playing a double game. He hated him, of course—why shouldn't he?—but he was right, too: Mundt *was* London's man. Fiedler was too powerful for Mundt to eliminate alone, so London decided to do it for him. But they also knew it was no good just eliminating Fiedler—he might have told friends, published accusations. They had to eliminate *suspicion*. Public rehabilitation, that's what they organized for Mundt.

"They told me to frame Mundt. They said he had to be killed, and

I was game. It was going to be my last job. So I went to seed, and punched the grocer and— You know all that."

"And made love?" she asked quietly.

Leamas shook his head. "But this is the point, you see. Mundt knew it all. He knew the plan. He had me picked up, he and Fiedler. Then he let Fiedler take over, because he knew in the end Fiedler would hang himself. My job was to let Fiedler think what in fact was the truth: that Mundt was a British spy." He hesitated. "Your job was to discredit me. Fiedler was shot and Mundt was saved, mercifully delivered from a Fascist plot."

"But how could they know we would come together?" Liz cried. "Heavens above, Alec, can they even tell when people will fall in love?"

"It didn't depend on that. They chose you because you were young and pretty and in the Party, because they knew you would come to Germany if they rigged an invitation. They knew I'd work at the library—that man in the Labour Exchange, Pitt, sent me there. Pitt was in the Circus during the war and they squared him, I suppose. They only had to put you and me in contact, even for a day, then afterward they could call on you, send you the money as if it came at my request, make it look like an affair even if it wasn't. An infatuation, perhaps. As it was, we made it very easy for them."

"Yes, we did." Then she added, "I feel dirty, Alec."

Leamas said nothing.

"Did it ease your department's conscience at all? Exploiting somebody in the Communist Party, rather than just anybody?" she continued.

Leamas said, "Perhaps. But they don't really think in those terms. It was an operational convenience."

"I might have stayed in that prison, mightn't I? That's what Mundt wanted, wasn't it? He saw no point in taking the risk—I might have heard too much, guessed too much. It seems odd that he let me go— even as part of the bargain with you," she mused. "I'm a risk now, aren't I? When we get back to England, I mean: a Party member knowing all this . . ."

"It gives him a chance to secure his position," Leamas replied. "He is going to use our escape to demonstrate to the presidium that there are other Fiedlers in his department who must be hunted down."

"And other Jews? Other innocent people? It doesn't seem to worry you much."

"Of course it worries me. It makes me sick with shame and anger and . . . But my life has been different from yours, Liz; I can't see this in black and white. People who play this game take risks. Fiedler lost and Mundt won. *London* won—that's the point. It was a foul, foul operation. But it's paid off, and that's the only rule." As he spoke his voice had risen until finally he was nearly shouting.

"You're trying to convince yourself," Liz cried. "They've done a wicked thing. How can you kill Fiedler? He was good, Alec; I know he was. And Mundt—"

"What the hell are you complaining about?" Leamas demanded roughly. "Your party's always sacrificing the individual to the mass. That's what it says. Socialist reality, fighting night and day—the relentless battle—that's what they say, isn't it? At least you've survived. I agree, yes I agree, you might have been destroyed. Mundt's a vicious swine; he saw no point in letting you survive. His promise—I suppose he gave a promise to do his best by you—wasn't worth a great deal. So you might have died in a prison in the worker's paradise. But I seem to remember that the Party is aiming at the destruction of a whole class."

Extracting a packet of cigarettes from his jacket he handed her two, together with a box of matches. Her fingers trembled as she lit them and passed one back to Leamas.

"You've thought it all out, haven't you?" she asked.

"We happened to fit the mold they needed for the operation," Leamas persisted, "and I'm sorry. I'm sorry for the others too—the others who fit the mold. But don't complain about the terms, Liz; they're Party terms. A small price for a big return. One sacrificed for many. It's not pretty, I know, choosing who it'll be—turning the plan into people."

She listened in the darkness for a moment, scarcely conscious of anything except the vanishing road before them and the numb horror in her mind.

"But they let me love you," she said at last. "And you let me believe in you and love you."

"They used us," Leamas replied pitilessly. "They cheated us both because it was necessary. It was the only way. Fiedler was bloody nearly home already. Mundt would have been caught, can't you understand that?"

"How can you turn the world upside down?" Liz shouted suddenly. "Fiedler was kind and decent, and now you've killed him. Mundt is a Nazi and a traitor, and you protect him. How can you . . . ?"

"There's only one law in this game," Leamas retorted. "Mundt is London's man; he gives them what they need. What do you think spies are: priests, saints and martyrs? They're a squalid procession of vain fools, pansies, sadists and drunkards. Traitors, too. Do you think they sit like monks in London, balancing the rights and wrongs? I'd have killed Mundt if I could, I hate his guts. But not now. They need him so that the great moronic mass you admire can sleep soundly in their beds at night."

"But what about Fiedler—don't you feel anything for him?"

"This is a war," Leamas replied. "It's graphic and unpleasant because it's fought on a tiny scale, at close range; fought with a wastage of innocent life sometimes. But it's nothing, nothing at all beside other wars—the last or the next."

"Oh Alec," said Liz softly. "You don't understand. You don't want to. It's far more terrible, what they are doing; to find the humanity in people, in me and whoever else they use, to turn it like a weapon in their hands, and use it to hurt and kill— That's far more wicked."

"Because I made love to you when you thought I was a tramp?" Leamas asked savagely.

"Because of their contempt," Liz replied. "Contempt for love, contempt for what is real and good. Only Fiedler didn't kick me about. The rest of you . . . all of you . . . treated me as if I was—nothing. Just currency to pay with. You're all the same, Alec."

"Oh Liz," he said desperately, "for God's sake believe me. I hate it. I hate it all. I'm tired. But it's the world, it's mankind that's gone mad. Everywhere's the same; lives thrown away, people shot and in prison, whole groups and classes of men written off for nothing. And you, your party—God knows it was built on the bodies of ordinary people."

As he spoke Liz remembered the drab prison courtyard, and the wardress saying, "This is a prison for those who slow down the march, for those who think they have the right to err."

Leamas was suddenly tense, peering through the windshield. In the headlights Liz discerned a figure standing in the road. In his hand was a tiny light which he turned on and off as the car approached. "That's him," Leamas muttered. He switched off the headlights and engine, and coasted silently forward. They drew up, and Leamas leaned back and opened the rear door. The man got in. Liz did not turn around to look at him. She was staring stiffly forward, down the road at the falling rain.

"YOU WILL DRIVE slowly, at thirty kilometers," the man said. His voice was taut, frightened. "I'll tell you the way. When we reach the place, you must get out and run to the Wall. The searchlight will be shining at the point where you must climb. Stand in the beam of the searchlight. When it moves away, begin to climb. You will have ninety seconds to get over. You go first, Leamas, and the girl follows. There are iron rungs in the lower part—after that you must pull yourself up as best you can. You'll have to sit on top and pull the girl up. Do you understand?"

"We understand," said Leamas. "How long have we got?"

"If you drive at thirty kilometers we shall be there in about nine minutes. The searchlight will be on the Wall at five past one exactly. The guards can give you ninety seconds."

"What happens after ninety seconds?" Leamas asked.

"They can only give you ninety seconds," the man repeated. "Otherwise it is too dangerous. Only one guard detachment has been briefed. They think you are being infiltrated into West Berlin. They've been told not to make it too easy. Ninety seconds are enough."

"I bloody well hope so," said Leamas dryly. "What time do you make it?"

"I checked my watch with the sergeant in charge of the detachment." A light went on and off briefly in the car. "It is now 12:48. We must leave at 12:55. Seven minutes to wait."

They sat in total silence save for the rain pattering on the roof. The cobblestone road reached out straight before them, staged by dingy streetlights every hundred yards. There was no one about. Above them the sky was lit with the unnatural glow of arc lights. Occasionally the beam of a searchlight flickered overhead, then disappeared. They were very near the end of the road.

"There is no turning back. No second chance," the man said. "He told you that?"

"I know," Leamas replied.

"If you fall or get hurt, don't turn back. They shoot on sight within the area of the Wall. You *must* get over."

"I know," Leamas repeated. "He told me."

"From the moment you get out of the car you are in the area," the man said.

"I know. Now shut up," Leamas retorted. And then he added, "Are you taking the car back?"

"As soon as you get out of the car I shall drive it away. It is a danger for me too," the man replied.

"Too bad," said Leamas. Again there was silence. Then Leamas asked, "Do you have a gun?"

"Yes," said the man, "but he said I shouldn't give it to you . . . that you were sure to ask for it."

Leamas laughed quietly. "He would," he said.

Leamas started the car. With a noise that seemed to fill the street it moved slowly forward.

They had gone about three hundred yards when the man whispered excitedly, "Go right here, then left." They swung into a narrow side street. There were empty market stalls on either side so that the car barely passed between them.

"Left here, now!"

They turned again, fast, this time between two tall buildings into what looked like a cul-de-sac. There was washing strung across the street. As they approached the dead end the man said, "Left again—follow the path." Leamas mounted the curb, crossed the sidewalk, and they followed a broad footpath bordered by a broken fence to their left and a tall building to their right. They heard a shout from above, a woman's voice, and Leamas muttered, "Oh, shut up," as he steered clumsily around a right-angle bend in the path and came almost immediately upon a major road.

"Which way?" he demanded.

"Straight across between the drugstore and the post office—there!" The man pointed, leaning so far forward that his face was almost level with theirs.

"Get back," Leamas hissed. "How the hell can I see if you wave your hand around like that?" Slamming the car into first gear, he drove fast across the wide road. Glancing to his left, he was astonished to glimpse the plump silhouette of the Brandenburg Gate and the sinister grouping of military vehicles at the foot of it. "Where are we going?" asked Leamas suddenly.

"We're nearly there. Go slowly now—left, left, go *left!*" the man cried, and Leamas jerked the wheel in the nick of time. They passed under a narrow archway into a derelict courtyard, at the other end of which was an open gateway. "Through there," came the whispered command, urgent in the darkness. "Then hard right. You'll see a streetlamp on your right. The one beyond it is broken. When you reach the second lamp, switch off the engine and coast until you see a fire hydrant. That's the place."

They passed through the gate and turned right into a narrow street.

"Lights out!"

Leamas switched off the car lights, drove slowly toward the first streetlamp. Ahead, they could just see the second. It was unlit. Switching off the engine, Leamas coasted silently past it until they discerned the dim outline of the fire hydrant. Leamas braked; the car rolled to a standstill.

"Look." The man pointed down a side street to the left. At the far end they saw a brief stretch of wall, gray-brown in the arc light. Along the top ran a triple strand of barbed wire.

"How will the girl get over the wire?"

"It is already cut where you climb. There is a small gap. You have three minutes to reach the Wall. Good-by."

They got out of the car, all three of them. Leamas took Liz by the arm, and she started from him as if he had hurt her.

"Good-by," said the German.

Leamas said, "Don't start that car till we're over."

Liz looked at the German for a moment in the pale light; she had a brief impression of a young, anxious face—the face of a boy trying to be brave.

"Good-by," said Liz. She followed Leamas across the road and into the narrow street that led toward the Wall.

As they entered the street they heard the car start up behind them, turn and move quickly away in the direction they had come.

THEY WALKED QUICKLY, LEAMAS glancing over his shoulder from time to time to make sure she was following. As he reached the end of the alley he stopped, drew into the shadow of a doorway and looked at his watch.

"Two minutes," he whispered.

She said nothing. She was staring straight ahead toward the Wall and the black ruins rising behind it. Before them was a strip thirty yards wide. Perhaps seventy yards to their right was a watchtower; the beam of its searchlight played along the strip. The thin rain hung in the air, so that the light from the arc lamps was sallow and chalky, screening the world beyond. There was no one to be seen; not a sound. An empty stage.

The searchlight began feeling its way along the Wall toward them, hesitant; each time it rested they could see the separate bricks and the careless lines of mortar hastily put on. The beam stopped immediately in front of them. Leamas looked at his watch.

"Ready?" he asked.

She nodded. Taking her arm, he began walking deliberately across the strip. Liz wanted to run, but he held her so tightly that she could not. They were halfway toward the Wall now, the brilliant semicircle of light drawing them forward, the beam directly above them. Leamas kept Liz very close to him, as if he were afraid that Mundt would not keep his word but would somehow snatch her away at the last moment.

They were almost at the Wall when the beam darted to the north, leaving them momentarily in total darkness. Still holding Liz's arm, Leamas guided her forward blindly, his left hand reaching ahead of him until suddenly he felt the coarse, sharp contact of the cinder brick. Now he could discern the Wall and, looking upward, the triple strand of wire and the cruel hooks which held it. Metal wedges, like climbers' pitons, had been driven into the brick. Seizing the highest one, Leamas pulled himself quickly upward until he reached the top of the Wall. He tugged sharply at the lower strand of wire and it came toward him, already cut.

"Come on," he whispered urgently, "start climbing."

Laying himself flat he reached down, grasped her upstretched hand and began drawing her slowly upward as her foot found the first metal rung.

Suddenly the whole world seemed to break into flame; from everywhere, from above and beside them, massive lights converged, bursting upon them with savage accuracy.

Leamas was blinded, he turned his head away, wrenching wildly at Liz's arm. Now she was swinging free; he thought she had slipped and he called frantically, still drawing her upward. He could see nothing—only a mad confusion of color dancing in his eyes.

Then came the hysterical wail of sirens, orders frantically shouted. Half kneeling astride the Wall he grasped both her arms in his, and began dragging her to him inch by inch, himself on the verge of falling.

Then they fired—single rounds, three or four, and he felt her shudder. Her thin arms slipped from his hands. He heard a voice in English from the Western side of the Wall:

"Jump, Alec! Jump, man!"

Now everyone was shouting, English, French and German mixed; he heard Smiley's voice from quite close:

"The girl, where's the girl?"

Shielding his eyes, he looked down at the foot of the Wall, and at last he managed to see her, lying still. For a moment he hesitated, then quite slowly he climbed back down the rungs until he was standing beside her. She was dead; her face was turned away, her black hair drawn across her cheek as if to protect her from the rain.

They seemed to hesitate before firing again; someone shouted an order, and still no one fired. Finally they shot him, two or three shots. He stood glaring around him like a blinded bull in the arena. As he fell, Leamas saw a small car smashed between great lorries, and the children waving cheerfully through the window.